THE ONE VS. THE MANY

THE ONE VS. THE MANY

MINOR CHARACTERS AND THE SPACE OF
THE PROTAGONIST IN THE NOVEL

Alex Woloch

PRINCETON UNIVERSITY PRESS PRINCETON AND OXFORD

Copyright © 2003 by Princeton University Press
Published by Princeton University Press,
41 William Street, Princeton, New Jersey 08540
In the United Kingdom: Princeton University Press,
3 Market Place, Woodstock, Oxfordshire OX20 1SY

Excerpt from "The Last Romantic" from *Wakefulness* by John Ashbery.
Copyright © 1998 by John Ashbery. Reprinted by permission of Farrar,
Straus and Giroux, LLC.

Library of Congress Cataloging-in-Publication Data

Woloch, Alex, 1970–
The one vs. the many : minor characters and the space of the protagonist
in the novel / Alex Woloch.
p.cm.
Includes bibliographical references and index.
ISBN 0-691-11313-0 (alk. paper)—ISBN 0-691-11314-9 (pbk.)
1. Characters and characteristics in literature. 2. European fiction—
19th century—History and criticism. 3. Realism in literature.
I. Title: One versus the many. I. Title.
PN3411.W64 2004
809.3'927—dc21   2003043333

British Cataloging-in-Publication Data is available

This book has been composed in Times Roman

Printed on acid-free paper.∞

www.pupress.princeton.edu

Printed in the United States of America

10   9   8   7   6   5   4   3   2   1

"I have met so many men," he pursued, with
  momentary sadness—"met them too with a certain—
  certain—impact, let us say . . ."
    —Joseph Conrad, *Lord Jim*

Contents

THE ONE VS. THE MANY

vast quantity of pain"—dramatically strains against its subordinate position, shattering the frame of the sentence through an almost ungrammatical bulge: "but [the dying soldiers] gave their bodies to be the delicate feasting of dogs, of all the birds." Finally, in an effort to rein in the uncontrollable drift of this image, the sentence invokes a teleotic order—"the will of Zeus was accomplished"—that motivates its own formal closure. Like the gods who famously step in to solve the plot complications in some Greek tragedies, Zeus seems to arrive here to set the syntactic problems of this *sentence* to rest. Resisting that drift from "the multitudes" of men to all of nature, the proem returns to Achilles. But the very repetition of "Achilles" within one sentence indicates that we have somehow left him. Now Achilles is depicted from the outside, delimited by a social relationship, "in division of conflict [with] Atreus' son, the lord of men."

This syntactic imbalance might be the key to the proem: the strange formulation of the sentence, torn between dominant and subordinate clause, dramatizes an essential aspect of the *Iliad* itself. The epic as a narrative whole, as much as its opening sentence, is divided between representing Achilles' singular experience and representing many other characters who—if only by the fact of this multiplicity—are configured as exterior, social, and *delimited* agents. Robert J. Rabel terms the *Iliad* "a double plotted work, with the wrath of Achilles furnishing the major plot, and with the Trojan War unfolding in tandem within a subplot" (26). Thus Zeus promises Thetis "to do honor to Achilles *and* to destroy many beside the ships of the Achaians" (1.558–59, emphasis added). Achilles' honor is produced through this destruction of the many, but such destruction can always potentially wrest attention away from the protagonist. The poet's point of view, although omniscient, is never secure. It wavers between representing individuals in terms of their own particularity and integrating them into a larger aesthetic structure that, finally, revolves around a singular personality. This play between the absorption of secondary characters into Achilles' central situation and the framing of Achilles himself within a much larger narrative field is an animating tension of the entire epic. We might say that there are two wars in the *Iliad*. Embedded within the Trojan conflict recounted in the tale we can find a battle on the discursive plane, not between the characters as individual soldiers on the field but between the characters as more or less important figures within the narrative structure. The formal clash between protagonist and minor characters redounds back on, and is motivated by, the clashing world of the story itself.

When Achilles Disappears: A Reading of Book 2

The *Iliad* only includes so many secondary characters because Achilles himself *withdraws* from the battle in Book 1. If Achilles' refusal to fight causes grave military and political problems for the Greek army, his retreat as a central protagonist also raises a series of *narrative* problems. Without a central protagonist to justify a limited focus, how can the epic begin to coherently represent the mass of humanity involved in a war? Book 2 introduces the range of these secondary characters and dramatizes the narrative crisis caused by Achilles' absence. This crisis is depicted in two essential and dialectically linked extremes in two famous set pieces of Book 2: the provocation by Thersites and the Catalogue of Ships. These scenes—which focus, respectively, on the singular individual and the innumerable crowd—are each significant in their own right but have never been read in terms of their close juxtaposition.

First there is Thersites, who disrupts the Greek social order through his egalitarian demands and embodies a vertiginous hyperindividualism:

> Now the rest had sat down, and were orderly in their places,
> but all alone Thersites, of the endless speech, still scolded,
> who knew within his head many words, but disorderly;
> vain, and without dignity, quarreling with kings
> with any word he thought might be amusing to the Argives.
> (2.211–15)

Thersites is perhaps the first truly minor character in Western literature. It is not simply that he has a subordinate narrative role, but that his striking fictional identity emerges *through*, and revolves around, this subordinated position. The collapse of authority signaled by Achilles' withdrawal seems to produce this narrative intrusion, this disruptive character. Thersites is so despicable because he refuses a delimited position; while others are "orderly in their place," even in the absence of Achilles, Thersites threatens to speak *endlessly* (ἀμετρο–), to drag the assembly (and the epic itself) in toward his own endless self. And, as with a minor character in Dickens, who will be one of the principal figures in this study, Thersites' disruptive position generates a sequence of heightened descriptive language. While the text is utterly dismissive of Thersites, it lavishes physical attention on him. The portrait of Thersites is actually *more* detailed than any physiognomy to this point in the poem, more precise than any description of Achilles or Agamemnon in Book 1.

> This was the ugliest man who came beneath Ilion. He was
> bandy-legged and went lame of one foot, with shoulders
> stooped and drawn together over his chest, and above this
> his skull went up to a point with the wool grown sparsely upon it.
> (2.216–19)

This detailed picture of Thersites is strangely linked to the thematic *subordination* of his disruptive political viewpoint. The text seems ironically able to dismiss him only by emphasizing him: pointing out his flaws also singles him out; he is not simply shameful and ugly but the *most* shameful and ugly of men (αἴσχοστς).[4]

Soon after, in the last third of Book 2, the Catalogue of Ships unfolds, tellingly chosen as the episode par excellence in Aristotle's discussion of epic
unity.[5] The Catalogue of Ships—clearly the widest representation of who is
involved in the war—exemplifies for Aristotle that element of the epic which,
because it lies beyond Achilles, "diversifies" the poem. It also lies beyond
the vision of the narrator himself, who breaks down in the face of such
human multiplicity:

> I could not tell over the multitude of them nor name them,
> not if I had ten tongues and ten mouths, not if I had
> a voice never to be broken and a heart of bronze within me,
> not unless the Muses of Olympia, daughters
> of Zeus of the aegis, remembered all those who came beneath Ilion.
> I will tell the lords of the ships, and the ships' numbers.
> (2.488–93)

There is a crucial relationship between the way Thersites exceeds, and threatens, the hierarchical framework of the Greek army camp and the way the
soldiers, en masse, exceed the empirical gaze of the poet. The two episodes,
together, precisely render the dialectical relationship between crowd and individual: the mass of soldiers is unspeakable *only as it is an aggregation of
distinct individuals*, while Thersites is threatening, *not merely as an individual*,
but insofar as his hostility might express (or become) the sentiment of a crowd.[6]
Thus the poet's inability to adequately represent the soldiers who have come
to Troy hinges on the distinction between seeing the *number* of soldiers and
being able to name them. As G. S. Kirk writes, "He is not able to tell who
were the troops, as he had with the leaders, . . . but rather how many they
were" (167). The distinction between counting and naming occurs precisely at
the fault line where an individual ceases to command attention as a qualitatively distinct being and begins to be viewed as a quantitative unit, absorbed
into a larger number even as the ordinary soldiers are encompassed by the
"lords of the ships" who represent them and do get named.

Both the obstreperous minor character and the nameless multitudes of soldiers enter the narrative in explicit relation to Achilles' absence, emphasizing
how the narrative threats of both the "endless" individual and the measureless
crowd (which are really interdependent) emerge out of the temporary lack of a
central, orienting narrative figure. Thersites thus motivates his speech—which
radically challenges Agamemnon's authority—with a reference to Achilles'
altercation with the king: "And now he has dishonored Achilles, a man much
better / than he is. He has taken his prize by force and keeps her" (2.239–
40). Similarly, the Catalogue of Ships ends by contrasting all the other troops
marshaled for battle with Achilles' idle camp, in a way which suggests that
but for Achilles' retreat there would be no need to list the mass of soldiers.
The shift to Achilles is folded within a complicated double comparison:

Tell me then, Muse, who of them all was the best and bravest,
of the men, *and the men's horses*, who went with the sons of Atreus.
Best by far among the horses were the mares of Eumelos
Pheres' son, that he drove, swift-moving like birds, alike in
texture of coat, in age, both backs drawn level like a plumb-line . . .
Among the men far the best was Telamonian Aias
while Achilles stayed angry, since he was far best of all of them,
and the horses also, who carried the blameless son of Peleus.
But Achilles lay apart among his curved sea-wandering
vessels, raging at Agamemnon. . . .
(2.761–772, emphasis added)

The belated inclusion of Achilles, which nullifies Ajax's superiority, oddly circles back to undermine the *previous* claim about the superiority of Eumelos's mares. The very mechanism of comparison, which underlies the Catalogue, is ushered in only through Achilles' absence, since his exalted status and distinctive superiority renders comparative judgments (and thus comprehensive catalogs) obsolete. As Seth Benardete notes, "As long as Achilles was in the field, the Trojans never ventured into the plain, and as long as Achilles fought no Achaean could hope to do anything of consequence" ("Aristeia of Diomedes," 26). Neither Thersites' propulsion into the narrative nor the indescribable Catalogue of Ships would occur, or be motivated, without the retreat and absence of the central protagonist.

The disappearance of Achilles also prompts the emergence of a third kind of character in Book 2, or, more precisely, a group of characters, who spring up right in between these two episodes and occupy a place in between the threatening singularity of Thersites and the dispersed multiplicity of the Catalogue. As though in response to this dual threat of overdefined individual and anonymous crowd, the circle of great Greek warriors first enters the narrative, hastily assembled by a worried Agamemnon:

[The king] . . . summoned the nobles and the best men of all the Achaians,
Nestor before all others, and next the lord Idomeneus,
next the two Aiantes and Tydeus' son Diomedes,
and sixth Odysseus, a man like Zeus himself for counsel.
Of his own accord came Menelaos of the great war cry
who knew well in his own mind the cares of his brother.
They stood in a circle about the ox and took up the scattering
barley. . . . (2.404–11)

Leadership—both social and narrative—devolves to this group of human beings, and it is precisely in their status *as* a group that they can anchor and sustain a distributed field of characterization that neither collapses into the one nor explodes out toward many. These characters—so memorable within the consciousness of European literature—exemplify the *Iliad*'s ability to present a variety of individual characters as fully realized and specific human personalities. The "foremost fighters" (*promachoi*) among the Greeks, this group forms a precarious and embattled middle space between the two extreme modes of characterization that this book will explore: the protagonist, whose identity rests on a narrative centrality that always threatens to take the form of wrath (erasing or absorbing all the other persons who surround him), and the minor characters who, simply through their subordinated multiplicity, hover vulnerably on the borderline between name and number. On the one hand, the qualities of each of these *promachoi* emerge only within a larger social, and narrative, structure. They are not only subject to but constituted through delimitation and juxtaposition. None of these characters can control or hope to anchor the entire formal or thematic architecture of the *Iliad*: we would never consider the epic as *essentially* about Diomedes or Odysseus. On the other hand, this delimitation does not corrode their distinctive independence. Each of the characters has enough narrative space to emerge as a unique and coherent individual. Such circumscribed uniqueness is most significantly expressed through the series of *aristeiai* that help organize the narrative structure of the *Iliad* and memorably define the various warriors.[7] (With Diomedes, ironically, it is his very frustration at *not* being able to command a certain kind of centrality that gives him a coherent and unique identity.)

In one of the most important twentieth-century theories of characterization (before the question *of* character, as I will discuss in the introduction, drops out of literary theory), Erich Auerbach argues that Dante transformed the nature of the literary character by making his fictional figures into the fusion of the particular and the essential, the transient and the permanent. The rich particularity of Dante's characters somehow erupts out of their atemporal destinies: the figures in the *Inferno* (the main locus for his theory) exist in a static world where time has essentially stopped, but are still paradoxically recognizable *as* their own secular, contingent selves.[8] Auerbach further suggests that Homeric characterization—which seizes on the essential characteristics of specific and varied individuals—anticipates the way that Dante will construct persons as both delimited *and* unique or complete.[9] But this dialectical configuration of character is most fully realized with the group of leading soldiers, each of whom is configured as a distinct, compelling personality even as he is embedded within a larger social, and narrative, context. The coherence of these characters relies on, and is indissociable from, their status as a finite, delimited group.[10] Coming together "in a circle," this assembly of individuals saves the epic narrative from the destabilizing possibilities that emerge out of Achilles' absence. The demiheroes, who will absorb most of the narrative's interest and attention until Achilles' return, work between the uncontrollable, endless Thersites and the indescribable masses. It is an astonishing narrative instantiation of aristocratic politics.[11]

The Death of Lykaon

Book 21 of the *Iliad* revolves around an unfair fight. Achilles, beginning his violent avenging of Patroklos's death, comes across a young nobleman named Lykaon fighting for Troy. Lykaon's poignant and unique fate is encapsulated in 125 lines near the beginning of the book. The compact space devoted to his fate is essential to our understanding of it, as the way Lykaon's tragic death gets squeezed into the episode forms an inherent aspect *of* the tragedy. And just as each line in the compressed scene develops Lykaon's encounter, as a fictional person, with Achilles, so each line modulates his configuration within the narrative—using various perspectives and shifting voices to intensify or diminish his narrative presence. If Book 2 illustrates the essential *structure* of the relationship between the one and the many, or the protagonist and the multitude of participants in the war, the Lykaon episode in Book 21 exemplifies how a particular encounter between one minor character and the protagonist is configured within this structure.

In the Lykaon episode, Homer threads a remarkable story into the epic: a fantastic instance of terrible luck that, in its very rarity, speaks powerfully to the essential nature of warfare. We quickly learn that Lykaon had been captured by Achilles only twelve days earlier and, in a rapid series of events, has been shipped from captor to captor until he is ransomed back by his wealthy Trojan family to enjoy a brief week and a half of freedom before reencountering his nemesis on the battlefield:

> For eleven days he pleasured his heart with friends and family
> after he got back from Lemnos, but on the twelfth day once again
> the god cast him into the hands of Achilles, who this time
> was to send him down unwilling on his way to the death god.
> (21.45–48)

Confronting this extraordinary destiny of Lykaon—which bursts into the poem from out of nowhere—the narrative is pulled in two inverse directions: toward the overwhelming pathos of Lykaon's subjective experience, as a discrete individual, and toward the function of Lykaon's strange doom within the development of Achilles' own story. The scene wavers between absorbing Lykaon's character into the narrative as a whole (centering on the foe who kills him) and rendering the particularity of this character's own life.

Real life is full of uneven matches, but fictional representation can uniquely amplify such disparities within the narrative form itself. While the representation of Achilles' personhood unfolds gradually, over the course of the narrative, Lykaon's whole being is squeezed into this one brief episode—he gets both ushered into and pushed out of the *Iliad* in this scene. Lykaon's *character-space* does not have nearly enough time to unfold, just as his character does not enjoy nearly enough freedom after captivity before he is pushed toward his strange death. There is a profound relationship between the story's events and the way these events get narratively structured—between the fate of Lykaon on the battlefield, as a weak individual overwhelmed by a strong soldier, and the fate of Lykaon as a subordinate character, within the tale, who gets absorbed into the plot of a strong protagonist.

Achilles' *aristeia* works like the wrath of the opening lines: it actualizes itself through the subsumption of other individuals. Just ten lines prior to his encounter with Lykaon, the poem offers a graphic image of this asymmetry: "[Achilles], when his hands grew weary with killing, / chose out and took twelve young men alive from the river / to be vengeance for the death of Patroklos, the son of Menoitis" (21.26–28). These twelve unnamed individuals gain no inflection into the narrative—and the compression of so many figures into one line is crucial to our sense of the violence that Achilles is here enacting.[12] Similarly, Achilles' response to Lykaon's plea absorbs Lykaon's discrete perspective into the larger, central perspective of the epic as a whole:

> So the glorious son of Priam addressed him, speaking
> in supplication, but heard in turn the voice without pity:
> "Poor fool, no longer speak to me of ransom, nor argue it. . . .
> So friend, you die also. Why all this clamor about it?
> Patroklos also is dead, who was better by far than you are.
> Do you not see what a man I am, how huge, how splendid
> and born of a great father, and the mother who bore me immortal?
> Yet even I have also my death and my strong destiny,
> and there shall be a dawn or an afternoon or a noontime
> when some man in the fighting will take the life from me also
> either with a spearcast or an arrow flown from the bowstring."
> (21.97–113)

The paragraph abstractly generalizes Lykaon's death and then relates it back to the more significant destiny of the epic's protagonist.[13]

But the unique unluckiness of Lykaon's destiny must also elude the parameters of how it functions in relation to Achilles; or, more precisely, it functions so effectively within Achilles' revenge only because of an irreducibly specific aspect of it. In contrast to the cold reply that ruthlessly subordinates Lykaon—making him into another unit like the twelve anonymous prisoners, who, en masse, will constitute the externalization of Achillean wrath—the episode is infused with Lykaon's specificity and inflects his subjective experience of his fate into the text. Thus the initial description of the two soldiers' previous encounter is strangely divided, flowing back and forth between Achilles' and Lykaon's consciousnesses, almost to the point of redundancy:

> And there he came upon a son of Dardanian Priam
> as he escaped from the river, Lykaon, one whom he himself
> had taken before and led unwilling from his father's garden
> on a night foray. He with the sharp bronze was cutting young branches
> from a fig tree, so that they could make him rails for a chariot,
> when an unlooked-for evil thing came upon him, the brilliant
> Achilles, who that time sold him as slave in strong-founded Lemnos
> carrying him there by ship, and the son of Jason paid for him. . . .
> (21.34–41)

The description begins from Achilles' perspective but unpredictably drifts into the consciousness of Lykaon. We arrive at the incident through the memory of Achilles, the captor, so that Lykaon enters into the *Iliad* as the protagonist recollects him, as someone whom Achilles "comes upon" and as "one whom he himself had taken before." Yet already with the mention of an "unwilling"(οὐκ ἐθέλοντα) Lykaon, the young man's memory of the event seems to impress itself onto the narrative. The middle of the sentence shifts away from Achilles toward Lykaon's own recollection, as though the experience of the captive always potentially lurks inside the captor's own consciousness. Only this shift justifies the strange repetition of Achilles, as the putatively remembering subject has become an object within the memory—"When an unlooked-for evil thing came upon him, the brilliant / Achilles, who that time sold him."

Again, when the poem shifts back into the present, it begins from Achilles' point of view.

> Now as brilliant swift-footed Achilles saw him and knew him
> naked and without helm or shield, and he had no spear left
> but had thrown all these things on the ground, being weary and sweating
> with the escape from the river, and his knees were beaten with weariness,
> disturbed, Achilles spoke to his own great-hearted spirit. . . .
> (21.49–53)

Once more the protagonist's external perception of Lykaon seems to drift into Lykaon's own interior feelings, moving from "he had no spear left" (something Achilles can plainly see) to "being weary and sweating" (something Achilles' could infer or sympathetically imagine) to "his knees were beaten with weariness" (an interior sensation that seems to intrude in on the description) until it finally returns to Achilles' own "disturbed" emotional state.

Even the final reply by Achilles—a death sentence that abolishes Lykaon within the text's overall hierarchy of character—is presented *through* Lykaon's consciousness, as the text adds the crucial detail: "but [Lykaon] heard in turn the voice without pity." And in Lykaon's own supplication we can trace a tension between his formulaic invocations and a deeper sense of bitterness and despair that penetrates through the rhetoric, bespeaking once more the singularity of what he is experiencing. In the compact presentation of Lykaon, every word counts—not simply as it unfolds the events, but as it continually modulates the configuration of Lykaon's *space* within these events. The *form* encapsulates and substantiates the essential crisis provoked by the avenging protagonist's encounter with a doomed minor character.[14] And this moral crisis is generated out of a larger social crisis. The particular intricacy of Lykaon's formed space within the epic emerges out of, and is amplified by, the governing narrative tension between the one and the many.

In constructing the idea of formal coherence, Aristotle performs a stunning act of alchemy: he transforms a work of art into a nearly sentient entity. The "resemblance" Aristotle draws between a unified composition and a "living organism" underlies the foundational premise of formalist criticism, which highlights the immanent unity of the aesthetic object as a closed and self-sufficient structure. This analogy allows us to imagine a beautiful kind of literary history. From the *Iliad* on, we can unfold the story of how each literary form comes to resemble a living organism, in a kind of supreme aesthetic entelechy. But there is that second question which we find in Aristotle's discussion as well: How can many people be contained within a single narrative? How do different narrative forms accommodate the surge of many people into a single story? How do they encapsulate and convey the impact of a human being—of varied human beings—within a coherent literary structure? In these questions we can see the outline of a different, almost inverted, history: a history that would trace not how the literary form, in its intricate coherence, is rendered into a living organism, but how living persons get rendered into literary form.

Introduction

Characterization and Distribution

> They told him there were too many characters
> in your novel, that the plot was still complicated, but still
> they keep coming on, there must have been a leak, wait, it's not even that,
> there are just too many people out there.
> —John Ashbery, "The Last Romantic"

> *"Done because we are too menny."*
> —Thomas Hardy, *Jude the Obscure*

Character-Space: Between Person and Form

Lykaon, Thersites, Achilles, Diomedes, Odysseus, the anonymous men fleetingly registered in the Catalogue of Ships: over and over again we are presented with different inflections of individuals into the total work of art. The rich diversity of these characters—the multitudinous ways in which the *Iliad* comprehends the human—depends on each character's structured position within the literary totality, or the narrative space that he occupies. In each instance, the character's referential personality—the unique sense and abiding impression that the character leaves us with—emerges in-and-through, not despite, his textual position and the descriptive configuration that flows out from this position.

"Now wol I stynte of Palamon a lite," writes Chaucer in "The Knight's Tale," registering the way that narrative progress always entails a series of choices: each moment magnifies some characters while turning away from—and thus diminishing or even stinting—others.[1] Such a process runs implicitly through any number of narratives and occasionally breaks out to the surface of the fiction itself. Consider these two quotations from Dostoevsky and Trollope. First, from *The Idiot*:

> Let us not forget that the motives behind human actions are usually infinitely more complicated and various than we assume them to be . . . do as we will, we are now under the absolute necessity of devoting to this secondary character in our story rather more space and attention than we originally had intended. (502)

And, from *Barchester Towers*, at the very end of chapter 3:

> Mr. Slope, however, on his first introduction must not be brought before the public at the tail of a chapter. (21)

Both of these passages explicitly render the novel's own awareness of the amount of narrative space allocated to a particular character. Squeezing a character into the end of a chapter creates a tension between our sense of the character as an actual human placed within an imagined world and the space of the character within the narrative structure. Trollope's example—a character who is too important to get pushed into the end of a chapter—is expanded into a general principle by Dostoevsky: *all* characters are potentially overdelimited within the fictional world—and might disrupt the narrative if we pay them the attention they deserve.[2]

Dostoevsky focuses on that gap between what he calls "motive" and "action"—or between the interior thoughts of a human being (which are "infinitely" complicated) and the finite, limited manifestation of this consciousness through external, social actions. If the narrative registers only action, it will elide the perspective of characters; if it attempts to register motive, it might lose the thread of narrative progression and have to devote too much "space and attention" to minor characters. That two novelists who represent such different extremes of nineteenth-century realism as Dostoevsky and Trollope share a similar ground for their systems of characterization speaks to the importance of this narrative process.

Trollope's comment about Mr. Slope and the tail of a chapter is so suggestive because it relies *both* on our ability to imagine a character as though he were a real person, who exists outside of the parameters of the novel, and on our awareness of such a highly artificial and formal aspect of the narrative structure as chapter divisions. The character-space marks the *intersection* of an implied human personality—that is, as Dostoevsky says, "infintely" complex—with the definitively circumscribed form of a narrative. It is the point where Mr. Slope can meet the "tail of a chapter." In this perspective the implied person behind any character is never directly reflected in the literary text but only partially inflected: each individual portrait has a radically contingent position within the story as a whole; our sense of the human figure (*as* implied person) is inseparable from the space that he or she occupies within the narrative totality.

The One vs. the Many seeks to redefine literary characterization in terms of this distributional matrix: how the discrete representation of any specific individual is intertwined with the narrative's continual apportioning of attention to different characters who jostle for limited space within the same fictive universe. We have seen how the dynamic flux of attention underlies important incidents and narrative strategies in the *Iliad*. Both the distorted physical description of Thersites and the partial, but ultimately elided, inscription of Lykaon's point of view flow out of the distributional pressures that inform these scenes. These examples are not rare. My study addresses and connects a series of questions that have never been conceptually formulated but that are provoked by, and often essential to, any number of narratives. What is the purpose or significance of a particularly marginal character? How much access are we given to a certain character's thoughts, and how does the partial enactment of this perspective or point of view fit into the narrative as a whole? Why and how are certain narratives divided between two or three central characters? How often, at what point, and for what duration does a character appear in the text? How does she enter and exit specific scenes? How does her delimited position intersect with the achieved representation of her speech, actions, or physiognomy? How are her appearances positioned in relation to other characters and to the thematic and structural totality of the narrative? Why does a particular character suddenly disappear from the narrative or abruptly begin to gain more narrative attention? How does the text organize a large number of different characters within a unified symbolic and structural system? As these questions flow into each other, I will begin to construct a new framework for interpreting both characterization itself—the literary representation of imagined human beings—and the design and significance of a number of nineteenth-century novels. My interpretive method rests above all in the combination of two new narratological categories which I will formulate and continually return to: the *character-space* (that particular and charged encounter between an individual human personality and a determined space and position within the narrative as a whole) and the *character-system* (the arrangement of multiple and differentiated character-spaces—differentiated configurations and manipulations of the human figure—into a unified narrative structure). In developing these categories through a series of nineteenth-century novels, I want to demonstrate the importance of distributed attention not just to the realist novel but to the vexed problem of characterization itself: a problem that lies at the heart of contemporary literary theory.

Characterization and the Antinomies of Theory

The literary character: so important to narrative praxis but ever more imperiled within literary theory. For a long time now, characterization has been the bête noire of narratology, provoking either cursory dismissal, lingering uncertainty, or vociferous argument. As Jonathan Culler writes, "Character is the major aspect of the novel to which structuralism has paid least attention and has been least successful in treating" (230). Other narrative theorists concur:

> It is remarkable how little has been said about the theory of character in literary history and criticism. (Chatman, 107)

> Whereas the study of the story's events and the links among them has been developed considerably in contemporary poetics, that of character has not. Indeed, the elaboration of a systematic, non-reductive but also non-impressionistic theory of character remains one of the challenges poetics has not yet met. (Rimmon-Kenan, *Narrative Fiction*, 29)

That no one has yet succeeded in constructing a complete and coherent theory of character is probably precisely because of this human aspect. The character is not a human being, but it resembles one. (Bal, 80)

Rimmon-Kenan's opposition between the "impressionistic" and the "systematic" signals the crux of a problem that characterization has posed within narrative theory. How does an interpretive practice that focuses on the syntax of narrative *as* a system conceptualize the implied resemblance between "the character" and "the human being"? Focusing on the character-system—and the character-spaces that it encompasses and puts into relation—highlights the way that the "human aspect" of a character is often dynamically integrated into, and sometimes absorbed by, the narrative structure as a whole. As this study will demonstrate, character-space draws on and redefines our understanding of both "impression" and "system," continually establishing a relationship between the referential elaboration of a character, as implied individual, and the emplacement of a character within a coordinated narrative structure.

By analyzing the distribution of attention within narrative, we can thus reconfigure a seemingly implacable conflict within theories of characterization: the tension between the authenticity of a character in-and-of-himself and the reduction of the character into the thematic or symbolic field. Harry Berger aptly summarizes such a problem in Spenser: "When the poet states or suggests that Woman A stands for Idea B, a dilemma is forced on us. Does Woman A disappear completely into Idea B? . . . Or is such sleight of hand impossible to a poet—doesn't a fable by its very nature have some elements of concreteness (belonging to the 'image of human life') that cannot be translated?" (120).[3] Mieke Bal's stress on the problematic "human aspect" of characterization comes out of a particular and highly influential perspective on this tension within twentieth-century literary theory. Beginning with the Russian formalists, the decoupling of literary characters from their implied humanness becomes the price of entry into a theoretical perspective on characterization. For instance, Boris Tomachevski analyzes the hero not as the central *person* whose story the literary text elaborates, but rather as a central device that acts as glue for the text itself, "a sort of living support for the text's different motifs." Tomachevski continues:

> The hero is hardly necessary to the story. The story, as a system of motifs, can entirely bypass the hero and his characteristic traits. The hero comes out of the transformation of the material in the discourse and represents, in one part, a means to tie together the motifs and, in another part, a personified motivation for the connection between the motifs. . . . The hero is necessary so that one can tie together anecdotes around him. (293–98)

French structuralists, poststructuralists, and new novelists return to and elaborate Russian formalism, arguing, even more insistently, against the anthropo-

morphic component of characterization. The attack on reference gets implicated in more ambitious schemes, whether ideological (Hélène Cixous and
Alain Robbe-Grillet), hermeneutic/semantic (A. J. Greimas and Philippe
Hamon), or both (Roland Barthes).[4] Thus while Cixous and others argue that
the referential basis of character underlies a particularly bourgeois notion of
personhood, Greimas tries to show that our very cognition of characters is
mediated through syntactic structures. Building on the earlier work of Vladimir
Propp, Greimas categorizes all characters within an "actantial" model, according to six positional functions that are homologous to syntactic elements.[5]

This model of criticism has both relied on, and continually generated, an
opposed perspective on characterization, which defines characters by their referential aspect. While formalists and New Critics attacked the psychological
and moralistic basis of character-criticism, some recent studies have been increasingly troubled by the excision of the human from narratology.[6] Throughout the twentieth century, analysis of character repeatedly seems to devolve
into polemics, where both sides ironically depend on the viewpoint that they
are dismissing. Such divisions fall into the more endemic alternations—and
altercations—between intrinsic and extrinsic criticism that have been identified
by Paul de Man and others as a kind of metastructure of twentieth-century
literary theory.[7]

Let me present two polemical passages that illustrate the nature of this division: on the one hand, L. C. Knights's famous 1933 attack on Shakespearean
character-criticism ("How Many Children Had Lady Macbeth?"); and, on the
other hand, Irving Howe's more recent broadside against the poststructuralist
attack on literary character:

> To examine the historical development of that kind of criticism which is mainly
> concerned with "character" is to strengthen the case against it. . . . Wherever we look
> we find the same reluctance to master the words of the play, the same readiness to
> abstract a character and treat him (because he is more manageable that way) as a
> human being. . . . The habit of regarding Shakespeare's persons as "friends for life"
> or, maybe, "deceased acquaintances," is responsible for most of the vagaries that
> serve as Shakespeare criticism. . . . Not only do we lose the necessary aloofness from
> a work of art (to be distinguished from an inability to respond imaginatively) but we
> lose the dramatic pattern and we are inhibited from the full complex response which
> a play of Shakespeare's can evoke. (Knights, 11 and 27–28)

> The sophisticated if just barely readable French theorist Hélène Cixous writes that a
> novel with mimetic characters turns into "a machine of repression," bourgeois repres-
> sion of course, since it presents a historical given as if it were everlasting and thereby
> thwarts all hope for transcendence. . . . There is something bizarre in the notion that
> fictional characterization is an agency of repression . . . this is to confuse narrative
> conventions with social categories. Where, in any case, have our strongest visions
> of possibility, as also our most telling social criticisms, come from if not the great

novelists—it is they who have given imaginative substance to what the young Marx called "the human essence," and far better and more fully than any social theorists. . . . The great fictional characters, from Robinson Crusoe to Flem Snopes, from Tess to Molly Bloom, cannot quite be "fitted" into or regarded solely as functions of narrative. *Why should we want to?* What but the delusions of system and total grasp do we gain thereby? Such characters are too interesting, too splendidly mysterious for mere functional placement. (Howe, 38 and 42)

These two starkly contrasting—and equally convincing—perspectives are typical of theoretical positions about characters: both Howe and Knights are urging the reader to *choose*. Ironically, the formalist and referential positions seem to rely on each other—both are generated only through the opposed position, which they configure into an extreme in order to reverse. Thus such debates circle around and around; as de Man argues "an undeniable and recurrent historical fact . . . this sort of thing happens, again and again, in literary studies" (*Allegories* 3–4).

In viewing these contrary positions as dialectically linked and strangely dependent upon each other, we can begin to see a single opposition—or antinomy—that structures and gives form to seemingly distinct, and irreconcilable, points of view. Characterization has been such a divisive question in twentieth-century literary theory—and has created recurrent disputes between humanist and structural (or mimetic and formal) positions—because the literary character is itself divided, always emerging at the juncture between structure and reference. In other words, a literary *dialectic* that operates dynamically within the narrative text gets transformed into a theoretical *contradiction*, presenting students of literature with an unpalatable choice: language *or* reference, structure *or* individuality. My study recasts theoretical conflict back into literary process. By interpreting the character-system as a distributed field of attention, we make the tension between structure and reference generative of, and integral to, narrative signification. The opposition between the character as an individual and the character as part of a structure dissolves in this framework, as distribution relies *on* reference and takes place *through* structure.[8] Thus the dimensions of both structure and reference—the scope of a complex, organizing formal system and the compelling human singularity of fictional individuals—become available to each other, rather than remaining mutually exclusive.

To link structure and reference in this way, in terms of distribution, brings out an inherently social dimension to narrative form as such. This socioformal dimension of a narrative is qualitatively distinct from (even if often related to) any social interactions that we might derive or extrapolate outside of the form, in the referenced social conflicts and relations between posited or implied persons within the imagined world of the story itself. For the character-system offers not simply many *interacting* individuals but many *intersecting* character-spaces, each of which encompasses an *embedded* interaction between the discretely implied person and the dynamically elaborated narrative form. While characters themselves might or might not gain a relationship, character-spaces inevitably do.[9] To put this differently, all character-spaces inevitably point us toward the character-system, since the emplacement of a character within the narrative form is largely comprised *by* his or her relative position vis-à-vis other characters. If the character-space frames the dynamic interaction between a discretely implied individual and the overall narrative form, the character-system comprehends the mutually constituting interactions among all the character-spaces as they are (simultaneously) developed within a specific narrative. None of these characters get elaborated in a vacuum, even if the particular configuration of a specific character can tempt the reader to consider him outside of or extract him from the coordinated narrative. There is never a *purely* isolated conflict between one character and the form—as in the image of Mr. Slope clashing against the edge of a chapter. Rather, the space of a particular character emerges only vis-à-vis the other characters who crowd him out or potentially revolve around him. It is precisely here that the social dimension of form emerges, revolving around the inflection rather than the simple reflection of characters.

This socioformal organization of individuals within the character-system allows us to approach the tension between representing and allegorizing *in terms of* the tension between focusing on one life and focusing on many. Thus, for example, A. Bartlett Giamatti, discussing perhaps the most traditional structure for elaborating a literary hero, argues that "[e]pic poems focus on that core of experience where our humanity is defined by the opposites it encompasses" (74–75). Facilitating this arrangement, a narrative can organize its discursive universe into a referential core—the central condition of the protagonist—and a symbolic field that elaborates and nuances this core: the peripheral representations of minor characters. Secondary characters—representing delimited extremes—*become* allegorical, and this allegory is directed toward a singular being, the protagonist, who stands at the center of the text's symbolic structure, or what Giamatti calls "the single and abiding visionary core."[10] Giamatti's version of the epic hero is far from incidental. The tension between the one and the many intrudes continually upon theories of epic poetics, which anticipate and lay the ground for questions of characterization that the realist novel will later face. Building on Giamatti's comments, we might consider the debate between single-plot and multiplot narrative that dominates Italian Renaissance literary criticism. William W. Ryding describes this argument in terms of two warring literary genres: holistic, often allegorical, texts that are embedded in the defensive unitarian framework of late medieval Christianity, and epic romances which privilege discrete and heterogeneous narrative strands that stem from, reflect on, and forward secularizing trends. The most influential criticism in this period attempts to establish a relationship between unity and heterogeneity, deriving an aesthetics that draws on the merits of both competing tendencies. Ryding distinguishes Tasso's synthetic approach to the dilemma between the parts and the whole "as by far the most lucid and thoughtful of those written during this period" (10). For Tasso, the epic poem, like the universe itself, is "a complex piece of machinery in which every gear and lever performs a necessary function with respect to the whole. Take out a part or change its position, and the machine is destroyed" (15). Tasso thus tries to construct an aesthetic framework at once heterogeneous and unified, and this model hinges precisely on the strength of *functionality*. Diverse "parts" can enter into a narrative, but only as they bear a useful relationship to a central whole. The very emergence of heterogeneity in Tasso's aesthetic rests conditionally on a countervailing process of function, or symbolic integration.[11]

This tension between the one and the many becomes particularly pressing in the realist novel, which has always been praised for two contradictory generic achievements: depth psychology and social expansiveness, depicting the interior life of a singular consciousness and casting a wide narrative gaze over a complex social universe. The novel's commitment to everyday life promotes an inclusive, extensive narrative gaze, while its empiricist aesthetics highlights the importance and authenticity of ordinary human interiority. In his canonical account of the connection between the English novel and the turn toward everyday life, Ian Watt describes a broad historical relationship between realist aesthetics and larger cultural and philosophical tendencies: "[B]oth the philosophical and the literary innovations must be seen as parallel manifestations of a larger change—that vast transformation of Western civilization since the Renaissance which has replaced the unified world picture of the Middle Ages with another very different one—one which presents us, essentially, with a developing but unplanned aggregate of particular individuals having particular experiences at particular times and at particular places" (31). The redundant profusion of "particulars" in Watt's sentence subtly illustrates the formal problem that arises out of the process he describes: once you are committed to "particularity," how do you curtail it? As Roland Barthes writes, "nothing could indicate why we should halt the details of the description here and not there; if it were not subject to an aesthetic or rhetorical choice, any 'view' would be inexhaustible by discourse: there would always be a corner, a detail, an inflection of space or color to report" ("Reality Effect," 145). Recasting Barthes's "reality effect," I want to argue that the realist novel is structurally destabilized not by too many details or colors or corners, but by *too many people*. It is the claim of individuals who are incompletely pulled into the narrative that lies behind the larger empirical precision of realist aesthetics.[12] As the logic of social inclusiveness becomes increasingly central to the novel's form—with the development of eighteenth-century empiricism and nineteenth-century omniscient social realism—this problem becomes more pressing. The novel gets infused with an awareness of its potential to *shift* the narrative focus away from an established center, toward minor characters.

In this inclusiveness, the realist novel never ceases to make allegorical (or functional) use of subordinate characters, but it does ferociously problematize such allegory, by more clearly and insistently putting it in juxtaposition with reference. Allegorical characterization now comes at a price: the price of the human particularity that it elides. In other words, the realist novel systematically reconfigures its own allegorical reduction of characters through a pervasive awareness of the distributional matrix. This awareness lies behind the "flatness" that E. M. Forster so insightfully conceptualizes: a flatness that would seem to go against the basic tenets of realism but, in fact, becomes essential to realism.[13] Flatness simultaneously renders subordinate characters allegorical and, in its compelling distortions, calls attention to the subordination that underlies allegory. Flat characters—or the flattening of characters—becomes a primary site for the dialectic *between* reference and allegory that is generated out of the distributional matrix.

If many previous genres flatten subordinate characters—highlighting the tension between allegory and reference—the omniscient novel is particularly conscious of this narrative process, integrating its awareness into the narrative fabric. Nineteenth-century realism—with its mobile and often impersonal narrators, its ambitions toward structural totality, and its commitment to an inclusive social representation—generates endless varieties of interaction between the discursive organization of minor and central characters and the essential social and aesthetic impulses of the genre as a whole. Here the very formal terms of the socionarrative matrix—inclusion and exclusion, hierarchy and stratification, abstraction, utility, functionality and effacement—are continually manifested as themes, concerns and "stories" of the novels themselves. It is often precisely in the interaction between character-spaces (rather than merely in the characters or stories themselves) that novels touch history—not least because the very dynamic tension between reference and structure is itself so socially significant, grounded in the problematic elimination or functionalized compression of real persons in the actual world. This is one reason why nineteenth-century social realism is a key literary site—perhaps the key site—for highlighting and conceptualizing character-system and character-space. On the one hand, the realist novel's mimetic ambitions and narrative strategies crystallize the referential stakes so often at play in the dynamic intersection of implied person and narrative form. On the other hand, social representation itself, which is so often stigmatized for an aesthetics of transparency that seeks to transcend or abolish form, emerges through the lens of character-space as an intricately and profoundly formal process. My readings of Austen, Dickens, and Balzac will offer more textured demonstrations of how crucial formal breakthroughs in fictional characterization, and character-space, are intertwined with the aesthetics of social realism. But before turning to the realist novel proper, or to the main authors of this study, I want to look at the preface to Henry James's *The Wings of the Dove*, written at the ebb of realistic poetics.

Here we find the novel quite literally reflecting on the processes of character-ization that this study will scrutinize. If the preface anticipates a network of issues this study will examine, it also reveals how heavily these problems weigh on the consciousness of the novel, at the end of the realist tradition.

"They Too Should Have a Case"

James constructs a dialectical relationship between "center" and "circumfer-ence" where the inner consciousness of the putative protagonist, perhaps as in the *Iliad*, constitutes only "half" of the narrative, as the story of Milly Theale inevitably gets intertwined with, and spills out toward, other human figures. It is through this intertwining that James justifies the provocative way that his novel *begins* with subordinate characters and tardily introduces the protagonist in the second section:

> If one had seen that her stricken state was but half her case, the correlative half being the state of others as affected by her (they too should have a "case," bless them, quite as much as she!) then I was free to choose, as it were, the half with which to begin. . . . [T]hough my regenerate young New Yorker, and what might depend on her, should form my centre, my circumference was every whit as treatable. (40)

The crucial parenthetic interjection lends a moral imperative to this narrative strategy: it shows how the novel's sense of the potential to shift narrative attention is intertwined with a specific notion of human right. In one sense, James shifts attention toward minor characters only in order to fully represent the space of the protagonist, as other people are incorporated into Milly Theale's narrative as exterior, social agents. James makes it clear that the narra-tive is *compelled* to pay attention to other characters because they are impli-cated in Milly Theale's own story.

> [O]ur young friend's existence would create rather, all round her, very much that whirlpool movement of the waters produced by the sinking of a big vessel or the failure of a great business; when we figure to ourselves the strong narrowing eddies, the immense force of suction, the general engulfment that, for any neighbouring object, makes immersion inevitable. I need scarce say, however, that in spite of these communities of doom I saw the main dramatic complication much more prepared *for* my vessel of sensibility than by her—the work of other hands (though with her own imbrued too, after all, in the measure of their never not being, in some direction, generous and extravagant, and thereby provoking). (39–40)

At first other characters are drawn into (or "engulfed" within) the novel in order to elucidate the "whirlpool movement" of the protagonist's decline and fall, much as Achilles' wrath leads immediately to its social consequences. But, crucially, James corrects himself, writing, "I saw the main dramatic complication much more prepared *for* my vessel of sensibility than by her—the work of other hands." This image of work is important, because it is precisely in their functional capacity that other characters enter into the narrative. But behind every hand is a heart and a head. Each of these narrative workers also has a "case," an orientating consciousness that, like the protagonist's own consciousness, could potentially organize an entire fictional universe. Thus once other characters have been incompletely brought into the story, through their functional importance, they inevitably threaten to destabilize the narrative, through the force of their unique consciousness. Such tension leads to what the preface trenchantly calls "the author's scarce more than half-dissimulated despair at the inveterate displacement of his general centre" (46–47).

The surrounding figures become competing centers-of-consciousness, which organize the narrative into a series of "blocks"—"a new block . . . by which I mean of course a new mass of interest governed from a new centre" (49). Not just occupying a certain quantitative proportion of the narrative, these centers, James insists, have a "mass" or qualitative weight. They are, he continues,

> sufficiently solid *blocks* of wrought material, squared to the sharp edge, as to have weight and mass and carrying power; to make for construction that is, to conduce to effect and to provide for beauty. Such a block, obviously, is the whole preliminary presentation of Kate Croy, which, from the first, I recall, absolutely declined to enact itself save in terms of amplitude. Terms of amplitude, terms of atmosphere, those terms, and those terms only, in which images assert their fullness and roundness, their power to revolve, so that they have sides and backs, parts in the shade as well as parts in the sun—these were plainly to be my conditions, right and left. (42)

This passage links together the mass of a character with "fullness and round-ness," anticipating—and perhaps inspiring—E. M. Forster's 1927 theory of the flat and the round. The pressure that secondary characters exert on the narrative frame is suggestively encapsulated in James's description of how the "preliminary" depiction of Kate Croy "declined to enact itself save in terms of amplitude." It is, in fact, the pull of Kate Croy's interiority, of her own point of view, that dilates the narrative; just as, describing the portion of the narrative devoted to Mrs. Lowder, a much more minor character, James notes how the reader is "saturated with her presence, her 'personality,' and felt all her weight in the scale" (44).

But what should we make of the phrase "squared to the sharp edge"? To square off "fullness and roundness" is to distort and limit it, to, literally, make a potentially round character flat. And, after invoking the idealistic hope that each character's inner consciousness can achieve a weight and a mass through the fictional construction, James focuses on the inevitable, and distressing, gaps between his fiction's sharp edges and the characters' rounded depths. The preface thus continues, much more pessimistically: "[T]hese were plainly to be my conditions, left and right, and I was so far from overrating the amount of expression the whole thing, as I saw it and felt it, would require, that to retrace the way at present is, alas, more than anything else, but to mark the gaps and the lapses, to miss, one by one, the intentions that, with the best will in the world, were not to fructify" (42). Here, James transforms a mimetic difficulty—the inability to fully represent human interiority—into an aesthetic difficulty—the failure of stylistic intent. These two registers—representation and style (or form)—are in fact confused and intertwined in the passage. Do the "intentions" that "fail to fructify" refer to the missing intentionalities of the fictional characters or to the artistic intention of the writer himself? The passage continues:

> I have just said that the process of the general attempt is described from the moment the "blocks" are numbered, and that would be a true enough picture of my plan. Yet one's plan, alas, is one thing and one's result another; so that I am perhaps nearer the point in saying that this last strikes me at present as most characterised by the happy features that *were*, under my first and most blest illusion, to have contributed to it. I meet them all, as I renew acquaintance, I mourn for them all as I remount the stream, the absent values, the palpable voids, the missing links, the mocking shadows, that reflect, taken together, the early bloom of one's good faith. (42)

Again, James writes on two different registers. The narrative "stream" that he invokes is a description of his premodernist impressionism, but "the absent values, the palpable voids, the missing links, the mocking shadows" is also a wonderful figuration of minorness, of the textual disruption caused by squaring a circle or reducing a head and a heart to a hand—of trying to fit the depths of human consciousness to the "sharp edges" entailed by a subordinated narrative position.[14] James continues his reflection on artistic failure, on the difference between describing and showing, by imagining Kate Croy's father as a frustrated minor character leaving the room:

> The image of her so compromised and compromising father was all effectively to have pervaded her life, was in a certain particular way to have tampered with her spring; by which I mean that the shame and the irritation and the depression, the general poisonous influence of him, were to have been *shown*, with a truth beyond the compass even of one's most emphasized 'word of honour' for it, to do these things. But where do we find him, at this time of day, save in a beggarly scene or two which scarce arrives at the dignity of functional reference? He but 'looks in,' poor beautiful dazzling, damning apparition that he was to have been; he sees his place so taken, his company so little missed, that, cocking again that fine form of hat which has yielded him for so long his one effective cover, he turns away with a whistle of indifference that nobly misrepresents the deepest disappointment of his life. One's poor word of honour has *had* to pass muster for the show. Every one, in short, was to have enjoyed so much better a chance that, like stars of the theatre condescending to oblige, they have had to take small parts, to content themselves with minor identities, in order to come on at all. (43)

This passage evokes the pathos and the *disappointment* of minorness, making the preface's strongest statement of the consequences that emerge from "squaring the sharp edges." It reads as a summary of how character-space is rendered within a fraught distributional field: characters get only partially inflected into the narrative universe, reduced to a "functional reference," and the "minor identities" that ensue produce "apparitions" which shadowily reflect the fullness that has been excluded. The minor character's impoverished position—in a "*beggarly* scene or two"—collapses into his own identity: "*poor beautiful dazzling.*"

Two Kinds of Minorness

James's preface calls attention to the gap between a minor character's implied being and the manifestation of this being in the fictional universe. The inwardness of a person—"her presence, her 'personality'"—gets expressed only through an exterior sign, in this case, "cocking again that fine form of hat." Narrative flatness, in fact, produces a disjunction between "personality" and "presence," dissociating the full weight of interior character from its delimited, distorted exterior manifestation. Forced to circumscribe the interior lives of many characters in the elaboration of a singular, central consciousness, the novel has to radically delimit and distort the exterior manifestation of "roundness and fullness."

The descriptive conventions that arise around minorness depict the symptoms of such disjunction, which takes two dominant forms: the *engulfing* of an interior personality by the delimited signs that express it and the *explosion* of the suffocated interior being into an unrepresentable, fragmentary, symptomatic form. We can consider these two typical descriptions from Dickens:

> He was not old, but his hair was white; his body was bent, or bowed as if by the weight of some great trouble: and there were deep lines in his worn and melancholy face. The fire of his eyes, the expression of his features, the very voice in which he spoke, were all subdued and quenched, as if the spirit within him lay in ashes. (*Dombey and Son*, 135–36)

> [H]is face was curiously twisted as by a spasm, but whether of paralysis, or grief, or inward laughter, nobody but himself could possibly explain. The expression of a man's face is commonly a help to his thoughts, or glossary on his speech; but the countenance of Newman Noggs . . . was a problem which no stretch of ingenuity could solve. (*Nicholas Nickleby*, 77)

In both these brief examples, the full actualization of human consciousness in a social, exterior form is blocked. One character's "spirit" is suffocated by his leaden exteriority, and one character's convulsive exterior is disjoined from any connection to a furious interior that cannot find adequate form.[15] (We can also note how these two passages begin to suggest a broader spectrum of contrasts, so that, for example, two different *modes of speech* reflect these two modes of being: the old man's "voice" gets "subdued and quenched," while Newman's "speech" no longer serves as a "glossary" for his thoughts.)

These two existential states lie behind the two pervasive extremes of minorness within the nineteenth-century novel: the *worker* and the *eccentric*, the flat character who is reduced to a single functional use within the narrative, and the fragmentary character who plays a disruptive, oppositional role within the plot. These two kinds of minorness—with all the narrative functions and descriptive conventions they motivate (to portray the characters' bodies, gestures, and speech)—are flip sides of one coin.[16] In one case, the character is smoothly absorbed as a gear within the narrative machine, at the cost of his or her own free interiority; in the other case, the minor character grates against his or her position and is usually, as a consequence, wounded, exiled, expelled, ejected, imprisoned, or killed (within the *discourse*, if not the *story*).[17] In both cases, the free relationship between surface and depth is negated; the actualization of a human being is denied.

The dialectical link between these two states is nicely illustrated in *Jane Eyre*, where one of the most famous *fragmentary* minor characters gets oddly shadowed by a more obscure *flat* one. Bertha Mason is, of course, an exemplary case of the minor character as "eccentric" or "opposer," an influential paradigm of one kind of minorness.[18] In Bertha, story and discourse interlock, as her narrative subordination is clearly linked to social subordination. Shut up in the story, in her literal confinement as "the madwoman in the attic," Bertha Mason is also shut up within the narrative discourse, revealed only in sporadic passages that present her in a fragmentary form. The denial of her own perspective, of her claims on Rochester, thus gets linked to her discursive configuration; the subordinated interiority explodes out in an alienated form, as the "continued *outbreaks* of her violent and unreasonable temper" (291, emphasis added).

At first, however, Jane mistakes this minor character's identity, and superimposes the disruptive presence of Bertha onto Grace Poole, a quite different minor character who seems flattened by the drudgery of her service:

> The door nearest me opened, and a servant came out—a woman of between thirty and forty; a set, square-made figure, red-haired, and with *a hard, plain face*: any apparition less romantic or less ghostly could scarcely be conceived. . . . Her appearance always acted as a damper to the curiosities raised by her oral oddities: hard-featured and staid, *she had no point to which interest could attach*. I made some attempts to draw her into conversation, but *she seemed a person of few words*: a monosyllabic reply usually cut short every effort of that sort. (99, 101, emphases added)

Grace Poole does not have too *much* emotion, like Bertha, but too little of it: her rigid exteriority drowns out an inner personality, so that her countenance and conversation (the two most direct manifestations of interior sentiment) yield nothing. Once again, these two kinds of minorness catalyze two different modes of inadequate speech, as Jane, still confusing Bertha with Grace, remarks: "There were days when she was quite silent, but there were others when I could not account for the sounds she made" (101). Here Jane conflates Grace's inexpressive "silence" and Bertha's inarticulate "sounds," each of which falls on one side of the *speech* that can translate interiority into social communication. The odd conflation makes dialectical sense as, between them, Grace and Bertha illustrate the double consequences of minorness. Only in their combination can we shift from the particular oddity of each minor character to the broad structure of domination and subordination, which conjoins the outbreaks of eccentricity and the monotony of functionality.[19]

Function and Alienation: The Labor Theory of Character

My study deploys this typology of minorness in place of the traditional classification in terms of function. The merit of these categories—the engulfed and the exploding—is that they take account of the essential dynamics of narrative subordination itself. A typology of characters based merely on the different ways that characters function or are described within a literary text can overlook the crucial process *of* functionalization within the narrative. As we can see in James's preface, novelists are often aware of, and can deliberately heighten, tensions between their interest in a character as a fictive individual and this character's reduction to, or compression within, a functional narrative role. The attempt to circumscribe a character within his or her delimited functionality is always potentially problematic—human beings take up more weight than they fill in this limited role, and it is difficult to separate their exterior function from their interior singularity. How can a human being enter into a narrative world and *not* disrupt the distribution of attention? Such a question might be the axiom of this entire study.

Function itself takes on new social meaning in nineteenth-century Europe, as industrialization and economic stratification harden a division of labor that constricts full human beings to increasingly specialized roles. Such specialization underlies both the engulfing and the exploding of minor characters, the worker and the eccentric, as both conditions result from the disjunction of (exterior) surface and (interior) depth. We have seen how James calls the delimited participation of subordinate characters in the protagonist's story the "work of other hands." In *The German Ideology*, Karl Marx draws a relationship between "utility" and individuality that casts light on the poetics of fictional characterization that emerges in the realist era. Marx attacks utilitarianism as an ideology that converts people, and the lived experience of social interaction, into functions, or the abstract expression of utility:

> The apparent stupidity of merging all the manifold relationships of people in the one relation of usefulness, this apparently metaphysical abstraction arises from the fact that, in modern bourgeois society, all relations are subordinated in practice to the one abstract monetary-commercial relation. . . . In Holbach, all the activity of individuals in their mutual intercourse, e.g. speech, love, etc. is depicted as a relation of utility and utilization. Hence the actual relations that are presupposed here are speech, love, the definite manifestations of definite qualities of individuals. Now these relations are supposed not to have the meaning peculiar to them but to be the expression and manifestation of some third relation introduced in their place, the relation of utility or utilization. . . . [O]ne sees at a glance that the category of "utilization" is first of all abstracted from the actual relations of intercourse which I have with other people (but by no means from reflection and mere will) and then these relations are made out to be the reality of the category that has been extracted from them themselves, in a wholly metaphysical method of procedure. (185)

In a similar way, the functionalization of minor characters effaces "the definite manifestations of definite qualities of individuals" (or what Watt labels "particular individuals having particular experiences at particular times and at particular places") and abstracts these qualities so that they lose *the meaning peculiar to them.*" The quality that has been extracted from lived experience is then turned into a category within which concrete, material relations are subsumed: "these relations are made out to be the reality of the category that has been extracted from them themselves."

The nineteenth-century novel's configuration of *narrative* work—within the context of omniscient, asymmetric character-systems—creates a formal structure that can imaginatively comprehend the dynamics of alienated labor, and the class structure that underlies this labor. In terms of their essential formal position (the subordinate beings who are delimited in themselves while performing a function for someone else), *minor characters are the proletariat of the novel*; and the realist novel—with its intense class-consciousness and attention toward social inequality—makes much use of such formal processes. A condensed, stylized enactment of this relationship between minorness and alienation—not in terms of an entire narrative, but rather in a single sentence—appears early in Proust's *Du côté de chez Swann*. The narrator in Combray is describing his grandmother's habit of walking in the garden:

> Elle disait: "Enfin, on respire!" et parcourait les allées détrempées—trop symétriquement alignées à son gré par le nouveau jardinier dépourvu du sentiment de la nature et auquel mon père avait demandé depuis le matin si le temps s'arrangerait—de son petit pas enthousiaste et saccadé, réglé sur les mouvements divers qu'excitaient dans son âme l'ivresse de l'orage, la puissance de l'hygiène, la stupidité de mon éducation

et la symétrie des jardins, plutôt que sur le désir inconnu d'elle d'éviter à sa jupe prune les taches de boue sous lesquelles elle disparaissait jusqu'à une hauteur qui était toujours pour sa femme de chambre un désespoir et un problème. (104)

[She would say, "At last one can breathe!" and would run up and down the soaking paths—too straight and symmetrical for her liking, owing to the want of any feeling for nature in the new gardener, whom my father had been asking all morning if the weather was going to improve—with her keen jerky little steps regulated by the various effects wrought upon her soul by the intoxication of the storm, the force of hygiene, the stupidity of my education and the symmetry of gardens, rather than by any anxiety (for that was quite unknown to her) to save her plum-coloured skirt from the spots of mud under which it would gradually disappear to a depth which always provided her maid with a problem and filled her with despair.][20]

In many ways, this distended sentence is emblematic of Proust's radically modern novelistic style. The density of the language interrupts our direct comprehension of what it describes, so that the sentence references the (fictional) writing subject more than the objects that he writes about. We should not, however, read the Proustian bulge simply as a reversal of realistic poetics: away from the observed object toward the observing subject, away from exterior description toward interior apprehension. The sentence's distention, I would argue, registers its problematic incorporation of two minor characters: the gardener, who extends the main ellipses in the sentence, and the maid, who adds on the final (and thus most disruptive) subordinate clause. The gardener and the maid are here the mechanisms for two of Proust's most essential stylistic devices: interruption and extension. Rereading the passage without these two clauses, we can see that the maid and the gardener lie *behind* this sentence's difficulty. The distorted syntax is caused, in both cases, by an inability to accommodate these peripheral characters within the normal flow of a sentence. Once again, if only through the contortion of its form, the passage conveys the elided consciousness, the compelling "case" of these characters. More specifically, the distended sentence leads us obliquely but inexorably to the basic dehumanizing structure of labor exchange. The servant disappears into his or her labor, is manifested only through a subordinate clause—an afterthought that considers the cause or result of a more central action. The grandmother's walk through the garden catalyzes these kinds of afterthoughts—who made the garden path prior to the walk? who cleans up the muddied dress after the walk?—until these afterthoughts, which are made manifest in the crevices and corners of the sentence, build up into the Proustian bulge.

For Marx, utilitarianism's theft of experience—which is a purely conceptual theft—results from the actual expropriation of the labor-power of the many by the few.[21] If exploitation directly extracts the worker's lived experience in an alien form, utilization abstractly engulfs the specificity of human experience into the generalized categories that it derives out of this experience. (As utiliza-

tion covers over the exploitation that inheres in the social structure, so charac-
ter-function effaces the narrative subordination that produces minor characters.) Marx then notes, however, that from the standpoint of the bourgeoisie,
utilization is not the destruction of lived experience but, on the contrary, the
condition for the development of the free human being, for the *bildungs* project
itself: "Holbach's theory is the historically justified philosophical illusion
about the bourgeoisie just then developing in France, whose thirst for exploitation could still be described as a thirst for the full development of individuals
in conditions of intercourse freed from the old feudal fetters. Liberation from
the standpoint of the bourgeoisie, i.e. competition, was, of course, for the 18th
century the only possible way of offering the individuals a new career for free
development" (186). Utility both expresses the structural contingency of the
bourgeoisie—in relationship to the exploitation of other human individuals—
and facilitates the "full development of individuals." Similarly, in the bildungsroman—the genre most essential to the development of the novelistic protagonist—the hero's progress is facilitated through a series of interactions with
delimited minor characters. Each encounter has a particular psychological
function within the interior development of the young protagonist, as minor
characters stand for particular states of mind, or psychological modes, that the
protagonist interacts with and transcends. In a novel like *Wilhelm Meister's
Apprenticeship* the free, full development of the central protagonist is contingent on the utilization, and delimitation, of minor characters (most notably
Werner, Mignon, and Philine). Georg Lukács thus notes how Wilhelm's development into a coherently integrated human being takes place through a dialectical interaction with other characters' "specialized" extremes:

> In this work Goethe depicts a whole tangle of individual lives which interweave with
> one another. He depicts those who, guilty or not, are tragically ruined; he portrays
> persons whose life dissolves into nothingness; he draws characters in whom the spe-
> cialization, brought about by the capitalist division of labour, ossifies one feature of
> their personality to the point of caricature, leaving the rest of their humanity to atro-
> phy completely. . . . The persons in this novel are grouped almost exclusively around
> the struggle for the ideal of humanism, around the problem of two false extremes:
> enrapturement and practicality. (*Goethe and His Age*, 55)

The bildungsroman organizes the novel's two modes of characterization, the
interior protagonist and the distorted minor character (whether eccentric and
"enraptured" or functional and overly "practical"), into a coherent and compelling whole. Franco Moretti has argued that the figure of the developing youth
that becomes the new locus of heroism in the nineteenth-century bildungsroman is a way to imaginatively comprehend and mediate the dynamics and
tensions of social mobility.[22] The asymmetric character-system allows the
novel to juxtapose this development with the conjoined processes of social
stratification. Structures of characterization that lock together protagonist and

minor character allow the realist novel to comprehend a relationship between the full, interior individual (the "ideal of humanism") and social disjunction. Thus E. M. Forster, disputing the claim that an overly flat character "falsifies life," insists on a larger *structure* of characterization that is mimetically significant: "[A] novel that is at all complex often *requires* flat people as well as round, and the outcome of their *collisions* parallels life more accurately than Mr. Douglas implies" (108, emphases added). Or as Dickens thematically brings together Forster's narrative model and Marx's social one: "It was a rude shock to his sense of property in his child, that these people—the mere dust of the earth, as he thought of them—should be *necessary* to him" (*Dombey and Son*, 70, emphasis added).

Realism, Democracy, and Inequality

> If we had a keen vision for all ordinary human life, it would be like hearing the grass grow and the squirrel's heart beat, and we would die of that roar which lies on the other side of silence.
> —George Eliot, *Middlemarch*

This study, like any analysis of genre, is located at an imprecise juncture between form and history: constructing a conceptual model for characterization within narrative poetics and analyzing a specific sequence of literary-historical circumstances. It would be a mistake to delimit the idea of "character-space" and "character-system" to the nineteenth-century European novel, even though the significance of narrative minorness, and the social and literary meaning of functionality, develop in specific ways in this period and place. I would instead suggest that the dynamics of distribution—and the tension between structure and reference that emerges in, and formulates, distribution—is inherent to narrativity as formal process. The specific focus on nineteenth-century fiction, however, is not a retreat from the consideration of this formal practice in its most essential dimensions, since the realist novel gives us a precise image or rendering of how this mode of narrative signification can function and become legible. The inclusive aesthetics of the nineteenth-century realist tradition— with its dual impulses to bring in a multitude of characters and to bring out the interiority of a singular protagonist—illuminates particularly well the tension between the structural and referential axes of characterization. The making of minor characters opens onto rich aspects of nineteenth-century fictions and social forms, and a concerted analysis of nineteenth-century fiction can highlight and elucidate a narrative process that is quite relevant to a broad spectrum of literature as well as to pictorial and cinematic art.[23]

I want to explore, more specifically, the relationship between what I will call an asymmetric structure of characterization—in which many are repre-

sented but attention flows toward a delimited center—and the nineteenth-century comprehension of social stratification. The dynamic interaction between flatness and roundness identified by Forster facilitates social realism's dual focus on psychological depth and social expansiveness. It also registers the competing pull of inequality and democracy within the nineteenth-century bourgeois imagination. In my reading of the realist aesthetic, a dialectical literary form is generated out of the relationship between inequality and democracy. The realist novel is infused with the sense that any character is a potential hero, but simultaneously enchanted with the freestanding individual, defined through his or her interior consciousness. In the paradigmatic character-structure of the realist novel, any character *can* be a protagonist, but only one character is: just as increasing political equality, and a maturing logic of human rights, develop amid acute economic and social stratification.[24] On the one hand, the asymmetric structure of realist characterization—which rounds out one or several characters while flattening, and distorting, a manifold assortment of characters—reflects actual structures of inequitable distribution. On the other hand, the *claims* of minor characters on the reader's attention—and the resultant tension between characters and their functions—are generated by the democratic impulse that forms a horizon of nineteenth-century politics. As C. B. Macpherson, writing about England, argues, "The extent and genuineness of the franchise became the central question because, by the early nineteenth-century in England, theorists were able to take for granted the rest of the framework of representative government: the constitutional provisions whereby legislatures and executives were periodically chosen, and therefore periodically replaceable, by the voters at general elections, and whereby the civil service (and the military) were subordinate to a government thus responsible to the electorate" (34).

Middlemarch—famously lodged between the era of the First Reform Bill (when it is set) and the Second Reform Bill (when it is written), two flashpoints in the struggle over the franchise's "extent and genuineness"—provides a magisterial example of the connection between the question of democracy and the distributed field of characterization. *Middlemarch*'s remarkable character-system achieves a precarious balance between different patterns of distribution. It can be read in terms of a singular protagonist (Dorothea), a pair of co-protagonists (including Lydgate), a series of principal characters (including Mary and Fred, Will, Rosamond, Casaubon, and Bulstrode) or a manifold group of characters, extending from principals to nearly anonymous figures, who all compete for attention within the narrative web. Eliot's desire to preserve a singular protagonist *and* to extend narrative attention to a broad mass of characters evocatively parallels John Stuart Mill's strange compromise position on universal suffrage, which idealistically insists on democratic principles (both morally and politically) *and* tries to preserve basic structures of class privilege. Mill imagines a franchise that is both stratified and universal: all citizens would receive voting power but to unequal degrees, just as *Middlemarch* includes many characters, while configuring them in various ways:

> First, then, in every system of representation which can be conceived as perfect, every adult human being, it appears to me, would have the means of exercising, through the electoral suffrage, a portion of influence on the management of public affairs. . . . But ought every one to have an *equal* voice? This is a totally different proposition; and in my judgment as palpably false, as the other is true and important. . . . If every ordinary unskilled labourer had one vote, a skilled labourer, whose occupation requires an exercised mind and a knowledge of some of the laws of external nature, ought to have two. A foreman, or superintendent of labour, whose occupation requires something more of general culture, and some moral as well as intellectual qualities, should perhaps have three. A farmer, manufacturer or trader, who requires a still larger range of ideas and knowledge, and the power of guiding and attending to a great number of various operations at once, should have three or four. A member of any profession requiring a long, accurate, and systematic mental cultivation—a lawyer, a physician, or surgeon, a clergyman . . . ought to have five or six. (322 and 324)

Middlemarch's intricate balances between protagonist and minor characters call into question, without repudiating, an asymmetric norm that had become an essential aspect of nineteenth-century omniscient narrative. This ambivalence is also conveyed in the Eliot epigraph to this section, which simultaneously registers the imperative to look at the masses of "ordinary life" and anxiously worries that the sight might be too much. In its hostility and its sympathy toward the ordinary life that, by being silenced, can only take the form of a roar, Eliot's passage captures the peculiar extremes of the realist imagination, caught between idealism and anxiety, between including and distorting minor characters, in the double pull of democracy and inequality.

Austen, Dickens, Balzac: Character-Space in the Nineteenth-Century Novel

"Only connect." It is of course the case that the nineteenth-century novel contains a greater quantity of characters than most previous literature—a huge variety of individuals who get crowded together into a single story. The omniscient totality of the nineteenth-century novel compels us to "connect" these individuals—to comprehend forms of social relation which can encompass the diverse populations that people these novels. By character-system, however, I don't mean the interlocking of a number of distinct fictional individuals within a narrative totality but rather the combination of different character-spaces or of various modes *through which* specific human figures are inflected into the narrative. The nineteenth-century novel also compels us to "connect" these often widely disparate character-spaces or modes *of* characterizing. We might think here of such complicated, rich, and varied character-systems as those we find in *Madame Bovary* or *Moby Dick*: these novels contain both a multitude of distinct individuals who are co-implicated within the story and a multitude of individuals who are *distinctively configured and positioned* within the novel as a whole. The integration of these varied modes of characterization into unified structures is a massive achievement of the nineteenth-century literary imagination. In novels like *Madame Bovary* or *Moby Dick*—or *Crime and Punishment*, or *Anna Karenina*—we need both to coordinate the large list of characters and to consider how each individual character-space is combined and differentially refracted through the narrative structure. The realist character-system is always oriented in two directions: toward each uniquely delineated character-space (and the implied human figure that it amplifies or obscures) *and* toward the unified structure, the symbolic or thematic edifice, the interconnected plot that is being constructed through—and often helping to delimit or distort—these character-spaces.

It is for this reason that I've concentrated on several novelists, and several novels, rather than a wider range of materials: precisely to show that attention to minor characters doesn't serve merely to disperse analysis centrifugally. In fact, almost every nineteenth-century novel is informed by the problematics of character-space: both in terms of the particular elaboration of a "hero" or central protagonist and in the inflection of inevitable (and often numerous) secondary figures. Furthermore, many novels offer interesting variations on these problems—both in the ironization of centrality (through an unconventional choice of protagonist or the dispersion of the major role into two, three, or four dominant figures) and in the innovative configuration, compression, or utilization of minor characters (through particularly compelling subordinate figures or in the organization of the overall character field). The problematics of distribution are at work in the genre as a whole, intersecting in countless ways with stylistic, structural, thematic, ideological, and sociohistorical dimensions of various nineteenth-century fictions. I have focused on some of those novels that best elucidate the very grounds of this problem: novels that confront key questions in characterization, offer new formulations of character, and elaborate the problematic of distribution *within* the fictional world itself.

My first chapter, an inductive analysis of *Pride and Prejudice*, attempts to formulate (rather than apply) the theory I have been discussing. The chapter temporarily puts aside the conceptual terms sketched in this introduction—the dual lenses of character-space and character-system—in order to gradually bring out these terms from within the aesthetic workings of the novel.[25] Crucially, I will offer a reading of the novel as a whole—in terms of both its entire diachronic progression and its full range of characterization. At the origin of both these planes—at the *beginning* of the story and at the *center* of its web of characters—are the five Bennet sisters, who share a single narrative situation:

an entailed estate that necessitates their entering into the competition among many women for a limited amount of wealth. This competition grounds the persistent nuance, and discrimination, of Austen's ironic voice. Ironic and omniscient, the narrator configures the five sisters' central situation into an asymmetrical structure, developing Elizabeth Bennet into a strong, central protagonist and making Lydia, Catherine, Mary, and Jane into different kinds of minor characters. Elizabeth's centrality emerges only in dynamic interaction with the development of these (and other) minor characters, so that the narrative price of her achieved interiority is the distortion of many other human figures.

My reading of *Pride and Prejudice* stands, in turn, at the origin of this study's two planes: at the center of my formal model and at the beginning of my historic analysis. On the one hand, my reading reveals the distributional matrix as it generates the two essential modes of realist characterization: a strong, rounded, fully realized central protagonist and a manifold group of delimited, "specialized" minor characters. At the same time, the tightly organized narrative structure of Austen's fiction suggests a new kind of novelistic coherence in which each part of the narrative—whether character, episode, or word—is integral to, and has a specific and contextualized position within, the fiction as a whole. The kind of novelistic coherence that Austen achieves has often been looked at apart from the social dynamics of her realist fiction. In fact, the closed formal structure of Austen's narrative fiction (relying, among other elements, on the impersonality of the omniscient narrator) suggests a radical interconnection between the two modes of character that the novels formulate, opening new horizons for social realism. The moral force of *Pride and Prejudice* has been traditionally located within Elizabeth Bennet's "full development." I will argue that it rests equally in the novel's refusal to stay *within* Elizabeth's development, in its insistence on showing how the protagonist's development rests on top of a system of utilization which fragments the fictional universe that surrounds her. In this sense the moral vision comes in the most negative form.

The critique implicit in the structure of characterization that Austen originates becomes more realized as the omniscient novel develops, even as the processes of competition and stratification that quietly underlie the enclosed social world (and stratified narrative system) of *Pride and Prejudice* get more directly represented. Later novelists write within the framework of asymmetry that Austen so successfully constructs while often straining, in various ways, to make more of minor characters. This effort can take many forms. I have already mentioned George Eliot's combination of a morally voluble omniscient voice and intricate narrative webs that link together many minor characters. A novel like Elizabeth Gaskell's *Mary Barton* (or, in a different sense, Zola's *Germinal*) tries to extend the parameters of character *topically*, through a focus on working-class individuals (who would traditionally appear only *as* minor characters), while in many ways preserving an asymmetric *form*.

Wilkie Collins's development of a perspectival narrative system—where our most basic comprehension of the story requires active concatenation of various, stratified narrative voices—is another, entirely different reworking of the tensions of asymmetry. In fact, the arrangement of protagonist and minor characters—within the story and the discourse—is a problem that almost any novel in this period must work through, becoming an essential field of narrative signification.

My study concentrates on Dickens and Balzac, the two novelists who make the most significant, and most imaginatively realized, contributions to the enlargement of the realist novel's franchise. Both novelists make more of minor characters, in radically different ways. Dickens's panoply of eccentrics and grotesques brings minor characters to the center of his novels by *increasing* their distortion. Balzac, in an attempt to give every character potential roundness, bursts apart the seams of *La Comédie humaine*, creating one vast and interconnected narrative universe. Chapter 2 breaks from analysis of a single narrative structure to examine Dickens's descriptive strategies as they manifest themselves in characters across different novels, from *The Pickwick Papers* to *Our Mutual Friend*. This follows from the logic of Dickens's own narrative organization, as his texts free minor characters from a structural position and concentrate their effect in the descriptive configuration itself. I consider *why* Dickens's characterization often de-emphasizes structure while overemphasizing local affect. The result is a more immediate historicity than Austen's: immediate in the sense that Dickens, time and again, makes direct and vivid links between a minor character's distortion and his or her subordination; but also in the sense that he is disinclined to pull back *from* these effects to dynamically represent the structures that produce such subordination. In chapter 3, I shift this analysis of Dickens's descriptive poetics to an interpretation of a single narrative, offering a close reading of *Great Expectations*, which, as in chapter 1, attempts to understand the character-system as a totality. While *Pride and Prejudice* features a strong protagonist, the intensity and vigor of whose personality seems to almost compel minorness all around her, *Great Expectations* features a weak protagonist, overwhelmed on all sides by various kinds of minor characters. With its child-protagonist who is also an adult narrator, *Great Expectations* gives concrete form to the narrative process that underlies all of Dickens's work: the central, but passive, protagonist who encounters the powerful, but distorted, minor character. Dickens subtly and intricately links this structure of characterization to the modern economic and social relations that extinguish Pip's expectations.

The very structure of Balzac's *La Comédie humaine* dramatically registers the problem of minor characters, and characterization, that this study concentrates on. The elephantine scope of *La Comédie* can be diagnosed, in one sense, as the price a novel must pay to avoid making certain characters minor. Rejecting a single closed narrative, Balzac develops a system of recurring characters and interconnected novels: we are always aware that a secondary character in one novel might become the protagonist in another. Tracing the strategy of narrative interconnection to the novel in which it originates, I analyze how *Le Père Goriot* also revolves around the complexities of *social* interconnection in a capitalist system, figured through the overlaid stories of the *pensionnaires* at the Maison Vauquer and directly embodied in Rastignac's youthful insecurity and ambition.

Le Père Goriot features neither a weak nor a strong protagonist but two competing co-protagonists. The three main novels in this study—*Pride and Prejudice*, *Great Expectations*, *Le Père Goriot*—thus illustrate three different and essential kinds of asymmetric narrative. These variations are not exhaustive, in the sense that they establish the bounds of the realist character-system, but, on the contrary, are meant to suggest how the process of permutation itself is a central aspect of character-system. If any character-system contains a constellation of intersecting and simultaneously unfolding character-spaces (minorness, after all, is partially developed *as* the attention rests on other figures), the character-system itself unfolds against the horizon of other possible configurations—not just configurations hypothetically or implicitly suggested within the narrative but achieved configurations forming the intertextual and generic conventions that any particular structural presentation of character is set against.[26] This kind of literary history is particularly relevant to *Le Père Goriot*, as the eponymous character's claim for centrality is intertwined with what is probably Balzac's most famous literary allusion: Goriot as an ironic version of King Lear. Examining the competing character-spaces of Rastignac and Goriot allows for, and indeed demands, a new interpretation of this ironic intertextuality, as the character-system of *King Lear*, with its radically centered protagonist, is the ground from which the permutation of *Le Père Goriot* departs.

The competition between Rastignac and Goriot—not as individuals within the story but in their discursive status *as* protagonists—is at the heart of *Le Père Goriot*'s character-system, and, in this sense, at the center of the interconnected narratives of *La Comédie humaine* (which are conceived *as* a totality in the writing of *Le Père Goriot*). I analyze the narrative rift that this competition between character-spaces creates in relation both to Balzac's powerful representation of social competition and to the poetics of characterization (the recurring personage, the social "type") that underlies his fictional project. This competition is essential to *Le Père Goriot* but perhaps more explicitly apparent in *Les Employés*, a relatively unremarked "scene from Parisian life" that is noteworthy for the number of dull, delimited characters it incorporates into the story. The problem of distributing attention to different characters—which literally threatens to turn this minor novel into disconnected theatrical scenes and social tableaux—is dramatized in the ruthless competition between the able protagonist, Rabourdin, and an incompetent coworker for a government promotion. And this personal competition—between two characters for one position—is intertwined with Rabourdin's attempt to transform the bureaucratic *structure*, as it generates a dispersed, and destructive, field of competition. A chapter heading of *Les Employés* thus offers the title for this chapter, but its question—"A qui la place?" (i.e., who gets the position?)—can apply back to *Le Père Goriot*, now not in terms of interacting characters (within the competitive world of Paris) but in terms of intersecting character-spaces (within the narrative discourse). After tracing *Le Père Goriot*'s character-system (which will shape the contours of the entire *Comédie*), I bring the two novels together around this question—reading the story of *Les Employés* through the discursive competition in *Le Père Goriot*, and the structure of *Le Père Goriot* through the bureaucratic competition that forms the narrative and thematic center of *Les Employés*.

The Minor Character: Between Story and Discourse

At first glance the interpretation of minor characters might seem to be nothing else than a repudiation of the text's own hierarchy of value, bringing to the critical foreground what has been subordinated to the narrative background. But how do we come to have this term "minor character" in the first place? The very occasion of the category suggests some dissonance between the character's delimited role and more extended impact. If "minor characters" were *literally* minor in the normative sense of this word—"Comparatively small or unimportant; not to be reckoned among the greater or principal individuals of the kind" (*Oxford English Dictionary*)—the term itself would never have been formulated or deployed so often in literary criticism and evaluation.

Minor characters exist *as* a category, then, only because of their strange centrality to so many texts, perhaps to narrative signification itself. But this is not to say that once we acknowledge the significance of the minor character, he suddenly becomes major, breaking out of his subordinate position in the narrative discourse. This would be to elide the very source through which the minor character signifies—and is made significant to the reader who strangely remembers. In one sense, certainly, the minor character stands out because the writer has done a lot with a little: illuminated that one scene, those few lines, that one pivotal moment in which the character appears. Or, in E. M. Forster's terms, lit upon that one memorable gesture.[27] (We can think here, for example, of Mercutio in *Romeo and Juliet*: the brevity of his life and his compressed space within the play seem to flow into the intensity and pressure of his language, producing that energy which catapults him right out of the plot.) But the minor character's interesting distinction cannot be based simply on the brief moment during which he stands out; in fact, it is precisely the opposite. The minor character is always drowned out within the totality of the narrative; and what we remember about the character is never detached from how the text, for the most part, makes us forget him. (Otherwise the minor character emerges only out of the *wreck* of the text as a whole, like the single gifted actor in a poor production, whose very talent calls our attention to the shoddiness of the show.)

The strange significance of minor characters, in other words, resides largely in the way that the character disappears, and in the tension or relief that results from this vanishing. These feelings are often solicited by the narrative, and it is the disappearance of the minor character (for *every* minor character does— by strict definition—disappear) that, finally, is integrated into his or her interesting speech or memorable gesture. We feel interest and outrage, painful concern or amused consent at what happens to minor characters: not simply their fate within the story (whether they marry or die, make their fortune or lose it, find a home or become exiled) but also in the narrative discourse itself (how they are finally overshadowed or absorbed into someone else's story, swallowed within or expelled from another person's plot).

This is simply, once again, to locate the minor character at the junction between implied person and narrative form, to read characterization in terms of the tension that narrative continually elicits between an individual who claims our interest and a fictional totality that forces this individual out of, or beneath, the discursive world. In this sense, the minor character, by calling attention to character-space, helps establish the relationship of "story" and "discourse"—the events in the novel and the rendition of these events in the narrative itself. The distinction between "story" and "discourse" is at the very crux of the interpretation of narrative and goes by many names: the tale and the telling; *histoire* and *discours*; *sjuzet* and *fabula*.[28] All these dichotomous terms refer, finally, to the essentially divided nature of the literary text, as it is torn between form and content; between the signified and the signifier; between the text's linguistic world—words, sentences, chapters—and the imagined world that we grasp at through the text. Discourse points us to the narrative's actual language and structure; story to the fictional events that we reconstruct through the narrative, to "the narrated events, abstracted from their disposition in the text and reconstructed in their chronological order, together with the participants in these events."[29]

The character-space provides a new framework through which we can apprehend an important mode of signification that is produced—like most narrative meaning—in the intersection of story and discourse. My specific employment of these terms is illustrated in passages from *Vanity Fair* and *Mansfield Park* where we see the same process, a subordinate character becoming so minor she is expelled from the novel, on these two different registers:

> But why speak about her? It is probable that we shall not hear of her again from this moment to the end of time, and that when the great filigree iron gates are once closed on her, she and her awful sister will never issue therefrom into this little world of history. (4)

> It ended in Mrs. Norris's resolving to quit Mansfield, and devote herself to her unfortunate Maria, and in an establishment being formed for them in another country—remote and private, where shut up together with little society, on one side no affection, on the other, no judgment, it may be reasonably supposed that their tempers became their mutual punishment. . . . She was regretted by no one at Mansfield. . . . Not even Fanny had tears for aunt Norris—not even when she was gone forever. (465)

In the first example, Jemima Pinkerton disappears from the narrative discourse, while in Austen's novel Mrs. Norris disappears from an imagined space within the story itself. And yet the two passages resonate with each other, employing the same spatial and temporal imagery. Thackeray's image of "the great filigree iron gates" that close on Jemima resembles the way Mrs. Norris and Maria end up "remote and private . . . shut up together." And Thackeray's admonishment that "she will *never* issue . . . into this little world of history" conveys the same finality as Austen's "even when she was gone *forever*." Such a conflation indicates a narrative process that flows smoothly from the imagined world into the narrative's discursive structure. The character-space always arises at the intersection of story and discourse.

We can see both kinds of expulsion densely intertwined in a third minor character, the crucial but marginal Bulkington in *Moby Dick*. If a minor character becomes significant only as he disappears, Bulkington quite literally vanishes (in the story itself), capturing attention precisely as he departs:

> I observed, however, that one of them held somewhat aloof, and though he seemed desirous not to spoil the hilarity of his shipmates by his own sober face, yet upon the whole he refrained from making as much noise as the rest. This man interested me at once; and since the sea-gods had ordained that he should soon become my shipmate (*though but a sleeping-partner one, so far as this narrative is concerned*), I will here venture upon a little description of him. . . . When the revelry of his companions had mounted to its height, *this man slipped away unobserved*, and I saw no more of him till he became my comrade on the sea. In a few minutes, however, he was missed by his shipmates, and, being, it seems, for some reason, a huge favorite with them, they raised a cry of "Bulkington! where's Bulkington?" and darted out of the house in pursuit of him. (23)

So big, but so anonymous: Bulkington becomes prominent only as he enters into obscurity, after he has "slipped away unobserved." And just as Bulkington, within the story, registers on his shipmates' consciousness only as he vanishes from them, so his subordination in the *discourse* will confer an important symbolic function on him. The narrator thus goes out of his way to note that Bulkington will be on board the ship *for the entire story* only to warn us that he will be "but a sleeping-partner . . . , so far as this narrative is concerned."[30]

The oversize Bulkington's disappearance, in both story and discourse, dramatizes how narrative subordination always involves some degree of vanishing. The minor character rests in the shadow-space between narrative position and human personality: an implied human being who gets constricted into a delimited role, but who has enough resonance *with* a human being to make us aware of this constricted position *as* delimited. The strange resonance of minor characters—the way that we so often come away from a novel, a drama, or a film remembering a marginal player, a side story, a fate only faintly illuminated or etched—stems from the intricacy of this narrative process; from the character who is *not* directly or fully represented in the narrative, and who comes to command a peculiar kind of attention in the partial occlusion of his fullness.

We could contrast this with Wayne Booth's meditation on narrative "fairness":

> Even among characters of equal moral, intellectual, or aesthetic worth, all authors inevitably take sides. A given work will be "about" a character or set of characters. It cannot possibly give equal emphasis to all, regardless of what its author believes about the desirability of fairness. *Hamlet* is not fair to Claudius. . . . But who cares? The novelist who chooses to tell this story cannot at the same time tell that story; in centering our interest, sympathy, or affection on one character, he inevitably excludes from our interest, sympathy, or affection some other character. (78–79)

Booth makes an acute observation here, only to retreat from the implication of his insight for fear of wrenching the text away from the author's own intention. But to contemplate and seek to externalize submerged perspectives within a narrative does not always mean reading against the text's own artistic organization. Couldn't one argue, in fact, that precisely the possibility of *telling more than one story at the same time* rests near the center of literary narrative as such? Novelists cannot "possibly give equal emphasis to all" characters; but narratives certainly do call attention to the process of emphasizing and the problems of "stinting" (to use Chaucer's term)—constantly suggesting how other possible stories, and other people's full lives, are intertwined with and obscured by the main focus of attention.

Booth's analysis, in other words, cuts short the generative tension between story and discourse: seeking to confirm the constructed achievement of the narrative design, he too quickly wards off a crucial way that narrative does signify. The distribution of attention to different characters, unfolding only through the intersection and entwinement of story and discourse, always generates a rich double vision: we have two superimposed patterns or arrangements that will rarely overlap or coincide and will frequently, and to great effect, diverge significantly. On the one hand, we have the polycentric arrangement of the story, the plot that pulls in many different individuals, each of whom has a unique (perhaps unelaborated) experience within the story and a unique (perhaps submerged) perspective on the story. On the other hand, we have the single, delimited, finite, and particular shaping of this story into a fixed discourse, the actual discourse that arranges such characters in a specific way. Here, the tendency is always away from a polycentric, or symmetrical, distribution, toward various forms of imbalance: all the characters still retain some position in the narrative discourse (else we could never place them in the story at all), but these are radically differentiated.

Neither one of these arrangements or narrative shapes has meaning exclusive of the other. To read characters in narrative, we need to read the dialectical tension between the formed distribution of attention within the discourse and the potential patterning of distribution within the story. This is far from a prescriptive aesthetics. I am not arguing that we need to assume a radical equality between all characters in a novel, and that, through this "proper" arrangement of how the story should be told, we can reinterpret narrative history, bending discourses formed in asymmetrical ways into a new, more symmetrical shape. This would mean that we begin with a "story" that is at a far remove from the text itself, and seek to impose this story back onto a narrative with an utterly different shape. Rather, I am arguing that narratives themselves allow and solicit us to construct a story—a distributed pattern of attention—that is at odds with, or divergent from, the formed pattern of attention in the discourse. This strikes near the essential openness of the literary text. The literary text solicits reinterpretation; it creates disjunctions between story and discourse that facilitate the production of meaning, the production of significance. It creates, more specifically, disjunctions between the attention the discourse grants certain characters and the attention that they would grant themselves and that the reader might grant them. This process takes a particularly acute and meaningful form in the nineteenth-century realist novel, with its complicated networks of characters, its varied techniques for registering the pull and possibility of interior consciousness, and its wide range of narrative structures that enact and represent both the premises of democratic equality and the pressures and consequences of social stratification.

This gives a more integrated perspective on the problem of narrative "fairness": a problem that is hard to grapple with because it remains so enmeshed within the tangled thicket of aesthetics, ideology, and ethics. We don't need to always choose between either admiring a text for the way it gives a character voice (by registering his or her perspective, point of view, and interior thoughts) or, in what clearly prompts Booth's frustration, attacking a text for unfairly excluding a character's voice. Frequently the character-system is more intricate than this, powerfully inscribing the very absence of voice that the distributional system produces. The minor character—that roundness squared to a sharp edge, that appearance of a disappearance—is so successful as a narrative type in precisely this way, as he enfolds the untold tale into the telling.

Chapter One

Narrative Asymmetry in *Pride and Prejudice*

Minor Characters in a Narrative Structure

Critics have always noted the presence of flat characters in Jane Austen's oeu-vre—and *Pride and Prejudice* particularly—but they have rarely insisted on analyzing this flatness. On the contrary, the distinction between flat and round characters helps *facilitate* critical analysis—by opening up a rich series of thematic antitheses—but is rarely subject to interrogation itself. Mary Craw-ford and Fanny Price; Emma Woodhouse and Jane Fairfax; or, in *Pride and Prejudice* itself, Collins against Wickham, Bingley against Darcy, Charlotte against Elizabeth, Mary and Lydia against each other: these oppositions are the grist that has kept the thematic mill running so strongly in Austen criticism for so many years. Critics, of course, use all sorts of characters in this way, but few characters—or character-groups—have proven themselves as useful as Austen's. To be a character in Austen is to get continually contrasted, juxta-posed, related to others, and, as such, to help build the thematic architecture that critics then discern. And if the weight of narrative signification seems to rest on all of these characters' backs, it is minor characters, in particular, who bear the heaviest portion: unequal partners in a dialectic that could not take place if attention were limited to the protagonist herself.

How does criticism respond to this multiplicity of persons who are so integral to the novels' thematic ambitions but who hold their place so strangely, and precariously, in the narrative world?[1] Most often readers have understood Aus-ten's flat characters as a reasonable imitation of actual life. If there are round and flat characters in Austen, this is an accurate representation of the real social universe—which has a few sympathetic people (always including the reader or critic him- or herself) and many simple and superficial people. For instance, Tony Tanner writes that "Elizabeth has a dimension of complexity, a questing awareness, a mental range and depth which almost make her an isolated figure trapped in a constricting web of a small number of simple people" (126). In this reading, minor characters such as Mary Bennet, Lydia Bennet, Mr. Collins, Mr. Wickham, *etc.*, are essentially verisimilar, and the novel is stocked with flat characters because there are so many "simple people" in real life.[2]

Other critics take an opposite tack, noting the way that Austen's minor char-acters are *clearly* distorted and, therefore, cannot be interpreted as the transpar-ent reflections of credible persons. For instance, D. W. Harding discusses a set of techniques that Austen uses again and again to effectuate caricature:

As a general rule attention is then concentrated on a few features or a small segment of the personality to the neglect of much that would make the figure a full human being, and the understanding is that the reader will accept this convention and not inquire too closely into the areas of behavior and personality that the author chooses to avoid. . . . [I]t works only because of an implicit agreement to ignore the greater part of any real personality in which the exaggerated features are embedded. (89)

Harding's comments invert the simple mimetic reading, but in both cases analysis of minor characters is cut off prematurely. Tanner's argument says, "Real people are actually like this"; Harding's says, "Well, they are not *supposed* to seem real" or "Obviously, no real people are actually like this." Both avoid analyzing narrative asymmetry itself: the dynamic narrative subordination of potentially full human beings.

To justify his model, Harding points to a "convention" that underlies the way we read, but does not provide any evidence for this shared "understanding," "rule," or "implicit agreement." What if we find that Austen's novels constantly, if subtly, call attention to the "areas of behavior and personality" that are distorted or effaced through characterization? How would a reading proceed that does "inquire . . . closely" into the "neglect[ed]" (and yet simultaneously "exaggerated") personality of minor flattened characters, not to bring into light what the "author chooses to avoid" but as these rejected potentialities and elided points of view also constitute part of the novel's achieved structure? In this chapter, I want to denaturalize asymmetry, using *Pride and Prejudice* to establish more general interpretive premises: both that many nineteenth-century novels sense the potential to shift the focus away from the established center, toward minor characters, and that novels often obliquely or emphatically represent this process, even while constructing strong distinctions between a central protagonist and a manifold field of minor characters. The more dynamic examples of asymmetric characterization do not simply represent these minor characters but represent characters *becoming* minor within a complex narrative system.

In a famous passage in *Middlemarch*, George Eliot criticizes precisely the reading model or "implicit agreement" to which Harding subscribes:

One morning, some weeks after her arrival at Lowick, Dorothea—but why always Dorothea? Was her point of view the only possible one with regard to this marriage? I protest against all our interest, all our effort at understanding being given to the young skins that look blooming in spite of trouble; for these too will get faded, and will know the older and more eating griefs which we are helping to neglect. In spite of the blinking eyes and white moles objectionable to Celia, and the want of muscular curve which was morally painful to Sir James, Mr. Casaubon had an intense consciousness within him, and was spiritually a-hungered like the rest of us. (253)

This passage argues for the approach I want to take to the realist novel, insisting that the balance between different kinds of characterization—and the asymmetrical space that different characters occupy within the novel—is relevant to the significance of the novel as a whole. The distributed pattern of characterization, Eliot suggests, is a dynamic narrative process that can be actively interrogated, rather than simply taken for granted. In other words, the question "why always Dorothea?" or Elizabeth Bennet, or Julien Sorel, is worth asking in the first place. This question, however, does not derive simply from a method of reading (Harding's convention or agreement) that we bring to bear on a text with its own, different concerns. Rather, I want to argue that the problem of distribution is motivated by, and emerges out of, the text's own mimetic and structural logic. In this sense, Eliot does not *impose* a moral problematic onto realist narration but rather theorizes or brings to the surface a dynamic literary process that has informed the realist novel all along.[3] Eliot's comment is an overt ethical intervention, certainly, but it also astutely identifies a literary structure, a central narrative procedure through which a literary text organizes itself.[4]

The question that Eliot asks is already profoundly elaborated—in its essential narrative and social dimensions—in Austen's early-nineteenth-century novels. The dynamic, asymmetrical balance between different characters—and between different modes of characterization—is not simply a thematic concern of Austen's novels, nor a moral or political question that we impose on the finished text, but rather a narrative process that is intertwined with, and unfurls out of, the novels' basic internal structure. This is most clear in *Pride and Prejudice*, because the tension between a protagonist who is interesting in-and-of-herself and minor characters who function only in relation to a central protagonist is dramatized through two competing registers of narrative attention: the five Bennet sisters *in general*, as a family unit faced with the same problem and attracting the same narrative interest, and Elizabeth Bennet *in particular*, the protagonist of the novel, who transcends the social context in which she has been placed to become the center of the narrative in-and-of-herself.

Pride and Prejudice has a peculiar double status within Austen's body of work. Many critics regard it as a less mature and perhaps less intricate novel than *Emma*, *Mansfield Park*, or *Persuasion*, but it is also the best-known and most canonically popular Austen text. It almost seems that *Pride and Prejudice* is *too* good a novel, partly because our awareness of its ingenious construction dilutes our engagement with the fictional universe that is depicted, producing a strange mixture of suspense and certainty. This exemplary narrative seems to hover on a border between novel and fairy tale: it is a fairy tale, perhaps, about the structure of "novelness" itself. *Pride and Prejudice* offers a paradigmatic marriage plot, a model of the omniscient narrator, the most exemplary of happy endings. Similarly, the development of Elizabeth's singularity in juxtaposition with her sisters' diminishing importance makes all of the characters memorable but is also a foundational example (and exploration) of a narrative structure. The fictional elaboration of the five sisters dramatizes the very tension of asymmetry, as much as the represented experiences of the story itself. This doesn't precisely make Elizabeth Bennet less interesting than subsequent protagonists Emma Woodhouse, Fanny Price, or Anne Elliot—each of whom has a very complicated position (and distinct kind of centrality) as the major figure within *Emma*, *Mansfield Park*, and *Persuasion*, respectively. On the contrary, it is the very strength of Austen's presentation of Elizabeth, the reader's sense that *this is exactly what it takes to be a novelistic protagonist*, that makes us aware of the text's constructedness and calls attention to Elizabeth's status *as* a protagonist, "the perfection of whose quality" (in Lionel Trilling's striking phrase) "needs no proof."[5] Like Stendhal's *Le Rouge et le noir*, *Pride and Prejudice* is a paradigm of the bildungsroman, not simply developing *a* young protagonist, but also developing *the protagonist* as an aesthetic construct. The "perfect qualities" of Elizabeth, as developing character, not only motivate but are ingeniously and inescapably ramified through her achieved centrality, as protagonist. And Austen's presentation of the protagonist qua protagonist is grounded in the novel's asymmetry.

To locate this asymmetry, we can ask a basic question: if *Pride and Prejudice* focuses on Elizabeth Bennet because she is the most interesting and complicated character, as most critics would argue, how do we account for the lingering presence of the other four Bennet sisters? It should not be immediately clear why these characters—depicted as much less interesting, less thoughtful, less cultured, and, ultimately, simply as *less*—have to be in the novel at all. Is it enough to say that the reason they are in the novel is, as Tony Tanner writes, to show "the relief with which an intricate person seeks out some solitude away from the miseries which can be caused by the constant company of more limited minds" (127)? Against the five Bennet sisters, we might compare the very limited role of Julien Sorel's two brothers in *Le Rouge et le noir*. When they are first described, Stendhal sets up precisely the same symbolic construction that Austen is at pains to establish in *Pride and Prejudice*:

> Approaching his mill, old Sorel yelled for Julien; nobody responded. He saw only his older sons, these hulking giants who, armed with heavy axes, were squaring off some trunks of pinewood which they were going to bring to the saw. Completely occupied with following exactly the black mark traced on the piece of wood, each blow of their axe separated enormous chunks of wood. . . . He looked vainly for Julien at the place where he should have been, on the side of the saw. He saw him five or six feet higher up, straddling one of the roof booms. Instead of attentively surveying all the workings of the machine, Julien was reading. Nothing was more distasteful to old Sorel: he could have pardoned Julien for his thin waist, little suited for physical work and so different from that of his older brothers, but that mania for reading was odious to him, since he didn't know how to read himself. (232)

This comic juxtaposition certainly dramatizes Julien's estrangement from his family and, more to the point, heightens our sense of his singularity by contrasting him with his two brothers. Thus the opening description of the protagonist emerges out of his juxtaposition with minor characters, as the details of Julien's own introduction are woven into, and become inseparable from, the overall configuration of the three brothers. The protagonist needs a contrast here in order to be fully individualized. Julien's singularity is symbolically thematized in the opposition between reading and mechanical repetition (thought and physical labor, consciousness and corporeality); literalized with his precarious perch "five or six feet higher up"; and then embodied in "his thin waist . . . so different from that of his older brothers." But having established this difference, and having shown the constraints that it imposes on Julien ("My brothers have always beaten me, don't believe them if they speak badly of me to you" [244]), the narrator, as much as Julien, is at pains to forget about these two "hulking giants" and get on with the center of interest—precisely, Julien himself.

In *Pride and Prejudice*, Elizabeth's sisters play a much more important role in the narrative, and it is more difficult to argue that they are there simply to represent the difficulty that they cause Elizabeth by being there. At the very least, Elizabeth's sisters—like Julien's two brothers—form the other pole of a semantic and symbolic field that is part of the novel's larger structure. Their role in the narrative cannot be assigned merely mimetic value—as the convincing representation of the "limited minds" that surround the protagonist—because they are also *used* by the narrative as points of signification within a dialectically charged symbolic field that revolves, as in *Le Rouge et le noir*, around the difference between thought and movement, depth and surface. But if their function in this larger semantic structure is simply to create a contrast with the more valorized symbolic register, it is still not clear why they are given such a central role. Julien's two brothers are just a passing motif within the symbolic elaboration of Julien's centrality; we could easily imagine Stendhal's novel (and Julien's character) without this little scene. Elizabeth's sisters are a continual presence in the novel: they are a constitutive part of the symbolic structure itself, despite, or, as I want to argue, because of their minorness. The combination of the sisters' continual subordination by the narrative *and* their resilient utility within it forces us to examine the logic behind a discursive system that repeatedly calls attention to persons, and modes of action, that it is interested only in dismissing, in order to elaborate a symbolic register that it is interested only in rejecting or destroying. In short, the sisters' importance on a thematic or structural level implies a logic that goes beyond—and in fact almost inverts—Tanner's model. In the story itself the sisters are, certainly, what Elizabeth needs to get away from in order to be her own singular self—but on the level of narrative discourse they are precisely what she needs to have around.

We can find an interesting enactment of this type of contradiction in the novel's ironic treatment of Lady Catherine's ridiculous snobbery. Lady Catherine's compulsive need to demonstrate her own superiority to those around her ends up making her comically dependent on the people whom she criticizes. Austen's harsh take on this master-slave relationship should make us wary of imposing Lady Catherine's problematic point of view onto the novel as a whole. From the start, the weakness of Lady Catherine's position—psychologically, morally, even politically—is revealed in the ironic way that her continual efforts to dismiss and belittle Mr. and Mrs. Collins, as well as Elizabeth herself when she visits Rosings, end up making her almost beholden to them:

> She enquired into Charlotte's domestic concerns familiarly and minutely, and gave her a great deal of advice, as to the management of them all; told her how every thing ought to be regulated in so small a family as her's, and instructed her as to the care of her cows and her poultry. Elizabeth found that nothing was beneath this great Lady's attention, which could furnish her with an occasion of dictating to others. (163)

> Now and then, they were honoured with a call from her Ladyship, and nothing escaped her observation that was passing in the room during these visits. She examined into their employments, looked at their work, and advised them to do it differently; found fault with the arrangement of the furniture, or detected the housemaid in negligence. . . . Elizabeth soon perceived that though this great lady was not in the commission of the peace for the county, she was a most active magistrate in her own parish, the minutest concerns of which were carried to her by Mr. Collins. (169)

Lady Catherine's desire to look down on other people's affairs leads her virtually to beg Elizabeth to stay longer at her estate. Although the first invitation to "dine at Rosings" is seen as a sign of "good fortune" and "condescension," positions have become reversed by the final visit:

> "But if that is the case, you must write to your mother to beg that you may stay a little longer. Mrs. Collins will be very glad of your company, I am sure."
> "I am much obliged to your ladyship for your kind invitation," replied Elizabeth, "but it is not in my power to accept it.—I must be in town next Saturday."
> "Why, at that rate, you will have been here only six weeks. I expected you to stay two months. I told Mrs. Collins so before you came. There can be no occasion for your going so soon. Mrs. Bennet could certainly spare you for another fortnight." (211)

Relentlessly trying to show how distant she is from her subordinates, Lady Catherine ends up dependent on them; her very longing for imperious singularity creates strong intersubjective structures. A similar pattern holds true for minor characters in the novel itself: they are continually belittled as the "simple" and "shallow" holding back and frustrating the profound and intricate, but, in terms of both the plot and the novel's larger semantic field, simple and intricate characters are locked into one overall structure that encompasses them both.

This leads to a pattern that we can see in most analyses of *Pride and Prejudice*. Many essays that aspire to interpret the significance of the novel as a whole at some point display a tension between evaluating Elizabeth and Darcy's developing relationship and evaluating all the other characters that surround this story. For instance, Marilyn Butler stops her influential account of Elizabeth about three-quarters of the way through her essay to remark that "Elizabeth's moral enlightenment accounts for about three-quarters of the novel," and then turns her attention toward the novel's other "minor characters" (213–14). The convergence is not coincidental: too often a structure that could be analyzed is instead reenacted, so that the asymmetry of the novel becomes naturalized, as though it exists outside of the novel's own parameters.

The pivot of analyses that focus primarily on Elizabeth and Darcy but also try to recognize the crucial presence of minor characters is often Austen's parody. Parody is extricated as a kind of freestanding rhetorical device that motivates the asymmetric structure: a way that the novel's asymmetry explains itself, so that critics don't need to explain it. Parody allows critics to contextualize or contain the narrative that doesn't explicitly concern Elizabeth and Darcy's "moral development" as the symbolic externalization of various paths that the protagonists avoid. For instance, according to Alistair Duckworth, the faults that Darcy will outgrow as he overcomes his pride are embodied, satirized, and dismissed through the subordinate characters: "The deficiencies of this view, evident enough in Darcy's own demeanor, are revealed in the parodies of it which appear in the novel. Everywhere in *Pride and Prejudice*, pompous gravity is laughed out of existence" (134). We'll want to hold on to Duckworth's language here, which subtly registers the consequential stakes of parody: the human vehicles for this satiric critique are not simply dismissed but "laughed *out of existence.*" For now we can note that such an answer— frequently employed by accounts of *Pride and Prejudice* that seek to isolate Darcy and Elizabeth's relationship as the thematic center of the novel—raises other questions. If we subsume minor characters under the umbrella of "parody," how is the trope of parody itself related to the narrative's overall structure? And why does parody in this novel hinge above all on the subordination and distortion of secondary characters? We are still facing the problem of Lady Catherine, now in a more formal context: the parodic narrative relies structurally on the very elements that it dismisses locally. More generally, if the achievement of a literary work lies in the unity of its semantic field, isn't it impossible to separate this unity into two sections—a dominant "three-quarters" of the text and a subordinate "one-quarter" that is only a distorted or parodic reflection of the dominant section?

The Double Meaning of *Character*

Pride and Prejudice does sometimes seem to stratify itself into two distinct
levels. It is as though the text encourages us to take in the increasingly intense
relationship between Elizabeth and Darcy on one register, while apprehending
the many memorable minor characters on another. However, analysis of the
novel needs to highlight the dialectical links between these two narrative registers, to bring out the textual logic that makes them coalesce into a unified
whole. We can see an early example of these two descriptive modes in the first
moment of detailed characterization in the novel, the depiction of Mr. and Mrs.
Bennet that ends chapter 1. This opening chapter consists mainly of quoted
dialogue between Mr. and Mrs. Bennet; after the first two sentences the narrator rarely intrudes (except to present indirect quotations or an occasional lighthearted comment). In the chapter's last paragraph, however, the narrator shifts
into a quite different tone, offering a summary judgment of the characters who
have been talking:

> Mr. Bennet was so odd a mixture of quick parts, sarcastic humour, reserve, and
> caprice, that the experience of three and twenty years had been insufficient to make
> his wife understand his character. *Her* mind was less difficult to develope. She was
> a woman of mean understanding, little information, and uncertain temper. When she
> was discontented she fancied herself nervous. The business of her life was to get her
> daughters married; its solace was visiting and news. (5)

Juxtaposed against the clipped conversation, this description announces the
omniscient narrator's analytic seriousness, showing us that the novel will not
be concerned simply with presenting surface appearances but will scrutinize
its characters' essential qualities. To read such a complex, intimate appraisal
of a character so early in a novel is jarring—the reader is forced to pause and
try to figure out what it means to describe a human being as "a mixture of quick
parts, sarcastic humour, reserve and caprice." This pause can be explained
technically and analyzed on a formal level: phonetically, through the lack of
assonance and the polysyllabic words; syntactically, through the heavy presence of abstract nouns; and semantically, through the simultaneous deployment
of both contradictions ("quick parts"/"reserve") and synonyms ("sarcastic humour"/"caprice"). But we also have to slow down because of *what* the language is describing, because of the startling way in which the narrator presents
a human being, encapsulating such a complicated person in only ten words
when "three and twenty years" is insufficient to reveal his "character" to his
wife. The formal qualities of the sentence are a reflection of the narrator's
insistence on accurately presenting the inner nature of Mr. Bennet's character.

This is an uncommon and original understanding of how to align a work of
literature with an individual life—of how a sense of the human can be refracted
through a literary text. As Raymond Williams writes:

In most drama and fiction the characters are already pre-formed, as functions of certain kinds of situation and action. "Creation" of characters is then in effect a kind of tagging: name, sex, occupation, physical type. In many important plays and novels, within certain class modes, the tagging is still evident, at least for "minor characters," according to social conventions of distribution of significance (the characterization of servants, for example). Even in more substantial characterization, the process is often the activation of a known model. . . . The detailed and substantial *performance of a known model* of "people like this, relations like this," is in fact the real achievement of most serious novels and plays. Yet there is evidently also a mode beyond reproductive performance. There can be new formations of "character" and "relationship," and these are normally marked by the introduction of different essential notations and conventions, extending beyond these specific elements to a total composition. Many of these new articulations and formations become, in their turn, models. But while they are being formed they are creative in the emergent sense. (*Marxism and Literature*, 208–9)

The description of Mr. Bennet is arguably part of a "new formation of character" in Austen, which is more psychological and analytic than that of previous British fiction. This new mode of characterization emerges in relation to Austen's strikingly original voice, perhaps the most notable use of omniscient narrative in the British novel since Henry Fielding, whose own omniscience is in quite a different mode. And part of the originality in Austen's omniscient, impersonal narrative is precisely what we see in this passage: the authority it gives her to probe the psychological workings of her characters.

Besides grounding stylistic or formal originality in the realm of characterization, Williams stresses that both "minor characters" and more rounded characters are subsumed under this creative model—that a signal method of narrative will somehow be directed toward both "character" *and* "relationship." How a novel finds new forms of representing individuals is connected, in other words, to how a novel "*distributes*" significance across a group of characters implicated within a single narrative. Austen's new style of omniscience also, crucially, intensifies this narrative relationship between characters, who are juxtaposed and concatenated within a closed and intricately organized discursive structure. What is so interesting about the closing paragraph of chapter 1 is not merely that Austen's intriguing description of Mr. Bennet absorbs us, but, also, that we are immediately forced to shift our attention elsewhere. While we expect the concise appraisal of Mr. Bennet's odd character to be elaborated, we are instead directed toward Mrs. Bennet's qualitatively different character. The shift is accomplished through the heavily emphasized "*her*": a use of italics that occurs throughout the novel to foreground a particular character. The narrator again unfurls her nuanced psychological vocabulary, but now a single characteristic emerges in different terms—"mean," "little," "uncertain." It is as though the language of precision—confronted with Mrs. Bennet's shallow mind—is drained of its own specificity.

We can already see a central tendency of the narrator: to closely link the description of an "intricate" mind with a counterpoised description of a "simple" one. Of course, it makes sense that descriptions of a husband and wife are placed side by side, but this overt motivation for the sentence does not fully explain the logic of the juxtaposition. The sentence places complexity and superficiality together in a way that will be repeated throughout the novel. Besides the two different characters who are linked by marriage, the paragraph suggests two linked modes of existence—and two registers of description that reflect these modes. And the abrupt shift from Mr. Bennet's depth to Mrs. Bennet's shallowness implies some kind of interconnection, some logic of "relationship," which governs both these modes of existence, and out of which they both emerge.

The achievement of Austen's narrative is to densely correlate two kinds of comparison—so that the abstract comparison between different personal qualities, or the discrimination of interior consciousness and personality, is grounded in the more concrete juxtaposition of different characters, or individuals, within a social field. "In understanding Darcy was the superior. Bingley was by no means deficient, but Darcy was clever" (16). These two short sentences are a very condensed example of a process that repeats itself over and over again in *Pride and Prejudice*. The passage establishes two kinds of comparison: the social distinction between two persons and the more conceptual, abstract distinction between two kinds of intelligence. This second relation— between "understanding" and "cleverness"—does not distinguish Darcy and Bingley per se but rather illustrates more general gradations of human consciousness through Darcy and Bingley. But the nuanced distinction between "understanding" and "cleverness," which concerns the interior realm of human character, is built in-and-through a social comparison that is necessarily exterior. The early juxtaposition of Mr. and Mrs. Bennet, set off at the end of chapter 1, is the novel's first major example of this process, as the interior comparison of different characteristics gets entangled with the exterior juxtaposition of different characters.

All of Austen's novels—and not least of all *Pride and Prejudice*—are full of these double comparisons: where an abstract elaboration is purchased through a social distinction. Here are two more examples, one subtly juxtaposing Elizabeth and Jane, and the other more harshly juxtaposing Mr. Darcy and Mr. Hurst.

> Elizabeth listened in silence, but was not convinced; their behavior at the assembly had not been calculated to please in general; and with more quickness of observation and less pliancy of temper than her sister, and with a judgment too unassailed by any attention to herself, she was very little disposed to approve them. (15)

> Mr. Darcy said very little, and Mr. Hurst nothing at all. The former was divided between admiration of the brilliancy which exercise had given to her complexion,

and doubt as to the occasion's justifying her coming so far alone. The latter was thinking only of his breakfast. (33)

In the first example we see the rich psychological distinction between "observation" and "temper" (a distinction that bears on the very crux of epistemology) getting constructed only in-and-through a social comparison. In the second example these two types of discrimination have been temporally separated, so that the psychological juxtaposition of "admiration" and "doubt" precedes the harsh social comparison between Mr. Darcy and Mr. Hurst. But the motivation of this second comparison, the reason that the narrative suddenly turns to Hurst, lies in the processes of the first comparison: it is an extension and an elaboration of Darcy's depth of character to compare his divided consciousness with Hurst's. And it is precisely in this moment, when the interior is being separated from the social, that we see a truly flattened character. Flatness and asymmetry enter into the novel through this dissociation; they are a residue of the denied relationship between thought and social being.

This dissociation of the two types of comparison helps account for the passages' different tones: the irony that is so clearly emphasized in the second passage is almost imperceptible in the first. This is due to the positions of Hurst and Jane within the asymmetrical character-structure of the narrative as a whole. Hurst is a quintessentially reduced and flattened caricature, while Jane is the character who more than any other seems to gloss over the very fact of asymmetry: the one sister who is not harshly juxtaposed with Elizabeth, who does not experience a radically different fate, and who might be minor but certainly does not suffer from this minorness. Remembering this difference, we can begin to see more clearly the similarity between the two passages. It makes sense that the social distinction which facilitates the first comparison (between "observation" and "temper") is hidden in a subordinate clause, while the second comparison (between Darcy's "admiration" and "doubt") is emphasized through a clipped second sentence and in the mode of comic juxtaposition. It is as though Mr. Hurst is *so* different from Mr. Darcy that he cannot even be assimilated into the same grammatical structure.[6]

All of these examples illustrate two different conceptions of character that coexist in Jane Austen: character as social being (a person *is* a character) and character as inner quality (a person *has* a character). The narrative structure that mediates between them is precisely asymmetry. Austen famously transforms the novel into a genre that abstracts, elucidates, and diagnoses human characteristics: facilitating contrasts between inner qualities like "observation" and "temper." This is most apparent in the well-known contrast of abstract nouns in the twin titles *Pride and Prejudice* and *Sense and Sensibility*. These two titles show how important such juxtapositions are. They alert us to a process of psychological analysis—built on the abstraction and dialectical comparison of characteristics—that runs throughout the novels, so that similar contrasts are continually rippling across and animating the text. These two titles suggest that the rich and complex texture of human interiority should be the subject of literature; and that the activity of the novelist revolves around discriminating between (and thus elucidating) different modes of thinking and feeling.

Characters, in this light, quickly become transformed into characteristics: the social relation of *individuals* rendered as the dialectical relationship between discrepant interior states. When Marianne criticizes Edward early in *Sense and Sensibility*, she says: "He admires as a lover, not as a connoisseur. To satisfy me, those characters must be united" (17). The specific point that Marianne is making is not nearly as important as the structure of feeling that she is enacting: the sense that human character can be neatly analyzed, categorized, divided—and that the ideal character will be some sort of synthesis, or nuanced modulation, rather than an exaggeration of one particular trait. Austen's novels hinge on transforming secondary characters—fictional human beings like Edward—into the repository of character—the internal and abstracted qualities of being human. The dual use of "character" thus lies at the heart of the birelational process we have been looking at, where the nuanced adumbration of inner qualities emerges only through the social juxtaposition of different people. This dichotomy is summed up in a crucial conversation among Bingley, Elizabeth, and Darcy:

> "I did not know before," continued Bingley immediately, "that you were a studier of character. It must be an amusing study."
>
> "Yes; but intricate characters are the *most* amusing. They have at least that advantage."
>
> "The country," said Darcy, "can in general supply but few subjects for such a study. In a country neighborhood you move in a very confined and unvarying society." (42–43)

What is continually enacted in particular instances throughout the novel is here more generally described: the psychological depth of "intricate" character is linked to the quantitative distribution of characters. The novel is full of more specific examples, such as when Elizabeth is received by the three Bingley siblings:

> She was received, however, very politely by them; and in their brother's manners there was something better than politeness; there was good humour and kindness. (33)

Again: the qualitative distinction between real politeness and what we might call *politesse* is constructed only through a social comparison. In a similar way, aesthetic criteria and distinctions are also not intrinsically grounded but rely on exterior juxtaposition. In another example, a classic juxtaposition of artificial and actual beauty, or "splendor" and "elegance," is socially inflected:

"Elizabeth saw, with admiration of his taste, that it was neither gaudy nor uselessly fine; with less of splendor, and more real elegance, than the furniture of Rosings" (246).

A dual process of discrimination—between physically real, specifically located persons and between abstract, immaterial gradations of character—is relentlessly repeated in Austen's universe.[7] Note how such a double comparison asserts itself into a sentence, surfacing, almost as in afterthought, in a subordinate clause: "To the civil enquiries which then poured in, and amongst which she had the pleasure of distinguishing the much superior solicitude of Mr. Bingley's, she could not make a very favourable answer" (35). This dual understanding of character does not just inform individual descriptions but underlies the larger structure of Austen's characterization. The process of interior character development—embodied in the titles *Sense and Sensibility* and *Pride and Prejudice*—is essentially a *via negativa*, a dialectical process of rejecting different extremes (too much pride, too much sensibility, etc.) to find a middle ground. This process accommodates itself perfectly with an asymmetrical structure of characterization, as various minor characters exemplify certain traits or ways of thinking that the protagonist must learn to discard. This is the pattern in all of Austen's novels: dialectical progress for the central protagonists, and the flattening, fragmentation, and dismissal of many minor characters who facilitate this progress as negative examples. The novels compel us not merely to aggregate the traits or qualities of mind that are exemplified (this is too "fine"; this is too "gaudy") but also to confront and evaluate what it means *to* exemplify, deriving these abstracted traits through persons. The dismissal of each individual character (along with the characteristics into which they are subsumed) points to a larger process—the dismissal of an entire mode of character for another, what we could see as the persistent transformation of characters as social beings into character as the reflection of internal, abstract qualities. This transformation, which we have seen in isolated sentences, is also enacted in the narrative *as a whole*: through the derealization of minor characters.

It is only in this context that specific instances of parody can be seen in their full significance. Parody is the site of a human drama in Austen's novels, the transformation of human beings as specific individuals into attributes, characteristics, aspects of existence. The term "character" is a privileged word in Jane Austen's novels, appearing sixty-four times in *Pride and Prejudice* alone, and nearly as frequently in *Mansfield Park*, *Emma*, and *Persuasion*. Nor is the term used incidentally; all of these novels have key passages involving the word, and it appears most often toward the end. In *Pride and Prejudice* the term is always employed in the second sense: never "character" as a way of denoting a person, but always character as, precisely, what can be derived *from* a person.[8] And yet it is in just this relentless transformation of social relationships (between concrete, discrete persons) into psychological comparisons (between abstracted interior states) that the social significance of Austen's narrative emerges. As Duckworth puts it, in terms that now become more suggestive to us, the parody which underlies Austen's abstraction means that certain characters are laughed "out of existence." In *Pride and Prejudice*, this kind of departure, or expulsion, does not only take place when a character actually leaves the narrative, but, on the contrary, also occurs through the very *integration* of a character into the narrative totality, as this integration is accomplished in relation to the character's abstraction. And by rigorously representing the transformation of human beings into abstract qualities—and enacting this through the derealization of minor characters who, en masse, facilitate the development of the protagonist—Austen frames the very construction of the interior realm of personality, the space of the protagonist, as part of a profoundly social structure.

The One vs. the Many

> "I think you said she was a widow, sir? has she any family?"
>
> "She has one only daughter, the heiress of Rosings, and of very extensive property."
>
> "Ah!" cried Mrs. Bennet, shaking her head, "then she is better off than many girls."
>
> —*Pride and Prejudice*, 67

In the first two sections I have tried to show how the distinction between flat and round characters is an organizing structure and not a contingent aspect of *Pride and Prejudice* and, by glancing at various examples from the novel, to show how this asymmetry contributes to a formal process in which characters, in juxtaposition with one another, are turned into interior characteristics. But why does the novel organize characterization in this way? What motivates this formal structure? If asymmetry is a means of recasting social relations within an abstracted psychological framework, Austen simultaneously shows us that the structure of asymmetry is itself a consequence and manifestation *of* social reality. In the next two sections I want to consider how the novel establishes a series of correspondences between the social world that underlies the fiction, the thematic interests of the novel, and this asymmetric narrative discourse.

Pride and Prejudice immediately creates two axes along which all the novel's events are oriented. These two axes focus, respectively, on the individual as she develops, in-and-of-herself, across time, and on the individual as she is developed, in relation to many other persons, across social (and narrative) space. It is the combination of these two narrative planes, as they unfurl and interact, that anchors each episode of the novel within a larger semantic structure. To begin an analysis of these two axes, we can look at Austen's famous beginning:

It is a truth universally acknowledged, that a single man in possession of a good fortune, must be in want of a wife.

However little known the feelings or views of such a man may be on his first entering a neighbourhood, this truth is so well fixed in the minds of the surrounding families, that he is considered as the rightful property of some one or other of their daughters.

The opening sentence, set off as an entire paragraph, is a well-known encapsulation of the marriage plot. After reading only one sentence, we immediately know what will be the chief problem of this novel—and can even anticipate the happy conclusion. The opening sentence lays the foundations for a linear narrative, for a story that will delay, obscure, and ultimately satisfy the "want"—both a desire and a lack—that is the governing subject of the marriage plot. In satisfying this want, the marriage plot centers on marriage not as a social process but as the fulfillment of individual desire. Social reality is incorporated into this individual marriage plot only in a strictly linear form: as the stable transmission of private property. "Possession of a good fortune" is the precondition for the "want of a wife" both because marriage requires property—only a wealthy man is an eligible husband—and because property requires marriage, as the stable form of its transmission.

The second paragraph of *Pride and Prejudice*, also just one complete sentence, introduces a second plot, a subplot, which, in interaction with the marriage plot, creates the vitality of the narrative as a whole. Here, too, there is a "want" that must be satisfied and an instability that must be resolved, although they are more subtly emphasized. The sentence hinges on the indefinite nature of the closing phrase—"some one or other of their daughters"—which puts the marriage plot in a specifically social context. The first sentence asks, "When will the single man marry?" while the second sentence expands this question to "Whom—among many different choices—will the single man marry?" The narrative that emerges out of the first sentence is singular and internal, and can be resolved over time; this second narrative is plural, intersubjective, and can be resolved only across a social space. Together they form the novel's two grids, a horizontal and a vertical plane, that assimilate a long list of dialectically charged terms—personal/public, temporal/spatial, psychological/social, diachronic/synchronic, metaphoric/metonymic. The first sentence anticipates Elizabeth, who will occupy the narrative space of the protagonist; the second sentence anticipates Elizabeth's four sisters, who will necessarily become minor characters.

These two different ways of looking at the same institution of marriage will soon become a governing logic of the text, embodied in the tension between Elizabeth Bennet, projected forward across time by her own developing internal consciousness, and the five Bennet sisters, represented as a single social (and narrative) group.

"Is he married or single?"

"Oh! single, my dear, to be sure! A single man of large fortune; four or five thousand a year. What a fine thing for our girls!"

"How so? how can it affect them?"

"My dear Mr. Bennet," replied his wife, "how can you be so tiresome! You must know that I am thinking of his marrying one of them." (3–4)

This snippet of dialogue emphasizes the social dimension of the marriage plot; the competition that had been alluded to generally in the second paragraph as between "some one or other of their daughters" is now placed more specifically within the Bennet family. Mrs. Bennet is concerned with the individual as part of a larger group: she sees marriage as exterior to the particular point of view or character of any one of her daughters. Later in the paragraph Mr. Bennet, as though responding to this polycentric drift, makes a counterclaim, organizing the marriage plot around Elizabeth.

"I dare say Mr. Bingley will be very glad to see you; and I will send a few lines by you to assure him of my hearty consent to his marrying which ever he chuses of the girls; though I must throw in a good word for my little Lizzy."

"I desire you will do no such thing. Lizzy is not a bit better than the others, and I am sure she is not half so handsome as Jane, nor half so good humoured as Lydia. But you are always giving *her* the preference."

"They have none of them much to recommend them," replied he; "they are all silly and ignorant like other girls; but Lizzy has something more of quickness than her sisters." (4–5)

This crucial paragraph positions Elizabeth as protagonist of the novel—and makes being the protagonist a position defined *only in juxtaposition with her sisters*, and a position that is contested from the start. Thus Mr. Bennet's suggestive comment that Elizabeth "has something more of quickness than her sisters" is a comparative understanding of Elizabeth's character—and this comparison is built into the very quality that Elizabeth possesses. Elizabeth isn't first described as having, like Mr. Bennet, "quick parts," but rather "something more of quickness"—a quality that is comparative *prior* to being descriptive. Thus Elizabeth's distinguishing quality, which will motivate her narrative centrality, emerges in a comparative context, a comparison that arises only because of the social problem of marriage. A social pressure catalyzes a cultural comparison out of which the protagonist emerges—who will then develop along a plotline that reverses these events, as she undergoes a cultural or interior education resulting in social stability.

To put it another way, Elizabeth is first singled out only because there is a social disequilibrium, an external pressure that forces the parents to make distinctions between their daughters. The social process of being "singled out" is then slowly transformed, over the course of the asymmetric narrative, into the lived experience of "singularity." Nancy Armstrong has noted the competitive nature of the marriage plot in *Pride and Prejudice*: "*Pride and Prejudice* presents the reader with a group of women who are daughters of polite country gentlemen and who compete among themselves in a matchmaking game. . . . The game of love decides which female virtues are the most advantageous in a woman aspiring to live the good country life. As a result, such traditional female attributes as chastity, wit, practicality, duty, manners, imagination, sympathy, generosity, beauty, and kindness are pitted against each other in the competition among the Bennet sisters and their friends" (50). *Pride and Prejudice* does not just demonstrate how marriage puts various female "attributes" in competition with one another. Rather, it suggests, that attribution itself is a result of competition. The analysis of a person in terms of a quality, the understanding of a quality as distinct and independent of the person, the engulfing of a person within this hardened, reified quality—all this emerges out of competition itself. The first evaluation of the Bennet daughters as individuals does not precede the social question of marriage but is necessitated by it. We are back to the crucial narrative and descriptive process that we discussed above: the transformation of characters into characteristics. And we can now see more clearly the social pressure that motivates this rhetorical process. It is not simply that Austen's narratives often depict social relationships in psychological terms. This incessant psychological comparison—which underlies the distinction between major and minor characters—revolves around a specific social problem, the tension between the one and the many. And in *Pride and Prejudice* this tension is condensed into, and finds its symbolic form in, competing representations of marriage as an individual experience and as a social institution.

The opening of *Mansfield Park* succinctly states the social problem that lies at the heart of *Pride and Prejudice*'s structure:

> She had two sisters to be benefited by her elevation; and such of their acquaintance as thought Miss Ward and Miss Frances quite as handsome as Miss Maria, did not scruple to predict their marrying with almost equal advantage. But there certainly are not so many men of large fortune in the world, as there are pretty woman to deserve them. (3)

All the asymmetry of Jane Austen's work flows out of this final sentence, out of her struggle to produce a closed and ordered fictional universe that reflects a fundamentally fragmented and disordered social one. The sly tone of the sentence, its lighthearted irony, softens but does not elide the grim central insight: that the *system* of marriage as it operates on a social level inevitably produces disequilibrium, even if the experience of the marriage plot, for a particular individual, might produce stability. This disequilibrium is inevitably generated by the competition among many human agents for a limited number of positions and resources, and is one of the essential phenomena of modern capitalism. This is Austen's great imaginative achievement: to represent the disequilibrium of the new, dynamic competition which is emerging in her period through her depiction of a sphere of life that was typically understood as sheltered from, and even an alternative to, these economic structures.

Balzac will present a similar disequilibrium at the center of his novels, summed up in a passage that we will return to later. As Vautrin says to Rastignac, in a description that, unlike Austen's, immediately moves to the violent effect of this system:

> "A quick fortune is the problem which needs to be solved at this moment by fifty thousand young men who all find themselves in your position. You are one of that number. Consider the efforts that you have to make and the bitterness of the combat. It's necessary that you eat up one another like spiders in a pot, since there aren't fifty thousand good positions."

> ["Une rapide fortune est le problème que se proposent du résoudre en ce moment cinquante mille jeunes gens qui se trouvent tous dans votre position. Vous êtes une unité de ce nombre-là. Jugez des efforts que vous avez à faire et de l'acharnement du combat. Il faut vous manger les uns les autres comme des araignées dans un pot, attendu qu'il n'y a pas cinquante mille bonnes places."] (*Le Père Goriot*, 144)

This disequilibrium—and the competition that it creates—has already insinuated itself into the formal structure of Austen's narratives. Asymmetry comprehends a system in which, as in this violent Parisian competition, the few with "very extensive property" are much "better off than [the] many girls" with none. Austen's formal system is necessary to this social comprehension; or, more precisely, Austen's narrative realizes this social problematic *as* a socionarrative one. Here the reality of social privilege is embedded into, indissociable from, the construction of narrated centrality; power is earned through attention, and attention, as we have seen, is intertwined with the essential analytic features of Austen's style: comparison, distinction, abstraction.

In an interesting summary of Austen's work, Raymond Williams writes, "The paradox of Jane Austen is then the achievement of a unity of tone, of a settled and remarkably confident way of seeing and judging, in this chronicle of confusion and change" (*English Novel*, 21). Williams locates this "confusion and change" in the social transformation that the novels describe, and thus, primarily, on the level of content or *histoire*. The stability of the narrative form, its "unity of tone," is set *against* the instability of the events that the narrative represents. Specifically, Williams commends Austen for depicting—within her "settled" and thus delimited "way of seeing and judging"—the essential conflict between a declining agrarian economy, rooted in a rigidly hierarchal social order, and an emergent mercantile capitalism linked to bourgeois politics and culture. "It is an active complicated sharply speculative process: of inherited and newly enclosing and engrossing estates; of fortunes from trade and colonial military profit being converted into houses and property and social position; of settled and speculative marriages into estates and incomes. It is indeed that most difficult world to describe, in English social history: an acquisitive high bourgeois society at the point of its most evident interlocking with an agrarian capitalism that is itself mediated by inherited title and by the making of family names" (21). Williams's insight is important, but limited, because he specifically balances the social content of the *histoire* against the unified form of the *discours*. In the form of the narrative itself, however, Austen also comprehends the inner experience of this "confusion and change," which inevitably results from the decline of fixed social identity and the chaos of social mobility. The disequilibrium of the marriage plot in Austen's narratives is an analogue to the transition that Williams describes, carrying these social pressures into the very dynamic elaboration of narrative form.

The uncertainty that the Bennet sisters face, grounded in the competition among many human agents for a limited number of positions and the collapse of rigidly defined social positions, is the direct result of the conflict between agrarian and bourgeois capitalism. In this unstable and mobile world, everyone imagines herself as becoming Miss Maria—even though she might recognize that Miss Ward and Miss Frances are "quite as handsome." Except for the propertied few, everybody must privately conceptualize their own future—their own temporal development—in terms of a singularity that it is impossible for them to generate internally.

Pride and Prejudice is situated squarely within this precarious state and links this psychological condition to the more general economic transition. Five daughters who are the product of a marriage between a landed husband ("an estate of two thousand a year") and an unlanded, middle-class wife ("her father had been an attorney") are facing an entail that makes each daughter entirely dependent on marrying into wealth that is clearly not available to everybody.[9] Of course, each of these daughters—Jane, Elizabeth, Mary, Lydia, and Catherine—is profoundly affected by the uncertainty of this condition! Austen conveys this uncertainty for all five individual characters, even while incorporating her presentation of each sister into the asymmetric structure which is configured by the larger economic environment that grounds their uncertainty in the first place. And Austen is careful to make the Bennet family—the combination of a gentry father, an unpropertied mother, and five daughters who are facing a wide spectrum of possible economic circumstances—a condensation of dominant economic tendencies of her period.

This becomes clearer when we look at her work as a whole. Despite the seemingly limited world of Austen's fiction, each of the major novels finds a different economic trajectory for the central character and configures the narrative totality—and character-system—*around* this trajectory (with a distinct *kind* of centrality for each protagonist). Character-system and economic situation change in tandem: from the upwardly mobile daughter of an economically imperiled household (Elizabeth Bennet) to the downwardly mobile daughter of a nobleman (Anne Elliot) to the lower-middle-class parvenue (Fanny Price) to the overly secure propertied woman (Emma Woodhouse) to the two sisters, Elinor and Marianne, who, *in their very unstable doubleness*, suggest a nascent middle class, without economic security, negatively defined against both the propertied and the working class.[10] Taken together, as a continuing aesthetic project, the novels present a complex, dynamic, and historically new spectrum of possibilities created in the transition away from a rigidly hierarchical agrarian economy to a more fluid, and potentially explosive, form of economic organization. Austen's ability to generate such unique but interrelated trajectories can only make us wonder what kinds of protagonists, and what structures of narrative totality, she would have developed in the 1820s and 1830s, as the anachrony that helps structure her narrative (and which is itself probingly thematized in *Persuasion*) became more apparent.

The conflict that Williams describes—the general transition away from agrarian capitalism and landed wealth—emerges in the novel through facts, descriptions, and events that are woven into the narrative (such as the frequent reference to levels of income). The subjective dislocation that accompanies these changes is primarily articulated through the narrative's form, and, more specifically, through the structure of asymmetrical characterization that we are examining.[11] This asymmetrical structure organizes the array of human beings in the novel and motivates the modes of describing these human beings that develop as the narrative unfolds. In the rest of this chapter, I want to analyze closely the two modes of description that control this narrative structure: the ever increasing narrative space of the protagonist, Elizabeth Bennet, and the distorted forms of minorness that develop alongside of her centrality.

Asymmetry: From *Discourse* to *Story*

"We must not be so nice. A few characters too many, must not frighten us."
—*Mansfield Park*, 131

The first chapter of *Pride and Prejudice* obscures the novel's central focus. Will the narrative continue to depict all the five sisters as a social group or orient itself around Elizabeth, whom Mr. Bennet claims has "something more of quickness"? This wavering continues a good way into the story. Austen's omniscience allows her to defocalize the novel, so that narrative attention drifts from person to person. Chapter 2 is set in an unspecified room in the Bennets' house, where Mr. and Mrs. Bennet and at least four of their daughters are talking. However, we do not find out that a particular daughter is present until Mr. or Mrs. Bennet actually speaks to her. The narrator simply follows the parents' wandering attention, as Elizabeth, Catherine, Mary, and Lydia are addressed before we are told that they are in the room. Throughout the chapter we have to repeatedly reconstitute our frame of reference to include more and more people:

> Observing his second daughter employed in trimming a hat, he [Mr. Bennet] suddenly addressed her. (6)

> Mrs. Bennet deigned not to make any reply; but unable to contain herself, began scolding *one of her* daughters.
> "Don't keep coughing so, Kitty, for heaven's sake!" (6, emphasis added)

> "What say you, Mary? for you are a young lady of deep reflection I know, and read great books, and make extracts." (7)

The five daughters are never explicitly located in the room; rather their presence seems to be simply assumed—as though the existence of *a* daughter implied the existence of *the* daughters. In fact, by the chapter's end all five sisters except Jane have been addressed and have spoken.[12] Furthermore, the group of daughters seems to *act* as a whole, so that the plural "they" or "the girls" is often the subject of a sentence, as in "[t]he girls stared at their father" (7) or, in the closing sentence (and paragraph) of the chapter: "The rest of the evening was spent in conjecturing how soon he would return Mr. Bennet's visit, and determining when *they* should ask him to dinner" (8, emphasis added). The sisters are presented primarily as a collective group, and the force of each character's own individuality is enough to arrest just the slightest narrative attention. Meanwhile, the conversation itself revolves around each girl's reaction to Mr. Bingley's arrival and the way that his presence precipitates the question of marriage. The precarious space of the daughters within the narrative discourse thus mirrors the tension that Mr. Bingley's arrival naturally provokes, since "there are certainly not so many men of large fortune in the world, as there are pretty woman to deserve them." Mrs. Bennet makes particular allusion to Lydia's especially difficult situation, as the youngest of the five daughters:

> "Lydia, my love, though you *are* the youngest, I dare say Mr. Bingley will dance with you at the next ball."
> "Oh!" said Lydia stoutly, "I am not afraid; for though I *am* the youngest, I'm the tallest." (8)

It is important to remember that if the narrative were to stop at this moment, Elizabeth would not stand out. The only bits of dialogue we hear from the daughter who has "something more of quickness" seem fairly banal:

> "But you forget, mama," said Elizabeth, "that we shall meet him at the assemblies, and that Mrs. Long has promised to introduce him." (6)

and:

> "When is your next ball to be, Lizzy?"
> "To-morrow fortnight." (6)

It is from this inconspicuous origin that Elizabeth will soon grow to engulf the entire form of the narrative. The narrator herself does not seem particularly interested in Elizabeth in this chapter—we get no sense of her emotions or thoughts. The narrator uses existential adverbs to describe Lydia and Catherine (" 'I do not cough for my own amusement', replied Kitty *fretfully*" and " 'Oh!', said Lydia *stoutly*" [emphases added]); and explicitly tells us what Mary is thinking: "Mary wished to say something very sensible, but knew not how." Elizabeth starts completely on the surface: lost among the rest of the family, making only an uninteresting comment about other people, *and* not attracting any of the narrative's own attention.

Chapter 3 continues to develop the novel's divided structure, and by the end of this section the essential armature of this structure is in place. At first glance, chapter 3 seems a bit scattered by exposition, since the narrator is concerned with introducing different characters and conveying background information. In fact, the tension between the one and the many unifies this chapter, getting thematized both on the level of narrative form and style and in the referenced world of the story. In this sense, the asymmetric discourse of characterization becomes intertwined with the social conditions that it is attempting to describe. This brief chapter, as much as any other section of *Pride and Prejudice*, grounds the novel's own *discours* within its *histoire*. And these overlapping registers of asymmetry are emphasized by the chapter's brevity, with sudden juxtapositions calling attention to thematic continuities.

The chapter starts with the announcement of a party at Bingley's, prompting Mrs. Bennet to make a sort of double wish that concisely exemplifies the contradiction we have been examining: " 'If I can but see one of my daughters happily settled at Netherfield,' said Mrs. Bennet to her husband, 'and all the others equally well married, I shall have nothing to wish for' " (9). Mrs. Bennet's wish occurs along two contradictory axes, united uneasily through the conjunction "and." She fluctuates between imagining the culturally privileged individual marriage plot—which must necessarily concern only "one of my daughters"—and recognizing the inadequacy of this structure for "all the others." Her statement wants to gloss over, but in fact calls attention to, the stubborn fact that if one daughter marries Bingley, it will be impossible for the other four to settle at Netherfield, and that there are not many other eligible husbands to be had. (And this tension among the five Bennet sisters is itself only the tip of the iceberg, since each family is also competing with the other "eligible" families.)

This asymmetry is presented more concretely, within the novel's visual field, when Mr. Bingley visits the Bennets and his singular presence is contrasted with the girls' plurality. In an image that encapsulates the inequality of social interaction, we see the five daughters look as a group at Bingley, as an individual, while he wishes, as an individual, to see them, as a group:

He had entertained hopes of being admitted to a sight of the young ladies, of whose beauty he had heard much; but he saw only the father. The ladies were somewhat more fortunate, for they had the advantage of ascertaining from an upper window, that he wore a blue coat and rode a black horse. (9)

This visual field—which blurs the sisters into a single mass while accentuating Mr. Bingley's individuality—is both a symbol for, and a consequence of, the asymmetrical nature of marriage as a system of social organization and property transmission.

Chapter 3 begins to focus on Mr. Bingley's ball, which is the field in which the struggle among many women for a little property is actually enacted. At the same time, descriptions in this chapter revolve around questions of "character." Mr. Darcy's introduction immediately positions him on the two different registers of character that we previously examined: "Mr. Bingley was good looking and gentlemanlike; he had a pleasant countenance, and easy, unaffected manners. His sisters were fine women, with an air of decided fashion. His brother-in-law, Mr. Hurst, merely looked the gentleman; but his friend Mr. Darcy soon drew the attention of the room by his fine, tall person, handsome features, noble mien; and the report which was in general circulation within five minutes after his entrance, of his having ten thousand a year" (10). Here Darcy's privileged *social* position within a large group of characters—the way he draws "the attention of the room"—is intertwined with the valorization of his internally grounded *characteristics*, his "handsome features" and "noble mien." Which comes first? If the passage suggests that Darcy's social presence in the room is contingent on his own internal characteristics (he draws attention *by means of* his own qualities), these characteristics are themselves linked to his social position—as his "person," "features," and "mien" seem to flow inevitably out of his privileged position of "ten thousand a year." In either case it is important that the final elaboration of Darcy's presence is represented spatially, in a way that is almost a staging of the narrative's own tactics. We could say that Mr. Darcy draws the attention of the room around him the way that Elizabeth has not yet, but soon will, draw the structure of the narrative around her.

A little later, as Bingley tries to prod Darcy out of his aloofness, their discussion turns on this same social asymmetry, with Darcy insisting that besides Bingley's sisters, " 'there is not another woman in the room, whom it would not be a punishment to me to stand up with' " (11). Bingley's response hovers on the fault line between the one and the many: " 'Upon my honour, I never met with so many pleasant girls in my life, as I have this evening; and there are several of them you see uncommonly pretty.' " Mr. Bingley's "and" is similar to Mrs. Bennet's conjunction at the beginning of the chapter. It juxtaposes his attempt to accommodate the multitude of "pleasant girls," as a group, with his need to distinguish "several of them" (e.g., Jane Bennet) as being, precisely, "uncommonly" pretty.

After the ball is over, we get another defocalized omniscient description of the five Bennet sisters as they are returning home. The tension that has shaped Bingley's ball once again is elaborated in the narrative discourse. The description is propelled forward not by any one individual's perspective but by the diffuse pull of all their perspectives, as sentence by sentence the narrator shifts point of view:

> The evening altogether passed off pleasantly to the whole family. Mrs. Bennet had seen her eldest daughter much admired by the Netherfield party. Mr. Bingley had danced with her twice, and she had been distinguished by his sisters. Jane was as much gratified by this, as her mother could be, though in a quieter way. Elizabeth felt Jane's pleasure. Mary had heard herself mentioned to Miss Bingley as the most accomplished girl in the neighbourhood; and Catherine and Lydia had been fortunate enough to be never without partners, which was all that they had yet learnt to care for at a ball. They returned therefore in good spirits to Longbourn, the village where they lived, and of which they were the principal inhabitants. (12)

Like the strange description of Mr. Bennet, this paragraph suggests a radical (if very different) understanding of how human life, human consciousness, or human character is inflected into literary form. The loose drift of the passage enacts—in a much more subdued form—the dizzying sense of competition that has saturated the ball. The drama of the paragraph arises from our anticipation of how a single, summarizing sentence will shape itself around each different character. Such a description is the purest form of a socially distributed narrative, presenting a varied group of individuals within a balanced structure of characterization. The paragraph, in other words, suggests a form that the novel *might have taken*; and it presents this option—which would shape narrative discourse equally around multiple characters—as essentially unsustainable. In fact, this dispersed paragraph is subtly shaped by asymmetry, squeezing together Catherine and Lydia and helping to develop Elizabeth's centrality. The one sentence about Elizabeth is qualitatively distinct from the other descriptions, despite its brevity. Her sensation is on a second order of apprehension, the consciousness of someone else's consciousness. Mrs. Bennet "sees" her eldest daughter; Jane is "gratified"; Mary "hears" herself mentioned; Catherine and Lydia "dance." But Elizabeth "feels" *Jane's* "pleasure"—so that, in the briefest of sentences, Austen depicts the essential process of consciousness moving beyond itself. We will see that it is this aspect of depth—ultimately a depth of *self*-consciousness, or a consciousness of her own consciousness (rather than, as in this passage, a consciousness of Jane's consciousness)—that is the underlying quality of Elizabeth's singularity.

At the paragraph's end the narrator comments, almost offhandedly, about "the village where they lived, and of which they were the principal inhabitants." All of a sudden, we see a larger social context for the chapter's asymmetrical patterns. All of the earlier manifestations of social asymmetry—

Mr. Bingley's juxtaposition with the five Bennet daughters who watch him from the window, Darcy's centrality in drawing the room around him, the problematic status of Elizabeth in relation to her other sisters, Mrs. Bennet's and Mr. Bingley's unsatisfactory *and*s—are abruptly linked to a broader social universe. The scrupulousness with which Austen has begun to dramatize the dynamics of inequality within the marriage plot spills out to this unsettling description. The text itself does not allow us to take its casual dismissal of the other people that live in "Longbourn" at face value. The excluded residents of Longbourn—whose inflection here serves just to underscore the Bennets' centrality—are, in a sense, the most minor of characters in the novel. A careful reading of asymmetry in *Pride and Prejudice* is ultimately directed toward this entirely absent mass of characters—not to recuperate something that the novel has excluded, but, on the contrary, to show how the text itself provokes us to read this invisibility as a social process, rather than an unalterable fact of inherent powerlessness.

At the end of chapter 3, Mrs. Bennet attempts to describe the ball to Mr. Bennet. Once again the problem of asymmetry comes to the surface, as we can read Mrs. Bennet's description as a particular mode of representation, which is radically distorted by multiplicity.

> "Oh! my dear Mr. Bennet," as she entered the room, "we have had a most delightful evening, a most excellent ball. I wish you had been there. Jane was so admired, nothing could be like it. Every body said how well she looked; and Mr. Bingley thought her quite beautiful, and danced with her twice. Only think of *that* my dear; he actually danced with her twice; and she was the only creature in the room that he asked a second time. First of all, he asked Miss Lucas. I was so vexed to see him stand up with her; but, however, he did not admire her at all: indeed, nobody can, you know; and he seemed quite struck with Jane as she was going down the dance. So, he enquired who she was, and got introduced, and asked her for the two next. Then, the two third he danced with Miss King, and the two fourth with Maria Lucas, and the two fifth with Jane again, and the two sixth with Lizzy, and the Boulanger—"
>
> "If he had had any compassion for *me*," cried her husband impatiently, "he would not have danced half so much! For God's sake, say no more of his partners. Oh! that he had sprained his ancle in the first dance!" (13)

Mrs. Bennet's speech exemplifies the type of unstructured, repetitive talk that Austen commonly uses to flatten many of her characters. Mrs. Bennet almost seems to flatten herself out while making this description: becoming more minor by the minute. Within the speech we also see flattened human figures, presented quite fleetingly—Miss King and Miss Lucas are fictional individuals rigidly positioned in a structure of multiplicity that drains them of any depth. (Note how Elizabeth also gets pushed into this structure. We can contrast the way her character will become completely "round" with the less fortunate narrative fate of Miss King.) But what elicits this flattening—in form and in content—is precisely the social disequilibrium that underlies the marriage plot. To gaze objectively at all of the women included as "some one or other of" the daughters of "the surrounding families" necessitates this type of catalog description. Mrs. Bennet's speech—so flat and monotonous—is really a strategy of representation, somewhat like the narrator's own catalog description of the five daughters returning from the ball. Mr. Bennet's impatience can then be seen as the pain that the consciousness of singularity experiences when confronted with the reality of multiplicity. To hear about all the girls at the ball makes Mr. Bennet uncomfortable, like a factory owner walking past an assembly line. This discomfort is displaced into his more superficial irritation with the *tone* of Mrs. Bennet's speech. It makes sense that Mrs. Bennet's description gives Mr. Bennet a headache. Mr. Bennet prefers Elizabeth and hates to talk about the entail that makes all his daughters' futures insecure; Mrs. Bennet favors Lydia and, of course, always talks about the entail. Their positions were already made clear in the double description that ends chapter 1. We now can start to more fully understand the last sentence of this description: "The business of her life was to get her daughters married; its solace was visiting and news." Mrs. Bennet's speech is flattened in the same way as her consciousness is here described: it becomes coequal with an exterior world governed by multiplicity, by other families, gossip, and the social understanding of the marriage plot.

Characterizing Minorness 1: Compression

"Cottager's wife!" cried Mr. Yates. "What are you talking of? The most trivial, paltry, insignificant part; the merest common-place—not a tolerable speech in the whole. Your sister do that! It is an insult to propose it."
—*Mansfield Park*, 134

At least forty-five characters appear in *Pride and Prejudice*, and another forty individuals are indirectly mentioned. A structural analysis of characterization should aim to account for all of these figures, to show how they are all positioned within the same asymmetrical configuration. Austen's tightly controlled narrative universe *does* anchor all of her characters within a unified character-system, governed by that tension, which begins in the opening two sentences, between a singular, central protagonist and ever more distorted, and diminished, minor characters. An analysis of characterization must begin with the five Bennet sisters, who are clearly the primary plane of asymmetry in *Pride and Prejudice*. Characterization in *Pride and Prejudice* essentially radiates out of this social group: the distinctions that the narrator makes among the Bennet sisters are extended to a wider group of characters but not qualitatively transformed.

The most common way of reading the Bennet sisters, associated with the more general trope of "parody," is to assume that each sister represents a different quality, and that their proximity to each other serves merely to juxtapose these contrasting traits. Jane represents a sort of uninspired kindness; Mary, a stultifying pedantry; Lydia, an excess of social and sexual energy. The worth of the central protagonist is then illustrated and delimited by these counterexamples of female sensibility. We can think of these minor or flat characters as synecdoches, as their outstanding quality is substituted for their entire personality, part for the whole. However, analysis that begins by looking at what each sister *stands for* has already missed (which is to say enacted) the novel's central trope: the conversion of characters into characteristics. We cannot consider what qualities the sisters represent without also examining how and why the text reduces all the sisters—except Elizabeth—to standing for an abstract quality. Between the minor character and the synecdoche into which she is absorbed is a narrative process that I will term compression. Compression underlies the distortion behind both "flatness" and the "synecdoche": just as the whole gets filtered through the essential part, so the full person is squeezed into the flat character, a flatness motivated and sustained by the *characteristic* that gets derived from the individual only to subsume her. This compression takes place at the intersection of two different narrative registers: the delimited position of each character within the novel as a whole (vis-à-vis all the other characters) and the distorted description of each sister herself. It is only the dynamic interaction between these two registers that produces compression: as the way in which a sister is positioned in relation to the other characters *collapses into* the representation of the sister in-and-of-herself.

Pride and Prejudice is saturated with comparisons among the five Bennet sisters. The novel does not simply assume a static fixed hierarchy among the five sisters but constantly reasserts, and modulates, the comparative judgments that privilege Elizabeth over the rest of the family. In other words, the asymmetrical organization that sustains the narrative is maintained only through a continual process of social judgment. Here are some examples, from different parts of the novel:

> The two youngest of the family, Catherine and Lydia, were particularly frequent in these attentions; their minds were more vacant than their sisters', and when nothing better offered, a walk to Meryton was necessary to amuse their morning hours. (28)

> Their sister's wedding day arrived; and Jane and Elizabeth felt for her [Lydia] probably more than she felt for herself. (315)

> To Elizabeth it appeared, that had her family made an agreement to expose themselves as much as they could during the evening, it would have been impossible for them to play their parts with more spirit, or finer success. (101–2)

Mrs. Gardiner . . . was an amiable, intelligent, elegant woman, and a great favourite with all her Longbourn nieces. Between the two eldest and herself especially, there subsisted a very particular regard. (139)

"Do not make yourself uneasy, my love. Wherever you and Jane are known, you must be respected and valued; and you will not appear to less advantage for having a couple of—or I may say, three very silly sisters." (231–32)

"The situation of your mother's family, though objectionable, was nothing in comparison of that total want of propriety so frequently, so almost uniformly betrayed by herself, by your three younger sisters, and occasionally even by your father.—Pardon me." (198)

As we have seen, these comparisons originate out of a concrete social context: the imbalance between the many daughters and the little property that is available to them through marriage. This relational grid—which is comparative and social—underlies the more static and abstract attributions that the text generates, where Mary comes to represent pedantry; Lydia, excessiveness, and so forth. The comparisons themselves are noticeably fluid. Sometimes the contrast is between Elizabeth and her two youngest sisters; sometimes between Elizabeth and Jane against the two youngest sisters; sometimes the two oldest are contrasted with all the three younger ones. Mr. Bennet compares Elizabeth and Jane to their "three very silly sisters," while Mr. Darcy's comparison includes Mr. Bennet himself. As we can see from these passages, Jane is the most difficult character to situate within a structure of asymmetry. While Elizabeth is often contrasted with her other three sisters, or with the entire family, a subordinate comparison elevates Elizabeth *and* Jane, against the rest. Jane's function is, precisely, to justify or disguise this structure, to lend a certain weight to the way Elizabeth balances out against the rest of the family. But the ultimate purpose of these comparisons, when understood as a network of intersecting judgments, is clearly to assure Elizabeth's central position in the narrative; a more subtle series of distinctions (some of which we have already encountered) serve to differentiate her from Jane.

These comparisons by themselves don't fix the asymmetrical contours of the novel; they simply force us to see characters in a comparative context and to get used to judging characters in a hierarchical framework. Asymmetry is fully achieved only through the distortion that takes place once these parameters have been established: in the way that the narrator's mode of representation changes because of a character's specific position within the narrative universe. In other words, the limitation of each sister's relative position within the overall narrative (grounded and justified through the fluid series of comparisons) becomes intimately linked to the specific way she is represented in-and-of-herself. For the more minor characters, a marginal narrative position collapses into various descriptive distortions. And it is finally out of this distortion that the synecdochal abstraction of the sister fully emerges: placing her limitation in functional relationship to the protagonist's depth.

This compression is most clear with Mary Bennet. The narrative accentuates the small attention that Mary attracts, or her marginal position within the novelistic totality, by always making the transitions toward her quite suddenly and cutting them off quickly. Mary never moves beyond the descriptive structure of chapter 2, where the narrative gaze rests for only an instant on each daughter. Mary fits into a simple opposition with Elizabeth: while the former has artificial knowledge, the latter has real intelligence; while Mary is learned, Elizabeth is both clever and thoughtful. This comparison serves to valorize qualities of Elizabeth that are at the center of her singularity: the quickness of her mind that leads to a vital self-consciousness. But Mary's fundamental importance rests not so much in establishing this quality in Elizabeth as in justifying the more general process of synecdochal representation that contains and flattens, or compresses, minor characters. Mary is the motivation for a strategy of characterization that extends far beyond her, though often in a more diluted form. Thus Austen quickly makes sure that the satire of Mary is linked to the overall reduction of her position in the novel. For this reason Mary's thoughts, and, in fact, Mary's entire being, are often reduced to a single sentence, which is also sometimes a single paragraph.

This containment occurs when Mary is first introduced, in a passage we have already seen in a different context:

> "What say you, Mary? for you are a young lady of deep reflection I know, and read great books, and make extracts."
>
> Mary wished to say something very sensible, but knew not how.
>
> "While Mary is adjusting her ideas," he continued, "let us return to Mr. Bingley." (7)

The curtailed description and the isolated paragraph are motivated by Mary's own stultifying character: she has nothing to say, so the narrator, like Mr. Bennet, moves on. The narrator's representational tactics seem justified by the character being depicted; we sense that the narrator *couldn't* say too much about Mary even if she wanted to. In a similar sense, Mary is rarely depicted for her own sake but almost always appears in a comparative context, as though she *would be of no interest by herself.* When Mary falls into the visual field at all, it is most often in relation to her other sisters, and frequently in a sort of double relation that compares her to Lydia and Kitty and then compares all three "younger sisters" to Elizabeth.

This contrast is quite clear in the symbolically charged scene that juxtaposes Mary's and Elizabeth's approaches to piano playing. This is the most extended description of Mary, and a rare instance where the narrator attempts to explain what is *behind* Mary's single-minded pedantry. The explanation, however, is

engulfed in and subordinated by the simultaneous construction of her opposition to Elizabeth:

> [Elizabeth's] performance was pleasing, though by no means capital. After a song
> or two, and before she could reply to the entreaties of several that she would sing
> again, she was eagerly succeeded at the instrument by her sister Mary, who having,
> in consequence of being the only plain one in the family, worked hard for knowledge
> and accomplishments, was always impatient for display.
>
> Mary had neither genius nor taste; and though vanity had given her application, it
> had given her likewise a pedantic air and conceited manner, which would have in-
> jured a higher degree of excellence than she had reached. Elizabeth, easy and unaf-
> fected, had been listened to with much more pleasure, though not playing half so
> well. (25)

We notice here the familiar trick of juxtaposing two types of comparison—
between characters (Elizabeth and Mary) and between characteristics (two different modes of application, "a pedantic air and conceited manner" against an
"easy and unaffected" style). Austen's depiction of Mary is unsparing and
precise: she notes not simply that Mary's defects outweigh her abilities, but
that this imbalance would persist with even "a higher degree of excellence."
The narrator's nuance, however, is directed toward the character's containment, while simultaneously, through the comparative nature of the description,
serving to expand our sense of *Elizabeth's* depth of character.

After this description the narrator spends even less time dwelling on Mary—
concentrating solely on the effect, and not the material cause, of her stultifying pretensions. The next few times Mary comes into the narrative, she once
again can attract only a single sentence that places her in comparison with the
other sisters and that emphasizes the one quality of "pedantry." When Jane
and Elizabeth return from Netherfield after Jane's illness, the narrative describes the other three sisters, beginning with Mary and quickly shifting to
Lydia and Kitty:

> They found Mary, as usual, deep in the study of thorough bass and human nature;
> and had some new extracts to admire, and some new observations of thread-bare
> morality to listen to. Catherine and Lydia had information for them of a different
> sort. (60)

She is next mentioned when the text describes each family member's reaction
to Mr. Collins's letter, and again she is isolated in a single comment:

> "In point of composition," said Mary, "his letter does not seem defective. The idea
> of the olive branch perhaps is not wholly new, yet I think it is well expressed."
>
> To Catherine and Lydia, neither the letter nor its writer were in any degree interest-
> ing. It was next to impossible that their cousin should come in a scarlet coat. (64)

The narrative can easily contain Mary's presence in these examples because Mary has already contained her own thoughts, encasing them in the leaden form of her moralistic epigrams. The clichés that Mary spins out make her a typical minor character because they collapse the distance between surface and depth, making Mary's own subjectivity equivalent to the monotonous (and constricted) way in which she expresses herself. Mary's recorded thoughts thus seem indistinguishable from her recorded speech:

> She rated his abilities much higher than any of the others; there was a solidity in his reflections which often struck her, and though by no means so clever as herself, she thought that if encouraged to read and improve himself by such an example as her's, he might become a very agreeable companion. (124)

> To this, Mary very gravely replied, "Far be it from me, my dear sister, to depreciate such pleasures. They would doubtless be congenial with the generality of female minds. But I confess they would have no charms for *me*. I should infinitely prefer a book."
>
> But of this answer Lydia heard not a word. She seldom listened to any body for more than half a minute, and never attended to Mary at all. (222–23)

If Mary compresses her own subjectivity within the banality of her "threadbare morality," becoming a dictionary of received ideas, she is also contained (within the narrative as a whole) by the way that other characters don't listen to what she says. Both her tendency to speak in epigrams and her complete isolation are reflected in the early passage where she sums up one of the book's own keywords:

> "That is very true," replied Elizabeth, "and I could easily forgive *his* pride, if he had not mortified *mine*."
>
> "Pride," observed Mary, who piqued herself upon the solidity of her reflections, "is a very common failing I believe. By all that I have ever read, I am convinced that it is very common indeed, that human nature is particularly prone to it, and that there are very few of us who do not cherish a feeling of self-complacency on the score of some quality or other, real or imaginary. Vanity and pride are different things, though the words are often used synonimously. A person may be proud without being vain. Pride relates more to our opinion of ourselves, vanity to what we would have others think of us."
>
> "If I were as rich as Mr. Darcy," cried a young Lucas who came with his sisters, "I should not care how proud I was. I would keep a pack of foxhounds, and drink a bottle of wine every day." (20)

Again, the narrative motivates its own technique of characterization—in this case its compression of Mary—by cutting her off from everyone else in the novel; in fact, Mary never says more than one sentence because she never actually has a *conversation* with anyone. If she is ignored here, the first time that she speaks, Elizabeth is similarly unresponsive the final time that we hear Mary speak:

> As for Mary, she was mistress enough of herself to whisper to Elizabeth with a countenance of grave reflection, soon after they were seated at table,
>
> "This is a most unfortunate affair; and will probably be much talked of. But we must stem the tide of malice, and pour into the wounded bosoms of each other, the balm of sisterly consolation."
>
> Then, perceiving in Elizabeth no inclination of replying, she added, "Unhappy as the event must be for Lydia, we may draw from it this useful lesson; that loss of virtue in a female is irretrievable—that one false step involves her in endless ruin—that her reputation is no less brittle than it is beautiful,—and that she cannot be too much guarded in her behaviour towards the undeserving of the other sex."
>
> Elizabeth lifted up her eyes in amazement, but was too much oppressed to make any reply. (289)

The narrative seems to follow Elizabeth's reaction and never bothers to quote Mary in the final one hundred pages.

We can see one final motivation for the novel's own compression of Mary into a flat, minor character in the middle sister's tendency never to leave the house. It's a tendency elaborated once more in contrast to other characters: "Lydia's intention of walking to Meryton was not forgotten; every sister except Mary agreed to go with her" (71); "Mrs. Bennet was not in the habit of walking, Mary could never spare time, but the remaining five set off together" (365). This immobility again functions as an extension of her own static personality but also lets the discourse confine her even more firmly into a cramped corner of the narrative. The stay-at-home sister, Mary has an equally limited space in both discourse and story. The passages I have quoted include almost every time that Mary is mentioned in the novel, give or take a couple of "grave reflections." But despite the character's flatness and simplicity, this is a shrewd and complicated characterization that ends up giving us a shocking sense of Mary's isolation. The discourse both elaborates and exaggerates Mary's immobility, turning her into a narrative satellite, with little effect on the plot and with an utterly marginalized textual position. If this character is pedantic, the text makes the "character-effect" seem almost autistic; if Mary has a tendency to stay at home, the text transforms this—on the level of discourse—into a virtual imprisonment. Only in the final description of Mary does the narrator once again present the concrete social and material conditions which underlie both Mary's personality and the textual distortions that this personality has catalyzed:

> Mary was the only daughter who remained at home; and she was necessarily drawn from the pursuit of accomplishments by Mrs. Bennet's being quite unable to sit alone. Mary was obliged to mix more with the world, but she could still moralize over every

morning visit; and as she was no longer mortified by comparisons between her sisters' beauty and her own, it was suspected by her father that she submitted to the change without much reluctance. (386)

Needless to say, Mary's remaining at home, which seems to have arisen so naturally out of her personality and the configuration of descriptive strategies that converge around her, is also the necessary result for "some one or other" of the daughters who cannot marry into the limited property available. And Mary's personality itself is shaped in the crucible of this socioeconomic situation, which indeed motivates the endless "comparison between her sisters' beauty and her own." To "remain at home": this final action (or inaction) by Mary needs to be understood on a socioeconomic, a psychological, *and* a narrative register; in the same way as Lydia's *displacement*, which I will now turn to, is both social and formal.

Lydia and Mary have nothing in common *except* their minor positions within this novel. Although they would not like to be in the same room together, the two sisters are often forced to share the same paragraph or sentence. In fact, the compression of Mary's character within short, ironic descriptions is often linked with a similar treatment of her younger sisters, Catherine and Lydia. Both Mary and Lydia are radically subordinated to Elizabeth, and in both cases their personalities are intimately tied to their narrative minorness. We have seen how Mary's containment within one paragraph, or one comment, grows out of her own static personality and actions. With Lydia, however, the narrator compresses not immobility and monotony but expansiveness, movement, and energy. The result is a markedly different, but just as delimited, narrative minorness. In fact, Lydia, along with Wickham, will become one of the two "major" minor characters in *Pride and Prejudice*.

Lydia is not simply a fragment of the multiplicity that the text avoids by centering the narrative on one character and the internally grounded marriage plot. Besides being one of the many characters who become subordinate to Elizabeth, in terms of the asymmetric structure, Lydia comes to embody the desire *for* multiplicity itself, within the thematic framework of the story. And this multiplicity—as in Mrs. Bennet's diffuse and illimitable description of the Netherfield ball—is ultimately rooted in the social asymmetry that comes to define the significance of marriage when it is framed in an institutional context. This conflation of minorness and multiplicity is first evinced in a passage that follows a comparison between Mary and Elizabeth, at the end of a long sentence that we have already partially analyzed:

> Elizabeth, easy and unaffected, had been listened to with much more pleasure, though not playing half so well; and Mary, at the end of a long concerto, was glad to purchase praise and gratitude by Scotch and Irish airs, at the request of her younger sisters, who with some of the Lucases and two or three officers joined eagerly in dancing at one end of the room. (25)

The passage flattens Lydia and Kitty both by associating them with Mary's shallowness, in comparison to Elizabeth's depth, and by pluralizing them into "her younger sisters" rather than giving their individual names. Suddenly the usually exact omniscient narrator becomes quite imprecise, telling us only that there were "two or three officers" and "some of the Lucases." These dancers— who clearly represent the excess of characters that are a fixture at these balls— are depicted right at the threshold where a group of distinct individuals becomes blurred into a crowd. The sentence concerns the same multiplicity that drives Mrs. Bennet's endless description of the first ball to Mr. Bennet. However, instead of being suggested by a rambling speech, the sense of multiplicity is now depicted spatially, as the characters are pushed to "one end of the room" and merged together.

This depiction is motivated by the original tension between the social and the individual marriage plot, which will soon begin to shape Elizabeth's singularity. Lydia has already been demarcated as the most disadvantaged sister within the competition for marriageable men, because she is the youngest. She occupies the other end of that spectrum—not the clear position of "the one of my daughters" that Mrs. Bennet wishes "happily settled at Netherfield," but the more crowded and imprecise position among "all the others equally well-married"; not picked out as a part of the "several" girls that Mr. Bingley sees "as uncommonly pretty," but rather among the "so many pleasant girls" that surround, and serve as a contrast to, this uncommonness. To return to the novel's opening sentences, Lydia is part of the social excess that remains after the marriage plot has produced a stable plot for "*a* single man" and "*a* wife"; she is one of the "other of their daughters" supplementing this individual marriage plot. Lydia's talent, almost her entire being in terms of the narrative, is to embrace, rather than flee from, the structure of multiplicity into which she is placed: unable to position herself within a stable, individual marriage plot, which would ensure a clear social position and the economic security that comes through transmission of property, Lydia becomes a magnet for a much larger, shifting, and fragmented social world that is the inevitable result of this stable transmission of property—a social world that the text equates with the principle of multiplicity itself. The crucial narrative effect in *Pride and Prejudice* is to translate this social structure of multiplicity into a *culture* of superficiality, which is contrasted with the privileged and singular depth of the protagonist.

This process is immediately foreshadowed in the sentence that follows the description of dancing: "Mr. Darcy stood near them in silent indignation at such a mode of passing the evening, to the exclusion of all conversation, and was too much engrossed by his own thoughts to perceive that Sir William Lucas was his neighbor, till Sir William thus began" (25). In this complicated sentence Darcy converts a spatial relationship (standing "near" to the other people) into a cultural relationship (distancing himself from the "mode" of their behavior) that is contrasted, by the passage itself, with his own mode of consciousness—a depth of thought that serves to cut him off from "his neighbor." If Darcy wants to change social space into thought, the narrative pushes in the other direction, showing how Darcy's thoughts take place in a social space, distorting his ability "to perceive" the people around him. The center of this description—of Darcy "too much engrossed by his own thoughts . . . to perceive his neighbor"—is precisely the mode of consciousness around which the space of the protagonist will be constructed in the novel, so that these two sentences are an early example of the conflict between the one and the many, between depth of interiority and social multiplicity, and between the protagonist and minor characters.

Returning to the descriptions of Mary, we can now see how the compression of the middle sister leads into the strikingly distinct containment, flattening, and devalorization of Lydia and Kitty, and through them, of social multiplicity itself.

> They found Mary, as usual, deep in the study of thorough bass and human nature; and had some new extracts to admire, and some new observations of thread-bare morality to listen to. Catherine and Lydia had information for them of a different sort. Much had been done, and much had been said in the regiment since the preceding Wednesday; several of the officers had dined lately with their uncle, a private had been flogged, and it had actually been hinted that Colonel Forster was going to be married. (60)

The same lens of satirical containment is applied to two opposite modes of being: the repetitive sameness of Mary, "as usual," and the overabundance of activity and gossip of Kitty and Lydia—the "much had been done" and "much had been said." We can imagine, similarly, the two distinct modes of speech that accompany this—Mary's frozen, carefully worded "observations," and the effusion of news suggested in the list of "information" that ends the paragraph. This news is centrifugal: it contains an overabundance of people that can be described only through the indefinite "several of the officers" and the anonymous "a private." Typically, this social mass then provides the context for the announcement of marriage. With Mary, Lydia, and Elizabeth the essential structure of the narrative has been established, and many different characters, and situations, will fall into this structure of characterization. More specifically, three plot strands will develop within this framework: the central, individually governed marriage plot (Elizabeth and Darcy), the plot of multiplicity and fragmentation (Wickham and Lydia), and the plot of banality and social containment (Mr. Collins, Catherine de Bourgh).

The Space of the Protagonist 1: Elizabeth's Consciousness

One of the most stunning achievements in *Pride and Prejudice* is the gradation that governs the way Elizabeth comes to be the center of the narrative and, simultaneously, becomes "revealed" as a character with more and more depth. The external tripartite plot structure is paced in terms of this construction of Elizabeth. The introduction of Mr. Collins comes at a particular point in this development of Elizabeth's space within the novel, and, similarly, her visit to Pemberley occurs at a specific and strategic moment within this trajectory. In the beginning of the novel, as we have seen, Elizabeth is de-emphasized: we are told about her qualities—her quickness—but this quickness has no bearing on the narrative's own form.

The first way in which Elizabeth begins to come to the foreground of the narrative is through the ironic displacement of attention toward Jane. Jane seems to be set up as the novel's protagonist: the "single man" whom everybody is talking about is attracted to her, and, within the *histoire*, Jane begins to receive an unusual amount of attention. But the very superfluity of Jane's experience allows Austen to subtly accentuate the depth of Elizabeth's consciousness. By separating the agent of experience from the agent of consciousness, Austen presents Elizabeth on a qualitatively different plane from the rest of the characters and slowly integrates Elizabeth's thoughts with the narrative's own point of view. It is precisely Elizabeth's distance from the events she is thinking about that first pushes her to a central position in the narrative.

We can compare two examples of this. The first one, in chapter 4, describes how Elizabeth is more skeptical of the Bingley sisters than Jane is, but then quickly shifts toward an omniscient description of the two sisters that is clearly not in Elizabeth's voice:

> Elizabeth listened in silence, but was not convinced; their behaviour at the assembly had not been calculated to please in general; and with more quickness of observation and less pliancy of temper than her sister, and with a judgment too unassailed by any attention to herself, she was very little disposed to approve them. They were in fact very fine ladies; not deficient in good humour when they were pleased nor in the power of being agreeable where they chose it; but proud and conceited. They were rather handsome, had been educated in one of the first private seminaries in town, had a fortune of twenty thousand pounds, were in the habit of spending more than they ought, and of associating with people of rank. (15)

The narrative here sets up a small place that obliquely externalizes Elizabeth's consciousness. The words that follow Elizabeth's silence are the first time her consciousness coincides with the text itself, as the narrative becomes indistinguishable from what Elizabeth is thinking: she "was not convinced; their behavior at the assembly had not been calculated to please in general . . . she was very little disposed to approve them." But this ripple of thought, presented as free indirect discourse, is interrupted by an omniscient comparison and gets quickly followed by a much longer omniscient description of the two sisters.

In the beginning of chapter 6 we have a more systematic integration of Elizabeth into the narrative discourse, again centering on her more profound awareness of the attention that Jane is receiving. We can also see here how this qualitative distinction between Elizabeth and Jane is put in the context of their difference from their other sisters. The quotation is a long one:

> The ladies of Longbourn soon waited on those of Netherfield. The visit was returned in due form. Miss Bennet's pleasing manners grew on the good will of Mrs. Hurst and Miss Bingley; and though the mother was found to be intolerable and the younger sisters not worth speaking to, a wish of being better acquainted with *them*, was expressed towards the two eldest. By Jane this attention was received with the greatest pleasure; but Elizabeth still saw superciliousness in their treatment of every body, hardly excepting even her sister, and could not like them; though their kindness to Jane, such as it was, had a value as arising in all probability from the influence of their brother's admiration. It was generally evident whenever they met, that he *did* admire her; and to *her* it was equally evident that Jane was yielding to the preference which she had begun to entertain for him from the first, and was in a way to be very much in love; but she considered with pleasure that it was not likely to be discovered by the world in general, since Jane united with great strength of feeling, a composure of temper and a uniform cheerfulness of manner, which would guard her from the suspicions of the impertinent. She mentioned this to her friend Miss Lucas. (21)

This paragraph is uniquely introspective up to this point in the narrative. Almost every sentence fits into the strategy of individuation. First, Elizabeth and Jane are distinguished from their mother and younger sisters. Next, Elizabeth's perception of the Bingley sisters is distinguished from Jane's perception. In the fifth sentence, Elizabeth's consciousness *of* Jane is singled out: she experiences her sister's experiences more profoundly than everyone else, seeing things that are not just "generally evident" and which can't be "discovered by the world in general." (The accentuation of Elizabeth in this contrast depends on the strength of italicization, the juxtaposition of the radical "to *her*" with this generality. As I mentioned before, italics come up repeatedly in *Pride and Prejudice* as a way of expressing a person's radical singularity—an extremely high proportion of italics in the novel are reserved for personal pronouns.)[13] Finally the paragraph offers an analysis of Jane's character that resembles the earlier omniscient description but is now clearly coming *from* Elizabeth's consciousness. This swallowing of the omniscient narrative is the final push in this passage's construction of Elizabeth's centrality, and it is made certain by the closing sentence in the paragraph, which confirms that the observations just recorded belong to Elizabeth and not the omniscient narrator. Thus the sentence "She mentioned this to her friend Miss Lucas" provides closure for the "plot" of this paragraph, as we have been reading it—a plot of the development of asymmetry, which is necessarily found only *between* the *histoire* and the *discours*. (And free indirect discourse—so often the "hero," as it were, in stylistic or formal analyses of Austen—is here functioning as merely an element within this larger process.)

   In the next crucial development of Elizabeth's central space within the narrative, the distance between Elizabeth and Jane—which has allowed the narrator to figure the depth of Elizabeth's consciousness—becomes externalized, when Jane is literally separated from the Bennets while she stays at Netherfield because of her illness. Just as Elizabeth's attention to Jane's pleasure has been emphasized over Jane's pleasure in and of itself, Elizabeth's trip to *visit* Jane is emphasized over Jane's illness. In an unexpectedly crucial paragraph, the narrative focuses on Elizabeth's walk to Netherfield, becoming more detailed at the precise moment when Elizabeth is separated from her two younger sisters:

> Elizabeth accepted their company, and the three young ladies set off together.
> "If we make haste," said Lydia, as they walked along, "perhaps we may see something of Captain Carter before he goes."
> In Meryton they parted; the two youngest repaired to the lodgings of one of the officers' wives, and Elizabeth continued her walk alone, crossing field after field at a quick pace, jumping over stiles and springing over puddles with impatient activity, and finding herself at last within view of the house, with weary ancles, dirty stockings, and a face glowing with the warmth of exercise. (32)

This passage functions as an externalization of Elizabeth's consciousness, so that her "something more of quickness" finds its corollary in her "quick pace" and her "impatient activity." The dilation of the description—as it drifts into the present tense through a series of participles ("crossing," "jumping," "springing," "finding herself")—is unique up to this moment in the text. In fact, this passage stands out within the narrative as a whole. It is a purely unplotted moment in this densely plotted novel, a free space in the narrative— or rather the only "plot" that it serves to advance is precisely the asymmetrical construction of Elizabeth as the center of narrative interest. The passage shows how a thought in *Pride and Prejudice*, a tendency of consciousness, can become gradually externalized. Within twenty pages we have moved from the simple comment that "Elizabeth felt Jane's pleasure," to the more intricate representation (in free indirect discourse) of Elizabeth's thoughts *about* Jane, to this physical description of Elizabeth running, with "quick pace," *toward* Jane. At the same time, when the text shifts from "continued her walk" to "crossing field after field," the change in verb tense subtly registers Elizabeth's *own* apprehension of her physical experience. No other character in the novel gets to feel things in this way.

   Elizabeth's increasingly central presence within the narrative discourse is then immediately dramatized when she enters Bingley's house:

> She was shewn into the breakfast-parlour, where all but Jane were assembled, and where her appearance created a great deal of surprise.

This surprise—which is next described and motivated on a psychological plane, with analysis of each individual reaction—is also the result of an uneasy interaction between Elizabeth's interior consciousness, which has just gained the attention of the narrative, and the more familiar polycentric social universe, which exerts a competing pressure on the narrative frame. This kind of grating, or tension, will occur frequently at moments when these two registers—the rapidly developing internal consciousness of the privileged protagonist and the unchanging texture of the external social world—overlap.

At the beginning of chapter 8 we see another, related sign of Elizabeth's centrality: when she leaves the frame of the narrative discourse, the other characters begin to talk about *her*. In one sentence Austen connects this with Elizabeth's concern *for* Jane, writing, "When dinner was over, she returned directly to Jane, and Miss Bingley began abusing her as soon as she was out of the room" (35). The next two pages follow a conversation about Elizabeth, until the narrative returns to directly reporting Elizabeth's actions.[14] The narrative develops the increasing centrality of Elizabeth's consciousness in yet another way in the next episode, again as she seemingly fades into the margins of the scene. Austen is careful to preface the whole scene by describing how Elizabeth will observe it, so that even as the dialogue is taken over by other characters, we have a sense that Elizabeth's unique consciousness is absorbing everything that occurs: "Elizabeth took up some needlework, and was sufficiently amused in attending to what passed between Darcy and his companion" (47). Through this sentence Austen moves Elizabeth closer to the narrative's own point of view: the events that the narrator is describing and the events that Elizabeth is herself apprehending begin to converge. In this sense, the protagonist increasingly becomes both the narrative's main object and its main subject; both a source of and the focal site for the narrative's point of view.

This more entrenched degree of centrality is further developed a few pages later, at the beginning of chapter 11. Again, Elizabeth's role becomes clear only over the course of a couple of paragraphs, when we *retroactively* discover that it has been Elizabeth, and not the narrator, who has been observing what has been described:

> When the ladies removed after dinner, Elizabeth ran up to her sister, and seeing her well guarded from cold, attended her into the drawing-room; where she was welcomed by her two friends with many professions of pleasure; and Elizabeth had never seen them so agreeable as they were during the hour which passed before the gentlemen appeared. Their powers of conversation were considerable. They could describe an entertainment with accuracy, relate an anecdote with humour, and laugh at their acquaintance with spirit.
>
> But when the gentlemen entered, Jane was no longer the first object. Miss Bingley's eyes were instantly turned towards Darcy, and she had something to say to him before he had advanced many steps. He addressed himself directly to Miss Bennet, with a polite congratulation; Mr. Hurst also made her a slight bow, and said he was "very glad;" but diffuseness and warmth remained for Bingley's salutation. He

was full of joy and attention. The first half hour was spent in piling up the fire, lest she should suffer from the change of room; and she removed at his desire to the other side of the fire-place, that she might be farther from the door. He then sat down by her, and talked scarcely to any one else. Elizabeth, at work in the opposite corner, saw it all with great delight. (54)

These two paragraphs seem so much like the omniscient narrative, in their elastic range and their analytic sensibility, that we might not notice the way they are firmly positioned as Elizabeth's observations, wedged between "Elizabeth had never seen them so agreeable" and "Elizabeth . . . saw it all with great delight." This retrospective comment is similar to the earlier passage, where the remark "She mentioned this to her friend" shows us that an analytic judgment of Jane, which might have simply been the narrator's, is actually Elizabeth's. But this passage is even more significant because it is not simply a thought belonging to Elizabeth but rather the apprehension of that external world which is in tension with her own centrality. Thus the very heterogeneity of this passage, its way of shifting from person to person merely because they are close together within a social or spatial field, does not challenge the centrality of a single consciousness but reinforces it. While Jane might no longer be able to be "the first object" within an intrinsically fluid social field, Elizabeth remains the first subject within the narrative field, filtering the omniscient description through her own perception.

This scene marks the end of the first phase of Elizabeth's development as the central protagonist, which is delimited by her return from Netherfield. The text is structured around three such trips—to Netherfield, to Rosings, to Pemberley—each of which pushes Elizabeth to the center of the narrative and gives us an increased sense of her depth as a person. (In other words, long after Elizabeth's *relative* centrality has been established, the nature and significance of this centrality continue to be dynamically elaborated, in relation to the asymmetric character-field.) The return home is always characterized by the return of multiplicity, mediated by an unpleasant encounter with her other sisters. This transition is emphasized in chapter 12, the book's shortest chapter, which starts with Elizabeth and Jane's decision to depart and ends with their arrival at home and the comments of their three sisters, which we have already examined. Chapter 13 begins the next phase of the narrative. Just as Elizabeth's interiority and narrative centrality have been extended and developed, so the construction of minorness also develops, with the introduction of Mr. Wickham and Mr. Collins.

Characterizing Minorness 2: Externality

Wickham and Collins both enter the novel belatedly, just at the point where the essential structure of asymmetry, and the organizing differentiation of the five sisters, have been established. The narrative calls attention to their nearly simultaneous entrance into the story, as the sisters themselves are first attracted by the radical strangeness, or externality, of each character. First Mr. Bennet announces "an addition to our family party . . . a gentleman and a stranger," and the conversation continues:

> "It is *not* Mr. Bingley," said her husband; "it is a person whom I never saw in the whole course of my life."
>
> This roused a general astonishment; and he had the pleasure of being eagerly questioned by his wife and five daughters at once. (61)

Wickham's arrival in the narrative, two chapters later, is described in similar terms:

> But the attention of every lady was soon caught by a young man, whom they had never seen before, of most gentlemanlike appearance, walking with an officer on the other side of the way. (72)

This externality helps develop our sense of these characters' minorness: throughout the novel we always look *at* these two men, from the outside, rather than sympathizing with their own point of view.[15] It is this condition of externality that allows Austen to push her techniques of characterization even further, so that Wickham and Collins exaggerate the types of minorness that we have already seen in Lydia and Mary, expanding the overall asymmetry of the novel. Wickham has the same excessive social energy as Lydia, while Collins's long-windedness is an exaggerated version of Mary's pedantry: it is as though he takes her compressed moral "extracts" and strings them together into his long speeches. More than Mary and Lydia, in fact, these men exemplify the two foundational kinds of minor character discussed in the introduction—the repetitive automaton and the unpredictable eccentric. These extremes are the dialectical results of one single process that flows out of asymmetry: the estrangement of surface from depth. This estrangement is, in this case, already formally suggested by the mere fact of the characters' externality. Again, as in compression, the characters' position within the novel's overarching structure, their exterior position vis-à-vis the Bennets, collapses into their representation in-and-of-themselves, as individual characters.

The two characters' externality from the Bennet family—who are always privileged as the primary and original source of narrative interest—exaggerates their minorness but does not diminish their importance in terms of plot, theme, or the novel's total structure. The rejected suitor is among the most crucial minor characters in the individual marriage plot, and in this story Collins and Wickham come to represent the Scylla and Charybdis of Elizabeth's navigation toward a successful marriage. Collins offers a potential marriage for money without any affection or desire; while Wickham elicits sexual desire without delivering the social advancement necessary for a good marriage. Elizabeth's

Ithaca is of course Pemberley, marriage for love and for money. But at the same time, Collins and Wickham, in their failed relationships with Elizabeth, continue to function as extensions of the two types of minorness that we have already seen embodied in Mary and Lydia. In rejecting Collins, Elizabeth distances herself further from the repetitive mode of pedantry that we have seen in Mary; in rejecting Wickham, Elizabeth distinguishes herself from the unpredictable mode of excessiveness that we have seen in Lydia. It is in this second stage of the narrative, with these two external figures, that minorness begins to be linked with subplots, which exist in clear tension with the central marriage plot. Wickham and Collins are thus the two figures that most evidently connect plot with characterization in the novel.

I will examine Wickham's singular place in the novel in a separate section but want to turn now to Mr. Collins, who clearly confronts us as a limit point of minorness in *Pride and Prejudice*. The narrator is unequivocal: "Mr. Collins was not a sensible man, and the deficiency of nature had been but little assisted by education or society" (70). Collins's caricatured personality, the symptom and sign of his minorness, emerges through three interrelated registers: the simple exaggeration of his faults, his incessant repetition of these faults, and the continual annoyance or disruption that these faults provoke. All three of these registers (his flaws, his repetitiveness, and his disruption) often manifest themselves through language. More than even Mary's, Collins's inner personality is distorted through his ridiculous way of speaking, which seems to have subsumed whatever was on his inside.

If the tension between surface and depth is commonly expressed through the reduction of a human being to a *function*, and, most literally, to his or her labor (the minor character as servant in the eighteenth-century novel or professional in the nineteenth-century novel or bureaucrat in the twentieth-century novel), a related process often reduces a character to his or her language or delimited way of speaking. Collins's subjectivity is, like Mary's, encased in and essentially subsumed by his long-winded, obsequious, and repetitive habits of communication. It is important, for this reason, that we don't see Mr. Collins until we have already judged him through his disembodied voice, revealed in his letter to Mr. Bennet. We learn much more about Collins from the letter's wording than from the information it conveys. Mr. Bennet, in fact, anticipates the main points of the omniscient narrator's own judgment:

> "Can he be a sensible man, sir?"
>
> "No, my dear; I think not. I have great hopes of finding him quite the reverse. There is a mixture of servility and self-importance in his letter, which promises well. . . ." (64)

Similarly, the narrator, in her most detached, omniscient description of Mr. Collins, will write that he was "altogether a mixture of pride and obsequiousness, self-importance and humility" (114).

If the essence of Mr. Collins's character is fully revealed through the mere surface of his language, a defining aspect of Collins's way of speaking is its repetitiveness. Chapter 13, which begins with Collins's letter, ends with an image of his long-windedness: "He begged pardon for having displeased her. In a softened tone she declared herself not at all offended; but he continued to apologise for about a quarter of an hour." This tendency is more than just another example of Collins's unseemliness or oversolicitousness. Collins's repetition consolidates the way that his inner being is effaced through the exterior of his language, reducing his personality, and even his consciousness, to one long monotony. The fifteen minutes of apology is just a symptom of a larger process. Collins really repeats himself during every moment in which he is present in the narrative, becoming a stunning example of narrative flatness.[16] As E. M. Forster notes, a key aspect of flatness is the inability to change or to surprise.

Collins's repetitiveness, even while it subsumes his personality, also helps create local disruptions across the text's surface. Repetition allows Mr. Collins to push his flaws to a foregrounded position in the narrative, even as it accentuates them. In this way Mr. Collins becomes ridiculous through the same process that makes him functionally significant—if only in a negative sense—as a source of narrative disruption. The primary example of this disruption is, of course, his preposterous but aggressive pursuit of Elizabeth, which is itself marked by repetition and failed communication. To put it schematically: Collins's pursuit of Elizabeth *diminishes* our sense of his character, since his repetitive stubbornness makes him seem very flat, even while it *expands* our sense of his importance in the novel, integrating him into the larger semantic field through which we understand Elizabeth.

Another example of this disruption is Mr. Collins's self-introduction to Darcy at the second ball, followed by his long speech about music playing. This example also works in a specifically formal sense: it dramatically represents a minor character trying to push up against the limited narrative space that has been allocated for him:

And with a low bow he left her to attack Mr. Darcy, whose reception of his advances she eagerly watched, and whose astonishment at being so addressed was very evident. Her cousin prefaced his speech with a solemn bow, and though she could not hear a word of it, she felt as if hearing it all, and saw in the motion of his lips the words "apology," "Hunsford," and "Lady Catherine de Bourgh."—It vexed her to see him expose himself to such a man. Mr. Darcy was eyeing him with unrestrained wonder, and when at last Mr. Collins allowed him time to speak, replied with an air of distant civility. Mr. Collins, however, was not discouraged from speaking again, and Mr. Darcy's contempt seemed abundantly increasing with the length of his second speech, and at the end of it he only made him a slight bow, and moved another way. (97–98)

This local example is itself informed by the dialectical relationship between Elizabeth's depth and Collins's flatness, so that *his* character flaws are inflected through *her* mortified perception of them. Collins's disruption is explicitly linked to the length of his speech, as his two drawn-out speeches are juxtaposed with Darcy's curt replies. This lengthiness erupts into the novel's *discourse* a few pages later, when Collins answers the request for someone to play music.

> "If I," said Mr. Collins, "were so fortunate as to be able to sing, I should have great pleasure, I am sure, in obliging the company with an air; for I consider music as a very innocent diversion, and perfectly compatible with the profession of a clergyman.—I do not mean however to assert that we can be justified in devoting too much of our time to music, for there are certainly other things to be attended to. The rector of a parish has much to do.—In the first place, he must make such an agreement for tythes as may be beneficial to himself and not offensive to his patron. He must write his own sermons; and the time that remains will not be too much for his parish duties, and the care and improvement of his dwelling, which he cannot be excused from making as comfortable as possible. And I do not think it of light importance that he should have attentive and conciliatory manners towards every body, especially towards those to whom he owes his preferment. I cannot acquit him of that duty; nor could I think well of the man who should omit an occasion of testifying his respect towards any body connected with the family." And with a bow to Mr. Darcy, he concluded his speech, which had been spoken so loud as to be heard by half the room.—Many stared.—Many smiled; but no one looked more amused than Mr. Bennet himself, while his wife seriously commended Mr. Collins for having spoken so sensibly, and observed in a half-whisper to Lady Lucas, that he was a remarkably clever, good kind of young man. (101)

Collins has been trying to ingratiate himself with Darcy, magnetized by his elevated social position. The scene relies on the social distance between the two characters but also subtly manipulates their distinct *narrative* positions. The way that Collins gets the room's attention is a parodic inversion of how Darcy "drew the attention of the room." Again, the exterior position and the interior being of this minor character become intertwined: the scene both magnifies our sense of Mr. Collins's flaws and suggests that these flaws are only becoming magnified, or growing more distorted, as he tries to gain a more central position in the narrative. The nature of Mr. Collins is inextricably entangled with the way he is presented—his individual character, striking on its own terms, is grounded in the narrative's larger asymmetric structure. This is often the case with minor characters: their own striking personalities (often striking only in their flaws) are subtly tied to their larger exclusion from the center of the narrative. Take Shakespeare's Falstaff, so often acknowledged as one of the playwright's most significant and certainly most popular characters. Can we understand his singular character outside of the plays' structure, and, more specifically, outside of his ultimate *exclusion* in *Henry IV*? The greatness of

Falstaff derives not simply from his grandiose excess but also from the way that his corpulent personality is ironically interwoven with his limited place in the dramatic universe. This is not to compare Mr. Collins to Falstaff, two characters who are perhaps as dissimilar as any in British literature. But, through this very dissonance, we can see a similar process of distortion that, in the final analysis, subsumes both extremes under the same narrative rubric. In each case, a particular mode of human excess is conditioned and shaped by a larger, asymmetric narrative structure.

Collins's speech is utterly banal; he ceaselessly exhibits an inert language that has become divorced from meaning. This minor character always speaks at length but signifies nothing. The speech seems motivated by the character as we understand him, and yet, simultaneously, we sense that its painful excess is propelled forward by the narrator's obsession with capturing, or configuring, the ridiculous. On one level, the speech is derived merely from Collins's individual character: it reflects on and emanates out of his personality. But it is also carefully situated in a specific context, which has as much to do with Collins's social, and narrative, position as with his internal qualities as a pedantic and obsequious bore. In this sense, the speech exists inside and outside our sense of Mr. Collins as a specific individual: it both highlights him and extinguishes him. This dual process can occur only in a complicated narrative structure, since the tension arises only as we are forced to contextualize a character who must exist—in every sense—on a subordinate level within the novelistic totality.

It has often been noted that a key trait of minor characters in Austen's novels is distorted or improper speech. Tony Tanner writes that "[t]he overriding concern of Jane Austen's novels—and of many of her heroines—is the nature of true utterance" (6); for *Pride and Prejudice* he proposes a typology based on the "different ways in which people use language" (126). "Some people," he continues, "employ it unreflectively as an almost automatic extension of their other behavior; they are unable to speak, as they are unable to think, outside their particular social situation. Others, by contrast, are capable of using language reflectively and not just as an almost conditioned response to a social situation." (It is testimony to the novel's asymmetric structure that Tanner privileges *incorrect* speech and then identifies proper speech only "by contrast.") Using similar criteria, Tanner claims that "Emma has a wider range of discourse than anyone else in the novel. She can out-talk, over-talk, everyone, and that includes Mr. Knightley, because she has a kind of energy of articulation" (181). These distinctions are very important, and an analysis of modes of discourse is one of the most probing ways in which critics have analyzed structures of asymmetry. The scenes with Mr. Collins that we have examined fit smoothly into this analysis, as Collins exemplifies many of the qualities that Austen associates with improper speech.

An analysis of language can also lead to the essential division between the development of the protagonist and the fragmentation of secondary characters, so that Tanner notes, "[A]ll of Jane Austen's novels portray a movement towards true seeing and true speaking. . . . [O]ne way or another all the heroines achieve the desired end. Those characters who do not either disappear into misery or continue blindly on in their confident unseeing and their empty words and meaningless stereotypical utterances" (6–7). This summation, despite its teleological slant, recognizes the essential division between the heroine's balanced achievement and the other characters' fragmented disappearance. In both Wickham's hypocrisy and Collins's repetitive obsequiousness, language becomes separated from meaning: we never know whether Wickham is honestly expressing himself, and we sense that Collins is really expressing nothing. Similarly, Wickham "disappear[s] into misery," and Collins "continue[s] blindly on." However we shouldn't view these two narrative fates, or these two minor characters, as simply embodiments of different ways of speaking. Too often analysis of how various characters have radically different speech patterns ends up subsuming the characters into a purely linguistic structure. Thus Tanner writes, "Almost exclusively the characters define themselves in their speech" (40). Pushing this analysis one step further, D. A. Miller writes, "To get rid of certain characters, however, is perhaps only a broad way of getting rid of what has *characterized the text* under their sponsorship, an insufficiently purposeful or wrongly opaque language" (77). Miller's brilliant analysis of narratability and closure in Austen elucidates the essential dialectical tension between centrality and fragmentation in Austen; his analysis diverges from the current one precisely in the way it subsumes characterization into language.

Helpers: Charlotte Lucas and the Actantial Theory

Il y a des hommes n'ayant pour mission parmi les autres que de servir d'intermédiaires; on les franchit comme des ponts, et l'on va plus loin.
—Flaubert, *L'Éducation sentimentale*

Miller's conflation of characters and the language they use plays into the narrative's own constant transformation of characters into characteristics. Elizabeth's rejection of Collins, soon after he comes on the scene, is certainly depicted as a cultural rather than a social rejection. Rather than dismissing an actual, living human being, Elizabeth's rejection of Collins functions as the dismissal of a certain type of person, a certain way of being or of speaking. Collins is such a caricature that Elizabeth never sees him except in terms of his ridiculous behavior, and for this reason she is not very much affected by having to turn down his marriage proposal (in sharp contrast to her rejection of Darcy, but also in contrast to the pain that Wickham later causes her). The only time that Elizabeth is prevented from articulating her opposition to Mr. Collins is when "[t]he idea of Mr. Collins, with all his solemn composure, being run away with by his feelings, made Elizabeth so near laughing that she could not use the short pause he allowed in any attempt to stop him farther" (105). Here Elizabeth stumbles not on Collins's status as a human being but precisely on his embodiment of the ridiculous.

However, the actual social context (and socionarrative consequence) that underlies this rejection is reinscribed into the text when Elizabeth finds out that Charlotte Lucas has consented to Mr. Collins's proposal. We can compare Elizabeth's casual rejection of Mr. Collins to her shock and surprise when she learns that Charlotte has accepted him:

> [T]hat Charlotte could encourage him, seemed almost as far from possibility as that she could encourage him herself, and her astonishment was consequently so great as to overcome at first the bounds of decorum, and she could not help crying out,
> "Engaged to Mr. Collins! my dear Charlotte,—impossible!" (124)

Charlotte Lucas is perhaps the most interesting figure within the novel's asymmetrical structure of characterization. She exists uneasily in a middle ground within this structure, illustrating the difficulties that inevitably occur when certain characters bear only a functional relationship to the protagonist. Charlotte Lucas is an ideal character to juxtapose against one of the most influential structuralist accounts of characterization—A. J. Greimas's functionalist "actantial" model. I want to draw out the limits of Greimas's method of interpretation by analyzing Charlotte's position within *Pride and Prejudice*: to read the actantial model through this minor character.

In the introduction, I have discussed how Greimas's model—which insists that all individual characters slot into six different narrative roles or functions—might start by rejecting the notion that individual characters represent human beings but ends up suggesting that a narrative's entire *structure* of characterization can serve as the reflection of a (single) human subject. Greimas's formal model does not finally reject mimesis per se but does imply that all narrative structures can represent only *one* subject, and that this subject ("le sujet") is necessarily oriented around desire. Greimas's entire actantial model thus accommodates the type of human subject that structures the *individual* marriage plot: internally grounded, not connected to other people in a meaningful way, oriented around a teleological desire that can unfold over time. We have also followed how Greimas, after noting the "secondary" nature of "helpers" ("adjuvants"), then makes two moves: describing helpers as the "adjectival" components of his semantic model, and claiming that "the helper and the opposer are only the projections of the will to act and the imaginary resistances of the subject himself, judged as beneficial or harmful in relation to his desire" ["l'adjuvant et l'opposant ne soient que des projections de la volonté d'agir et des résistances imaginaires de sujet lui-même, jugés bénéfiques ou maléfiques par rapport à son désir"] (180).

With Charlotte Lucas, Austen shows just how a fictional character can get placed in such a secondary, functional, symbolic position, and then shows the problematic limitations of this construction. When we first see Charlotte, she is quite explicitly positioned as a "helper" of Elizabeth, as that character who— in the *story*, and not simply the *discourse*—allows Elizabeth to externalize her own viewpoints. Charlotte is first introduced at the beginning of chapter 5, and from the start she is placed in relation to Elizabeth: "They had several children. The eldest of them, a sensible, intelligent young woman, about twenty-seven, was Elizabeth's intimate friend" (18). Although Charlotte is immediately positioned as one of "several children," the dynamic between her and the other Lucas sisters is never developed. Instead, Charlotte's next several appearances in the novel place her in a firmly responsive mode, reacting to or modifying Elizabeth's thoughts (even while these thoughts are, of course, simultaneously functioning as a crucial element in the development of Elizabeth's achieved centrality). In this way, as we have seen, the first rehearsal of free indirect discourse, in the passage describing Elizabeth's perspective on the Bingley sisters, concludes by noting that "[s]he mentioned this to her friend Miss Lucas" (21), while the next scene begins with Elizabeth *questioning* Charlotte: " 'What does Mr. Darcy mean,' said she to Charlotte, 'by listening to my conversation with Colonel Forster?' " (24). Soon after, Charlotte prompts Elizabeth to strike up a conversation with Darcy: "On his approaching them soon afterwards, though without seeming to have any intention of speaking, Miss Lucas defied her friend to mention such a subject to him, which immediately provoking Elizabeth to do it, she turned to him and said . . ." (24). In the ensuing conversation, Elizabeth uses Charlotte's comment to display her own energetic wit, overshadowing her friend in front of Darcy.

Already Charlotte has played numerous *different* roles for the protagonist: the vehicle for Elizabeth to articulate her (narratively privileged) thoughts about the Bingleys; the sounding board for Elizabeth's questions about Darcy; the "provoking" motivation for Elizabeth's actions at the ball. Charlotte's role in externalizing Elizabeth's own consciousness is demonstrated most clearly the next time she is mentioned, after Elizabeth has met Wickham and become angry at Darcy for keeping Wickham away from the ball:

> But Elizabeth was not formed for ill-humour; and though every prospect of her own was destroyed for the evening, it could not dwell long on her spirits; and having told all her griefs to Charlotte Lucas, whom she had not seen for a week, she was soon able to make a voluntary transition to the oddities of her cousin, and to point him out to her particular notice. (90)

This passage, beginning with an explication of Elizabeth's character, puts Charlotte in a purely functional position, as the human being who provides the link in the "transition" *within* Elizabeth's own consciousness, from her attachment to Wickham to her distaste for Collins. The configuration of this transition, however, already begins to motivate the way that Charlotte's functional bearing on Elizabeth's consciousness will soon exceed this purely psychological or cognitive role—leading Charlotte to get mixed up with Collins herself. Charlotte's interaction with Collins begins quite literally as the residue of the assistance she lends to Elizabeth, who completes her "transition" from one topic to another by "point[ing Collins] out" to Charlotte's "particular notice." In a scene that soon follows, Charlotte provides a different kind of "transition," one equally useful to the protagonist, by enabling Collins to transfer *his* attention toward *her*. This is again depicted in terms of the relief it provides Elizabeth: "He scarcely ever spoke to her, and the assiduous attentions which he had been so sensible of himself, were transferred for the rest of the day to Miss Lucas, whose civility in listening to him, was a seasonable relief to them all, and especially to her friend" (115).

It is from this position, as the pivot of both Collins's and Elizabeth's emotional "transitions" (of attention) that Charlotte comes to replace Elizabeth as the object of Collins's proposal. In a certain sense this marriage just continues to develop Charlotte's functional role of helping the protagonist: she fully diverts Collins's attention away from Elizabeth, coming to represent a type of marriage that Elizabeth rejects. Charlotte thus becomes the embodiment and limit point of a possibility that Elizabeth refuses to pursue, "une projection . . . du sujet lui-même" that the text can fully contain. Thus the narrator first describes Elizabeth's surprise about Charlotte's action in terms of Elizabeth's own *self-understanding*: "that Charlotte could encourage him, seemed almost as far from possibility as that she could encourage him herself."

At this point we can discern three different but interrelated ways in which Charlotte functions as a helper or an *adjuvant*, each more embedded in the narrative's symbolic structure. Most superficially, she facilitates *plot* developments that will help bring Elizabeth together with Darcy, by inciting Elizabeth to challenge Darcy and by taking Mr. Collins's attention away from Elizabeth. This type of utility extends to many minor characters. For instance, Charlotte's father, William Lucas, functions in a similar way in the scene where he encourages Darcy and Elizabeth to dance.

> He paused in hopes of an answer; but his companion was not disposed to make any; and Elizabeth at that instant moving towards them, he was struck with the notion of doing a very gallant thing, and called out to her,
>
> "My dear Miss Eliza, why are not you dancing?—Mr. Darcy, you must allow me to present this young lady to you as a very desirable partner.—You cannot refuse to dance, I am sure, when so much beauty is before you." And taking her hand, he would have given it to Mr. Darcy, who, though extremely surprised, was not unwilling to receive it, when she instantly drew back, and said with some discomposure . . . (26)

Notice how Sir William's own consciousness arrests brief narrative attention ("he was struck with the notion") only as it is circumscribed *within* this functional role vis-à-vis the protagonist's marriage plot. Such containment of this character's perspective is mirrored by the way that Sir William's unmistakable instrumentality is itself contained. His "gallant" suggestion doesn't directly help bring Darcy and Elizabeth together—actually prompting the future partners to dance—but inadvertently helps by, precisely, pulling them apart. (It is as though the marriage plot needs to ward off *too* meaningful an integration of a Sir William into its eventual conclusion.)

Charlotte, on the other hand, helps the protagonist in explicitly more consequential ways—beyond the vagaries of the plot—during the scenes in which she enables Elizabeth to articulate or develop her thoughts. Unlike the first type of narrative help, this role as confidante is reserved for only a few characters in the novel, primarily Charlotte, Jane, and Mrs. Gardiner. But this more skillful kind of psychological help is not finally distinct from Charlotte's plot function. Since the plot *itself* hinges on what Marilyn Butler calls "Elizabeth's moral enlightenment," all plot-helpers are ultimately contributing to the development of Elizabeth's consciousness. Charlotte simply makes this link more apparent: she actualizes the way that every minor character within the discourse variously serves a structure which effectuates the growth of Elizabeth's mind. Finally, Charlotte performs another kind of help, thematically significant, by actualizing a possibility that Elizabeth rejects when she marries Collins to secure economic comfort. Charlotte's marriage to Collins is a crux of the novel's thematic architecture and is thus the final instance of her functionality, of her secondary position, vis-à-vis Elizabeth's centrality, within the narrative universe. The absorbing interest of this character might depend in part on the way that the depiction of Charlotte strikingly condenses three distinct kinds of narrative help that could be abstracted as a general interpretive model: the *plot-helper*, who facilitates external developments within the story itself; the *psychological-helper*, who more directly helps to elaborate the protagonist's interiority within the story, often as a friend, interlocutor, or confidante; and the *thematic-helper*, who functions within the overall semantic field of the narrative discourse, as this discourse itself elaborates the symbolic identity (and centrality) of the protagonist. (The actantial model subsumes all of these under one essential narrative rubric, but there are significant differences and potential interactions among the three, which could be applied to the analysis of different genres and historical periods as well as individual works.)

If these multiple and interlocking modes of "assistance" establish Charlotte as an exceptional helper in a novel with many different kinds of helper, her unique position in the novel rests, finally, in the problematic misalignment between her status as character and her elaborate thematic and psychological utility.[17] Elizabeth feels too close to Charlotte to simply view this marriage as a negative example that redefines the more elevated qualities of her own consciousness. This type of judgment is easy enough to pursue with her sisters, still simpler with Collins, but much more difficult with her friend. Thus Elizabeth's surprise about Charlotte takes two forms: one that continues to revolve around Charlotte's functional role in defining Elizabeth's own qualities and one that stumbles against the actual subjective experience of her friend:

> She had always felt that Charlotte's opinion of matrimony was not exactly like her own, but she could not have supposed it possible that when called into action, she would have sacrificed every better feeling to worldly advantage. Charlotte the wife of Mr. Collins was a most humiliating picture!—and to the pang of a friend disgracing herself and sunk in her esteem, was added the distressing conviction that it was impossible for that friend to be tolerably happy in the lot she had chosen. (125)

This conjunction, "and to the pang . . . was added," lies at the fault line of the novel's asymmetrical construction. How is it possible to "add" together the utilization of Charlotte's choice vis-à-vis Elizabeth's own development and Charlotte's actual experience of the choice? The first half of the sentence moves toward Elizabeth, and, more specifically, toward Elizabeth's increasing moral centrality within the narrative, while the second half of the sentence moves away from her, and toward the plurality of subjective experiences that together compose the system of marriage, understood as a social phenomenon. This is a contrast that will not be allowed in the more extreme, and disruptive, case of Lydia and Wickham. These two are *fully developed* minor characters because their embodiment of the socially grounded marriage plot effaces their subjectivity, pushes them outside the limits of the story, and constructs their being on a purely functional level—as the rejected embodiments of the sexual, economic, and psychological residue that Elizabeth and Darcy's individual marriage plot produces.

Charlotte exists on the threshold of effacement: Elizabeth wants to push her away but knows her too well. Out of this tension emerges one of the most curious and interesting spaces in the narrative. Charlotte can be neither included nor excluded in the text, just as she cannot be compressed into the role of "narrative helper."

> Between Elizabeth and Charlotte there was a restraint which kept them mutually silent on the subject; and Elizabeth felt persuaded that no real confidence could ever subsist between them again. Her disappointment in Charlotte made her turn with fonder regard to her sister. (127–28)

> Elizabeth soon heard from her friend; and their correspondence was as regular and frequent as it had ever been; that it should be equally unreserved was impossible. Elizabeth could never address her without feeling that all the comfort of intimacy was over, and, though determined not to slacken as a correspondent, it was for the sake of what had been, rather than what was. (146)

> Elizabeth in the solitude of her chamber had to meditate upon Charlotte's degree of contentment, to understand her address in guiding, and composure in bearing with her husband, and to acknowledge that it was all done very well. (157)

In these passages we see the social undercurrent that structurally informs the narrative *adjuvant* but which is elided in Greimas's actantial model. If Charlotte represents an exemplary narrative helper, she also shows the limitation of (and dynamic contradictions within) this model by dramatizing the intricate tension between a character's functionality and her own implied personhood. Charlotte's subjectivity *does* enter into the plot, as do the conditions that motivated her choice:

> Charlotte herself was tolerably composed. She had gained her point, and had time to consider of it. Her reflections were in general satisfactory. Mr. Collins to be sure was neither sensible nor agreeable; his society was irksome, and his attachment to her must be imaginary. But still he would be her husband.—Without thinking highly either of men or of matrimony, marriage had always been her object; it was the only honourable provision for well-educated young women of small fortune, and however uncertain of giving happiness, must be their pleasantest preservative from want. This preservative she had now obtained; and at the age of twenty-seven, without having ever been handsome, she felt all the good luck of it. The least agreeable circumstance in the business, was the surprise it must occasion to Elizabeth Bennet, whose friendship she valued beyond that of any other person. (122–23)

In this crucial passage we again see how Elizabeth's centrality is intricately linked to the more general tension between the individual and the social marriage plot. Thus Charlotte's quite different understanding of marriage is articulated even as Elizabeth is presented suddenly from the outside, with the uncommon and subtly jarring use of her full name.

The social conditions that ground Charlotte's choice are even more starkly emphasized in a telling conversation between Elizabeth and Jane:

> "The more I see of the world, the more I am dissatisfied with it; and every day confirms my belief of the inconsistency of all human characters, and of the little dependence that can be placed on the appearance of either merit or sense. I have met with two instances lately; one I will not mention; the other is Charlotte's marriage. It is unaccountable! in every view it is unaccountable!"
>
> "My dear Lizzy, do not give way to such feelings as these. They will ruin your happiness. You do not make allowance enough for difference of situation and temper. Consider Mr. Collins's respectability, and Charlotte's prudent, steady character. Remember that she is one of a large family; that as to fortune, it is a most eligible match; and be ready to believe, for every body's sake, that she may feel something like regard and esteem for our cousin."
>
> ". . . you must feel, as well as I do, that the woman who marries him, cannot have a proper way of thinking. You shall not defend her, though it is Charlotte Lucas. You

shall not, for the sake of one individual, change the meaning of principle and integrity, nor endeavour to persuade yourself or me, that selfishness is prudence, and insensibility of danger, security for happiness." (135–36)

Elizabeth's sudden juxtaposition of "one individual" against "the meaning of principle and integrity" touches upon the novel's central mechanism of characterization: the way that individuals are converted into "principles," into discrete units of meaning that function only in relationship to the protagonist. We are back to the two understandings of character, and the way that the novel constructs an ideal set of characteristics through the manipulation of a set of characters. "Darcy, on the contrary, had seen a collection of people in whom there was little beauty and no fashion" (16). The understanding of abstractions like "beauty" and "fashion" is purchased by the deindividualization of human beings into "a collection of people." Elizabeth attempts to convert Charlotte into a caricature, into another example of "the inconsistency of all human characters," but the effort is halfhearted. Elizabeth can produce caricatures— it is one of the central qualities of her quickness—but Charlotte simply won't fit into her mold.

It is also a mistake to recognize how *Pride and Prejudice* is uncomfortable about the position of Charlotte's subjective viewpoint within the narrative and then to understand this subjectivity on only a metaphoric register—to see the general principles that Charlotte stands for but forget the way that these principles are embodied in a specific fictional human being. Charlotte's viewpoint can be understood as "realistic," pragmatic, pessimistic, or cynical. Her controlled and measured understanding of the system of marriage emerges out of the text's presentation of her character: in its description of her as "sensible" and "intelligent," and indeed in her considered responses to Elizabeth's own problems. We have also seen how Charlotte's own decision to marry Collins snakes out of her secondary, functional position as a catalyst, buffer, and method of "transition" for Elizabeth. One conventional way to understand how Austen links this alternative perspective on marriage to the character of Charlotte is through the modality of repression. In this reading, the confinement of Charlotte to the margins of the narrative is really about the circumscription of the *viewpoint* that she represents. This is how critics have often recuperated the importance of minor characters in general. According to this reading, Austen inscribes the negation of her own romantic model into the text but then limits or represses this negation. The critic can in turn deconstruct the repressed master narrative and reconstruct the alternatives presented within the text. This type of reading is famously demonstrated in Gilbert and Gubar's *The Madwoman in the Attic*, which, beginning with the title, often insightfully emphasizes the importance of minor characters within the nineteenth-century novel. Looking at all of Austen's novels, and focusing on Catherine de Bourgh in *Pride and Prejudice*, they discover the "representation of a series of extremely powerful women each of whom acts out the rebellious anger so successfully repressed by the heroine and the author," who "quietly and forcefully undercuts her own moral" (169).

A more intricate example of this analysis occurs in Mary Poovey's reading of Austen in *The Proper Lady and the Woman Writer*. Poovey interprets narrative distribution in terms of ideology: a key "narrative technique" in Austen is thus "shifting between different levels or planes of the fiction so that the problems or contradictions raised at one level can be symbolically 'resolved' by foregrounding another, nonproblematic level. . . . In *Pride and Prejudice* [this resolution] . . . consists in foregrounding romance conventions in order to displace complexities raised by the introduction of realistic social and psychological details" (229). This shift is facilitated, more specifically, by the way that Austen foregrounds a successful marriage at the center of her novels, while "shifting" attention away from more problematic marriages: "The fact that almost all of the peripheral marriages in her novels are dissatisfying in one way or another seems to indicate that Austen recognized both the social liabilities that Wollstonecraft identified and the psychological complexities that Shelley intuited. Nevertheless, and especially in *Pride and Prejudice*, the most idealistic of all of her novels, marriage remains for Austen the ideal paradigm of the most perfect fusion between the individual and society" (203). Poovey incorporates Charlotte Lucas's peripheral status under this interpretive rubric: Charlotte embodies a problematic critique of *Pride and Prejudice*'s dominant ideology or "value system," but this critique is carefully contained. "It is through the value system developed in the overall action of the novel that Austen hopes to counter the relativism that the localized ironies might permit. We can see this principle at work in Charlotte Lucas's argument about marriage. . . . The closure of *Pride and Prejudice* is thus aesthetically successful, but whether it ensures a comparable ideological resolution is doubtful" (205).

This type of reading can often become a simple inversion of the traditional model, which views minor characters only as inferior, incomplete reflections of the protagonist. In both cases, Charlotte Lucas becomes reduced to abstract qualities or to a general ideology for which she stands. In the traditional reading the overplot is always correct: Charlotte Lucas should be seen simply as Elizabeth presents her, as too pragmatic or concerned with material goods, and lacking the human spirit that prevents Elizabeth from marrying for money. In the more deconstructive reading the underplot is always correct: Charlotte's insight is the real realism that would shatter the ideologically suspect romance plot and so must be written out of the narrative. Both views understand characterization in a purely thematic or metaphorical sense, and (ironically) reduce Charlotte to an entirely functional role. They both miss a central dramatic axis of the text: the incomplete effacement of Charlotte, *as* a fictional human being, into her narrative function. But this very reduction, which underlies both interpretations, might be more significant than either. The ideological interpretation suggests that Austen abandons social realism when she writes Charlotte Lucas out of the narrative, concentrating on the fairy-tale marriage of Elizabeth and Darcy. However, I would argue that as concerns Charlotte we need to consider the question of realism, above all, in terms of the asymmetric structure encompassing *both* Elizabeth's "romance" plot and Charlotte's "realist" plot. *Pride and Prejudice* presents a world shaped by the dissolution of a clear social hierarchy and a fixed set of values, allowing an overproduction of different stories and different social experiences. Elizabeth's plot, embedded in a complex narrative structure, is "realistic" insofar as it represents those lucky self-made persons who are guaranteed no property but end up with a lot of it. Charlotte's plot is also a "real" one—accurately representing the many people who have to make an essential compromise in their most basic values or aspirations in order to ensure material self-sufficiency. But what is more significant than either of these two individual stories, or individual plotlines, is the dynamic social structure that has produced them both and that cleaves the two characters' friendship apart. This structure is formally registered by the striking position of Charlotte within the novel as a whole, and by the way she is encased in, but not subsumed by, her narrative function. The ambiguous effacement of Charlotte from the narrative—grounded in the novel's asymmetrical structure—is not the moment when the text turns away from material reality or inscribes its own evasion. On the contrary, it is here, as much as anywhere, that the text powerfully registers the derealization, the dehumanization inherent to Austen's world, and inherent to the emergent economic modalities that structure this world.

The Space of the Protagonist 2: Elizabeth's Self-Consciousness

> "I am the happiest creature in the world. . . . I am happier even than Jane; she only smiles, I laugh.
> —*Pride and Prejudice*, 382–83

When Elizabeth returns from visiting Netherfield, she has already become, in many ways, the central character in the novel. Specifically, the novel pays more attention to her consciousness and suggests that she has a depth of consciousness which is qualitatively different from that of the other characters. Occasionally the narrative discourse, rather than simply representing Elizabeth's thoughts, seems to emanate out of her thoughts, so that we have trouble distinguishing omniscient descriptions from Elizabeth's observations. Elizabeth's space within the narrative, however, has not become entirely elevated above all the other characters. Elizabeth's thoughts get temporarily de-emphasized when Wickham arrives on the scene (I will look at this process more closely below), and chapter 17 ends with another catalog description. The description is more ironically inflected, but it still suggests that the novel's plot is not yet completely focused on Elizabeth:

If there had not been a Netherfield ball to prepare for and talk of, the younger Miss Bennets would have been in a pitiable state at this time, for from the day of the invitation, to the day of the ball, there was such a succession of rain as prevented their walking to Meryton once. No aunt, no officers, no news could be sought after;— the very shoe-roses for Netherfield were got by proxy. Even Elizabeth might have found some trial of her patience in weather, which totally suspended the improvement of her acquaintance with Mr. Wickham; and nothing less than a dance on Tuesday, could have made such a Friday, Saturday, Sunday and Monday, endurable to Kitty and Lydia. (88)

Just as I haven't strictly analyzed the function or thematic significance of Mary's, Lydia's, or Mr. Collins's character but rather tried to examine how this abstracted significance works to justify their position *as* minor characters, I don't want to analyze the significance of Darcy's and Elizabeth's prolonged courtship on a semiotic or thematic level: in terms of how it facilitates a synthesis of the two negative ideas in the title, or two other ideas, or how it represents a model of "moral enlightenment." Instead, I want to examine how Elizabeth's position *as* central character becomes consolidated in-and-through this courtship. Chapter 11 ends by recording Darcy's thought: "He began to feel the danger of paying Elizabeth too much attention" (58). Darcy's increasing attention is a sign of their evolving relationship, but their relationship also facilitates attention, the continually deepening attention that the narrative pays to Elizabeth.

Elizabeth's position in the novel changes qualitatively during her second trip away from home, when she visits Mr. Collins and Charlotte at Rosings. In this episode Elizabeth becomes less focused on Jane and begins to think more directly about her own situation. At the same time, and accompanying this inward turn of Elizabeth's thoughts, the text starts to construct a clearly defined symbolic space that represents, and enacts, the depth of Elizabeth's consciousness. Just as Elizabeth's quickness and free consciousness are externalized when she runs over to visit Jane at Netherfield, so at Rosings Elizabeth's consciousness becomes equated with various insides—a room, a book, a solitary walk—that are interrupted by constant intrusions from the outside.

Chapter 32 begins with an image of this solitude, and this consciousness:

Elizabeth was sitting by herself the next morning, and writing to Jane, while Mrs. Collins and Maria were gone on business into the village, when she was startled by a ring at the door, the certain signal of a visitor. As she had heard no carriage, she thought it not unlikely to be Lady Catherine, and under that apprehension was putting away her half-finished letter that she might escape all impertinent questions, when the door opened, and to her very great surprise, Mr. Darcy, and Mr. Darcy only, entered the room. (177)

The dramatic tension in this paragraph stems precisely from Elizabeth's endangered solitude, which is now equated with her consciousness. Elizabeth's thoughts are still ostensibly directed toward her sister, as she is "writing to Jane," but Jane's role is here much more marginal, overshadowed by the activity of writing itself. When Elizabeth puts away her "half-finished letter," we get a full sense of the interruption: an interruption experienced from the perspective of Elizabeth's consciousness, even as the very term "half-finished" subtly stems from, and reflects on, Elizabeth's own thoughts, like a tiny ripple of free indirect discourse.

The description of the letter as "half-finished," in fact, begins to develop an eventually crucial narrative tension between Elizabeth's own subjective sense of time—here indicated simply through the activity of writing—and the external, social, or objective passage of time as it is unconnected with Elizabeth's consciousness. This tension is reiterated in the next chapter:

> She was engaged one day as she walked, in re-perusing Jane's last letter, and dwelling on some passages which proved that Jane had not written in spirits, when, instead of being again surprised by Mr. Darcy, she saw on looking up that Colonel Fitzwilliam was meeting her. Putting away the letter immediately, and forcing a smile, she said . . . (182)

Again the narrative focuses on a seemingly insignificant moment, as this long, intricate sentence emphasizes and lingers on the transition between two plotted events, the letter from Jane and the conversation with Fitzwilliam. But this transition itself "plots" Elizabeth's developing position within the narrative's overall structure. The focus on Elizabeth is once more linked to her solitude, and to the temporal rhythm of her consciousness, as she is "*dwelling* on some passages" in the letter. If "dwell," like most of the verbs in this passage, is in participial form, it also distinctively captures a salient aspect of the participle itself: *all* participles, we might say, dwell on the action they describe.[18] The unpleasant "surprise," in turn, stems from the need to change temporal registers, to "immediately" put away the letter. At the end of the conversation, Elizabeth is once more alone, and as she had been rereading, or "re-perusing," Jane's letter, she now begins to review the events of the day: "There, shut into her own room, as soon as their visitor left them, she could think without interruption of all that she had heard" (186).

These passages begin to formulate what will become two dominant narrative effects of Elizabeth's centrality: the equation of consciousness with solitude, symbolically figured by an inside that is endangered by various interruptions from the outside; and the development of two modes of temporality, one private and authentic, one social and not pertinent to the "real" or experiential unfolding of human consciousness. The next chapter, 34, concerns Darcy's first proposal. It starts with a scene in which Elizabeth—for the third time—

is interrupted while she reads or writes. Notice how the narrative splits itself between emphasizing the content of Jane's letter and the *activity* of reading:

> When they were gone, Elizabeth, as if intending to exasperate herself as much as possible against Mr. Darcy, chose for her employment the examination of all the letters which Jane had written to her since her being in Kent. They contained no actual complaint, nor was there any revival of past occurrences, or any communication of present suffering. But in all, *and in almost every line of each*, there was a want of that cheerfulness which had been used to characterize her style, and which, proceeding from the serenity of a mind at ease with itself, and kindly disposed towards every one, had been scarcely ever clouded. *Elizabeth noticed every sentence* conveying the idea of uneasiness, *with an attention which it had hardly received on the first perusal*. Mr. Darcy's shameful boast of what misery he had been able to inflict, gave her a keener sense of her sister's sufferings. . . . She could not think of Darcy's leaving Kent, without remembering that his cousin was to go with him; but Colonel Fitzwilliam had made it clear that he had no intentions at all, and agreeable as he was, she did not mean to be unhappy about him.
>
> While settling this point, she was suddenly roused by the sound of the door bell. (188, emphasis added)

This paragraph is divided between revealing the extent of Jane's suffering and representing the depth of Elizabeth's apprehension, thus highlighting the activity of *her* consciousness. Once again, Elizabeth's centrality is filtered through Jane: the narrative emphasizes Elizabeth's reexamination of Jane's letters, not the revelation about Jane that this reexamination provides. Elizabeth's rereading gives "her a keener sense of her sister's sufferings," but it also reiterates, once again, that Elizabeth has a keener sense *than* her sister, and in fact, than every other character in the novel.

If Elizabeth will soon be profoundly shocked and agitated by Darcy's first marriage proposal, it is only because she has the depth of consciousness to be so seriously affected. Again, the representation of her agitation after Darcy's proposal is also a representation, and construction, of her depth of consciousness, and of how this consciousness functions in time:

> The tumult of her mind was now painfully great. She knew not how to support herself, and from actual weakness sat down and cried for half an hour. Her astonishment, as she reflected on what had passed, *was increased by every review of it*. (193, emphasis added)

Darcy's proposal continues to intensify and, as it were, lengthen Elizabeth's consciousness—rereading phrases, reviewing events, she has a consciousness that constructs itself through its own activity rather than simply being shaped through perception of the outside world. Darcy's proposal also facilitates the symbolic opposition between Elizabeth and the outside world, between the operation of her consciousness alone and inside, and the relentlessly obtrusive social world. Chapter 34 thus ends: "She continued in very agitating reflections till the sound of Lady Catherine's carriage made her feel how unequal she was to encounter Charlotte's observation, and hurried her away to her room" (194). The proposal chapter is thus simultaneously a turning point of the plot and a turning point in our perception of Elizabeth as a singular protagonist within the plot.

The new configuration of Elizabeth's singularity—as a consciousness lodged within a sheltered solitude that becomes intensified by turning in on itself—is stated more explicitly a few chapters later:

> Reflection must be reserved for solitary hours; whenever she was alone, she gave way to it as the greatest relief; and not a day went by without a solitary walk, in which she might indulge in all the delight of unpleasant recollections. (212)

Darcy's long letter becomes the pivotal object for this recollection and catalyzes Elizabeth's tendency to reread, to linger, to dwell on the objects of her apprehension: "Mr. Darcy's letter, she was in a fair way of soon knowing by heart. She studied every sentence" (212). At the same time this letter endows Elizabeth with precisely those contradictory sentiments, that heterogeneous consciousness, which is typical of the literary protagonist: "[I]t may be well supposed how eagerly she went through them, and what a contrariety of emotion they excited. Her feelings as she read were scarcely to be defined" (204). This sense that the protagonist's thoughts exist outside the scope of the novel's range of description, that their intensity and complexity exceed the narrative's finite parameters, becomes hardened into an opposition between Elizabeth's hidden depth and the constricted superficiality of the social world.

The narrative sums up this opposition right as Elizabeth is about to return to her family; significantly, Elizabeth's thoughts are now directly quoted, in opposition to Maria Lucas's words:

> "We have dined nine times at Rosings, besides drinking tea there twice!—How much I shall have to tell!"
>
> Elizabeth privately added, "And how much I shall have to conceal." (217)

When Elizabeth returns home the second time, her position in the narrative has been consolidated and expanded. In direct reaction to her younger sisters, Elizabeth's thoughts are again directly quoted, at the beginning of chapter 39. " 'Yes,' thought Elizabeth, '*that* would be a delightful scheme, indeed, and completely do for us at once. Good Heaven! Brighton, and a whole campful of soldiers, to us, who have been overset already by one poor regiment of militia, and the monthly balls of Meryton' " (220).

After her second return home Elizabeth has a clearly central status: she has become the consciousness around which the novel—as a totality—is oriented. In the book's final third this centrality motivates increasing attention and specificity toward Elizabeth's subjective apprehension of time:

Upon the whole, therefore, she found, what has been sometimes found before, that an event to which she had looked forward with impatient desire, did not in taking place, bring all the satisfaction she had promised herself. It was consequently necessary to name some other period for the commencement of actual felicity; to have some other point on which her wishes and hopes might be fixed, and by again enjoying the pleasure of anticipation, console herself for the present, and prepare for another disappointment. (237)

In passages like this one, Elizabeth could be the hero of a Stendhal novel, in which the temporal experience of the hero's own consciousness is always more authentic than his relationship to the object-world; where the "pleasure of anticipation" is stronger than the pleasure of gratification; where, finally, the outside world is experienced only through anticipation and regret, the prospective and retrospective measurements of a consciousness that is separate from, and can never be precisely aligned with, external reality. Elizabeth's subjective experience of time flows into the temporal pace of the overall narrative; as we become more aware of her sense of time, the plot grows increasingly suspenseful. Thus Elizabeth's impatience, structured by the experience of anticipation and agitated by the pathos of regret, also contributes to the reader's suspense and involvement. As Elizabeth rushes home after she learns of Lydia's elopement, the narrator comments that "the misery of her impatience was severe" (280), while the narrative itself gives structure to this impatience, so that the plot is aligned to the particular temporal rhythm of Elizabeth's consciousness.

This convergence of narrative suspense and Elizabeth's personal experience of time is also apparent in seemingly unimportant, transitional passages, such as the short paragraph wedged between Jane's two letters about Lydia:

Without allowing herself time for consideration, and scarcely knowing what she felt, Elizabeth on finishing this letter, instantly seized the other, and opening it with the utmost impatience, read as follows . . . (274)

This link between Elizabeth's sense of time and the larger rhythm of the plot in general is just another example of how our perception of Elizabeth's character is intertwined with her changing space within the narrative totality. If Austen chooses a fairly typical symbolic system—representing human consciousness through the imagery of enclosed, sheltered spaces—she dynamically introduces this symbolic register at a specific moment within the narrative and then develops it in a way that coincides with the narrative's own structural unfolding. The symbolic order of *Pride and Prejudice* does not exist prior to the narrative structure but, on the contrary, is configured in-and-through this narrative. Elizabeth's increasing centrality within the narrative is inseparable from our sense of her increasing depth as a character, so that we come to see her psychological depth as a character and her narrative space as the protagonist as connected and mutually supportive. This is the same process that we have observed for minor characters: their subordinate position as characters within a larger narrative structure slides into our understanding of them in-and-of-themselves.

Wickham: "How He Lived I Know Not"

George Wickham is the final elaboration of asymmetry in *Pride and Prejudice*. Without this character the novel's semantic field would be entirely different; the novel needs him but also needs to exclude him. In fact, these two aspects of the character cannot be strictly separated: Wickham's centrality emerges only in-and-through his marginalization, just as his importance finally manifests itself through his disappearance. Wickham's problematic presence in *Pride and Prejudice* is the strongest link between the narrative center—Elizabeth's "moral enlightenment" through Darcy's courtship—and the position of minor characters and subplots, en masse. Wickham facilitates the marriage plot, certainly, but more importantly he helps shape the thematic contours of the novel, which hinge on a contrast between him and Darcy.

If a structural analysis of the novel can never accept the distinction between a dominant "three-quarters" of the narrative and a subordinate final quarter, the text more specifically links the representation of Darcy's character to the representation of Wickham, despite Darcy's insistence on his individually grounded moral qualities. As Elizabeth responds to Jane's attempt to "seek to clear one, without involving the other":

> "This will not do," said Elizabeth. "You never will be able to make both of them good for any thing. Take your choice, but you must be satisfied with only one. There is but such a quantity of merit between them; just enough to make one good sort of man; and of late it has been shifting about pretty much. For my part, I am inclined to believe it all Mr. Darcy's, but you shall do as you chuse." (225)

In this passage Elizabeth casts light on the economy of characterization in *Pride and Prejudice*. Her comment is essentially an image of asymmetry: as a greater "quantity of merit" flows into one character within the novel, a corresponding quantity must disappear from somebody else.

In a brief but insightful essay on *Pride and Prejudice*, Karl Kroeber comments, "What we know about a character is how his or her personality contrasts against others" (146). Even when all the "quantity of merit" shifts to Darcy, this merit is still contingent on his juxtaposition with Wickham. Darcy's character does not stand alone simply because, when judging this merit, Elizabeth is "inclined to believe it all Mr. Darcy's." His goodness only exists in contrast to Wickham's lack of goodness, just as Elizabeth's "quickness" was constituted only in relationship to her sisters' comparative slowness. Moreover, Darcy's very presence within the narrative (grounded and justified only in terms of his goodness) is contingent on Wickham's absence (grounded and justified only in terms of his wickedness).

This is the crucial conflation of quality and character in Elizabeth's comment that there is "just enough to make one good sort of man." We can read this in a moral sense, "one *good* sort of man," or in a social sense, "*one* good sort of man." The phrase encompasses and condenses the double meaning of character, imbricating moral quality and social presence. Wickham's representation in the novel is the final point of convergence between the two terms. He disappears as a character, or social presence, in confirming Darcy's character, or interior qualities.

From Darcy's letter:

> I thought too ill of him, to invite him to Pemberley, or admit his society in town. In town I believe he chiefly lived, but his studying the law was a mere pretence, and being now free from all restraint, his life was a life of idleness and dissipation. . . . After this period, every appearance of acquaintance was dropt. How he lived I know not. (201)

This passage has often been interpreted as showing the limit of Jane Austen's mimetic ability or interest: faced with "idleness and dissipation," Austen's pen can no go further, and Wickham's disappearance is a sign of, and a motivation for, this repression. For example, Marvin Mudrick writes: "It is with Wickham, nevertheless, that Jane Austen's directing and organizing irony . . . begins to fail; and the area of failure . . . is the sexual experience outside marriage. . . . [T]hough the nature of her subject makes an approach to the sexual experience inevitable, Jane Austen will not allow herself . . . to assimilate extra-marital sex to her characteristic unifying irony. . . . She must truncate, flatten, falsify, disapprove, all in the interests of an external morality" (110–11). But isn't it also possible that Austen manipulates the semes of idleness and dissipation to justify the disappearance of Wickham, a disappearance—or "truncating" or "flattening"—that is crucial to the asymmetrical, metonymic structure of the narrative? Going back to Elizabeth's statement, I want to emphasize her suggestion that there is just enough quantity of merit to "make *one* good man" rather than to "make one *good* man." The moral symbolism of *Pride and Prejudice* is used to ground and justify its metonymic structure. It is this asymmetric structure that first organizes the text around the tension between "a single man" and "a wife" and "some one or other of their daughters."

I would argue that the novel stages a symmetrical, semantic opposition between Darcy and Wickham which it can resolve only through its asymmetrical structure of characterization. Critics read the text backward and conclude that the final level of significance lies in the abstract and balanced conflict between two sets of values "represented" by Darcy and Wickham. Darcy's property, stability, honesty, sincerity, and sexual decorum are juxtaposed with Wickham's poverty, instability, dishonesty, hypocrisy, and sexual dissipation. Elizabeth's own choice mediates between these two sets of values, and her evolving relationship with Darcy, and devolving relationship with Wickham, become the main narrative mechanisms for hierarchically arranging the two sets of values. Thus when we first see Wickham, Elizabeth immediately notices the interaction of Darcy and his former servant:

> Mr. Darcy corroborated it with a bow, and was beginning to determine not to fix his eyes on Elizabeth, when they were suddenly arrested by the sight of the stranger, and Elizabeth happening to see the countenance of both as they looked at each other, was all astonishment at the effect of the meeting. Both changed colour, one looked white, the other red. Mr. Wickham, after a few moments, touched his hat—a salutation which Mr. Darcy just deigned to return. (72–73)

At the end of this passage the two men are indistinguishable: the text gives us no clue about whether Darcy is the "one" who turns white or "the other" who turns red. Caught under the specular astonishment of Elizabeth, the text begins with a blurred antithesis, and the rest of the novel is spent undoing what Roland Barthes would call the transgression of this antithesis: "[T]he antithesis is the battle between two plentitudes set ritually face to face [l'antithèse est le combat de deux plenitudes, mises rituellement face à face] like two fully armed warriors; the Antithesis is the figure of the *given* opposition, eternal, eternally recurrent: the figure of the inexpiable. Every joining of two antithetical terms, every mixture, every conciliation,—in short, every passage through the wall of the Antithesis—thus constitutes a transgression" (*S/Z*, 34).[19] It is this sense of transgression that Elizabeth immediately feels when she sees how "both changed colour," wondering to herself, "What could be the meaning of it?—It was impossible to imagine; it was impossible not to long to know." The rest of the novel establishes the difference between Darcy and Wickham, rips the two men apart from this mutually astonished doubling, and enacts a series of antithetical equations that could be mapped out in a semantic reading of the text. However, this metaphoric juxtaposition cannot itself be motivated or resolved on the metaphoric level but is inevitably narrated, and worked through, on a metonymic, social plane. All the abstract questions of value in *Pride and Prejudice* are left undecidable outside of this social, and narrative, context.

If Charlotte Lucas exemplifies but also problematizes Greimas's theory of narrative helpers, we can gain insights into Barthes's important theory of *personnage* and *figure* in *S/Z* by examining Wickham's representation and function in *Pride and Prejudice*. Barthes's privileging of the *figure* or *caractère* over the *personnage* takes the double meaning of character to its most general hermeneutic limits. For Barthes, the *personnage* in a novel always goes toward the dispersed "semes" that are collected under its locality, and these semes are specifically *adjectives*:

The seme (or the signified of connotation, properly speaking) is a connotator of persons, places, objects, of which the signified is a *character* [un *caractère*]. Character is an adjective, an attribute, a predicate (for example, *unnatural, shadowy, star, composite, excessive, impious*, etc.). . . . [W]hat is constant is that the seme is linked to an ideology of the person (to inventory the semes in a classic text is therefore merely to observe this ideology): the person is no more than a collection of semes. . . . What gives the illusion that the sum is supplemented by a precious remainder (something like individuality, in that, qualitative and ineffable, it may escape the vulgar bookkeeping of compositional characters) is the Proper Name [le Nom Propre], the difference completed by what is proper to it. The proper name enables the person to exist outside of the semes, whose sum nonetheless constitutes it entirely. (196–97)

What Barthes's analysis eschews is not simply the understanding of an individual—dismissing the connection of characters to actual people as purely ideological—but rather, and more importantly from a formalist perspective, a trope that is inherent to the process of reading itself. In *Pride and Prejudice*, the "person" of Wickham is *turned into an adjective*, and to have already consigned all "proper names" to this adjectival state is to overlook one of the great dramatic axes of the novel. The question of Wickham's status, as a person, becomes equated with the question of Darcy's status, in terms of character.

Thus when Elizabeth questions Darcy about Wickham, it is to reflect on the nature of Darcy's inner qualities:

> "I remember hearing you once say, Mr. Darcy, that you hardly ever forgave, that your resentment once created was unappeasable. You are very cautious, I suppose, as to its *being created*."
> "I am," said he, with a firm voice.
> "And never allow yourself to be blinded by prejudice?"
> "I hope not."
> "It is particularly incumbent on those who never change their opinion, to be secure of judging properly at first."
> "May I ask to what these questions tend?"
> "Merely to the illustration of *your* character," said she, endeavouring to shake off her gravity. "I am trying to make it out." (93)

On the next page, Miss Bingley makes this equation even clearer:

> "I do not know the particulars, but I know very well that Mr. Darcy is not in the least to blame, that he cannot bear to hear George Wickham mentioned, and that though my brother thought he could not well avoid including him in his invitation to the officers, he was excessively glad to find that he had taken himself out of the way."

Here a person is balanced against another person's quality, as Miss Bingley's catalog equates Darcy's blamelessness with the very mention of Mr. Wickham. The lack of "blame" on Darcy's part thus somehow requires the complete absence of Wickham. Hence her next words: "His coming into the country at all, is a most insolent thing indeed." Wickham here turns into a "seme"; he becomes transformed from a noun into an adjective, or, to put it another way, his reality as a person, as a "character," is meaningful only as a register of "character," of quality, or the lack of quality, of the "insolence" that can be balanced against Darcy's lack of "blame."

The conversation develops this distinction between the social realness of Wickham as an actual person and the meaningfulness of Wickham within an abstract schema of quality. It is precisely the distinction that Barthes makes in his section titled "Personnage et Figure":

> When identical semes traverse the same proper name several times and appear to settle upon it, a character is born [il nait un personnage]. Thus, the character is a product of combinations. . . . The proper Name acts as a magnetic field for the semes; referring virtually to a body, it draws the semic configuration into an evolving (biographical) tense. . . . The figure is altogether different: it is not a combination of semes concentrated in a legal Name, nor can biography, psychology, or time encompass it; it is an illegal, impersonal, anachronistic, configuration of symbolic relations. . . . As a symbolic ideality [comme idéalité symbolique], the character has no chronological or biographical standing; he has no Name, he is nothing but a site for the passage (and return) of the figure. (S/Z, 74–75)

In their ensuing conversation, Elizabeth accuses Miss Bingley, as one might criticize Barthes, of privileging Mr. Wickham's "symbolic ideality" over his "biographical standing":

> "His coming into the country at all, is a most insolent thing indeed, and I wonder how he could presume to do it. I pity you, Miss Eliza, for this discovery of your favourite's guilt; but really considering his descent, one could not expect much better."
>
> "His guilt and his descent appear by your account to be the same," said Elizabeth angrily; "for I have heard you accuse him of nothing worse than of being the son of Mr. Darcy's steward, and of *that*, I can assure you, he informed me himself." (94–95)

The double meaning of character reaches its most significant form in the tension between Wickham's metaphoric significance, "his guilt," and biographical standing, "his descent." In both Wickham's and Darcy's main account of their tumultuous history the reader gets a clear sense of Wickham's almost unquenchable resentment of Darcy's privilege. Elizabeth's and Wickham's conversation thus begins with Wickham's knowledge of Darcy's finances:

> "He is a man of very large property in Derbyshire, I understand."
>
> "Yes," replied Wickham;—"his estate there is a noble one. A clear ten thousand per annum. You could not have met with a person more capable of giving you certain information on that head than myself. . . ." (77)

We have seen how Elizabeth first notices Darcy and Wickham locked together
in an indistinguishable embarrassment, a shared sense of discomfort. The central metaphoric antithesis between the two characters begins in this moment,
becoming clarified as Darcy's virtue and Wickham's guilt are developed. We
can find a precise equivalent of this doubling in Wickham's description of their
childhood lives:

> "We were born in the same parish, within the same park, the greatest part of our
> youth was passed together; inmates of the same house, sharing the same amusements,
> objects of the same parental care." (81)

"[T]he same . . . the same . . . together . . . the same . . . sharing . . . the same
. . . the same": this sentence conveys a sense of absolute, almost mythic equality. Their indistinguishable childhood is equivalent to the initial blurring of
their metaphoric significance, just as the increasing disparity of their social
(and narrative) fortunes coincides with, and cannot be separated from, the development of their semantic opposition.

Another minor character in *Pride and Prejudice* helps cast light on the links
between Wickham's outraged sense of injustice and the development of the
novel's semantic field. Colonel Fitzwilliam's brief role in the novel replicates,
in a much milder form, Wickham's oppositional relationship to Darcy. Like
Wickham, Fitzwilliam is a potential rival for Elizabeth's affection and gives
Elizabeth information that turns her against Darcy. Of course, his rivalry is
relatively trivial. While Elizabeth says of Mr. Wickham that "he is, beyond all
comparison, the most agreeable man I ever saw" (144), she sees Fitzwilliam
precisely in comparison: "Elizabeth was reminded by her own satisfaction in
being with him, as well as by his evident admiration of her, of her former
favourite George Wickham" (180). But, as with Wickham, Fitzwilliam's status
as an "opposer" of Elizabeth's marriage to Darcy is linked to his social inferior-
ity to Darcy. In a striking passage, Fitzwilliam discusses the resentment that
accompanies his friendship toward Darcy:

> "Do you certainly leave Kent on Saturday?" said she.
> "Yes—if Darcy does not put it off again. But I am at his disposal. He arranges the
> business just as he pleases."
> "And if not able to please himself in the arrangement, he has at least great pleasure
> in the power of choice. I do not know any body who seems more to enjoy the power
> of doing what he likes than Mr. Darcy."
> "He likes to have his own way very well," replied Colonel Fitzwilliam. "But so
> we all do. It is only that he has better means of having it than many others, because
> he is rich, and many others are poor. I speak feelingly. A younger son, you know,
> must be inured to self-denial and dependence." (183)

In this passage we can again see the social underpinnings of characterization
within the marriage plot: Darcy's status as a rounded character—which de-

pends on his "power of choice"—is placed within a dynamic contrast between him and the "many others" who are poor. But Fitzwilliam's resentment is relatively mild and a little tongue-in-cheek; Elizabeth responds by questioning the extent of his deprivation:

> "In my opinion, the younger son of an Earl can know very little of either. Now, seriously, what have you ever known of self-denial and dependence? When have you been prevented by want of money from going wherever you chose, or procuring any thing you had a fancy for?"
>
> "These are home questions—and perhaps I cannot say that I have experienced many hardships of that nature. But in matters of greater weight, I may suffer from the want of money. Younger sons cannot marry where they like."

Fitzwilliam is more a friend than a rival of Darcy, and his class status links him with, more closely than it divides him from, his friend. We could say that Fitzwilliam is four-fifths like Darcy and one-fifth like Wickham, suggesting in a much milder form the functional role that Wickham will play.[20] Wickham also speaks feelingly, complaining to Elizabeth about "a sense of very great ill usage, and most painful regrets at his being what he is" (78).

Darcy's own explanation of their troubled history, while shifting blame and responsibility, reinforces our sense that Wickham's struggle against Darcy is rooted in and takes form through a struggle over property and money. Wickham is the son of "a very respectable man, who had for many years the management of all the Pemberley estates," and Darcy's "father supported him at school, and afterwards at Cambridge" (199–200). Darcy's father's affection takes a purely material form, so that he bequeaths "a valuable family living" and "a legacy of one thousand pounds" to Wickham. Darcy begins to separate himself from Wickham through another financial transaction: "The business was therefore soon settled. He resigned all claim to assistance in the church, were it possible that he could ever be in a situation to receive it, and accepted in return three thousand pounds. All connection between us seemed now dissolved" (201).

This connection, dissolved through a financial transaction, completely separates the two men, so that Darcy both claims uncertainty about what Wickham was doing, and insists on specifying exactly what type of character he became: "In town I believe he chiefly lived, but his studying the law was a mere pretence, and being now free from all restraint, his life was a life of idleness and dissipation. For about three years I heard little of him" (201). The two men fall into a clearer conflict that is once again essentially material: "He had found the law a most unprofitable study, and was now absolutely resolved on being ordained, if I would present him to the living in question. . . . His resentment [upon Darcy's refusal] was in proportion to the distress of his circumstances" (201). Once more, Wickham drifts off into obscurity, prompting the passage we already looked at: "After this period, every appearance of acquaintance was dropt. How he lived I know not." The two men are brought together for a final time, now in complete enmity with each other, when Wickham attempts to seduce Darcy's sister. Darcy himself acknowledges the financial context that motivates Wickham's action: "Mr. Wickham's chief object was unquestionably my sister's fortune, which is thirty thousand pounds; but I cannot help supposing that the hope of revenging himself on me, was a strong inducement" (202).

These episodes from Wickham's past provide the background for the qualitative distinction between Wickham and Darcy, shifting all the "quantity of merit" toward Darcy. At the same time we can see how each episode that establishes the two characters' abstract qualities is also informed by their concrete social positions. To the modern reader, of course, Darcy's aristocratic behavior could easily fall under the chief "semes" that are tacked onto Wickham: "idleness and dissipation." Such a judgment is not that far removed from Fitzwilliam's own cynical understanding of Darcy's privileged "power of choice." Again, this judgment—deciding which of these men is really more idle and dissipated—is not a question that can be conclusively answered. The "merit" of the novel shifts to Darcy in large part because of the other process that is enacted in the passages we are examining: the configuration of Wickham's minorness.

Darcy's letter duplicates a central process of the novel as a whole: associating Wickham's immoral actions with his drift into an epistemologically imprecise territory, outside of Darcy's purview. We can really see three interrelated processes: Wickham's moral decline is associated with both increased financial difficulties and an increasingly marginal position in relation to Darcy. What occurs in Darcy's letter also holds for the novel as a whole: as Elizabeth's opinion of Wickham begins to sink, Wickham himself starts to run up the debts that will eventually drive him from Netherfield, and, simultaneously, begins to make increasingly sporadic appearances within the narrative. This is the other side of that estrangement between surface and depth that is the chief quality of minor characters: while Mr. Collins's repetitive exterior drowns out any sense of his inner self, Mr. Wickham's own inner desires cannot accommodate themselves to social forms or be fully contained within the narrative form. While the narrator equates Mr. Collins's inner consciousness with the superficial tone he takes in the letter, Mr. Wickham's *character* is precisely rendered distinct from any outer form: "As to his real character, had information been in her power, she had never felt a wish of enquiring. His countenance, voice, and manner, had established him at once in the possession of every virtue" (206). The precise registers within which Mr. Collins's suffocating personality is limited—his countenance, voice, and manner—become irrelevant for understanding, or representing, Mr. Wickham. Thus Wickham experiences the second type of ending that Tanner identifies for minor characters: *disappearing* into misery. Wickham's flight with Lydia, which is the final sign of his dissipation and the final result of his financial insecurity, is also the paradigmatically *unnarratable* event. We approach this event only through its chaotic effects on everyone else in the novel. It is an event that is both highly significant and fundamentally invisible. Lydia and Wickham disappear into their dissipation, succumbing to a fate that is extremely common for minor characters in the realist novel.

Wickham makes only one more, extremely contained, appearance in the novel, and this appearance is presented as an interruption. The scene begins after a long paragraph describing Elizabeth's thoughts, of which I will quote only the end:

> She was even sensible of some pleasure, though mixed with regret, on finding how steadfastly both she and her uncle had been persuaded that affection and confidence subsisted between Mr. Darcy and herself.
>
> She was roused from her seat, and her reflections, by some one's approach; and before she could strike into another path, she was overtaken by Wickham. (327)

The conversation consists, essentially, of Elizabeth's attempt to get Wickham to shut up ("Elizabeth hoped she had silenced him; but he soon afterwards said . . ."), while walking as quickly to the house as she can in order "to get rid of him." At the end of the conversation the narrator suggests that they never speak seriously again, noting that Elizabeth "was pleased to find that she had said enough to keep him quiet."

This reduction of Wickham's place within the story is the narratological equivalent of the "truncating" or "flattening" that Mudrick associates with Austen's treatment of Lydia and Wickham's extramarital relationship. But to fully understand Wickham's truncated position at the narrative's end, we have to look more carefully at the way he is represented before his elopement with Lydia. The conflict between Darcy's wealth and Wickham's poverty—which ends with Wickham's truncation and disappearance—is itself only part of the larger conflict between singularity and multiplicity that is the governing structure of the text as a whole. This structure mediates between the symmetric, metaphoric conflict of Darcy and Wickham and the asymmetric, metonymic relationship of the two characters. Darcy at once *stands for* a sense of singularity and is *positioned in* a singular place within the novel's structure of characterization. Similarly, Wickham both stands for multiplicity and is placed within a structure of multiplicity that shapes and delimits his representation within the novel. I want to argue that the final "seme" which Wickham represents is neither sexual promiscuity, financial speculation, nor even the "dissipation" that encompasses both of these activities. This dissipation is itself subsumed by Wickham's excessiveness, an excess that the narrative connects to the excess inherent in social multiplicity.[21]

We have noticed how Wickham's introduction into the novel immediately puts him in a doubled relationship to Darcy, which, under the astonished gaze of Elizabeth, will grow into the novel's central metaphorical division. Even before this encounter, however, Wickham is positioned in a very particular space within the narrative. His first appearance occurs when all the sisters are walking into town, and is at first juxtaposed with Mr. Collins's stultifying behavior:

> In pompous nothings on his side, and civil assents on that of his cousins, their time passed till they entered Meryton. The attention of the younger ones was then no longer to be gained by *him*. Their eyes were immediately wandering up in the street in quest of the officers, and nothing less than a very smart bonnet indeed, or a really new muslin in a shop window, could recall them.
>
> But the attention of every lady was soon caught by a young man, whom they had never seen before, of most gentlemanlike appearance, walking with an officer on the other side of the way. The officer was the very Mr. Denny, concerning whose return from London Lydia came to inquire, and he bowed as they passed. All were struck with the stranger's air, all wondered who he could be, and Kitty and Lydia, determined if possible to find out, led the way across the street, under pretence of wanting something in an opposite shop, and fortunately had just gained the pavement when the two gentlemen turning back had reached the same spot. Mr. Denny addressed them directly, and entreated permission to introduce his friend, Mr. Wickham, who had returned with him the day before from town, and he was happy to say had accepted a commission in their corps. (72)

Wickham's very presence is immediately the subject of two different registers of perception: "the attention of the younger ones," who are "in quest of the officers," and "the attention of every lady," which obviously includes Elizabeth. The narrator emphasizes this split: "*All* were struck with the stranger's air, *all* wondered who he could be, and *Kitty and Lydia*, determined if possible to find out, led the way across the street" (emphasis added). Elizabeth's perception—which has been increasingly emphasized in the course of the narrative—gets drowned out in this introduction: her observation is indistinct from those of a larger group, while Kitty's and Lydia's points of view are singled out.

The description that follows is curiously unspecific: "This was exactly as it should be; for the young man wanted only regimentals to make him completely charming. His appearance was greatly in his favour; he had all the best part of beauty, a fine countenance, a good figure, and very pleasing address." It is impossible to tell whether this is the narrator's voice, the collective judgment of "every lady," the dual sentiment of Kitty-and-Lydia, or, more subtly, the emerging opinion of Elizabeth herself. It makes sense that Lydia's and Kitty's perception is emphasized, because Wickham fits comfortably into their field of vision. Like Lydia, Wickham seems inherently social, oriented toward motion, multiplicity, and the surface.

> "It was the prospect of constant society, and good society," he added, "which was my chief inducement to enter the ——shire. . . . Society, I own, is necessary to me. I have been a disappointed man, and my spirits will not bear solitude. I *must* have employment and society." (79)

In the most general terms, minor characters in *Pride and Prejudice*, as a group, form a structure of multiplicity that is overshadowed by the protagonist's compelling singularity. Wickham condenses this multiplicity within his own individuality: his motion, his agitation, his sociability, and his superficiality become an embodiment of social multiplicity, which necessarily transcends a single individual.

We have seen how Lydia's and Kitty's multiple desires for many different officers function as a desire for multiplicity, in-and-of-itself. When Wickham arrives, their desire is immediately displaced and finally focused: "She had been watching him the last hour, she said, as he walked up and down the street, and had Mr. Wickham appeared Kitty and Lydia would certainly have continued the occupation, but unluckily no one passed the windows now except a few of the officers, who in comparison with the stranger, were become 'stupid, disagreeable fellows' " (74). This passage suggests that Kitty and Lydia don't simply rate Wickham higher than each individual officer they see; rather, they compare Wickham to "a few of the officers" as a group. Wickham enters the novel after its asymmetrical structure is fully developed. The text has already begun to elevate Elizabeth, and, simultaneously, to push more and more characters to the margin. Wickham does not become merely another fragment of "the many" juxtaposed against Elizabeth's "oneness." Instead, Wickham comes to represent fragmentation and multiplicity itself. The constant comparisons of Wickham to the other officers do not make Wickham qualitatively distinct from the many other people he is compared to, as do all the comparisons involving Darcy. On the contrary, Wickham's exceptionality hinges on his association with the other officers he is compared to. Wickham is always presented *within*, not against, a social field, and his singularity emerges out of the way he exemplifies and condenses social multiplicity. Thus the first introduction of Wickham as "walking with an officer on the other side of the way" is repeated throughout the text:

> With such rivals for the notice of the fair, as Mr. Wickham *and the officers*, Mr. Collins seemed likely to sink into insignificance. (76, emphasis added)

> [S]ome of the officers always made part of it, of which officers Mr. Wickham was sure to be one. (142)

> When Denny, and Wickham, and Pratt, and two or three more of the men came in . . . (221)

It is not only Lydia and Kitty who are attracted to Wickham vis-à-vis his association with a crowd of other officers. Elizabeth's desire for Wickham also hinges on comparing him to the many other officers whom he is around, on this singularity-within-multiplicity. "Elizabeth entered the drawing-room at Netherfield and looked in vain for Mr. Wickham among the cluster of red coats there assembled" (89). Wickham catalyzes a type of desire that is outer directed, that ties up the different parties in a common bond of circumstances. Again, we see the form of Elizabeth's desire: "The officers of the ——shire were in general a very creditable, gentlemanlike set, and the best of them were of the present party; but Mr. Wickham was as far beyond them all in person, countenance, air, and walk as *they* were superior to the broad-faced stuffy uncle Philips, breathing port wine, who followed them into the room" (76). The text emphasizes the nature of Elizabeth's desire for Wickham by showing how it brings her closer to the many other woman who also are attracted to him. If Wickham's attractiveness is linked to multiplicity, it also draws in *many* admirers: "Mr. Wickham was the happy man towards whom almost every female eye was turned, and Elizabeth was the happy woman by whom he finally seated himself" (76). And if Wickham acts as a double for Darcy, Elizabeth's desire for Wickham naturally is doubled with Lydia's desire, as is made clear in a witty passage that follows the two examples we have just examined:

> Mr. Wickham did not play at whist, and with ready delight was he received at the other table between Elizabeth and Lydia. At first there seemed danger of Lydia's engrossing him entirely, for she was a most determined talker; but being likewise extremely fond of lottery tickets, she soon grew too much interested in the game, too eager in making bets and exclaiming after prizes, to have attention for anyone in particular. (76–77)

And, much later, Elizabeth remembers:

> When first he entered the corps, she was ready enough to admire him; but so we all were. Every girl in, or near Meryton, was out of her senses about him for the first two months; but he never distinguished *her* by any particular attention. (285)

As the coin of *Pride and Prejudice* is so often "attention," it makes sense that Lydia's inability "to have attention for anyone in particular" becomes transformed into Wickham's failure to "distinguish by any particular attention." The subtle permutation of "particular" and "attention" in these two phrases again glosses that crucial device of the narrative: social or exterior dispersion ("attention for *anyone* in particular") gets manifested as cultural or interior superfice ("any particular attention"). But precisely in this way, too, the particular attention that Elizabeth gains in this narrative is, simultaneously, attention in particular.

All of these passages suggest a different way of organizing the relationship among Elizabeth, Lydia, Darcy, and Wickham. The parallels and doublings we have just traced find a common link in the tension between the one and the many. Wickham is the double of Darcy: the narrative starts by blurring the two men and revolves around establishing a stable difference; Wickham is the exemplification of multiplicity, while Darcy exemplifies singularity;[22] Wickham's attractiveness arises within a structure of multiplicity (standing out within a crowd), whereas Darcy's attractiveness arises against a structure of multiplicity (standing apart from a crowd). Elizabeth's attraction to Wickham emerges in relation to both her attraction to Darcy and Lydia's attraction to Wickham: Lydia's desire for Wickham exemplifies the attraction toward multiplicity, while Elizabeth's desire for Darcy exemplifies the attraction toward singularity; Elizabeth's marriage to Darcy, finally, is the marriage of a singular individual attracted to another singular individual, in-and-of-themselves, apart from any larger social structure. We navigate ourselves through multiplicity; this multiplicity is condensed, critiqued, and contained in the characters of Lydia and Wickham; and we rearrive at the opening sentence: "It is a truth universally acknowledged, that a single man in possession of a good fortune, must be in want of a wife."

However, there is still an excess, which has been developed (just as the individuals in the marriage plot have developed) into its ultimate form within a structure of asymmetry. What began as "some one or other of their daughters" has been developed into various stages of minorness, through compression, externality, fragmentation. The final end of this development is actual disappearance, a disappearance that occurs only in-and-through agitation. Austen brilliantly condenses Lydia and Wickham's fate into one final sentence: "They were always moving from place to place in quest of a cheap situation, and always spending more than they ought" (387). We can, if we want, throw up one last argument against the values expressed in this sentence, attacking the wrong-minded morality of "ought," protesting that they certainly spent less than the Darcys. Such a protest is drowned out, however, by the sheer *narrative* brilliance of the sentence: the way it conflates Wickham and Lydia's financial dislocation—within the story—with their narrative dislocation. This is one of the great endings written for minor characters, if only because of the infinity of implied disintegration. "They lived shoddily ever after." Wickham and Lydia suffer a fate worse than death, perhaps because Austen's rigorous sense of interconnection will not allow such an easy way out. Death would imply the end of asymmetry, would unhinge the centered individual marriage plot from its contingent position vis-à-vis social disintegration.

There is still a question of how the novel can finally end and close off the system of asymmetry. To highlight the fragmented disappearance of the minor characters might create an inappropriate balance between *histoire* and *discours*. But Austen will not, even in the final moment, simply settle into the centrality of her protagonists, despite having convincingly represented how their achieved centrality is ultimately contingent. Instead, the novel ends ingeniously on a middle ground: neither with the stability of the protagonist nor with the fragmentation of the most important minor characters:

> With the Gardiners, they were always on the most intimate terms. Darcy, as well as Elizabeth, really loved them; and they were both ever sensible of the warmest gratitude towards the persons who, by bringing her into Derbyshire, had been the means of uniting them. (388)

This last sentence stresses, for the final time, that the central marriage plot is inseparable from the larger social (and narrative) structure in which it is embedded. By ending on characters who help Darcy and Elizabeth to unite—rather than with Darcy and Elizabeth themselves, sheltered within a state of union—the conclusion highlights the social process that underlies the value system constructed through the marriage. If the protagonists have required helpers, the narrative has needed to reduce certain characters to being "the means of" other characters' development. The Gardiners are poised at the pinnacle of the asymmetrical system: they are described as necessary to the Darcys' final union, while reminding us of all the other characters who have also played a functional role vis-à-vis the central marriage plot. In this sense, the Gardiners act as a bridge between the two directions of the narrative: subsumed under the sign of their utility, they are positioned between the closed space of the protagonist that they have "been the means of" constructing and all the other characters who have also helped construct this marriage plot while being themselves pushed to the perimeter of the novel.

Minor Minor Characters: Representing Multiplicity

> Mr. Woodhouse considered eight persons at dinner together as the utmost that his nerves could bear—and here would be a ninth.
> —*Emma*, 292

Toward the beginning of chapter 27, Elizabeth is riding in a coach with Sir William Lucas and his daughter, and comparing them unfavorably to Wickham: "Her fellow-travellers the next day, were not of a kind to make her think him less agreeable. Sir William Lucas, and his daughter Maria, a good humoured girl, but as empty-headed as himself, had nothing to say that could be worth hearing, and were listened to with about as much delight as the rattle of the chaise" (152). If Lydia and Wickham are minor characters who, through their very minorness, are central to the novel's semantic field, how can we account for most of the minor characters in *Pride and Prejudice*, who are not thematically significant? It is an error to concentrate on how Wickham and Lydia come to *represent* multiplicity in contrast to Darcy's and Elizabeth's singularity and forget that this opposition is effective only because of the larger structure of multiplicity in which all four characters are embedded. Lydia and Wickham disappear into a fragmented world evoked in the narrative itself, through the many flattening descriptions of more peripheral minor characters. The totality of asymmetry exists through its dispersion, which seems paradoxical until we remember that the vanished and fragmented *content* of multiplicity implies a simple and totalized *process* of organization. In other words, the cohesion of asymmetry's form relies on the dispersion of its content. The periphery of *Pride and Preju-*

dice's universe is made up of these fragmented characters, but the form of fragmentation is always the same: caricature, containment at the margins of the story and the narrative's own visual field, functionalization, abstraction, repetition or unpredictability, the emphasis of physical features over cognitive perceptions—in short, the disjunction of surface and depth.

The reduction of Sir William Lucas to the rattling of a chaise—which entraps the human being within his machinelike repetitiveness—is linked to other passages that reduce him to a purely instrumental role in the narrative, such as his failed effort to get Darcy and Elizabeth to dance or his later interruption of a conversation between Darcy and Elizabeth:

> "Mr. Wickham is blessed with such happy manners as may ensure his *making* friends—whether he may be equally capable of *retaining* them, is less certain."
>
> "He has been so unlucky as to lose *your* friendship," replied Elizabeth with emphasis, "and in a manner which he is likely to suffer from all his life."
>
> Darcy made no answer, and seemed desirous of changing the subject. At that moment Sir William Lucas appeared close to them, meaning to pass through the set to the other side of the room; but on perceiving Mr. Darcy he stopt with a bow of superior courtesy to compliment him on his dancing and his partner. . . .
>
> "Sir William's interruption has made me forget what we were talking of." (92–93)

Passages like this provoke the reader to make limitations, to organize the fictional universe in an asymmetrical pattern. Only through these minor minor characters does the text create a structure of characterization—a character-system—that is then crucially entwined with the more important thematic conflicts between Elizabeth and Darcy and Wickham and Lydia.

This is also the case for the most basic structure of multiplicity that we have been examining: the Bennet sisters themselves. While we have touched on Elizabeth, Jane, Lydia, and Mary, how can we understand the function of Catherine, the most minor of all the five sisters? Catherine is precisely the character who breaks down a traditional reading that insists on looking only at what each sister *stands for* and ignores the social process which underlies this signification. If we look at the characters only in this sense, there is no reason for Catherine's place in the novel; she is an additional sister within the Bennet family but does not add anything to the novel's semantic plane. After all, Catherine doesn't represent any fixed quality or "seme" but latches on to the qualities of those around her. For most of the novel she acts like Lydia, but not because these qualities are somehow intrinsic to her:

> Elizabeth had frequently united with Jane in an endeavour to check the imprudence of Catherine and Lydia. . . . Catherine, weak-spirited, irritable, and completely under Lydia's guidance, had been always affronted by their advice; and Lydia, self-willed and careless, would scarcely give them a hearing. They were ignorant, idle, and vain.
> (213)

This passage, like most such descriptions up to this point, links Catherine and Lydia together and then categorizes them in terms of abstract characteristics: as "ignorant, idle, and vain." But the description itself presses against this abstraction, since it shows the particular social structure that mediates between Catherine and these qualities. Thus at the end of the novel, Catherine begins to be assimilated to her older sisters, rather than her younger one:

> Kitty, to her very material advantage, spent the chief of her time with her two elder sisters. In society so superior to what she had generally known, her improvement was great. She was not of so ungovernable a temper as Lydia, and, removed from the influence of Lydia's example, she became, by proper attention and management, less irritable, less ignorant, and less insipid. From the farther disadvantage of Lydia's society she was of course carefully kept. (385)

If Austen includes the other, minor sisters merely as counterexamples that serve to valorize Elizabeth, why does she need four sisters to fill three semantic positions? While passages in the text set up clear, symbolic distinctions between Elizabeth and Mary, Elizabeth and Lydia, and Elizabeth and Jane, there is never a symbolic relationship constructed between Catherine and Elizabeth. This helps explain why Catherine, and Catherine alone, crosses over the dominant semantic divide in the novel, when she starts to follow Elizabeth and Jane instead of Lydia. By insisting on this fifth sister, Austen transcends a purely symbolic depiction of the Bennet sisters that would center the narrative on Elizabeth, and forces us to take into account the metonymic, social dimensions of all the characters' significance.

Of course, one could insist that hers is just another type of personality, that Catherine *stands for* malleability, but this would ignore the way she is presented within the text's structure. If Catherine is always outside of or irrelevant to the novel's semantic field (as though all the positions in this semantic field were already *filled up* by the other sisters), she is also the daughter who seems most drowned out within the family itself. Catherine is simply there, hovering around after all the other daughters have been qualified. She is just "one of the daughters," as when she is first introduced ("Mrs. Bennet . . . began scolding one of her daughters"), or as the surplus in the scene when Collins asks Mrs. Bennet about Elizabeth:

> On finding Mrs. Bennet, Elizabeth, and one of the younger girls together, soon after breakfast, he addressed the mother in these words,
> "May I hope, Madam, for your interest with your fair daughter Elizabeth, when I solicit for the honour of a private audience with her in the course of this morning?"
> Before Elizabeth had time for any thing but a blush of surprise, Mrs. Bennet instantly answered,
> "Oh dear!—Yes—certainly.—I am sure Lizzy will be very happy—I am sure she can have no objection.—Come, Kitty, I want you upstairs." (104)

In classical Chinese landscape painting there is a rule that you can never place more than five trees in the foreground, as though five were the largest number of units that can be individually distinguished by a human mind. With any more than five units we will start to blur individuals into some larger group. So with the Bennet sisters Catherine embodies the sheer weight of their social being; she is like the fifth tree, hovering uneasily between foreground and background, already beginning to lose a defined individual essence. Catherine is thus meaningful precisely *because* all the fixed semantic positions have already been filled by the other sisters. If Catherine's lack of personality seems to make her into the equivalent of a "floating signifier," her reduction to this state is itself very significant. Catherine is a representation of how we perceive or constitute people at the periphery, when our main focus is taken up by other individuals, and her variable personality seems to flow out of this specific social (and narrative) position.

If asymmetry relies on dispersion, we might find a similar pattern for the novel as a whole. Catherine's very insignificance (in the literal sense of lack of a clear signifying status and also in the colloquial sense of unimportance) ironically elucidates the larger structure of the five sisters' characterization; similarly, we could expect that there would be a multitude of human figures at the perimeter of the narrative, literally shrinking into nothingness, or, more specifically, into signifying nothing. Only such a metonymic structure of containment, distortion, and effacement could "close" off an asymmetric totality. The figures who are placed in this position are the servants.

Servants have always been used to exemplify minor characters: they have a unique and privileged position, both because they embody (within the story) that narrative functionality which is central to the construction of minor characters, and because, in the development of the nineteenth-century novel, they come to stand for members of the working class, who are often excluded from the narrative but are a constitutive part of the real social structure that shapes asymmetry in the first place. In the most probing analysis of this process, Bruce Robbins insists that the importance of servant figures in British nineteenth-century fiction is increased through their very marginality within the plot.[23] Robbins, however, argues that these minor characters embody a register of meaning that is necessarily outside the text's own unity or totality. For Robbins, analysis of minor characters begins precisely where a conception of the text as a unified structure ends. Thus he prefaces his analysis of the figure of the servant in British fiction by suggesting that his area of interest *necessitates* an incomplete reading:

> Finally, neither the originality of the authors nor the organic wholeness of individual texts could be respected. As the common property of any novelist willing, en bon bricoleur, to make use of available materials, the literary servant is too repetitive for treatment by author, just as it is too minor, fragmentary, and marginal to any given

text to be treated by work. Getting it on the map at all means forgoing the completeness of the "reading" and forcing the literary canon off-center. (xii)

In *Pride and Prejudice*, however, servants are the final extension of the text's
system of characterization: through their fragmentation they ensure, precisely,
the "completeness" of the novel's asymmetric structure.

Servants are first represented on the opening page of the novel, soon after the
initial opposition of "a single man" and "some one or other of their daughters."
Echoing the imprecision of "some one or other of their daughters," Mrs. Bennet describes how Mr. Bingley will soon move into the neighborhood: "[H]e
is to take possession before Michaelmas, and some of his servants are to be in
the house by the end of next week." Mr. Bingley's "possession" is elaborated
through the imprecise status of these servants. We get a sense of *his* wealth
precisely through their impoverished representation.

Throughout the novel, servants hover at this imprecise periphery of the narrative, marking the limit point of the text's distortion of minor characters. First,
servants are reduced to a purely functional position within the novel's plot structure; second, they are reduced to a purely exterior and physical plane of description. The servant vanishes into the duty he or she performs—on both the semantic and the descriptive planes of the novel.[24] The narrator sometimes stresses a
servant's functionality by tying his or her labor—within the *histoire*—to a specific discursive function within the plot's elaboration. Thus a servant will often
act as a sort of human bridge from one subplot to another, becoming the ultimate
example of how the dominant plot—Elizabeth's marriage to Darcy—is facilitated only through the participation of many other human agents.

In an early passage a footman helps shift attention from Lydia to Jane, mediating between the sisters' respective romantic situations.

> "Mama," cried Lydia, "my aunt says that Colonel Forster and Captain Carter do
> not go so often to Miss Watson's as they did when they first came; she sees them
> now very often standing in Clarke's library."
>
> Mrs. Bennet was prevented replying by the entrance of the footman with a note
> for Miss Bennet; it came from Netherfield, and the servant waited for an answer.
> Mrs. Bennet's eyes sparkled with pleasure, and she was eagerly calling out, while
> her daughter read.
>
> "Well, Jane, who is it from? what is it about? what does he say? Well, Jane, make
> haste and tell us; make haste, my love." (30)

As far as the narrative is concerned, this servant is still waiting for a reply.
The final character introduced in the novel is also a servant whose only place
within the novel is in an intermediate position between Elizabeth and Jane:

> He came, and in such very good time, that the ladies were none of them dressed. In
> ran Mrs. Bennet to her daughter's room, in her dressing gown, and with her hair half
> finished, crying out,

"My dear Jane, make haste and hurry down. He is come—Mr. Bingley is come.—
He is, indeed. Make haste, make haste. Here, Sarah, come to Miss Bennet this moment, and help her on with her gown. Never mind Miss Lizzy's hair." (344)

The servants in these passages dramatize what occurs, in more subtle ways, at
every level of the narrative—minor characters function only vis-à-vis other
characters and are, consequently, pushed into a limited place within the novel
that distorts our sense of them as full, rounded persons. The limited function
of servants is intertwined with their limited place. In one scene Elizabeth and
Jane directly dismiss a "waiter" from the room, but we are not told he is in the
room *until* they tell him to leave:

"Now I have got some news for you," said Lydia, as they sat down to table. "What
do you think? It is excellent news, capital news, and about a certain person that we
all like."

Jane and Elizabeth looked at each other, and the waiter was told that he need not
stay. Lydia laughed, and said,

"Aye, that is just like your formality and discretion. You thought the waiter must
not hear, as if he cared! I dare say he often hears worse things said than I am going
to say. But he is an ugly fellow! I am glad he is gone. I never saw such a long chin
in my life. Well, but now for my news: it is about dear Wickham. . . . " (220)

The waiter gets into the text only through his dismissal from the room, but the
narrator then seems to go out of her way to include a description of the "ugly
fellow" with his "long chin."

This logic applies to the narrative as a whole: the narrator seems entirely
dismissive of the novel's many servants but consistently makes sure to mention the role they play as intermediaries, messengers, and go-betweens. We
can thus trace the disappearance of human agency into a smaller and smaller
represented space. In this passage the waiter's limited narrative position
allows in only a "long chin," approaching the most reductive type of synecdoche. Later, one of Darcy's servants is reduced to his mouth: "Mr. Gardiner
expressed a wish of going round the whole Park, but feared it might be beyond a walk. With a triumphant smile, they were told, that it was ten miles
round" (253). The servant's smile, the only fragment of his being that is inflected into the narrative, complicates what would otherwise be a passive
construction. Even beyond this, servants become reduced to their names, or
equated with material objects: "The dinner was exceedingly handsome, and
there were all the servants, and all the articles of plate which Mr. Collins had
promised" (162).

These passages could be interpreted as the symptoms of an ideology that
simply does not take into account the humanity of servants. I would argue
that the narrative does not merely dismiss servants, or shut them out of the
novel, but rather represents the process of their disappearance, integrating

these flat characters into the more general structure of asymmetry. This asymmetric structure—which always makes a character's representation contingent on his or her narrative position—extends from the most marginalized servants to the most "elevated" characters in the novel. In one interesting passage, Austen suddenly brings these two extremes uncomfortably together. Elizabeth has just learned of Lydia and Wickham's disappearance and must break off her visit with Darcy:

> "I beg your pardon, but I must leave you. I must find Mr. Gardiner this moment, on business that cannot be delayed; I have not an instant to lose."
>
> "Good God! what is the matter?" cried he, with more feeling than politeness; then recollecting himself, "I will not detain you a minute, but let me, or let the servant, go after Mr. and Mrs. Gardiner. You are not well enough;—you cannot go yourself."
>
> Elizabeth hesitated, but her knees trembled under her, and she felt how little would be gained by her attempting to pursue them. Calling back the servant, therefore, she commissioned him, though in so breathless an accent as made her almost unintelligible, to fetch his master and mistress home, instantly. (276)

Darcy quickly substitutes a servant for himself, transforming what would have been an action growing out of and elaborating the novel's emotional center into a mundane, meaningless duty. The strange doubling—"let me, or let the servant"—reveals a sudden similarity between two characters who exist at the poles of the narrative's asymmetric structure. In this brief moment we can see what the system of characterization usually distorts but ultimately relies on: the radical continuity, or similarity, of all human agents. The dramatic cohesion of *Pride and Prejudice* rests in the way that Darcy and the servant—who are ultimately not dissimilar—become separated and represented in utterly different manners.

Servants illustrate in the crudest form what has been a central process of the narrative: the utilization of minor characters within the semantic field hinges on a distorted representation that radically flattens them. The way in which servants are reduced to sending messages in *Pride and Prejudice* is similar to the way that the younger Bennet sisters are reduced to standing for abstract qualities against which the protagonist is juxtaposed. Servants are so completely reduced as characters that they hardly make an impact on the semantic or the *thematic* register of the novel, functioning only on the more superficial register of plot. But, as we have seen with Charlotte Lucas, the plot is ultimately not distinguishable from the semantic drive of the novel—helpers who deliver messages and helpers who symbolize the marital possibilities that Elizabeth rejects are both, finally, helping to construct the singularity of Elizabeth Bennet. However, as we established in the first section of this analysis, this does not mean that the narrative privileges Elizabeth over everyone else in the novel. If every other character is reduced to functioning in this way, it is conversely the case that Elizabeth's singularity is contingent upon every other character in the novel, no matter how minor.

———

To understand the characters in *Pride and Prejudice* as linked together within a common, although asymmetrical structure helps us to understand the complicated relationship between the form of Austen's novel and the emergent social structure that is both a source and end point of this narrative form. The same system of characterization that produces the beautifully rounded Elizabeth Bennet produces a diffuse series of distorted characters—from her less fortunate sisters, to the antithetically odious Mr. Wickham and Mr. Collins, to the fragments of personality and motion that hover around the narrative's periphery. Their minorness is built into her centrality; their functionality is built into her freedom. In *The Economic and Philosophical Manuscripts of 1844*, Karl Marx describes how the exploitative nature of production in capitalism is similarly organized around a structure of contingency that produces radically asymmetrical results for the laborer and the capitalist:

> The worker puts his life into the object and this means that it no longer belongs to him but to the object. . . . So the greater the product the less he is himself. . . . [T]he more the worker produces the less he has to consume, the more values he creates the more valueless and worthless he becomes, the more formed the product the more deformed the worker, the more civilized the product the more powerless the worker, the more cultured the work the more philistine the worker becomes. . . . Labour produces works of wonder for the rich, but nakedness for the worker; it produces beauty, but cripples the worker; it replaces labour by machines but throws a part of the workers back to a barbaric labour and turns the other part into machines. (79)

Considering the problem of the literary character from a structuralist perspective, Tzvetan Todorov has noted how a system of characterization, which places the characters in seemingly discordant and discrepant relation with one another, can often help shape the *ideological* contours of the narrative. "Ideological writing does not establish a direct rapport among the unities that constitute it, but these appear to our eyes as so many manifestations of the same idea, a single law. It becomes necessary sometimes to push abstraction far enough to discover the rapport between two actions whose copresence at first glance seems purely contingent. . . . In this way, isolated and independent actions, *often accomplished by different characters*, reveal the same abstract rule, the same ideological organization" (*Qu'est-ce que c'est la structuralisme?* 72, emphasis added). Todorov's point is quite pertinent to the problem we have seen in interpretations of *Pride and Prejudice*. Structuralism moves beyond the "copresence" of disparate elements that "at first glance seem purely contingent," and these disparate elements will often be, precisely, "different characters." The system of characterization in *Pride and Prejudice* shows that Austen is not simply using secondary characters to reflect back on the real center of interest, Elizabeth and Darcy, but rather that Elizabeth, Darcy, and all the secondary characters fit into one unified, although asymmetric field, which is the controlling structure and final representation of the novel. This field of characterization rigorously links the protagonist's interior development to the dispersion and fragmentation of the many other minor characters, producing a textual structure homologous to the social structure of capitalism. "The more formed the product the more deformed the worker." What makes *Pride and Prejudice* a representation of, rather than simply a derivative reproduction of, this structure is precisely the way that we recognize minor characters *as* caricatures. At the root of caricature is an implied standard that organizes the interpretive process. Our sense that these characters are distortions implies, if only in a negative form, a radical sense of human commonality. Beneath the fragmentation and dispersion inherent in Austen's asymmetry is a controlling vision of human equality, without which the poetics of the narrative system would not coalesce. The alienating nature of the structure she is depicting, however, makes the notion of equality invisible, persisting only as the receding assumption of an ineluctably human quality. Only this assumption causes the caricatures in *Pride and Prejudice* to appear as ironic, rather than purely descriptive. The disturbing recession of equality to the invisible horizon of Austen's narrative shows the profound and perhaps unique way in which she grasped the emergent structure of modern capitalism and represented it on the literary plane.

Chapter Two

Making More of Minor Characters

A full analysis of minor characters must examine not simply the specific descriptions of particular characters but also how these characters are inflected into a complex narrative system. Such analysis highlights the *intersection* of description and structure, elucidating how particular stylistic configurations emerge out of and flow into the larger, dynamic construction of dominant and subordinate elements within the narrative totality. Charles Dickens, however, immediately confronts the reader with a radically distinct formulation of the minor character, so striking that it can pull attention away from the structural dynamics of character-system. If Dickens's characters are all anchored within a specific narrative system, they famously tend to resemble one another, accruing features that thus seem to transcend any particular structure. Before even looking at a total character-system, we need to pause and consider the radical stylistics of characterization that run through and *across* all of Dickens's novels and rest near the center of his literary achievement.

Reading Dickens, we are often won over by the stunning array of comic and grotesque minor characters, but, surprisingly, critics rarely linger on these parts of the novels or make his deeply influential methods of characterization the focal point of analysis. In this chapter, I want to consider both the essential significance of Dickens's distorted and exaggerated minor characters and the *over*-significance of minor characters within the novels. I begin this analysis by examining how minor characters claim so much imaginative space within Dickens's novels. This will provide a context for my discussion of the descriptive syntax that Dickens develops in his representation of minorness. Then, in chapter 3, I will reintegrate this analysis of minor characters into a comprehensive reading of one Dickens novel, looking at both individual character-spaces and the character-system in *Great Expectations*.

Distorted Characters and the Weak Protagonist

[I]n *David Copperfield* Dickens creates some of his most memorable characters—Micawber, Uriah Heep, Steerforth. . . .

Around his central story of Nicholas Nickleby and the misfortunes of his family, Dickens weaves a great gallery of comic types.

> In no other of his novels [than *Bleak House*] is the canvas broader, the sweep more inclusive, the linguistic and dramatic texture richer, the gallery of comic grotesques more extraordinary.

These three blurbs, culled from the back of Penguin Classics, illustrate the paradoxically central role of minor characters—comic, grotesque, eccentric— in Dickens's novels. More than with any other nineteenth-century novelist, minor characters are at the heart of Dickens's fictional achievement. As George Orwell memorably writes, "Dickens is obviously a writer whose parts are greater than his wholes. He is all fragments, all details—rotten architecture, but wonderful gargoyles" (65). The type of intrinsic readings that emerge out of formalism and New Criticism, however (the type of readings that we might find in the *front* of a Penguin Classic), tend to stress the unity of Dickens's work—the overall "architecture"—even while trying to account for the manifest importance of minor characters. In fact, critics often overload minor characters with metaphoric significance. In one recuperation of a clearly minor character, Alan Wilde claims:

> Mr. F's Aunt makes only five appearances in the course of *Little Dorrit*, and it may seem disproportionate to consider at such length a character who appears with relative infrequency in so massive a novel. In fact, the old woman is at the heart of the book; she is the analogical center of the chaotic forces that pervade it, the genuine contrast to Little Dorrit, who is the symbolic center of the forces for and of good. (34)

This minor character is thus made *doubly* symbolic: she is a synecdoche for (or the "analogical center of") a metaphor itself, a thematic conflict that structures the novel as a whole. This critical operation on Mr. F's Aunt might stand in for any number of interpretations of Dickens, and many other novelists, that locate thematic significance in a marginalized character. We need to linger further on the very "disproportion" that underlies this critical movement: not merely interpreting the novel through the thematically significant minor character, but simultaneously considering the significance *of* this strange and discordant thematic significance. In another example of such complete thematic recuperation, Lawrence Frank argues: "Silas Wegg's comic embodiment of the danger of dispersal, of fragmentation, is matched by his equally comic inclination to paralysis, to petrification. . . . Inevitably, in the art of analogy Dickens so skillfully employs, Wegg's comic predicament comments upon the serious plights of other characters" (27). Under Frank's watchful critical eye, the comic predicament—that territory of the minor character—is *absorbed into* the more "serious" thematic totality of the novel. And so criticism "inevitably" moves from the comic to the serious, from the narrative's caricatured surface to its significant depth. (And as Mr. F's Aunt, Silas Wegg, and many other subordinated figures get bound to the symbolic, they are also bound to the central characters whom they reflect on and refract.)

The thematic recovery of secondary characters is usually motivated by a larger aesthetics of formal coherence that underlies most intrinsic criticism. As Edgar Lohner describes formalism in its Russian, German, and Anglo-American contexts, "It is primarily a question of uncovering the unity which is inherent in a work of art, and demonstrating to what extent the relationship of the various parts to each other contributes to the achievement of the whole" (164). J. Hillis Miller's *Charles Dickens: The World of His Novels* offers a seminal example of this type of criticism, identifying its goal as "the revelation of that presiding unity hidden at the center, but present everywhere within his novels and partially revealed there in the embodied disguises of particular characters, actions, interiors, landscapes, and cityscapes" (x). "Particular characters" has the first place in Miller's list of parts, and most of the chapters in the book (each organized around a specific novel) include a mapping of minor characters into an ordered thematic field.[1]

This interpretive stance asks what specific minor characters stand for in Dickens's novels, in place of another fundamental question: *why are minor characters made to stand for so much in the first place*? In fact, a minor character's very importance, as an affective space within the novel, might work *against* his or her incorporation into the larger thematic or analogic structure. As Irving Howe notes about comic characters:

> Such a character bursts through the frame of the novel, grabbing more space and attention than the conception of the novel might warrant. . . . [W]e persist in taking pleasure in the notion that a character, fresh with energy, can overturn a writer's formative plan. Thoughts such as these come freely when reading Dickens. It's as if there is a deeper Dickens, an ur-Dickens more anarchic and free, who thrusts his way past the Dickens who manufactures those tiresome plots. . . . In such portions of Dickens's work we sense an abandonment to the demons of creation, as if the impulse to literary representation has overpowered theme, plot and purpose. (74)

Dickens's minor characters certainly fulfill the most common functions of narrative helpers, opposers, or *ficelles*. They are used to map social relations (we can think immediately of *Dombey and Son*), to externalize different psychological aspects of the protagonist (perhaps most clearly in the first-person novels *Great Expectations* and *David Copperfield*), and to present a range of variations within a thematic field (as in the vicissitudes of selfishness in *Martin Chuzzlewit*). Foils, displacements, projections, and doubles abound. But these instrumental, narrativized functions don't sufficiently absorb the strange interest, and impact, of the minor characters through whom they are enacted. Instead, while performing these narrative duties, Dickens's minor characters compel intense attention, in-and-of-themselves, through the configuration of their personalities and physiognomy, the texture of their speech, and their immediate and direct interaction with the protagonists.[2] This is the fundamental achievement of Dickens's depiction of minor characters: he dramatizes the

écartement between a minor character's function and his or her own fictional
being, showing how the very subordinated nature of minor characters catalyzes
new kinds of affective presence. It is a liberating moment in the development
of the European realist novel, unleashing a whole new sequence of narrative
techniques and descriptive strategies.

Look at the first arrival of Mr. Grimwig in *Oliver Twist*:

> At this moment, there walked into the room, supporting himself by a thick stick,
> a stout old gentleman, rather lame in one leg, who was dressed in a blue coat, striped
> waistcoat, nankeen breeches and gaiters, and a broad-brimmed white hat, with the
> sides turned up with green. A very small-plaited shirt frill stuck out from his waist-
> coat, and a very long steel watch-chain, with nothing but a key at the end, dangled
> loosely below it. The ends of his white neckerchief were twisted into a ball about
> the size of an orange; the variety of shapes into which his countenance was twisted,
> defy description. He had a manner of screwing his head on one side when he spoke;
> and of looking out of the corners of his eyes at the same time, which irresistibly
> reminded the beholder of a parrot. In this attitude, he fixed himself, the moment he
> made his appearance, and holding out a small piece of orange-peel at arm's length,
> exclaimed, in a growling, discontented voice,
>
> "Look here! do you see this! Isn't it a most wonderful and extraordinary thing that
> I can't call at a man's house but I find a piece of this cursed poor surgeon's-friend
> on the staircase? I've been lamed with orange-peel once, and I know orange-peel
> will be my death at last. It will, sir; orange-peel will be my death, or I'll be content
> to eat my own head, sir!"
>
> This was the handsome offer with which Mr. Grimwig backed and confirmed
> nearly every assertion he made; and it was the more singular in his case, because,
> even admitting for the sake of argument, the possibility of scientific improvements
> being ever brought to that pass which will enable a gentleman to eat his own head
> in the event of his being so disposed, Mr. Grimwig's head was such a particularly
> large one, that the most sanguine man alive could hardly entertain a hope of being
> able to get through it at a sitting—to put entirely out of the question, a very thick
> coating of powder. (147)

Mr. Grimwig is a fundamentally peripheral character because his position in
the novel is as an adjunct to another character; he appears only in scenes with
Mr. Brownlow, while Mr. Brownlow can operate independently of his "old
friend" (146). And Grimwig has a symbolic function in the novel as a foil *to*
Mr. Brownlow, someone who always suggests a more cynical interpretation
of events. But this character function is drowned out by the "more singular"
characteristics through which it is enacted. Mr. Grimwig plays a small role
within the totality of the novel but is memorable because of the eccentric way
this role is configured. The character becomes larger than—and stands out
against—his instrumental role in the novel's "theme, plot and purpose."

The affective force of these "gargoyles"—which often interrupts and over-shadows their metaphoric or symbolic function within the overall narrative—is linked to their status as *minor* characters. The comic moments that Howe identifies in Dickens almost always originate with secondary characters. As I have suggested, E. M. Forster's discussion of "flatness" relies on the conver-gence of two different processes, minorness *and* caricature, which are often conflated in the nineteenth-century novel. Flatness is the consequence of narra-tive distortion, a distortion that takes place in relation to minorness. In other words, there are strong connections between a character's position within the novel's overall structure and his or her local representation on the stylistic plane. Dickens's forceful caricature—his insistent distortions of secondary characters—is the wellspring of their affective force. It is as though he has followed the process of asymmetry to the point where it turns in on itself. Making people minor produces more and more distortion and flatness, until that distortion becomes so extreme that it begins to call attention to itself. In this way the minor character's significance rests in—not against—his insig-nificance; his strange prominence is inseparable *from* his obscurity. The surg-ing forth of minor characters within Dickens's novels always takes place in relation to this socionarrative condition: the character's presence (visually, af-fectively) is intricately linked to his or her simultaneous effacement (structur-ally, axiologically).

The crucial techniques of Dickens's caricature—highly distinctive speech patterns, emphasis of an eccentric gesture or habit, concentration on specific physical features or body parts—are all rooted in, or motivated by, the human being's constriction to an extremely reduced space. Grimwig's singularity thus emerges *out of* his flatness, his delimitation. The first paragraph in the passage (before his exclamatory speech) emphasizes Grimwig's isolated body parts (the "thick stick" that substitutes for his lame leg and his "manner of screwing his head on one side"); the way his clothing doesn't fit him (the "shirt frill stuck out from his waistcoat, and a very long watch-chain . . . dangled loosely below it"); and a unique, inimitable contortion ("the variety of shapes into which his countenance was twisted, defy description"). In all these cases it is as though Mr. Grimwig cannot wholly or comfortably fit into the space he is allocated.[3]

All of these distortions drive the description forward and mark Mr. Grimwig as a minor character. We sense Grimwig's minorness not so much through his dynamic positioning within the novelistic totality as from the descriptive distortions that his position catalyzes. Compared to characterization in Austen, minorness here has become more of an absolute given in the narrative universe, has become more deeply embedded as an essential narrative principle. We no longer see the process of characters *becoming* minor; we see merely the results of that distortion which springs from their minorness. And it is this distortion that claims our attention and begins to reverse the flow of asymmetry.

In a later passage in *Oliver Twist*, Dickens explicitly emphasizes how Grimwig's eccentricity pulls more narrative attention toward him, when he describes the friends' dissimilar responses to Oliver's sudden return. Before Oliver enters, Brownlow and Grimwig are placed in direct comparison:

> The servant soon returned, to beg that she would walk upstairs; and following him into an upper room, Miss Maylie was presented to an elderly gentleman of benevolent appearance, in a bottle-green coat. At no great distance from whom, was seated another old gentleman, in nankeen breeches and gaiters; who did not look particularly benevolent, and who was sitting with his hands clasped on the top of a thick stick, and his chin propped thereupon. (369)

As always Grimwig enters the scene in a subordinate capacity, as a modifying supplement to the description of Brownlow. The description turns on the comparative phrase "*another* old man . . . who did not look particularly benevolent," and the eccentric description that follows ("sitting with his hands clasped on the top of a thick stick, and his chin propped thereupon") seems to flow out as a consequence of this negative comparison, if only because of the weight of the semicolon as the chief division in the sentence. On the next page this eccentricity bursts out of its comparative, secondary position, when Oliver finally enters:

> "I shall surprise you very much, I have no doubt," said Rose, naturally embarrassed; "but you once showed great benevolence and goodness to a very dear young friend of mine, and I am sure you will take an interest in hearing of him again."
>
> "Indeed," said Mr. Brownlow. "May I ask his name?"
>
> "Oliver Twist you knew him as."
>
> The words no sooner escaped her lips, than Mr. Grimwig, who had been affecting to dip into a large book that lay on the table, upset it with a great crash, and falling back in his chair, discharged from his features every expression but one of unmitigated wonder, and indulged in a prolonged and vacant start; then, as if ashamed of having betrayed so much emotion, he jerked himself, as it were, by a convulsion into his former attitude, and looking out straight before him emitted a long deep whistle, which seemed, at last, not to be discharged on empty air, but to die away in the innermost recesses of his stomach.
>
> Mr. Brownlow was no less surprised, although his astonishment was not expressed in the same eccentric manner. (369–70)

Grimwig exceeds his secondary position here—or, more precisely, accrues narrative attention *through* his secondary position, which, we remember, underlies his eccentricity. The ironic imbalance between the brief paragraph describing Brownlow and the long paragraph devoted to Grimwig demonstrates how the Dickensian minor character can pull the narrative focus away from a more important character, reconfiguring the contours of the novel. The description of Mr. Grimwig ebulliently dilates, accumulating clause after clause, and in the middle of this, with the comment, "he jerked himself, as it were, by a convulsion into his former attitude," we see a vocabulary that connects to numerous passages from Dickens's work, forming a web of metonymic images that links the eccentric features of many characters across different novels.[4]

The contrast between the detailed and brief paragraphs signals the narrator's own awareness of Grimwig's affective force. Such self-consciousness about the minor character's strange ability to compel attention (even while remaining minor) is also evident in the description of Flora Finching's introduction to Mr. Dorrit in *Little Dorrit*, where highly eccentric minor characters have by now become an essential convention of Dickens's novels.

> Flora, putting aside her veil with a bashful tremor upon her, proceeded to introduce herself. At the same time a singular combination of perfumes was diffused through the room, as if some brandy had been put by mistake in a lavender-water bottle, or as if some lavender-water had been put by mistake in a brandy-bottle.
>
> "I beg Mr. Dorrit to offer a thousand apologies and indeed they would be far too few for such an intrusion which I know must appear extremely bold in a lady and alone too, but I thought it best upon the whole however difficult and even apparently improper though Mr. F's Aunt would have willingly accompanied me and as a character of great force and spirit would probably have struck one possessed of such a knowledge of life as no doubt with so many changes must have been acquired, for Mr. F. himself said frequently that although well educated in the neighborhood of Blackheath at as high as eighty guineas which is a good deal for parents and the plate kept back too on going away but that is more a meanness than its value that he had learnt more in his first years as a commercial traveller with a large commission on the sale of an article that nobody would hear of much less buy which preceded the wine trade a long time than in the whole six years in that academy conducted by a college Bachelor, though why a Bachelor more clever than a married man I do not see and never did but pray excuse me that is not the point."
>
> Mr. Dorrit stood rooted to the carpet, a statue of mystification.
>
> "I must openly admit that I have no pretensions," said Flora, "but having known the dear little thing which under altered circumstance appears a liberty . . ." (680)

Through another contrast between a long and a clipped paragraph—Flora's expansive speech, Mr. Dorrit's shocked reaction—Dickens inscribes the sensation he expects characters like Flora to elicit in the reader. Her comic monologue interrupts the novel and compels *our* attention, like the entranced (and silenced) Mr. Dorrit's, in a way distinct from the rest of the narrative, upsetting the balance, or the proportion, between a minor character's place in the *histoire* and in the *discours*. Flora's eccentricity, more than Grimwig's, is rooted in her language, but the compelling strangeness of this "disjointed and voluble" (315) idiolect also emerges out of its flatness.[5] Flora's words roll over any syntactic qualifiers so that the speech simultaneously becomes grammatically one-dimensional and conveys how Flora cannot fit her thoughts—or her perspective—into the language she is accorded. In other words, her eccentric speech—like minor characters in Dickens's novels—is compressed but not at all concise.

As we might expect, the affective presence of minor characters registers on the other side of the asymmetric structure, namely, in the weakening of the protagonist's affective centrality. Dickens's novels rarely break from a central protagonist, just as the forceful presence of his minor characters does not alter their position *as* secondary characters. The novels almost all retain the superficial shell of asymmetry, but the actual content has been massively shifted. From Samuel Pickwick, Oliver Twist, and Nicholas Nickleby to Arthur Clennam, Pip, and John Harmon, Dickens's central figures are overshadowed by the minor characters who surround them.[6] If Mr. Grimwig pulls attention away from Mr. Brownlow and thus from the central focus on Oliver's homecoming in this scene, he is only one among many strong minor characters who *together* configure the narrative in such a way as to make Oliver himself an extremely weak protagonist, most clearly in terms of his passive role within the plot. A metaphoric center—"I wished to show, in little Oliver, the principle of Good surviving through every adverse circumstance" (33)—Oliver's "survival" is almost continually reactive, responding to plot twists that he rarely generates. (Even Oliver's request for a little more gruel—the paradigmatic act of agency that both distinguishes Oliver in the first place and catalyzes the narrative—is the result of the more active, and distorted, minor character who prompts a lottery).[7] More importantly, Oliver's passive status is elaborated through the delimited space of his interiority within the overall narrative. Notice how this early passage moves away from Oliver's interior perspective out toward the caricatured, polycentric surface:

> Not having a very clearly defined notion of what a live board was, Oliver was rather astounded by this intelligence, and was not quite certain whether he ought to laugh or cry. He had no time to think about the matter, however; for Mr. Bumble gave him a tap on the head with his cane to wake him up, and another on the back to make him lively, and bidding him follow, conducted him into a large, whitewashed room where eight or ten fat gentlemen were sitting round a table, at the top of which, seated in an arm-chair rather higher than the rest, was a particularly fat gentleman with a very round, red face. (53)

This passage functions as both a representation and a literary enactment of consciousness itself. Both Oliver's distraction in reaction to the cane "taps" and the narrative's own shift of attention away from Oliver's emotions toward the confusion surrounding him are quite typical. All of Dickens's protagonists are sometimes "unable to think," because the narrative relentlessly moves away *from* their thoughts, from their interiority, toward the external events, and minor characters, who overwhelm them (thus *shaping* their thoughts). This configuration of consciousness is diametrically opposed to what we have seen in *Pride and Prejudice*. In Austen, a strong interiority grapples with the outside world and absorbs it into categories of consciousness. This process leads to the broader structure of the narrative, to the conversion of characters into characteristics (and, through the narrator's ironic omniscience, to the total structure of narrative asymmetry that is at once objective and subjective). In Dickens, the protagonist's interiority is overwhelmed by the very exterior content that it attempts to process, and this condition also underlies the structure of the character-system, motivating the strong minor characters who are, in one sense, the distorted consequence of the protagonist's incomplete processes of consciousness and perception.[8]

Between Jingle and Joe: Asymmetry and Misalignment in *The Pickwick Papers*

In his influential analysis of *The Pickwick Papers*, Steven Marcus singles out one early passage, which he praises as "something entirely new to the novel of his day" (15). Marcus invokes the passage to explain *The Pickwick Papers'* remarkable popularity, but the hyperbole suggests that he is also brooding on the very nature of Dickens's originality. The passage derives its vitality from precisely what we have been examining: an eccentric minor character's encounter with a weak protagonist, which attracts our attention because of its singular distortion.

> "Heads, heads—take care of your heads!" cried the loquacious stranger, as they came out under the low archway, which in those days formed the entrance to the coach-yard. "Terrible place—dangerous work—other day—five children—mother— tall lady, eating sandwiches—forgot the arch—crash—knock—children look round—mother's head off—sandwich in her hand—no mouth to put it in—head of a family off—shocking, shocking! Looking at Whitehall, sir?—fine place—little window—somebody else's head off there, eh, sir?—he didn't keep a sharp look-out enough either—eh, sir, eh?" (78–79)

Mr. Jingle is the first important minor character in Dickens, and he immediately grabs attention, pulling the narrative away from the novel's supposed center. In the early chapters of *The Pickwick Papers* we can see the essential way that Dickens makes more of minor characters: not by rounding out their flatness or reducing their distorted nature, but, on the contrary, by extending their flatness in such a compelling way that it focuses the reader's interest. It is worth paying close attention to these early scenes in *The Pickwick Papers*, not simply because they famously generated an unprecedented literary celebrity for Dickens, but also as they establish the durable paradigm for Dickensian minorness.

Crucially, the turn toward Jingle does not shift attention completely away from the central protagonist. Jingle arrives on the scene as a helper *to* Pickwick,

someone who can extricate him from an unruly crowd. And we approach Jingle's speech *through* the protagonist's observation of him, although the process
of Pickwick's observation has become displaced—de-emphasized by the interesting person whom he observes. Thus Jingle's striking monologue is continually addressed toward Pickwick, so that his distorted speech is woven through
Pickwick's shocked silence: " 'Heads, heads—take care of your heads! . . .
somebody else's head off there, eh, sir . . . eh, sir, eh?' "

In fact, Mr. Jingle is not the first narrative helper in the novel, or the
first minor character, despite his early appearance. He walks into a structure
that has already begun to crystallize. The narrative begins, after a first chapter in the form of the Club's minutes, with Pickwick's determination to penetrate "beyond . . . Goswell Street," or beyond the limited space of his own
consciousness:

> That punctual servant of all work, the sun, had just risen, and begun to strike a light
> on the morning of the thirteenth of May, one thousand eight hundred and twenty-
> seven, when Mr. Samuel Pickwick burst like another sun from his slumbers, threw
> open the chamber window, and looked out upon the world beneath. Goswell Street
> was at his feet, Goswell Street was on his right hand—as far as the eye could reach,
> Goswell Street extended on his left; and the opposite side of Goswell Street was over
> the way. "Such," thought Mr. Pickwick, "are the narrow views of those philosophers
> who, content with examining the things that lie before them, look not to the truths
> which are hidden beyond. As well might I be content to gaze on Goswell Street for
> ever, without one effort to penetrate to the hidden countries which on every side
> surround it." (72–73)

The mock-heroic tone of this passage doesn't lessen its accurate anticipation of
the novel's trajectory, which will chart Pickwick's excursions into the larger
social world. The tone derives in part from the particular vantage point that
informs Pickwick's quest: the position of a wealthy, elderly gentleman. Thus
the incantation of "Goswell Street" and the image of Pickwick looking "out
upon the world *beneath*" both grow out of his established domesticity. *The
Pickwick Papers* is often taken as a kind of picaresque novel, with its episodic
structure built around misadventures that occur as the protagonist tours the
countryside. Pickwick, however, is a wildly inappropriate hero for the picaresque novel, which typically tracks an active protagonist, unpropertied, socially
or materially ambitious, often young, someone who has the world "ahead of"
rather than "beneath" him. By focusing on an elderly man, Dickens foregrounds
the *passive* element of picaresque fiction, the dependence of the quester on
other, more delimited, and thus more colorful individuals to bring him adventure, rather than the ability of the quester to dynamically generate adventure.[9]

Pickwick's idea of a quest outside of Goswell Street is defined, from the
inception, in terms of his passive consciousness; adventure is constituted
merely through the registering of disparate external events. When the hero sets

out, the narrator details his instruments of perception: "Mr. Pickwick, with his portmanteau in his hand, his telescope in his great-pocket, and his note-book in his waistcoat, ready for the reception of any discoveries worthy of being noted down, had arrived at the coach stand in St. Martin's-le-Grand" (73). This suggests the essential rhythm of the novel, in which Pickwick's inquisitive consciousness is constantly overwhelmed by what it observes. Throughout the novel, Pickwick is depicted in a passive, specular relationship to these outside events; as "astonished," "surprised," and "amused" by characters who are defined as "extraordinary," "curious," "strange," and, most of all, "*singular*":

> As the little old man concluded, he looked round on the attentive faces of his wondering auditors with a smile of grim delight.
> "What strange things these are you tell us of, sir," said Mr. Pickwick, minutely scanning the old man's countenance, by the aid of his glasses. (362)

> "That's the most extraordinary case I ever heard of," said Mr. Pickwick, with an emphatic blow on the table.
> "Oh, that's nothing," said Jack Hopkins; "is it, Bob?"
> "Certainly not," replied Mr. Bob Sawyer.
> "Very singular things occur in our profession, I can assure you, sir," said Hopkins. (527)

> "It got us in trouble last time," said the woman, turning into the house; "I woan't have nothin' to say to 'un."
> "Most extraordinary thing I ever met with in my life," said the astonished Mr. Pickwick. (137)

> "Stop a bit," replied Sam, suddenly recollecting himself. "Yes; there's a pair of Wellingtons a good deal worn, and a pair o' lady's shoes, in number five."
> "What sort of shoes?" hastily inquired Wardle, who, together with Mr. Pickwick, had been lost in bewilderment at the singular catalogue of visitors. (205)

> "Here is my card, sir," replied Mr. Pickwick, much amused by the abruptness of the question, and the singular manner of the stranger. (381)

All of these examples flow out of the narrative's episodic structure, so that strangeness or singularity always originates with a minor character.[10] Minor characters *generate* the picaresque structure of the narrative, at the expense of the protagonist's interiority, but also at the price of their *own* distortion.[11]

Distortion is first conflated with minorness almost immediately in the narrative, as Pickwick stands on St. Martin's-le-Grand:

> "Cab!" said Mr. Pickwick.
> "Here you are sir," shouted a strange specimen of the human race, in a sackcloth coat, and apron of the same, who with a brass label and number round his neck, looked as if he were catalogued in some collection of rarities. This was the waterman.

This instrumental character's singularity, as a "strange specimen of the human race," is conditioned by his sudden appearance and quick exit from the novel. In a certain sense this is a perfect minor character, or, more precisely, a perfect condensation of minorness and caricature. Such distortion—the natural result of containing a human being within two sentences—is connected with his reduced, purely functional existence, a reduction signaled by the very brevity of the second, final sentence. The waterman's strangeness thus emerges both through his abrupt entrance into and departure from the novel and through his contrast to Pickwick's social standing, which, as we have already seen, is connected to Pickwick's passive, specular relationship to the events around him.[12]

Immediately afterward we see a more concrete instance of Pickwick's curiosity, as his colloquy with the cabman is also formed, or deformed, through their class distance. Curiosity soon generates more adventure than Pickwick bargains for: his scribbling down information in the cab immediately leads to an altercation with the cabman, who accuses Pickwick of being an informer and taking down his cab number. Pickwick's surprised reactions to the cabman's answers do not differ from his reaction to the cabman's hostility:

"What!" ejaculated Mr. Pickwick, laying his hand upon his notebook. (73)

"Weeks," said Mr. Pickwick in astonishment—and out came the note-book again. (74)

What was the learned man's astonishment, when that unaccountable person flung the money on the pavement, and requested in figurative terms to be allowed the pleasure of fighting him (Mr. Pickwick) for the amount! (74)

"I didn't want your number," said the astonished Mr. Pickwick. (74)

Pickwick's "astonishment" connects his questions to the cabman with the more unruly adventures that follow. The interview, the chaos it sparks, and the angry crowd that results all become part of the "discoveries" Pickwick originally set out to find. But if Pickwick's astonishment integrates the diverse events in the chapter, it is only the passive register of these events, revealing his essentially contingent position. The protagonist still remains at the center of the novel, but the *weight* of interest has shifted away from him, flowing off into the astonishing margins of the text. Pickwick's very passive curiosity helps generate the external phenomena that overwhelm him: his "astonishment" works like a match, flaring up the excessive action of other, minor characters. Jingle seems to be spontaneously generated out of this process, suddenly arriving at the end of a long sentence that describes, precisely, the increasing volatility of the *crowd*, as it shifts from a state of passivity to hyperactivity:

The mob had hitherto been passive spectators of the scene, but as the intelligence of the Pickwickians being informers was spread among them, they began to canvass with considerable vivacity the propriety of enforcing the heated pastry-vendor's proposition; and there is no saying what acts of personal aggression they might have committed had not the affray been unexpectedly terminated by the interposition of a new comer.

"What's the fun?" said a rather tall thin young man, in a green coat, emerging suddenly from the coach yard.

"Informers!" shouted the crowd again.

"We are not," roared Mr. Pickwick, in a tone which, to any dispassionate listener, carried conviction with it.

"Ain't you, though—ain't you?" said the young man, appealing to Mr. Pickwick, and making his way through the crowd by elbowing the countenances of its component members. (75)

Like Wickham, in *Pride and Prejudice*, Jingle springs up from the excesses of the crowd, rather than acting as a foil *to* these excesses. If he immediately extricates Pickwick from the scene, diffusing the threat of mob violence, he also extends and consolidates the energies that have just been associated with social multiplicity. Thus the narrator immediately stresses Jingle's unpredictability, following the phrase "unexpectedly terminated" with the somewhat redundant "emerging suddenly." Jingle is like a lightning rod of the crowd, able to navigate himself through it because he has mastered its essential rhythms, "elbowing the countenances of its component members," presumably with a series of short, quick jerks, the physical counterpart to what will soon emerge as his highly distinctive manner of speech. Even while moving the protagonist out of the anonymous crowd, Jingle thus reiterates its aggressive challenge to him, responding to his indignant claim not like "any dispassionate listener" but with an abrupt denial, "Ain't you, though—ain't you?"

If Jingle's speech about "heads" a few pages later is the first achieved caricature of the novel (and in all of Dickens), its singularity is generated in the structured relationship between Pickwick's passive interiority and social exteriority. Jingle's eccentric characteristics thus flow out of his specific narrative position within the character-system; they are an elaboration *of* the exterior energies of the crowd as both generated by and incompletely registered through Pickwick's central consciousness. But this condensation all takes place very quickly: the novel has barely gotten underway. Thus at the virtual outset of the narrative we are confronted with what is more gradually developed in *Pride and Prejudice*, the disjunction between surface and depth. It is this disjunctive process that underlies the strong connection between minorness and caricature—minorness implies the effacement of a character's interiority within the narrative totality, while caricature dramatizes and embodies this effacement on the local, descriptive plane.

Jingle's fragmented speech stems from the misalignment of thought and language; the distinctive gaps and elisions mark a kind of semiarticulation, the noise we might expect from "that roar which lies on the other side of silence."

At the same time, Jingle's wild swerving from phrase to phrase condenses the chaotic energies of the crowd. Right after Jingle's first monologue we get a description of the "new acquaintance," filtered through Pickwick's passive consciousness and organized around the tension between Jingle's body and his clothing, another key trope for the disjunction of surface and depth:

> While his three companions were busily engaged in proffering their thanks to their new acquaintance, Mr. Pickwick had leisure to examine his costume and appearance.
>
> He was about the middle height, but the thinness of his body, and the length of his legs, gave him the appearance of being much taller. The green coat had been a smart dress garment in the days of swallow-tails, but had evidently in those times adorned a much shorter man than the stranger, for the soiled and faded sleeves scarcely reached to the wrists. It was buttoned closely up to his chin, at the imminent hazard of splitting the back; and an old stock, without a vestige of shirt collar, ornamented his neck. His scanty black trousers displayed here and there those shiny patches which bespeak long service, and were strapped very tightly over a pair of patched and mended shoes, as if to conceal the dirty white stockings, which were nevertheless distinctly visible. His long black hair escaped in negligent waves from beneath each side of his old pinched up hat; and glimpses of his bare wrists might be observed between the tops of his gloves, and the cuffs of his coat sleeves. His face was thin and haggard; but an indescribable air of jaunty impudence and perfect self-possession pervaded the whole man. (77–78)

Just as Jingle's thoughts can't fit into the regular flow of language, his body now strains against his clothing. There is an essential misalignment between his actual person and that "costume and appearance" which are the modes of Pickwick's examination. The misfit is apparent in the way Jingle strains the fabric of his clothing, almost "splitting the back" of his jacket and wearing away his now "patched and mended shoes." Everywhere we look we see bits and pieces of his body peeping out of the spaces where he doesn't align with his clothes: the sleeves that "scarcely reached to the wrist," "the dirty white stockings, which were nevertheless distinctly visible," "the long black hair" that "escaped in negligent waves from beneath each side of his old pinched up hat," and, again, the "glimpses of his bare wrists . . . between the tops of his gloves and the cuffs of his coat sleeves." (It is an inversion of the way that Grimwig's clothing is misaligned, so that his "shirt frill stuck out from his waistcoat.") These details don't suggest a stable wholeness lurking beneath, misrepresented in a fragmented form. Mr. Jingle himself seems penetrated by this disjunction, and the passage's last sentence shifts to this more essential register, noting that "an indescribable air of jaunty impudence and perfect self-possession pervaded the *whole man*."

These two somewhat contradictory qualities—jaunty impudence and self-possession—would also make a good description of Wickham, or, more precisely, of Darcy's hostile vision of Wickham, which is eventually adopted by the novel. As with Wickham, these qualities leave Jingle "indescribable," the final result of the way inner being exceeds, or cannot be aligned with, exterior parameters. "How he lived I know not." If Wickham's elusive character cannot be registered through "his countenance, voice, and manner," Jingle is both hidden and revealed through these parameters. As we have seen, there is a relation between his physical appearance and his speech: just as his body bursts out of his threadbare clothes, his consciousness pokes out through fragments of language, and, I am suggesting, his character itself emerges sporadically, within the truncated limits of his minorness. A few chapters later Jingle's staccato idiolect is also described as rendering him indescribable:

> "Come," replied the stranger—"stopping at Crown—Crown at Muggleton—met a party—flannel jackets—white trousers—anchovy sandwiches—devilled kidneys—splendid fellows—glorious."
>
> Mr. Pickwick was sufficiently versed in the stranger's system of stenography to infer from this rapid and disjointed communication that he had, somehow or other, contracted an acquaintance with the All-Muggletons, which he had converted, by a process peculiar to himself, into that extent of good fellowship on which a general invitation may be easily founded. His curiosity was therefore satisfied, and putting on his spectacles he prepared himself to watch the play which was just commencing. (163)

Again, Mr. Jingle's eccentric, fragmented outside—his "rapid and disjointed communication"—makes his inside inscrutable, so that Pickwick can only "infer" that Jingle had "somehow or other," "by a process peculiar to himself," ingratiated himself with yet another group of people. In this sense Mr. Jingle is simultaneously reduced and expanded—the fragments of his speech and shreds of his clothing encase his thoughts and body within a limited, distorted form, but they also generate an inimitable singularity, a mode of being "peculiar to himself." (In a similar way, Grimwig's twisted countenance is said to "defy description.")

In Jingle we see the culmination of one of the two forms of minorness that structure the nineteenth-century novel as a whole: the minor character as eccentric—as outcast, criminal, madman, or troublemaker. His fragmented speech pattern and physical appearance, as well as his sudden entrances and exits throughout the novel, all stress the way his "singular" personality cannot be stably aligned with external social forms *or* a fixed social position. Soon after Jingle's appearance, the novel generates the antithesis of this fragmentation, presenting a minor character as worker or helper, whose inner being has been engulfed within a hardened, exterior form (even as the character has been confined within a delimited and static role). This figure is, of course, Joe, the obese, narcoleptic servant. Corpulence and sleepiness: his only remaining qualities are almost a paradigm for this kind of minorness, as the very weight of his exteriority seems to dull his thoughts, pushing him toward catatonic slumber.

As with Jingle (as well as Mr. Grimwig and Flora), the importance of Joe's character within the novel can be measured only in an affective sense, as he inevitably attracts the reader's attention beyond, and because of, his marginal role. Throughout the presentation of Joe, Dickens emphasizes his social, and narrative, minorness, while also emphasizing his singularity. Thus in his first appearance Joe comes at the *end* of a long catalog description of an "open barouche" (which I will not fully quote), and this belatedness is motivated by his reduction to a purely functional role:

> Fastened up behind the barouche was a hamper of spacious dimensions—one of those hampers which always awakens in a contemplative mind associations connected with cold fowls, tongues and bottles of wine—and on the box sat a fat and red-faced boy, in a state of somnolency, whom no speculative observer could have regarded for an instant without setting down as the official dispenser of the contents of the before-mentioned hamper, when the proper time for their consumption should arrive.
>
> Mr. Pickwick had bestowed a hasty glance on these interesting objects, when he was again greeted by his faithful disciple. (121)

As in the opening description of the "strange specimen of the human race," this scene condenses minorness, caricature, and functionality. Joe's somnolency, which will soon become the key to the famous caricature, is intertwined with his reduced position "as the official dispenser of the contents," and with the way he is filtered through other people's consciousness: the "speculative observer" who is invoked in the original sentence and then dramatized in Mr. Pickwick's "hasty glance." Just as Mr. Jingle erupts out of a specific structure of chaotic multiplicity (which he soon, however, leaves behind) Joe's configuration as an individual character is intertwined with his subordinated functionality. His character emerges out of his character-space, shaped by the way he is reduced to his job, placed at the end of a catalog description, and positioned in an exterior space vis-à-vis a central interiority. (And the implied "speculative observer" is also the presumed beneficiary of Joe's services.) Joe thus occupies a typical nexus of minorness: presented only as he registers on the protagonist's consciousness, confined to a functional role (and here the most essential role of servant), and defined in terms of limited character traits. These three coordinates are, indeed, interdependent.

If Jingle's eccentricity is measured through the way his singular personality fragments his exterior being—his speech, clothes, and body—Joe's inner self is buried underneath his corpulent body. However, like Jingle, Flora, and Mr. Grimwig, Joe's very minorness creates the conditions for his momentary centrality; he soon grabs the attention of the protagonist and of the novel itself:

> "Damn that boy," said the old gentleman, "he's gone to sleep again."
> "Very extraordinary boy, that," said Mr. Pickwick, "does he always sleep in this way?"

"Sleep!" said the old gentleman, "he's always asleep. Goes on errands fast asleep, and snores as he waits at table."

"How very odd!" said Mr. Pickwick.

"Ah! odd indeed," returned the old gentleman; "I'm proud of that boy—wouldn't part with him on any account—he's a natural curiosity! Here, Joe—Joe—take these things away, and open another bottle—d'ye hear?"

The fat boy rose, opened his eyes, swallowed the huge piece of pie he had been in the act of masticating when he last fell asleep, and slowly obeyed his master's orders—gloating languidly over the remains of the feast, as he removed the plates, and deposited them in the hamper. The fresh bottle was produced, and speedily emptied: the hamper was made fast in its old place—the fat boy once more mounted the box—the spectacles and pocket-glass were again adjusted—and the evolutions of the military recommenced. (127–28)

This glance at Joe is prompted by the novel's underlying structure, in which Pickwick's innate curiosity, his "love of the truths which are hidden beyond," propels him to investigate the outside world. In this sense, Joe, like all the other characters in *The Pickwick Papers*, enters into the novel only in-and-through Pickwick's consciousness. In this example such a process is made more explicit, when Pickwick turns toward the fat boy and says, "Very extraordinary boy, that, does he always sleep in this way?" However, the host does not really answer Pickwick's question as to whether Joe sleeps "in this way" but, seizing on the word "sleep," merely informs Pickwick that Joe *always sleeps*, repeating the word three times. Pickwick cannot find out the specifics about the *way* Joe sleeps. Pickwick's probing curiosity is overwhelmed by the sheer extraordinariness of Joe's somnolence, so that the protagonist can utter about this minor character only, "How very odd!" If Austen's novels hinge on the transformation of characters into characteristics, we can note an inverse process in this passage: the protagonist's natural curiosity, arguably his most *essential* interior characteristic, gets overshadowed by the minor character, as someone who actually *is* "a natural curiosity."

This shift is elaborated in the next, dilated sentence, which is one of those comic descriptions that burst out of the narrative frame, making more of minor characters. Again, I am dwelling on these first minor characters because Dickens seems to be actively formulating his own creative perspective, a process that drives the rhythm of the sentence, as the narrator adds clause after clause to increase our focus on Joe: "The fat boy rose, opened his eyes, swallowed the huge piece of pie he had been in the act of masticating when he last fell asleep, and slowly obeyed his master's orders—gloating languidly over the remains of the feast, as he removed the plates, and deposited them in the hamper." In Austen we would not find a sentence whose content was so hostile to a minor character—nor whose form was so sympathetic. But the final accomplishment of this character portrayal rests in the next sentence, which, rather than being propelled toward the sentimental or grotesque, reminds us of the socionarrative position that first produces Joe's minorness. Thus the abrupt shift toward a different, fragmented, syntax is combined with a sudden inversion of Joe's position, which now renders him as purely functional: "The fresh bottle was produced, and speedily emptied: the hamper was made fast in its old place—the fat boy once more mounted the box—the spectacles and pocketglass were again adjusted—and the evolutions of the military recommenced." The two adjacent sentences present dialectically opposite relations between Joe and his labor. In the first sentence Joe is the grammatical subject whose characteristics are brought out more fully through the objects of his labor, as he "*slowly* obeyed his master's orders—*gloating languidly* over the remains of the feast." In the following sentence, the objects of his service have become the grammatical subjects of the narrative—"The fresh bottle was produced . . . the hamper was made fast," while Joe's labor is only implied in the passive syntax and his personality suddenly effaced from the narrative, as suddenly as it had just erupted. The two sentences shouldn't be read as contradictory, though; rather, they suggest, together, that Joe's singular personality, which shines out in one sentence, is produced in-and-through that effacement into his labor which hides him in the other sentence.

Precisely like Jingle, this minor character's appearance is thus strangely linked to his disappearance: both of these minor characters (the first important ones in Dickens) encapsulate the essential structural, and narrative, problematic that Dickens confronts: the surging forth of subordinated characters because of their minorness. This is reiterated at the end of the chapter, which, by closing with an image of the fat boy, emphasizes the affective pull of minor characters, while also associating Joe's affective force with his reduced inflection into the narrative:

> "That's it," said the old gentleman. "I don't let you off, mind, under a week; and undertake that you shall see everything worth seeing. If you've come down for a country life, come to me, and I'll give you plenty of it. Joe—damn that boy, he's gone to sleep again—Joe, help Tom put in the horses."
>
> The horses were put in—the driver mounted—the fat boy clambered up by his side—farewells were exchanged—and the carriage rattled off. As the Pickwickians turned round to take a last glimpse of it, the setting sun cast a rich glow on the faces of their entertainers, and fell upon the form of the fat boy. His head was sunk upon his bosom; and he slumbered again. (128)

First Joe is flattened—reduced to the already repetitive trait of falling asleep—and in the familiar cry, "damn that boy, he's gone to sleep again," this flattening is linked specifically to his functional position as a servant. However, this flattening has distorted Joe in a way that makes him interesting—if the natural curiosity has captured Pickwick's attention, Joe's affective force becomes naturalized at the chapter's close, coordinating the very glow of the setting sun.

The last sentence then emphasizes that this attention is linked to his reductive habit of falling asleep, so that the same character trait which elevates Joe within the text also obscures him, reducing him to an inexpressible cipher, "His head . . . sunk upon his bosom." The final sentence thus melds Joe's affective force with his functional passivity—his singularity emerges through his reduction, through the very blankness of his subordinated subjectivity. Somnolency is merely the descriptive encapsulation of this reduction.[13]

Seeing into Sight: Mr. Elton and Uriah Heep

The Pickwick Papers offers an important paradigm for Dickensian asymmetry. Not merely surrounding the weak, central character with a manifold group of eccentric and distorted secondary figures, *The Pickwick Papers* revolves around the charged interactions *between* the protagonist and this world of minorness. Pickwick continually perceives and confronts a world that overwhelms his cognitive and sensory faculties, a world that in being observed inevitably turns back, ferocious, upon the observer.[14] The protagonist's passivity allows a crowd of minor characters to flood into the novel, accruing attention through their compelling singularity. Yet we must note a crucial limit to Pickwick's narrative weakness. The protagonist might be continually overwhelmed, but, as long as he holds on to his position as central character, the world of minorness never *completely*, or substantially, overwhelms him. In all of Dickens's novels, minor characters persistently wrest attention away from any privileged, central figure—but they never *succeed* in destroying the asymmetric structure that condemns them to minorness. Dickens's novels thus present the reader with a very particular kind of stasis. An asymmetric world has begun to collapse—to literally *revolve*—but this revolution is incomplete, or, in fact, frozen in place. "A character, fresh with energy, can *overturn* a writer's formative plan," writes Irving Howe. And already in the prefatory first chapter of *The Pickwick Papers*, the narrator writes:

> Travelling was in a troubled state, and the minds of coachmen were unsettled. Let them look abroad, and contemplate the scenes which were enacting around them. Stage coaches were upsetting in all directions, horses were bolting, boats *were overturning*, and boilers were bursting. (71, emphasis added)

We must pay attention to the abundance of participles here, as they suspend those actions that seem related above all by their very immediacy (to upset, bolt, overturn, burst). The world of minorness can't go any further than in Dickens's novels—it is about to overturn the observing faculties of the protagonist. But it is never able finally to do so. The central character has been discredited, weakened, rendered invalid, submerged or (in *Our Mutual Friend*) even drowned; but he still never loses the distinct space *of* centrality, with all of its implications for the narrative structure.

Above all, centrality in Dickens has become (epistemologically and psychologically) *passive*, posterior to the characters—and characteristics—it observes. Such posteriority underlies this passage's distribution of energy away from the members' faculties of "contemplation" to the viewed events *that* they are contemplating, "the scenes which were enacting around them." It's a telling phrase for *The Pickwick Papers*, and perhaps for all of Dickens, and its distinctive sense rests upon that keyword "enacting." This term restages the epistemology of Boz's *Sketches* (which have already theatricalized social viewing), to subtly shift the *agency* of the "scene" from the viewer or beholder to the viewed or beheld (which, crucially, seems to *surround* the contemplative viewer). It is a model for Dickens's radical social epistemology, which inscribes an excess into the things we see, consider, or partially comprehend. "The mist was heavier yet when I got out upon the marshes, so that instead of my running at everything, everything seemed to run at me." The latent priority of the observed over the observer in the opening of Dickens's first novel is hyperbolically literalized in this much later passage, from the beginning of *Great Expectations*. But even here the very attention *to* the protagonist's beleaguered comprehension of "everything" still elaborates, and thus confirms, centrality in relationship to interiority. After all, these events that "enact themselves around" the Pickwickian observers (like the world that rushes at Pip) are comprehended not as events but merely as "scenes" (or, in other words, *viewed* events). In this sense the verb "enact" splits between (threatening) action and (theatrical) acting, doing and seeming, unraveling the very generative agency that overwhelms the central beholder by elaborating this agency only *as* it is understood to overwhelm contemplation, or understanding, itself. Likewise, the central, observing consciousness still maintains its grip on the narrative structure, underlying the minorness that surrounds it on all sides. Minor characters, in turn, flood into the narrative, in transfixed and permanent states of distortion. En masse, they have collectively facilitated a vast displacement of attention, and yet, individually, they suffer from a narrative compression and distortion that can never be transcended.

This incomplete overturning has an important place within the history of the novel, and, more specifically, within the development and elaboration of narrative asymmetry. In one sense, as I have suggested, Dickens's novels pursue the dynamics of asymmetry that we have seen in *Pride and Prejudice* to its logical extreme. Austen's narratives forcefully integrate minor characters' specifically *subordinated* positions into the achieved structure and representation of the novels as a whole. Minor characters are not simply ornamental and cannot be analyzed as merely a supplement of or colorful counterpoint to the main plot and central characters because the overriding metaphoric structure, the "theme, plot and purpose" that we can map out of the thickness of the narrative, is built *through* the minor characters, and, more saliently, through their very minorness, and the processes of compression, externalization, abstraction, distortion, and fragmentation that underlie the asymmetric character-system. Dickens follows the pressures and consequences of this kind of narrative asymmetry a step further: minor characters are now a threat *to* the overall semantic structure. His novels canonically establish the connection between minorness and caricature that produces flatness, making minor characters a central part of the achieved fictional universe.

But the very affective force of Dickens's minor characters—who call attention to themselves at the expense of narrative coherence—can weaken the relationship between a character and his or her dynamic position within the organized narrative totality. In Austen, a minor character's individual configuration inevitably flows into and is circumscribed by his or her integration into the narrative's overall structure. Her narratives thus generate processes such as compression and externalization that dynamically entwine a character's local configuration with his or her subordinated narrative position. The transition from characters to characteristics is not assumed but actually enacted in these novels, motivating the continual discrimination that underlies a shifting network of relations. In Dickens, such compression and externalization have already occurred; they are a *given* in the narrative universe. The moment Mr. Grimwig arrives he disrupts the narrative, because his flatness is already fully developed. As Esther says of Mr. Jellyby's defining eccentricity in a telling line in *Bleak House*, "I suppose he had been more talkative and lively once; but he seemed to have been completely exhausted long before I knew him" (477). Minor characters are often not established or motivated in Dickens's novels; they simply appear. Mr. Jingle's characteristics on the descriptive plane are, from his first instant in the novel, a spectacular exaggeration of what Mr. Wickham becomes within the total narrative structure of *Pride and Prejudice*. For this reason, the question we began with in chapter 1—Eliot's query about "why always Dorothea?"—is in an important sense much less urgent in Dickens than in many other Victorian novels. There is no chance that Joe will pull the narrative too closely around him, or that the novel will become a reflection of his consciousness. And the same holds for Mr. Grimwig, Mr. F's Aunt, Mr. Jingle, Newman Noggs, Mr. Pancks, Flora Finching, Silas Wegg, *etc*.

I want to make a brief excursion back into Jane Austen to elaborate this comparison:

> She was, in fact, beginning very much to wonder that she had ever thought him pleasing at all; and his sight was so inseparably connected with some very disagreeable feelings, that except in a moral light, as a penance, a lesson, a source of profitable humiliation to her own mind, she would have been thankful to be assured of never seeing him again. She wished him very well; but he gave her pain, and his welfare twenty miles off would administer most satisfaction. (*Emma*, 182)

As he sat on the sofa, with his long knees drawn up under his coffee-cup, his hat and gloves upon the ground close to him, his spoon going softly round and round, his shadowless red eyes, which looked as if they had scorched their lashes off, turned towards me without looking at me, the disagreeable dints I have formerly described in his nostrils coming and going with his breath, and a snaky undulation pervading his frame from his chin to his boots, I decided in my own mind that I disliked him intensely. It made me very uncomfortable to have him for a guest, for I was young then, and unused to disguise what I so strongly felt. (*David Copperfield*, 437)

These passages both describe the same asymmetrical moment: a minor character inflected through the hostile consciousness of the central protagonist. But there is a telling difference between Mr. Elton's position in *Emma* and Uriah Heep's presence in *David Copperfield*. In *Emma*, Elton is flattened through the course of the narrative; he becomes a minor character. Uriah Heep is presented as "formerly described"; he is always already flat, eccentric, exaggerated, a parody of himself.

Even more than in *Pride and Prejudice*, the omniscient totality of *Emma* is built around the space of the protagonist, engendering an asymmetrical narrative structure. On the one hand, the ironic narrator is endlessly critical of her central protagonist. In the only novel named after a single character, Austen immediately highlights egoism or self-love as Emma's central character flaw: "the real evils indeed of Emma's situation were the power of having rather too much her own way, and a disposition to think a little too well of herself" (3). This allows Austen to make the form of the novel—and its method of characterization—utterly relevant to the story she is trying to tell. *Emma*'s plot—the *histoire*—revolves around challenging and ultimately destroying Emma's complacent sense that she is the center of the social universe. At the same time, we must juxtapose this plot of decentering with Emma's unchanging position at the center of the fictional, *discursive* universe. However much irony is lodged at Emma's own self-centered viewpoint, this irony does not serve to dislodge her from the center of the narrative itself. The *histoire* interrogates Emma's egoistic worldview, while the *discours* externalizes this self-centeredness into the very fabric of the narrative structure. Emma's relative centrality within the *histoire* and the *discours* are developed in parallel, so that a careful reading of the novel reveals a shrewd and telling examination of what it means to have a central protagonist—at all—within a realist narrative.[15] And this generates the tense asymmetry of the novel, organized around the memorable and intricate character-spaces of figures such as Harriet Smith, Jane Fairfax (one of the most suggestively submerged characters in Austen), Miss Bates, Mr. Knightley, Mr. Woodhouse, Robert Martin, and the anonymous gypsies.

As with these other characters, Mr. Elton's position is developed at the juncture between Emma's limited consciousness—as an organizing narrative perspective—and the omniscient totality that challenges but never fully displaces this perspective. Attempting to propose to Emma while she tries to arrange a marriage between him and Harriet, Mr. Elton plays the paradigmatic minor role of rejected suitor. The collapse of the distance between Harriet and Emma that results from the confusion over Elton is the first major challenge to the protagonist's self-centeredness (after the removal of her beloved governess). Elton's misdirection of desire complicates Emma's highly ordered class perspective and disrupts her technique of mediating her own sexual desires through her friend.[16] Emma's misjudgment or misperception of Elton thus flows directly out of her own central character flaw (a character flaw, I would argue, that is intimately tied to *centrality* itself). This is made clear during the scene in which Harriet falls ill and Emma tries to persuade Elton to stay with Harriet, skipping a dinner party that Emma herself will attend:

> Mr. Elton looked as if he did not very well know what answer to make; which was exactly the case; for though very much gratified by the kind of care of such a fair lady, and not liking to resist any advice of her's, he had not really the least inclination to give up the visit;—but Emma, too eager and busy in her own previous conceptions and views to hear him impartially, or see him with clear vision, was very well satisfied with his muttering acknowledgement of its being "very cold, certainly very cold," and walked on, rejoicing in having extricated him from Randalls, and secured him the power of sending to inquire after Harriet every hour of the evening. (110)

At this point—before the crisis when Elton directly confronts Emma—there is a clear distinction between who Elton really is and how Emma perceives him. Thus "Mr. Elton looked" a certain way, but Emma cannot "see him with clear vision." The ironic structure of the passage depends on the reader's gaining access to Elton's own thoughts, which are presented in free indirect discourse and serve to contradict Emma's central, organizing perspective. In this sense, Elton is not yet a fully developed minor character.

The narrative, however, will elaborate Emma's lack of vision until it becomes more externally realized. The passage that I juxtaposed with *David Copperfield*, which occurs after Emma has been unpleasantly confronted with the actual nature of Elton's desires, functions as the turning point in Elton's narrative configuration. Now it is not Emma's misperception but the substantial, although distorted, reality of Elton's presence that is highlighted. The process of Emma's inaccurately "see[ing]" Elton gets collapsed into the term "his sight"—a verbal noun that objectifies and lends external validity to Emma's subjective perception, as Elton cannot now emerge as separate from Emma's interior "feelings." This shift—from the depiction of Emma "seeing" Elton to the "sight" of Elton as it is connected with Emma's interior feelings— encapsulates how the description and exaggeration of characters is often only the externalization of a social relationship, a mode of vision. Elton has become a minor character and will remain one for the rest of the novel—functioning only through the repression that he catalyzes. This function is made explicit in the rest of the sentence, which continues "except in a moral light, as a penance, a lesson, a source of *profitable* humiliation to her own mind, she would have been thankful to be assured of never seeing him again" (emphasis added). Elton is here abstracted into a symbolic and instrumental relationship with the protagonist, becoming merely a displaced externalization of the misjudgment that stems from her own self-centeredness, who must be confined to the story's margins. And while this description is also in free indirect discourse, so that we can draw an ironic distance between the protagonist and the omniscient narrator, Emma's perspective is confirmed by the narrative as a whole. Her wish is essentially satisfied—Elton does not move twenty miles away in the story but he no longer plays an important role in the discourse, except in further disturbing Emma through his marriage to another of the protagonist's foes. His own thoughts are never again represented, even in free indirect discourse. In the "development" of Elton, as minor character, we can trace a three-step process: the protagonist's misperception (not seeing Elton); the hardening of this misperception into an external form (the *sight* of Elton); and the functionalization of Elton's newly unpleasant (but now receding) form vis-à-vis the protagonist's own developing consciousness. As though constrained by *Emma*'s hyperasymmetric structure, the narrative shifts from representing the process of misperception to displacing this misperception onto the visual object itself.[17]

In Dickens, this displacement has become complete. Like a verb turning into a noun, the socionarrative *process* that always underscores the *substance* of minor characters in Austen has essentially disappeared. The introductory description of Uriah Heep in *David Copperfield* thus anticipates David's subsequent rendering of his opponent, his distortions fully apparent from the beginning.

> When the pony-chaise stopped at the door, and my eyes were intent upon the house, I saw a cadaverous face appear at a small window on the ground floor (in a little round tower that formed one side of the house), and quickly disappear. The low arched door then opened, and the face came out. It was quite as cadaverous as it had looked in the window, though in the grain of it there was that tinge of red which is sometimes to be observed in the skins of red-haired people. It belonged to a red-haired person—a youth of fifteen, as I take it now, but looking much older—whose hair was cropped as close as the closest stubble; who had hardly any eyebrows, and no eyelashes, and eyes of a red-brown, so unsheltered and unshaded, that I remember wondering how he went to sleep. He was high-shouldered and bony; dressed in decent black, with a white wisp of a neckcloth; buttoned up to the throat; and had a long, lank skeleton hand, which particularly attracted my attention. (275)

Heep's minorness (figured through his distant position "in a little round tower that formed one side of the house") and his distorted *body* (registered through the "cadaverous face") are simultaneously depicted. Or nearly simultaneously.

The narrative does suggest that Heep's eccentric features bear a relation to David's *distance* from him, so that Heep first only appears "at a small window" that calls attention to his strange head. But it immediately separates the character from this mediating frame: "[T]he face came out. It was quite as cadaverous as it had looked in the window." What is the function of this narrative stutter-step if not to literally collapse the structure through which Heep is apprehended into his eccentric physiognomy itself? This physiognomy then becomes the ground for all of David's observations. When the protagonist's animus reaches a peak in the later passage, as Uriah sleeps in the next room, his hostile description merely reiterates earlier passages, singling out "the disagreeable dints *I have formerly described* in his nostrils coming and going with his breath." These dints are, in fact, already suggested in Heep's introduction (with his "cadaverous face") and in an extended image in the following chapter, well before the night they spend together in David's apartment: "[F]ollowing up the lines with his forefinger, I observed that his nostrils, which were thin and pointed, with sharp dints in them, had a singular and most uncomfortable way of expanding and contracting themselves—that they seemed to twinkle instead of his eyes, which hardly ever twinkled at all" (291).

Partial Visibility and Incomplete Vision: The Appearance of Minor Characters

> "You look at him, and there he is. You look at him again, and—there he isn't."
> —*Barnaby Rudge*, 128

All of Dickens's novels tend to convert seeing into "sights," processes into substances, diseases into symptoms. Dickens consistently replaces incomplete vision with distorted visibility, hardening a social process into a substantive physical phenomenon. In a similar way, the narrative processes that underlie asymmetry are not as evident in Dickens, drowned out by the substantialized bearing of the minor characters themselves. Consider the dynamic that underlies such a modest observation as this one offered by Raymond Williams: "[Dickens's] way of seeing characters, in their brief fixed appearances, defined by certain phrases, is a way of seeing that belongs to the streets: to faces and gestures briefly seen . . . in the crowded passage of men and women in the city" ("Introduction" 28). I point to this comment merely to note how Williams enacts the transition from process to substance, as "brief fixed appearances" come to stand in for "faces and gestures briefly *seen*." Such a "fixed appearance" has the distinction of showing both more *and* less than the "men and women" who actually crowd the street: less because the person is only briefly, or partially, seen; more because this circumscribed view becomes "fixed" and, as with the Dickensian minor character, intensified through its very circumscription. In fact, I want to argue that this "fixity" already inheres within the term "appearance"; or, to put this another way, that in Dickens all *three* of Williams's terms—"brief," "fixed," "appearance"—mean the same thing, suggest the same conjunction of manifestation and effacement. And this conjunction is the very locale for Dickens's minor characters.

At the beginning of book 3, halfway through *Our Mutual Friend*, Dickens writes:

> It was a foggy day in London, and the fog was heavy and dark. Animate London, with smarting eyes and irritated lungs, was blinking, wheezing, and choking; inanimate London was a sooty spectre, divided in purpose between being visible and invisible, and so being wholly neither. (479)

The strange phrase—"divided in purpose between being visible and invisible"—is an invaluable reference point for Dickens's organization of the visual field. Things are continually presented as half-visible in Dickens's novels, but what underlies this half-visiblity is the transformation of incompletely *seeing* into eccentric or obscure *sights*. The conjunction of "visible" and "invisible" suggested in *Our Mutual Friend* is most fully developed and gains sustained thematic elaboration in *Bleak House*. The famous opening, also concerned with London as a whole, links another vision-obscuring fog with the city's fragmented multiplicity:

> London. Michaelmas term lately over, and the Lord Chancellor sitting in Lincoln's Inn Hall. Implacable November weather. As much mud in the streets, as if the waters had but newly retired from the face of the earth, and it would not be wonderful to meet a Megalosaurus, forty feet long or so, waddling like an elephantine lizard up Holborn Hill. Smoke lowering down from chimney-pots, making a soft black drizzle with flakes of soot in it as big as full-grown snowflakes—gone into mourning, one might imagine, for the death of the sun. Dogs, indistinguishable, in mire. Horses, scarcely better; splashed to their very blinkers. Foot passengers, jostling one another's umbrellas, in a general infection of ill temper, and losing their foot-hold at street-corners, where tens of thousands of other foot passengers have been slipping and sliding since the day broke (if this day ever broke).

In this paragraph's sequential chain the mud, soot, and darkness seem to *cause* "tens of thousands" of people to "lose their foot-hold." But what determines this loss of visibility is the sheer fact of urban multiplicity, the social structure that makes us "jostle one another's umbrellas" and stumble on the tracks of "other foot passengers." In other words, the rhetorical logic of the passage reverses social cause and effect: the mud and mire and lack of light are, in fact, the visual *consequences* of this chaotic urban field, rather than its origin. This imagery then saturates the novel's descriptive field ("Fog everywhere," the next paragraph begins), so that it appears to be the source of the processes that have generated it.

Dickensian objects can become half-visible or obscure for any number of reasons: the dirt on a window; the faint illumination of dusk or dawn; a half-lifted mist, haze, or fog; a dimly lit interior; the play of sunlight and shadow; or a flickering source of illumination. Here are examples of all of these, with particular emphasis on *Bleak House*:

> [A]t length his eyes wandered to a little dirty window on the left, through which the face of the clerk was dimly visible. (*Nicholas Nickleby*, 67)

> Although the morning was raw, and although the fog still seemed heavy—I say seemed, for the windows were so encrusted with dirt, that they would have made Midsummer sunshine dim . . . (*Bleak House*, 95)

> I recollect that it was neither night nor day, that morning was dawning, but the street-lamps were not yet put out; that the sleet was still falling, and that all the ways were deep with it. I recollect a few chilled people passing in the streets. (*Bleak House*, 867)

> It was a cold, dry, foggy morning in early spring, a few meager shadows flitted to and fro in the misty streets, and occasionally there loomed through the dull vapour the heavy outline of some hackney coach wending homewards, which drawing slowly nearer, rolled jangling by, scattering the thin crust of frost from its whitened roof, and soon was lost again in the cloud. (*Nicholas Nickleby*, 344–45)

> The confined entrance was so dark that it was impossible to make out distinctly what kind of person opened the door; but it appeared to be an old woman. (*Little Dorrit*, 375).

> The perspective was so long, and so darkened by leaves, and the shadows of the branches on the ground made it so much more intricate to the eye, that at first I could not discern what figure it was. (*Bleak House*, 563)

> Jingling and clattering, till distance rendered its noise inaudible, and its rapid progress only perceptible to the eye, the vehicle wound its way along the road, almost hidden in a cloud of dust: now wholly disappearing, and now becoming visible again, as intervening objects, or the intricacies of the way, permitted. (*Oliver Twist*, 321)

> Presently we lost the light, presently saw it, presently lost it, presently saw it, and turned into an avenue of trees, and cantered up towards where it was beaming brightly. (*Bleak House*, 112)

What do these descriptions have to do with minor characters in Dickens? They shape a visual field in which human beings themselves emerge only partially, substantializing the way that subordinate characters, in their intrinsically submerged narrative position, are half-visible. These descriptions are almost all generated out of London's fragmented multiplicity and often devolve down toward one distorted figure: "at first I could not discern what figure it was";

"impossible to make out what kind of person opened the door; but it appeared to be an old woman"; "the face of the clerk was dimly visible." In the place of a strong narrative structure that motivates minorness and caricature, we have this strong descriptive field.

In the opening of *Bleak House* we can grasp a connection between the "tens of thousands of . . . foot passengers," the individual person who loses his "foot-hold," and the mire and fog that become the objectification of half-visibility. Later, when Esther comments on "an unearthly fire, gleaming on all the unseen buildings of the city and on all the faces of its many thousands of wandering inhabitants" (484), she draws a subtle link between "unseen" and "many thousands." In a third passage, the site of caricature springs directly from this urban multiplicity, which has already itself been connected to an indistinct visual field: "I admired the long succession and varieties of streets, the quantity of people already going to and fro, the number of vehicles passing and repassing, the busy preparations in the setting forth of shop windows and the sweeping out of shops, and the extraordinary creatures in rags, secretly groping among the swept-out rubbish for pins and other refuse" (97). What structures the narrative flow of the early passage in *The Pickwick Papers* (from the excited crowd to the extraordinary Mr. Jingle) or in the comment by Raymond Williams (from a flow of people "briefly seen" to "brief fixed appearances") is here synchronically enacted, and in this mature novel the image of "extraordinary creatures" would immediately remind readers of Dickens's minor characters. Half-visibility is, in fact, the necessary consequence of social multiplicity, and such multiplicity is narratively enacted by the variously "extraordinary" minor characters who are crowded into every Dickens novel and who signify their subordination in their distortion, fragmentation, and eccentricity.

Returning to the speech by Mr. Jingle that Steven Marcus identifies as the seminal passage in Dickens, we can see a fascinating correlation between content and form, as though Dickens has grasped, in this one explosive passage, the essential contours of his own originality. It is no accident that Mr. Jingle's fragmented monologue also tells a story *of* physical fragmentation, circling around the image of a person losing her head: "Heads, heads—take care of your heads! . . . Terrible place—dangerous work . . . mother—tall lady, eating sandwiches—forgot the arch—crash—knock—children look round—mother's head off—sandwich in her hand—no mouth to put it in." The separation of the head from the body is a graphic enactment of the fragmentation that can result from that narrative subordination which makes characters both visible and invisible, there and not there: it violently registers the disjunction of surface and depth that occurs when a person's "head"—or interior consciousness—becomes estranged from her "body" or her exterior, socially configured position. The full person behind every minor character is squeezed into an inadequate space even as the "tall lady" is too large for the "terrible place" in which she finds herself.

The strange motif of losing one's head that is introduced in Jingle's staccato anecdote recurs frequently in *The Pickwick Papers*. In the briefest example, the isolation of the single word ("heads") calls attention to its thematic centrality. " 'Jump up in front, Sammy,' said Mr. Weller. 'Now Villam, run 'em out. Take care o' the archvay gen'lm'n. "Heads" as the pieman says. That'll do Villam. Let 'em alone.' And away went the coach up Whitechapel, to the admiration of the whole population of that pretty-densely populated quarter" (383). Mr. Weller's pithy statement connects directly to Jingle's initial story of decapitation: both characters imagine an endangered person who's not minding where he or she is going. (This very connection between two scenes of violent *dis*connection, and the further relation between this compressed decapitation and the way that Tony Weller compresses the gentlemen into "gen'lm'n," speaks to much of *The Pickwick Papers'* comic logic). In fact, decapitation, which ushers in Jingle's eccentric minorness and Dickens's comic innovation, seems to pervade this novel.[18] In later novels, Dickens continues to play on the resonance of this image, in its full range from a verbal expression, to a mode of looking, to an actually violent event. If he can write, in *Martin Chuzzlewit*, that "there was such a skirmishing, and flouting, and snapping off of heads, in the metaphorical sense of that expression" (52), he will also sometimes physicalize this metaphor:

> Mr. Sparkler's head peering over the balcony looked so very bulky and heavy that it seemed on the point of overbalancing him and flattening the unknown below. (*Little Dorrit*, 763)

> "Don't be frightened!" said Mr. Guppy, looking in at the coach-window. "One of the young Jellybys been and got his head through the area railings!"
>
> "O poor child," said I; "let me out, if you please!"
>
> "Pray be careful of yourself, miss. The young Jellybys are always up to something," said Mr. Guppy.
>
> I made my way to the poor child, who was one of the dirtiest little unfortunates I ever saw, and found him very hot and frightened, and crying loudly, fixed by the neck between two iron railings, while a milkman and a beadle, with the kindest intentions possible, were endeavoring to drag him back by the legs, under a general impression that his skull was compressible by those means. As I found (after pacifying him) that he was a little boy, with a naturally large head, I thought that, perhaps, where his head could go, his body could follow, and mentioned that the best mode of extraction might be to push him forward. (*Bleak House*, 84)

Most often, however, Dickens carefully makes the image hover between the figural and literal: a separation between the body and head doesn't actually take place but only seems to have occurred because a whole person *is* in fact half-visible. In particular, Dickens often shows a character's head entering into the scene (and into the narrative) before his or her body.

[T]he door opened, and a somewhat forbidding countenance peeped into the room. The eyes in the forbidding countenance looked very earnestly at Mr. Pickwick, for several seconds, and were to all appearances satisfied with their investigation, for the body to which the forbidding countenance belonged, slowly brought itself into the apartment, and presented the form of an elderly individual in top-boots— not to keep the reader any longer in suspense, in short, the eyes were the wandering eyes of Mr. Grummer, and the body was the body of the same gentleman. (*Pickwick Papers*, 414–15)

The call being repeated, Gride looked out again so cautiously that no part of the old man's body was visible, and the sharp features and white hair appearing alone above the parapet looked like a severed head garnishing the wall. (*Nicholas Nickleby*, 871)

Raising his eyes thus one day, he was surprised to see a bonnet labouring up the step-ladder. The unusual apparition was followed by another bonnet. He then perceived that the first bonnet was on the head of Mr. F.'s Aunt, and that the second bonnet was on the head of Flora, who seemed to have propelled her legacy up the steep ascent with considerable difficulty. (*Little Dorrit*, 313)

Mr. Sparkler, who had merely put in his head and looked round the room without entering . . . (*Little Dorrit*, 448)

They were not a little startled by the unexpected obtrusion into that sanctuary of genius, of a human head which, although a shaggy and somewhat alarming head in appearance, smiled affably upon them from the doorway, in a manner that was at once waggish, conciliatory, and expressive of approbation. . . . "If that is Mr. Pinch," cried Tigg, kissing his hand again, and beginning to follow his head into the room. (*Martin Chuzzlewit*, 98–99)

[Kate] was quite terrified by the apparition of an old black velvet cap, which, by slow degrees, as if its wearer were ascending a ladder or pair of steps, rose above the wall dividing their garden from that of the next cottage, (which, like their own, was a detached building,) and was gradually followed by a very large head, and an old face, in which were a pair of the most extraordinary grey eyes, very wild, very wide open, and rolling in their sockets with a dull, languishing and leering look, most ugly to behold. (*Nicholas Nickleby*, 620)

Here seven different minor characters from four different novels all enter into the consciousness or sight of a more central character. If their fragmentation is generated through this asymmetrical relation, the effect is, once again, to displace the process of perception onto the object being viewed. A visual, and social, relationship becomes absorbed into the strange image of the characters themselves, who seem in some real sense "beheaded." If it is the protagonist's specific point of view that creates this disjunction, we are not told about *their* vision but instead see exaggerated images of the minor character's eyes: "the wandering eyes," the head that "looked round," and, of course, "the most extraordinary grey eyes, very wild, very wide open, and rolling in their sockets with a dull, languishing and leering look."

Repetition and Eccentricity: Minor Characters and the Division of Labor

Let's return to the description of Mr. Jellyby: "I suppose he had been more talkative and lively once; but he seemed to have been completely exhausted long before I knew him." We might make a similar comment about nearly *every* minor character in Dickens: they enter the novel after something terrible seems to have already happened—and produced one or another kind of eccentric and disturbing "completeness." Nor do we sense that this transformation has just occurred; as Esther muses, Mr. Jellyby could have been a different kind of person only "long before" she encountered him. In a similar way, Wegg didn't *always* have a wooden leg, but *Our Mutual Friend* inscribes only to conceal the mysterious history behind this emblem of Dickensian minorness:

> "How did you get your wooden leg?"
> Mr. Wegg replied, (tartly to this personal inquiry), "In an accident."

This passage teasingly calls attention to a past that we hardly learn more of—except in one other elliptical reference to a "hospital amputation" (83). The history of Wegg's disfigurement remains obscure even as the result of that history is stunningly apparent. This example, like the sudden distortion of Uriah Heep, occurs when the character is first brought into the narrative, and in its very mode of staging the minor character's opening appearance, Dickensian narrative works to both substantialize and dehistoricize the character's minorness. Characters barrel into the novel with the immediate effects of their minorness fully apparent; and while they might change or progress in the story-world, they rarely escape or climb out of their minorness. As Audrey Jaffe writes, "Dickens's characters are famously marked: eccentric in appearance and character, doomed in general to repeat the same phrases, whistle the same tunes, twitch the same twitches throughout their lives as characters, *even if and when they exhibit a capacity for change*" (14, emphasis added). Such change, in other words, does not occur on the level of narrative structure, rarely loosening a "doom" that obtains in the strict coordinates of their subordinated delimitation, regardless of their fate in the story-world itself.

From where does this doom derive? In *Little Dorrit*, Mr. Plornish tries to address the impoverished conditions in Bleeding Heart Yard: "Well, he couldn't say how it was; he didn't know as anybody *could* say how it was; all he'd know'd was, that so it was" (183). Plornish's futile explanation of his present conditions offers a striking parallel to Esther's comment on Jellyby's flatness. In the face of his impoverished conditions, Mr. Plornish's effort to comprehend history seems to collapse, tautologically, into a single existential verb ("all he'd know'd was, that so it was"). In a similar way, the very eccentric and distorted "singularity" of Dickens's minor characters obscures the history—or the dynamic narrative structuration—underlying this distortion: incomplete seeing turns into the distorted "sight"; briefly seen persons become "brief, fixed appearances." And it is the very "completeness" of Mr. Jellyby's current exhaustion that makes it hard to imagine anything else.

In *Pride and Prejudice* the dynamic elaboration of the character-system, I argued, suggests a distinctively transitional historical period, what Raymond Williams calls "this chronicle of confusion and change" (*English Novel*, 21). This transition is suffused into the very dynamics of Austen's novelistic form, which is remarkably active: integrating, effacing, functionalizing, subordinating, discriminating, distorting. In Dickens's novels, the essential structures of an industrial and urban world seem to be already deeply embedded. Most significantly, a troubling stratification has long set in and defines the (markedly asymmetrical) social geography within which the novels unfold. As I have been stressing, the novels are concerned not primarily with representing the transformation of characters into minor figures but rather with constantly dramatizing the distortion that is a consequence of minorness. In the same way, social stratification—along with the division of labor that underlies and is produced by social inequality—is already deeply entrenched, always present ("and so it was"), not actively formulating itself. Another gloss on the static "doom" of Dickens's minor characters might be found in Friedrich Engels's brief sketch of how class distinction changed between 1800 and 1845, Austen to Dickens: "There was now no possibility that the workers would ever improve their position and rise out of their social group. Craftsmanship was now replaced by factory production. There was a strict division of labour. . . . The proletariat now became a definite class in the population whereas formerly it had only been a transitional stage towards entering into the middle classes. Today he who is born a worker must remain a worker for the rest of his life" (24–25). And Dickens's minor, flat characters always remain flat.

In fact, the division of labor, so central to nineteenth-century social and economic theory, is also the social process most profoundly implicated in the character-systems of nineteenth-century fiction. The importance of flat characters to the modern novel, which E. M. Forster so shrewdly places at the center of characterization, becomes consolidated at the same time that numerous disciplines conceptualize and confront the problem of specialization, the radical delimitation of human activity—and even human agency—to ever more narrow, and segmented, parameters. If Engels's workers are trapped in their class as Dickens's minor characters are trapped in their minorness, Dickens's circumscription of characters (squeezed into "brief fixed appearances" or "doomed . . . to repeat the same phrases . . . tunes . . . twitches throughout their lives") echoes so seminal an account of the division of labor as Adam Smith's opening to *The Wealth of Nations*:

> [T]he division of labour, by reducing every man's business to some one simple operation and by making this operation the sole employment of his life, necessarily increases very much the dexterity of the workman. . . . I have seen several boys under twenty years of age who had never exercised any other trade but that of making nails, and who, when they exerted themselves, could make, each of them, upwards of two thousand three hundred nails in a day. . . . But in consequence of the division of labour, the whole of every man's attention comes naturally to be directed towards some one very simple object. (7–9)

As a single operation becomes the "sole employment of [the worker's] life," E. M. Forster will base his theory of characterization on flat characters who are "constructed round . . . a single quality"(103) and "unalterable"(106).

Both Austen and Dickens—the two nineteenth-century British writers who perhaps most profoundly shape the contours of novelistic characterization—confront the phenomenon of the division of labor. In *Pride and Prejudice* we see the reduction of whole individuals into restricted roles as part of a larger total process: the transformation of certain characters into delimited characteristics is linked to the rise of the central protagonist's nonspecialized, more human interiority. We thus see specialization developing and taking root over the course of the novel; we sense it as an inherently dynamic *process* of discrimination, as a structure or system of relations, rather than as a substance, or an individually experienced condition. In Dickens, as we have seen, the minor character appears—like Jingle, Heep, Jellyby—already distorted, and doomed to stay that way. This hardening—and substantialization—of stratification has an actual social basis, as Engels's polemic suggests. But just as there is a profound relationship between a *structural* stasis in Dickensian narrative (that suspended moment of overturning) and the *descriptive* stasis that dooms individual characters, so we need to understand the "fixity" associated with the division of labor as more than simply a historical reflection of the way that class boundaries have set in. If Dickens's novels register the rigid segmentation that sustains specialization ("There was now no possibility that the workers would ever improve their position"), they also comprehend the rigidity that inheres *within* specialization itself ("the whole of every man's attention comes naturally to be directed towards some one very simple object"). This kind of experienced stasis is the essential consequence of the very division of labor that itself seems to be intractable.

Many of Dickens's best critics have discerned a pervasive pessimism in Dickens's novels, beginning perhaps with George Orwell's seminal reconsideration of the novelist. Anticipating an essential strategy in Dickens criticism, Orwell stages a kind of argument with himself that reflects the contradictory valences of Dickens's political vision. In one crucial passage, Orwell notes the fatalism, and even acquiescence, that seem to be inextricably intertwined *with* Dickens's powerful social critique:

> [G]iven the existing form of society, certain evils cannot be remedied. . . . In every page of his work one can see a consciousness that society is wrong somewhere at the root. It is when one asks "Which root?" that one begins to grasp his position.
>
> The truth is that Dickens's criticism of society is almost exclusively moral. Hence the utter lack of any constructive suggestion anywhere in his work. He attacks the law, parliamentary government, the educational system and so forth, without ever clearly suggesting what he would put in their places. . . . It would be difficult to point anywhere in his books to a passage suggesting that the economic system is wrong as a system. (5)

For Orwell, Mr. Plornish's comment would express an important aspect of Dickens's own historical consciousness.[19] In one sense, as critics have since argued, this can be read as a retreat from the very sociological frame that seems inevitably suggested by the strength of the novel's own investigations.[20] But Orwell's essay lingers on the complicated descriptive and stylistic consequence of Dickens's historical sense, coming to rest on the same problematic of the "appearance" and the "sight" that we have already seen:

> The last thing anyone ever remembered about these books is their central story. On the other hand, I suppose no one has ever read them without carrying the memory of individual pages to the day of his death. Dickens sees human beings with the most intense vividness, but he sees them always in private life, as "characters," not as functional members of society; that is to say, he sees them statically. Consequently his greatest success is *The Pickwick Papers*, which is not a story at all, merely a series of sketches. . . . As soon as he tries to bring his characters into action, the melodrama begins. . . . Of course it would be absurd to say that Dickens is a vague or merely melodramatic writer. Much that he wrote is extremely factual, and in the power of evoking visual images he has probably never been equaled. When Dickens has once described something you see it for the rest of your life. But in a way the concreteness of his vision is a sign of what is missing. For, after all, that is what the merely casual onlooker always sees—the outward appearance, the non-functional, the surfaces of things. . . . Wonderfully as he can describe an *appearance*, Dickens does not often describe a *process*. (46–47, Orwell's emphasis)

Orwell here connects his sense of Dickens's historical consciousness to what I have analyzed as the transition from incomplete vision to partial visibility. The privileging of "appearances" over "processes" reflects the terrible rigidity of social circumstances in Britain. This tendency is stylistic, its consequences social: if the novels accept stratification as a kind of tragic precondition (so that, "given the existing form of society, certain evils cannot be remedied"), the discourse instantiates minorness and flatness as *narrative* preconditions. Each subordinate character, in his or her starkly delimited configuration, bears witness to a much larger social process—the very sort of process that Orwell suggests seems to be elided *by* appearance.

This privileging of the "half-visible," "fixed," or "concrete" appearance is linked to the hardening of minor characters as always already flat, or specialized. Orwell's essay holistically grasps the relation between Dickens's pessimistic stance and the privileging of appearance.[21] We have seen how Dickensian asymmetry itself itself suggests a kind of frozen world, hovering on the brink of an "overturning" that never occurs. This fraught structural stasis flows into a descriptive stasis that penetrates the core of almost all of Dickens's minor characters. Sometimes, of course, Dickens expresses the connection between a minor character's fixity and social specialization more overtly, as in the description of Mr. Chivery, the Marshalsea turnkey in *Little Dorrit*, whose flatness actually unfurls out of his working conditions: "It has already been remarked that he was a man of few words; and it may be here observed that he had imbibed a professional habit of locking everything up. He locked himself up as carefully as he locked up the Marshalsea debtors. Even his custom of bolting his meals may have been a part of an uniform whole; but there is no question that, as to all other purposes, he kept his mouth as he kept the Marshalsea door" (345–46). In this case, Chivery's flatness is directly rooted to his specialized working conditions; his physical being takes on the qualities of his job. The division of labor is also occasionally highlighted in a plot or subplot, as in Richard Carstone's futile rebellion against specialization throughout *Bleak House*. Typically, however, Dickens does not offer a taxonomic representation of the division of labor—in which an individual's characteristics reflect a specific kind of work—but rather continually configures the essential social and psychological effects of specialization. The social grounding of a minor character's "reduced" being is not explicitly linked to his or her specialized vocation but is narratively comprehended in the unbreakable connection between narrative flatness and descriptive distortion.

Such a conjunction between flattening and distortion might remind us not so much of Adam Smith as of Friedrich Schiller, the seminal diagnostician of specialization's discontents. While Smith argues that industrialization inevitably produces more narrowly defined economic agents, Schiller's 1795 *On the Aesthetic Education of Man* meditates on the consequences of the division of labor for human interiority. Segmentation into different functions leads to the reification of different interior "faculties," and a restricted "occupation" produces a "specialized knowledge" that circumscribes and distorts an individual's full humanity.

> With us ... the image of the human species is projected in magnified form into separate individuals—but as fragments, not in different combinations, with the result that one has to go the rounds from one individual to another in order to be able to piece together a complete image of the species. With us ... the various faculties

appear as separate in practice as they are distinguished by the psychologist in theory, and we see not merely individuals, but whole classes of men, developing one part of their potentialities, while of the rest, as in stunted growths, only vestigial traces remain. . . . Everlastingly chained to a single little fragment of the Whole, man himself develops into nothing but a fragment, everlastingly in his ear the monotonous sound of the wheel that he turns, he never develops the harmony of his being, and instead of putting the stamp of humanity upon his own nature, he becomes nothing more than the imprint of his occupation or of his specialized knowledge. (33–35)

Schiller's insistent conjoining of segmentation and distortion suggests the social logic by which Dickensian flatness inevitably gets manifested as eccentricity. The very terms of Williams's description of characters as "brief fixed appearances" resembles Schiller's depiction of human beings as "fragments" and "stunted growths." We have seen how the violent topos of decapitation—where such fragmentation becomes dangerously literal—dramatizes the dispersion inherent in constricted "appearance," as it disjoins exterior surface and interior depth. These visual scenes of beheading are only part of Dickens's poetics of misalignment, where flat characters are depicted as inevitably distorted, just as Schiller claims that specialization inevitably leads to stunted growth, destroying the potential "harmony" of human beings. Similar disjunction is also apparent in the configurations of Mr. Jingle and Joe, in Grimwig's eccentricities or Flora's strange idiolect. Dickens will often describe a mismatch between person and clothing, perhaps most briefly in this description of one of Jellyby's children: "Everything the dear child wore, was either too large for him or too small" (*Bleak House*, 236). Here Dickens is obviously concerned not with the precise shape of the misalignment but with its dialectical nature; the disjunction between surface and depth can take place because human interiority has been rendered either "too large" *or* "too small." In *Nicholas Nickleby* (written fifteen years earlier) two contrasting passages about misaligned buttons show this dialectical sensibility already at work:

[A] little page, so little indeed that his body would not hold, in ordinary array, the number of small buttons which are indispensable to a page's costume, and they were consequently obliged to be stuck on four abreast. (339)

[A] suit of clothes (if the term be allowable when they suited him not at all) much the worse for wear, very much too small, and placed upon such a short allowance of buttons that it was quite marvelous how he contrived to keep them on. (67)

Such misaligned buttons reappear in *Our Mutual Friend* (ten years after *Bleak House*), where they are assimilated into a broader configuration of narrative distortion:

Of an ungainly make was Sloppy. Too much of him longwise, too little of him broadwise, and too many sharp angles of him angle-wise. One of those shambling male human creatures, born to be indiscreetly candid in the revelation of buttons; every button he had about him glaring at the public to a quite preternatural extent. A considerable capital of knee and elbow and wrist and ankle, had Sloppy, and he didn't know how to dispose of it to the best advantage. (249)

The consideration of Mrs. Boffin had clothed Mr. Sloppy in a suit of black, on which the tailor had received personal directions from Rokesmith to expend the most cunning of his art, with a view to the concealment of the cohering and sustaining buttons. But, so much more powerful were the frailties of Sloppy's form than the strongest resources of tailoring science, that he now stood before the Council, a perfect Argus in the way of buttons: shining and winking and gleaming and twinkling out of a hundred of those eyes of bright metals, at the dazzled spectators. . . . Some special powers with which his legs were endowed, had already hitched up his glossy trousers at the ankles and bagged them at the knees; while similar gifts in his arms had raised his coat-sleeves from his wrists and accumulated them at his elbows. (390–91)

The opposition between the character's "frailties" and the "strongest" resources of tailoring presents Sloppy's misalignment as the consequence of a more general disjunction between the exterior surface and the individual human form. At the same time, the specific image of buttons becomes metonymically linked, in both passages, to "knee and elbow and wrist and ankle." Following the inevitable tracks of Dickensian minorness, we can find an early image of *these* dispersed, disconnected body parts in *The Pickwick Papers'* description of Bob Sawyer: "Bob did look dampish inasmuch as the rain was streaming from his neck, elbows, cuffs, skirts and knees" (811). The same concentration on fragmented extremities informs Esther Summerson's description of the Jellyby children: "our attention was distracted by the constant apparition of noses and fingers" (88). Sometimes, this dispersion is directly implicated with a minor character's interiority, most often through laughter: "The internal laughter occasioned by the triumphant success of his visit, which had convulsed not only Mr. Weller's face, but his arms, legs and body also."[22]

Both major kinds of minor characters in the nineteenth-century novel—the functional worker and the deviant eccentric—can be structured by, or emerge as a consequence of, the division of labor. Thus Schiller always notes *two* different results of specialization, either a disconnected excess of interiority *or* the stultified containment of interiority:

Once the increase of empirical knowledge, and more exact modes of thought, made sharper divisions between the sciences inevitable, and once the increasingly complex machinery of State necessitated a more rigorous separation of ranks and occupations, then the inner unity of human nature was severed too, and a disastrous *conflict* set its harmonious powers at variance. The intuitive and the speculative understanding now withdrew in hostility to take up positions in their respective fields. . . . While in the one a riotous imagination ravages the hard-won fruits of the intellect, in another the spirit of abstraction stifles the fire at which the heart should have warmed itself and the imagination been kindled. (33–35)

This intellectual divide flows out of the contradictory social results of the division of labor, and, most starkly, mechanized industrial labor. On the one hand, alienated labor *reduces* individuals, whether through the increasing segmentation and mechanization of the labor process itself; the increasing length of the working day, which can restrict human activity to work and sleep; or the material confinement of poverty and, more directly, overcrowded and inadequate housing. As Elizabeth Gaskell writes in *North and South*, attempting to encapsulate this conception of work: "They labour on, from day to day . . . never speaking or lifting up their poor, bent, downcast heads. The hard spade-work robs their brain of life; the sameness of their toil deadens their imagination; they don't care to meet to talk over thoughts and speculations, even of the weakest, wildest kind, after their work is done; they go home brutishly tired, poor creatures! Caring for nothing but food and rest" (306). On the other hand, alienated labor simultaneously produces dislocation and dispersion, through the psychological stress inherent in the drudgery of mechanized labor (which even Gaskell's description subtly gestures toward when imagining thoughts of "the weakest, *wildest* kind"); through the fluctuations in employment built into the industrial business cycle that lead to unstable alternations between enforced work and enforced idleness; and, finally, through the rebellious or "deviant" response to these conditions that produces insurgent working-class resistance.

In other words, the two types of minor characters that structure the omniscient, asymmetric novel, the functional automaton and the deviant eccentric, are *both* the results of the division of labor. For Marx, of course, both repetition and dislocation are finally embedded in the very rhythm of industrial labor itself. And Victorian accounts of working-class poverty, as much as Marx's theory of alienation, frequently suggest that working-class life is structured by an alternation between drabness and chaos, stultification and dissipation. For example, the relationship between deviance and work—which underlies the association of functionality and eccentricity—emerges dramatically in this passage from Henry Mayhew's 1861 *London Labour and the London Poor*:

According to the Criminal Returns of the metropolis . . . labourers occupy a most unenviable pre-eminence in police history. One in every twenty-eight labourers, according to these returns, has a predisposition for simple larceny: the average for the whole population of London is one in every 266 individuals; so that the labourers may be said to be more than 9 times as dishonest as the generality of people resident in the metropolis. In drunkenness they occupy the same prominent position. One in every 22 individuals of the labouring class was charged with being intoxicated in the year 1848; whereas the average number of drunkards in the whole population of London is one in every 113 individuals. Nor are they less pugnaciously inclined; one in every 26 having been charged with a common assault of a more or less aggravated form. The labourers of London are, therefore, 9 times as dishonest, 5 times as drunken, and 9 times as savage as the rest of the community. . . . While the Government returns show the labourers generally to be extraordinarily dishonest, drunken and pugnacious, their vices cannot be ascribed to the poverty of their calling; for, compared with other occupations, their vocation appears to produce fewer paupers than the generality of employments. (233)

Mayhew's graphic image maps social deviance to a specific class of individuals. Lawrence Frank has suggestively read Dickens's representations of reduction and dislocation as psychological projections, used to bolster, by negative assertion, efforts to construct a unified self: "The Faustian self, moving toward an integration never to be fully achieved, vacillates between the two poles of fragmentation and paralysis . . . the disintegration of the self in pure debauchery, or . . . the paralysis of the self in a form of sodden, self-satisfied inertia. For Dickens . . . the two poles of the living self remain fragmentation or paralysis" (26). A strictly psychological interpretation can elide the way that social deviance is spatially mapped in the Victorian imagination. Holding Frank's distinction in mind, we can see how Mayhew connects work itself to social deviance: both paralysis and disintegration are rooted in the division of labor. Interior agency either is engulfed by drudging, mechanistic labor or erupts out, manifesting itself in a socially deviant or "savage" form.

In *The Condition of the Working Class in England*, Engels insistently makes the same connection between labor and social deviance, writing about industrial workers: "They are goaded like wild beasts and never have a chance of enjoying a quiet life. They are deprived of all pleasures except sexual indulgence and intoxicating liquors. Every day they have to work until they are physically and mentally exhausted. This forces them to excessive indulgence in the only two pleasures remaining to them" (111). Later, Engels refers to how alienated labor leads to *two* choices, the equivalents of "paralysis" and "fragmentation." The passage, in fact, fluidly incorporates several different modes of fragmentation and paralysis, demonstrating the importance of this opposition itself, as it is formulated against the model of a free, actualized human interiority:

The extent to which the workers are degraded may be seen from the conduct of those who submit passively to this state of affairs. Some of them submit to their fate and exist as best they can as respectable law-abiding citizens. . . . Other workers are content to take their chance in the new industrial world. Since they have lost not merely economic security but also moral stability, they lead a hand to mouth existence, drink too much gin and run after the girls. *Whether they submit passively to their fate or take to drink*, they are equally no more than animals. The behaviour of this section of the working classes is the main cause of that "rapid increase in vice" which so disgusts the sentimental middle classes, although they are themselves actually responsible for the conditions which inevitably give rise to it.

Another reason why the workers are demoralised is the fact that they are condemned to a lifetime of unremitting toil. . . . No worse fate can befall a man than to
have to work every day from morning to night against his will at a job that he ab-
hors. . . . If only because his hours of labour are so long and so dismally monotonous,
the worker must surely detest his job after the first few weeks, assuming that he
possesses a spark of humanity. The division of labor has intensified the brutalizing
effects of forced labour. In most branches of industry the task of the worker is limited
to insignificant and purely repetitive tasks which continue minute by minute for every
day of the year. How much human feeling or ability can a man of thirty expect to
retain if since childhood he has spent twelve hours a day or more daily making pin
heads or filing cogwheels, and in addition has dragged out the normal existence of a
member of the English proletariat? The introduction of steam-power and machinery
has had the same results. . . . [A] job of this kind gives the worker no scope for
exercising his intelligence, since the operator must pay some attention to the machine
to ensure that nothing is going wrong, and so he is prevented from thinking about
anything else. It is obvious that a man must be degraded to the level of a beast if he
is condemned to work of this kind. . . . *Once more there are only two courses open
to the worker.* He may submit to his fate and become a "good worker," "faithfully"
serving the interests of the middle classes—and if he does so he is absolutely certain
to become a mere animal—or he can resist and fight for his rights as far as is humanly
possible and that necessarily involves the most strenuous opposition to the middle
classes. (133, emphasis added)

This passage continually works to link together the "functionality" and the
"eccentricity" that underlie the two principal types of minor character in nineteenth-century fiction. Engels configures a choice between two kinds of disjunction: capitalist production either extinguishes the last "spark of humanity"
in the worker or sets off destructive forms of dissipation. The "dismally monotonous" inertia of work has at least three different (though interrelated) aspects:
the simple length of the workday; the division of labor under which "the task
of the worker is limited to insignificant and purely repetitive tasks"; and the
consequent mechanization of work through the "introduction of steam-power
and machinery." Engels also posits *various* kinds of human deviance, or eccentricity, that contrast with—even as they are embedded within—this dismal
monotony. In this passage the original contrast the worker faces between "submit[ing] passively to [his] fate or tak[ing] to drink" gets notably transformed
into "submit[ing] to his fate" or entering into "the most strenuous opposition
to the middle classes." This last choice, in turn, is suggestively echoed in
E. M. Forster's description of the dangerous *narrative* choice that characters
pose for the novelist (a choice underlying the very division between flat and
round): "[I]f they are given complete freedom they *kick the book to pieces*,
and if they are kept *too sternly in check*, they revenge themselves by dying,
and destroy it by intestinal decay" (102, emphasis added).

In this analysis of the division of labor we can see a kind of social grounding for the two forms of psychological failure that Lawrence Frank identifies. More powerfully than any previous novelist, Dickens integrates both, contradictory aspects of specialization into the distortion that marks his minor characters—characters whose very doomed circumscription *into* minorness, on the level of the narrative discourse, registers the nature of mid-nineteenth-century social stratification. A key achievement of Dickensian characterization rests in the uncanny combination of these two discrepant modes. Consider how Dickens sums up one of his most eccentric (and memorable) minor characters, in *Little Dorrit*:

> The major characteristics discoverable by the stranger in Mr. F's Aunt were extreme severity and grim taciturnity; sometimes interrupted by a propensity to offer remarks in a deep warning voice, which, being totally uncalled for by anything said by anybody, and traceable to no association of ideas, confounded and terrified the mind. (199)

In this dullness interrupted by occasionally disconnected fragments, Mr. F's Aunt dramatizes two different consequences of specialization: the *reduction* of her personality to "extreme severity and grim taciturnity" and the *dislocation* of her personality in fragmented expressions, "totally uncalled for by anything said by anybody, and traceable to no association of ideas." The first description of Mr. F's Aunt, a page earlier, itself has a strangely mechanistic air:

> There was a fourth and most original figure in the Patriarchal tent, who also appeared before dinner. This was an amazing little old woman, with a face like a staring wooden doll too cheap for expression, and a stiff yellow wig perched unevenly on the top of her head, as if the child who owned the doll had driven a tack through it anywhere, so that it only got fastened on. Another remarkable thing in this little old woman was, that the same child seemed to have damaged her face in two or three places with some blunt instrument in the nature of a spoon; her countenance, and particularly the tip of her nose, presenting the phenomena of several dints, generally answering to the bowl of that article. A further remarkable thing in this little old woman was, that she had no name but Mr. F's Aunt. (198)

If Mr. F's Aunt is herself depicted as a mechanical object—who is "wooden," "stiff," and has "dints"—she also seems to have been *through* a mechanical process, so that her disfigurement is caused by a "tack" and a "blunt instrument" resembling a spoon. (The "tack" that the narrator imagines as piercing her is an emblem of industrial production, similar to Smith's "nails" and Engel's "pinheads.") But the result of this distortion (also clearly linked to her minorness) is again presented as both paralysis and fragmentation: she is already taciturn (frozen like "a staring wooden doll too cheap for expression") *and* off-balance (with "a stiff yellow wig perched *unevenly* on the top of her head"). The sentence with these two clauses anticipates the syntactic logic of the next description, in which her "severity" and "taciturnity" are "interrupted" by disconnected phrases. This same pattern is repeated in other scenes:

> A momentary silence that ensued was broken by Mr. F's Aunt, who had been sitting upright in a cataleptic state since her last public remark. She now underwent a violent twitch, calculated to produce a startling effect on the nerves of the uninitiated and with the deadliest animosity observed:
>
> "You can't make a head and brains out of a brass knob with nothing in it. You couldn't do it when your Uncle George was living; much less when he's dead." (319)

In Mr. F's Aunt, repetition (the catalepsy) produces and absorbs eccentricity and fragmentation (the violent twitch). Conversely, Dickens often transforms eccentricity into repetition. Everytime that Mr. Jingle or Flora appears, they repeat their same, eccentric idiolect, until this mechanical repetition seeps into the very rhythms of their speech itself. Other times Dickens makes fragmentation, or the jerking or misalignment of a single body part, the vehicle *of* repetition, as with the "red-haired man" in *The Pickwick Papers* "with a bird-like habit of giving his head a jerk everytime he said anything" (381). In the following passages he combines these two modes, so that a character's physical fragmentation is correlated with speech patterns: " 'I—certainly—did—NOT,' said Coavinses, whose doggedness in utterly renouncing the idea was of that intense kind that he could only give adequate expression to it by putting a long interval between each word, and accompanying the last with a jerk that might have dislocated his neck" (*Bleak House*, 127). Coavinses's eccentric mode of speech (which is inadequate as expression) produces an eccentric and *repetitive* gesture, which, however, climaxes in a singular "jerk" that calls attention to his almost "dislocated" head.

The total effect of these caricatures is to represent constricted specialization as *simultaneously* reductive and dislocating. Social repetition produces its opposite, eccentric singularity, while the singular always loses itself in a structure of repetition. This process is encapsulated in the brief appearance of a casino worker operating the roulette table in *Nicholas Nickleby*:

> He did it all with a rapidity absolutely marvelous, never hesitating, never making a mistake, never stopping and never ceasing to repeat such unconnected phrases as the following, which, partly from habit, and partly to have something appropriate to say, he constantly poured out with the same monotonous emphasis, and in nearly all the same order, all day long. (751)[23]

"[R]epeat[ing] . . . unconnected phrases" and "monotonous emphasis": these two paradoxical expressions give us terms to express the convergence of repetition and eccentricity we have been examining, a crucial aspect of both Dickensian characterization and the social structure that is grasped through this characterization.

"Monotonous Emphasis": Minorness and Three Kinds of Repetition

Repetition is the horizon and boundary of Dickensian minorness—like the shock inflicted by an invisible fence, each repetitive gesture by a minor character both presses up against *and* confirms the very limits of their subordinated circumscription. Repetition in Dickens is also, crucially, a hinge connecting (narrative) structure and (physical) description. As I have noted, minor characters (like Jingle or Grimwig) tend to intrude upon the text, bursting in immediately with their flatness, as it were, fully developed. Here is a gestural or descriptive monotony emanating from the characters themselves. But this is never the end of the story. They then proceed to burst in *again*, and again. The repetition that Jaffe points to, for example, is twofold—characters are "doomed to *repeat* the *same* phrases, whistle the same tunes, twitch the same twitches." In other words, Dickensian repetition is both local and intervallic: the minor character will typically repeat himself (saying or doing the "same" things) several times in a single scene (most dramatically in his first appearance), and then repeat this repetition when he appears again. These two kinds of repetition stretch across the boundary between story and discourse: what is a physical or gestural recurrence, literally enacted in the story-world, is amplified as a discursive repetition, tracked along the very seams of the character's narrative minorness (as coordinated by these different scenes). Repetition thus bridges the structural emplacement of the minor character (doomed to a series of delimited and recurring appearances) and the descriptive disarticulation of the minor character *within* any scene.

How can a character express himself in such a structure? The descriptions of Coavinses in *Bleak House* and the casino worker in *Nicholas Nickleby* both focus on a character's speech, and Dickens's configuration of minor characters often produces verbal fragmentation, whether in the form of Mr. Jingle's "rapid and disjointed communication" or in the snippets of speech by Mr. F's Aunt that are "traceable to no association of ideas." In Coavinses's case, gesture arises only when speech has failed, in the literal intervals between words that register speech as "inadequate expression." Such "inadequate" or "disjointed" expression, however, merely literalizes the minor character's isolation, an isolation that is finally "traceable" to his narrative circumscription. The almost inevitably iterated appearance of the Dickensian minor character is not merely repetitive—it is also fragmentary. By definition, the sporadically appearing character is disjoined from himself. The affective flush of the character's reappearance is purchased—like the head without the body—only against the backdrop of an extended disappearance. "You look at him, and there he is. You look at him again, and—there he isn't." This quotation, which encapsulates the way Dickens's characters are "divided . . . between being visible and invisible," also aptly describes the *discursive* condition of any recurring minor character (there he is in one scene and there, in several subsequent scenes, he—isn't). Here, too, we can see a convergence between discourse and story, since, as we have examined, the character's referenced gestures *within* any scene also uncannily combine repetition and fragmentation. Consider once more Jaffe's terms: phrase, whistle, twitch. There is an inevitable progression here, away from the normative to the eccentric. In a certain sense, all repetition relies on fragmentation, but this paradox is brought home with particular force in Dickens's novels, with their unique conjunction of monotony *and* eccentricity, of manifestation and obscurity.

We can see how Dickens associates failed expression, eccentric speech, and (both kinds of) repetition in the story of an extremely minor—and unnamed—character in *Little Dorrit*, the obsessed prisoner of Marshalsea whom Arthur Clennam meets on his first visit:

> The keeper of a chandler's shop in a front parlour, who took in gentlemen boarders, lent his assistance in making the bed. . . . He boasted that he stood up litigiously for the interests of the college; and he had undefined and undefinable ideas that the marshal intercepted a "Fund," which ought to come to the collegians. He liked to believe this, and always impressed the shadowy grievance on new-comers and strangers; though he could not, for his life, have explained what Fund he meant, or how the notion had got rooted in his soul. He had fully convinced himself, notwithstanding, that his own proper share of the Fund was three and ninepence a week; and that in this amount he, as an individual collegian, was swindled by the marshal, regularly every Monday. (128)

In this passage, the prisoner's notion is both radically singular (as it is literally "rooted in his soul") and disconnected from a clear social meaning ("undefined and undefinable"). However, repetition also underlies both the content and expression of this notion: the prisoner "*always* impressed the shadowy grievance on new-comers and strangers" and insists that he gets "swindled by the marshal, *regularly every* Monday." This is structurally reiterated when the grievance itself is repeated much later in the novel. After some three hundred pages, the "textual life" of this very minor character is doubled, when he suddenly appears again.[24] But what is the consequence of having such a radically truncated character-space, of being confined to two widely separated appearances that—like the complaint itself—are both disconnected (by the amount of narrative time that has passed) and repetitive (since the only way we can *remember* the minor character is through his reentering in a similar guise)? In fact, only by his reappearance does the minor character become truly flattened, reduced now to the single characteristic of this obsession.

This repetition of the prisoner's complaint comes at a structurally privileged moment: in the middle of a catalog description of all the prisoners who observe the Dorrits' release, at the end of part 1. In this description, we see the character's inarticulateness embedded in multiplicity, shaped by the way that he has become simply one among many indistinguishable prisoners. I need to quote most of the catalog description to demonstrate how this strange prisoner works as a pivot, within the passage, between individuals and groups:

> In the yard, were the Collegians and turnkeys. In the yard, were Mr. Pancks and Mr. Rugg, come to see the last touch given to their work. In the yard, was Young John making a new epitaph for himself, on the occasion of his dying of a broken heart. In the yard, was the Patriarchal Casby, looking so tremendously benevolent that many enthusiastic Collegians grasped him fervently by the hand, and the wives and female relatives of many more Collegians kissed his hand, nothing doubting that he had done it all. In the yard, was the man with the shadowy grievance respecting the Fund which the marshall embezzled, who had got up at five in the morning to complete the copying of a perfectly unintelligible history of that transaction, which he had committed to Mr. Dorrit's care, as a document of the last importance, calculated to stun the Government and effect the Marshall's downfall. In the yard, was the insolvent whose utmost energies were always set on getting into debt, who broke into prison with as much pains as other men have broken out of it, and who was always being cleared and complimented; while the insolvent at his elbow—a mere little, snivelling, striving tradesman, half dead of anxious efforts to keep out of debt—found it a hard matter, indeed, to get a Commissioner to release him with much reproof and reproach. In the yard, was the man of many children and many burdens, whose failure astonished everybody; in the yard, was the man of no children and large resources, whose failure astonished nobody. There were the people who were always going out tomorrow, and always putting it off; there, were the people who had come in yesterday, and who were much more jealous and resentful of this freak of fortune than the seasoned birds. (478)

In *"copying . . . a perfectly unintelligible history,"* the prisoner's action is at once monotonous and emphatic (he hopes to "stun" the authorities). The phrase encapsulates both the repetitive and the radically singular, inexpressible nature of his grievance. The strangely monotonous manifestation of this unrepresentable subjectivity (with its "shadowy grievance") occupies the most space in the passage, despite the character's seeming insignificance. It also works as a hinge: on one side, we find individuals (Pancks, Rugg, John Chivery, Casby) and on the other anonymous, typical, and finally multiple persons ("the insolvent," "the insolvent at his elbow," "the man of many children," "the man of no children," "people who were always going out tomorrow," "people who had come in yesterday").

While narrative subordination in Dickens seems to produce an eccentricity that is expressly idiosyncratic, minorness, on the level of narrative structure, is intrinsically and necessarily collective. No novel—and certainly no Dickens novel—can have merely one minor character. In fact, all of Dickens's novels coordinate a series of figures each of whom, taken out of context, appears to epitomize a kind of experience, and finally a kind of suffering, rooted in the individual. In this sense, Dickens's minor characters are both typical and peculiar, a paradoxical conjunction ultimately inseparable from the way that, as we have seen, minor characters conjoin repetition with eccentricity and link together emphasis with obscurity. Consider Mr. Vuffin's comment in *The Old Curiosity Shop*: "Look at wooden legs. If there was only one man with a wooden leg what a property *he*'d be!" (149). But, in fact, as this passage suggests, the man with a wooden leg—an emblem of idiosyncrasy—always belongs to a larger group, even as the many descriptively or physically disjoined appendages in Dickens's novels (including, frequently, wooden legs) belong to characters whose minorness, actualized by their "singular" prosthetic distortion, is contingent on the much wider group they belong to. As a contrast to Vuffin's comment, we can find this description of specialization in *Hard Times*: "He and some one hundred and forty other schoolmasters had been lately turned at the same time, in the same factory, on the same principles, like so many pianoforte legs." Repetitive production ("the same . . . the same . . . the same") ends with a subtly disjunctive metonymy: of course, Dickens chooses only the piano *legs*. Or consider the opening description of Mr. Nandy, in *Little Dorrit*:

> Anybody may pass, any day, in the thronged thoroughfares of the metropolis, some meagre, wrinkled, yellow old man . . . creeping along with a scared air, as though bewildered and a little frightened by the noise and bustle. This old man is always a little old man. If he were ever a big old man, he has shrunk into a little old man; if he were always a little old man, he has dwindled into a less old man. *His coat is a colour, and cut, that never was the mode anywhere, at any period. Clearly, it was not made for him, or for any individual mortal.* Some wholesale contractor measured Fate for five thousand coats of such quality, and Fate has lent this old coat to this old man, as one of a long unfinished line of many old men. *It has always large dull metal buttons, similar to no other buttons.* This old man wears a hat, a thumbed and napless and yet an obdurate hat, which has never adapted itself to the shape of his poor head. His coarse shirt and his coarse neckcloth have no more individuality than his coat and hat; they have the same character of not being his—of not being anybody's. (413, emphasis added)

The description undermines its own general assertion that Mr. Nandy has "no . . . individuality," when the very uniformity of Mr. Nandy's clothing seems to produce a kind of radical singularity: a coat "that never was the mode anywhere." This paradox is most evident in the uneasy play between the singular and the plural, in the shift from "five thousand coats of such quality" to "this old coat." The next sentence—"It has always large dull metal buttons, similar to no other buttons"—suggests that Mr. Nandy's coat is unique, but such inimitability is undermined by the "always," which conserves a strong sense of generalization. It is really not clear, from the sentence's syntax, whether the five thousand coats have a distinct kind of button, or whether Mr. Nandy's

buttons, *in particular*, are "similar to no other buttons." This contradiction—
between singularity and repetition—is also apparent in the phrase "a long unfinished line of many old men." Here the strong adjective "unfinished" seems
to modify, in contradictory ways, both "line" and "old men." While "unfinished
line" suggests an ever more redundant social uniformity, "unfinished old men"
suggests a kind of individual incompleteness that is necessarily singular.

In this sense we need to consider three different kinds of repetition: a minor
character repeats a phrase, whistle, or twitch *within* a given scene (until it is
exposed as a defining, limiting habit); the character appears repeatedly (and
sporadically) within the narrative discourse; and, finally, the character's minorness is repeated in the other subordinate characters who surround him and
whose presence, ultimately, produces the first two kinds of repetition. I want
to investigate these interrelated modes of repetition (gestures, narrative appearances, and, finally, *persons*) by considering *David Copperfield*'s Mr. Barkis, a
celebrated minor character who, in Robert Golding's words, "is one of that
legion of Dickens characters who achieves immortality though uttering
scarcely more than a dozen lines in the book, all of which are torn out of his
own inarticularity" (136). The interplay between Barkis's (discursive) "scar-
city" and (affective) "immortality" returns us, with obviously different terms,
to our starting point: the disjunction or "disproportion" underlying a subordinate character's narrative claim. How can a character be scarce and immortal,
memorable and minor, monotonous and emphatic? "You look at him, and there
he is. You look at him again, and—there he isn't."

As Golding's study of Dickensian idiolect suggests, Barkis's durability, as
minor character, is rooted in his speech, and more specifically in those unique,
eccentric phrases (most notably "Barkis is willing!") that he *repeats* over and
over again. The double nature of Barkis's speech—repetitive, eccentric—is
also manifested on a structural level. As with so many Dickens characters,
Barkis appears in a series of scenes and the fictional individual emerges only
as we are able to reconstruct a complete personality out of these sporadic
entrances and exits. Like the unnamed prisoner in *Little Dorrit*—whose minorness is written across the two (widely separated) scenes in which he appears—the development of Barkis as a minor character within the narrative
totality relies on both repetition and disconnection: Barkis's intermittent appearances rest upon his disappearances, as the negative space between the
scenes, or the disconnection produced *by* Barkis's narrative subordination, is
just as important as the various connecting threads that (necessarily) link the
passages together.

In one early passage, Dickens gives a genealogy of, and motivation for, Barkis's idiolect, rather than just presenting it in its symptomatic fullness. Crucially,
Barkis's repeated expression derives *out of* his inscrutable singularity; his
pinched manner of communication is produced by the protagonist's inability to
fathom his interiority. In this way Barkis's "inarticularity" is a dramatic embodi-

ment of George Eliot's dialectic between subjectivity and exteriority, illustrating one way that the "roar which lies on the other side of silence" gets incompletely filtered out. Barkis literally emerges out of his silence in the text, since his identification *as* Barkis, rather than simply as "the carrier," occurs in-and-through a reference to a previous scene where he is characterized by *not* talking:

> "Are you only going to Yarmouth then?" I asked.
> "That's about it," said the carrier. "And there I shall take you to the stage-cutch, and the stage-cutch that'll take you to—wherever it is."
> As this was a great deal for the carrier (whose name was Barkis) to say—*he being, as I observed in a former chapter*, of a phlegmatic temperament, and not at all conversational—I offered him a cake as a mark of attention, which he ate at one gulp, exactly like an elephant, and which made no more impression on his big face than it would have done on an elephant's. (114, emphasis added)

In the previous scene we have not yet identified Barkis *as* a character; or, more precisely, we have been able to see him only in a purely functional position, as something like the "waterman" in *The Pickwick Papers*. The earlier passage, at the opening of chapter 3, makes this clear:

> The carrier's horse was the laziest horse in the world, I should hope, and shuffled along, with his head down, as if he liked to keep people waiting to whom the packages were directed. I fancied, indeed, that he sometimes chuckled audibly over this reflection, but the carrier said he was only troubled with a cough.
> The carrier had a way of keeping his head down, like his horse, and of drooping sleepily forward as he drove, with one of his arms on each of his knees. I say "drove," but it struck me that the cart would have gone to Yarmouth quite as well without him, for the horse did all that; and as to conversation, he had no idea of it but whistling. (77)

Barkis's silence is related to his specifically minor position within the novel, which here motivates both his ascribed resemblance to the horse and his classification three times in three sentences as "the carrier." Just as "the utter vacancy of the fat boy's countenance" (*Pickwick Papers*, 172) is related to the simultaneous configuration of Joe's minorness, functionality, and caricatured surface, Barkis's silence is a sign *of* his inscrutability, which in turn stems from his reduction to a functional position (within the story) and a minor position (within the discourse). The absurd comparison to the elephant—in the passage where Barkis reappears—serves to reinforce our inability to read Barkis's inside ("the cake . . . made no more impression on his big face") and connects this inscrutability to comic caricature, or reduction.

In the scene I want to examine more closely, Barkis enters the narrative under these same conditions: as a "carrier" who is inscrutable to David. "Mr. Barkis came into the house for Peggotty's boxes. I had never known him to pass the garden-gate before, but on this occasion he came into the house. And

he gave me a look as he shouldered the largest box and went out, which I
thought had meaning in it, if meaning could ever be said to find its way into
Mr. Barkis's visage" (190). *Can* meaning enter into Barkis's visage? Does he
have an interiority as actual as the narrator's own? The narrative says both
yes and no, and Barkis's disconnected speech, which begins as the passage
continues, is a manifestation of this inscrutability. Again, the fitful words are a
version of that internal "roar" filtered through "silence"—in this case a silence
grounded in Barkis's role as a minor character and a worker. (In the same way,
the look that both does and does not communicate "meaning" takes place only
when Barkis *leaves* the house he had "never" entered before and "as he shoulder[s] the largest box" in his capacity as "carrier.")

> So long as she remained in this condition, Mr. Barkis gave no sign of life whatever.
> But when she began to look about her, and to speak to me, he nodded his head and
> grinned several times. I have not the least notion of whom, or what he meant by it.
> "It's a beautiful day, Mr. Barkis!" I said, as an act of politeness.
> "It ain't bad," said Mr. Barkis, who generally qualified his speech, and rarely
> committed himself.
> "Peggotty is quite comfortable now, Mr. Barkis," I remarked, for his satisfaction.
> "Is she, though?" said Mr. Barkis.
> After reflecting about it, with a sagacious air, Mr. Barkis eyed her, and said:
> "*Are* you pretty comfortable?"
> Peggotty laughed, and answered in the affirmative.
> "But really and truly, you know. Are you?" growled Mr. Barkis, sliding nearer
> to her on the seat, and nudging her with his elbow. "Are you. Really and truly
> pretty comfortable? Are you? Eh?" At each of these inquiries Mr. Barkis shuffled
> nearer to her, and gave her another nudge; so that at last we were all crowded together
> in the left-hand corner of the cart, and I was so squeezed that I could hardly bear it.
> (190–91)

In this scene, Dickens gives us a kind of history of his caricature—we see an
idiolect grow up before our eyes, as Barkis's eccentric repetition of his question
is not simply presented to us but derived out of his silence ("Mr. Barkis gave
no sign of life whatever," "Mr. Barkis . . . rarely committed himself") and his
inscrutability to David ("I have not the least notion of whom, or what he meant
by it"). In other words, Barkis exhibits the same reduction and dislocation as
Mr. F's Aunt, but now this is motivated by, rather than simply causing, the
protagonist's inability to understand him.

In the same passage David continues:

> I could not help observing that he seemed to think he had hit upon a wonderful
> expedient for expressing himself in a neat, agreeable and pointed manner, with-
> out the inconvenience of inventing conversation. He manifestly chuckled over it for
> some time. By and by he turned to Peggotty again, and repeating, "Are you pretty

comfortable though?" bore down upon us as before, until the breath nearly edged out of my body. (191)

In his attempts to be particularly lucid, Mr. Barkis was so extremely mysterious, that I might have stood looking in his face for an hour, and most assuredly should have got as much information out of it as out of the face of a clock that had stopped. (192)

In both of these passages David connects Barkis's eccentric mode of speaking with his inscrutability, and this relationship between the minor character's interiority and his speech occurs at the juncture between reduction and dislocation, so he might be characterized, as is Mr. F's Aunt, by a "taciturnity" (or silence) interrupted by a speech that is "traceable to no association of ideas," or, as David puts it, is not "conversation" and does not convey "information." If the development of Barkis's eccentricity is dwelt on more suggestively than with most of Dickens's minor characters, the strange specifics of his idiolect soon overshadow the context from which they emerge. Barkis's affective presence—the strange way we remember his elliptical expressiveness—shifts him to that plane of achieved distortion that runs throughout Dickens's novel, and which I have been analyzing as a kind of totalized, symptomatic representation of specialization and its discontents.

Such specialization is always a mass phenomenon, as is made clear, most simply, by the way in which characters flood into the narrative en masse in all of Dickens's novels. Thus we can see Barkis's distortion in a more exaggerated form in another neighboring scene from *David Copperfield*, when David is traveling to his aunt's house and goes into a pawnshop to sell his jacket. The scene begins with an image of half-visibility that quickly produces a distorted human figure, whose own face is also only half-visible: "Into this shop, which was low and small, and which was darkened rather than lighted by a little window, overhung with clothes, and was descended into by some steps, I went with a palpitating heart; which was not relieved when an ugly old man, with the lower part of his face all covered with a stubbly grey beard, rushed out of a dirty den behind it, and seized me by my hair" (239). This descriptive (and narrative) context immediately collapses into the character's grotesque singularity:

"Oh, what do you want?" grinned this old man, in a fierce, monotonous whine. "Oh, my eyes and limbs, what do you want? Oh, my lungs and liver, what do you want? Oh, goroo, goroo!"

I was so much dismayed by these words, and particularly by the repetition of the last unknown one, which was a kind of rattle in his throat, that I could make no answer; hereupon the old man, still holding me by the hair, repeated:

"Oh, what do you want? Oh, my eyes and limbs, what do you want? Oh, my lungs and liver, what do you want? Oh goroo!"—which he screwed out of himself, with an energy that made his eyes start in his head. (240)

Here we have a final convergence of eccentricity and reduction, of repetition *and* dislocation, as the character's speech fixates on the meaningless word "goroo," which is obviously detached from any sense. David is thus dismayed "particularly by the *repetition* of the last *unknown* [word]" so that its dislocation from meaning and its monotonous repetition are simultaneously registered in their affective force. David himself repeats his *own* use of the term "repetition" when he says the old man "repeated: 'Oh what do you want?' " but if this second speech by the old man is in some ways redundant, the final and thus most redundant "goroo" is "screwed out of himself, with an *energy* that made his eyes start in his head." This strange relationship between repetition and energy is already suggested in the first description of "a fierce, monotonous whine," two adjectives whose striking juxtaposition captures the complicated nature of alienation. What makes monotony fierce? And not just for Dickens, but for Schiller ("man himself develops into nothing but a fragment, everlastingly in his ear the monotonous sound of the wheel that he turns"), and for Engels ("because his hours of labour are so long and so dismally monotonous, the worker must surely detest his job after the first few weeks").

In some ways the old man is merely a consolidation of what we have seen in Barkis's combination of repetition and inscrutability. Like the pawnbroker, Barkis seems to pull his strange expression out of himself. And if David can't understand Barkis's elliptical phrases, or knowing looks, this has become exaggerated in the objectively incomprehensible "goroo." Repeating this sound seems to generate the same kind of physical fragmentation we have seen in many of Dickens's passages, as the "eyes [which] start in his head" is developed in subsequent descriptions of his hands, eyes, and head, reinforcing the pawnbroker's own references to "my eyes" and "my limbs."

> With that he took his trembling hands, which were like the claws of a great bird; and put on a pair of spectacles, not at all ornamental to his inflamed eyes. (240)

> "Oh my lungs and liver," cried the old man, "no! Oh, my eyes, no! Oh, my limbs, no! Eighteenpence. Goroo!"
>
> Every time he uttered this ejaculation, his eyes seemed to be in danger of starting out; and every sentence he spoke, he delivered in a sort of tune, always exactly the same, and more like a gust of wind, which begins low, mounts up high, and falls again, than any other comparison I can find for it. (240)

> "Oh, go—roo!" (it is really impossible to express how he twisted this ejaculation out of himself, as he peeped round the door-post at me, showing nothing but his crafty old head); "will you go for fourpence?"
>
> I was so faint and weary that I closed with this offer; and taking the money out of his claw, not without trembling, went away, more hungry and thirsty than I had ever been, a little before sunset. (242)

If Barkis's weird personality can perhaps be assimilated to a metaphoric register, this man's metonymic configuration overshadows any possible metaphoric significance. The qualities that we might derive from his character—like "greed" or "penury"—are overwhelmed by the means through which we derive them, and, most of all, by the "innumerable Goroos interspersed" (241). The Goroos—which unite repetition and eccentricity—are the crux of this minor character's representation, which then produces, typically, an idiolect (one that can be described only through an imperfect natural comparison) and the fragmented images of his head, eyes, and hands. But, in a more complete analysis of *David Copperfield*, this scene would be important precisely because it would highlight the metonymic aspects of *other* idiolects, most significantly the scenes we have looked at with Barkis (which take place in the previous monthly installment) and in Betsey Trotwood's repeated use of "Janet! Donkeys!" (which she first says in the same chapter as this incident), as well as in the slightly less distinctive idiolects of Heep and Mr. and Mrs. Micawber. Finally, we can see how the local association of minor characters with repetition through speech tags like "Barkis is willin'," "Goroo!," and "Janet! Donkeys!" is developed into a *structure* of repetition, through the frequent (and often surprising or disruptive) reappearances of minor characters in *David Copperfield*. In precisely this way we have seen how Barkis's speech—both repetitive and disconnected—is related to his structural position as a minor character who appears in a series of repeating, but disconnected, scenes. These recurring characters, so manifold in *David Copperfield*, elaborate the tension between eccentricity and repetition on a structural level, in terms of the episodic poetics of the bildungsroman. This brings us back to the larger narrative totality within which Dickens's configuration of his misaligned characters occurs. If we rush too quickly to thematize minor characters, to absorb them back into the totality of the narrative, we lose sight of their rich metonymic significance. But this tendency—to reabsorb the eccentric flatness of minor characters back into its proper, peripheral (and metaphorical) place—is enacted not just by critics but by virtually all of Dickens's novels themselves. In the next chapter, I want to shift to this register, looking more closely at how minor characters fit into the overall narrative structure, and intersect with the problematic space of the protagonist, in *Great Expectations*.

Chapter Three _____

Partings Welded Together: The Character-System
in *Great Expectations*

Between Two Roaring Worlds: Exteriority
and Characterization

> Beingless beings. Stop! Throb always without you and the throb always within.
> Your heart you sing of. I between them. Where? Between two roaring worlds
> where they swirl, I. Shatter them, one and both. But stun myself too in the blow.
> —James Joyce, *Ulysses*

A novel's character-system consists not merely in the interlocking of a large
group of distinct fictional individuals but also in the combination of different
kinds of character-*spaces*, the various modes through which specific human
figures are inflected into the narrative. Each fictional individual emerges only
within a larger narrative framework, shaped by the particular space he or she
occupies within a complicated structure. This space is formed through the
dynamic interaction, or jostling, among numerous characters who share a
limited, and unevenly distributed, amount of narrative attention. The implied
person is transformed in this process: whether pushed to the side or fondly
rendered, a character's relative position within the totality flows into his or
her specific representation as an individual. Arising at this juncture between
person and narrative position, the fictional individual gets elaborated in numerous ways: by how often and in what manner she exits and enters the
narrative; by the degree to which we sense her interior consciousness; through
the kind of figurative language she motivates or is encased in. Certainly, the
flat or minor character is inflected into the narrative universe in a qualitatively
different way from a fully rounded protagonist. But this is not the only distinction. A friend, a servant, a criminal, and a parent can all surround, and be
compressed by, a central protagonist and, in each case, get incorporated into
the total narrative in a particular way, with specific bearing on her fictional
identity. In *Pride and Prejudice*, for instance, we've seen how the five Bennet
sisters occupy five different kinds of narrative space: the protagonist's central
position and four distinct forms of minorness. In these multifarious realist
novels we don't coordinate just a large list of characters but also many different kinds of character-space, each shaped through the warp and woof of a
complex organizing system.

Dickens absorbs and transforms the traditionally asymmetric structuring of character-system and character-space. He grasps and problematizes this crucial paradox: minor characters tend to become more distorted as they get obscured (or "stinted" of narrative attention), and then become more memorable as they get distorted. In his biography of Dickens, Peter Ackroyd notes that as the author moved from house to house, he obsessively carried certain objects to place on his writing desk, including a bronze image of "a dog fancier, with the puppies and dogs swarming all over him" (503). We can see how Dickens might love this piece, as the scene confirms his imaginative patterning of characterization. The Dickensian character-system is driven by this overwhelming of the protagonist, who gets swarmed by the very minorness that he creates through his centrality.

The distinction of *Great Expectations*, within Dickens's oeuvre, lies in the novel's rendering of this affective structure, its depiction of the sense of centrality *itself* as it becomes besieged. While many of Dickens's novels feature a weak protagonist, *Great Expectations* magisterially represents what it feels like to *be* a weak protagonist, as Pip is constantly overwhelmed by the marginal characters who surround him. If we have a more immediate relationship to Pip's vulnerability as a protagonist, this is in large part because he is one of the author's few first-person narrators. But in a strange way, *Great Expectations* is a masterpiece of the *omniscient* imagination. Like almost all of Dickens's third-person novels, *Great Expectations* revolves around a weak protagonist, distorted minor characters, and an intricately organized plot that brings all the characters together. As Pip navigates through the challenges of the provinces and London, these challenges continually reflect and flow back into the *discursive* pressures—of centrality, subordination, caricature, distortion—that we examined in chapter 2. In this sense, we are granted direct psychological access to the narrating central character precisely as he experiences and responds *to* the peculiar pressures of Dickensian asymmetry. *Great Expectations*, we might say, is the story of a first-person narrator stuck in a third person narrative world—a world in large part shaped by the structures and logic of Dickens's own earlier omniscient novels.

A first-person narrative necessarily makes a qualitative distinction between the human figure who narrates the story (and is thus presented as an *agent* or subject of perception) and the characters he writes about (mere *objects* of perception).[1] In this sense we might say that the asymmetric structure of the character-system in first-person narration is intrinsic and unavoidable. Of course, many kinds of first-person narratives look for ways to circumscribe the fictional narrator's distinctive character-space: perhaps through a framed structure (the first-person narrator tells a story within which there is a *different* protagonist), an unreliable narrator (whose narration leads the reader to confer more importance on other characters within the story), or a rotating structure of multiple narrators (as in *As I Lay Dying*), which bestows first-person status on a number of characters. All of these different strategies amount to a certain reshuffling of the deck, attempting to compensate in one way or another *for* the structural imbalance that is compelled by first-person narrative. But Dickens puts pressure on the distinction of the first-person protagonist in a quite different way. *Great Expectations* does not collapse or weaken the dissimilar positions of narrator and minor characters, but heightens their divergence—exaggerating *both* the narrator's interiority and the exteriority of all the other characters. While we never get a description of what Pip looks like, we receive magnified, distorted images of the minor characters whom he apprehends. If the social world is essentially fragmented, elaborated only through its grotesque distortions, the space of the protagonist is also limited: never able to actualize itself as exterior, and continually overwhelmed and agitated by the fragmented world that assaults it. In this sense, the *priority* of the narrating protagonist—as the subject who apprehends the entire content of the narrative, the entire world of the fiction—is disrupted in *Great Expectations*. If Pip's consciousness necessarily precedes the other characters who form the field of his perception, it also depends upon these other characters, is beholden to them, is vulnerable in front of them. And such a reversal speaks not only to Dickens's vision of the "self" but also to his idea of narrative: Pip's weak centrality enacts and dramatizes the affective force of minorness that we see throughout Dickens's novels. It is as though, in *Great Expectations*, the fundamental difference that marks the first-person narrator in terms of the narrative *discourse* has completely infiltrated the fictional world he inhabits.

Pip's weakness as a protagonist is spectacularly represented in the opening scene. In his terrifying encounter with Magwitch, we are plunged into a narrative universe shaped by the reversed flow of asymmetry:

> "Hold your noise!" cried a terrible voice, as a man started up from among the graves at the side of the church porch. "Keep still, you little devil, or I'll cut your throat!"
>
> A fearful man, all in coarse grey, with a great iron on his leg. A man with no hat, and with broken shoes, and with an old rag tied around his head. A man who had been soaked in water, and smothered in mud, and lamed by stones, and cut by flints, and stung by nettles, and torn by briars; who limped, and shivered, and glared, and growled; and whose teeth chattered in his head as he seized me by the chin. . . .
>
> The man, after looking at me for a moment, turned me upside-down, and emptied my pockets. There was nothing in them but a piece of bread. When the church came to itself—for he was so sudden and strong that he made it go head over heels before me, and I saw the steeple under my feet—when the church came to itself, I say, I was seated on a high tombstone, trembling, while he ate the bread ravenously. (36)

This opening scene anticipates the essential structure of *Great Expectations*'s character-system: the central, interior consciousness who is powerless and the marginal, exterior figures who—in their very bewildering distortion—are extremely powerful. Magwitch's effect on Pip is registered most memorably in terms of Pip's interiority: not only is Pip's body turned upside down, but this flip, "so sudden and strong," disorders Pip's perception of what is around him. Who has the advantage here? Pip is certainly weak and vulnerable, but the scene, like any in first-person narrative, also depicts him in terms of his consciousness—as an agent defined through his perception and thought. Magwitch is powerful and strong, but the text inflects him only as an exterior agent, entering the narrative as he intrudes onto Pip's terrified consciousness. Pip gets flipped upside down, but Magwitch is viewed as *though* he were upside down.

This division between the protagonist's vulnerable interiority and minor characters' fragmented exteriority recalls an important comment in Georg Lukács "historico-philosophical" *Theory of the Novel*. Lukács describes how the genre is situated between mutually incomplete forms of both the (central) individual and the (surrounding) social world: "The contingent world and the problematic individual are realities which mutually determine one another. . . . This self-destruction of reality . . . appears in two different ways. . . . First, as disharmony between the interiority of the individual and the substratum of his actions. . . . Second as the inability of the outside world, which is a stranger to ideals and an enemy to interiority, to achieve real completeness; an inability to find either the form of totality for itself as a whole, or any form of coherence for its own relationship to its elements and their relationship to one another" (79). The qualitative distinction between Pip ("the problematic individual") and Magwitch ("the contingent world," which becomes "an enemy to interiority") that Dickens manipulates in this scene is, I've been arguing, an inherent aspect of first-person narration. And many first-person novels begin with an encounter between the protagonist and an egregiously minor character, perhaps in order to configure the specific nature of this distinction. For instance, Lesage's picaresque novel *Gil Blas* (1715) has a memorable scene at the start of chapter 2, when Gil is first riding away from home and encounters a beggar:

There I was outside of Oviedo, on the road to Pennaflor, in the middle of the countryside, master of my actions, of a poor mule and of forty good ducats, without counting the rials that I had stolen from my honorable uncle. The first thing I did was to let my mule walk as he pleased, that is, very slowly. I put the bridle around his neck, and taking the ducats from my pocket I began to count them and recount them inside my hat. I had never seen so much money. I couldn't stop looking at it and handling it. I must have counted it for the twentieth time when, all of a sudden, my mule, lifting up his head and pricking up his ears, stopped in the middle of the highway. I supposed that something had frightened him; I looked up to see what it could have been. I perceived on the ground a turned-up hat in which there was a rosary with large beads and at the same time I heard a lamentable voice say these words:

"You, sir, who are passing-by [Seigneur passant], have pity for a poor maimed soldier; please throw some coins into that hat and you will be compensated in the other world." I quickly turned my eyes to the side from which the voice came; I saw, at the root of a bush, some twenty or thirty feet from me, a kind of soldier who, upon two cross sticks, supported the barrel of a carbine which seemed to me longer than a pike, and with which he seemed to make me a target. At this view, which made me quake for the Church's money, I stopped suddenly, and quickly pocketing my ducats, took out some rials and, approaching the hat that was set up to receive the charity of frightened people, I threw them in one after another, to show the soldier that I was treating him well. He was satisfied with my generosity, and gave me as many benedictions as I gave kicks to the side of my mule to take me quickly away from him [pour m'éloigner promptement de lui]. (9–10)

This passage integrates its first-person perspective into the charged symbolic structure of the social encounter. Gil's position, in the *story*, depends on the emergent socioeconomic forms that give shape to the picaresque genre in the first place.[2] As Gil starts out on his adventures, the opening lines of the chapter convey the sense of freedom, mobility, economic ambition, and interiority which structures the kind of "everyday adventure" that inheres in picaresque fiction.[3] Gil feels like the "master of [his] actions," and his decision "to let [his] mule walk as he please[s]" externalizes this free sense of anticipation and links it to a more specifically *physical* mobility. As his mule moves forward, the protagonist turns inward, his consciousness revolving around the money that he obsessively counts, and the narrative itself revolving around his consciousness. The encounter with the beggar halts Gil's mobility and disrupts his stream of thoughts. If Gil's adventure is sustained by his subjective sense of freedom and economic possibility, the beggar is the negative object of this same economic mobility. When he addresses Gil as "Seigneur *passant*," the wounded soldier captures the essential asymmetric structure of the scene, which symbolically encompasses both sides of social mobility. Propelled forward on a specific socioeconomic trajectory, Gil passes by the inevitable residue of this trajectory, and the episodic nature of the encounter is crucial to the characters' two linked positions. The structure of novelistic asymmetry—which first finds a form in the episodic poetics of the picaresque—controls this scene, pushing the protagonist forward and leaving the distorted minor character behind.[4] Thus Gil's perception of the beggar is shaped by the way he is "passing-by": he notices first only exterior fragments, the hat and the voice, while his *own* interior apprehension is highlighted: "I supposed [je jugeai]," "I looked," "I perceived," "I heard," "I quickly turned my eyes," "I saw . . . twenty or thirty feet from me," and, finally, "I gave kicks . . . to take me quickly away from him [je donnai de coups de pieds . . . pour m'éloigner promptement de lui]." Our sense of Gil as a mobile subject, or agent of perception and cognition, is intertwined with the impoverished soldier's delimited inflection as a wounded object.

In many ways, these early scenes from *Gil Blas* and *Great Expectations* are quite similar. Pip notes how "a man started up," while Gil writes, "all of a sudden my mule stopped [tout à coup ma mule . . . s'arrêta]." The "poor wounded soldier" resembles the limping convict, and while the soldier demands money, Magwitch empties Pip's pocket. Magwitch, like the soldier, is first simply a "terrible voice," and just as Gil then infers a person only peripherally, through the hat on the ground, Pip also focuses on isolated, fragmented articles of clothing instead of the full person, noticing the "broken shoes" and "old rag." Like the wounded soldier, Magwitch is a kind of human residue ("soaked," "smothered," "lamed," "cut," "stung," and "torn") cast in opposition to the protagonist—and, more specifically, intruding onto, and posited against, his interiority. However, as we have seen, Gil develops his faculties of apprehension in-and-through this encounter and soon leaves the beggar behind. Pip's consciousness, on the other hand, is disordered by the encounter with the convict, and he never fully leaves Magwitch behind. This is borne out, of course, in the forms of the two narratives: the open, episodic composition of *Gil Blas* and the tightly organized structure of *Great Expectations*, divided into three volumes and hinging on the convict's return.[5] What happens to the picaresque novel when it is turned in on itself, when it cannot leave behind transient episodes and peripheral characters? What happens to the first-person voice when it finds itself living (and narrating) in an omniscient universe?

The disruptive impact of Magwitch—grounded in the problematic relationship between narrating protagonist and minor character—resonates in the descriptive norms of *Great Expectations*. The novel abounds with caricatured portraits and descriptions of fragmented persons, portraits and descriptions that take shape within and are motivated by the misaligned character-system as a whole. Caricature confers affective presence onto secondary characters, generating that eccentric singularity which is itself the product of narrative subordination. Distortion arises out of the misalignment between implied person and delimited narrative role, a misalignment that is the consequence, in *Great Expectations*, of a first-person narration, and, implicitly, of narrative centrality itself. We can pick up this descriptive tendency almost anywhere in the novel: "exterior" and fragmentary descriptions occur on many different narrative registers, at crucial turning points and as insignificant asides. The structural imbalance at the heart of the character-system, in other words, gets endlessly reiterated, saturating even inessential and peripheral details in the story itself. Consider how Pip describes Joe's eyes, in a narratorial aside that punctuates Joe's speech about his parents:

> "[A]s I was saying, Pip, it were my intentions to have had it cut over him; but poetry costs money, cut it how you will, small or large, and it were not done. Not to mention bearers, all the money that could be spared were wanted for my mother. She were in poor elth, and quite broke. She weren't long of following, poor soul, and her share of peace come round at last."
>
> Joe's blue eyes turned a little watery; he rubbed first one of them, and then the other, in a most uncongenial and uncomfortable manner, with the round knob on the top of the poker.

"It were but lonesome then," said Joe, "living here alone, and I got acquainted
with your sister. . . ." (77–8)

Instead of simply noting that "he rubbed his eyes," Pip makes the more lingering observation that "he rubbed first one of them, and then the other." This is
typical of Pip's visual imagination.[6] Pip highlights Joe's exterior as it is in the
process of coming apart; and the understated dissociation of Joe's two eyes is
related to the exaggerated emphasis on "the round knob on the top of the
poker." We see the distorted surface of the world here, rising into Pip's interior
consciousness. The image is similar to a cluster of descriptions of one-eyed
people in Dickens that, like the recurring wooden legs and oversized or dislocated heads, are part of the network of physical distortions that ramify and
substantialize the misalignment of surface and depth.

This misalignment is emphatically configured at many other points in *Great
Expectations*, and particularly in volume 1, which establishes the specific
asymmetric contours of childhood experience: a youthful subject confronting
a world that is always much larger than he is, that comes at him on all sides, in
distorted and fragmentary parts, in enlarged dimensions and at oblique angles.

She was most noticeable, I thought, in respect of her extremities; for, her hair always
wanted brushing, her hands always wanted washing, and her shoes always wanted
mending and pulling up at heel. (74)

"Camilla, my dear, it is well known that your family feelings are gradually undermining you to the extent of making one of your legs shorter than the other." (115)

One was a taller and stouter man than the other, and appeared as a matter of course,
according to the mysterious ways of the world both convict and free, to have had
allotted to him the smaller suit of clothes. (248)

After dinner the children were introduced, and Mrs. Coiler made admiring comments
on their eyes, noses and legs. (215)

Like Pip's description of Joe's eyes, these four passages are not essential to
the progression of the narrative, but they do help construct the ubiquitous visual norm that emphasizes human exteriority (as configured in an asymmetric
narrative field) in terms of fragmentation. This norm underlies the otherwise
disparate images of ill-fitting clothing, mismatched legs, and the "extremities"
that seem to almost pull away from Biddy's body.

We see the same process comically enacted in an earlier passage about Mr.
Pocket's son:

His manner was so final and I was so astonished, that I followed where he led, as if
I had been under a spell.

"Stop a minute, though," he said, wheeling round before we had gone many paces.
"I ought to give you a reason for fighting, too. There it is!" In a most irritating manner

he instantly slapped his hands against one another, daintily flung one of his legs up behind him, pulled my hair, slapped his hands again, dipped his head, and butted it into my stomach. . . .

"Laws of the game!" said he. Here, he skipped from his left leg on to his right. "Regular rules!" Here he skipped from his right leg on to his left. "Come to the ground, and go through the preliminaries!" Here, he dodged backwards and forwards, and did all sorts of things while I looked helplessly at him. (119)

Herbert seems to come apart right in front of the protagonist, as Pip's attention to the hands and legs breaks down further, skipping back and forth between "left leg" and "right leg." Many other subordinate characters get compressed in a similar way—everywhere Pip sees dangerously mobile "extremities," mouths, heads, or limbs.

A tremulous uncertainty of the action of all her limbs soon became a part of her regular state. (150)

But she shook her head to that extent when she was shown it, that we were terrified lest in her weak and shattered state she should dislocate her neck. (151)

At the same time, he hugged his shuddering body in both his arms—clasping himself, as if to hold himself together—and limped towards the low church wall. (38)

The other, with an effort at a scornful smile—which could not, however, collect the nervous working of his mouth into any set expression—looked at the soldiers, and looked about at the marshes and at the sky. (68)

These passages don't just present us with fragmented parts but with the very process of fragmentation—minor characters who are coming apart, getting dislocated, shuddering, clasping, failing to "collect" their nervous selves. Significantly, Biddy's fragmented appearance makes her more "noticeable." Throughout *Great Expectations*, minor characters' exaggerated exteriority lends them an affective force—they capture attention *because* of their distortion. Another passage links Pip's "amazement" with a minor figure's extraordinary gesture that, characteristically, focuses on his head and hands: "To my unutterable amazement, I now, for the first time, saw Mr. Pocket relieve his mind by going through a performance that struck me as very extraordinary, but which made no impression on anybody else, and with which I soon became as familiar as the rest. He laid down the carving-knife and fork—being engaged in carving, at the moment—put his two hands into his disturbed hair, and appeared to make an extraordinary effort to lift himself up by it" (215). Mr. Pocket's affective presence captivates Pip's attention, shifting the narrative focus toward him. What happens to the protagonist's own identity when his consciousness is carried away by a minor character's fragmentation? If Mr. Pocket causes "*unutterable* amazement," Pip is literally silenced by forceful minor characters at other points in the novel. Magwitch says, "Hold your noise!" (36); Mrs. Gargery commands, "ask no questions" (45); and later Pip writes, "I was squeezed in at an acute angle of the table-cloth . . . I was not allowed to speak" (56), and "I received strict charge to keep in the rear and to speak no word after we reached the marshes" (64). As often Pip is effectively silenced because forceful minor characters simply confound or petrify him, rendering him *unable* to speak: "My heart was beating so fast, and there was such a singing in my ears, that I could scarcely stammer I had no objection" (165); "I could not have spoken one word, though it had been to save my life" (337). In these cases Pip's inability to speak, as with his "unutterable amazement," is a symptom of his disordered consciousness. Occasionally the text directly emphasizes this: "in my astonishment I had lost my self possession" (334); "I tried to collect my thoughts but I was stunned" (339); "I remained too stunned to think" (340); "all these things I saw without knowing that I saw them, for I was in an agony of apprehension" (62).[7]

Once again, all of these passages need to be read as they help to constitute the central protagonist's subjective experience of Dickensian asymmetry itself. The novel further literalizes the way that minor characters can overwhelm the protagonist (with the energy and force generated through their very subordination), when Pip gets shaken and abused by the adults who form his world. Here, too, a narrative relationship seems to travel relentlessly into the fictional story. Such physical interaction is immediately established in the first two chapters, when Pip is dramatically harassed by Magwitch and Mrs. Gargery:

> After darkly looking at his leg and me several times, he came closer to my tombstone, took me by both arms, and tilted me back as far as he could hold me; so that his eyes looked most powerfully down into mine, and mine looked most helplessly up into his. . . . After each question he tilted me over a little more, so as to give me a greater sense of helplessness and danger. . . . He tilted me again. . . . He tilted me again. . . . He tilted me again. . . . He gave me a most tremendous dip and roll, so that the church jumped over its own weather cock. (37)

> My sister, Mrs. Joe Gargery, was more than twenty years older than I, and had established a great reputation with herself and the neighbours because she had brought me up "by hand". . . . My sister, Mrs. Joe, throwing the door wide open, and finding an obstruction behind it, immediately divined the cause, and applied Tickler to its further investigation. She concluded by throwing me—I often served as a connubial missile—at Joe. (39, 41)

In these early chapters, Pip may be at the center of the narrative universe, but his centrality only brings him together with stronger minor characters who aggressively, and often physically, silence or overwhelm him. The young Pip ironically has *less* control of himself the more he is at the center of events, as he makes clear when describing the dinner party of Mr. Pumblechook, Mr. Wopsle, and Mr. and Mrs. Hubble:

> I should not have minded . . . if they would only have left me alone. But they wouldn't leave me alone. They seemed to think the opportunity lost, if they failed to point the conversation at me, every now and then, and stick the point into me. I might have been an unfortunate little bull in a Spanish arena, I got so smartingly touched up by these moral goads. (56–57)

> For, it inscrutably appeared to stand to reason, in the minds of the whole company, that I was an excrescence on the entertainment. And to make it worse, they all asked me from time to time—in short, whenever they had nothing else to do—why I didn't enjoy myself. (133)

These guests amplify the structure that puts minor characters in violent relationship with the protagonist, simply insofar as they are a *group* of individuals. The narrative emphasizes the multiplicity of these dinner guests, who are first described arriving en masse—"I opened the door to the company . . . I opened it first to Mr. Wopsle, next to Mr. and Mrs. Hubble, and last of all to Uncle Pumblechook" (55). Their dramatic intrusion on Pip's poor consciousness relies on this multiplicity; the silencing and scolding reaches a crescendo here *because* Pip is surrounded on all sides.

If the force of these minor characters is linked to their plurality, each individual character-space is framed within this crowded field, emphasizing the misaligned body:

> Mr. Wopsle, united to a Roman nose and a large shining bold forehead, had a deep voice which he was uncommonly proud of. . . . (55)

> Uncle Pumblechook, a large hard-breathing middle-aged slow man, with a mouth like a fish, dull staring eyes, and sandy hair standing upright on his head . . . (56)

> I remember Mr. Hubble as a tough high-shouldered stooping old man, of a sawdusty fragrance, with his legs extraordinarily wide apart. . . . (56)

There is not enough space for a full person here: each individual instead gets compressed, respectively, into "a Roman nose and a large shining bold forehead," "a mouth like a fish, dull staring eyes, and sandy hair standing upright," or "legs extraordinary wide apart." Needless to say, these details, and particularly the "Roman nose," recur frequently in this episode and other early scenes. "I think the Romans must have aggravated one another very much, with their noses. Perhaps, they became the restless people they were, in consequence. Anyhow, Mr. Wopsle's Roman nose so aggravated me, *during the recital of my misdemeanours*, that I should have liked to pull it until he howled" (59, emphasis added). Pip's observation occurs *as* he is listening to Mrs. Gargery's lecture, conjoining two kinds of aggravation experienced by the young child.

At other points, Wopsle and Pumblechook are directly aggressive toward Pip, and as these scenes unfold, the same eccentric gestures and isolated body parts are repeatedly mentioned.[8] Wopsle and Pumblechook leave an indelible impression on the reader although they are not necessary to the story. The dinner guests play an important role in the formation of the character-system in volume 1, as minor characters who, because of their multiplicity, offer the most exaggerated version of the war between Pip's consciousness and social exteriority. One passage makes it clear that Pumblechook's flatness is rooted in his particular, stultifying role in the village economy.

> In the early morning, I discovered a singular affinity between seeds and corduroys. Mr. Pumblechook wore corduroys, and so did his shopman; and somehow, there was a general air and flavour about the corduroys, so much in the nature of seeds, and a general air and flavour about the seeds, so much in the nature of corduroys, that I hardly knew which was which. The same opportunity served me for noticing that Mr. Pumblechook appeared to conduct his business by looking across the street at the saddler, who appeared to transact *his* business by keeping his eye on the coach-maker, who appeared to get on in life by putting his hands in his pockets and contemplating the baker, who in his turn folded his arms and stared at the grocer, who stood at his door and yawned at the chemist. (83–84)

This passage contextualizes Pumblechook's strange personal configuration: his distorted body is embedded within, and motivated by, his circumscribed social position. Now, instead of his being reduced to "a mouth like a fish [and] dull staring eyes," his clothing becomes stained by the material of his work; and instead of confronting Pip as part of the "larger company" of guests (Mr. Pumblechook, Mr. Wopsle, Mr. Hubble, Mrs. Hubble), he's portrayed as part of a social network of small tradesman (seedsman, saddler, coachmaker, baker, grocer, chemist). Again, flatness is linked to the division of labor, and we might speculate that Pumblechook's aggressive social ambition (like Pip's) is a reaction to the dullness of economic life in a small village. But this brief social motivation of Pumblechook's character is clearly less significant (and less memorable) than the descriptive configuration that connects the young Pip's vulnerability (as child and as protagonist) with Pumblechook's violence and aggression, and links this aggression to Pumblechook's distorted minorness. An entire universe with its own phenomenological rules is taking shape before our eyes, with this comic fragmentation of Pumblechook. The dinner company, and especially Mr. Pumblechook, function much like Mary in *Pride and Prejudice*: not central to the plot, reduced to a simple opposition with Pip, Pumblechook is both an elaboration of and a motivation for the overall configuration of the novel's character-system. Mary justifies the deeply rooted structures of asymmetry in *Pride and Prejudice*, and Pumblechook naturalizes *Great Expectations*'s insistent condensation of exteriority, specialization, fragmentation, minorness, and violence.

The Structure of Childhood Experience

All the objects among which they crept were so huge in contrast with their
wretched boat, as to threaten to crush it.
—*Our Mutual Friend*, 219

If Pip finds himself in an asymmetric world that reflects the very shape of
narrative discourse in all of Dickens's novels, this asymmetry also suggests
the specific nature of childhood experience. The Dickensian child, like the
weak protagonist or focalizing agent, both apprehends the world and is overwhelmed by the world. This connection between the child's structural position
(within the *story*) and the narrating protagonist's structural position (within the
discourse) brings out an important aspect of Dickens's radically original interest in childhood and child characters. Of course, the multifaceted relationship
between Dickens's novels and childhood—from the emphasis on childhood
experience to the status of Dickens's own work as children's literature—has
many sources and consequences.[9] One way to understand this relationship is
in terms of the asymmetric character-system. I want to suggest that the attention to childhood is in part motivated by the formal arrangement it allows and
elucidates: the weak protagonist and the strongly distorted, but still powerful,
minor character. The child, like the weak protagonist, finds himself a strangely
embattled center; he comes into consciousness by observing, apprehending,
and grappling with a group of characters—with, in fact, an entire social
world—that is both extensively and intensively too large. The achieved and
celebrated depiction of childhood in *Great Expectations* is thus related to the
represented experience of omniscience itself, as it is understood by and wreaks
havoc upon the weak protagonist.

We might consider here the interesting formal congruity between the three
narratives that first establish the contours of Dickensian asymmetry: *Sketches
by Boz*, *The Pickwick Papers*, and *Oliver Twist*. Whether the focalizing agent
is an inquisitive urban flaneur-cum-journalist, a benign and wealthy elderly
man, or an impoverished and vulnerable young orphan, we are confronted with
the same underlying discursive structure. Each focalizer—journalist, old man,
and child—both apprehends and is overwhelmed by the reality he observes,
until, finally, observation revolves around the very apprehension of the overwhelming. This surplus of sensory observations is clear, first of all, on a syntactic level. *Sketches by Boz* is full of distended sentences that register—in the
strain of the phrase itself, torn between hypotaxis and parataxis—the fundamental plentitude of urban reality. From "Greenwich Fair":

The road to Greenwich during the whole of Easter Monday, is in a state of perpetual
bustle and noise. Cabs, hackney-coaches, 'shay' carts, coal-waggons, stages, omni-
buses, sociables, gigs, donkey-chaises—all crammed with people (for the question

never is, what the horse can draw, but what the vehicle will hold), roll along at their utmost speed; the dust flies in clouds, ginger-beer corks go off in volleys, the balcony of every public-house is crowded with people, smoking and drinking, half the private houses are turned into tea-shops, fiddles are in great request, every little fruit-shop displays its stall of gilt gingerbread and penny toys; turnpike men are in despair; horses won't go on, and wheels will come off; ladies in 'caravans' scream with fright at every fresh concussion, and their admirers find it necessary to sit remarkably close to them, by way of encouragement; servants-of-all-work, who are not allowed to have followers, and have got a holiday for the day, make the most of their time with the faithful admirer who waits for a stolen interview at the corner of the street every night, when they go to fetch the beer—apprentices grow sentimental, and straw-bonnet makers kind. Every body is anxious to get on, and actuated by the common wish to be at the fair, or in the park, as soon as possible. (137)

To enter into the fray—of narrative, of urban strolling, of social observation itself—is to risk a kind of cognitive dissipation: there is always much more to the world than is dreamt of in the narrator's projected frame of observation. This urban plentitude derives ultimately from the plentitude of humanity itself, as the city is, like the vehicles in this description, "all crammed with people." Underneath the mass of vehicles, or of languages and sounds,[10] or of places and things, are the *people* who have shaped and are shaped by these material objects and sensory processes. As Boz writes in "Seven Dials": "If the external appearance of the houses, or a glance at their inhabitants, present but few attractions, a closer acquaintance with either is little calculated to alter one's first impressions. Every room has its separate tenant, and every tenant is, by the same mysterious dispensation which causes a country curate to 'increase and multiply' most marvelously, generally the head of a numerous family" (94). To cross the threshold of a house or locale—the fundamental physical and epistemological activity of the narrator in *Sketches by Boz*—is to confront this "marvelous" process of multiplication; in every room we find a separate tenant, and behind *each* separate individual a numerous group of other persons. In another revealing passage, the narrator suggests how this social multiplicity underlies his own reflexive attraction to the eccentric or the singular:

> The row of houses in which the old lady and her troublesome neighbour reside comprises, beyond all doubt, a greater number of characters within its circumscribed limits, than all the rest of the parish put together. As we cannot, consistently with our present plan, however, extend the number of our parochial sketches beyond six, it will be better, perhaps, *to select the most peculiar*, and to introduce them at once without further preface. ("The Four Sisters," 29, emphasis added)

The crowding of people into the "circumscribed limits" of a cluster of houses seems to shift, imperceptibly, into the crowding of characters into the sketches themselves, which, like the houses, are also limited in number (and size). Here we seem to once again face the recognizable opposition between narrative coherence and descriptive extent: to register the "action and motive" of all the neighborhood's residents (to use Dostoevsky's phrase) is to risk the destruction of narrative form itself, which gets unraveled in the dispersion of its "space and attention." If Dickens had "but world enough and time," perhaps he could avoid condensing the crush of humanity into its "most peculiar" element. But this equation is not quite right. Marvell's baleful formula—which becomes, of course, the epigraph to Erich Auerbach's *Mimesis*—seems somewhat inappropriate to Dickens. Auerbach means to register the necessarily limited form of all the different modes of social representation that *Mimesis* traces. But the restriction of Boz's narrative to only the "most peculiar" elements does not merely suggest the text's failure to encompass the larger world. The narrator's compression of an extensive number of characters into the most idiosyncratic is also motivated by the actual compression of many people into the circumscribed row of houses, and, more generally, into London itself, and its houses, streets, and vehicles "all crammed with people."

If the delimitations of, and the peculiarities within, the *Sketches* don't necessarily fail to comprehend London, the first two novels that spring from this literary confrontation with London do dissolve the overly confident observer in *Sketches by Boz*—a jocose avatar of Auerbach's realist narrator—into the Janus-faced personae of the old man and the orphaned child. The early Dickensian protagonist walks on three legs or on four legs but least of all on two, seeming to avoid the dominant location of heroism in the nineteenth-century novel.[11] Like the urban narrator, the child stares in shock at the (adult) world that has preceded and created him, and at all the adults who, as in the extreme case of an orphan, refuse to take responsibility for their creation. In the later first-person novels (*Bleak House*, *David Copperfield*, and *Great Expectations*), childhood always begins with the narrating protagonist's troubled contemplation of his or her origin, highlighting the belated relationship each character has to a world that both has given rise to *and* only exists in-and-through his or her consciousness. These three novels all draw a strong connection between the way a child faces the adult world—which both precedes and towers over him—and the way a first-person narrator faces *the narrated world*, a world that is simultaneously the source, background, and object of narratorial consciousness. In this sense, the very predicament of orphanhood canonically exemplified in the third-person *Oliver Twist* becomes a *discursive* condition for Dickens's later first-person narrators.

When Pip travels to London, across the seams of volumes 1 and 2, the structure of childhood experience gets embedded within asymmetry's original social and urban ground. In this crucial shift, *Great Expectations* brings its configuration of childhood—in which Pip is overwhelmed by the minor characters who populate, and overpopulate, his provincial youth—to bear upon the asymmetry of modern, urban social relations. Volume 1 has established both the problematic relationship of the child to an adult world that precedes and towers over him, and the problematic relationship of the narrator (and protagonist) to the (distorted) narrated world. Volume 2 elaborates this problematic in new, socially expansive terms: the vexed relationship of the "gentleman"—the mysteriously propertied individual—to the many people who produce and underlie this wealth. How much goes into the making of one gentleman? This is, perhaps, the most important question that *Great Expectations* asks and one that it elaborates on a narrative dimension by the following question: How much goes into the making of a single protagonist? After all, consider how Dickens emphasizes the strange amount of activity involved in the making of a single *cup of tea*:

> I rang for the tea, and the waiter, reappearing with his magic clue, brought in by degrees some fifty adjuncts to that refreshment, but of tea not a glimpse. A teaboard, cups and saucers, plates, knives and forks (including carvers), spoons (various), salt-cellars, a meek little muffin confined with the utmost precaution under a strong iron cover, Moses in the bulrushes typified by a soft bit of butter in a quantity of parsley, a pale loaf with a powdered head, two proof impressions of the bars of the kitchen fireplace on triangular bits of bread, and ultimately a fat family urn: which the waiter staggered in with, expressing in his countenance burden and suffering. After a prolonged absence at this stage of the entertainment, he at length came back with a casket of precious appearance containing twigs. These I steeped in hot water, and so from the whole of the appliances extracted one cup of I don't know what, for Estella.
> The bill paid, and the waiter remembered, and the ostler not forgotten, and the chambermaid taken into consideration . . . we got into our post-coach and drove away. (288)

This costly cup of tea—which is delayed by and then "extracted" from the strange adjuncts that are problematically implicated in its production—is an analogue for the protagonist himself, for the "gentleman" who is produced through a social system that at all points exceeds him, and finally comes to overwhelm and engulf him. Pip stumbles around in a world that always has a mysterious priority over his actions—a priority first signaled in his estranged relationship to his own birth. In the middle of this description of the single cup of tea is an inscription of this birth story: like "Moses in the bulrushes," each individual's biological origin—as well as the modern "gentleman's" *social* origin—is already implicated in a complicated mediated structure (expressed here through the unknown hands that bring the baby to the river). Earlier, Dickens inscribes a parodic version of this into his novel as well, recounting how the youngest baby of the Pockets seems literally brought up by hand (or hands): "[B]y and by Millers came down with the baby, which baby was handed to Flopson, which Flopson was handing to Mrs. Pocket, when she too went fairly head-foremost over Mrs. Pocket, baby and all, and was caught by Herbert and myself" (211).

Behind the "fifty adjuncts" to the cup of tea we find the forlorn waiter: an irrelevant minor character and narrative "helper" who "stagger[s] in . . . expressing in his countenance burden and suffering." This worker is only *one* of the persons involved; the scene ends as Pip pays off the others: "waiter," "ostler," "chambermaid." These peripheral characters clearly resemble the various and dispersed adjuncts that seem strangely, and troublingly, necessary to the cup of tea; here the activity of these hotel workers forms a literal residue of the cost of this meal ("the bill paid, *and* the *waiter* remembered, the ostler not forgotten"). This comic scene thus gives us an economic model for the character-system, one that might recall an earlier passage describing all the new people who will be involved in dressing Pip in clothes that suit a gentleman: "After this memorable event, I went to the hatter's and the bootmaker's and the hosier's, and felt rather like Mother Hubbard's dog whose outfit required the services of so many trades" (178–79). The making, or clothing, of one person here requires the activity of many people; and not just many people but many *trades*, or discrete activities demanding specialized work from these various persons. In other words, as a single individual becomes *more* of a gentleman (getting a new hat, and then new boots, and then new stockings, etc.), increasing numbers of people become *less* whole, confined within a particular activity or function that is necessary to this single (and now singular) person. Clothes are a particularly apt commodity to figure this kind of economy, since they form a sort of meeting ground between a person in his own right and the objects a person owns. In fact, all the objects that Pip commands through his wealth are a form of clothing; all the social attributes that now make him a "gentleman" are similar to these hats, boots, and stockings. In *Great Expectations*, clothing stands in for the various contingent aspects of a person—his property, wealth, or social privileges—that seem to become essential to him (to his personhood) even while depending, in actuality, on the specialized work of *other* persons: "My guardian then took me into his own room, and . . . informed me what arrangements had been made for me. . . . Also, I was told what my allowance was to be—it was a very liberal one—*and* had handed to me from one of my guardian's drawers the cards of certain tradesmen with whom I was to deal for all kinds of clothes, *and such other things* as I could in reason want" (194, emphasis added). Here we see both the actual and figurative clothing that wealth commands—the cards of tradesman who will make his hats, boots, and stockings are connected to Pip's new allowance *in general*, and the clothes that he can now purchase get included among "such other things as I could in reason want." To have "all kinds of" clothes requires, of course, all kinds of tradesmen, and each tradesman is reduced to his specialized function within this social production, just as he is here represented by a simple card handed to the protagonist.

Behind each "separate tenant," in *Sketches by Boz*, is a "numerous family," and behind each tradesman—and each article of clothing that Pip buys—are other people who are necessary to this social production. The clearest example of this in *Great Expectations* is one of its more memorable minor characters, "Trabb's boy," whose diminutive appellation obviously defines him by his trade, and, more specifically, by his subordinated position *within* a trade. (After all, he is merely a boy *to* "Trabb," who is himself reduced to his professional name). The narrative later comically acknowledges the inadequacy of this moniker, when Trabb's boy helps rescue Pip during his climactic conflict with Orlick: "Trabb's boy—Trabb's overgrown young man now—went before us with a lantern" (441). We don't actually get the *real* name of Trabb's boy here, but we do find out that the still nameless character no longer fits into, is in fact too large for, the diminutive appellation under which the novel has placed him. (Here Trabb's status in the *story*—we might suddenly picture a "young man" who has grown bigger—gets cunningly intertwined with his space in the *discourse*, which the newly helpful character has likewise outgrown.)

The restriction of this unnamed (and yet strangely overnamed) character to the truncated identification of "Trabb's boy" fits precisely into the character's social and narrative position within *Great Expectations*. Trabb's boy comes into the novel just as Pip's new social status requires a widened range of labor to clothe him; and his entire, so comically *specialized*, existence in the novel revolves around his resentment toward Pip, who used to be his equal and now commands his subordinated functionality. Mr. Trabb's suddenly obsequious behavior toward Pip is thus followed by the abrupt introduction of Trabb's boy into the novel:

> "My dear sir," said Mr. Trabb, as he respectfully bent his body, opened his arms, and took the liberty of touching me on the outside of each elbow, "don't hurt me by mentioning that. May I venture to congratulate you? Would you do me the favour of stepping into the shop?"
>
> Mr. Trabb's boy was the most audacious boy in all that countryside. When I had entered he was sweeping the shop, and he had sweetened his labours by sweeping over me. He was still sweeping when I came out into the shop with Mr. Trabb, and he knocked the broom against all possible corners and obstacles, to express (as I understood it) equality with any blacksmith, alive or dead.
>
> "Hold that noise," said Mr. Trabb, with the greatest sternness, "or I'll knock your head off! Do me the favor to be seated sir. Now this . . . is a very sweet article. I can recommend it for your purpose, sir, because it really is extra super. But you shall see some others. Give me Number Four, you!" (To the boy, and with a dreadfully severe stare: foreseeing the danger of that miscreant's brushing me with it, or making some other sign of familiarity). (177)

This emergence of Trabb's boy aptly demonstrates how a minor character can get introduced into a novel at a specific and specifically significant moment within the narrative development: a moment that will then shape both his configuration and his position within the novel as a whole. The tension between the protagonist's social elevation in the first paragraph and Trabb's boy's social subordination in the second is further developed when each of Trabb's respectful gestures toward Pip the gentleman is matched by a command toward his "boy," who acts as a go-between to fetch the clothes that Trabb sells. "Hold that noise!" Trabb yells, uncannily echoing the very first command shouted at the young Pip (by the convict), and the silencing of Trabb's boy is inseparable from his labor, as a necessary, but strictly subordinated, "adjunct" to the production of a gentleman's clothes. Trabb's boy stands in, in this sense, for *all* the anonymous labor that rests behind one gentleman's clothes:

> So, Mr. Trabb measured and calculated me, in the parlour, and gave himself such a world of trouble that I felt that no suit of clothes could possibly remunerate him for his pains. When he had at last done and had appointed to send the articles to Mr. Pumblechook's on the Thursday evening, he said, with his hand upon the parlour lock, "I know, sir, that London gentlemen cannot be expected to patronise local work, as a rule; but if you would give me a turn now and then in the quality of a townsman, I should greatly esteem it. Good morning, sir, much obliged.—Door!"
> The last word was flung at the boy, who had not the least notion what it meant.

The opening of the door, to let the gentleman out of the shop where he has bought the clothes, is here emblematized as an essential "unit" of labor, a discrete action, summoned by a single "flung" word. But this single command suggests all the surplus activity that surrounds exchange and implicates ever more people in the gentleman's world. Trabb's boy doesn't actually make or sell the clothes in this scene but is involved only in the peripheral work that rests behind the production of clothes, just as multiple trades are necessary to clothing a single gentleman; or the ostler, chambermaid, and waiter rest behind the cup of tea.[12]

Interpreting the Character-System: Signification, Position, Structure

The previous analysis of Trabb's boy has edged back into the thematic: we've grasped at the economy of *Great Expectations* through a kind of critical swoop-and-dive that extracts a single minor character who, as a tailor's assistant, can illustrate the novel's symbolic use of clothing. But the significance that we derive through Trabb's boy must be understood in relation to the totality which not only radically delimits but in an important sense constitutes his achieved character-space. We have already looked at the specific way that Mr. Pumblechook (as well as the unnamed tailor's assistant) enters into the character-system in volume 1. Just as Pumblechook's aggression and distortion are initially associated, in the *story* itself, with a group of other secondary characters (Wopsle, Hubble), so his conspicuous character-space emerges only as one of a group of character-*spaces* that "swarm" into the narrative discourse in volume 1. Throughout *Great Expectations* there is a surplus of minorness. To read the narrative we must attempt to track the significance of the *many* varied characters through whom Pip's story is woven. The excessive meaning of any particular character tends to lead into or out toward the entrance of another character. Minorness, in this sense, always seems to elicit more minorness; the young Pip is surrounded, as we've seen, on all sides.

Pumblechook (as well as Trabb's boy) both contributes to, and emerges within, the larger character-system that organizes all these different figures around the protagonist's bewildered consciousness. As much as any nineteenth-century novel, *Great Expectations* prompts us to actively coordinate the significance and impact of numerous minor characters. The inflection of any particular character into a narrative might be usefully approached in the form of a riddle: Why does this character need to make an appearance, and why does he or she appear at this point, and in this way? We need to distinguish between the kind of reading that pauses at this question—in order to open up the dynamic relationship between a character's implied personhood, his position as it (necessarily) emerges in relation to many other characters, his descriptive configuration, and the thematic and semantic constructions into which he is absorbed—and one that moves immediately to obtain interpretive value out of the subordinated character, simply deriving the *significance* of this character for the novel as a whole.

Of course, there are different, quite productive ways that we *can* wrest such interpretive value out of the character-field. Perhaps most commonly, the arrangement of characters within a narrative structure facilitates psychological, aesthetic, thematic, or ideological interpretations. Thus the character-field is often translated into a psychological matrix, where various tendencies, inclinations or fears of the protagonist are presented in an exaggerated form through minor characters—and often contained or devalorized.[13] (As we will see, this mapping of character-system is particularly suitable to *Great Expectations*.) Alternatively, the arrangement of characters can be read in terms of competing aesthetic or generic registers, as when, for example, a potential literary tendency of a novel itself (toward the gothic, the comic, a more politically subversive story) is inscribed through a subordinate figure.[14] Perhaps most pervasively, the organization of secondary characters helps build a novel's thematic architecture. Contrasts between characters illustrate larger conceptual or philosophical conflicts—divergent characters become the perennial two "sides" that constitute the single thematic coin.[15] Finally, the arrangement of characters can be read in relation to competing ideologies or, more intricately, as itself an ideological construct.[16]

But even as a character-system can be read to derive any of these (or other) kinds of interpretation, such signification itself relies on certain common processes: the shifting distribution of attention that structures each individual character-space; the tension between the character as implied person and the character as symbolic or textual element; the more or less asymmetric opposition between the one and the many; the distortion, exaggeration, functionalization, effacement, abstraction, or caricature that often accompanies minorness. These underlying (but so often instrumentalized) processes don't necessarily shut down other possible interpretations of the character-system but, on the contrary, can be productively integrated *back into* psychological, aesthetic, thematic, and ideological readings. This study is therefore centered on narratives that transformatively reiterate the formal problematics of character-space and character-system within the story itself. *Pride and Prejudice*, for example, both employs narrative asymmetry in constructing its intricate and radically original character-system and continually reflects *on* asymmetry in its own fictional world.

Similarly, returning to our interpretation of Trabb's boy, there is a correlation between the referenced and thematized social economy that underlies the newly made gentleman and the asymmetric arrangement of character-spaces within the narrative economy itself. Trabb's boy suggests a structure in which labor is both integrated into the attributes that constitute the gentleman's wealth, and escapes him, hovering outside (whether in the aggressive movements of the assistant or the obsequious measurements of the tailor himself). Likewise, on the level of discourse, minor characters (in their functionality and fragmentation) are both integrated into and exceed the protagonist's achieved centrality (and the wealth of attributes that might flow from this centrality). Such a convergence of story and discourse helps explain Trabb's boy's appeal—his memorable and comic aggression (spurred by his subordinated functionality) must be understood on the level of character-*space* and not merely character.

This tension between integration and excess strikes at a central dynamic of the minor character more generally—a dynamic that is particularly well illustrated in Dickens's novel. As with many narratives, the entire character-system of *Great Expectations* can be interpreted as an ever more elaborate and achieved representation of the protagonist's subjectivity. The first-person narrative structure continually leads us back to Pip's interiority, and it is no surprise that *Great Expectations* has generated some of the best psychological and psychoanalytic character-criticism on Dickens. In these readings, every scene seems to reflect on, and point us back toward, Pip's conscious or unconscious drives.[17] When we organize the character-system in relationship to Pip's consciousness, minor characters can play a functional role within Pip's psychological development or be cast as symbolic and thematic reiterations of his psychological conflicts. There is ample use of minor characters both functionally and symbolically in *Great Expectations*: as foils and as projections.[18]

However, as we have seen, Pip's own psychological condition revolves around the way he is overwhelmed *by* all the characters who surround him.

And in *Great Expectations*, the continuous absorption of secondary characters into a thematic or functional relationship to the protagonist does not negate the way that the same characters also stand as potential, if submerged, forces of narrative interest and agency, bearing upon and cast in relation to Pip's *centrality* rather than his interior personality. The often manifest subordination of minor characters in a novel does not compel a static character-field locked into place around the dominant perspective; as the Russian formalist Yuri Tynianov has argued, the very "sensation of [literary] form" itself might inhere in the dynamic interaction *between* the "dominant" and the subordinated elements that it both generates and becomes embedded within. Tynianov writes:

> The unity of the work is not a closed, *symmetrical* intactness, but an *unfolding, dynamic integrity....* Dynamic form is not generated by means of combination or merger (the often-used concept of "correspondence"), but by means of interaction, and, consequently, the pushing forward of one group of factors at the expense of another. In so doing, the advanced factor deforms the subordinate ones. The sensation of form is always the sensation of the flow (and consequently of the alteration) of correlation between the subordinating, constructive factor and the subordinated factors. It is not obligatory to introduce a temporal nuance into the concept of flow, or "unfolding." Flow and dynamics may be taken as such, outside of time, as pure movement. (33, emphasis added)

Tynianov's distillation of the dynamic, synchronic tension between dominant and subordinate elements offers a definition of literary form which suggestively accommodates the interaction between protagonist and minor character that this study is tracing. In particular it casts light on how *Great Expectations* consciously develops the tension between minor characters as symbolic elaborations of or psychological foils for the protagonist's interiority *and* as competing centers of interest and agency that radically contextualize the protagonist (if only through the affective force generated *in* their subordination).

This divide is powerfully illustrated in the configuration of Magwitch within the total character-system. We have noted how both Trabb's boy's and Pumblechook's personalities are inextricably connected *to* their minorness—and how both minorness and personality emerge out of the larger, dynamically elaborated character-system in volume 1. The novel's first chapters also introduce Magwitch, who, more than either of these two, is implicated into the essential structure of the asymmetric character-system. As Peter Brooks notes, in his influential structural analysis of *Great Expectations*, "Pip's experience of and with Magwitch [is] to be the central energy of the text" (*Reading for the Plot*, 137). Brooks's reading offers a strong version of the psychologized character-system, one that pays unusually close attention to the structural nature of characterization in the novel. The totality of the character-system, in this reading, is anchored to the psychological conflict at its center, a conflict that by necessity attaches to the novel's own central character. But Magwitch's disruptive force—

so central, as Brooks argues, to the text's structural energies—is keenly linked to his minorness. Magwitch's forceful presence impinges on the narrative center, even while he is clearly placed at the margin, as a social outcast, and as a figure who quickly disappears from the narrative. In this sense, Magwitch is torn between two narrative dimensions that potentially inhere within any minor character. As an implied person, Magwitch hovers outside or at the margins of the fictional world: first appearing furtively at the outskirts of Pip's village (and in nameless, distorted guise), Magwitch then gets literally exiled to the farthest reach of the British Empire (while vanishing entirely in the narrative discourse). But when cast in relation to Pip's own psychological conflicts, Magwitch is quickly absorbed into the symbolic center of the narrative. In other words, Magwitch is both outside society (with a marginal position in the socionarrative formation of the character-system) and *inside* Pip (getting absorbed into the center of the narrative's symbolic architecture).[19]

Magwitch is such a key minor character because his profound effect on Pip unfolds in direct relation to his configured marginality. As the character-system develops between Magwitch's disappearance from the text and his return at the climax of volume 2, the narrative elaborates the tension between Pip's psychological and social relationships to subordinate characters. In the original disruptive excess of Magwitch, the convict both serves as a symbolic aspect of Pip's own interiority and stands radically outside the protagonist's ambit. The rest of the novel hinges on the convict's return, as it disrupts the intentional focus of Pip's consciousness: his union with Estella. In the conflict between the return of Magwitch and Pip's pursuit of Estella, we see a structured elaboration of the tension between the psychological functionality and the social positionality of minor characters. Pip wants to establish a psychological connection to Estella, but their relationship ends up being elaborately mediated through a social chain, so that Pip and Estella are ultimately brought together only through the intervention of Wemmick, Jaggers, Molly, Compeyson, and Magwitch. The narrative starts to develop two distinct kinds of character-space that organize these two subplots and which come into conflict with each other through the return of Magwitch. While one narrative plane presents multiple characters in contiguous (metonymic) relationship with one another, a second narrative plane organizes minor characters in symbolic (metaphoric) relationship to the protagonist.

Metaphor, Metonymy, and Characterization

The distinction and interaction between metaphor and metonymy as two kinds of literary and linguistic figuration has an important place in twentieth-century literary theory.[20] I want to try to reconfigure these terms in relation to what we have been discussing as a foundational tension within the character-system:

the interplay between the structured *position* and the thematic *significance* of any character within the narrative totality. Subordinate characters are particularly likely to get squeezed into a presentation that takes on symbolic or psychological significance; my study insists that we incorporate *the way* that they are squeezed into the meaning that we extract from them.[21] (Once again, without denying the multifarious thematic, ideological, aesthetic, or psychological consequences of the character-system, we need to focus on a certain grid of circumstances through which all of these various arrangements occur.) *Great Expectations* highlights the split between metaphor and metonymy that is implicit within the character-system as signifying field. The first-person narrative structure again allows for a brilliant "inside" depiction of omniscience itself: Pip's struggle to make sense of the world—as an overwhelmed, vulnerable child—dramatizes the effort that omniscient narrative makes to knit together its component parts.[22] This struggle revolves, above all, around the tension between the (metonymic) positionality and the (metaphoric) significance of minor characters, as they respectively confirm or challenge the protagonist's centrality.

The narrative positionality of a minor character—his or her literal and delimited placement within a larger narrative structure—is itself thematized and symbolized within the story of *Great Expectations*. If, as we've seen, narrative position helps build thematic implication, Dickens chooses symbolic images that represent the very nature of narrative (and social) positionality itself. Chief among these symbols is a network of contiguous associations—chain, iron, file, leg, hand, finger—that come to thematically signify contiguity itself. This chain of associated images (of chains) is rooted in the dynamics of subordination and distortion that begins with Magwitch's excessive role and takes form through the total construction of the asymmetrical character-system. When Pip first sees Magwitch, he describes him as "[a] fearful man, all in coarse grey, with a great iron on his leg" (36). The manacled leg orients Pip's observation, so that Pip notes how "he limped towards the low church walls" and was "like a man whose legs were numbed and stiff" (38). The leg and manacle also exert a hold on Pip's consciousness when he returns home: "I thought I heard the voice outside, of the man with the iron on his leg" (44); "I tried it with the load upon my leg (and that made me think afresh of the man with the load on *his* leg)" (45); "I was in mortal terror of my interlocutor with the ironed leg" (46). When he leaves home again to give Magwitch the file, Pip focuses once more on the convict's leg, now joined to the iron and thus radically detached *from* the full person: "But he was down on the rank wet grass, filing at his iron like a madman, and not minding me or minding his own leg, which had an old chafe upon it and was bloody, but which he handled as roughly as if it had no more feeling in it than the file" (52). The separation of Magwitch's leg from his body, the proximity of the leg to the iron and the file, and the homologous shape of the leg and the file begin a metonymic chain that will structure the novel's character-system. The metonymic plane makes a series of connections between characters based on actual physical contiguity and represents individual characters through a fragmented body part (synecdoche). The leg-iron-and-file are metonymic objects par excellence, since, beside their overdetermined proximity, their actual *function* is to form and break chains.

In chapter 10, Pip goes to the Jolly Bargeman and encounters a stranger, and his perception of this new minor character relies on a series of metonymic configurations:

> He was a secret-looking man whom I had never seen before. His head was all on one side, and one of his eyes was half shut up, as if he were taking aim at something with an invisible gun. He had a pipe in his mouth, and he took it out, and, after slowly blowing all his smoke away and looking hard at me all the time, nodded. (103)

> The strange man . . . nodded at me again when I had taken my seat, and then rubbed his leg—in a very odd way, as it struck me. (104)

> [T]hen he made his shot, and a most extraordinary shot it was.
> It was not a verbal remark, but a proceeding in dumb show, and was pointedly addressed to me. He stirred his rum-and-water pointedly at me, and he tasted his rum-and-water pointedly at me. And he stirred it and he tasted it: not with a spoon that was brought to him, but *with a file*. (106)

Again, this detached device exerts a hold on Pip's consciousness, so that at night, "I was haunted by the file too. A dread possessed me that when I least expected it, the file would reappear . . . in my sleep I saw the file coming at me, out of a door, without seeing who held it, and I screamed myself awake" (108). The reappearance of the file is now linked to the other metonymy in the description of the stranger: "His head was all on one side, and one of his eyes was half shut up." This image of the dislocated head recurs when another stranger appears at the Jolly Bargeman, and, through a process particular to metonymic association, now brings with it new contiguous associations:

> Then, and not sooner, I became aware of a strange gentleman leaning over the back of the settle opposite me, looking on. There was an expression of contempt on his face, and he bit the side of a great forefinger as he watched the group of faces. (160)

> He stood with his head on one side and himself on one side, in a bullying interrogative manner, and he threw his forefinger at Mr. Wopsle—as it were to mark him out—before biting it again. (161)

> [H]e still could not get rid of a certain air of bullying suspicion; and even now he occasionally shut his eyes and threw his finger at me. (166)

Jaggers has his "head on one side," just as Magwitch's friend's "head was all on one side." He shuts his eyes and throws his finger at Pip, as the convict had "one of his eyes . . . half shut up, as if he were taking aim at something." And now the finger, which Jaggers continually bites and points throughout the scene, occupies the same spatial position as the file. However, the finger also motivates a new association through its contiguity with Jaggers's hands, which are further embedded within the metonymic chain through their previous association with Jaggers's head, when Pip first sees him in Miss Havisham's house: "He was a burly man of an exceedingly dark complexion, with an exceedingly large head and a corresponding large hand" (111). This hand, of course, becomes a key image for the novel as a whole; and, more generally, "hand" or "hands" are mentioned over 450 times in *Great Expectations*, an average of almost once a page. As such they are the end point of the novel's metonymic logic, the most common way in which narrative attention is deflected from an entire person to an exterior aspect of the person.[23]

The interconnection of Magwitch, his friend, and Jaggers is established through an exemplary metonymic chain of images, which goes something like this:

> **a.** Magwitch's leg—
> **b.** the iron and the file—
> **c.** the file reappearing—
> **d.** the stranger's leg—
> **e.** the stranger's one eye—
> **f.** the stranger's head on one side—
> **g.** Jaggers's head on one side—
> **h.** Jaggers's one finger—
> **i.** Jaggers's large hand.

The binding together of Magwitch, his friend, and Jaggers is one of the most elaborate figurations *of* a character-system in the nineteenth-century novel: everywhere we look, the discursive relationship between (mutually constituting) subordinate character-spaces is inscribed within the story itself. In other words, this chain of associations physicalizes (and thematizes) the experience of tracking and connecting an excess of characters—an experience that is central to our comprehension of nineteenth-century novels. Such tracking relies on both connection (the different ways we link or bind these characters to one another) and dissociation (as each character, through the force of Dickensian metonymy, is reduced to a state of fragmented exteriority, the implied person represented merely through a leg, a file, and a chain; or a file, an eye, and a head; or a finger, a large hand, and a large head). Thus minor characters are simultaneously torn away (from their own full selves) and bound up (to other social fragments).

The exteriority of these minor characters is also linked to their strong affective pull, which, of course, flows into the narrative's general affective structure: the way our attention is compelled by those characters who are at the periphery. Both Jaggers's and the stranger's exterior configurations are thus motivated by their externality within the story itself, as both men are introduced—much like Wickham and Collins in *Pride and Prejudice*—as mysterious outsiders. However, while in *Pride and Prejudice* this externality contributes to the minor characters' *subordination* within the novelistic totality, the externality of Jaggers and the mysterious stranger heightens their affective importance. Jaggers's compelling space as a character is thus part of the larger, systematic configuration of Pip's weakness as a central protagonist who is always overwhelmed by what is exterior to him. An imbalanced narrative totality, an asymmetrically organized field of fictional human beings, results, finally, in specific descriptive patterns, in the orientation of the novel's *language* toward metonymic construction.

Jaggers's affective presence is dramatically represented during his interrogation of Mr. Wopsle at the Jolly Bargeman, when he first enters the novel. This pivotal scene, a comic high point in the novel, hinges on the connection between Jaggers's eccentricity (itself linked to his position as a stranger who encroaches, simultaneously, on the small village and the undeveloped plot) and his affective force. The interrogation of Mr. Wopsle holds the reader's attention through its exemplary metonymic structure—the pattern of question-and-answer leads us to anticipate each of Mr. Wopsle's protestations and each of Mr. Jaggers's grim rejoinders, which are often literally linked through a repeated word or phrase. The scene handily illustrates Roman Jakobson's famous identification of prose with forward-driving metonymic structure. As Victor Erlich writes, " 'Verse,' wrote Jakobson, 'rests upon association by similarity; the rhythmical affinity of individual lines is an indispensable prerequisite for our perception of verse. The rhythmical parallelism is further strengthened whenever it is accompanied by the sense of similarity on the level of imagery.' Not so prose narrative. Here the motive force is not similarity, but association by contiguity, which lies at the core of metonymy. 'As the narrative unfolds, its focus shifts from an object to its neighbor (in terms of physical space—time or causality, that is). Consequently,' Jakobson concluded, 'for verse the line of least resistance is metaphor; for artistic prose, metonymy' " (231). In the interrogation scene, this rhetorical pattern is intertwined with the images we have been examining, as descriptions of Jaggers's fingers, hands, and head are woven into the dialogue. The passage below, which begins the scene, emphasizes these anatomical details, the repeated phrases that link Jaggers's questions and Wopsle's replies (thus moving the narrative forward, from a phrase to "its neighbor"), and the references to Jaggers as a stranger:

> Then, and not sooner, I became aware of *a strange gentleman* leaning over the back of the settle opposite me, looking on. There was an expression of contempt on his face, and *he bit the side of a great forefinger* as he watched the group of faces.
>
> "Well!" said *the stranger* to Mr. Wopsle, when the reading was done, "You have settled it all to your own satisfaction, I have no doubt?"

Everybody started and looked up, as if it were the murderer. He looked at every-body coldly and sarcastically.

"*Guilty*, of course?" said he. "Out with it. Come!"

"Sir," returned Mr. Wopsle, "without having the honour of your acquaintance, I do say *Guilty*." Upon this, we all took courage to unite in a confirmatory murmur.

"*I know you do*," said the stranger; "*I knew you would. I told you so. But now I'll ask you a question. Do you know, or do you not know*, that the law of England supposes every man to be innocent, until he is proved—proved—to be *guilty*?"

"Sir," Mr. Wopsle began to reply, "as an Englishman myself, I—"

"Come!" said *the stranger, biting his forefinger* at him. "Don't evade the question. *Either you know it, or you don't know it*. Which is it to be?"

He stood with *his head on one side* and himself on one side, in a bullying interroga-tive manner, and he *threw his forefinger* at Mr. Wopsle—as it were to mark him out—before biting it again.

"Now!" said he. "*Do you know it, or don't you know it?*"

"*Certainly I know it*," replied Mr. Wopsle.

"*Certainly you know it*. Then why didn't you say so at first? Now, I'll ask you another question. . . ." (161, emphases added)

Aptly illustrating the way these different narrative registers function together, this scene demonstrates how the character-system's metonymic drive is linked to, and intertwined with, more strictly verbal structures.

If the convict, the first stranger, and Mr. Jaggers provoke this kind of met-onymic association in Pip, and in the narrative structure itself, a different kind of association has also been developing. Analysis of *Great Expectations*'s char-acter-system needs to take close account of Miss Havisham, who, whatever quantitative space she occupies in the narrative, certainly has one of the most qualitatively distinctive positions. Miss Havisham also enters the text through this surplus of minorness: as the excessive significance of individual minor characters (such as Pumblechook and Magwitch) seems to motivate the arrival of still more minor characters who, in turn, create even a greater surplus of "unfixed" significance. In his seminal, thematically driven explication of *Great Expectations*, J. Hillis Miller draws an interesting parallel between Miss Havis-ham and Magwitch, as the most important of "several characters in *Great Expectations*" who "try to 'make' other characters in their own image" (255). This interpretation is quite convincing, but the parallel between the two charac-ters should not overshadow the unique, highly charged narrative *space* that Miss Havisham occupies, which makes it difficult to draw strong connections between her and other characters (especially, as we will see, Magwitch). In other words, as is often the case, a *thematic* parallel between Magwitch and Miss Havisham is complicated by the specific configuration of Miss Havis-ham's character-space (and Magwitch's) within the novel as a whole.

Miss Havisham is perhaps the novel's most imaginative figure, a character whose eccentric configuration exceeds whatever thematic interpretive frame we scramble to erect around her. When Pip visits Satis House, Miss Havisham's "strangeness" is, in fact, the controlling aspect of his observation, which begins: "In an arm-chair, with an elbow resting on the table and her head leaning on that hand, sat the strangest lady I have ever seen, or shall ever see" (87). If Miss Havisham's strangeness exemplifies the narrative's imagination, Pip's encounter with Satis House—an encounter that changes his life—is depicted in no uncertain terms as the sudden explosion of imagination into the story itself. This defamiliarization is soon more concretely described:

> I saw that everything within my view which ought to be white, had been white long ago, and had lost its lustre, and was faded and yellow. I saw that the bride within the bridal dress had withered *like the dress*, and *like the flowers*, and had no brightness left but the brightness of her sunken eyes. . . . Once, I had been taken to see some ghastly waxwork at the Fair, representing I know not what impossible personage lying in state. Once, I had been taken to one of our old marsh churches to see a skeleton in the ashes of a rich dress, that had been dug out of a vault under the church pavement. Now, waxwork and skeleton seemed to have dark eyes that moved and looked at me. (87, emphasis added)

Here the chain of associations—between the dress and the flowers, the old woman, and the waxwork and skeleton—is constructed not through physical proximity but through a seme that is abstracted from them all: faded youth. The skeleton, like the waxwork, "represents" the person who once lived; while the "bride" does not really resemble the "bridal dress" or the flowers, but only shares the same connotative significance. Miller's thematization of Miss Havisham seems premature, since what is going on in this scene is the very birth of the "thematic" within Pip's consciousness, the sudden ability to see an external object not in-and-of-itself but as "a subject of artistic representation, an implicit or recurrent idea, a motif" (*American Heritage Dictionary*, s.v. "theme").[24] In Satis House, physical objects are metaphors, designed to signify not through their physical contiguity but through the similarity of their connotations. But the translation of an object into an abstraction is precisely the kind of activity, inhering within figuration, that takes on heightened significance in relation to literary characters.

Satis House catalyzes Pip's own mode of metaphoric apprehension, and the text soon begins to generate typical, romantic metaphors: "She seemed much older than I, of course, being a girl, and beautiful and self-possessed; and she was as scornful of me *as if* she had been one-and-twenty, and a queen. . . . But she answered at last, and her light came along the dark passage *like* a star. . . . She put the mug down on the stones of the yard, and gave me the bread and meat without looking at me, as insolently *as if* I were a dog in disgrace" (86, 89, 92, emphases added). The representation of people in terms of other physical objects (like a queen, like a star, like a dog) is matched by Pip's growing ability to read signification into the physical landscape, and, particularly, to see everything as a symbol of Estella's presence:

> But she seemed to be everywhere. For, when I yielded to the temptation presented by the casks, and began to walk on them, I saw her walking on them at the end of the yard of casks. She had her back towards me, and held her pretty brown hair spread out in her two hands, and never looked round, and passed out of my view directly. So, in the brewery itself—by which I mean the large paved lofty place in which they used to make the beer, and where the brewing utensils still were. When I first went into it, and, rather oppressed by its gloom, stood near the door looking about me, I saw her pass along the extinguished fires, and ascend some light iron stairs, and go out by a gallery high overhead, as if she were going out into the sky. (93)

Pip then goes on to locate a specific change in his own processes of apprehension, discovering a new ability to project so much signification onto the landscape as to literally, if only transiently, change it. He finds the process, in other words, of imagination: "It was in this place, and at this moment, that a strange thing happened to my fancy. I thought it a strange thing then, and I thought it a stranger thing long afterwards. I turned my eyes—a little dimmed by looking up at the frosty light—towards a great wooden beam in a low nook of the building near me on my right hand, and I saw a figure hanging there by the neck" (93–94).

We have come full circle, here, from the depiction of Pip encountering Miss Havisham as the "strangest lady" to the "strange thing" that Pip generates out of his own fancy. Miss Havisham's strangeness is, in fact, indissociable from the more specific process of metaphoric signification, an imaginative method that Pip carries with him when he leaves Satis House. This is reiterated in the next chapter, through the fanciful chain of events that Pip invents when he is asked about Satis House:

> "Now, boy! What was she a doing of, when you went in today?" asked Mr. Pumblechook.
>
> "She was sitting," I answered, "in a black velvet coach."
>
> Mr. Pumblechook and Mrs. Joe stared at one another—as they well might—and both repeated, "In a black velvet coach?"
>
> "Yes," said I. "And Miss Estella—that's her niece, I think—handed her in cake and wine at the coach-window, on a gold plate. And we all had cake and wine on gold plates. And I got up behind the coach to eat mine, because she told me to."
>
> "Was anybody else there?" asked Mr. Pumblechook.
>
> "Four dogs," said I.
>
> "Large or small?"
>
> "Immense," said I. "And they fought for veal cutlets out of a silver basket." (96–97)

The extravagance of Pip's answers ("Large or small?" "Immense") captures the sense of an imagination that is still generating itself, exploring the wonderful possibilities it has glimpsed in Satis House, where people can be transformed into stars, or queens, or waxwork, or hanging figures, or dogs.

At the same time, Pip's visit to Satis House provokes a radical reconceptualization of himself. " 'He calls the knaves, Jacks, this boy!' said Estella with disdain, before our first game was out. 'And what coarse hands he has! And what thick boots' " (90). Estella's criticism of Pip, which will haunt him for years to come, turns on the metaphoric significance of Pip's own hands and boots. These physical entities are abstracted into the adjectives tacked onto them, absorbed into the "coarseness" or "thickness" that they represent for Estella. Now the "hand" is configured not in relation to the rest of the body, or in contiguous relationship to something or somebody that it can grasp, but only in terms of its abstract, metaphoric import. By the chapter's end Pip is already repeating these judgments: "I set off on the four-mile walk to our forge; pondering, as I went along, on all I had seen, and deeply resolving that I was a common labouring-boy; that my hands were coarse; that my boots were thick; that I had fallen into a despicable habit of calling knaves Jacks; that I was much more ignorant that I had considered myself, and generally that I was in a low-lived bad way" (94). While this is in some ways a painful self-abnegation, there is also an extravagance to Pip's criticism, rooted in the protagonist's sheer ability to make such metaphoric claims, to conceptualize himself in abstract, albeit negative, terms. Thus Pip links his fanciful lies to Estella's criticism, explaining to Joe that "she had said I was common, and that I knew I was common, and that I wished I was not common, and that the lies had come out of it somehow, though I didn't know how" (99). The ability to abstractly conceptualize himself is also clearly connected to his desire for Estella, which, as in the original scene, is elaborated through the oversignification of the landscape:

> Whenever I watched the vessels standing out to sea with their white sails spread, I somehow thought of Miss Havisham and Estella; and whenever the light struck aslant, afar off, upon a cloud or sail or green hill-side or water-line, it was just the same.—Miss Havisham and Estella and the strange house and the strange life appeared to have something to do with everything that was picturesque.
>
> One Sunday . . . I lay on the earthwork for some time with my chin on my hand, descrying traces of Miss Havisham and Estella all over the prospect, in the sky and in the water. (137)

In this passage the protagonist externalizes his own interior consciousness; he swallows up what is physically around him, transforming it into an elaboration of what is inside him. His desire for Estella is essentially an outgrowth or symptom of this cognitive process: unity with Estella facilitates a more essential unity between mind and world, in which external reality will conform to the parameters of his own consciousness. As he describes Satis House later on:

> The candles that lighted that room of hers were placed in sconces on the wall. . . . As I looked round at them, and at the pale gloom they made, and at the stopped clock, and at the withered bridal dress upon the table and the ground, and at her own awful figure with its ghostly reflection thrown large by the fire upon the ceiling and the wall, *I saw in everything the construction that my mind had come to, repeated and thrown back at me.* (321, emphasis added)

Here the series of metaphoric correspondences between Miss Havisham's faded youth and the objects she has surrounded herself with, literalized as the "ghostly reflection" of shadow and light in the dimly illuminated room, manifests itself, finally, as the reflection of Pip's consciousness. Still later, when Pip tries to describe the intensity of his love to Estella, he reveals how this desire has always been an elaboration of the symbolizing process, which transforms the exterior into a reflection of one's own interiority:

> "You will get me out of your thoughts in a week."
> "Out of my thoughts! You are part of my existence, part of myself. You have been in every line I have ever read, since I first came here, the rough common boy whose poor heart you wounded even then. You have been in every prospect I have ever seen since—on the river, on the sails of the ships, on the marshes, in the clouds, in the light, in the darkness, in the wind, in the woods, in the sea, in the streets. You have been the embodiment of every graceful fancy that my mind has ever been acquainted with. (378)

In this way, *Great Expectations* inscribes and dramatically contextualizes the psychological dimension of its character-system, which, like Pip in these last passages, positions minor characters as the projective "embodiments" of Pip's fancy and continually directs us back to the "constructions" of the protagonist's mind.

Getting to London

In the previous section I have tried to show how both the metaphoric and metonymic drives of the novel are structured through and motivated by the larger character-system. By this I don't mean simply that we can decode these tropes in terms of persons or in relation to specific characteristics of persons. Such one-to-one translation is a common, perhaps necessary, element of literary analysis and tends to be a two-way street. (If Rodolphe is characterized *by* outsized symbols of masculinity in *Madame Bovary*, he also is used *to* represent a certain kind of masculinity within a larger thematic field: who can say which form of signification comes first or second?) But such analysis still places the process *of* encoding and decoding as prior to, and outside the ambit of, the configuration of character. I want to suggest, on the contrary, that these very laws of figuration (how the text substitutes a figure *for* a person or for the characteristic of a person) are motivated by, and take on significance in relation to, the character-field. A strictly linguistic or figurative analysis of *Great Expectations* cannot fully explain the elaboration of and intersection between its metaphoric and metonymic drives. The syntax of figuration itself is animated by and derives out of the character-system, which is constituted by the unfolding of multiple and colliding character-spaces, each of which gains a specific figurative charge. The confrontation with the implied person, and the novel's dynamic elaboration of many persons within the narrative structure, have deep ramifications for the arrangement of images (all those depictions of misalignment), themes (the elaborated motif of chains), even of words (the repetitions that drive Jaggers's interrogation of Wopsle).[25]

The character-system does not compel us merely to connect a variety of individuals but to concatenate the narrative's varied ways *of* characterizing individuals. In particular, *Great Expectations* explores and dramatizes two essential, conflicting dimensions of the minor character: as symbol, subordinated and thematically instrumentalized in relation to the dominant protagonist, and as a competing center of narrative interest, defined by his social positionality. In *Great Expectations*, the metonymic distortion that underlies so much of Dickensian characterization—and generates the relentless combination of fragmentation and repetition that we examined in chapter 2—is dramatically set against Pip's countertendency of symbolic reduction, abstraction, and absorption. Attempting to elaborate the metaphoric faculties that have been awakened by Miss Havisham and then Estella, Pip confronts a series of minor characters in terms of their exteriority, starting with Magwitch, the mysterious stranger, and Jaggers. The flow of these minor characters to the center of *Great Expectations*—both on the descriptive, affective plane and in terms of the plot—takes place in opposition to Pip's attempts to organize the exterior world metaphorically. This opposition is crystallized in the contrast between Magwitch's and Estella's competing holds on Pip's (and the reader's) attention. The crux of the narrative is the triumph of Magwitch's hold over Estella's. The individuals are not as important as the structures of relationship that they imply. Pip does establish a connection to Estella, but not in terms of his own interiority (as in his imperative, "you cannot choose but remain part of my character" [378]). Instead, their relationship is elaborately mediated through an exterior chain of social associations that necessarily put Magwitch, and all that he represents, between Pip and Estella. In this sense, *Great Expectations* is a profoundly unromantic love story. The full development of this metonymic chain occurs in volume 2 and revolves around Pip's relationship to Jaggers and Wemmick. Not coincidentally, in the story itself, these characters are positioned at the hub of a social network that seems to include, by degrees of separation, the entire London underclass.

Jaggers's position in this social chain—which develops the field of metonymic associations that we analyzed in volume 1—is immediately emphasized at the start of volume 2, when Pip first arrives in London. Before Pip meets *directly* with Jaggers, the powerful lawyer is connected to the coachman, who warily refuses to overcharge Pip: " 'I don't want to get into trouble. I know *him!*' He darkly closed an eye at Mr. Jaggers's name, and shook his head" (188). The naming of Jaggers by this social intermediary (who is literally transporting Pip) seems to automatically elicit another winking eye and another shaking head. Pip's access to Mr. Jaggers is further disrupted as he enters the law offices and comes across two other figures.

> I went into the front office with my little portmanteau in my hand and asked, Was Mr. Jaggers at home?
>
> "He is not," returned the clerk. "He is in Court at present. Am I addressing Mr. Pip?"
>
> I signified that he was addressing Mr. Pip.
>
> "Mr. Jaggers left word would you wait in his room. He couldn't say how long he might be, having a case on. But it stands to reason, his time being valuable, that he won't be longer than he can help." With those words, the clerk opened a door, and ushered me into an inner chamber at the back. Here, we found a gentleman with one eye, in a velveteen suit and knee-breeches, who wiped his nose with his sleeve on being interrupted in the perusal of the newspaper.
>
> "Go and wait outside, Mike," said the clerk.
>
> I began to say that I hoped I was not interrupting—when the clerk shoved this gentleman out with as little ceremony as I ever saw used, and tossing his fur cap out after him, left me alone. (188)

Between Jaggers and Pip are "the clerk" and the disfigured one-eyed client who is "shoved . . . out" of the "inner chamber." Pip's encounter with Jaggers cannot take place directly because of the social structure; it cannot even be triangulated. The minor minor character, typically Dickensian in his distortion, is thus crucial to the scene. Pip emphasizes the rude treatment of this individual, and Wemmick's unceremonious dismissal of Mike might remind us of Dickens's thematization of "moving on" in *Bleak House* and "Podsnappery" in *Our Mutual Friend*. Such dismissiveness is reiterated when Jaggers returns and pushes away more people hovering around his office: "First he took the two men . . . waving his hand at them to put them behind him. . . . 'And now *you!*' said Mr. Jaggers, suddenly stopping, and turning on the two women with the shawls. . . . 'Say another word—one single word—and Wemmick shall give you your money back' " (190–91). While Mike occupies a specific position in the configuration of Pip's mediated encounter with Jaggers in his office, he is also assimilated to the larger representation of stragglers outside of Jaggers's office, here once again pushed away through Wemmick's intercession.

The obstacles (i.e., *persons*) that render Pip's encounter with Jaggers so indirect at the opening of volume 2 are embedded within a larger socionarrative structure, as Jaggers's office itself works as a buffer between Pip and the source of his expectations. In the opening scene, Jaggers's law office literally generates personnel to take Pip to his "destination":

> He said it was not worth while, I was so near my destination; Wemmick should walk round with me, if I pleased.
> I then found that Wemmick was the clerk in the next room. Another clerk was rung down from up-stairs to take his place while he was out, and I accompanied him into the street, shaking hands with the guardian. (194)

The inessential detail here, "another clerk was rung down from up-stairs to take his place while he was out," subtly bridges story and discourse, connecting Wemmick's actantial narrative function (à la Greimas), as the mediator or helper bringing Pip to a projected "destination," to the *social* chain that requires another clerk to step in and take up Wemmick's subordinate role in Jaggers's office (even as Pip's arrival in the waiting room has forced Mike out).

Walking Pip to his "destination," Wemmick again emphasizes the nature of London as a social and spatial field (a field that mirrors the spatial organization of the character-system that is unfolding simultaneously):

> "Is it a very wicked place?" I asked, more for the sake of saying something than for information.
> "You may get cheated, robbed, and murdered, in London. But there are plenty of people anywhere, who'll do that for you."
> "If there is bad blood between you and them," said I, to soften it off a little.
> "Oh! I don't know about bad blood," returned Mr. Wemmick; "there's not much bad blood about. They'll do it, if there's anything to be got by it."
> "That makes it worse."
> "You think so?" returned Mr. Wemmick. "Much about the same, I should say."(195–96)

Pip's comments attempt to subsume this new, intimidating urban space under metaphoric categories (a "wicked place," "bad blood"), while Wemmick punctures these abstractions with blunt, literal comments. Crucially, the syntax of his statement—"[b]ut there are plenty of people anywhere, who'll do that for you"—verges on attributing crime in London to the sheer fact *of* social multiplicity. The plentifulness of people, implied here as the material ground for social disorder, amplifies (and indeed thematizes) the multiplicity that is already embedded into the narrative progression: the clients hovering outside Jaggers's office; the one-eyed man who is "shoved out" of Jaggers's inner chamber; the clerks who come between Pip and his lawyer. In all cases the new urban space that Pip has entered is depicted as overcrowded, and thus inevitably hinging on the incomplete social mediation of people who are reduced to their function, value, or disruptiveness.[26]

Wemmick himself, of course, is also locked into a functional, mediating position, leaving the scene when he has delivered Pip to his destination (as the coachman has already delivered him to Jaggers's office):

> "You don't want me anymore?"
>
> "No, thank you," I said.
>
> "As I keep the cash," Mr. Wemmick observed, "we shall most likely meet pretty often. Good day." (197)

It is this delimited socio*narrative* position within a larger network (remember that the "destination" is not merely physical but also narrative—functioning as part of the trajectory that will lead the protagonist to his donor), not just Wemmick's referenced status as a clerk, that underlies this minor character's famously distorted physiognomy. Wemmick's physical configuration is, of course, highly metonymic, emphasizing and growing out of the clerk's functionalized place within a large and interconnected social field (ultimately generated by that "plentifulness" of people within London as a whole):

> Casting my eyes on Mr. Wemmick as we went along, to see what he was like in the light of day, I found him to be a dry man, rather short in stature, with a square wooden face, whose expression seemed to have been imperfectly chipped out with a dull-edged chisel. There were some marks on it that might have been dimples, if the material had been softer and the instrument finer, but which, as it was, were only dints. (195)

> He wore his hat on the back of his head, and looked straight before him: walking in a self-contained way as if there were nothing in the streets to claim his attention. His mouth was such a post-office of a mouth that he had a mechanical appearance of smiling. We had got to the top of Holborn Hill before I knew that it was merely a mechanical appearance, and that he was not smiling at all. (196)

I will discuss Wemmick's crucial position in the character-system below, but for now we can note how the two similes—the expression that "seemed to have been . . . chipped out with a dull-edged chisel" and the "post-office of a mouth"—both stress a physical process (with a "chisel" that reminds us of that other tool, the iron file) and physical resemblance. They also both emphasize the fragmented surface of Wemmick's being: flattened out and, like one of Schiller's stunted growths, constricted to a "mechanical appearance."

Dickens organizes the entire scene—Pip's introduction to London—in widening rings that unfold out of the metonymic configuration of exteriority already developed in the provinces. Volume 2 continues to transform the distorted, physical images that organize volume 1 into this more achieved representation of a mediated social network. In Pip's next visit to the law offices, the narrative begins by emphasizing Jaggers's affective pull, again linked to that metonymic configuration motivated by his radical exteriority:

"More than that, eh!" retorted Mr. Jaggers, lying in wait for me, with his hands in his pockets, his head on one side, and his eyes on the wall behind me; "how much more?" . . . This strongly marked way of doing business made a strongly marked impression on me, and that not of an agreeable kind. Mr. Jaggers never laughed; but he wore great bright creaking boots, and, in poising himself on these boots, with his large head bent down and his eyebrows joined together, awaiting an answer, he sometimes caused his boots to creak, as if *they* laughed in a dry and suspicious way. (221)

Once more the structure of mediation is emphasized: " 'Wemmick!' said Mr. Jaggers, opening his office door. 'Take Mr. Pip's written order, and pay him twenty pounds.' " As we have noted, Jaggers is *himself* merely an intermediary between Pip and his secret donor, while Wemmick, called in only to intercede between Jaggers and Pip, leads Pip through other clerks in the office. "In the front first floor, a clerk who looked something between a publican and a rat-catcher—a large pale puffed swollen man—was attentively engaged with three or four people of shabby appearance, whom he treated as unceremoniously as everybody seemed to be treated who contributed to Mr. Jaggers's coffers. 'Getting evidence together,' said Mr. Wemmick, as we came out, 'for the Bailey' " (222). The description pushes in two directions: toward both discrete caricature ("a large pale puffed swollen man") and opaque imprecision ("three *or* four people of shabby appearance"). In this visit to Little Britain, then, the link between Pip and his anonymous donor incrementally expands, as more and more people come between him and the benefactor he still assumes to be Miss Havisham.

1. Pip—donor (Miss Havisham)
2. Pip—Jaggers—donor
3. Pip—Wemmick—Jaggers—donor (" 'Wemmick!', said Jaggers, opening his office door")
4. Pip—"a large pale puffed swollen man" / "three or four people of shabby appearance . . . who contributed to Jaggers's coffers"—Wemmick—Jaggers—donor.

Both the intermediaries within Jaggers's office and Jaggers's own position as intermediary between Pip and the donor are further emphasized in a later scene from volume 2, as we can observe in a series of passages when Pip comes into control of his finances:

I received an official note from Wemmick, informing me that Mr. Jaggers would be glad if I would call upon him at five in the afternoon of the auspicious day. (305)

In the outer office Wemmick offered me his congratulations . . . and motioned me with a nod into my guardian's room. (305)

I looked about me, but there appeared to be now no possible escape from the inquiry, "Have—I—anything to receive, sir?" On that Mr. Jaggers said, triumphantly, "I thought we should come to it!" and called to Wemmick to give him that piece of paper. Wemmick appeared, handed it in, and disappeared. (306)

"Now take this piece of paper in your hand. You have got it? Very good. Now, unfold it and tell me what it is." (306)

"Now, that handsome sum of money, Pip, is your own. . . . That is to say, you will now take your money affairs entirely into your own hands, and you will draw from Wemmick one hundred and twenty-five pounds per quarter, until you are in communication with the fountain-head, and no longer with the mere agent. As I told you before, I am the mere agent. I execute my instructions, and I am paid for doing so." (307)

But he insisted on walking home with me, in order that I might make no extra preparation for him, and first he had a letter or two to write, and (of course) had his hands to wash. So, I said I would go into the outer office and talk to Wemmick. (309)

The social chain is here narrativized on three intertwined registers. First, Pip gets shuttled from the "outer" office with Wemmick to Jaggers's "inner" office and then back to the "outer" office with Wemmick. These rooms spatialize the mediated social relations that the law firm relies on. However, Pip does not establish a direct connection with Jaggers even when he does find himself in the interior office, in the middle of this sequence. Instead Wemmick is called in by Jaggers to act as a sort of gratuitous intermediary, delivering the financial papers to Jaggers, who in turn gives them to Pip. Jaggers's insistence on bringing in Wemmick, only to dismiss him, incorporates the very extreme delimitation *of* Wemmick ("he appeared, handed it in, and disappeared") into the communication between lawyer and client. Finally, in this communication itself, Jaggers describes a scenario to Pip in which a "fountain-head" communicates with the "mere agent" (Jaggers) who communicates with his own agent (Wemmick), who makes the actual quarterly disbursements to Pip.

Three Narrative Workers and the Dispersion of Labor in *Great Expectations*

"A bit of a poacher, a bit of a labourer, a bit of a waggoner, a bit of a haymaker, a bit of a hawker, a bit of most things that don't pay and lead to trouble, I got to be a man."
—*Great Expectations*, 361

Now, in groping my way down the black staircase I fell over something, and that something was a man.
—*Great Expectations*, 342

[W]hen is a man not a man?
—James Joyce, *Finnegans Wake*

Wemmick as Helper (the Functional Minor Character)

Imagine a Hall of Fame for minor characters—ranging from Pylades to Lucky and Pozzo, with a handful of Mercutios and Fridays in between—where fictional creations were suddenly plucked from their relative obscurity within the dramas and narratives that they enchant.[27] The egregiously divided George Wemmick would certainly have a distinguished place; Dickens's unforgettable clerk is in many ways the emblematic minor character of the nineteenth-century novel. Clearly a secondary *adjuvant*, Wemmick also strikes many readers as profoundly important to the novel. As one critic comments, "*Great Expectations* would be unimaginable without him" (Sell, 186). This brief comment, however, suggests two possible interpretations, which go to the heart of Wemmick's divided identity. Would the novel be impossible to conceive without Wemmick because of the functions that he performs within it (in other words, because he is so deeply *integrated into* the narrative totality), or, on the contrary, because of the way that he remains freestanding and memorable in-and-of-himself?

Wemmick, like Charlotte Lucas in *Pride and Prejudice*, is poised at the pinnacle of the text's character-system, encased in but not subsumed by his narrative function. While certain minor characters are more clearly central to the two novels (Lydia and Wickham, Miss Havisham and Magwitch), Wemmick and Charlotte occupy that tantalizing, intermediate position between discrete representation and functional distortion: not fully reducible to their integrated position within the total narrative structure, but unimaginable outside of it. (The two share this tension even though Charlotte Lucas is at the realistic extreme of minor characters while Wemmick is at the most parodic, fanciful pole.) Wemmick (like Charlotte) thus condenses a problem that structures the interpretation of character in the novel more generally: the double necessity of delimiting minor characters to their functional position in relation to other points in the text (organized around the protagonist) and of reading them as independent, freestanding personages. Or more simply put, the way readers inevitably encounter characters both as they are embedded in the text and as they escape from it.

Needless to say, this *discursive* division, which Wemmick exemplifies by his highly functional position within the narrative, is elaborated through his famously divided character, with his Little Britain self and his Walworth self, his "moat" and "castle," his post-office mouth and aged P. Dickens thus represents the utility of the "narrative helper" in its symptomatic fullness, making Wemmick's individual character indissociable from his structural position and function within the character-system. When we think carefully about Wemmick's function, it leads toward his specific character; and when we contemplate his character, as a fictional human being, we see how it is anchored (functionally) in the larger character-system. Wemmick's narrative help, like Charlotte's, occurs on a wide range of narrative registers. We have already seen him as a "plot-helper," as an instrumental link in the metonymic chain that ties Pip to his "donor" and "destination." Wemmick's depiction in this chain emphasizes his constricted functionality (through such terse, directed phrases as "Wemmick appeared, handed it in, and disappeared"), and this functionality, embodied in his clerkship, motivates the mechanistic "flattening" of his character, the typical highlighting of an eccentric physical gesture that is then repeated whenever he appears:

> His mouth was such a post-office of a mouth that he had a mechanical appearance of smiling. (196)

> Wemmick was at his desk, lunching—and crunching—on a dry hard biscuit; pieces of which he threw from time to time into his slip of a mouth, as if he were posting them. (221)

> By degrees, Wemmick got dryer and harder as we went along, and his mouth tightened into a post-office once again. (232)

> Wemmick tightened his post-office and shook his head, as if his opinion were dead against any fatal weakness of that sort. . . . I could have posted a newspaper in his mouth, he made it so wide after saying this. (309–10)

Dickens has thus found the perfect discursive equivalent for the type of flattening that stems from his depiction of the division of labor, so that Wemmick's Schilleresque self-division, his hardened, caricatured exteriority, and his actantial position as a narrative helper are intertwined and mutually reinforcing.

But Wemmick also becomes a psychological helper to Pip, increasingly acting as a friend or confidant who, by providing hidden information and offering speculative insights, allows Pip to reconstruct the past interactions and relationships of Magwitch, Molly, Compeyson, Miss Havisham, and Estella. Most specifically, he warns Pip to stay home because he is being followed by Compeyson's henchman, helps hide Magwitch and orchestrate the escape attempt, and gives Pip important information about Jaggers's past relationship with Molly. In these actions (mostly in volume 3) Wemmick acts more like a confidant than a functional plot-helper; both the private nature of the information Pip is seeking and the mode of their conversation emphasize how Wemmick facilitates Pip's own increasing self-awareness. Wemmick even occasionally becomes (like Charlotte) a sounding board, so that Pip, ostensibly receiving information, can actually work through what he already knows by saying it to somebody else:

> But I told him, after a little meditation over the fire, that I would like to ask him a question, subject to his answering or not answering, as he deemed right, and sure that his course would be right . . . he nodded once to me, to put my question.

"You have heard of a man of bad character, whose true name is Compeyson?"
He answered with one other nod.
"Is he living?"
One other nod.
"Is he in London?"
He gave me one other nod, compressed the post-office exceedingly, gave me one
last nod, and went on with his breakfast. (383–84)

When Wemmick gives Pip such information, he continually emphasizes a more
intimate side of his personality, saying, for instance, as he tells Pip about Magwitch's endangered position, "we are in our private and personal capacities"
(382) and "I have probably done the most I can do, but if I can ever do more—
from a Walworth point-of-view, and in a strictly private capacity—I shall be
glad to do it" (386). These passages suggest that the shift from plot functionality to psychological help follows the shift from Wemmick's hardened, caricatured personality to his more rounded, Walworth self. However, Wemmick
can offer this help not because he transcends his Little Britain personality but
precisely because of his self-division. Every piece of information that he gives
Pip in his Walworth capacity he has been able to obtain only in his Little
Britain, post-office-mouth capacity, so, to use the same example, he notes
about his knowledge of Magwitch and Compeyson, "I accidentally heard, yesterday morning, being in a certain place where I once took you . . ." (382).
Rather than moving beyond this division, Pip relies on Wemmick's alienation;
once again, we see how Wemmick's individually configured character is perfectly integrated into the overall narrative structure.

This helps explain how the novel provokes strong empathy toward and appreciation of Wemmick without diluting our recognition of his essentially
stunted and distorted personality. As James Phelan astutely notes, "Although
Wemmick is more successful than Pip in living in both spheres, the very division of his personality indicates that his solution is less than ideal" (127).
Wemmick's division is certainly represented quite differently from Charlotte
Lucas's, but Austen's minor character is also marked by a similar division, in
this case between her personal desire and the economic imperative to marry
Collins. Most importantly, Charlotte's self-division is similarly integrated into,
and inseparable from, her narrative position as a subordinate helper. By elaborating Wemmick's narrative division through the celebrated figure of the bureaucrat divided between his constricted, dehumanizing labor and his sealed-
off and protected home life, Dickens ingeniously integrates the tension of the
character-system into the social tensions depicted in the *histoire.* If *Great Expectations* is unimaginable without Wemmick, we should also remember that
Wemmick is unimaginable outside of *Great Expectations*'s character-system,
and, more specifically, outside of his *minorness.* Only this minorness deepens
and sustains the wonderful and haunting self-division that Dickens observes,

a self-division that makes Wemmick an emblem of both Dickensian representation and nineteenth-century character-space. With Wemmick, as with many minor characters, less is more.

Magwitch's Return (the Marginal Minor Character)

Magwitch's return is the defining event of the novel, and much of the novel's power derives from the way this dramatic episode encapsulates and substantializes one of Dickens's underlying narrative tendencies: making more of minor characters. Magwitch's return occurs at the end of volume 2 and is conditioned by, and elaborates, the metonymic structure I have been tracing. When he announces himself to Pip, Magwitch thus immediately collapses the mediating chain that has been elaborately constructed throughout the volume:

> "Put it," he resumed, "as the employer of that lawyer whose name begun with a J., and might be Jaggers—put it as he had come over sea to Portsmouth, and had landed there, and had wanted to come on to you. 'However, you have found me out,' you says just now. Well! However did I find you out? Why, I wrote from Portsmouth to a person in London, for particulars of your address. That person's name? Why, Wemmick." (336–37)

Pip is, once again, overwhelmed, and his shock is directly reminiscent of the affective overwhelming of the protagonist that structured volume 1:

> I could not have spoken one word, though it had been to save my life. I stood, with a hand on the chair-back and a hand on my breast, where I seemed to be suffocating—I stood so, looking wildly at him, until I grasped at the chair, when the room began to surge and turn. He caught me, drew me to the sofa, put me up against the cushions, and bent on one knee before me: bringing the face that I now well remembered, and that I shuddered at, very near to mine. (337)

By making the climax of the novel Pip's confrontation with Magwitch, Dickens once again de-emphasizes the putatively central marriage plot. We have already seen how the metonymic and metaphoric planes of characterization vie for narrative centrality, and at various points in volume 2 Pip more explicitly describes a conflict between his interest in Estella and his interactions with Jaggers and Wemmick. His chance encounter with Wemmick, which is firmly situated in the metonymic chain, thus prompts this strong contrast: "While my mind was thus engaged, I thought of the beautiful young Estella, proud and refined, coming towards me, and I thought with absolute abhorrence of the contrast between the jail and her. I wished that Wemmick had not met me, or that I had not yielded to him and gone with him, so that, of all days in the year on this day, I might not have had Newgate in my breath and on my clothes. I beat the prison dust off my feet as I sauntered to and fro" (284). Earlier in volume 2, when Jaggers unexpectedly appears at Satis House while Pip visits, he stresses how Jaggers's *physical proximity* is discomforting:

> What I suffered from, was the incompatibility between his cold presence and my feelings towards Estella. It was not that I knew I could never bear to speak to him about her, that I knew I could never bear to hear him creak his boots at her, that I knew I could never bear to see him wash his hands of her; it was, that my admiration should be within a foot or two of him—it was that my feelings should be in the same place with him,—*that*, was the agonizing circumstance. (264)

This is more than a simple conflict between two people: Pip contrasts his interior "feelings towards Estella" with Jaggers's simple presence, so that his discomfort revolves around the tension between the two modes of apprehension we have been examining. This is reiterated when Pip emphasizes his unhappiness "that my *feelings* should be in the same *place* with him," as though he is forced to see his feelings as positioned, rather than as purely interior, through Jaggers's compelling presence.

In the climax of the conflict between the two plots, the narrative more overtly depicts the tension between Magwitch's and Estella's relative centrality to Pip, not simply as two distinct narrative threads, but rather as two separate narrative registers: "theme" and "event." The chapter right before Magwitch returns is thus framed by these two, linked passages:

> A great *event* in my life, the turning point in my life, now opens on my view. But, before I proceed to narrate it, and before I pass on to all the changes it involved, I must give one chapter to Estella. It is not too much to give to the *theme* that so long filled my heart.

> And now that I have given the one chapter to the *theme* that so filled my heart, and so often made it ache and ache again, I pass on, unhindered, to the *event* that had impended over me longer yet; the event that had begun to be prepared for, before I knew that the world held Estella, and in the days when her baby intelligence was receiving its first distortions from Miss Havisham's wasting hands. (318, 330, emphases added)

Just as Pip's visit to Miss Havisham's marks the explosion of the thematic into the novel—through the process of metaphorically transmogrifying exterior reality into the substantial reflection of interior sentiment—so Pip now labels his entire relationship with Estella a "theme," while defining his interaction with Magwitch as an "event." The distinction is crucial to the entire organization of the novel, and to its self-conscious reflection on the divided nature of literary characterization. If the previous passage contrasted Pip's "feelings" with Jaggers's "position," the subordinated "theme" is here associated with feelings, metaphors, and interiority, while the dominant "event" is necessarily exterior, taking place outside of Pip, and thus intersubjective. The description of the encounter—of Magwitch "bringing the face that I now well remembered, and that I shuddered at, very near to mine"—emphasizes this intersubjective structure.[28] Pip does not confront here an externalized version of that aspect of his interiority which he has repressed, but rather the very fact of exteriority itself, irreducible to symbolization.

However, the status of the "event" as exterior and intersubjective, in contrast to the "theme," is elaborated not primarily through the local description of Magwitch's face and hands in this return scene but in the essential status of his return in relation to the narrative as a whole. Descriptive details are (once again) generated by the larger structure of minorness, and by Magwitch's marginal position in the discourse (disappearing from the narrative while manifesting his influence through other detached agents) and in the story (as a fringe member of society, a criminal who is literally exiled). Thus Magwitch emphasizes the distance he has traveled: "many a thousand mile of stormy water off from this" (335); "I've been sea-tossed and sea-washed, months and months" (339).

At the same time, this distance elaborates Magwitch's exteriority in a specific sense: in narrative terms, Magwitch is not simply exterior to Pip but fundamentally minor, both subordinated within the novel's totality and crucial to its plot and thematic architecture. The link between Magwitch's important function and his marginal narrative position develops the tension that has already been elaborated through Wemmick's self-division. There is an inverse relationship between Magwitch's minorness and his plot function: he moves to the center of the text in receding away from it. This narrative process reflects a specific social relationship. As Magwitch says in the next paragraph, "I lived rough, that you should live smooth; I worked hard, that you should be above work." Magwitch's exteriority is motivated by his social marginality, and if this marginality is generally depicted as criminality, this passage, as well as the narrative structure as a whole, reveals it as, more fundamentally, modern *labor*: which is to say, the production of wealth through the same process that fragments and marginalizes the worker in relation to what he produces. Thus Pip's preface to the climactic scene continues:

> I pass on, unhindered, to the event that had impended over me longer yet. . . . In the Eastern story, the heavy slab that was to fall on the bed of state in the flush of conquest was slowly wrought out of the quarry, the tunnel for the rope to hold it in its place was slowly carried through the leagues of rock, the slab was slowly raised and fitted in the roof, the rope was rove to it and slowly taken through the miles of hollow to the great iron ring. *All being made ready with much labour*, and the hour come, the sultan was aroused in the dead of the night, and the sharpened axe that was to sever the rope from the great iron ring was put into his hand, and he struck with it, and the rope parted and rushed away, and the ceiling fell. So in my case; all the work, *near and afar*, that tended to the end, had been accomplished; and in an instant the blow

was struck, and the roof of my stronghold dropped upon me. (330, emphases added)

This extended analogy alludes directly to Magwitch's distant work and indirectly to the entire series of circumstances that form a complicated web around Pip's life. Here we see, underneath the fairy tale, a hidden story of labor—a story that, perhaps, must be hidden because labor itself is constituted, most essentially, by the very way that it *is* hidden. Pip lives in a world where "the work, near and afar, was already done," and where the "blow" occurs as the subject—the narrating protagonist—is forced to recognize himself in-and-through this work of others, as a product of this work.

Pip's own stronghold—his own achieved sense of self—is built through a social chain to which he doesn't have full access. As Pip writes, "the roof of my stronghold dropped upon me," but this collapse of his stronghold, of his self-sufficiency, is implicated in the chain of labor that leads up to the collapse: the heavy slab that was wrought, the tunnel that was dug, and so forth. Here we have a gulf between work and product, between the concentrated result and the dispersed activity that lies behind this result. We can't fully absorb the work that has gone into the product, just as we can't fully absorb the affective force of minor characters who, certainly in *Great Expectations*, have produced the central protagonist.

The narrative integrates Magwitch's labor into his minorness, or, in other words, gives this labor a specific narrative and social form. In the *discours*, Magwitch's early impact on Pip is indissociable from his disappearance from the text. Similarly, in the *histoire*, Magwitch literally disappears to a work colony where he produces the wealth that undergirds Pip's social mobility. Magwitch, like *Jane Eyre*'s Bertha Mason, is a triumph of characterization within an asymmetric narrative system, fully realizing the Victorian novel's rich and complicated development of minorness. The novel thus powerfully connects Magwitch's production of Pip's wealth with his own disappearance from the text in a way that harks back again to Marx's notion of contingency: "The more the worker produces the less he has to consume, the more values he creates the more valueless and worthless he becomes, the more formed the product the more deformed the worker."

One of the key insights of *Great Expectations* is its strong association of criminality with labor, its insistent effort to understand Magwitch's social deviancy in class terms. While Magwitch is not strictly a worker, he comes into life as the residue of what the structure of capitalist labor produces.

"This is the way it was, that when I was a ragged little creetur as much to be pitied as ever I see (not that I looked in the glass, for there warn't many insides of furnished houses known to me), I got the name of being hardened. 'This is a terrible hardened one,' they says to prison wisitors, picking out me." (361)

"Tramping, begging, thieving, working sometimes when I could—though that warn't as often as you may think, till you put the question whether you would ha' been over-ready to give me work yourselves—a bit of a poacher, a bit of a labourer, a bit of a waggoner, a bit of a haymaker, a bit of a hawker, a bit of most things that don't pay and lead to trouble, I got to be a man." (361)

These passages might remind us of the more insistent interconnections that a text like Orwell's *Down and Out in Paris and London* draws among petty thieving, tramping, temporary jobs, and working-class life. Moreover, this connection between criminality and labor is elaborated in the novel's discursive structure, as Magwitch's minorness is linked to both marginalization and utility. The criminal who is expelled from the narrative system (and Pip's village) at the beginning of volume 1, Magwitch returns as the *worker* who has built up Pip's fortune (and the narrative plot) at the end of volume 2. Both "hardened" and fragmented ("a bit of . . . a bit of . . . a bit of"), the double elaboration of Magwitch's minorness also reiterates the essential poetics of Dickens's caricature, which connects hardened repetition with fragmented eccentricity.[29]

The key scene in the story, and the crux of the narrative structure, is Magwitch's return, and this return functions symbolically as the return of the estranged worker to claim the wealth that he has produced. Magwitch's return links the worker (and minor character) to his labor, and this is expressed symbolically through the guilty relationship of the upwardly mobile gentleman (and protagonist) to the criminal element from which he has attempted to distinguish himself. The dramatic centrality of this return scene resides not simply in the spectacle of social interconnection but in the interconnection of a radically stratified social network. As Pip says, "It has almost made me mad to sit here of a night and see him before me, *so bound up* with my fortunes and misfortunes, *and yet so unknown to me*" (358, emphases added). In this line we approach the paradoxical crux of minorness: how do you represent the terribly asymmetrical contingency of social interconnection, or, in different terms, fully depict the effacement of human personality into labor?

Of course, Dickens's novels increasingly revolve around the structure of social interconnection, and the three late omniscient masterpieces all build interconnected plot edifices and overtly thematize this interconnection:

What connexion can there be, between the place in Lincolnshire, the house in town, the Mercury in powder, and the whereabout of Jo the outlaw with the broom, who had that distant ray of light upon him when he swept the churchyard-step? What connexion can there have been between many people in the innumerable histories of this world, who, from opposite sides of great gulfs, have, nevertheless, been very curiously brought together! (*Bleak House*, 272)

Thus, like the tides on which it had been borne to the knowledge of men, the Harmon Murder—as it came to be popularly called—went up and down, and ebbed and flowed, now in the town, now in the country, now among palaces, now among hovels, now among lords and ladies and gentlefolks, now among labourers and hammerers and ballast-heavers, until at last, after a long interval of slack water it got out to sea and drifted away. (*Our Mutual Friend*, 74)

"Yet," looking fully upon her, "you may be sure that there are men and women already on their road, who have their business to do with you, and who will do it. Of a certainty they will do it. They may be coming hundreds, thousands of miles over the sea there; they may be close at hand now; they may be coming, for anything you know or anything you can do to prevent it, from the vilest sweepings of this very town." (*Little Dorrit*, 64)

One tendency of these passages is to render social interconnection as static and symmetrical; and sometimes in Dickens's novels social interconnection undergirds thematic interconnection, a stable and closed semantic field. However, Dickens also often accentuates the radically asymmetrical nature of interconnection, the paradoxical way that people can be "so bound up with my fortunes . . . and yet so unknown to me." It is not simply that a large network of people are mutually implicated, but that this relationship results in the dispersion, fragmentation, marginalization, disappearance, and expulsion of many of these persons. It is harder, of course, to erect a traditionally thematic edifice over such a metonymic field. While one passage creates a series of paratactic equivalences between "palaces" and "hovels," and "gentlefolks" and "laborers," another passage shows how this network is implicated in a process of distanciation: the physical distance, "[from] hundreds, thousands of miles over the sea," that is quickly transformed into *social* distance, "from the vilest sweepings of this very town." Physical distance becomes, at bottom, the symbolic representation of social distance, or, more specifically, the social stratification that accompanies the division of labor. We have seen how Magwitch's distance from Pip is related to his hidden production of Pip's wealth, as is made explicit in this passage: " 'I've been a sheep-farmer, stock-breeder, other trades besides, away in the new world,' said he, '*many a thousand mile of stormy water off from this*' " (335, emphasis added). As Magwitch is positioned "many a thousand mile" away while plying these different trades that ultimately prop up Pip as a gentleman, Pip refers to the labor "near and afar" in the short "Eastern story" that encapsulates the essential narrative structure of *Great Expectations* itself.

We all depend on labor near and afar, on work that we don't have access to, that's invisible or, more problematically, partially visible. As Pip says to Herbert, as he gets more entangled in the mysterious source of his wealth, "how dependent and uncertain I feel, and how exposed to hundreds of chances" (269). In the return of Magwitch, Pip glimpses the unthinkable presence of hidden labor, the way his life is implicated with so many others, in these complicated social chains. "All the truth of my position came flashing on me" (336). Dickens's structure amplifies and gives form to this moment: to the "flash" or the "blow" in which the protagonist, as it were, momentarily perceives the minorness on which his centrality rests. The "truth of [his] position" must come only as a flash, since the position itself would begin to dissolve if such awareness of minor characters was to be sustained.

Earlier, in a crucial passage of the novel, Joe bids farewell to Pip across both spatial and class lines:

> "Pip, dear old chap, life is made of ever so many partings welded together, as I may say, and one man's a blacksmith, and one's a whitesmith, and one's a goldsmith, and one's a coppersmith. Diwisions among such must come, and must be met as they come. If there's been any fault at all to-day, it's mine. You and me is not two figures to be together in London. . . ."
>
> The fashion of his dress could no more come in its way when he spoke those words, than it could come in its way in Heaven. He touched me gently on the forehead, and went out. As soon as I could recover myself, I hurried out after him and looked for him in the neighbouring streets; but he was gone. (246–47)

Joe plays exquisitely with two radically different senses of "parting"—two senses that the novel suggests are ultimately interrelated: parting as leave-taking and parting as *division*, and, specifically, that hardened division of labor which separates individuals into specialized functions that are socially stratified and disconnected. In the flow of Joe's metaphor these two senses almost inconspicuously merge into each other, but there is a forceful intelligence behind that shift from "life is made of ever so many partings welded together" to "and one man's a blacksmith, and one's a whitesmith." Suddenly a painful, personal leave-taking comes to resemble nothing less than the very structure that holds together—*and separates*—society. It's so difficult to grasp society in this way, as at once radically whole—"welded together"—and constituted through fragmentation. "As soon as I could recover myself, I . . . looked for him in the neighbouring streets; but he was gone."

The rich structure of this novel's character-system—with so many memorable minor characters who somehow coexist within a dense and tightly organized narrative structure—is nothing less than "partings welded together": both in the sense that the narrative encompasses all of these heterogeneous *parts* into a narrative whole (as in Aristotle's notion of formal unity) and as the novel demonstrates how a *parting*—an absence or leave-taking—always lies *underneath the part*. For as we have seen, the minor character in taking a role (or playing a part) in the narrative (whether as helper, opposer, double, foil, projection, etc.) is not fully incorporated, in his own rich selfhood, into the narrative but rather must both *depart from* the narrative (as Joe literally leaves Pip's neighborhood in this scene and as all minor characters take leave of a novel) and come *apart in* the narrative (as in Wemmick's self-division or the escaped prisoner who needs to clasp "himself as if to hold himself together"). Joe's vernacular analogy—which finds its rhetorical material in the very social specialization that it conceptualizes—provides, in fact, a shorthand theory of minor characters, who in becoming parts within a great whole also enact endless varieties of parting. At the same time, this statement of Joe's—that life is nothing other than "partings welded together"—encapsulates the essential social structure that emerges in the shift from Pip's overwhelmed childhood to his precarious position as a London gentleman. The wealth of society is also composed not simply of many parts but many partings—work that is done but also lost, economic divisions and partitions that result in social effacement and the forceful estrangement of people from their productions. Joe's phrase sums up both alienation—as labor too often becomes a series of "partings" or self-separations—*and* the wealth that is extracted from this alienated work, which "welds together" multiple partings into a coherent, and now valuable, whole.

Orlick and Social Multiplicity (the Fragmented Minor Character)

By interpreting Magwitch's shocking return as the symbolic claims of alienated labor to be reconnected with the wealth it has produced, we situate his individual character, much as we have positioned Wemmick's individual character, in terms of the narrative as a whole. *Great Expectations* (like the realist novel in general) provokes us to do this, by unfurling the narrative within a complex, synchronic organization of domination and subordination. We have seen how Wemmick's famously divided self is organically connected with his divided narrative function, or his self-division as a narrative helper. This is elaborated by the way in which his participation in Pip's narrative progress depends on both sides of his split personality. Wemmick makes sense only *as* a minor character: as a functional agent within a larger narrative totality that compels our attention outside of his specific participation. Similarly, Magwitch becomes fully realized only through *his* minorness: as a *marginalized* agent within the larger narrative. But while these two characters occupy distinct modes of minorness within the narrative (and literally never meet), Wemmick's functionality and Magwitch's marginality are both aspects of the structured depiction of alienated labor, the comprehension of which organizes the metonymic field as a whole. This field dominates volume 2, which begins with Pip's arrival in London and at Jaggers's office and ends with Magwitch's return. If volume 1 details how Pip's fragile interiority is overwhelmed by incomplete modes of exteriority, volume 2 moves from a phenomenological to a social register, showing how Pip is inevitably caught in the middle of a larger social field defined by its radically asymmetric contingency. Society relies on distance: Wemmick helps Pip, but at the price of his own self-division; Magwitch builds Pip's fortune, but at the price of his own marginalization. Through his tightly controlled poetics of misalignment Dickens narratively dramatizes the crucial, demystifying statement by Magwitch: "I lived rough, that you should live smooth; I worked hard, that you should be above work."

If Magwitch's return is the "great event" of the novel, and embodies the narrative's essential social vision, how is this event, and this knowledge, developed in volume 3? Ironically, the more detailed representation of Magwitch's story risks collapsing the broader contours of the character-system: more, in this case, can be less. In chapter 42 we have the notable inclusion of Magwitch's own life history, told in his own words. This information begins to break apart the strong connection between *histoire* and *discours*: it reveals the extent of Magwitch's social minorness in the fictional universe, while making him a much rounder character in the narrative universe. The crucial connection between criminality and labor that gets detailed in Magwitch's narration disrupts the discursive elaboration of his minorness. The narrative risks becoming oversentimental, fictitiously transcending the real phenomenon of social stratification through an imaginary solution. The more inclusive representation of Magwitch suggests a general paradox of realist aesthetics: how do you fully represent social stratification, or structures of alienation and inequality that, insofar as they are grasped as totalized structures, are built in-and-through fragmentation and distortion? The poetics of distortion and imprecision arises through the same socio-epistemological aesthetics that leads to typification and detail—two foundations of realist narrative. The tension between these two tendencies is, in fact, the governing structure of volume 3, which continually elaborates a dialectical movement between assimilation and expulsion.

This movement is built into Pip's rapprochement with Magwitch, which is facilitated by both his actual relationship with his benefactor and his intellectual pursuit of knowledge about Magwitch's past. Pip's central discovery in volume 3—of the tangled interconnections among Compeyson, Magwitch, Molly, Miss Havisham, and Estella—functions in two contradictory ways. It massively disorders the narrative, by bringing in the fragmented lives of Molly and Compeyson, and it allows Pip to constitute a new, metaphoric order based on the opposition of Magwitch and Compeyson. The complicated past history of these characters is inevitably confusing; even after we have read the novel a number of times, and grasp the relations that Pip discovers, the *presentation* of these relations is fragmentary and disorientating. (We might reconstruct the back story but it is extremely difficult to reconstruct the order in which Pip *himself* slowly ties together the different evidentiary strands of the story.) Furthermore, Compeyson and Molly, as figures within the narrative, are distorted and presented imprecisely, so that Magwitch's minorness is, to a large extent, displaced onto them. Together they again embody the two main qualities of minorness that have been developed through the metonymic plane of characterization: the human figure defined as a fragmented synecdoche or in terms of exterior positionality. Molly has already been memorably, and forcibly, reduced to her hands.[30] And in volume 3, Compeyson begins to shadow Pip, hovering outside his range of perception. His exteriority is emphasized in the scene where Pip meets Mr. Wopsle after a performance:

> "I had a ridiculous fancy that he must be with you, Mr. Pip, till I saw that you were quite unconscious of him, sitting behind you there, like a ghost." . . . I cannot exaggerate the enhanced disquiet into which this conversation threw me, or the special and peculiar terror I felt at Compeyson's having been behind me. . . . I put such questions to Mr. Wopsle as, When did the man come in? He could not tell me that; he saw me, and over my shoulder he saw the man. (398–99)

This passage dramatizes the sheer fact of Compeyson's exteriority vis-à-vis Pip, summed up in the phrase "he saw me, and over my shoulder he saw the man." This exteriority is formally elaborated in Compeyson's shadowy position within the narrative as a whole: we never see him too clearly, and we learn about his relationship to Magwitch and Miss Havisham only indirectly. However, the radical spatial differentiation in this scene is counterbalanced by the text's insistence on creating a closed opposition between Magwitch and Compeyson. This tension is already anticipated in the opening chapters, by the way that Compeyson is depicted both as exterior to Magwitch and Pip and as locked in a symbolic and closed opposition with Magwitch.

Look at the first time Pip sees Compeyson:

> I thought he would be more glad if I came upon him with his breakfast, in that unexpected manner, so I went forward softly and touched him on the shoulder. He instantly jumped up, and it was not the same man, but another man!
>
> And yet this man was dressed in coarse grey, too, and had a great iron on his leg, and was lame, and hoarse, and cold, and was everything that the other man was; except that he had not the same face, and had a flat broad-brimmed low-crowned felt hat on. (49)

In this introduction, the novel immediately positions the two convicts in contradictory relationships: "it was not the same man, but another man" and "this man . . . was everything that the other man was." This is reiterated during the two passages that describe Magwitch's and Compeyson's fights, at the novel's beginning and end:

> Water was splashing, and mud was flying, and oaths were being sworn, and blows were being struck, when some more men went down into the ditch to help the sergeant, and dragged out, separately, my convict and the other one. Both were bleeding and panting and execrating and struggling; but of course I knew them both directly. (67)

> He added that he did not pretend to say what he might or might not have done to Compeyson, but, that in the moment of his laying his hand on his cloak to identify him, that villain had staggered up and staggered back, and they had both gone overboard together; when the sudden wrenching of him (Magwitch) out of our boat, and the endeavour of his captor to keep him in it, had capsized us. He told me in a whisper

that they had gone down, fiercely locked in each other's arms, and that there had been a struggle under water, and that he had disengaged himself, struck out, and swum away. (456)

Both of these passages draw a strong correspondence between the two men precisely so as to distinguish them. In the first passage, the two convicts' similarity ("[b]oth were bleeding and panting and execrating and struggling") leads immediately into Pip's recognition ("of course I knew them both directly"). In the second passage, Magwitch is able to "disengage himself" (and kill Compeyson) only as they go overboard "together" and become "fiercely locked in each other's arms." The parallels and the distinction between Compeyson and Magwitch are not in opposition but rather work together in contrast to the more radical differentiation of social exteriority.

However, Compeyson is an undeveloped minor character in *Great Expectations*: which isn't to say that he is not a "round" character, but, on the contrary, that his *minorness* isn't developed. Compeyson's metonymic configuration— either through local descriptions or through his positioning in relation to other characters—is usually static and metaphoric, except for the brilliant scene where he is depicted as lurking around Pip: "he saw me, and over my shoulder he saw the man." It is as though Dickens relies too heavily on the symbolic juxtaposition of Magwitch and Compeyson—which is so crucial to the novel's metaphoric stability—to develop the disruptive (positional) aspect of Compeyson's minorness. Instead, Magwitch's opponent becomes simply an archvillain, manipulating society from above, penetrating everywhere: a symbolic force rather than an actual person. But the social weight of Compeyson's position— as the bad disruptive criminal in juxtaposition with whom Magwitch's own fugitive subjectivity is assimilated into the narrative—is displaced onto Dolge Orlick, who finds his last career, after working for Joe, Miss Havisham, and Drummle, as Compeyson's henchman. Compeyson sets Orlick to work (as Jaggers sets Wemmick to work) mediating between himself and Pip, and this position is amplified by the overall construction of Orlick's position in the novel. Thus when Magwitch first arrives at Pip's house, he is trailed by another mysterious person, and Pip's encounter with Orlick in this passage is the pinnacle of the text's development of minorness:

> I was fain to go out to the adjacent Lodge and get the watchman there to come with his lantern. Now, in groping my way down the black staircase I fell over something, and that something was a man crouching in a corner.
> As the man made no answer when I asked him what he did there, but eluded my touch in silence, I ran to the Lodge and urged the watchman to come quickly: telling him of the incident on the way back. (342–43)

Like the representation of Compeyson hovering over Pip's shoulder, this scene positions a minor character as radically exterior to the focalizing protagonist.

But now this exteriority is more fully developed: Orlick becomes a "thing," a dehumanized object, and Pip's collision is an encounter with the very fact of dehumanization. This passage exemplifies and condenses the reversed flow of asymmetry that lies at the heart of Dickens's characterization. We turn other people into objects, society pushes people into the margin or "a corner," but then, far from watching them disappear as they do in Jane Austen's narrative universe, we collide with the now distorted forms; "groping" through our own troubled lives, we "fall over something" and realize, finally, that the "something" is in fact "a man." However, the force of this passage derives from its position in the narrative totality. Volume 3 has just begun, and Pip has just arrived at the decision "to take precautions to ensure (so far as I could) the safety of my visitor" (342). In other words, the mechanism of assimilation is just getting underway when Pip immediately runs into Orlick, balancing the narrative's integration of Magwitch with a countervailing instance of exclusion. Thus his conversation with the watchman:

> "I don't call to mind another since about eleven o'clock, when a stranger asked for you."
>
> "My uncle," I muttered. "Yes."
>
> "You saw him, sir?"
>
> "Yes. Oh yes."
>
> "Likewise the person with him?"
>
> "Person with him!" I repeated.
>
> "I judged the person to be with him," returned the watchman. "The person stopped, when he stopped to make inquiry of me, and the person took this way when he took this way."
>
> "What sort of person?"
>
> The watchman had not particularly noticed; he should say a working person to the best of his belief, he had a dust-coloured kind of clothes on, under a dark coat. The watchman made more light of the matter than I did, and naturally; not having my reason for attaching weight to it. (343–44)

No sooner does Pip try to convert the "stranger" into his "uncle" than *another* figure is produced, even more radically exterior than Magwitch had been, and described simply as a "working person." The scene gains additional resonance because this new figure turns out to be Orlick, a character whom the novel, well before volume 3, has been carefully positioning within the totality of the character-system.

In *Pride and Prejudice*, Catherine as the "fifth" sister, the many servants, and other minor minor characters form the final ring of the character-system, structuring the more central conflict between Elizabeth's increasingly profound interiority and the increasingly fragmented and superficial exteriority of the other characters. The same use of minor minor characters occurs in *Great Ex-*

pectations: our already stratified apprehension of such discrepant character-spaces as Miss Havisham, Jaggers and Wemmick, Magwitch, and Mr. Pumblechook is elaborated through much more clearly secondary characters. As in *Pride and Prejudice*, these "tertiary" characters motivate the essential structure of asymmetry. Catherine is more clearly situated in a strictly metonymic position than Lydia, Mary, or Wickham, whose metonymic subordination can be overshadowed by their thematic and metaphoric significance. Similarly, Wemmick's and Magwitch's thematic significance is grounded in their narrative subordination, but the thematic configuration of the characters is so compelling in itself that we can decontextualize them, interpreting them only on the semantic plane that we extrapolate from the narrative. Almost as a corrective against this tendency, volume 3 elevates the importance of Dolge Orlick, who, more than any other character, confirms the links between exteriority, (narrative) subordination, and alienated functionality. Thus while Orlick can certainly be interpreted on a psychological or metaphoric register—as a symbolic externalization of certain unconscious tendencies within the protagonist—it is difficult to interpret him solely on that register, because the specific mode of his appearance in the novel is so particular. If Magwitch is depicted as a tramp—"They both led tramping lives, and this woman . . . had been married . . . to a tramping man" (405)—Orlick literally tramps through the narrative, suddenly popping up and then quickly disappearing, a narrative nomad with no fixed place. Orlick, in fact, is a compelling paradigm of this kind of vanishing character: a character who prompts us, perhaps in frustration, to chase after his significance, only to realize that his significance is largely constituted in this chase itself.

Crucially, Orlick occupies a specific point in the figurative chain made of those contiguous associations between Magwitch's leg, file, and iron, which, as we have examined, are integrated into—and stand as an emblem *for*—the larger metonymic character-chain. Just as the character-system produces fragmentation (or "partings") even as it welds itself together, so the novel's figurative chain is fractured—as the murder of Mrs. Gargery takes place in the space that opens up through the broken iron: "And on the ground beside her, when Joe picked her up, was a convict's leg-iron which had been filed asunder" (148). Much later, Orlick repeats the same fractured image, referring to "the leg-iron wot Old Orlick had picked up, filed asunder . . . and wot he kept by him till he dropped your sister with it" (439). The significance of this fractured image is elaborated when Pip immediately assimilates it *to* the character-system: "For I believed one of two other persons to have become possessed of it, and to have turned it to this cruel account. Either Orlick, or the strange man who had shown me the file" (148). As the broken leg iron fragments the narrative's figurative chain, so Orlick (in his alienation) fragments the chain of contiguous associations that organizes the novel's character-system. Once again, the novel's rigorous metonymic trajectory is subsumed in its structure of characterization. The separation of the "leg iron . . . filed asunder" from the "strange man who had shown me the file" is simply the literary mapping of a process that is finally simultaneous: the fragmentation and the extension of the social chain, its extension in-and-through its fragmentation. By representing Orlick, Dickens also makes his narrative more complete, capturing even the fragmented excess produced through the metonymic architecture. Orlick is truly a "parting" welded into the discursive totality, as his very disappearance is absorbed into the overall narrative structure.

Orlick's narrative identity is defined by this metonymic position: that most unstable position of the broken link in the chain. For this reason his appearances are disjointed and sporadic; he often takes Pip by surprise.

> Being at last touched on the shoulder, I started and turned. I started much more naturally then, to find myself confronted by a man in a sober grey dress. The last man I should have expected to see in that place of porter at Miss Havisham's door.
> "Orlick!" (254)

But just as importantly, as Orlick makes the sporadic appearance, he is simultaneously shown in the capacity of a laborer and as an intermediary between Pip and other characters. Here he is the porter at Miss Havisham's, literally mediating between Pip and his most metaphoric relations: Miss Havisham and Estella. Earlier, Orlick first enters into the text only in-and-through his labor function—more precisely, through the inevitable intrusion of capitalist forms of labor into the precapitalist order of the Gargerys' home and village: "Now Joe kept a journeyman at weekly wages whose name was Orlick" (139). Orlick is the human excess that encroaches onto the archaic, guildlike economy of Joe's small village (just as, crucially, he enters the character-system only after it has begun to develop, in chapter 15), and the reduction of his labor to a "weekly wage" seems to inevitably correlate with his self-estrangement.

So Pip continues:

> He pretended that his christian name was Dolge—a clear impossibility—but he was a fellow of that obstinate disposition that I believe him to have been the prey of no delusion in this particular, but willfully to have imposed that name upon the village as an affront to its understanding. . . . He never even seemed to come to his work on purpose, but would slouch in as if by accident. . . . He lodged at a sluice-keeper's out on the marshes, and on working days would come slouching from his hermitage, with his hands in his pockets and his dinner loosely tied in a bundle round his neck and dangling on his back. On Sundays he mostly lay all day on sluice gates, or stood against ricks and barns.

This passage enacts the legitimist critique of capitalism that associates the decline of feudal socioeconomic norms with the destruction of organic human life. The description draws a series of oppositions: the "christian" name against the dehumanizing professional name (we see this again with "John" and

"Wemmick," with "Abel" and "Magwitch," even with "Trabb"); purposeful vocation against purposeless, "accidental" wage-labor; a real home against rented lodging (emphasized through Pip's ironic use of "hermitage"); and, finally, the grotesque devolution of Sunday as a day of rest. In all these cases, Orlick's social exteriority is ripped apart from his own interiority, and his interiority, finally, is reduced to the unhappy consciousness of its own denial: "He always slouched, locomotively, with his eyes on the ground; and, when accosted or otherwise required to raise them, he looked up in a half resentful, half puzzled way, as though the only thought he ever had, was, that it was rather an odd and injurious fact that he should never be thinking" (140). The description moves from Orlick's status as a wage-laborer to a series of social oppositions that derive from this status, to the most existential rendition of this opposition, in the contrast between thought and exteriority. "Half resentful" and "half puzzled," Orlick is a condensation of alienated consciousness, and the text is unforgiving toward him. Unlike the configurations of both Magwitch and Wemmick, the two other most important representations of social dispersion, the novel never moves beyond this portrayal of Orlick. In this sense, a superficial critique could be mounted against Dickens, for the negative valorization of working-class consciousness. Such a critique, however (like the criticism of Austen's representation of Charlotte Lucas), works only by ripping a character out of the narrative totality, rushing too quickly to confirm an ideological valence detached from the novel's most significant formal and social logic. Orlick, as much as any character, is meaningless outside the narrative totality, both because of the elaboration of his position in relation to Wemmick and to Magwitch, and because of the absolutely exterior position he occupies within the novel as a whole.

This exteriority (as with Magwitch's marginality and Wemmick's functionality) is brilliantly developed in both the story and the discourse. Orlick's exteriority is enacted structurally (through his sporadic appearances) and descriptively (through his representation in specific scenes), as is exampled in this passage where Pip encounters Drummle:

> I saw [Drummle] through the window, seizing his horse's mane, and mounting in his blundering brutal manner, and sidling and backing away. I thought he was gone, when he came back, calling for a light for the cigar in his mouth, which he had forgotten. A man in a dust-coloured dress appeared with what was wanted—I could not have said from where: whether from the inn yard, or the street, or where not—and as Drummle leaned down from the saddle and lighted his cigar and laughed, with a jerk of his head towards the coffee-room windows, the slouching shoulders and ragged hair of this man, whose back was towards me, reminded me of Orlick. (371–72)

Orlick's fragmentary appearance in the narrative (so that Pip "could not have said from where" he emerges) devolves to the descriptive field, as he becomes reduced to "the slouching shoulders and ragged hair" that Pip sees from the back. (And here this convergence of description and emplacement takes place at another "calling" for a single increment of labor: Drummle summons Orlick to bring a light as Jaggers calls "Wemmick!" or Trabb shouts out "Door!") A similar description occurs at the beginning of the conflict at the lime-kiln, as Pip writes, "As the sparks fell thick and bright about him, I could see his hands and touches of his face, and could make out that he was seated and bending over the table, but nothing more" (434). This fragmentation is grounded in Orlick's radically exterior position within the narrative totality. A kind of narrative excess, the representations of Orlick (like the descriptions of servants in *Pride and Prejudice*) work to convey the distortion inevitably produced by the containment of the many people who are "so bound up" in a social structure "and yet so unknown."

Orlick is only the most symbolically central of a host of human figures who, when we become alert to the text's socionarrative structure, begin to surge forward in *Great Expectations*, especially in volume 3. We have already considered how the clients and "suppliants" lingering outside of Jaggers's office enact this kind of dispersion. Similarly, servants are themselves positioned as occupying marginal, and thus disruptive, positions; as in *Pride and Prejudice* they are often inflected into the text only through their very dismissal from it:

> "Then you can go about your work, Mary Anne," said Wemmick to the little servant; "which leaves us to ourselves, don't you see, Mr. Pip?" he added, winking, as she disappeared. (382)

> The impossibility of keeping him concealed in the chambers was self-evident. It could not be done, and the attempt to do it would inevitably engender suspicion. True, I had no Avenger in my service now, but I was looked after by an inflammatory old female, assisted by an animated rag-bag she called her niece. . . . They both had weak eyes, which I had long attributed to their chronically looking in at keyholes; indeed that was their only reliable quality besides larceny. (342)

As we have seen, Orlick, in his capacity as Miss Havisham's porter and Drummle's footman, also works as a servant, and his position suggests that the disruptive aspect of servants is structural: based not on the personal "quality" of individuals but on the inevitable disruption caused by the partial, and thus distorted, inflection of other human beings into purely functional positions within a social structure.

As Pip writes about a maidservant at Miss Havisham's (and only this mention brings her into the text at all): "We dined very well, and were waited on by a maid-servant whom I had never seen in all my comings and goings, but who, for anything I know, had been in that mysterious house the whole time" (263). *We don't know who is around us*, this passage suggests, and once again this sense of overpopulatedness is presented in specifically social terms: not merely that a city has an unimaginable number of individuals all packed into the same physical space, but that the social order creates strong structures of integration—pulling people into close relation with each other—while also relying on fragmentation. Like the all the great realists, Dickens configures multiplicity in its social dimensions, not simply as a neutral quantitative category. Dickens is fond of inserting, toward the end of his novels, new minor characters who grind against the mechanisms of closure. In *Our Mutual Friend*, for instance, the Reverend Frank Milvey and his wife are interrupted while on their way to marry Eugene and Lizzy, a marriage that obviously contributes to closing off the multiplot novel. The new minor character is inflected into the novel entirely in terms of this frustrating delay, while, characteristically, her own distorted flatness is quickly sketched out: "That worthy couple were delayed by a portentous old parishioner of the female gender, who was one of the plagues of their lives, and with whom they bore with most exemplary sweetness and good-humour, notwithstanding her having an infection of absurdity about her, that communicated itself to everything with which, and everybody with whom, she came in contact. She was a member of the Reverend Frank's congregation, and made a point of distinguishing herself in that body, by conspicuously weeping at everything, however cheering" (817). Scenes like this convey the sense that the novel is already full, or overcrowded, and doesn't have room for a new character. Minorness is thus juxtaposed against—even as it is shaped by—the closing off of the narrative.[31] As the spouses explain to Lizzy and Eugene: " 'Detained at the last moment by one who had a claim upon me,' was the Reverend Frank's apology to Lightwood, taking no thought of himself. To which Mrs. Milvey added, taking thought for him, like the championing little wife she was, 'Oh yes, detained at the last moment. But *as* to the claim, I must say that I *do* think you are *over*-considerate sometimes, and allow *that* to be a *little* abused' " (818, Dickens's emphasis). This explanation extends the narrative half-life of the otherwise tangential character, now absorbed into the thematics of sympathy and interconnection. These "late" minor characters, usually stunningly compressed and quickly dismissed, remind us that the mechanics of closure in Dickens's novels does not alter the fundamental misalignment that gives rise to the narrative's modes of caricature in the first place. For this reason it is important that the minor minor characters, besides being quickly dismissed, embody Dickens's poetics of distortion (so that, in this example, the parishioner has an "infection of absurdity" and always weeps even when she should smile).

The sense of overpopulatedness in volume 3 of *Great Expectations* is most significantly conveyed through the scenes when we see Compeyson hovering at Pip's shoulder and Orlick hovering on his stairway, because these characters' thematic conflict with the protagonist is integrated into their structured exteriority. However, Dickens also throws new minor minor characters into the gears of closure. Thus the obstacle to Herbert's marriage with Clara appears quite late in the novel, and is depicted in highly distorted terms and as a frame to Pip's visit with Magwitch:

> Clara returned soon afterwards, and Herbert accompanied me up-stairs to see our charge. As we passed Mr. Barley's door, he was heard hoarsely muttering within, in a strain that rose and fell like wind, the following Refrain; in which I substitute good wishes for something quite the reverse.
>
> "Ahoy! Bless your eyes, here's old Bill Barley. Here's old Bill Barley, bless your eyes. Here's old Bill Barley on the flat of his back, by the Lord. Lying on the flat of his back, like a drifting old dead flounder, here's your old Bill Barley, bless your eyes. Ahoy! Bless you."
>
> In this strain of consolation, Herbert informed me the invisible Barley would commune with himself by the day and night together; often while it was light, having at the same time, one eye at a telescope which was fitted on his bed for the convenience of sweeping the river.
>
> In his two cabin rooms at the top of the house, which were fresh and airy, and in which Mr. Barley was less audible than below, I found Provis comfortably settled. . . . it struck me that he was softened—indefinably, for I could not have said how, and could never afterwards recall how when I tried; but certainly. (390)

> We thought it best that he should stay in his own rooms, and we left him on the landing outside his door, holding a light over the stair-rail to light us down stairs. Looking back at him, I thought of the first night of his return when our positions were reversed, and when I little supposed my heart could ever be as heavy and anxious at parting from him as it was now.
>
> Old Barley was growling and swearing when we repassed his door, with no appearance of having ceased or of meaning to cease. (392)

Barley's typically Dickensian reduction to a "monotonous emphasis"—"growling and swearing . . . with no appearance of having ceased or of meaning to cease"—is unusually literalized through his radically contained position in the *histoire*. Shut up in his room, reduced to the aggravating voice that filters out, "passed" and "repassed" by Pip, Barley's constricted personality is intertwined with his circumscribed and marginal position in the narrative. More importantly, his dismissal or imprisonment is clearly juxtaposed with Magwitch's assimilation. It is as though Pip's very sense that Magwitch has "softened"—or that he has become less marginal, less flat, and more fully human—generates the radical exteriority of this new character, whose voice still filters in, "less audible . . . than before," during Pip's conversation with the convict. In this sense, the scene emblematically stages the dialectic between containment and expulsion that characterizes volume 3. Bill Barley's moans and groans are less communication than a pure (and thus unintelligible) expression of his interiority, and his expendable role in the novel suggests the more general pressures produced by competing subjectivities within an asymmetric narrative structure. The novel's ability to accommodate Magwitch's subjectivity is thus entwined with the denial of sympathy to, and the very distortion of, Bill Barley.

Still closer to the final resolution, during Magwitch's escape attempt, another strangely distorted, disruptive minor character is inflected into the narrative:

> Leaving the rest in the boat, I stepped ashore, and found the light to be in a window of a public-house. It was a dirty place enough, and I dare say not unknown to smuggling adventurers. . . . No other company was in the house than the landlord, his wife, and a grizzled male creature, the "Jack" of the little causeway, who was as slimy and smeary as if he had been low-water mark too.
>
> *With this assistant*, I went down to the boat again, and we all came ashore, and brought out the oars, and rudder, and boat hook, and all else, and hauled her up for the night. (450, emphasis added)

> While we were comforting ourselves by the fire after our meal the Jack—who was sitting in a corner, and who had a bloated pair of shoes on, as interesting relics that he had taken a few days ago from the feet of a drowned seaman washed ashore—asked me if we had seen a four-oared galley going up with the tide? . . . He spoke in a slushy voice, as if much mud had washed into his throat. . . . In the infinite meaning of his reply, and his boundless confidence in his views, the Jack took one of his bloated shoes off, looked into it, knocked a few stones out of it on the kitchen floor, and put it on again. He did this with the air of a Jack who was so right that he could afford to do anything. (451)

> The Jack at the Ship was instructed where the drowned man had gone down, and undertook to search for the body in the places where it was likeliest to come ashore. His interest in its recovery seemed to me to be much heightened when he heard that it had stockings on. Probably, it took about a dozen drowned men to fit him out completely; and that may have been the reason why the different articles of his dress were in various stages of decay. (456)

All of these descriptions of the Jack are quite distracting, pulling us away from the novel's climax. Echoing the crucial line—"I fell over something, and that something was a man crouching in the corner"—the Jack is depicted as a "grizzled male *creature*" who is "sitting in a corner." The narrative stresses, as usual, the misalignment between surface and depth, voice and thought, contrasting, as with the representation of Barkis in *David Copperfield*, his blurred articulation ("he spoke in a slushy voice") and his private, incommunicable certainty ("the infinite meaning of his reply"). The Jack's fragmented surface is more directly linked to dehumanization—to our sense of him as a "grizzled . . . creature"—through the morbid description of his mismatched clothing, taken from "a dozen drowned men" and "in various stages of decay." Here Dickens takes his frequent trope of ill-fitting clothing on minor characters (already employed on Mr. Jingle at the beginning of *The Pickwick Papers*) and melodramatically literalizes its suggestion of fragmentation and dehumanization. At the same time, the Jack acquires this clothing only through his job, just as his integration into the *narrative* comes through his functional utility to Magwitch's escape: "With this assistant, I went down to the boat again."

A brief intertextual addendum on this minor character. An interesting and particular "surplus" of significance adheres to the Jack, who is himself, of course, both narratively and socially superfluous. If this character is utterly minor, straining at the limits of the novel's character-system, a similar figure becomes the first character in Dickens's subsequent novel. The opening sentence of *Our Mutual Friend* thus describes "a boat of dirty and disreputable appearance, with two figures in it," who make their living towing in drowned bodies. Suddenly we can see the next triple-decker novel emerging out of this most peripheral character in *Great Expectations*. A fine example of how novelists think alternative, or future, stories through a secondary character, the Jack's association with a more significant character in the next novel only increases his disruptive *minorness* in *Great Expectations*.[32] Our retrospective knowledge of *Our Mutual Friend* enhances the thematic significance of this minor figure at the end of *Great Expectations*, and this thematic import grates against his distorted personality and contained position within the narrative. And, once again, this thematic dimension is not distinct from his metonymic configuration but revolves around the same issues of dehumanization, fragmentation, labor, and social dispersion that are structured through the character-system. The drowned corpse dredged up by Lizzy and Gaffer Hexam in these first lines of *Our Mutual Friend* itself turns out to be *both* the novel's central protagonist and its most minor character: both the strangely submerged hero John Harmon and the utterly peripheral, but narratively crucial, George Radfoot. But this relationship between Harmon and Radfoot leads us astray, quickly absorbing us into the shadowy events at the center of *Our Mutual Friend* and the complicated nexus of character-spaces—Harmon, Rokesmith, Radfoot, Riderhood, and Hexam—at the heart of this novel's own intricate and revealing character-system.[33]

Returning to the fragmented residue at the end of *Great Expectations*, we can find another example of the interplay between closure and expulsion in a scene at Jaggers's law office, which, in volume 2, has already been shown to rely on the harsh exclusion of the human concerns, and thus the human beings, who depend on his services. Here social exclusion is explicitly linked to narrative closure, as Wemmick and Jaggers "re-establish their good understanding" by viciously dismissing Mike's feelings and, more literally, expelling Mike himself:

> I had never seen them on such ill terms; for generally they got on very well indeed together.

But, they were happily relieved by the opportune appearance of Mike, the client with the fur cap and the habit of wiping his nose on his sleeve, whom I had seen on the very first day of my appearance within these walls. This individual, who, either in his own person or in that of some member of his family, seemed to be always in trouble (which in that place meant Newgate), called to announce that his eldest daughter was taken up on suspicion of shop-lifting. As he imparted this melancholy circumstance to Wemmick, Mr. Jaggers standing magisterial before the fire and taking no share in the proceedings, Mike's eyes happened to twinkle with a tear.

"What are you about?" demanded Wemmick, with the utmost indignation. "What do you come snivelling here for?"

"I didn't go to do it, Mr. Wemmick."

"You did," said Wemmick. "How dare you? You're not in a fit state to come here, if you can't come here without spluttering like a bad pen. What do you mean by it?"

"A man can't help his feelings, Mr. Wemmick," pleaded Mike.

"His what?" demanded Wemmick, quite savagely. "Say that again!"

"Now, look here my man," said Mr. Jaggers, advancing a step, and pointing to the door. "Get out of this office. I'll have no feelings here. Get out."

"It serves you right," said Wemmick, "Get out."

So the unfortunate Mike very humbly withdrew, and Mr. Jaggers and Wemmick appeared to have re-established their good understanding. (426–27)

This scene suggests how volume 3's dialectic between closure and fragmentation continues to develop the overarching tension between the interior and the exterior within the novel. In volume 1, the exterior world continually overwhelms Pip's interiority, and in volume 2, the protagonist's vulnerability is linked to his position within a complex, radically dispersed social chain. This social field uneasily coexists with and finally disrupts Pip's attempt, in his courtship of Estella, to configure exterior reality in terms of his own interior desire. In volume 3, the interior realm is reconstituted, but only at the price of the exclusion and fragmentation of human figures in the social field. In this sense, Jaggers's dismissal of Mike does not deny feeling but rather *constitutes* feeling, as something abstract from material, social beings. Thus Wemmick actually responds *with* feeling, with "the utmost indignation" and "quite savagely." He converts Mike's exclusion from a metonymic to a metaphoric process: from the actual, *social* exclusion of a real person to the psychological rejection of "feeling." As in the contrast between Pip's "feelings" and Jaggers's place, or the "theme" of Estella and the "event" of Magwitch, Jaggers ends by saying, "I'll have no feelings *here*," spatializing an abstraction that really can't exist "here" or "there," while abstracting the human being who only *can* exist in (social) space. If Jaggers's office has always been depicted at the heart of the London social order, this gesture embodies the most essential dynamic of capitalism, which abstracts a human being into function (which it utilizes) and feeling (which it dismisses).[34]

The Double: A Narrative Condition?

If Orlick is the lightning rod for all the other minor minor characters (the servants, Bill Barley, Mike, and the Jack) who surge forward in volume 3, the narrative enfolds Pip's conflict with Orlick as a penultimate climax that leads up to the final clash between Magwitch and Compeyson. In their struggle at the lime-kiln, Orlick confronts the protagonist not primarily as an externaliza-tion (and return) of Pip's psychological tendencies but rather through his insis-tence on Pip's own exteriority. This is an important, but underrecognized, nar-rative dimension of the doppelgänger in nineteenth-century fiction, whose purely *exterior* configuration (are the thoughts of a double ever narratively articulated?) forces the protagonist to confront or conceptualize himself as an object rather than a subject, as a *social* rather than merely psychological being (and thus as a minor rather than central character). This play between exteri-ority and interiority seems intrinsic to the very structure of the doppelgänger plot: if the double can *never* attract any free indirect discourse, for instance, the anxious protagonist *must*; in fact, this is precisely what differentiates dou-ble *from* original (so that it is, ultimately, a strictly narrative difference that we are here confronting).

The double's highly specific socionarrative position has been relatively ne-glected in criticism of this crucial character-type, which, perhaps more than any other kind of figure, has always bolstered the psychological model of character-criticism. Such criticism reinforces the protagonist's centrality by adjudging the double in strict relation to the hero, most often as a psychological or symbolic projection of the hero (a projection that emanates, precisely, out of the protagonist's own ample interiority). But I would argue that a double nearly always creates a narrative crisis by inscribing the potential minorness *of* the central figure into the storied world—a minorness linked, above all, to the double's categorical (narrative) exteriority. The asymmetric relationship between protagonist and double posited in a psychologized model (where the double represents a problematic side or aspect of the protagonist, whose very fullness is amplified through this partial critique) begs the question. Insofar as the double's only *difference* from the protagonist rests in his exaggerated exteriority (an exteriority that is narratively grounded but can then take other forms, as in the trope of replication itself or, as I've suggested with Orlick, social marginality), it would seem that all the remaining *similarity* between the two characters almost necessarily calls the protagonist's centrality itself into question (and, in this *narrative* sense, then works to undermine the charac-ter's identity).

This exteriorization of the hero is crucial to Dostoevsky's *The Double*, a seminal exploration of the character-type that forms a compelling intertext with *Great Expectations*. Dostoevsky's novella wastes no time in describing its hero Golyadkin, in the opening sentence, as "a minor civil servant" and goes on to paint a devastating portrait of how the bureaucratic system, with its cruel blend of homogeneity and competition, drowns out individuals while also preventing collective consciousness. The protagonist's arrival at work after the double first appears makes this problem of exteriority clear: Golyadkin's anxiety, presumably caused by the shocking appearance the night before, is simply an exaggerated version of his *usual* response to the mixture of anonymity and competitiveness that accompanies his work:

> At last, by means of such arguments, Mr. Golyadkin salved his conscience completely, and justified himself in advance against the reprimand he might expect from Andrey Filippovich for neglecting his work. In all such situations our hero was very fond of justifying himself in his own eyes by various irrefutable arguments, and so salving his conscience completely . . . he sprang up from the sofa . . . quickly washed, shaved and combed his hair, dragged on his uniform jacket and other things, and grabbing some papers, shot off to the office.
>
> Timidly, Mr. Golyadkin entered his section, trembling in anticipation of something extremely nasty, with an expectancy which, if unconscious and vague, was at the same time unpleasant. Timidly he seated himself at his usual place next to Anton Antonovich Setochkin, the chief clerk. Without looking round or allowing himself to be distracted, he buried himself in the papers before him. . . . [D]espite his promise not to become involved whatever happened, and to keep aloof from everything, no matter what it was, Mr. Golyadkin kept raising his head, furtively and ever so slightly, to take a sly peep at the faces of his colleagues to left and right, in an attempt to decide whether anything new or special concerning him was for some improper reason being concealed. (46–47)

This social context is crucial to the poetics and logic of the character-system. The "minor civil servant," cast into an unfulfilling and insecure social role, experiences a continual disjunction between his own subjectivity and his constricted—but *also* precarious—social position. It is precisely this exterior aspect of himself that he does confront in a double: a person who is exactly the same as Golyadkin but is now legible to him only *from* the outside.

The story's opening lines have already focused on the cramped and dispiriting social role that Golyadkin finds himself in: "It was a little before eight when Yakov Petrovich Golyadkin, a minor civil servant, came to, yawned, stretched, and finally opened his eyes wide after a long night's rest. For two minutes or so he lay motionless in bed, like a man as yet uncertain whether he is awake or still asleep, whether all at present going on about him is reality or a continuation of his disordered dreams" (3). As he confronts his double, we continually see signs of this "uncertainty," of Golyadkin's inability to harmonize internal consciousness with external action or role. Hesitating at a doorway (of his superior), unable to decide whether to ring the bell or walk away, Golyadkin finally acts and almost *simultaneously* defines himself in opposition to this action: "Suddenly Mr. Golyadkin pulled the bell; it tinkled and footsteps

were heard within. At this juncture Mr. Golyadkin cursed himself for his bold-
ness and precipitation" (77). With his double, however, Golyadkin is forced to
see himself strictly as an exterior agent. For this reason the crisis of doubling
centers on his work, that aspect of his social existence which is most constricting and alienating: "No sooner had Mr. Golyadkin decided that the whole
thing was impossible, than all of a sudden Golyadkin junior came flying into
the room, with papers in both hands and under both arms" (71). This double
is here no more than a hypostatized version of Golyadkin's lingering sense of
his own exteriority. Naturally, our hero tries to make a *metaphoric* opposition,
which, like the distinction between Pip and Orlick, is based on character: "That
Golyadkin's a blackguard. Don't you take any notice of him, and don't mix
him up with the other one who's honest, virtuous, gentle and forgiving, who's
very reliable at work and deserves promotion" (79). But what is at stake is not
the particular status of each Golyadkin's conscience but rather, as we have
seen, the "original" Golyadkin's ability *to* "justify himself by his own eyes,"
or in terms of his interior subjectivity.

Of course, Orlick's status as a double has been well investigated: in fact,
rarely has a Dickensian minor character proved more thematically useful,
dramatizing elements of Pip's unconscious that, embodied in a discrete and
delimited character, are now abstracted, or understood as thematic. The seminal study here, Julian Moynahan's "The Hero's Guilt: The Case of *Great Expectations*," is worth examining, more generally, as a model of interpreting
character-system. Like this analysis, Moynahan's insists that Orlick *can't*
merely be "considered by himself" (153); that his character necessarily
emerges within, and takes shape in relation to, the larger narrative structure.
For Moynahan, this structure leads to a specific and delimited frame of interpretation: rather than considering the minor character in-and-of-himself, we
need to "consider Orlick in his connections with Pip" (154). The essay deploys
numerous images of the minor character as it makes the argument that "Orlick
is bound to the hero by ties of analogy." Orlick is described as a "parallel"
(154), "a parody" (154), "a distorted echo" (154), "a distorted and darkened
mirror-image" (156), "a monstrous caricature" (156), "a sort of double, alter
ego, or shadow" (156), "a shadow image" (159), and an "objective correlative"
(159) of Pip. All of these images work to incorporate the minor character
within the elaborated interiority of the protagonist—a process that concludes
when Orlick gets absorbed, quite literally, into what Moynahan calls "a complex unity—we might call it Pip-Orlick." This dyad, merging together protagonist and radically subordinate character, functions, of course, to comprehen-
sively render the intentional and unconscious aggression of the protagonist.
What separates the protagonist from the minor character, *within* this constructed unity, is precisely a fundamental difference of interiority: "several of
Orlick's charges are justified, and it is only in the assumption that Pip's *motives*
are as black as his own that he goes wrong" (155, emphasis added).[35]

In the conflict at the lime-kiln, however, Orlick confronts Pip not as an externalization of his own hidden motives but by demanding that Pip see himself as an exterior agent. We remember that *Great Expectations* never gives us a precise physical description of the protagonist, withholding a sense of what Pip actually looks like. As Orlick's vulnerable prisoner, however, Pip becomes painfully aware of his own exteriority: "His enjoyment of the spectacle *I furnished*, as he sat with his arms folded on the table, shaking his head at me and hugging himself, had a malignity that made me tremble" (435, emphasis added). Orlick insists on the spectacle of Pip's physicality, saying, "I'll have a good look at you" (437), and viscerally imagining Pip's death in terms of his bodily remains.[36] Pip is all too aware of his exteriority, most painfully signaled through his wounded arm, which makes him "faint and sick" (434) and which, he says later, "was violently swollen and inflamed, and I could scarcely endure to have it touched" (441). At the same time Orlick's attack makes Pip's *mind* race, and he seems torn between the (interior) reality of his spinning thoughts and the (exterior) actuality of Orlick's physical presence, describing a kind of double consciousness: "In the excited and exalted state of my brain, I could not think of a place without seeing it, or of persons without seeing them. It is impossible to over-state the vividness of these images, and yet I was so intent, all the time, upon him himself—who would not be intent on the tiger crouching to spring!—that I knew of the slightest action of his fingers" (438). With the conflict at the lime-kiln we return fully to the phenomenological register of volume 1. Pip's consciousness of Orlick's exteriority provokes consciousness of his own exteriority *and* consciousness of his own consciousness. Once again, Pip is between two roaring worlds, depicted in their purest terms as the "excited and exalted state of my brain" and "the slightest action of his fingers." This reconfiguration of exteriority and interiority simultaneously continues to express the social dynamics that were elaborated in volume 2. The final resolution entwines the expulsion of Orlick, the reconstitution of Pip's interiority, and the assimilation of other, exterior figures:

> It was only my head and my legs that I could move, but to that extent I struggled with all the force, until then unknown, that was within me. In the same instant I heard responsive shouts, saw figures and a gleam of light dash in at the door, heard voices and tumult, and saw Orlick emerge from a struggle of men, as if it were tumbling water, clear the table at a leap, and fly out into the night.
>
> After a blank, I found that I was lying unbound, on the floor, in the same place, with my head on some one's knee. My eyes were fixed on the ladder against the wall, when I came to myself—had opened on it before my mind saw it, and thus as I recovered consciousness, I knew that I was in the place where I had lost it.
>
> Too indifferent at first, even to look round and ascertain who supported me, I was lying looking at the ladder, when there came between me and it, a face. The face of Trabb's boy!

"I think he's all right!" said Trabb's boy, in a sober voice; "but ain't he just pale though!"

At these words the face of him who supported me looked over into mine, and I saw my supporter to be —

"Herbert! Great Heaven!" (440–41)

The contradiction between Pip's interiority and Orlick's exteriority finds a synthesis in the "responsive shouts" that "respond to the force . . . that was within me" and more completely in the image of "my head on some one's knee." The second paragraph repeatedly describes the moment of coming to consciousness—"I found that I was lying unbound," "when I came to myself," "as I recovered consciousness"—in a way that connects back to the original configuration of Pip's interiority on the opening page. However, if the novel's opening associates Pip's very possession of consciousness with his sense of radical separation, this revision posits consciousness through the connection to others. Thus the protagonist rests his "head" on someone's "knee" and is "supported" by a "face" that looks into his face. At the same time Orlick's expulsion from the narrative—integrated into this reconfiguration of Pip's consciousness—is associated with a backward chain of events in the novel. As Orlick emerges "from a struggle of men" and flies "out into the night," we can remember his own fragmentary appearances throughout the narrative, the other minor minor characters who have been expelled or contained in volume 3, the marginalization of Magwitch, the self-division of Wemmick. In other words, while Orlick's expulsion is one of the final signs of the conservative thrust of volume 3— which pulls away from the radical vision of volume 2 to reconstitute Pip's own sense of self—it also becomes part of the more totalized representation of alienation that develops alongside the relatively happy ending. In terms of the plot, Pip's conflict with Orlick solidifies the development of his own interiority, his transformation into a more mature, detached personality. In terms of the character-system, Orlick's narrative ejection contributes to the overarching depiction of social contingency: first presented through the existential terror of a child; then in the more expansive comprehension of London as an overpopulated and stratified urban field; and finally in the guise of a "maturity" that can produce its own stability only through a series of expulsions. On the one hand, we are left with the novel's memorable image of Pip's compromise: "I must not leave it to be supposed that we were ever a great House, or that we made mints of money. We were not in a grand way of business, but we had a good name, and worked for our profits, and did very well" (489). On the other hand, we are left with a lingering memory of the narrative system, of the partial inflections of Miss Havisham, Mr. Pumblechook, Wemmick, Magwitch, Orlick, and all the other characters who have been so dynamically represented. This memory, this sense of an organizing system, further leaves us with the ambition to build a whole out of these disparate fragments. The narrative ends with a realistic representation of psychological retreat—retreat from both ambition and social knowledge—while embedding this retreat in a larger representation of the complex social structure that has both catalyzed and extinguished Pip's expectations. Dickens himself follows Joe's wise adage; like life itself—and like the social system that structures and is reflected in *Great Expectations*—this narrative is nothing so much as these "partings welded together."

Chapter Four

A qui la place?: Characterization and Competition in *Le Père Goriot* and *La Comédie humaine*

Typification and Multiplicity

The Problem: Who Is the Hero?

> Ces deux lignes sont des asymptotes qui ne peuvent jamais se rejoinder.
> —*Le Père Goriot*, 120

Who is the hero of *Le Père Goriot*: Rastignac or Goriot? As Pierre Barbéris succinctly asks, "is the subject the martyrdom of a father or the initiation of a young man into the mysteries of social life" (20)? The novel seems to tell two stories at once; or, more precisely, it unfolds a whole series of events that can revolve around two different centers of interest. Depending on where we look, we can find a classical tragedy of "the death of the father [la mort du père]" (the original title of the last section) superimposed onto a modern narrative form or a prototypical bildungsroman about Rastignac's "entrance into the world [l'entrée dans le monde]" (the original title of section 2). Deciding the relative centrality of Rastignac and Goriot has been a component element of this novel's critical history but has rarely been explicitly examined.[1] Most interpretations base their argument on one of the two characters, while critics who acknowledge the choice as a problem often shift from this fragmented character-field to a unified thematic one.[2]

Highlighting a stable thematic center too swiftly leaves no room for examining the competition between alternative character centers. The problem of Goriot's and Rastignac's relative centrality comes prior to thematic interpretation; not merely an aspect of critical analysis, it helps condition the grounds for analysis. For example, before we can interpret the thematic significance of Rastignac's social education, we have to assess his position within the novel as a whole. Is the story of Rastignac's development the governing focus of the entire novel? Does the text essentially collapse into this inset bildungsroman? But if it does, how should we interpret the novel's strange title? And why does the novel initially position Rastignac as a mere witness to the central story, rather than as the central story himself?

> But for his inquisitive observations [observations curieuses] and the facility with which he knew how to get himself into the salons of Paris, this story would not be

colored with its tone of reality, that it owes without doubt to his alert spirit and to his desire to penetrate the mysteries of a terrible situation as carefully hidden by those who had created it as by the victim himself. (51)[3]

In this chapter I don't want to provide an answer to "who is the hero?" but rather consider why this *question* is at the center of Balzac's novel. Examining the riddle of Hamlet's delay, Lev Vygotsky once cautioned against trying to eliminate the riddle by solving it through a psychological explanation: "[A] veil has been thrown over the picture, but in trying to lift it in order to examine the picture beneath we discover that the veil is painted into the picture itself. . . . By depriving the tragedy of its riddle, the critics deprive the play of its most essential element" (168). Similarly, I don't want to resolve or explain away the problem of the protagonist in *Le Père Goriot* but to elaborate its inscrutability. Once we eschew identifying who the protagonist is, we come across other questions, which this chapter *will* attempt to answer: Why does Balzac arrange this novel around two incomplete protagonists? How does this undecidable tension contribute to the formal structuration of the novel? What are the historical and ideological implications that emerge from a reading that highlights this tension?

This last question is important because of the overt sociological interests of *Le Père Goriot*, and its centrality within the construction of social realist aesthetics. The weight of Rastignac and Goriot within the novel as a whole does not simply facilitate a psychological conflict between the two figures, as individuals, but also dynamically juxtaposes them, as character-spaces, within the overall narrative. Because *Le Père Goriot* claims to present a total picture of Parisian reality, the competition between Goriot and Rastignac as potentially central characters gains new significance, and new aesthetic charge. Their competitive jostling for position within the narrative totality is inseparable from their changing positions within the Parisian totality, a social framework that informs the novel's stylistic, thematic, and structural contours.

Novels that feature competing co-protagonists are an interesting subset within the broader development of stratified character-fields that call attention to the distribution *of* attention. A wide range of nineteenth- and twentieth-century novels feature dual (and sometimes dueling) protagonists, from *Sense and Sensibility*, *Anna Karenina*, and *Daniel Deronda* to *The Wings of the Dove*, *Ulysses*, and *Blood Meridian*.[4] Other novels, as dissimilar as *The Moonstone*, *The Sound and the Fury*, and *Buddenbrooks*, display a similar tension through a *series* of potential protagonists (obviously deployed in very different ways), while the Victorian multiplot novel hypostatizes competing characters into distinct but connected story lines. Other novels, still more closely akin to *Le Père Goriot*, associate a split or problematic division between two potentially central characters with attention to social problems and sociological realism. For instance, in *Mary Barton*, Elizabeth Gaskell's main subject—how the poverty of working-class urban England leads to radical and violent class conflict—gives rise to an interesting balance between Mary and John Barton as two competing centers of narrative interest. Similarly, in *Sister Carrie*, Theodore Dreiser's attempt to represent the social dynamics of turn-of-the-century United States capitalism generates a division between Carrie, who begins as a clearly dominant protagonist organizing the contours of the narrative, and Hurstwood, who starts as a minor character but gains more and more narrative attention, becoming the focus of the reader's interest by the end of the novel. In this chapter I will analyze more precisely how and why these two processes fit together in *Le Père Goriot*: how the formal division of the narrative between Goriot and Rastignac relates to the novel's sociological framework. The vital association between a novel's backgrounded social content and its dynamic configuration of character-spaces—intuitively clear in *Mary Barton*, *Sister Carrie*, and *Le Père Goriot*—helps elucidate the relationship between literary form and social realism. Social reality is not simply reflected in an immediate correspondence between fictional text and real world; rather, we have to read the sociological landscapes that the three novels paint *through* the prism of the character-system, and, more precisely, through the interaction between two distinct characters—and distinctively formulated character-spaces—within the narrative totality.

Character, Type, Crowd

Our attention is divided between Goriot and Rastignac for a specific reason: their shared residency at the Maison Vauquer. Their division is elaborated in the formal organization of the narrative discourse, but it is motivated by the story's setting. The co-protagonists are, in fact, only two members of a larger group: the seven residents who find themselves living together in a dilapidated boardinghouse. "At the epoch when this story begins, the full-time boarders numbered seven. . . . A similar consideration influenced all these beings randomly brought together" (50, 51). *Le Père Goriot*'s urban lodging house—in which individuals are simultaneously disconnected and radically proximate—is a memorable realist topos, crucial to the novel's social and narrative framework. Like the five sisters in *Pride and Prejudice*, *Le Père Goriot*'s seven boarders (who are introduced *as* a group near the novel's opening) form an emblematic character-field. In both cases, the limited number of people suggests that *each* be taken seriously. For every character who falls into this central narrative field, the novel feels an imperative to partially represent his or her particular consciousness and to incorporate this consciousness into the texture of the achieved omniscient universe. The stratified attention that each character receives then intersects with this imperative, shaping the actual structure of the character-system.

To understand the character-system in *Le Père Goriot*, we need to look closely at the social environment in which it is embedded. The framework of the urban hotel and its strangely connected boarders does more than motivate the juxtaposition of the two co-protagonists with five other individuals. It configures each character's own individuality, or the way that he asserts himself against the background of the other residents, as part of a larger social process. The narrator notes: "The wallspace between the barred windows offers to the *pensionnaires* the scene of the feast given to the child of Ulysses by Calypso. For forty years this painting has provoked jokes from the young *pensionnaires*, who think themselves superior to their position by scoffing at the dinner to which poverty has condemned them" (47). On the one hand, a person's individuality is here purchased only through extravagant negation: the young man looks around the dinner table at the other boarders and believes himself to be superior. On the other hand, in the context of Paris as a whole, the assertion of one's individual superiority against a multiple field is itself typical: the young man falls into the very crowd he is trying to evade, becoming simply one of many young men over the last forty years who reacts this way.

This kind of process goes far beyond a single hotel: it embeds the intercourse among the seven characters in the boardinghouse within a larger structure of social relationships. The unthinkable multiplicity of nineteenth-century urban social life—which both creates new, extravagant forms of individuality and threatens to drown individuality out—is not caused by the dilapidated Maison Vauquer but produces such a residency. "Sera-t-elle comprise au-delà de Paris? le doute est permis," Balzac famously writes ("Could this be understood outside of Paris? It's doubtful") (44). And references to the specific nature of *Parisian* reality abound in *Le Père Goriot*. Paris creates places like the Maison Vauquer, which in turn creates this group of residents, which will, finally, condition the specific *narrative* relationship between Goriot and Rastignac. Paris is an ocean: "He had then fifteen months of leisure to sail through the ocean of Paris [Il avait ainsi quinze mois de loisirs pour naviguer sur l'océan de Paris]" (124). Paris is a battlefield: "This life in Paris is a perpetual combat [Cette vie de Paris est un combat perpétuel]" (123). The story is an "obscure but frightening Parisian tragedy [obscure, mais effroyable tragédie parisienne]" (129). But how, precisely, is an ocean like a battlefield? Behind both these images we can find social multiplicity. Paris is like a sea, "un véritable océan" (54), because of its vastness and depth. This oceanlike vastness, however, does not refer to the amount of physical space in the city but to the number of people, or individual interests, crammed into this space. And Paris is a battlefield for the same reason: because of the struggle among so many individual centers of interest, which occurs because there *are* so many centers of interest. While Goriot's and Rastignac's formal conflict as co-protagonists is embedded in the larger group of seven hotel lodgers, this group is itself only an emblem, and a product, of Parisian reality—conceived as the unthinkable juxtaposition of innumerable individuals, all fighting on "the battlefield of Parisian civilization [le champ de bataille de la civilisation parisienne]" (114).

To grasp the competition between Rastignac and Goriot (so as to analyze that central riddle of *Le Père Goriot*), I must now take a major detour, toward Paris. Paris, that is, as the horizon of Balzac's social imagination, and as the (less obvious) ground of his narrative poetics. Balzac's narrative ambitions had, from their inception, revolved around the confrontation with Parisian reality; and Balzac, more than any previous novelist, grasps the reality of Paris in terms of social multiplicity. An earlier version of the famous line from *Le Père Goriot* ("Could this be understood outside of Paris?") appears in *Ferragus*, which anticipates the thematization of Paris as a unique area of inquiry:

> These observations, incomprehensible outside of Paris, will no doubt be understood by those men of study and of thought, of poetry and of pleasure, who know how to collect, while strolling through Paris, the mass of sensations which float, at all hours, between the city walls [la masse de jouissances flottantes, à toute heure, entre ses murailles]; by those for whom Paris is the most delicious of monsters: there, a pretty woman; further away, an old and poor man; right here, all new like recently minted currency; in that corner, elegant like a fashionable woman [là, jolie femme; plus loin, vieux et pauvre; ici, tout neuf comme la monnaie d'un nouveau règne; dans ce coin, élégant comme une femme à la mode]. (28)

Here the story that Balzac will tell is linked with a specific kind of observation that is "incomprehensible outside of Paris." More particularly, the passage suggests that Paris generates a specific mode of observing *human beings*. Balzac carefully grounds the fragmented nature of perception in urban space—"la masse de jouissances flottantes, à toute heure, entre ses murailles"—in its fundamental social origin: the juxtaposition of many different *people* in radically heterogeneous positions. Balzac's passage shows how we relentlessly make human beings into something else, into abstractions—"pretty," "old and poor," "all new," "elegant"—while also showing the social structuration of these abstractions. Thus the abstractions are locked together with spatial terms that coordinate the flaneur's observations—"there," "further away," "here," "in that corner." It is impossible to visualize simultaneously, within a single frame, these four dispersed figures: Paris is here not merely a stable taxonomic system (the new, the old, the poor) but a jangled conglomeration of competing perspectives.

And the flaneur himself? How can we understand "[the man] of study and of thought" who makes these observations, transforming the human beings that crowd in on his field of vision into abstractions of themselves? This machine of interiority—who can harvest or collect ("récolter") the multiple instances of human reality that he encounters walking through Paris—is himself positioned in a multiple field. He is not the man of study and thought but only *one of* "those men of study and of thought." Perhaps he is a poor student lodging at the Maison Vauquer, imagining his exceptionality in precisely the same way as all the other struggling students around Paris. The description seems to divide humans into two modes of being: those who are presented through their interiority, as apprehending what is around them, and those who offer themselves to the world in an exterior form. But the mass classification of "those men of study and of thought" positions the implied perspective in a social context, while the dispersion effected by the four position-markers hints at the weight of these counter-perspectives. These positions are not disruptive simply because of the visual disorder they create (in the same way as any four *objects* would be disordered) but also because of our sense that each of these four fleeting observations is a human being who could look back, further disaggregating the scene into four additional perspectives. It is the weight of these four figures who compose the fragmented visual field as implied human *subjects* that makes the image so unstable.

If the Parisian street in *Ferragus* teems with too many passersby, *La Fille aux yeux d'or*, another early story that precedes *Le Père Goriot*, amplifies this image into a representation of Parisian social life as a whole. The ambitious opening of the story runs through the individuals who compose each rung of the social ladder: the workers, the petite bourgeoisie, the professionals, the artists, and the aristocrats. Before this segmented description, however, is a general image of the structure that conditions these divisions themselves:

> Paris: isn't it a vast field incessantly agitated by a tempest of interests under which a harvest of men are blown around. . . . There everything smokes, everything burns, everything glows, everything trembles, everything flames up, evaporates, disperses, relights, sparks, shines and consumes itself. Never, in any country has life been so ardent, nor so ferocious. This social nature always in fusion seems to say to itself after every piece of work is finished—on to another! [Cette nature social toujours en fusion semble se dire après chaque oeuvre finie:—*A une autre!*] (357–58)

This last sentence succinctly encapsulates the poetics of characterization in *La Comédie humaine*. Social instability, which stems from the overspilling competition of individual interests, generates narrative instability. The story of any one individual character thus brings in a flood of other characters who, through their filiation with other diverse novels, bring in a flood of other, separate stories. Like Paris, *La Comédie humaine* is "toujours en fusion," propelled forward by the need to constantly turn attention "à une autre."

The spatial dispersion in the scene from *Ferragus* and the narrative problem posed by *La Fille aux yeux d'or* both highlight the literary repercussions of representing social multiplicity. How do you represent ten people who share the same living conditions, or ten thousand people who all belong to the same social class? You can find common traits and conjure up a single individual who exemplifies much more widespread characteristics. In this way, as Georg Lukács notes, social characteristics are realized only as they are inevitably embodied in a particular individual, while an individual is anchored, in an essential but not overdetermined fashion, to the social position that shapes him. Christopher Prendergast writes, "The centrality, indeed the prestige, which the notion of the type has acquired in modern critical thinking about literary realism can scarcely be over-emphasized, and is in the main due to the hugely influential work of Lukács" (32). But this dialectic between the particular and the general—which Lukács places as the key to Balzac's sociological vision and artistic humanism—does not necessarily account for the underlying multiplicity of the larger group of people. Between a particular individual and a general social category is a mass of discrete persons, that quantitative plurality which Balzac emphasizes through his gesture to the dispersed mass of fleeting sensations—rooted in actual people—that constitutes Parisian uniqueness.

We have seen how Rastignac's individuality is generated through a process that simultaneously links him with so many other young Parisian men. Similarly, any typical character in Balzac shares his or her qualities with a large mass of people. And as with Rastignac, this shared quality often bears a direct relationship *to* the fact of multiplicity. Typification has two different modes that are temporally distinct but get condensed together. First, there is the grasping of a social characteristic—the analytic moment when we suddenly see a relationship between a large group of individuals. As Prendergast continues, "the characteristic or 'essential' features of the social process are picked out and gathered into *a single expressive moment* of a peculiarly intense and concentrated kind" (32, emphasis added). This is an instantaneous realization: we are thinking about a group of persons and at a particular point become aware of a quality that they commonly possess. Out of this abstraction a synthetic character emerges, transcending the group from which he is sprung.[5] This clear image, though, which grasps social characteristics through a character, can get dissolved back into the larger group of people who share it, getting fractured into a thousand and one component parts.

The typical character in Balzac is ontologically unstable. On the one hand, he is pressed into that static fusion of the particular and the general, a fusion representing not so much an individual or a group as a particular moment of consciousness—that lucid instant when we synthesize the mass of individuals around us. On the other hand, he is drowned out by the actual plurality of individuals who compose this social group. In the most common formula of this division Balzac will introduce characters with a static, unchanging portrait and then immerse them within a dynamic, unsettled narrative. The most typical fate of Balzacian characters is to get torn from *a state of timelessness* into a destructive narrative, and the most aggressive examples of typification usually occur near the beginning of the novel, or when a new character is first introduced. This introduction, where the character is parceled out into a series of abstract qualities, artistically embodies the analytic instant of classification. What follows—the plot, the disastrous series of events, the highs and lows, the flood of interventions by other self-interested people, the astounding coincidences—shows the dispersion of the type back into the social plurality from which it is sprung.

A clear example of the conflict between portraiture and plot is *César Birotteau*: the more unchanging and static the central character, the more the world he inhabits is tempestuous and dynamic. And between César's banal stability and the mysterious motions of social life is a crowd, *une foule*, the concrete, dispersed milieu that he inhabits. Certainly, the novel is larded with static descriptions, social analogies, and generalizations about the main character, becoming a showcase for the most aggressive kind of Balzacian typification. In one set piece, the narrator begins by describing César's external appearance, which is reduced to a series of static signs:

> The work that he performed in manufacturing had left him with a few premature wrinkles and added a touch of silver to an abundant head of hair, polished around his skull by the pressure of his hat. His hair, which, by the way in which it was fixed, came down in five points across his forehead, announced the simplicity of his life. . . . His broad and hairy hands, the fat knuckles on his wrinkled fingers and his big, square fingernails would have attested to his origin, if vestiges of it did not remain on every part of his person. (89)

Each characteristic of César is grounded in a larger social circumstance: his "premature wrinkles" indicate "the work that he performed in manufacturing"; his unfashionable haircut attests to the "simplicity of his life"; his large hands suggest his origin, which is, in fact, implicated "on every part of his person." César becomes reduced to this series of characteristics, which are necessarily fixed because they are in strict correlation with a larger social environment. Thus as the description unfolds, it begins to enumerate César's gestures and habits, confining him to a mechanized routine: "Habitually in speaking he crossed his hands behind his back. When he thought that he had said something gallant or witty, he rose imperceptibly on the tip of his toes, twice, and then fell back heavily on his heels, as if to underline what he said. . . . His long experience of commercial business had given him habits considered obsessive by some people" (90). Reduction and correlation necessarily go together, facilitating the continuity of the type across the different registers of body, habits, clothing, gestures. As the passage continues, "The manner of dress he adopted corresponded to his manners and his physiognomy" (91).

César's static characteristics are intertwined with, and motivated by, the character's social typicality. The qualities that Balzac is describing—César's gullibility, his lack of control over events—ironically justify typification, as César is precisely the "type" of person who is subsumed *by* larger circumstances: the type of person who could become a type. The novel makes it quite clear that César *represents* a much larger group of people. We have seen how Rastignac's individuality is generated through a process that simultaneously links him with so many other young Parisian men. The protagonist of *César Birotteau* is more clearly an unexceptional individual, a character who becomes "le jouet des événements [the plaything of events]" (252). But this passivity is itself not merely psychological; it's embedded in a larger social environment, connected to a larger mass of individuals.

> Such was César Birotteau, a worthy man whom the mysterious powers that preside over the birth of men had denied the faculty to judge politics and life as a whole [juger l'ensemble de la politique et de la vie] or to rise above the social level in which the middle class [la classe moyenne] lived, and who followed in all things the vagaries of routine: all his beliefs had been given to him from outside and he applied them without examining them. . . . Let this history be the poem of those bourgeois vicissitudes that no voice has dreamed of, which seem so denuded of grandeur but at the same time are immense: this is not about a single man, but about an entire suffering people [il ne s'agit pas d'un seul homme ici, mais de tout un peuple de douleurs]. (91–92, 93)

The passage attributes César's inability to comprehend the larger currents of social life to an utterly particular essence—the mysteries of birth. At the same time it drowns César within a much larger social group—the middle class—that, in its name alone, is structurally situated in the same relation to "l'ensemble de la politique" as César. We can begin to see that César does not merely *represent* the quality of passivity that he shares with a large group of people (as we first assume upon reading, "il ne s'agit pas d'un seul homme ici"), but that the sheer extent of so many people crammed into this specifically intermediate social position produces the quality of passivity. The middle class cannot seize awareness of economic life because of its essential position within the economic structure, not merely because of the mysteries of individual fate. But even social position is too abstract: an individual only finds himself in this particular "social position" because of all the other individuals who jointly constitute it.

César motivates the most static kind of Balzacian typification, as his interior consciousness is rigidly linked to physical appearance, physical gesture, material possession. At the same time, the novel shows how the qualities connecting César to a larger, abstract social category emerge out of the specific social position that he occupies, *a position shaped by the plentitude of other people who share it with him*. When the narrator later writes that César, "like all the people in small Parisian business, was ignorant of the manners and the men of high finance [comme tous les gens du petit commerce parisien, ignorait les moeurs et les hommes de la haute Banque]" (262), he renders César typical (or representative) of a larger group of people. But the typification gets turned inside out when we realize that the particular quality César exemplifies—being ignorant of the manners and the men of high finance—is nourished and developed only because there are *so many* "gens du petit commerce parisien."

César thinks in terms of multitudes; when he ambitiously imagines success, it is through rising to a social class that teems with other individuals: " 'Conducting myself with prudence, I can make an honorable place among the bourgeoisie of Paris, like those who have done so in the past, and set up the Birotteaus, like the Kellers, the Jules Desmarets, the Roguins, the Cochins, the Guillaumes, the Lebas, the Nucingens, the Saillards, the Popinots, the Matifats—who all make a mark, or have made a mark, in their neighborhoods' ['En m'y conduisant avec prudence, je puis faire une maison honorable dans la bourgeoisie de Paris, comme cela se pratiquait jadis, fonder les Birotteau, comme il y a des Keller, des Jules Desmarets, des Roguin, des Cochin, des Guillaume, des Lebas, des Nucingen, des Saillard, des Popinot, des Matifat qui marquent ou qui ont marqué dans leurs quartiers']" (51). Here César's desire, the same desire that provokes his habitualized behavior, is embedded in a large social context. Similarly, we should note the expansive description of César's circle of friends.

> M. and Mme Ragon, their predecessors, their uncle Pillerault, Roguin the lawyer, the Matifats, druggists on la rue des Lombards and suppliers of *la Reine de Roses*, Joseph Lebas, textile merchant and successor of Guillaume at the *Chat-qui-Pelote*, one of the shining lights of la rue Saint-Denis, the judge Popinot, brother of Mme Ragon, Chiffreville, of the firm Protez and Chiffreville, M. and Mme Cochin, clerks at the Treasury and the sleeping partners of Matifat, the Abbé Loraux, confessor and director of the pious people in this group, and several other people, composed the circle of their friends [et quelques autres personnes, composaient le cercle de leurs amis]. (76)

Balzac purposely holds off the organizing clause of this list—"composaient le cercle de leurs amis"—until the end of the sentence, forcing the reader to confront these names without any unifying principle. The effect of putting the *catalog* before the *category* is to represent social reality in its essentially multiple configuration, and to link the qualitative and quantitative aspects of the Birotteau circle. The presentation of the petite bourgeoisie thus works on two distinct registers, describing the group's characteristics and its *size* (which shapes the characteristics that then serve to unify it). This can be seen in the catalog's oscillation between listing each person and qualifying his social position. The descriptions work to harness individuals into their specific social roles, either defining them simply by their profession ("Roguin the lawyer") or allowing them into the catalog because of their economic link to César's business ("the Matifats, druggists on la rue des Lombards and suppliers of *la Reine de Roses*"). A store owner is necessarily implicated in larger chains of commerce: most materially through suppliers and consumers, but also through lawyers and accountants, who function in the financial and legal system that embeds specific sequences of material exchange; other tradesmen, who make a commercial neighborhood viable; and even a priest, who can make this area

"respectable." The novel as a whole insistently foregrounds these larger economic processes, focusing most intently on the rise of modern advertising in
Restoration Paris. But the novel conveys this economic intercourse in material
terms, suggesting the overflowing group of individuals who are necessarily
implicated in the structures of commerce and finance it conceptualizes. Even
as each individual is carefully located in a specific social position, the cumula-
tive effect of the catalog is a sense of confusion and overcrowdedness. In
the catalog's final entry this dynamic confusion clearly wins out over rigid
classification. The "quelques autres personnes" are depicted only in terms of
their multiplicity, with no hint of their specific social function. By putting this
clause at the end of such a long catalog (which still has not been explained),
Balzac creates the sense of a social vanishing point, of a network of people
too large for each individual to be fully comprehended.[6] (Similarly, as I will
discuss below, Balzac titles the section of *Les Employés* that describes the
office of bureaucrats as "Quelques employés vus de trois-quarts," making explicit the connection between social multiplicity and partial representation.)

César's conflict with the tempestuous world models the dynamic nature of
typification in Balzacian realism. Typification, which seems to subsume many
different individuals under a single taxonomic rubric, also represents individual characteristics and emotions as they emerge in-and-through collective
structures. Balzacian typification moves from stating that a large number of
people share a given characteristic with a particular individual to suggesting
that this characteristic—for the particular individual, and others—is shaped by
the existence *of* a large number of people. There is a sudden inversion of figure
and ground. The effect of reading in Balzac is to slowly be turned inside out in
this way, to see, before your eyes, results mysteriously transmuted into causes.

Describing the barren environment of the Maison Vauquer, Balzac writes:
"There, the pavements are dry, the gutters have neither mud nor water, the
grass grows along the walls. The most carefree man gets sad just like all passersby, the noise of a vehicle becomes an event there, the houses are gloomy,
the walls seem like a prison. . . . No neighborhood in Paris is more horrible,
or, let us say it, more unknown" (45). The typifying gesture here—that even
the most carefree pedestrian feels the same way as all passersby—also conveys
a sense of multiplicity that in fact underlies the generalization. This man has
the same emotion as many other passersby in part because the emotion is
derived from there *being* so many men, creating these zones of anonymity.
Again, the Maison Vauquer is made emblematic—"the Maison Vauquer is one
of those curious monstrosities [La Maison Vauquer est une de ces monstruo-
sités curieuses]" (54) that explorers of Paris will encounter—and it is not just
that the hotel is monstrous like many other hotels, but that it is monstrous in
part because there are so many other hotels like it. Earlier, Balzac writes about
"that yellowish color which gives an ignoble character to nearly all the houses
of Paris [cette couleur jaune qui donne un caractère ignoble à presque toutes

les maisons de Paris]" (46). Here too we have a reversal of figure and ground, or cause and effect. The cause—a somber color—creates an effect of "ignobility" that is emphasized by its frequency, occurring on "nearly all the houses of Paris." But this final modifier is also the origin of the ignobility, rather than merely a consequence.

This process also underlies Balzac's depiction of individuals. Rastignac's ambition to distinguish himself is not, as we have seen, a unique (or a distinguished) ambition. The narrator describes Rastignac's thoughts as he walks: "He walked during nearly all the afternoon, a prey to that brain fever which all young men affected by too lively hopes have known [Il flâna pendant presque toute la journée, en proie à cette fièvre de tête qu'ont connue les jeunes gens affectés de trop vives espérances]" (171). On the one hand, this "fever" is emblematic of a larger social category, but, again, his thoughts are so feverish only because of the overabundance of other hopeful *jeunes gens*, who make rapid success so difficult. How many of the qualities that Rastignac shares with so many other young men are shaped by the fact that there are so many young men? And how many of the secret troubles experienced by Goriot are generated by the conditions of secrecy in which they are obscured?

Balzac's Double Vision

The juxtaposition of two kinds of typification—static and dynamic—is reflected both in Balzac's own varied conceptions of *La Comédie humaine* and in the structure of interpretation that has developed over the years. The famous French debate over realism in the 1960s—which is intertwined with the emergence of *le nouveau roman*—often centered more specifically on Balzacian typification. And if *le nouveau roman* might not have achieved its anticipated promise as a central postmodern literary genre, the ideological framework of *le nouveau roman* has been central to poststructuralist aesthetics. The contradiction between the static and dynamic aspects of typification is reflected in divergent opinions by Robbe-Grillet, the practitioner and theorist of *le nouveau roman*, and Georg Lukács, who first formulated the centrality of Balzacian typification.

The narrative, as our academic critics conceive it . . . represents an order. This order, which we may in effect qualify as natural, is linked to an entire rationalistic and organizing system, whose flowering corresponds to the assumption of power by the middle class. In that first half of the nineteenth century which saw the apogee—with *The Human Comedy*—of a narrative form which understandably remains for many a kind of paradise lost of the novel, certain important certainties were in circulation: in particular the confidence in a logic of things that was just and universal.

All the technical elements of the narrative—systematic use of the past tense and the third person, unconditional adoption of chronological development, linear plots, regular trajectory of the passions, impulse of each episode toward a conclusion, etc.—everything tended to impose the image of a stable, coherent, continuous, unequivocal, entirely decipherable universe. (Robbe-Grillet, 32)

Take the depiction of the typical in Balzac's *Le Père Goriot*. In this novel Balzac exposes the contradictions in bourgeois society, the inevitable inner contradictions appearing in every institution in bourgeois society, the varied forms of conscious and unconscious rebellion against the enslavement and crippling of the institutions in which men are imprisoned. Every manifestation of these contradictions . . . is intensified to an extreme by Balzac and with merciless consequence. Among his characters he depicts men representing ultimate extremes: beings lost or in revolt, thirsting for power or degenerate: Goriot and his daughters, Rastignac, Vautrin, the Viscountess de Beauséant, Maxime de Trailles. The events through which these characters expose themselves follow upon each other in an avalanche that appears incredible if the content is to be considered in isolation—an avalanche impelled by scarcely credible explosions. . . . And yet, or rather precisely on account of this rush of events, the novel provides the effect of a terrifyingly accurate and typical picture of bourgeois society. (Lukács, *Writer and Critic*, 49–50)

Where Robbe-Grillet sees "order," "certainties," and an "apogee" of bourgeois narrative that "imposes" a "stable, coherent, continuous, unequivocal" picture of the world, Lukács finds an "avalanche," "explosions," and a "rush of events" providing a "terrifyingly accurate" picture of "the inevitable inner contradictions . . . of bourgeois society."

This divergence mirrors a tension that informs *La Comédie humaine* itself. Do immutable human types precede the specific, dynamic structure of nineteenth-century Parisian social life, or do character-types (and even typification itself) emerge only out of this social structure? In other words, does *La Comédie humaine* ground its own practice of typification within the social environment it attempts to represent? In the 1842 preface to *La Comédie humaine* Balzac describes his style of characterization as an objective science that is imposed on and independent of the social universe he is depicting. The type is merely "the unification of traits from several homogenous characters [la réunion des traits de plusieurs caractères homogènes]" (11). And these characteristic traits are not shaped in-and-through a dynamic social structure but precede this structure, as the inevitable and immutable categories of humanity. Balzac thus compares his novel cycle to work by biologists and zoologists who classify physical reality: "There have existed, there will exist in all times, Social Species just as there are Zoological Species. If Buffon made a magnificent work by trying to represent in a book the categories of zoology, isn't there a work of this kind to make for Society?" (8). Characterization is here a taxonomic enterprise, involving the division of human beings into static categories, "Espèces Sociales," which are as fixed and rigid ("there will exist in all times") as zoological species. The immense and intricate nature of social interconnection does not complicate this taxonomic structure but undergirds it: "It is not a small task to paint the two or three thousand striking figures of an epoch, for this is, surely, the sum of types which each generation presents and which the Human Comedy will consist of. This number of figures, of characters, this multitude of existences requires some frames, and, forgive the expression, some galleries. From this comes the natural divisions, already well known, of my work into Scenes of private life, provincial life, Parisian life, political life, military life and country life" (18). In this passage the very weight of multiplicity compels its own taxonomic organization. The series of novels are not an interconnected network so much as a gallery of distinct social portraits organized by the macrocategories, much as animals are organized into families, genera, and species.

Balzac's 1842 preface, however, offers only one version of his narrative method; and his reliance on the taxonomic model for the official introduction to his collected works seems related to the politics of the preface, which insistently gestures toward the need for a restored monarchy. A different picture of *La Comédie humaine* emerges in the 1839 preface to *Une Fille d'Eve*, another important autocommentary that is best known for its statements about recurring characters. At times Balzac emphasizes the same synthetic, taxonomic principles, writing:

[T]he business of the author is principally to arrive at a synthesis through analysis, to depict and bring together the elements of our life, to pose themes and work them out all in one arrangement, finally, to trace the immense physiognomy of a century by painting its principal characters.

[L'affaire de l'auteur est-elle principalement d'arriver à la synthèse par l'analyse, de dépeindre et de rassembler les éléments de notre vie, de poser des thèmes et de les prouver tout ensemble, de tracer enfin l'immense physionomie d'un siècle en peignant les principaux personnages.] (261)

However, this preface simultaneously suggests the extraordinary complexity of the society depicted; and, inherent in this complexity, the dynamic, fragmentary structure of social life. The largeness of the work is now related directly to the "immense" multiplicity of social life: "This book will contain more than a hundred distinct works, the *Thousand and One Nights* was not so considerable; but then again, our civilization is immense in details, while 'society' did not exist in the Orient that recounted for us these Arab fables [Ce livre contiendra plus de cent oeuvres distinctes, *Les Milles et Une Nuits* ne sont pas si considérables; mais aussi notre civilisation est-elle immense de détails, tandis que *la société* n'existait pas dans l'Orient que nous racontent les fabulations arabes]" (262).

The technique of characterization is also, like the scale of the work, historically specific: "Other periods were simplified by the institutions of monarchy; characters were clearly demarcated: a bourgeoisie, a merchant or artisan, a nobleman entirely free, an enslaved peasant—there you have the old society of Europe. It provides few incidents for the novel. . . . Today, Equality has produced in France infinite nuances. Previously, social caste gave to everyone a physiognomy which dominated the individual; today, the individual does not draw his physiognomy from society, but from himself." Furthermore, and most importantly, these "infinite nuances," besides being historically specific, are dynamically constituted within the present moment.

> He is the historian, that is everything. He glories in the grandeur, the variety, the
> beauty, the fecundity of his subject, however deplorable is the confusion caused by
> things in extreme opposition, by the abundance of materials, by the impetuosity of
> movements, when considered from a social point of view. This disorder is a source
> of beauties.

This passage is saturated with terms that undermine the notion of a synthetic classification of society: taxonomy is made impossible by the "confusion," "abundance of materials," "movements," and "disorder." The two passages stand in stark contrast: how is it possible to "synthesize" the inherent "confusion" of "things in extreme opposition"? How can the author "bring together the elements of our life" when this life is in part defined by "infinite nuances" and "the impetuosity of movements"? Or "pose themes and work them out all in one arrangement" when the story is always spilling out toward an insurmountable "abundance of materials"? Finally, if society can be summed up only in terms of its "disorder," how is it possible to "trace" the "physiognomy of a century by painting its principal characters"? The debate between Lukács and Robbe-Grillet is anterior to *La Comédie humaine* itself; Balzac's own work structures the polarities of its critical reception.[7]

The polemical positions exemplified by Lukács and Robbe-Grillet might not be mutually exclusive. The Balzacian "type" seems to be both static and dynamic, just as, more generally, Balzacian style is both unitary and disordered, and Balzac criticism has famously divided the author into "visionary" and "realist."[8] Thus Albert Béguin, the best-known critic of the "visionary" Balzac, is always quite clear that his reading does not negate the realistic dimension of *La Comédie humaine*. On the contrary, the very tendency toward realism helps heighten the visionary quality that Béguin observes.

> The singular impression that one gets—*and I speak here of the novels which are
> most down-to-earth, not even to mention the fantastic stories or the mystical books*—
> come precisely from the way that everything simultaneously conforms to our habitual
> image of the world and its reassuring norms and seems surrounded by a strangeness
> through which enter the divine and the demonic. Reality is there—solid, concrete,
> immovably established in its equilibrium of familiar matter; men's faces appear in
> broad daylight; their gestures, their desires are maintained in those moderate mea-
> sures which give quotidian life its reassuring banality. And yet, these blocks of the

real, exactly as they would when we are in the least bit dreaming, seem to emerge here out of a large shadow, out of an immense sea of nocturnal water, the waves of which surround from all sides the unchanging appearances of things. (42–43)

Béguin's distinction can easily be assimilated into the antimimetic school of Balzac criticism. Certainly, in the motion from "blocks of the real [ces blocs du réel]" to "a large shadow [une grande ombre]" we can read the familiar trajectory of defamiliarization in which the literary text becomes estranged from and distinct from external or social reality. However, the dynamic shifting that Béguin identifies can also, itself, reflect on, and get generated in relation to, the complexity of social reality. The impingement of these large shadows on "solid" or "immovable" reality might not suggest a dissolution of mimetic form but rather indicate two distinct yet complementary modes of confronting the same crowded, dispersed, competitive social world. The two styles register that same double vision which generates the static and dynamic aspects of Balzacian typification. In *Ferragus*, for example, Balzac moves seamlessly from describing the boundless explosions of individual interests to the shadowy landscape highlighted by Béguin.

> Every door yawns and turns on its hinges like the articulations of a huge lobster, invisibly operated by thirty thousand men and women, each one of whom lives in six square feet, which has a kitchen, a workspace, a bed, some children, a garden; who cannot see clearly and yet has to see everything. Imperceptibly these joints begin to crack, movement is passed on from one to another, the streets are filled with talk. At noon, everything is living, the chimneys smoke, the monster eats; then it roars and its thousand legs get agitated. A wonderful sight! But, O Paris: whoever has not admired your somber landscapes, pierced with only glimmers of light, your silent and profound cul-de-sacs; whoever has not heard your murmurings, between midnight and two in the morning, knows nothing still of your true poetry and your bizarre and large contrasts. (29)

The *éclatement* of individual interests leads to a blurring of vision, so that no one can clearly see through to the totality of this mass of people. The obscurity that Béguin eloquently describes flows out of the dispersion inherent in social stratification, just as the end of the passage couples the "true poetry" of Parisian life with the "bizarre and large contrasts" of social inequality. The description thus fuses the realistic and visionary elements of Balzac, and reveals the connection between these two modes to be the boundlessness, or invisibility, of Paris's social multiplicity. Like Béguin, other critics of Balzac have noted this double vision, with contrasts between "unity" and "division," a "single tendency" and "a series of complex oppositions," or a "totalizing intention" and a "kaleidoscopic explosion."[9]

What I have termed the reversal of figure and ground in Balzac is thus a switch-point for two tendencies in Balzacian style. This reversal occurs when the "type" in Balzac shifts from embodying a specific quality, shared by a large group of people, in a single character to registering how an individual character's qualities emerge through his or her position in relation to a large group of people. This transformation captures an essential tension within literary characterization, as a character both encompasses a series of referents— Barthes's bundle of extratextual qualities or "semes"—and occupies a narrative position dynamically integrated into the discursive totality. In this way a character is simultaneously projected *outside* the discourse and embedded *within* a narrative structure. This doubleness is strikingly realized in the particular "double vision" of Balzac, at once realistic and visionary, unified and fragmentary, static and kaleidoscopic. Look again at the description of four characters in *Ferragus*: "[L]à, jolie femme; plus loin, vieux et pauvre; ici, tout neuf comme la monnaie d'un nouveau règne; dans ce coin, élégant comme une femme à la mode." On the one hand, the character "over there" is defined by the concise abstraction "pretty woman." On the other hand, her spatial demarcation gives her a narrative *position*, in relation to the other three characters, that affects the way we receive this specific seme. In this example, spatial position is equivalent to syntactic position, and since the anonymous characters do not appear again in the novel, syntactic position is equivalent to narrative position. We have also seen how the extended catalog in *César Birotteau* creates a tension between the description of each character and each character's position, within a multiple group, that grows as the sentence continues on and on. But how could we extend this kind of tension back to *Le Père Goriot*, and the way we comprehend the characters of Rastignac and Goriot in relation to narrative positions that are elaborated not in terms of a single sentence but in terms of the novel as a whole?

The Character-System in *Le Père Goriot*

La belle loi de soi pour soi

In this discussion I want to root the essentially *formal* problem of the balance between Rastignac and Goriot as organizing centers of the narrative in the competitive organization of Paris as a social totality. Rastignac's and Goriot's histories are precariously situated within a greater whole, unfolding within a massive social structure that puts individuals into social categories and can always subsume each individual within the larger group forming this category. This social instability, as we have seen, creates narrative instability, generating a storytelling structure that needs to constantly turn attention "à une autre." The specific spaces that Rastignac and Goriot occupy are charged with this more general conflict. This doesn't mean that the literary configuration of this conflict is simply a discursive elaboration of an ideological problem. The social

pressures that animate the tension between Rastignac and Goriot do not somehow corrode the formal coordinates of the character-system. On the contrary,
these social pressures come alive only *because* of the dynamic workings of
literary form, within which the relative domination and subordination of particular characters is meaningful.

What is specific about Paris, as we have seen, is the mass competition between individual interests. In his 1842 preface Balzac notes "the beautiful law
of *every man for himself* on which rests the unity of the composition [la belle
loi de *soi pour soi* sur laquelle repose l'unité de composition]" (8). The paradoxical formation of narrative *unity* through fragmented and conflicting individual interests reiterates the way that the social structure is itself formed
through these interests; as Balzac writes in *La Cousine Bette*, "civilization
is impossible without the continual grating of personalities and interests [la
civilisation est impossible sans le frottement continuel des esprits et des inté-
rêts]" (246). This *frottement* governs the "tempest of interests [tempête d'inté-
rêts]" crowded together in Paris, assuring that the story of any individual character will always spill out toward other characters.

Parisian reality is defined by multiplicity, and, more specifically, by the continual grating and misalignment of individual private interests. This tempest,
ocean, or battlefield of interests inevitably results in inequality: "Everywhere,
and in all things, inequality of conditions bursts out in Paris, in this country
drunk with equality [Partout, et en toute chose, éclate à Paris l'inégalité des
conditions, dans ce pays ivre d'égalité]" (*Le Cousin Pons*, 334). Or, as the
aggrieved title character claims in *La Cousine Bette*, "Adeline and me, we are
of the same blood, our parents are brothers, but she is in a mansion, and I am
in a garret" (58). Similarly, the Maison Vauquer is not simply lost within the
crowded grid of Parisian neighborhoods but distinctively poor: "No neighborhood in Paris is more horrible, or, let's say it, more unknown [Nul quartier de
Paris n'est plus horrible, ni, disons-le, plus inconnu]" (45). Paris bursts with
inequality because of the competitive structure that organizes the interaction
of individual interests. As we have seen, the double nature of the Balzacian
type revolves around the way that an individual both subsumes a social category and can always get drowned within it. This is because any such "category"
is the abstraction of the many real individuals competing for position.

In *Le Père Goriot*, a novel that equates itself with Parisian reality, and one
that gives birth to Balzac's strategy of recurring characters, there are constant
allusions to this structure of competition, most famously in Vautrin's monologues to Rastignac.

"I have the honor to make you further observe, that there are only twenty Attorneys
General in France, and that you aspirants to that position are twenty thousand. . . . A
quick fortune is the problem which needs to be solved at this moment by fifty thousand
young men who all find themselves in your position. You are one of that number.

Consider the efforts that you have to make and the bitterness of the combat. It's necessary that you eat up one another like spiders in a pot, since there aren't fifty thousand
good positions. . . . You can find that for every million of this herd of human cattle
there are ten sharp ones who put themselves above it all, even the laws. . . .' (143–46)

Three times in his central speech Vautrin punctuates his diatribe about morality
to offer these specific quantitative equations. Unlike other aspects of Vautrin's
perspective, this description of Parisian reality is never called into question.
The same asymmetric formula occurs at other points in the text, and also in
other novels, such as the lines near the beginning of *Les Employés* describing
the competition for a place to work (in Paris) or a passage in *Le Cousin Pons*
detailing competition for a place to live (in Paris):

Célestine honestly believed herself a superior woman. . . . But in the social order, just
as in the natural order, there are more young shoots than there are trees, more young
fry than fish that arrive at their full development: most potentials, like Athanase Gran-
son, must therefore die, suffocating, like grains which fall onto a naked rock. . . . many
called and few elected is a law of the City as well as of the Heavens. (40)

You can't realize what contortions are inspired by every place which gives residence
in Paris. To live in Paris is a universal desire. For every sale of a tobacco-license, or
a postal-license, one hundred women get up like a single person and make moves so
that their friends can get it for them. (241)

It is this structure of competition that puts each character amid many others,
creating the agitation of the story itself. Thus Mme de Langeais, whose knowledge of high society mirrors Vautrin's demystified perspective on society as a
whole, cynically downplays the significance of Goriot's troubles: " 'Oh! My
God!' said Mme de Langeais, 'yes, that seems pretty horrible, and yet. . . . don't
we see this tragedy taking place every day? [Ne voyons-nous pas cette tragédie
s'accomplisant tous les jours?] Here [ici], the daughter-in-law is completely
impertinent to the father-in-law, who has sacrificed everything for his son. Further along [plus loin], a son-in-law puts his mother-in-law at the door . . .' "
(114–15). Mme de Langeais drifts away from Goriot's particular story with
the same spatial coordinates we have seen before: "ici . . . plus loin. . . ." The
simultaneity of these tragic stories is simply another example of overcrowdedness, of "la lutte" that takes place among individual interests at all levels of
social life. The social fusion that "semble se dire après chaque oeuvre finie: à
une autre" radically contextualizes both a momentary scandal (when Vautrin is
uncovered) and an individual's entire life (when Goriot passes away):

If at first the diners talked about Vautrin and the events of the day, they soon obeyed
the serpentine path of the conversation, and started to talk about duels, about penal
servitude, about justice, about laws to reform, about prisons. Then they found themselves a thousand paces from Jacques Collins, Victorine and her brother. . . . The

habitual carelessness of this egotistical world which, the next day, would have in the quotidian events of Paris another prey to devour, resumed its usual sway. (240)

"One of the privileges of this good city of Paris is that a person can be born here, live here, die here without anybody paying attention to you. Let us profit from the advantages of civilization. There were sixty deaths today, do you want to pity the entire Parisian hecatombs?" (309)

If Mme de Langeais suggests that such a superimposition of stories drowns out the particular tragedy of Goriot—"don't we see this tragedy taking place every day"—I want to argue that the way Goriot's death is drowned out *generates* Balzac's novelistic tragedy. The precariousness of the individual story—and of the individual—in the face of "social fusion" is emphasized early in *Le Père Goriot*, right after the reference to the novel's specifically Parisian setting. We have already been told that the Maison Vauquer is a site where a multitude of people (and perspectives) converge: "A bourgeois hotel . . . between the Latin Quarter and the Faubourg Saint-Marceau . . . admitted equally men and women, young people and old men." The Maison Vauquer is composed of many intersecting points of view, or what we might more accurately call *points of interest*, all positioned in relation to each other, just as the hotel itself is located only "between" different neighborhoods. This relativity and multiplicity are then extended to the entire city: "Could this be understood outside of Paris? It's doubtful. The particularities of this scene full of observations and of local colors could not be appreciated except between the hills of Montmartre and the heights of Montrouge, in this illustrious valley of rubbish incessantly about to fall and of black streams of mud; a valley full of real suffering, of often false joys, and so terribly agitated that it requires something unimaginably outrageous to produce a sensation of any duration" (44). The description centers on the phrase "valley full of real suffering [vallée remplie de souffrances réelles]," where we can see, again, a two-way link between suffering and multiplicity. The quantity ("full [remplie]") is both an appurtenant attribute of the suffering (the suffering is worse because there is so much of it) and an originary cause *of* the suffering—sensations can't last long precisely because each individual case of suffering is conditioned by, and emerges in, the crowded structure that pushes us "à une autre." Social fullness entails this suffering, through the fragmentary multiplicity it generates, so that "la vallée remplie de souffrances" must be situated in the "tempest of interests" constituting Parisian life. This tempest creates a superabundance of individual cases, and, out of this superabundance, an overflow of suffering due to the inevitable misalignment of individual interests within the seething whole. This foregrounding of the social multiplicity that threatens the stability of each individual experience helps explain the narrator's two uses of "between [entre]" in the opening paragraph—"between the Latin Quarter and the Faubourg Saint-Marceau," and, expanding from here, "between the hills of Montmartre and the heights of Montrouge." These prepositions do not simply give an approximate geographical location but suggest that *any* location within the city is approximate, dependent on the *frottement*, or social fusion, that constantly destabilizes fixed positions.

If this area is full ("remplie") of suffering, it is also full ("pleine") of images to observe. In other words, the social reality that threatens the individual story also generates narrative plenitude, in "the particularities of this scene full of observations and of local colors [les particularités de cette scène pleine d'observations et de couleurs locales]." Through this phrase the passage subtly connects *descriptive* fullness with *social* multiplicity, so that the plenitude of observations and local colors—in other words, a fullness of meaning—is linked to the social fullness of the Parisian landscape, or the multiplicity of human beings. Peter Brooks has identified this kind of semantic fullness as central to Balzacian realism: "Here we touch on the core of the Balzacian project and aesthetic: to make the plane of representation imply, suggest, open onto the world of spirit as much as can possibly be imagined; to make the vehicles of representation evocative of significant tenors. . . . Hence the 'pressure' applied to the surface of the real, the insistence of the recording glance, striving toward that moment where, as Albert Béguin has put it, 'view becomes vision.' Balzacian description is regularly made to appear the very process of investing meaning in the world, demonstrating how surface can be made to intersect with signification. . . . Everything in the real—facades, furniture, clothing, posture, gesture—must become sign" (*Melodramatic Imagination*, 125). The passage from *Le Père Goriot* embeds this signifying process within a specific social context. By juxtaposing "pleine d'observations" and "remplie de souffrances réelles," the passage creates a dialectic between two distinct kinds of fullness, between oversignificant *meaning* and overcrowded *social ground*.

This dialectic is an elaboration of the more general conflict between interior and exterior. Meaning, in the opening pages of *Le Père Goriot*, is what can be abstracted out of social reality, presented as "observation" and inflected through an interior sensibility. The fullness of observation depends on an observing consciousness; it implies the very fullness of individual interiority that ultimately makes social multiplicity so problematic. Already, in the invocation of "les particularités de cette scène pleine d'observations et de couleurs locales," the narrative voice is trying to negotiate a vantage point, a position within the story from which to view a *social* fullness that is characterized by the way it engulfs any discrete perspective. In this sense, the passage dramatizes the particular efforts of the narrative voice to find a space for interiority, from which signification can take place. After noting how rare are "sensations of any duration," the narrative continues: "However, one encounters here and there those woes which the accumulation of vice and virtue renders grand and solemn [Cependant il s'y rencontre çà et là des douleurs que l'agglomération des vices et des vertus rend grandes et solennelle]" (44). Again, we can see a dialectic between the quantitative dispersion of real human beings (implied through the "ça et là") and the qualitative (abstract) accumulation of "vice and virtue."

The pressure of the distinction between social and descriptive fullness soon pushes the narrative to a different reference point: the implied reader, who is specifically invoked as the observer of the scene. Now the reader, like the narrator, must be inside the system, inside Paris, to "understand" the story, but also outside Paris, able to inflect this multiplicity, this social field, through his own interior consciousness: "This drama is neither a fiction, nor a novel. *All is true*, it is so realistic, that anyone could recognize the elements in himself, in his own heart perhaps" (44). Here "the heart" is an emblem for the meaningful, for the sentimental, for the interior or metaphorical; it can unify, without getting absorbed by, social plurality. This heart converts "*particularities*" into "*elements*," or, in Brooks's terms, forces "the plane of representation to yield, to deliver the plane of signification" (126). However, the introductory paragraph also depicts the heart in an inverse fashion, as precisely the fragile, powerless interior that, no matter how sheltered, will inevitably be broken by social plurality: "The chariot of civilization . . . barely delayed by a heart less easy to pulverize than the others and which halts its wheel, quickly shatters it and continues its glorious march. [Le char de la civilisation . . . à peine retardé par un coeur moins facile à broyer que les autres et qui enraye sa roue, l'a brisé bientôt et continue sa marche glorieuse.]" The essence of the opening passage is embodied in these two extremely different descriptions of "the heart" (which elaborate the two different kinds of "fullness"): the interior sensibility that filters social reality while developing the coherency of its own subjective perspective, and the interior which is shattered in-and-through the social world that it both subsists in and stands in contrast to. This contrast establishes the coordinates that will organize the positions of the novel's two co-protagonists, even before they are introduced. To account for the mysterious division between Goriot and Rastignac, we need to read their intertwined stories through this dialectic between subjective interiority and social exteriority, which is established in the novel's opening pages, and which, in a different form, resides at the heart of Balzacian characterization itself.

Goriot: The Interior as Exterior

From the beginning of the novel, from his name, Père Goriot is depicted as a man who suffers above the common mark, but whose suffering is apprehended only through exterior forms. There is an insurmountable distance between Goriot's subjective experience of suffering and the representation of this suffering in the novel. This distance is created through the mediation of social perception, which turns any emotion, however subjective, into an object. While Vautrin, in the first introduction of the characters, "se disait ancien négociant [called himself an old merchant]" and Rastignac "se nommait-il [gave his name]," our co-protagonist "se laissait nommer [let himself be called] le père Goriot" (50–51). His externally given name is indissolubly bound up with his internal pain, but only as this pain *manifests itself* through Goriot's physical and economic decline. Besides pitying Goriot's pain, we come to pity the way it is expressed, getting drained of its own interiority.

After the opening description of the Maison Vauquer and Paris, the narrator soon introduces the seven main residents, ending with Père Goriot. It makes sense that Goriot comes last, since he is introduced only in-and-through the reactions of the others:

> Among the eighteen fellow diners there could be found . . . a poor snubbed creature, a scapegoat on whom rained pleasantries. . . . This sufferer was the retired vermicelli-merchant, Old Goriot, on whose head a painter would, like the storyteller, have made the light of his painting fall. By what chance had the oldest lodger been struck with this half hateful contempt, this persecution mixed with pity, this nonrespect toward unhappiness? (58)

Here the narrator both signals (and spatializes) the textual attention that Goriot merits and casts "the light" of narrative interest in his direction only *through* the other residents. The exterior presentation of Goriot's pain is clarified in the next description, when the narrator writes, "His physiognomy, which secret troubles [des chagrins secrets] had insensibly rendered more sad from day to day, seemed the most desolate of all those who surrounded the table" (68). This sentence makes Goriot's obscure interior sufferings, or "chagrins secrets," *doubly* exterior: first as they manifest themselves in "his physiognomy" and then as this physiognomy is multiply refracted, put in relation to (and implicitly observed by) "all those who surrounded the table." This distinction is important, since it shows how Balzac carefully combines the *physically* exterior and the *socially* exterior, the simply external and the explicitly multiple—a convergence that is at the heart of his system of typification.

The objectification of Goriot's pain is developed in the next few pages, as the man's suffering, already translated as his decline ("more sad from day to day"), is rendered through material, external signs: "When his stock of clothes was worn out, he bought calico at fourteen sous per ell to replace his fine linen. His diamonds, his gold snuffbox, his chain, his jewels disappeared one by one. . . . He became progressively thinner; his calves shrank; his face, swollen with the contentment of a happy bourgeois tradesman, got excessively lined; his forehead became wrinkled; his jaw stood out" (69). This passage continues to intertwine two aspects of Goriot's suffering—its manifestation on the exterior, physical plane, and the way that these physical effects lend themselves to interpretation by all the other lodgers—until these two aspects seem almost indistinct. In fact, their combination shows how Balzac's system of typification is linked to social interconnection. Thus: "His blue eyes, once so lively, took on a sad, leaden gray tint, they had faded, moistened no more, and their red edges seemed to ooze blood. To some, it caused horror; to others, it provoked pity" (69). Here the *direct* emotions—"horror" and "pity"—are reserved for the anonymous "uns" and "autres" who observe Goriot, while his own subjective experience is rendered only through the physical, external condition of his eyes.

Throughout this introductory passage, Goriot is emphasized as the object of other people's analysis, of "those who observed him superficially [ceux qui l'observaient superficiellement]" (69). And these observers, because of the generally fragmented nature of Parisian social life, cannot accurately understand him: "As for other people, the particular pull of Parisian life made them forget, when leaving the rue Neuve-Sainte-Geneviève, the poor old man whom they mocked [Quant aux autres personnes, l'entraînement particulier de la vie parisienne leur faisait oublier, en sortant de la rue Neuve-Sainte-Geneviève, le pauvre vieillard dont ils se moquaient]" (70). If their flawed observation of Goriot is linked to the general pull of Parisian life—which always compels everyone toward another *oeuvre* or person—these limited observations constitute the fulcrum of the story itself, as the narrator breaks from his descriptive frame to self-consciously refer to the narrative: "And so toward the end of November 1819, the period when this drama burst forth, every one in the hotel had well-fixed ideas about the poor old man [Aussi, vers la fin du mois de novembre 1819, époque à laquelle éclata ce drame, chacun dans la pension avait-il des idées bien arrêtées sur le pauvre vieillard]" (70). While the narrator has introduced Goriot only after all the other pensionnaires, this sentence restores our sense of his centrality to the novel. But this centrality is now paradoxically mediated through the attention of "chacun dans la pension," and, more specifically, through their fragmented and multiple external observations. Thus Goriot's centrality is, from the introductory section of the novel, facilitated through the very incompleteness of its representation.

Rastignac: The Exterior as Interior

Rastignac's elevation as the novel's potential protagonist occurs gradually during this introductory section. In the first catalog description of the seven boarders the narrative does not emphasize Rastignac, except in placing him together with Victorine Taillefer: "two figures formed a striking contrast with the mass of boarders and familiars [deux figures y formaient un contraste frappant avec la masse des pensionnaires et des habitués]" (54). This distinction is somewhat attenuated because it is shared by two people and does not immediately motivate heightened attention toward Rastignac. In fact, the first description of him within the seven-part catalog is the briefest of all the boarder sketches, and consists mostly of external and sociological details:

Eugène de Rastignac had a typically southern face, a pale complexion, black hair, blue eyes. His appearance, manners and his habitual bearing indicated that he was the child of a noble family, where education had concerned above all the traditions of good taste. If he practiced economy in his dress, if on ordinary days he wore his clothing from a year ago, nevertheless he could go out occasionally looking like an elegant young man. Ordinarily he wore an old coat, a shabby waistcoat, the student's wretched, black, faded, badly knotted tie, worn-out pants and boots that had been resoled. (55–56)

While this passage can certainly be read for important themes—especially the crucial contrast between (and imbrication of) wealth and poverty—its *position* within the overall narrative works against this. The short descriptive passage, following the more extensive portrait of Victorine and preceding the more intensive passage on Vautrin, does not attract the reader's attention (or, to use the narrator's own metaphor, establish the young man as the place where a painter's light would fall). It is as though we are asked to quickly move past Rastignac, so that the description itself becomes weighted down toward the exterior plane, rather than focusing in on Rastignac's own character.

Rastignac appears in two other contexts in the introductory section. Significantly, he is mentioned as a witness to Goriot, and, more specifically, Goriot's suffering. His own emerging centrality is thus linked with, and subordinated to, the importance of the other co-protagonist. We have already seen the passage that attributes the story (of Goriot) to Rastignac's "inquisitive observations." Rastignac's perception is also woven into the general descriptive process we examined above, in which Goriot's suffering is simultaneously emphasized *and* rendered only on the exterior plane. Looking at the full introduction of Goriot, we can see how Eugène's perspective, in particular, is threaded into the collective observations about the older man: "A similar reunion must offer, and did offer in miniature, the elements of a complete society. Among the eighteen fellow diners there could be found . . . a poor snubbed creature, a scapegoat on whom rained pleasantries. At the beginning of his second year, this figure became for Eugène de Rastignac the most outstanding of all those in the company of whom he was condemned to live for another two years. This sufferer was the retired vermicelli-merchant, Old Goriot." First described cursorily, and then only in relation to the other co-protagonist, Eugène is finally presented, at the end of this introductory section, from the perspective that will dominate the rest of the narrative and motivate his increasing centrality within the novel. This third description focuses on his interior desire, which has been, and will continue to become, heightened by the dynamic pull of Parisian society. This description of Rastignac's consciousness initially places him in a social context. The narrative has not yet collapsed its own perspective into Rastignac's inflamed desire; rather, it attempts to describe the growth of this desire from a distanced and objective point of view. Starting from this distanced perspective, however, the narrative seems affected by the object it is describing, especially in the long sentence detailing all the circumstances that provoke Rastignac's desire:

> In his successive initiations he gradually loses his greenness, widens the horizon of his life, and finishes with some perception of the layers of human beings which compose society. If he began by admiring the carriages parading the Champs-Elysées on a sunny afternoon, he soon begins to covet them. . . . His childish illusions, his provincial ideas disappear . . . his father, his mother, his two brothers, his two sisters, and an aunt whose fortune consisted of annuities, all lived on the small Rastignac estate. . . . The sight of the constant distress which had been generously hidden from him, the comparison that he was forced to make between his sisters, who seemed quite beautiful to him in his childhood, and the women of Paris, who had realized for him a beauty he had dreamed of, the uncertain future of that numerous family which counted on him, the parsimonious attention which he saw them take for the smallest affairs, the wine which his family drank which was made from the dregs of the wine-press, in short, a crowd of circumstances futile to record here exponentially increased his desire [décuplèrent son désir] to succeed and gave him thirst for distinctions. (71–72)

In this last sentence the narrative itself starts to "décupler," so that the external description of circumstances flows seamlessly into Rastignac's consciousness of these circumstances, as the rhythm of the sentence begins to resemble the way a person contemplates "a crowd of circumstances." In other words, the form of the sentence responds to the pressures of what it is describing, until the narrator seems to have forgotten himself, pulling abruptly away from the list of concerns that are "futile to record here"—and which he has already spent too much time enumerating. This formal distention is directly related to what I've termed the space of the protagonist: both in the simple quantitative sense that the force of Rastignac's desire motivates a lengthy sentence, and in the way that the omniscient narrative voice moves toward, and nearly gets swallowed up in, Rastignac's own point of view.

The sentence is important because it *dramatizes* Rastignac's narrative centrality, making this centrality a contingent element within the novelistic totality rather than a fixed perspective organizing the narrative as a whole. And it equates Rastignac's centrality with his interior consciousness, so that the narrative perspective qualitatively changes when it represents this consciousness. The pull of the narrative voice toward Rastignac becomes clear again at the fault line between his story and the more general narrative frame, when, at the end of the paragraph, the narrator suddenly abandons his focus on Rastignac.

> Several days after his return to Paris, Rastignac sent the letter of his aunt to Mme Beauséant. The Viscountess responded with an invitation to a ball on the following evening [une invitation de bal pour le lendemain].

Such was the general situation of the boardinghouse at the end of November 1819.
Several days later, Eugène, after having gone to Mme Beauséant's ball, returned toward two o'clock at night [Quelques jours plus tard, Eugène, après être allé au bal de Mme de Beauséant, rentra vers deux heures dans la nuit].

The shift from Eugène to the Maison Vauquer causes a change in time frames, from the subjectively perceived "lendemain" to the objectively measured "fin du mois de novembre 1819." As though to emphasize the inherent tension between these two temporal scales, the next sentence *returns* to a subjective register, in continuing Eugène's story, "quelques jours plus tard . . . *vers* deux heures dans la nuit."

Georges Poulet has described the way narrative attention can get pulled across from an objective to a subjective point of view: "The external judgment about an objective work is replaced by participation in the purely subjective movement that this work reveals and communicates. . . . [T]his has as its end point the revelation of an interior [Le jugement externe sur une oeuvre objective est remplacé par la participation au mouvement purement subjectif que cette oeuvre révele et communique. . . . [E]lle a pour fin de réveler l'homme intérieur]" (23). This kind of dissonance, exemplified in the double shift of time frames, is reminiscent of Stendhal's strategy in *Le Rouge et le noir*, where the tension between private and public temporal modes also helps create a sense of the protagonist's detached singularity. Both Stendhal's novel—an exemplary site of the strong protagonist in nineteenth-century French fiction—and *Le Père Goriot* construct their young protagonist's centrality in-and-through a heightened sense of his interiority. "*Except* for the passion of the hero," Stendhal writes in the preface to *Lucien Leuwen*, "a novel must be a mirror" (761). Like Julien's secure space in *Le Rouge et le noir*, the more contested centrality of Eugène de Rastignac in *Le Père Goriot* is indissociable from the focalization of his consciousness or interiority. Eugène's interior perspective—his emotions, thoughts, and desires—is threaded into the formal, thematic, and plot structure of *Le Père Goriot*; pull it out and you unravel the entire novel. However, if Goriot's interior suffering is apprehended only in its exteriority—as the external signs registered by a multiple social field—Rastignac's consciousness, which is represented in its interior fullness, is completely shaped by interactions with this Parisian social world. The narrator famously writes: "Rastignac had one of those heads full of powder which exploded at the slightest shock [Rastignac avait une de ces têtes pleines de poudre qui sautent au moindre choc]" (136). The consciousness that we watch become the central interiority of *Le Père Goriot* is simply this series of explosions, always sparked by encounters on "le champ de bataille de la civilisation parisienne."

A typical description of Eugène's interactions with Mme de Beauséant and M. d'Ajuda:

Mme de Beauséant rose, and called him over to her, without paying the least attention to Eugène, who stood, overwhelmed by the dazzle of a marvelous wealth, believing in the reality of the *Arabian Nights*, and not knowing where to hide in finding himself in the presence of this woman without being noticed by her. The Viscountess had lifted the index finger of her right hand, and by a pretty movement had indicated to the marquis a place in front of her. There was in this gesture such a violent, despotic passion that the marquis let go of the door handle and came. Eugène watched him, not without envy.

"So there," he said to himself, "is the man with the brougham! But is it necessary, then, to have prancing horses, servants in livery and oceans of money to obtain the glance of a woman in Paris?" The demon of luxury gnawed at his heart, the fever for profit seized him, thirst for money dried up his throat. He had one hundred and thirty francs for his trimester. His father, his mother, his brothers, his sisters and his aunt didn't spend two hundred francs a month, among all of them. This rapid comparison between his present situation and the goal which it was necessary to move toward ended up stupefying him.

"Why," said the viscountess laughing, "*can't you* come to the Italiens?" (107–8)

What a striking difference between Eugène's inconsequential place in the story and the attention that the narrative lavishes on him! In this short passage, the narrator attempts to fully represent one of Eugène's "shocks" by spanning a range of different voices, from omniscient description of Eugène's consciousness ("Eugène watched him, not without envy") to direct quotation (" 'So there,' he said to himself, 'is the man with the brougham!' ") to free indirect discourse ("[h]e had one hundred and thirty francs for his trimester"). Goriot never motivates such a dense cluster of narrative techniques in this novel, nor does any other character. Critics have not sufficiently noted how Rastignac's claim for centrality is based not primarily on what happens to him but on the way his consciousness is represented.

Unlike the narrator, who organizes the entire scene around Eugène's mortified thoughts, the characters in the story do not pay "the least attention to Eugène" and continue their own conversation. In the *discours*, Rastignac is at the center of things; in the *histoire*, he is unnoticed. However, Eugène's consciousness is not itself removed from the social situation but, on the contrary, completely shaped by it. This is an essential distinction from Julien Sorel. Rastignac remains fixated on the scene in front of him, his thoughts spurred by the right index finger of Mme de Beauséant. The omniscient sentence that bridges the direct narration of Eugène's thoughts and the more intimate free indirect discourse sums up what is controlling this interiority: "The demon of luxury gnawed at his heart, the fever for profit seized him, thirst for money dried up his throat." Eugène's interiority is structured by what is outside him, even as the representation of his interiority is disrupted by this intrusive omniscient sentence. And if Eugène's interiority can flare up through the miserable comparison to those around him, it can also quickly die down. The description of his thoughts ends because the thoughts themselves seem to have ended:

> This rapid comparison between his present situation and the goal which it was necessary to move toward ended up stupefying him.
> "Why," said the viscountess laughing, "*can't you* come to the Italiens?"
> "Business. I am dining with the English ambassador."
> "Throw him over."
> Once a man lies, he is inevitably compelled to pile deception on top of deception.

The rapid workings of Eugène's consciousness, which orients the narrative perspective, is itself shaped around the social gap between his present condition and his ambitions, a gap that stupefies him. Within one sentence we go from the quickness of Eugène's interiority to its stupefaction, which then leads us back into the external, social scene that he is watching. The next narrative intervention ("Once a man lies . . .") comes from an omniscient, and aphoristic, perspective, entirely removed from Eugène's interior point of view.

Between the Exterior and the Interior

In Goriot and Rastignac, then, we have two opposed character-spaces that will shape the structure of the narrative as a whole. The narrative's messiness—its rapid shifts between scenes, its jumpy pace, its tangled plotlines, its emphasis on transitional passages and on in-betweenness—comes out of the central tug-of-war between Eugène and Goriot, a conflict between them not within the *histoire* but rather as competing kinds of central character-spaces within the total form of the novel. This tug-of-war highlights the estrangement of interiority and exteriority, an estrangement that is rooted in the story's larger social "background": the competitive structure of Parisian multiplicity that is so memorably highlighted in the novel's opening. If the introductory section establishes Goriot's exteriorized interiority and Rastignac's interiorized exteriority, the novel dramatizes this opposition in the scene immediately following the introductory exposition, which, we have already seen, begins with Rastignac returning to the Maison Vauquer from the Faubourg Saint-Germain "vers deux heures dans la nuit." The narrator follows Rastignac's return from Mme de Beauséant's ball, once again drifting from an external description into the rhythm of Rastignac's own consciousness. The split between this consciousness and the exterior social world is first figured in the opposition between Rastignac's silent pensiveness upon his return to the Maison Vauquer and Christophe's noisiness:

> Rastignac arrived at this moment and was able to go up to his room without making any noise [sans faire de bruit], followed by Christophe, who was making a great deal. Eugène undressed, put on his slippers and an old coat, lit up his turf fire, and nimbly

prepared himself for work, while the clatter of Christophe's heavy boots still covered the slight noise of his preparations. Eugène rested thoughtfully [Eugène resta pensif] for a few minutes before plunging into his law books. He had become aware [il venait de reconnaître] that Mme la vicomtesse de Beauséant was one of the queens of Parisian fashion, and that her house was one of the most charming in the whole Faubourg Saint-Germain. (73)

We should note two related aspects of this passage: the narrative shift from an exterior to an interior presentation of Rastignac and the interaction between Rastignac and Christophe. The passage turns on the foregrounding of Eugène's thoughts, in the development from "without making any noise" to "Eugène rested thoughtfully" to "He had become aware." By the end of the passage the narrative has started to focus on Eugène's subjective reprocessing of the evening, so that the first, crucial excursion into the Faubourg Saint-Germain is retrospectively narrated, filtered through Rastignac's consciousness. The narrative shift at the end of our passage, "il venait de reconnaître," continues for several pages, modulating from Eugène's memories (still rooted in the external world) to his emotions, and finally taking on the exclamatory syntax of desire, that brain fever "which all young men affected by too lively hopes have known":

To be young, to be thirsty for society, to be hungry for women, and to see open for him two houses! To plant a foot in the Faubourg Saint-Germain in the house of the Vicomtesse de Beauséant, and fall on his knees in the house of the Comtesse de Restaud! To take one quick look, and then dive into the best houses in Paris, one after the other, and believe himself a handsome enough young man to find aid and protection in a woman's heart! To feel himself ambitious enough to strike a magnificent stride over the tightrope on which he must walk with the assurance of an acrobat in order not to fall, and to have found in a charming woman the best of balance poles! (75)

This description is a turning point in this novel, and, one could argue, in the nineteenth-century European novel more generally. As in the description of Elizabeth Bennet's trip across the muddy field to visit her ailing sister, it is crucial to note not simply what the protagonist is thinking but how the protagonist's thoughts have come to occupy such a central space in the narrative universe, and how they converge with the omniscient voice at this particular juncture. In both *Pride and Prejudice* and *Le Père Goriot* the protagonist's increasing centrality facilitates thematic progress, but, at the same time, any thematic developments help motivate the protagonist's centrality: a centrality that itself is constructed through, and lends dramatic content to, the larger narrative structure. In other words, these scenes vividly show how the protagonist's centrality is not just a way to focus the narrative but can itself become the focus *of* the narrative.

This dramatization of the protagonist's very centrality is developed by the second process we can trace in our original passage: Christophe's opposition to Rastignac. First positioned in a purely functional, instrumental context, Christophe opens the door fortuitously at just the moment that Rastignac walks in. It has to be a coincidence: does a servant exist in the narrative if he opens a door and nobody appears to walks through it? This subordinate position is literalized in the next sentence and gets organized, like George Eliot's aphorism, around an opposition between silence and noise: Rastignac climbs "up to his room without making any noise, followed by Christophe, who was making a great deal." As we have seen, the narrative's focus on Rastignac is grounded in the emphasis of his interiority, which here is associated with physical silence. The opposition is extended—hammered home, as it were—when Rastignac's wandering thoughts ("Eugène . . . nimbly prepared himself for work. . . . Eugène rested thoughtfully") are interrupted by Christophe's noisiness: "the clatter of Christophe's heavy boots still covered the slight noise of his preparations." Christophe's inflection into the scene, as minor character, allows the narrative to once again contextualize its own developing focus on Rastignac. The emphasis on Eugène's interiority occurs within a larger social field, is positioned within a larger narrative structure. This is made clear at the end of this long enactment of Eugène's thoughts, when his interiority is again interrupted by the external world: "With such thoughts and before this woman who rose sublimely from the fire of peats, between his legal Code and his poverty, who would not, like Eugène, have imagined the future, who would not have decorated it with successes? His wandering thoughts anticipated so eagerly his future joys that he thought he was at the side of Mme de Restaud, when a sigh similar to the weary breath of Saint Joseph troubled the silence of the night, seizing the heart of the young man in a manner which made him take it for the groan of a dying man" (75). Here the other co-protagonist is reintroduced into the scene, now assimilated to the same shallow, external, noisy plane as Christophe. Again, Goriot's inner emotions are expressed only externally, pressed into a sigh that intrudes on the silence of Rastignac's thoughts. Again, Rastignac is interrupted, shocked out of his reveries by another person outside himself. The sentence, hovering both inside and outside Rastignac's consciousness, summarizes the dramatic structure of the entire narrative, as it presents both protagonists in their essentially incomplete nature: Goriot, whose intense suffering is here manifested in a purely external form, condensed into a sigh that floats into the next room; and Eugène, whose own consciousness, that "pensée vagabonde," appears as essentially insufficient, beholden to the exterior, and unsettled by the kind of interruption that will dog him throughout the novel. The passage develops this relationship, presenting Goriot's desperate emotions as filtered through the young student's apprehension:

He gently opened his door, and, when he was in the corridor, he perceived [il aperçut] a line of light under the door of Père Goriot. Eugène feared that his neighbor was indisposed; he moved his eye [il approcha son oeil] toward the keyhole, looked into the room [regarda dans la chambre], and saw [et vit] the old man busy at work which appeared to him [qui lui parurent] so criminal in nature that he could not help but render a service to society in examining carefully [en examinant bien] what the so-called vermicelli-manufacturer was up to in the night. Père Goriot, who without a doubt had a silver tray and a vessel like a soup tureen on the crossbar of a table flipped upside-down before him, was winding a kind of rope cable around these richly carved objects, twisting them with such great force that he was bending them, apparently to convert them into ingots [en les serrant avec une si grande force qu'il les tordait vraisemblablement pour les convertir en lingots]. (75–76)

The two long sentences narrate the same scene—Rastignac observing Goriot converting his wealth—but they split along the fault line of perception. The first sentence highlights the subjective process of apprehension. Beginning with "aperçut" in the preceding sentence, we don't simply see Goriot through Rastignac's eyes but more directly see Rastignac seeing Goriot. The sentence is punctuated with these references to the process of vision: "il approcha son oeil . . . regarda . . . vit . . . lui parurent . . . examinant bien." The second sentence follows this sight to the external object that is being seen, and once again highlights the transference of Goriot's interior emotions to the physical plane: "en les serrant avec une si grande force qu'il les tordait."[10]

This dual configuration of the co-protagonists continues throughout the novel. The next night Rastignac describes the scene to Bianchon, and once more we see Goriot's interior suffering reduced to its symptomatic exteriority: "I saw him that night twisting silver plate as if it were made of wax, and in that moment the expression on his face betrayed extraordinary emotion [Je lui ai vu cette nuit tordre un plat de vermeil, comme si c'eût été de la cire, et dans ce moment l'air de son visage trahit des sentiments extraordinaires]" (93). On the same page, we find another interior description of Rastignac, again revolving around his thoughts about the social field. As before, the narrative follows the rhythm of Rastignac's consciousness, becoming loose and distended at precisely the moment that it describes how Rastignac "exercises his thoughts": "The next day Rastignac dressed himself elegantly and went, toward three o'clock in the afternoon, to Mme de Restaud's, giving himself up to, during the walk, those mad, foolish thoughts which render the life of young men so full of beautiful emotions. . . . Eugène walked with a thousand precautions to not splatter himself with mud, but as he walked he thought about what he would say to Mme Restaud, he shaped witty comments, he invented clever rejoinders to an imaginary conversation, he prepared his polished words, his phrases after Talleyrand, in thinking of the smallest circumstances which would improve the declaration on which he would found his future" (93).

Rastignac walks as he thinks, and what he contemplates are simply imaginary, or interior, versions of anticipated social actions.

The dynamic interaction between these two character-spaces is dramatized in the next major scene, when Rastignac visits Mme de Restaud. Hurtling forward in his advancement into the Faubourg Saint-Germain, Rastignac discovers Goriot being ushered in through the backdoor. The passage brings out Rastignac's interiority and turns Goriot into an external spectacle:

> He returned to the dining room, walked through it, followed the servant, and got back into the main living room where he rested, still, in front of the window, becoming aware that it had a view of the court [en s'apercevant qu'elle avait vue sur la cour]. He wanted to see whether this Père Goriot was actually, in truth, his Père Goriot. His heart beat inside of him strangely. (95)

The subtle use of "s'apercevoir" highlights the reflexivity that is always latent within perception. In the intimate representation of Rastignac, seeing leads into thinking, or, in the root sense of "s'apercevoir," seeing to oneself, or becoming aware of what one has seen (or is seeing). It is this shift—from perception to the reflexivity of perception—that structures the emphasis of Rastignac's perspective over Goriot's; while the former is presented in terms of his consciousness, the latter is reduced to a symptomatic plane.[11] (Rastignac's perception, in other words, is rendered reflexive, while Goriot's reflections are only perceived.)

In Rastignac's visit to Mme de Restaud, his consciousness is emphasized through his perception and his apprehension, through his consciousness *of* Goriot, while Goriot himself is inflected into the scene only as a rapidly passing sight. Goriot's suffering is manifested in a negated form, as it exists *outside* of himself, or, more precisely, as it exists *inside* of Rastignac. Rastignac precipitously stumbles through the wrong door trying to get to Mme de Restaud's drawing room and hears, at a distance, Goriot's voice. Returning to the reception room, he rushes to the window, which overlooks the court, and sees Goriot leaving just as Maxime de Trailles rides in.

> At this moment, Père Goriot appeared through the door that opened from the little staircase into the court, near the carriage entrance. The old fellow was carrying his umbrella and preparing to use it, not paying attention to the great door, which had opened to allow a tilbury driven by a young man wearing the ribbon of a decoration to enter. Père Goriot had barely time to throw himself backward to avoid being run over. The spread of silk had frightened the horse and it shied before dashing forward toward the steps. The young man turned his head angrily, looked at Père Goriot, and, before jumping out, gave him a greeting which carried the constrained courtesy shown to usurers when their services are needed, or the conventional show of respect for a man with a tarnished reputation, which will be blushed for later. . . . These events followed one another with the rapidity of lightning. Too attentive to notice that he wasn't alone, Eugène suddenly heard the voice of the countess. (95–96)

Not physically harmed, Goriot is emblematically humiliated, and the near miss with the horse might remind us of that opening image of Paris's terrible destructiveness: "Le char de la civilisation, semblable à celui de l'idole de Juggernaut, à peine retardé par un coeur moins facile à broyer que les autres et qui enraye sa roue, l'a brisé beintôt et continue sa marche glorieuse" (44). And yet this suffering, this near miss, is somehow converted into the lightning-quick shock of events as they are received by Rastignac.

We remember in *The Trial* when Joseph K. accidentally stumbles upon a backroom in the office and, hearing a sigh from behind the door, hesitates, then rushes into the room to see two functionaries (and exemplary minor characters) getting beaten. Shocked by this brutal episode—which has the strange feeling of a digression, or interlude, from the main story—we are more shocked by K.'s return the next day, where he comes upon the exact same scene:

> As he passed the lumber-room again on his way out he could not resist opening the door. And what confronted him, instead of the darkness he had expected, bewildered him completely. Everything was still the same, exactly as he had found it on opening the door the previous evening. The files of old papers and the ink bottles were still tumbled behind the threshold, the Whipper with his rod and the warders with all their clothes on were still standing there, the candle was burning on the shelf, and the warders immediately began to wail and cry out "Sir!" At once K. slammed the door shut and then beat on it with his fists, as if that would shut it more securely. (111)

The suffering that is only outside of K., in the first encounter, is disturbing enough, but more terrifying still when it is trapped inside K., "real" only in terms of his interior processing of it. The Whipper and his two victims wait, night after night, for K. to enter the room, and the violence exists only in-and-through his perception of it, when he swings open the door as one might pop open one's eyes. This phenomenology of suffering is already structuring the scene in *Le Père Goriot*. As in "The Whipper," Goriot's shame is not represented in its interior actuality but is converted into what Rastignac hears, then what he sees, and then his stunned comprehension, and reprocessing, of these events.

But there is a difference. Goriot is not simply a minor character, a functionary who has an instrumental role in relation to Rastignac; he remains alive in the text as the potential hero. This makes his inflected position in the novel all the more effective. The tragedy of *Le Père Goriot* lies not only in the respective fates of Rastignac and Goriot, as characters, but also in the configuration of each of them, as character-spaces, within the novel's totality. There is a double tragedy: not simply Goriot's decline and death, but his effaced position within the novel, a narrative space that, by veiling his interiority, is at all points intertwined with the actual death. Critics have often noted the superficial resemblance between *Le Père Goriot* and *King Lear*, but the interpretive significance of this resemblance has proved puzzling. In both cases fathers are fatally dispossessed by two selfish daughters; get treated cruelly by their sons-in-law; undergo a gradual and then precipitous decline. However, this connection should not be viewed in terms of direct influence or as merely the adoption of a Shakespearean plot by Balzac. As Pierre Barbéris has pointed out, more minor, contemporaneous plays have closer links to the specific plot content of Balzac's novel.[12] Nor can a meaningful comparison stop, as some criticism does, with idle speculation about the absence of a Cordelia figure in Balzac's novelistic version of *Lear*. Rather, the connection with *King Lear* rests in the essential tragic structure of the two works. We can gain keen insight into Goriot's double tragedy—both his decline into death and the way that his interior experience of decline gets obscured in the narrative and social totality—by considering how differently the experience of Lear is amplified and dramatized through the play as a whole.

What would the tragedy of *King Lear* look like if Lear became a minor character? This odd question is at heart of the relationship between Balzac's novel and its dramatic precursor, not merely because of Goriot's strangely "obscure" tragedy but because of the remarkable character-space of Lear himself. *King Lear* might be considered a tragedy of interiority—and centrality—par excellence. Like *Le Père Goriot*, *King Lear* has a rich, multilayered system of characterization, with a manifold group of uniquely configured character-spaces. However, all aspects of characterization in *King Lear*, and all the episodes in the play, serve to elaborate and enhance Lear's centrality within the tragic structure. Certainly, Lear does not share the interest of the play in a structural sense, as Othello shares his play with Iago, or as the division between Antony and Cleopatra organizes their tragedy as a whole. But more to the point, Shakespeare deploys a distinctive series of techniques and devices to keep this play, in particular, revolving around its central character. In the subordinate story of Gloucester and his sons, we find what is often taken to be Shakespeare's most fully realized example of the double plot—in which the experience of a secondary character gets folded into the central experience of the protagonist.[13] With the onset of the storm, we encounter Shakespeare's most spectacularly realized objective correlative, as Lear's internal suffering gets symbolically externalized, becoming, quite literally, the background and landscape of the play. This use of the storm and of the Gloucester double plot are only the two dominant and most apparent devices that formulate each instant of the play in relation to the protagonist. In a unique way for Shakespeare, the central character in this play dominates and coordinates the tragic form. Nearly every human being in *King Lear* is subsumed by Lear's interiority. Social multiplicity—embodied in Kent's subordinate political role and Gloucester's subordinate plot—is contained in relation to the central story of Lear's interior suffering. Similarly, Lear's Fool's mysterious disappearance is often interpreted in relation to the disintegration of the king's own personality, just as this extraordinary minor character acts to constantly refract and reflect

Lear's consciousness when he *is* onstage, in the drama's early acts. And just as every other character's fate is inextricably bound up in, and casts light back upon, Lear's suffering, so the totality of the play exists as an extension of, and not in tension with, the protagonist's interiority. At almost every moment—with the storm, Lear's madness, the cataclysm of deaths in the final act, and the stilted, unsatisfying denouement—the tragic structure seems to be directly shaped by the impact of Lear's centrality.

Lear's powerful character-space usefully contrasts with the strange minorness of Goriot and the precarious foregrounding of Rastignac. In *The Western Canon*, Harold Bloom approvingly quotes and glosses a line from Hegel's *Aesthetics* as "the best critical passage on Shakespearean representation yet written": " 'While doing so, however, he confers on them [his characters] intelligence and imagination; and by means of the image in which they, by virtue of that intelligence, contemplate themselves objectively, as a work of art, he makes them free artists of themselves.' Overhearing their own speech and pondering these expressions, they change and go on to contemplate an otherness in the self, or the possibility of such otherness" (70). Hegel and Bloom focus on the artistic externalization of consciousness. As a character "overhears" himself, blurring the line between his interior cognition and its "object," so *King Lear* externalizes Lear's tragic consciousness, representing the protagonist in the fullness of both objectivity and subjectivity. The two central destinies in *Le Père Goriot* are cut apart in the dissolution of this kind of artistic synthesis, so that we are left with *Rastignac incompletely overhearing Goriot.* père Goriot suffers, but his interiority is never elaborated within the textual universe; Rastignac's contemplation is elaborately unfolded, but there is no authentic interiority for him to ponder. Shakespearean centrality—which can produce a consciousness that is confirmed and amplified by the character-system—splits apart in the divide between these two protagonists, as we watch Rastignac listen to Goriot (in a sentence that might sum up the novel): "Le père Goriot se retira en balbituant quelques paroles dont Eugène ne saisit pas le sens [Père Goriot withdrew into his room, muttering some words of which Eugène could not grasp the sense]" (124). In both co-protagonists consciousness is prevented, in the texture of the work of art, from freely externalizing, or actualizing, itself. To find the real tragedy in *Le Père Goriot*, we do not need to determine which co-protagonist is the hero; rather, we must understand how the question itself, in its unanswerable impact, organizes the tragic structure, and essential human significance, of the novel.

In *King Lear*, the protagonist's initial decline is marked by the loss of his men, whom Goneril and Regan reduce from a hundred to fifty to twenty-five to none. Goriot suffers a similar decline, in one of the most important parallels between the two texts, reducing his payments to Mme Vauquer, because of "a gradual diminution of fortune" (65), from twelve hundred francs a year to nine hundred to forty-five francs a month. He also begins to sell off his goods, and we see him twisting personal property into ingots in the encounter with Rastignac. For Lear, his men are a direct manifestation of his power, and when they abandon him, their disloyalty is a transparent, immediate sign of his decline. This resembles Xavier Rabourdin's vision of prebureaucratic government under a monarchy, in *Les Employés*: "In early times, under the monarchy, the armies of bureaucrats simply did not exist. Of small number, government workers obeyed the prime minister who was always in communication with the sovereign, and thus almost directly served the king. In this way, the least point of the circumference attached itself directly back to, and received its life from, the center" (44). The signifying relationship between men and king confirms Lear's centrality even when it might indicate the decline of his power. The men whom Lear loses still emanate from him; even Oswald, who so fiercely betrays Lear, seems connected to him, in the very moral disintegration that this betrayal entails. These men, with or without Lear, "attach themselves back to him" and "receive life" from him.

Goriot, on the other hand, converts his wealth into money—a universal solvent—and this money has no relationship to him; it does not carry the force of his personality, nor does it gesture back to his central interiority. For Goriot, then, the sign through which we register the decline is, in itself, constitutive of the decline, just as the novel's shrouding of his suffering is embedded in the nature of this suffering. Like the novelistic discourse—which conveys Goriot's decline even while obscuring it—the economic structure through which Goriot declines, veils him. The instant that money is transferred, it loses any signification of its previous owner. In the first overview of the pensionnaires Balzac writes about "the faces cold, hard, effaced like those on old, withdrawn currency [des faces froides, dures, effacées comme celles des écus démonétisés]" (52). This ironic invocation of the real faces originally on money can take place only through a *negative* comparison, in reference to effaced visages on withdrawn money. It is vain to search for an authentic connection between money and the face inscribed on it; by referencing this mythic representation of a face on a coin, Balzac points to the relationship that the monetary economy relentlessly denies.[14] In actuality, these "faces" are "effaced" *because* of money, because of "that misery without poetry: an economic misery, concentrated and shabby [la misère sans poésie; une misère économe, concentrée, râpée]" (49). Ultimately, you cannot possess (or lose) money the way Lear possesses (and then loses) his men because coins, unlike men, have no intrinsic value.

We have looked at the text's mediated presentation of Goriot's suffering when Rastignac observes him, legible only as it is expressed externally and symbolically through the old man's contortion of his silver household goods. At the precise moment that we lose sight of Goriot's authentic interiority, we *also* see this other kind of mediation: the transformation of personal objects whose value is rooted in their particular relationship to a particular individual

into commodified objects that bear no relationship to the person. The effacement of Goriot's interiority so skillfully achieved within the character-system
precisely reflects the fate of Goriot within the novel's economic structure, that
Parisian totality which, because of competitive interests, always directs us "à
une autre."

The relationship of monetary wealth to the effacement, and the destruction,
of the human personality is a constant concern of the novel. We have already
seen how the structure of competition within which Rastignac's development
is embedded leads people "to eat up one another like spiders in a pot." This is
exemplified in the novel's famous parable of killing the old mandarin: a death
(and a fortune) that are posited precisely in terms of having no knowledge of
the person who is being killed. We will see how Goriot dies and is forgotten,
and how the forgetfulness is implicated in the death itself. In her letter to
Rastignac, his mother talks about the sacrifice his aunt has made to raise money
for his Parisian enterprises: "You must act as wisely as a grown man, the
destinies of five persons who are dear to you rest on your shoulders. . . . My
dear Eugène, you must love your aunt, I won't tell you what she has done for
you until you have succeeded, otherwise the money would burn your fingers
[son argent te brûlerait les doigts]. You do not know, you children, what it is
to sacrifice your memories. . . . This good and upstanding woman would have
written to you herself if she didn't have gout in her fingers [la goutte aux
doigts]" (130). Two reasons are given for the effacement of what Rastignac's
aunt has done: how she earned her money is indescribable, and she can't write
because her fingers hurt. A systematic gap between human action and wealth
is replaced by a symptomatic one. Instead of a connection between two people
we have the negation of a handshake: his fingers which wouldn't be able to
touch the letter that her fingers couldn't write. Like the worn-out face on the
coins, like the old mandarin who must die an anonymous death to confer
wealth upon someone, and most of all like Père Goriot, this minor minor character exemplifies how the gap between interiority and exteriority is economically structured.

These thematic elaborations unfurl out of and lead the reader back into the
novel's central, animating focus—the characters, and character-spaces, of Rastignac and Goriot. We have seen how Balzac understands the economic process
of commodification in material terms: as the ultimate result of countless individuals who collectively form a structure of multiplicity and competition that
destroys them. At the center of this novel is the gap between Goriot and Rastignac, a gap that resembles the economic rift between Rastignac and his aunt but
runs through, and animates, the entire text, making it impossible to organize the
novel around either one of the characters. This gap both expresses the fracturing of an actualized interiority into two component parts (related to each other
but radically separate) and highlights the economic structure that converts personal worth into exchange value. These two planes of the same problem are

condensed in the scene where Goriot converts his family property into silver ingots while his interior suffering is converted into Rastignac's external observations. In both the action and its representation, interiority is transformed into, and confronted with, a radically alien version of itself.

Rastignac himself cannot fully sense the continuity between what Goriot is doing to his property and his own interaction with the old man. There is a relationship between Goriot and Rastignac that never actually takes place between the two characters but is realized through the character-spaces within the novel's totality. It is configured, precisely, in the continual development of Goriot and Rastignac as mutually incomplete narrative centers. The transference of wealth from Goriot to Rastignac—which is the novel's master plot—is defined through the splintering of a full, central protagonist into these two incomplete co-protagonists. Balzac's disenchantment with this kind of economic arrangement comes across not simply in the story he tells—how a young man gains entrance into the world of Paris in relation to an old man's death—but in the relative configuration of these two human beings at each moment in the narrative. The *narrative* gap between the two co-protagonists exemplifies the disjunction between a person's interior being and the "valuation" of this interiority on the social, exterior plane. This disjunction is shaped by the mass structure of competition: a structure that inevitably converts use value into exchange value, that makes men into tools, and that pushes us on toward the next story.

Interiority and Centrality in Le Père Goriot and King Lear

This reading of *Le Père Goriot* has used Lear's centrality as the lever against which Goriot's modern tragedy—*in* its very obscurity—takes shape. But Shakespeare's play itself uses the protagonist's formal centrality as a point of contrast *with* social and dramatic tensions that are comprehended through this asymmetric form. Turning away for a moment from Balzac's novel, I want to amplify the contrast and relationship between Lear's and Goriot's status as central character with a brief consideration of the dynamics of character-space and character-system in Shakespeare's play. If the structure of *King Lear* has proved crucial to Balzac's elaboration of Goriot's Parisian minorness, we might also read the asymmetric character-system of the play through this social realist novel. As we have seen, *King Lear* generates a unique sequence of devices that continually amplify the protagonist's centrality (the paradigmatic double plot, the storm that seems to sweep out of the protagonist's heart to engulf the stage, etc.). I want to argue that Shakespeare motivates these devices in relation to Lear's specific status as monarch. Unlike Hamlet, Othello, or Macbeth, who all aspire to greater political power, Lear starts the play as king and seems to *have been* king for as long as any character has political memory.

If the protagonist in certain forms of narrative has absolute centrality—controlling the narrative's structural dimension—so the monarch qua monarch has an achieved form of political centrality: the state as a whole, as well as *each* individual subject within the state, takes on identity only vis-à-vis the king.[15] But even while externalizing the power of kingship through its dramatic structure (through the double plot, the storm as objective correlative to the central character's interiority, etc.), *King Lear* revolves around the destruction of Lear's political power and the way this destruction estranges his thoughts—his interiority—from their social actualization. In this sense, Shakespeare's play, as much as Balzac's novel, relies on the tension *between* formal and social centrality. *King Lear* depicts the explosion of a monarchical ideology within a *character-system* that remains resolutely monarchical.

We have examined how character-space in *Le Père Goriot* is organized around that fault line between the exterior and interior. Balzac's character-system, indeed, helps consolidate the conventions of nineteenth-century narratives, which so often realize centrality in terms of interiority (and vice versa). In Shakespeare's play as well, the king's central authority (along with the protagonist's very centrality) depends on both the effectuation of thought as language (Lear's ability to directly translate his consciousness into speech) and the effectuation of language as action (the direct, and *immediate*, enactment of the king's words as law). These two processes fold into one another: the world of *King Lear*, prior to the political crisis that in fact begins the play, presupposes the uncontested unity of the king's thought, speech, and action. In articulating his thoughts through words, and in enacting his language through command, the protagonist offers his subjects nothing less than a unified world, in which speech, thought, and deed are organically related rather than in tension or open conflict. But in the fragmentation of the state that begins Shakespeare's drama, thought, speech, and action become problematically disaggregated. The hollow words of Regan and Goneril—words entirely unrelated to thought—prompt Cordelia to sadly insist that "my love's more ponderous than my tongue" (1.1.77–78) and "I cannot heave my heart into my mouth" (1.1.91–92). These words are so painful to Lear not simply for the love that is denied but for the way they signal and register an essential linguistic problem apparently ushered in by the problem of inheritance (connected now to the kingdom's fragmentation). If Cordelia points to the way that words and thoughts have become problematically distinct, Lear soon chastises Kent for coming "betwixt my sentence and my power." The sentence of law and the verbal sentence split apart here: the king suddenly faces a world where his language is, for the first time, rendered as distinct *from* power—even as Cordelia has exposed how language is itself distinct from thought.

This crisis is salient to our concerns because of its profound relationship to the formulation of the character-system as a whole. Like the protagonist whose achieved centrality is contingent on the exteriorized minor characters surrounding him, the king derives his own identity in relation to the subjects who serve him, subjects who enable Lear to translate his interiority (or "intent") into a kind of language that is immediately realized (as action or law) in the world at large. But as Lear puts it: "Where's my fool? Ho, I think the world's asleep" (1.4.47)—and we can notice that the world falls asleep as a consequence of Lear's unanswered call. This despairing line comes in the middle of act 1, scene 4, an episode that forcefully dramatizes monarchical power as it is in the process of disintegrating, and, as much as any scene in the play, configures this political process in relation to the social and formal intricacies of the character-system. Before returning to Balzac's novel, I want to consider the first hundred lines of this fascinating scene as they highlight the disjunctive relationship between Lear as strong protagonist and failing king.

Scene 4 begins not with Lear but with a secondary character, and Kent's soliloquy addresses the problem that he faces *as* a secondary character within this play, as the protagonist's most loyal subject suddenly confronting a new political world.

> If but as well I other accents borrow
> That can my speech diffuse, my good intent
> May carry through itself to that full issue
> For which I razed my likeness.
> (1.4.1–4)

Kent has two related goals: to reconstruct his shattered identity by reestablishing a self in direct relation to Lear, and to successfully translate his good "intent" into full "issue." For Kent, fixing his own identity in relation to the king is nothing more nor less *than* reestablishing a connection between interiority and circumstance (or "intent" and "issue"). As Kent has spoken earlier, "Royal Lear / Whom I have ever honoured as my king, / Loved as my father, as my master followed, / As my great patron thought on in my prayers" (1.1.140–43). There is no possibility that Kent is lying here or even exaggerating, even if these lines are strategically aimed at convincing Lear to act more reasonably. The speech is sealed *to* the thought just as the relationships described all serve to seal the subordinate "man" to the "king"—relationships that precisely take both exterior form (to follow and to honor) and interior form (to love and to think). In scene 4, however, this effort by Kent to heal the world, to stitch "intent" back together with "issue," is embedded within a structure of disguise, emerging, imperfectly, only through borrowed accents and a razed likeness. Kent is fighting a losing battle right from the start, striving to re-create a direct relationship to the king (and the protagonist) through indirection.[16]

If Kent depends on Lear—as person and as king—to confer an identity upon him, the king similarly depends on the subjects whom he rules. Lear's own intent gets issued into sentences that are directly translated into power, and the king finds himself only in-and-through this responsive world. Consider the conversation in scene 4 that occurs immediately after Kent's opening monologue:

LEAR: [*to his Knight*]: Let me not stay a jot for dinner; go, get it ready.
   [*to Kent*] How now, what are thou?

KENT: A man, sir.

   (1.4.8–10)

LEAR: What art thou?

KENT: A very honest-hearted fellow, and as poor as the King.

LEAR: If thou be'st as poor for a subject as he's for a king, thou art poor enough.
   What wouldst thou?

KENT: Service.

LEAR: Who wouldst thou serve?

KENT: You.

LEAR: Dost thou know me, fellow?

KENT: No, sir; but you have that in your countenance which I would fain call master.

   (1.4.18–28)

The dispatched Knight is crucial to the scene, as he places Lear, at the very start of the episode, in a suspended zone *between* intent and issue, between sentence and power, forced to "stay" and wait for the Knight to return, thereby confirming his command, or realizing his words as action. As the scene progresses, Lear is, then, waiting not merely to receive dinner but to reestablish his own (monarchical) self through the response of the world to his language. From this point on, Lear is trapped in the interrogative mode: asking questions of the world. In fact, Lear's first fourteen speeches in the scene all end with a question. But these questions are also commands: commands for the world to speak *to* him, to respond, and thus, again, to transform his words into actions. In twice asking Kent, "What art thou?"—demanding that Kent tell Lear who he is—Lear also seeks to glimpse himself: he needs to confirm that Kent is a subject who takes on identity only through the king. Both simply by answering the king *and* in the answer that he gives (that his identity is based upon the king), the subject reaffirms, and in a certain sense momentarily creates, the identity of the king himself. In this way Lear's questions about Kent remarkably come back *toward* Lear, ending with an explicit plea for Kent not to reveal his *own* identity ("What art thou?") but to identify Lear himself ("Dost thou know *me*?").

   Lear's questions continue—"What's that?" "What services canst thou do?" "How old art thou?"—each one momentarily extending the suspension of his identity. The brief space between each question and answer, we might say, mirrors the longer "stay" during which Lear is waiting for a minor character to more explicitly enact his command. At this point in scene 4, then, Lear is locked into relationships with two other characters; and each relationship (with the Knight who has been sent offstage, and with Kent) directly bears on the king's effort to actualize his interiority into social circumstance. Now things become even more complicated and confusing as *three* more relationships between king and subjects converge, with more minor characters quickly entering the scene:

LEAR: Follow me, thou shalt serve me; if I like thee no worse after dinner, I will not part from thee yet. Dinner, ho, dinner! Where's my knave, my fool? Go you and call my fool hither. [*Exit 2 Knight*]
   Enter Oswald.
You, you, sirrah, where's my daughter?
OSWALD: So please you—*Exit*
LEAR: What says the fellow there? Call the clotpoll back.
   [*Exit 3 Knight*]
Where's my fool? Ho, I think the world's asleep.
   Enter 3 Knight
How now, where's that mongrel?
KNIGHT: He says, my lord, your daughter is not well.
LEAR: Why came not the slave back to me when I called him?
KNIGHT: Sir, he answered me in the roundest manner, he would not.
LEAR: He would not?
   (1.4.40–54)

The string of questions continues, and in his frustrated query to the third Knight—"Why came not the slave back to me when I called him?"—we see a failed command literally return as a question. Lear's lines play with and break down the difference between these two seemingly distinct modes of speech: they point to the interrogative that always lurks behind the imperative, and the demand that we can find beneath any question. The third Knight steps into the breach created by Oswald's disobedience, and Lear's command ("come back to me") now becomes a *question* about this command ("Why came not [he] back to me when I called him?"). Oswald himself, however, is also a messenger—a human agent who is meant to render the king's call immediate. Messengers need to be particularly loyal since they simultaneously function as *any* servant to (or finally any subject of) the king does—externalizing the king's intention into action, transforming his questions into commands—and, more literally, work to carry the king's language into the world (and toward potentially competing authorities). Thus messengers expose the king's language *as* social, as unfolding in-and-through a mediated social structure. Oswald, ignoring the king's question about his daughter's whereabouts, precisely separates Lear's sentence from his power. A messenger's failure to return—like the Knight who *still* has not brought back Lear's dinner—leaves the king's words aimlessly echoing without getting socially effectuated, and leaves the king's identity in suspension. " 'Tis strange that they should so depart from home / And not send back my messenger" (2.2.193–94). As Lear descends into this mediated situation in act 1, scene 4, he chases after more removed objects: not now *directly* commanding his Fool, but sending someone to "call my fool hither"; not instructing his daughter, but commanding Oswald to tell him where his daughter is, and then commanding the third Knight to tell him why *Oswald* wouldn't tell him where his daughter is. "The world," so unresponsive to the immediacy of Lear's command, really does seem "asleep."

In such a context, the third Knight can affirm Lear's self-conception—performing the essentially circular structure of monarchical authority—only by ironically confirming the very way Lear's authority is disintegrating (just as we have seen that Kent's directness has taken the form of a disguise):

> KNIGHT: My lord, I know not what the matter is, but to my judgment your highness is not entertained with that ceremonious affection as you were wont. There's a great abatement of kindness appears as well in the general dependents as in the Duke himself also, and your daughter.
>
> LEAR: Ha? Sayst thou so?
>
> KNIGHT: I beseech you pardon me, my lord, if I be mistaken, for my duty cannot be silent when I think your highness wronged.
>
> LEAR: Thou but rememberest me of mine own conception. I have perceived a most faint neglect of late, which I have rather blamed as mine own jealous curiosity than as a very pretence and purpose of unkindness. I will look further into't. But where's my fool? I have not seem him this two days.
>
> (1.4.55–70)

In that most ineffectual, and final, question—"Ha? Sayst thou so?"—Lear has entirely ceded agency to the third Knight; the imperative is now fully translated into the interrogative. In response to his query as to why Oswald no longer listens to his command, Lear now gains his own conception from his Knight. Reminded of his own interior *thought*—a "conception" that revolves around his very lack of self-command—Lear seems forced to comprehend his own actual conception, his birth or emergence as a self, through other people's actions. "But where's my fool?"

This tragic disintegration of the protagonist's subjectivity—who now ironically conceives of his very loss of authority through his servant—accelerates with the return of Oswald as the scene continues. Just as Lear asked Kent, "Dost thou know me, fellow?" he calls out to Oswald, "Who am I, sir?" and, later in the scene, will finally utter, "Does any here know me? . . . Who is it that can tell me who I am?" (1.4.217, 1.4.221).

> LEAR: O you sir, you, come you hither, sir: who am I, sir?
>
> OSWALD: My lady's father.
>
> LEAR: My lady's father? My lord's knave, you whoreson dog, you slave, you cur!
>
> (1.4.77–80)

With Oswald, Lear can gain an answer to his question ("Who am I, sir?") precisely if Oswald does "come . . . hither." He will have his authority reconfirmed, and his question, through the force of Oswald's obedience, could be transformed back into a command. Lear would then *be* the person toward whom Oswald comes, the person whom you come toward when he asks you a question. But Oswald refuses to enter into this relationship with Lear; his response—that Lear is only "[m]y lady's father"—instead asserts a primary relationship with a person other than the king. Lear's response to this response is quite strange. In his very effort to starkly deny Oswald's assertion, Lear becomes entangled in his rebelling servant's language, labeling Oswald only through the term that Oswald has used to label him. (For this reason Lear's "my lord's knave" becomes tellingly confused with what may be the more strictly accurate "*your* lord's knave"). Even as he asserts his radical centrality over Oswald, and Oswald's utter lack of wealth, he can't help but name himself through Oswald's disobedient perspective. Lear quickly enters into this accusatory stance—"you whoreson dog, you slave, you cur!"—but the initial grammatical ambiguity wonderfully registers the depth of the king's confusion.[17]

This episode encapsulates the way that the play embeds Lear's confusion—which erupts when kingship no longer functions—within a character-structure that, as we have seen, consistently centers Lear. Only at the play's end are audience members, and the surviving characters, left to contemplate the disjunction between story and discourse: between the death of a king and the dramatic form that has resolutely granted the king centrality. Thus the play famously ends with the very specter of historical differentiation. While Albany urges Edgar and Kent to "[r]ule in this realm and the gored state sustain" (5.3.319), Edgar's more troubling lines conclude, "The oldest hath borne most; we that are young / Shall never see so much, nor live so long" (5.3.324–25). *Le Père Goriot*—in its decentering of Goriot's tragic experience—picks up on these last lines, as, in the structure of modern Parisian society, it becomes impossible to "see so much" of Goriot as we have seen of Lear. The way that Balzac's story is told, Goriot's inner feelings are only partially rendered. But this is also what the story is *about*—the gap between Goriot's inner feelings and the articulation they find in the modern, Parisian social structure. What would *King Lear* look like if Lear were a minor character? Perhaps this question is impossible to answer—except in terms of a novel like *Le Père Goriot*, and a social world like Balzac's Paris.

The Shrapnel of *Le Père Goriot*

Recurring Characters, Le Père Goriot, *and the Origins of* La Comédie humaine

In *The Interpretation of Dreams*, Freud writes about the unfathomable center of every dream: "There is at least one spot in every dream at which it is unplumbable—a navel, as it were, that is its point of contact with the unknown" (143). The irresolvable relationship between Goriot and Rastignac as competing protagonists might be considered the "navel" of *Le Père Goriot*, and the very tension between the two offers the novel an important "point of contact" with the structure of nineteenth-century Parisian life that is its overarching concern. The navel of the dream, for Freud, is also generative of the dream's network of associations, so he continues: "At that point there is a tangle of dream thoughts which cannot be unravelled. . . . The dream-thoughts to which we are led by interpretation cannot, from the nature of things, have any definite endings; they are bound to branch out in every direction into the intricate network of our world of thought. It is at some point where the meshwork is particularly close that the dream-wish grows up, like a mushroom out of its mycelium." In a similar way, *Le Père Goriot* generates the intricate network of *La Comédie humaine*, its tangle of intersecting narratives and recurring characters. *La Comédie humaine*, itself, emerges out of the gap between Rastignac and Goriot, a modern-day *Thousand and One Nights* that flows from the fracturing of interest inherent in modern economic exchange and condensed into the space of these two co-protagonists.

Certainly, critics have noted the centrality of *Le Père Goriot* within Balzac's novel cycle. As Albert Béguin writes, arguing against the tendency to see this novel as an isolated masterpiece: "In reality, *Le Père Goriot* is, in the entirety of Balzac's creating, a sort of mother-cell [une sorte de cellule-mère], from which are developed the countless lines that organically form some seventy novelistic works, the chapters of one immense novel with many, inextricable episodes" (171). In his 1838 preface to *Les Employés*, Balzac writes, "To indicate the disasters produced by the change of customs is the only purpose of books [Indiquer les désastres produits par le changement des moeurs est la seule mission des livres]" (895). The typical, foundational disaster of *La Comédie humaine* might be that tragedy which emerges *between* Rastignac and Goriot, and which helps structure *Le Père Goriot*, the "cellule-mère" of Balzac's oeuvre. This tragedy cannot be apprehended simply through the story of the two characters' relationship—Rastignac pursuing, through Nucingen, money that is taken from Goriot—but also springs from the configuration of their relationship as character-spaces. This is made clear by the way that Balzac will later clarify the actual economic basis of the story in *Gobseck* and *La Maison Nucingen*. Spilling beyond the boundaries of a single novel, this clarification occurs only through a confusing presentation of the facts in the intercalated and fragmented literary form that Balzac slowly forges. The connection between *Le Père Goriot* and these two novellas is one of the most important creative pulsations of *le retour des personnages* and shows how this narrative strategy arises out of the specific social and economic concerns of *Le Père Goriot*. And these concerns—about the complicated relationship between Rastignac's economic adventurism and the financial difficulties of the Goriot daughters—are themselves embedded in the central relationship between the two co-protagonists.

In this sense the stylistic contours of Balzac's realism (as he conceptualizes a network of interconnecting novels) emerge in relation to the fascinating—and finally tragically fractured— character-system of *Le Père Goriot*. Tracing the socionarrative conflict between Goriot and Rastignac, Balzac generates literary techniques that will help define *La Comédie humaine*. Consider the intersecting narrative and thematic registers in the brief scene describing Rastignac's walk in the Luxembourg Gardens. Here, Balzac simultaneously develops Rastignac's incomplete interiority (which is always connected to his nervous strolling); thematically elaborates this relationship between interiority and exteriority through the crucial parable of the old mandarin; and extends the contours of the character-system that is both framing and emerging around this central situation, through the foregrounding of Bianchon. This is the young doctor's most important moment in the novel, and we can see how Balzac's paradigmatic recurring character is born at the same instant in which the clearest moral analogy for Rastignac's tragic behavior is elaborated, while both the minor character and the parable are brought into the text because of Rastignac's nervous walking.

> Rastignac left promptly to go to the law school, he wanted to stay as little time as possible in this odious house. He strolled during nearly all the afternoon, a prey to the brain fever which all young men affected by too lively hopes have known. Vautrin's reasoning had him reflecting on the social order, at the moment in which he met his friend Bianchon in the Luxembourg Gardens.
>
> "Where did you get the grave look?" asked the medical student, while taking his arm to walk in front of the palace.
>
> "I'm being tormented with bad ideas."
>
> "Of what kind? You know these take care of themselves, these ideas."
>
> "How?"
>
> "By succumbing to them."
>
> "You're laughing, without knowing what it's about. Have you read Rousseau?"
>
> "Sure."
>
> "Do you remember that passage where he asks his reader what he would do in the case where he could enrich himself by killing in China, by his sheer will, an old mandarin, without leaving Paris?"
>
> "Yes."
>
> "Well?"
>
> "Bah! I'm already on my thirty-third mandarin."
>
> "Don't joke. Come on, if it were really proved to you that the thing was possible and that a single sign of your head would suffice, would you do it?"
>
> "And he's really old, this mandarin . . . Bah! young or old, paralyzed or healthy, my God . . . Damn! Very well, no." (171–72)

The encounter between Bianchon and Rastignac is a fine example of how juxtaposed characters can be used to present competing worldviews.[18] The passage also clearly juxtaposes a dominant and a subordinate character, creating the kind of dynamically integrated range of characterization discussed by Philippe Hamon in *Texte et idéologie*. Hamon's interest in a character-field is exemplified in this scene, because we are dealing not simply with two characters, or even two character-spaces, but with *modes* of characterization that transcend this novel, becoming the cornerstone of *La Comédie humaine* and, as Prendergast suggests, of literary realism.

Rastignac's particular kind of modern centrality is exemplified in the passage: both by the connection between walking and thinking that is developed throughout the novel and by the sudden encounter in a public place, graphically emphasized in the detail about Bianchon "taking his arm." Bianchon's position as a foil to Rastignac's radically incomplete centrality in turn consolidates his own character: it is in this moment that Bianchon's morality, so succinctly linked to his professional role as a medical student, is actualized. Both these character-spaces are developed in relation to the parable about killing the mandarin, which thematizes, in the most essential terms, the process of competition underlying modern Parisian reality. The scene exemplifies the rich possibilities of the realist character-system, operating on at least four different levels simultaneously: developing Bianchon as a character-type and foil; highlighting Rastignac's interiority and centrality; actualizing the density of Parisian social life through an emphasis on the suddenness of the encounter in this public space; and thematizing the structure of Parisian social life through the controlling analogy of the old mandarin.

The scene itself is framed in relation to the other co-protagonist, so that a fifth element—Goriot's vanishing centrality—is negatively implied. Rastignac's morning begins a page earlier immediately after a reaffirmation of Goriot's narrative importance—"the old man began to assume a constantly growing friendliness for his neighbor, without which it would, without doubt, be impossible to know the dénouement of this story" (170). And when Rastignac returns to the boardinghouse, right after his walk, he immediately reencounters Goriot: "When Eugène returned to the boardinghouse, he found Père Goriot, who was waiting for him" (173).

The scene in the Luxembourg Gardens shows how Bianchon's emergence in *Le Père Goriot* is embedded within the more general structure of the character-system, revolving around the problematic relationship between Rastignac and Goriot. We have also briefly noted how two intercalated stories immediately arise out of the central, but obscured, economic history of Rastignac and the Goriot daughters, fragmenting this material foundation of the plot into discrete narrative centers (each of which brings more and more characters into the economic situation). More generally, it is in *Le Père Goriot* that Balzac first fully conceives and employs the idea of recurring characterization, and we can see an achieved relationship between this narrative breakthrough, the central topos of the Parisian boardinghouse, the sweeping comprehension of Parisian

competition and overcrowdedness, and the tension between Rastignac and Goriot as competing centers around which the narrative universe is organized.

Balzac stresses the polycentric composition of the Maison Vauquer in catalog lists structured around divided attention among the various boarders:

> The student went back up to his room. Vautrin departed. A few moments later, Mme
> Couture and Victorine got up in a hackney coach that Sylvia had found them. Poiret
> offered his arm to Mlle Michonneau, and the two of them went to walk in the Jardin
> des Plantes, during the two fine hours of the afternoon. (88)

> "Ah bah! They've all left. Mme Couture and her young person went to think about
> the good Lord at Saint-Etienne at eight o'clock. Père Goriot left with a package. The
> student won't come back until after his classes, at ten o'clock. I saw them all leaving
> while washing the stairs." (78)

Such catalog scenes often focus, as in these two examples, on the crowd of
boarders *dispersing*, so that the narrative flattening implicitly emphasizes the
characters' uncontainable individuality. Significantly, Balzac's use of recurring
characters often occurs in similar passages, through a long list of discrete individuals who are each pulled in different directions. While the boarders each
go off to a different part of Paris, the recurring characters go off to a different
story or novel.

We have already seen a good example of this in the passage from *César
Birotteau*: "En m'y conduisant avec prudence, je puis faire une maison honorable dans la bourgeoisie de Paris, comme cela se pratiquait jadis, fonder les
Birotteau, comme il y a des Keller, des Jules Desmarets, des Roguin, des Cochin, des Guillaume, des Lebas, des Nucingen, des Saillard, des Popinot, des
Matifat qui marquent ou qui ont marqué dans leurs quartiers" (51). The thickness of this catalog description in which César compares himself to other *petits
bourgeois* is exponentially increased by our knowledge, or at least potential
knowledge, of the figures who fleetingly enter the narrative. To even begin to
order these intertwined narratives—to trace out the general impression that
some of the more familiar names, such as Keller, Guillaume, or Nucingen,
leave us with, and analyze how these connections should influence our understanding of *César Birotteau*—would radically disrupt the effective weight of
this sentence within the novel as a whole.

Recurring characters, in this context, do not work to anchor the fictional
universe into a clear analytic framework but rather function as an *effect of*
the fragmented, disordered nature of social multiplicity. Lukács thus connects
Balzac's two main narrative strategies: typification, which grants a certain narrative roundness to each character, *produces* recurring characterization, as individuals cannot be contained within clear narrative parameters:

> [E]very cog in the mechanism of a Balzacian plot is a complete, living human being
> with specific personal interests, passions, tragedies and comedies. The bond which

links each character with the whole of the story is provided by some element in the make-up of the character itself, always in full accordance with the tendencies inherent to it. As this link always develops organically out of the interests, passions, etc. of the character, it appears necessary and vital. . . . Such a conception of the characters necessarily causes them to burst out of the story. Broad and spacious as Balzac's plots are, the stage is crowded by so many actors living such richly varied lives that only a few of them can be fully developed within one story.

This seems a deficiency in Balzac's method and composition; in reality it is what gives his novels their full-blooded vitality and it is also what made the cyclic form a necessity for him. His remarkable and nevertheless typical characters cannot unfold their personality fully within a single novel. . . . [T]hey protrude beyond the framework of one novel and demand another, the plot and theme of which permit them to occupy the centre of the stage and develop to the full all their qualities and possibilities. . . . The cyclic interdependence of Balzac's novels derives from his urge to develop every one of his characters to the full. (*Studies in European Realism*, 54)

In this interpretation, the impulse to represent individuals fully necessarily leads to narrative fragmentation. Recurring characters create a kind of narrative static between different texts within the novel cycle. Some critics take a more conservative view on the relation between characterization and narrative cohesion. For instance, Anthony Pugh, who has written the most comprehensive account of Balzac's recurring characters, argues for the unifying function of these characters within *La Comédie humaine*: "the need to unify his oeuvre [le besoin d'unifier son oeuvre] was for Balzac a pressing need and . . . the system of recurring characters—a means to satisfy this need—imposed itself on him as a necessity" ("Personnages reparaissants," 217). But just as Balzacian typification can be both static and dynamic, this narrative strategy works at times to unify and just as frequently to fragment the totality of Balzac's oeuvre. As Peter Brooks points out, "[t]he device of the 'retour des personnages' is . . . both complicating and clarifying" (*Melodramatic Imagination*, 145).

Vincent Descombes has elaborated this distinction. Presumably the "unity" of the novel cycle would be advanced only if we could draw up coherent, or unified, representations of the characters who are dispersed throughout *La Comédie humaine*. In this sense, the growing coherence of individual characters would go hand in hand with the growing coherence of the entire novel cycle. In fact, we have unity of the one at the expense of unity of the other:

Taken then to its limit, this procedure would require the authors [of an index to Balzac's characters] to rewrite the entire opus in a different order, grouping the information scattered throughout ninety-one novels into as many biographical entries as there are identifiable characters. *Le Père Goriot*, for instance, would be dismantled and its contents redistributed among the entries devoted to Rastignac, Bianchon, Nucingen, and so forth. In other words, the inconvenience of the labyrinth would have proved impossible to turn to advantage, and the labyrinth would simply have to be eliminated in favor of a kind of monadology in which the 2,472 monads (apparently) of Balzac's universe could be reciprocal expressions of one another. (193)

Descombes's essay, by highlighting the abstract modes of organization that recurring characterization provokes, moves us to think about the *effect* of this narrative strategy. Recurring characters do not directly fragment or unify *La Comédie humaine*, but *signify* unification or fragmentation in different contexts. It is very rare that a narrative's actual plot will be determined by specific material derived from other novels and revealed by recurring characterization. Far more frequently, our abstract knowledge of recurrence supplements our understanding of the plot, helping establish the thematic field within which signification takes place. This signifying function is particularly prominent in those passages when Balzac compresses *many* recurring characters into a single crowded context, as in the scene from *César Birotteau*. On the one hand, we cannot be expected to work through all of the specific connections between the recurring characters and their intertexts. The fact of recurrence does not, in this context, promote a direct, denotative process, where a particular character immediately refers either to another specific narrative (in which he appears) or to certain fixed characteristics (which we associate with him). This denotation is impossible because of an overload of information, an excessive amount of referential thickness crowded into a short narrative passage. On the other hand, our very sense that there are all of these denotative connections which cannot be worked out *does* connote a sense of misalignment between the characters and the space they occupy in the narrative, which is integrated into, and amplifies, the general sense of social multiplicity that these crowd scenes convey.

The germination of recurring characterization in *Le Père Goriot* involves precisely such a catalog: the strategy is conceived not in terms of a single, clear intertext but through a jumble of *many* intertexts. The first crucial example, which takes place as Rastignac remembers his eventful night in the Faubourg Saint-Germain, ushers in a slew of recurring personalities:

> He had the happiness to meet a man who did not laugh at his innocence, an unpardonable crime in the eyes of the famous, haughty men of that period, those men like Malincour, Ronquerolles, Maxime de Trailles, de Marsay, Ajuda-Pinto, Vandenesse, who were there in the glory of their fatuousness and mingled with the most elegant women, Lady Brandon, the Duchess of Langeais, The Countess of Kergarouet, Mme de Sérizy, the Duchess of Carigliano, the Countess Ferraud, Mme de Lanty, the Marquise of Aiglemont, Mme Firmiani, the Marquise of Listomère and the Marquise of Espard, the Duchesse of Maufrigneuse and Grandlieu. (74–75).

The confusing proliferation of names, in-and-of-themselves, captures Rastignac's bewildered plunge into social ambition, which hinges upon his acute consciousness of an overflowing multiplicity of individuals. And this sense of expansiveness is reiterated and extended in the confusing proliferation of intertexts—in this case the reference to various characters from *Histoire des treize*—all squeezed into one long sentence. However, this moment marks the consolidation of Balzac's narrative strategy, not only because it is the greatest quantitative use of recurring characters to this point. As Anthony Pugh points out in his comprehensive study, the name of the protagonist himself emerges out of this flood of minor characters. Until this draft, Balzac was using Massiac for the name of his young co-protagonist, and "les Rastignac" appeared in the catalog list right after "les Vandenesse." Pugh explains: "After his first ball, Massiac went to visit Mme de Beauséant, and while they were talking, Mme de Langeais called. Here Balzac had a new inspiration. The young hero will be, not Massiac, but Rastignac. The pages of the novel already written have to be changed slightly: Rastignac's name must disappear from the list of dandies, and the date must be moved back five years to allow the young student of *Le Père Goriot* time to mature into the worldling of *La Peau de Chagrin*" (*Balzac's Recurring Characters*, 78–79). The name "Rastignac" is first buried in a crowd of recurring characters and then gets transferred onto the protagonist who observes this crowd. Besides linking recurring characterization to multiplicity (we don't have simply one recurring character but many), this passage has an important effect on the status of the young co-protagonist. First of all, the centrality of this character is enhanced. When "Massiac" is changed into "Rastignac," the ideal reader of Balzac (who has, in 1835, already read *La Peau de chagrin*) is presented with an important intertext that gives the figure—who is still assumed to be only a secondary witness to Goriot—a depth that exceeds the novel's parameters. At the same time, the singular protagonist is embedded in, and originates out of, the crowd that he observes. The crowd of recurring characters, who come into being through the consciousness of the protagonist as he "enters into the world," also generate the protagonist. When the signifier "Rastignac" crosses over from the crowd to the protagonist—at the exact moment when Balzac associates a crowd of people with recurring characterization—it confers heightened importance onto the scene, linking the turn toward a young, socially ambitious protagonist with the development of *le retour des personnages*.

The Social Representation of Death: **Le Père Goriot** *and* **Le Cousin Pons**

I have tried to show how recurring characterization, which helps make *Le Père Goriot* "une sorte de cellule-mère" of *La Comédie humaine*, emerges out of social multiplicity, which itself is generated out of the structure of competition that organizes the novel and underlies the double configuration of Rastignac and Goriot as incomplete protagonists. The overspill that destroys Goriot, and destroys the *representation* of his destruction, also produces the overflow of characters spilling out past the parameters of the novel, and of all the other novels that Balzac will write.

"Don't we see this tragedy taking place every day?" asks Mme de Langeais, in a passage we have already examined. The attentive reader of *Le Père Goriot* must finally realize that the commonality of Goriot's situation does not obscure, but rather generates, its tragic dimension—not merely because we take his individual fate as "representative" of a widespread experience, but also because his particular fate, in-and-of-itself, is constituted through the structure of multiplicity that underlies commonality. Balzac stresses the more widespread social structure that both generates and amplifies Goriot's tragedy in two different ways. First, he embeds Goriot's death within a larger thematic framework that constantly echoes his particular situation. The parable of the old mandarin who is killed to generate wealth for a distant stranger; the murder of Taillefer to secure his inheritance for Victorine; even the story of the aunt who sacrifices her essential being to get some money to Eugène—all of these stories parallel the central tragedy of how Goriot's life is destroyed in-and-through the extraction of his life's savings by his prodigal daughters. But this thematic elaboration would not succeed by itself—since it would risk making Goriot into merely a metaphoric exemplum of a larger social process. At the same time the narrative veiling of Goriot's decline—motivated by the larger structure of multiplicity shaping the character-system—becomes a constitutive element of the decline (just as the economic medium through which his decline can be traced is implicated in its genesis).

This second narrative process continues in the later parts of the novel, through, and even beyond, Goriot's actual demise. If the novel's early sections reduce Goriot's suffering to its exterior signs, he becomes more completely effaced as the narrative continues. Rastignac moves from overhearing him (which reduces Goriot's being to its exterior manifestation) to not understanding him (which highlights the disjunction *between* this exterior manifestation and Goriot's actual interiority) to forgetting him (which engulfs both his objective and his subjective being in oblivion). The end of the novel continually returns to Rastignac's sudden memory *of* his forgetfulness:

> The young people were so avid about their little pleasures, that they had nearly forgotten Père Goriot. . . . nevertheless, around four o'clock, the two lovers thought of Père Goriot . . . Eugène realized that it would be necessary to get to the old man very quickly, if he was sick, and he left Delphine to run to the Maison Vauquer. (275)

> They left. Eugène remained silent during a part of the trip.
>
> "What's on your mind?" she asked him.
>
> "I hear the troubled breathing of your father," he responded with a tone of annoyance. (282)

The novel naturalizes the connection between Rastignac's forgetfulness and the death scene that he is forgetting; in fact, the link beween death and forgetting highlights, once again, how the experience that Goriot undergoes and the *representation* of this experience within the narrative totality are inseparable. This intensifies as Goriot's death approaches. Like King Lear, Goriot dies of heartbreak, or of a psychological breakdown that precipitates a physiological crisis. Emanating from his disordered consciousness, Goriot's death, like Lear's, is a fatality of interiority par excellence. In Lear's death, however, the disintegration of his subjectivity is directly manifested in the disintegration of language that punctuates the final scene ("Howl! Howl! Howl!"; "Never, never, never, never, never"; "Look on her, look, her lips, look there, look there!"). Goriot, on the other hand, becomes reduced to a clinical, diagnostic object of study; his suffering—which the very first scene introduces in terms of its symptomatic manifestation—is finally converted into symptomatology: "This morning, while you were sleeping, we had a grand consultation. A pupil of Doctor Gall's was here, and the senior physician from the Hôtel-Dieu, and our own chief. These gentleman thought there were unusual features in the case, and we are going to study the progress of the disease, *in order to throw some light on several rather important scientific problems.* One of the doctors holds that the pressure of the brain-serum, as it weighs on one organ more than another, should develop certain particular effects" (289, emphasis added). Could we imagine King Lear as the object of medical inquiry?

The obscuring of Goriot's interiority is elaborated forcefully even after his death, in the arrangements that must be made for his burial. As Bianchon and Rastignac descend from the death chamber, Balzac immediately embeds what has happened to Goriot within a larger structure of multiplicity:

> For goodness' sake, gentleman," cried the tutor, "leave Père Goriot for a while, and let's not chew on him any more [et ne nous en faites plus manger], because he had the last sauce applied an hour ago. One of the privileges of this good city of Paris is that a person can be born here, live here, die here without anybody paying attention to you. Let us profit from the advantages of civilization. There were sixty deaths today, do you want to pity the entire Parisian hecatombs? If Père Goriot is dead, so much the better for him! If you adore him, go and have a vigil over the corpse, and let us eat tranquilly [et laissez-nous manger tranquillement], the rest of us." (309)

This passage, as we have seen, stresses once more the synchronous mulitiplicity of Parisian life. Balzac seems particularly interested in framing the event of death in a context of multiplicity, perhaps because it is an event so essentially defined in relation to an individual. Already at the end of *Ferragus* we see the origin of this scene, when Jacquet asks the undertaker where he can find Mme Jules's grave:

"Monsieur," Jacquet said to him, "we want to know where Mme Jules has been interred."

"*Which* Mme Jules?" he asked. "In the last eight days we've had three Mme Jules." (163)

The radical contextualization of Goriot's death is carefully placed around the dinner table at the Maison Vauquer, the original site of multiplicity in the novel. The schoolmaster's comments are framed by two references to the *group* of people who are eating the meal: "ne nous en faites plus manger . . . et laissez-nous manger tranquillement, nous autres." In the grotesque figural movement from eating Goriot to eating their meal, the speech linguistically mimics the essential process of obliterating Goriot—by making him into a disposable story—which this group of pensionnaires, *because* they are a group, have been assigned throughout the narrative. In the same way, the novel displaces the growing coldness around Goriot's body onto the food the group is eating, in the jump cut that occurs at the moment when his death is pronounced:

"Yes, he is definitely dead," said Bianchon, coming down the stairs.

"Come on, gentleman, to the table, said Mme Vauquer, "the soup is going to get cold." (308)

The two passages link Goriot's literal bodily disintegration with the continuation of business at the boardinghouse, a business that the novel has consistently defined in terms of multiplicity. Thus the sentence describing the residents' descent back into the quotidian makes sure to include a specific *quantitative* detail: "The *fifteen* boarders began to chat as they ordinarily did" (309).

As the funeral services for Goriot progress, they are at all points marked by financial constraints: "They had to measure the last duties owed to the old man in terms of the little money that they could spend. . . . Eugène and Bianchon calculated that if the relatives of the dead man did not want to be at all involved, they could scarcely cover minimal expenses. . . . Bianchon, obliged to be at his hospital, had written a note to Rastignac to inform him of what he had arranged with the church. The intern told him that a mass would be too expensive, that it was necessary to content themselves with a less costly service, and that he had sent Christophe with a note to the undertakers" (309–11). The economic exchange swirling around Goriot's funeral is even inscribed into the written record that this funeral produces, as Bianchon and Rastignac talk of writing on the gravestone, "Here lies M. Goriot, father of the Countess de Restaud and the Baroness of Nucingen, buried at the expense of two students [Ci-gît M. Goriot, père de la comtesse de Restaud et de la baronne de Nucingen, enterré aux frais de deux étudiants]" (310). This melodramatic equation of money and death gains force because of the structure of multiplicity in which it is embedded. The abstraction entailed in the valuation of a commodity is only the end result in a long process that begins with actual human beings and, more particularly, takes shape through the overcrowded organization of human beings within a competitive society. This abstraction is made apparent in Goriot's death through the connection between the cost of a funeral and the earlier comment that "there were sixty deaths today." Similarly, the funeral scene incorporates Christophe, once again, as a radically external figure, who shadows Rastignac: "He was alone with Christophe, who thought himself obliged to pay final respects to a man who had given him several very nice tips [qui lui avait fait gagner quelques bons pourboires]" (311). In the very last moment of the scene these two registers—the funeral's economic valuation and Christophe's inclusion—combine, once more demonstrating how Balzac configures the abstract question of economic value in relation to the material terms of social multiplicity:

> When the two grave-diggers had thrown several scoops of earth on the coffin to cover it, they climbed back up, and one of them, turning to Rastignac, asked him for their tip [lui demanda leur pourboire]. Eugène searched in his pocket and couldn't find anything, so was forced to borrow twenty sous from Christophe. This event, so small in itself, gave Rastignac a feeling of horrible sadness [Ce fait, si léger en lui-même, détermina chez Rastignac un accès d'horrible tristesse]. (312)

The passage completes the grim economic cycle: in return for throwing some scoops of dirt onto the grave, the grave-diggers want to be thrown several coins; Rastignac, whose payment for the funeral could be inscribed onto the tombstone, needs to turn to Christophe to provide his *pourboire*, while Christophe is attending the funeral only because of the tips *he* has received from Goriot. These social coordinates of the novel's final economic exchange are highlighted by the intense sadness it causes Rastignac to turn to Christophe, who has already been represented as the radically excessive, and thus exterior, functionary within the economic structure. Rastignac measures a disproportion between the act—"so small in itself [si léger en lui-même]"—and the horrible sensation of grief it provokes. While the co-protagonist does not know why this should make him so sad, Balzac's readers may have a better idea: the scene snakes back to that first nighttime encounter with Goriot, which contained the seeds of the tragedy that has just transpired, and in which Christophe again played the role of an excessive third between the two co-protagonists.

This representation of death is repeated, in an even more extended and persuasive manner, in *Le Cousin Pons*; I want to turn to the end of that novel both for its connection to *Le Père Goriot* and for the way it links together the economics of death, social multiplicity, and minor characters. *Le Cousin Pons*, in the typical mode of late style, revisits and transforms Balzac's achieved fictional vision, bearing a particularly clear relationship to *Le Père Goriot*. If this chapter has tried to demonstrate how Goriot's death is narratively embedded within a structure of multiplicity that we must finally see as implicated in the death itself, *Le Cousin Pons* more directly attributes the old man's death to such a structure. Pons is killed not by one person but, quite literally, by many; and Balzac carefully delineates how many discrete (and utterly avaricious) individual interests contribute to Pons's death, while only their collective interaction is truly fatal. This study is not the place for a detailed analysis of how *Le Cousin Pons* synthesizes individual interest and collective structure, but I will cite one encapsulating motif of this process, when Pons on his sickbed is *surrounded* by the group of people who are doing him in: "Here begins the drama, or, if you prefer, the terrible comedy of the death of a bachelor sent away by the force of circumstances, because of the rapacity of the greedy souls who stood in a group around his bed [des natures cupides qui se groupent à son lit]" (225). Later Balzac continues, "It was a spectacle to break the heart, that of these four different kinds of greed [de ces quatre cupidités différentes], imagining the inheritance during the sleep of him whose death was the subject of all their attentions" (284). The terror of the social situation is represented only through the novel's rapid crosscutting among the four "cupidités *différentes*." Each one is radically separate; but they become linked together because of a single, singular consequence—the death of Pons—that has no one intentional cause.[19]

If Pons's death is caused by the overcrowded field of individual interests— which consistently degrades human activity by converting it into monetary worth—Pons's funeral, like Goriot's, is shockingly reduced to its economic value. This funeral scene again demonstrates Balzac's use of the economic abstraction of death to suggest that death (or the destruction of human interiority) is caused by economic abstraction, and by the overcrowding of actual human beings that generates such abstraction. We remember how Pons's true friend, Schmucke, is dragged from station to station, through the entire funerary industry, at each point assaulted by someone trying to make a profit off the corpse. This commodification is systematically integrated into the multiple deaths within Paris. Thus the first reevaluation of Pons as a thing is juxtaposed with the uniqueness of the experience for Schmucke:

> It was this terrible woman who closed the eyes of the poor, expired musician; then, with the familiarity of a deathbed nurse, an occupation she had performed over the last ten years, she undressed Pons, stretched him out, put his hands on either side of his torso, and lifted the blanket all the way up to his nose, exactly as if she were preparing a package in a store.
>
> "We need a shroud to wrap him in, where can we get one?" she asked Schmucke, whom this spectacle had struck with terror.
>
> After having seen the religious procession with his profound respect for the creature destined for such a great future in the sky, it caused a sadness which dissolved the coherence of his thoughts, this kind of packing job where his friend was treated like an object.
>
> "Do as you like," Schmucke mechanically replied.
>
> This innocent creature had seen a man die for the first time. And this man was Pons, his only friend, the only soul who had understood him and loved him! (330)

This is the first in a series of events in which Pons's death is treated as a routine economic exchange, a process here contrasted with Schmucke's "first" direct experience of death and with his grief over his "only" friend, the "only" being who loves him. Schmucke's sense of Pons's uniqueness ties into the narrative's own construction of Pons as a central protagonist, and Schmucke's crisis over the cruel economic reduction of Pons's death mirrors the narrative crisis that occurs when a central protagonist dies. A notable concern in the several pages of *Le Père Goriot* that take place after the co-protagonist's death, this narrative problem is dramatically extended in *Le Cousin Pons*, which continues for fifty-five pages after Pons dies.

As Schmucke gets run through the Parisian funerary machine, the chapter titles themselves highlight Balzac's concern with contrasting the actual and ideal responses to death: "Death as it really is [La mort comme elle est]" (465); "Where you learn how one dies in Paris [Où l'on apprendra comment l'on meurt à Paris]" (468); "Death is a drinking-trough for a good number of people in Paris [La mort est un abreuvoir pour bien des gens à Paris]" (470). More extensively than in *Le Père Goriot*, Balzac here traces each step in burying the dead and each particular economic interest that corrupts this process. And once again, Balzac inscribes the *multiplicity* of Parisian deaths into this array of interests:

> Rémonencq was forced to take Schmucke out of the coach and hold his arm in order to get him all the way to the Office of Registry for civil affairs, where Schmucke had gotten married. Schmucke had to wait his turn, because, by one of these random coincidences that frequently occur in Paris, the head clerk had five or six other death certificates which he needed to fill out. (335)

Pons's fate inverts the normal relationship of death to funerals: if a funeral should emphasize the uniqueness of the individual life by bringing together *many* people around *one* burial, Pons has only a handful of people attend to his interment, while his own death is as one small part of a larger group of deceased Parisians. As in *Le Père Goriot*, the structure of the narrative as a whole leads us to conceptualize the etiology of the protagonist's death in terms of the fragmented human multiplicity that here degrades his funeral. And the protagonist's tragic death is linked to the problematic status of Pons *as* a protagonist—a problem that is intensified when we shift from the complex representation of Pons's subjectivity to the residual impact, and continued devaluation, of his individuality once he has died.

The final similarity I want to draw between the death scenes in *Le Père Goriot* and *Le Cousin Pons* is the inclusion of a minor character within the funeral, as the only accompaniment to Rastignac or Schmucke. *Le Cousin Pons* actually takes this a step further, introducing a minor character whom we have never seen before (but who has been peripherally involved in Pons's life):

"If only two other persons were to come," said the master of ceremonies, "all four tassels would be alloted."

Just then there arrived the indefatigable salesman of the Sonet firm, followed by the only man who had remembered Pons, who had thought to pay him his last respects. This man was a hired assistant at the theater, the underling who had to lay out the parts on the orchestra music stands, whom Pons had given every month a five-franc tip, knowing that he was the father of a family.

"Ah, it is Topinard!" exclaimed Schmucke, recognizing the odd-job man from the theater. "You at any rate love Pons." (346)

Like Christophe, Topinard decides to attend the funeral because of the tips he has previously been given. Introduced from out of nowhere, Topinard suddenly becomes a principal player at the novel's end, as the narrative gives him a role in the plot and, more significantly, goes out of its way to incorporate his particular circumstances and point of view into the story. The narrative emptiness caused by the protagonist's death helps motivate this sudden arrival of another point of view; while the abrupt shift to Topinard's concerns and interests (already hinted at in the remark that Pons tipped him because he knew he had a family) complements the emphasis on human multiplicity underlying Pons's death.

Topinard's precarious narrative place in the story mirrors his precarious social position in Paris, as a peripheral worker within the theatrical economy, struggling (as Pons suspected) with a large family and overburdened by financial obligations. This struggle and these burdens get inflected into the novel as much as Topinard's own character, expanding the already wide range of "interests" that *Le Cousin Pons* has incorporated. Topinard's particular ambition for a better job within the subworld of Parisian stagehands parodies the more extravagant, and selfish, competition for "place" and "position" that we have already witnessed.[20] Throughout the novel, Balzac has carefully linked Pons's decline and fall to the "frottement" of individual interests, summarized by the different characters (or "cupidités différentes"), each with his or her own particular point of interest, who surround Pons on his sickbed and are responsible for his death. At the novel's end, Balzac focuses similarly on the particular position in which Topinard finds himself, and this shift allows a new emphasis on the impoverished quarters of Paris. More than any other character in the novel, Topinard has real material needs and experiences the difficulties of working-class life. The focus on Topinard, which completely subverts the the closure expected to follow the protagonist's death, simultaneously widens the narrative's sociological scope:

Schmucke followed Topinard like a sheep, who conducted him into one of those frightful neighborhoods which one might call the tumors of Paris. It was known as the Cité Bordin . . . the *cité* merged into an inner street running across it and forming a T. These two streets, laid out like this, are surrounded by some thirty houses of six or seven floors; the inner courts and all these buildings contain warehouses, workshops and factories of all kinds. . . . Dirty but productive like industry itself, always full of people coming and going, thronged with barrows and handcarts, this passage has a repelling aspect, and its teeming population is in harmony with the locality and the objects within it. . . . Topinard stayed in this flourishing industrial *cité* because the rents were low. He lived in the second building on the left as one enters. (366–67)

This description is typical of our received notions of the realist imagination: it connects narrative scope with the ability to see into the poorer sections of society; it sweeps in from a geographic and "objective" framework to a more individual case; it equates the character of human beings with the character of their surroundings. What is distinctive about the passage is its *position* within the novel, following in the wake of a supplementary figure who strains the perimeter of the novel just when things should be winding down. Topinard's excessive role within the plot both recasts the relationship between individuality and multiplicity configured through the representation of Pons's death and motivates this widening of the narrative's sociological framework. The inflection of Topinard's perspective, in other words, mediates between the representation of the funeral and the representation of this neighborhood, and the inflection of this perspective—at such an unlikely moment in the narrative—suggests the most radical and democratic potentiality of Balzacian realism. Topinard, a sketchily drawn character who, at such a late point in the novel, cannot be significantly developed, does not compel the reader in-and-of-himself; *nor* does he stand as a social "type" of the kind that bothers Robbe-Grillet. He stands as a product of radical inclusiveness, as a representation of the included consciousness par excellence—of the insistent way that additional human perspectives assert themselves, and work themselves into, the fabric of social life.

Cogs in the Machine: Les Poiret between Le Père Goriot and Les Employés

We can see a clear connection between Topinard's role as a supplemental character within *Le Cousin Pons* and the more global strategy of recurring characterization. Like Topinard, who does not appear in any other novel, Balzac's recurring characters lead us to take the implied perspective, position, and interests of a minor character seriously, to sense the weight of his or her point of view as something that might exist *elsewhere* within *La Comédie humaine* and could come rushing in *here and now*. Balzac often explicitly thematizes this insertion of a character's perspective by introducing a new character at a cost to narrative flow. Details about a character are introduced as a *necessity* to the story:

Here, perhaps, it becomes necessary to give the history of the stuttering and the deafness of Grandet. (*Eugénie Grandet*, 116)

But, to fully understand the secret of the trepidation which afflicted the gentleman, it is necessary to give a slight sketch [donner une légère esquisse] of the president. (*Le Cousin Pons*, 84)

Motivated by the need to convey pertinent facts about a character who plays a functional role in the larger narrative, such interruptions do not always fit comfortably into the space they are allocated. The narrator's ambition to "donner une *légère* esquisse" betrays an anxiety that any such digression will disrupt the story line, tempting the narrator to turn his attention toward the distinct, individual perspective of the new character. Thus the narrator in *Le Cousin Pons* must carefully select the moment to delve into details about Mme Cibot:

Mme Cibot, the concierge of the building, was the pivot on which the two Nutcrackers' ménage turned, but she plays so important a role in the drama which broke up this dual existence, that it is better to postpone her description until she is about to walk into this Study. (72)

Now, to understand the revolution that the return of Pons at this hour to his apartment was going to cause, the promised explanations on Mme Cibot are here necessary. (95)

These narrative interruptions highlight the tension between exteriority and interiority that animates the system of characterization in Balzacian realism. On the one hand, characters in *La Comédie humaine* are continually reduced to an instrumental, exteriorized role that negates their own subjectivity. As a character remarks in *La Cousine Bette*: "It is necessary to consider people in the society as tools which serve you, which you take up and let go according to their utility [Il faut considérer les gens dans le monde comme des ustensiles dont on se sert, qu'on prend, qu'on laisse selon leur utilité]" (240). On the other hand, to fully understand a character's functional role, the narrative must elaborate the details of his or her situation, which cannot be accomplished if the character's own *comprehension* of this situation is elided.

Before Vautrin is arrested in *Le Père Goriot*, the narrator makes a comment about two different terms for the human head:

Since Mlle Michonneau didn't understand, Gondureau explained to her the two slang terms which he had just used. *Sorbonne* and *tronche* are two energetic expressions in the language of thieves, who, above everyone else, felt the necessity to consider the human head under two aspects. *Sorbonne* is the head of the living man, his resolution, his thoughts. *Tronche* is a contemptible word designed to express how the head becomes a worthless thing when it is cut off. (221)

This double definition of the head encapsulates the sustained tension between exteriority and interiority that is dramatized in the conflict between Rastignac and Goriot *as* character-spaces, a tension which is expressed most succinctly, perhaps, by Vautrin: " 'What is a man to me? *This!*' he said, snapping his thumbnail under one of his teeth. 'A man is everything or nothing [Un homme est tout ou rien]. He is less than nothing if he is called Poiret: you can crush him like a bug, he is flat and stinks. But a man is a god when he resembles you: he is no longer a machine covered in skin, but a theater where the most beautiful sentiments are played out, and I live only for sentiments. A sentiment: isn't it the world in a thought!' " (196). A man is everything or nothing: either an interior sensibility who can engulf the entire world within his head, or someone who exists only on the outside, as a social object. In this second sense, the character's head is cut off—like *la tronche*—in the same way that Dickens figuratively cuts off so many of his minor characters' heads, to express the disjunction between exterior surface and interior depth. Vautrin's example of Poiret's nothingness—or the vacuity of his interiority—is linked to his functional role, as part of the human flotsam produced by modern economic organization. Notice how the first description of Poiret (in the catalog of seven descriptions that begins the novel) logically moves from his "shriveled" physiognomy to the enervating social milieu in which he works, and which, by necessity, includes many other people:

> M. Poiret was a kind of automaton. Seeing him moving along one of the pathways at the Jardin des Plantes like a gray shadow, his head covered with a limp, old cap, scarcely holding his cane with its ivory yellow knob, letting float the crumpled skirts of his frock coat which barely hid his nearly empty pants . . . many people would ask themselves if this outlandish apparition belonged to the bold race of the sons of Japhet who flutter under the sun on the Boulevard Italien. What work could have shriveled him like this? What passion could have darkened his bulbous face, which, appearing in a caricature, would have seemed too exaggerated to be true? What had he been? [Ce qu'il avait été?] Perhaps he had been employed at the Ministry of Justice, in the office where the public executioners send their expense accounts, the cost of the supply of black veils needed for the parricides, the sawdust for the guillotine baskets, cord for the knives. Perhaps he had been a receiver at the door of a slaughterhouse, or a subinspector for Sanitation. Finally, this man seemed to have been one of the mules who pull our great social mill wheel, one of those Parisian Rats who pulls other people's chestnuts out of the fire but never finds out who eats them; some pivot around which revolved the dirty and unpleasant parts of public affairs; in sum, one of those men about whom we say when we see them: "all the same, fellows like this are necessary [enfin l'un de ces hommes dont nous disons, en les voyant: *Il en faut pourtant comme ça*]. (53–54)

These *peut-être*'s—after the question "[c]e qu'il avait été?"—effectively convey the lack of specificity of Poiret's labor. More than just showing that his work does not have any distinctive features, it makes the way that many other people are performing similar kinds of work in Paris *into* a distinctive feature, defining Poiret's work in terms of multiplicity. For this reason, we cannot grasp what Poiret does specifically. Whatever he *does* do, it is only as one of many: "*one of* the mules who pull our great social mill wheel," "one of those Parisian Rats," and "*one of those* men about whom we say . . . 'fellows like this are necessary.' " By now we can see that these phrases are not simply representing a general condition through this individual but rather showing how this individual's particular condition is essentially configured through his position within a larger mass of human beings. As the last phrase makes clear, this multiplicity—which drowns out Poiret's individuality, converting him into a barely human specimen—is linked to its *supplemental position* within the economic structure.

Poiret, like so many other people, does not make anything but is *necessary* to the system (like those characters whom it is "necessary" for the narrative to expand upon). His job does not directly provide anything for other people but rather springs into being in the wake of other people's work. The dispiriting image of providing the inventory of an execution (which again separates the head from the body) encapsulates this kind of alienated labor. In this example, Poiret's work is abstractly implicated in the most violent administration of justice but utterly divorced from this activity in its particularity. As the criminal is separated from his *tronche*, in a wrenching division of interior and exterior, so the worker is separated from the labor he performs: here inventorying that very separation. Balzac uses bureaucratic work in this passage as a figure for a more general depiction of labor, where the gap between intentionality and functionality has become complete, and middlemen appear, in huge numbers, doing work that is not directly productive but of which "*il en faut pourtant comme ça.*" Such a job is unthinkable until it actually exists, in the same way as Poiret's face would seem too exaggerated to be in a caricature. In this way his individual personality is directly linked to his social role.

Right before Vautrin invokes the fifty thousand young men fighting like spiders in the pot, he mentions Poiret again: "Then, what will you do? Will you work? Working, understood as you now can comprehend it, yields, in old age, an apartment at mother Vauquer's for fellows with the force of Poiret. A quick fortune is the problem which poses itself before fifty thousand young men at this moment" (144). Poiret here becomes the limit of everything that Rastignac avoids, and, more specifically of the common fate—due to the pressure of so many people competing to rise above this fate—that he will manage to avoid. Poiret is a nothing, or even a *less than nothing*, because he is one of the 49,999 against whom Vautrin juxtaposes Rastignac's singularity. It is this economy—supplementary excess and meaningless, routinized work for the many, juxtaposed with singular success and power for the few—that conditions the division with which we began: "Un homme est tout ou rien."

I hope to have demonstrated the way that this division is realized in the fictional structure of the realist novel's character-system, where, at the intersection of story and discourse, the novel can divide itself between a protagonist who is everything—because the entire narrative amplifies his central story—and minor characters who are nothing outside of their relationship, which could be functional or thematic, to this central story. Despite the stark differences between Elizabeth Bennet, Pip, and Eugène Rastignac, the realization of each of these profoundly influential protagonists takes place within a narrative system that hinges (each, again, in a different way) on the integration, effacement, or distortion of other characters. My readings of *Great Expectations*, *Pride and Prejudice*, and *Le Père Goriot* might suggest that the nineteenth-century novel's very accomplishment rests on the exclusion—the derealization—of characters as much as on its achieved widening of social representation. This study began by suggesting that the inert argument between two warring models of the literary character—structural and referential—might be understood, instead, as a dynamic process central to characterization itself. In the nineteenth-century European novel, the socionarrative competition between the one and the many offers a particularly important elaboration of this vital relationship between the structural and referential bases of characterization. The fraught conflict between the one and the many, we might say, is the very animating subject of the novel, the "story" that the form of the realist novel tells. I want to finish this chapter with a reading of Balzac's 1844 *Les Employés*, a novel that explicitly confronts the world of work, and the problem of those 49,999 Poirets, and embeds this problem within a dispersed character-field that highlights the endangered space of the protagonist. Building on—but also departing from—the readings I have offered of *Pride and Prejudice*, *Great Expectations*, and *Le Père Goriot*, I want to undertake a metafictional analysis of *Les Employés*, hoping to discover a self-conscious fictional confirmation of the model I have been developing. *Les Employés*, a generally unregarded work within Balzac criticism, will emerge, in these pages, as a commentary or meditation by Balzac on the enterprise of characterization in *La Comédie humaine*.

In another stab at portraying Poiret, Balzac explains his obsequiousness (toward the police investigator M. Gondureau) by noting: "Office life produces its own kind of passive obedience [Les bureaux ont leur obéissance passive], just as the army produces its own. It is a system which strangles the conscience, can annihilate a man, and finishes, with enough time, by adapting him into the role of a tiny gear within the machine of government. M. Gondureau, who felt that he knew something about men, quickly saw in Poiret one of these bureaucratic fools [ces niais bureaucratiques]" (199). This description of "les bureaux" and "ces niais bureaucratiques" anticipates the central subject matter of Balzac's later novel. *Les Employés* does not have many direct filiations to "la cellule-mère" of *La Comédie humaine*, but it is the only other novel to prominently feature another Poiret.[21] In other words, no other character links the two novels closely, while *Le Père Goriot* is not significantly linked, *through* Poiret, to any other novel. It is almost as though Balzac wishes to identify the seed of his bureaucratic novel in this brief passage from *Le Père Goriot*. Poiret's brother in *Les Employés* shares the same "mechanical" character, which, again, is rooted in his stultifying labor in *les bureaux*:

> Poiret Jr., to distinguish him from his elder brother, Poiret Sr.—who was retired in the Maison Vauquer, where Poiret Jr. sometimes would go for dinner—was planning, himself, to retire soon, after thirty years of service. Nature is not as invariable in its cycles as this poor man was in the routines of his life: he always put everything on his desk in exactly the same place, put down his pen on the same strip of wood, sat down at his place at the same time every day, and warmed himself at his stove at the same minute, for his only vanity consisted of carrying an infallible watch, which he checked, moreover, every day against the Hôtel de Ville, in front of which he passed walking toward the rue du Martroi. (134)

Like his brother, the younger Poiret's character is forged in *les bureaux*. If Balzac emphasizes the older brother's vacuity, he emphasizes the younger brother's uniformity, the highly regulated habits that are rooted, as we can see in this passage, in the overly regulated nature of his work. This then extends to his routinized life outside of work, which is further elaborated in the rest of the portrait and brilliantly epitomized in his obsession *with* the perfectly accurate watch. Even the idiosyncratic way Poriet measures time, now configured as a hobby or "vanity," is, itself, subordinate to the routines and temporality of work, since Poiret meticulously checks his watch against a clock that he passes on his standard route to work.

If Poiret's fictional character is forged in *les bureaux*, the representation of his character literally occurs in the first chapter of part 2 of *Les Employés*, entitled "Les Bureaux." And, just as the elder Poiret's character is structured by the shared space he occupies with many other Parisian bureaucrats, so the *portrait* of this younger brother is only one of the many serial portraits constituting the bulk of this important chapter. This chapter is crucial to the novel as a whole both because it explicitly concerns itself with the social environment shaping the eponymous heroes of *Les Employés*, and because it showcases, and parodies, many of the central techniques of characterization employed in *La Comédie humaine* more generally. This larger framework leads us away from the individual character of Poiret to the novel as a whole, and the position of this strange chapter within it.

Competition and Character in Les Employés

Is *Les Employés* a novel about failure or merely a failed novel? Certainly, the novel has been criticized. "There are those works of Balzac which are not well known, and among them is *Les Employés* [Il y a des oeuvres de Balzac mal connues, et, parmi elles, *Les Employés*]," begins an introduction by Anne-

Marie Meininger, who edited the novel's Pléiade edition (7). *Les Employés* is understood as one of the novels required by the totalizing exigencies of *La Comédie humaine*: a text that fills in a hole, that slots into a specific position. Just as the human individuals in the novel are reduced, like Poiret, to being simply "the bureaucrats," so the text itself is reduced to being a novel *about* office workers or about bureaucrats. As Herbert J. Hunt writes, in terms that could as easily apply to Poiret, "According to Balzac's own testimony, the readers of *La Presse* found *Les Employés* boring and insipid" (190).

Part of this novel's seeming weakness originates in the weakness of its character-system, which lacks a strong central figure to retain the interest of the narrative and drive the plot forward. In trying to tell a story about its hero, Xavier Rabourdin, the novel drifts away from his point of view and gets scattered among too many different characters. Most notably, when the narrator enters *Les Bureaux* in part 2, plot becomes subordinated to social observation, and the narrative literally dissolves into a strange form of drama, offering several "scenes" of office life that feature unremarkable individuals in banal conversation. These two flaws both stem from the problematic relationship of the protagonist to minor characters, rendering manifest the difficulty of coordinating many character-spaces. Confronting the multiplicity inherent in bureaucratic work leads to the static portraits of many individuals crammed into a little space, and submerges the central character, who cannot control or anchor his novel's aesthetic form, just as he is unsuccessful in controlling his fate *within* the novel. Spending too much time shifting attention from one employee to another, the narrator kills the story itself, so that the well-made plot falls victim to excessively close observation of monotonous work. This "death" of the story might put a new, narratological spin on George Eliot's rejoinder: "If we had a keen vision of all ordinary human life . . . we should die of that roar which lies on the other side of silence."

The formal problems of this minor novel are distinctly ones of characterization. These problems are exemplified in Balzac's shift from the original title of *Une Femme supérieure* to *Les Employés*, which moves from the singular to the plural, from distinction to flatness, and from a protagonist to minor characters. Balzac calls attention to this shift from Célestine to the bureaucrats in his preface to *Les Employés*, which he begins with a strange tone of regret: "Here are three fragments which, later, will find themselves in their place within *Les Études de moeurs*. The first had the misfortune to be called *La Femme supérieure*, a title which no longer expresses the subject of this Study, in which the heroine, as much as she might be superior, is now only an accessory figure, instead of the principal character" (879). Most of the preface that follows this depreciation of his own novel does not concern the narrative itself but rather deplores the conditions in which authors must work. Balzac implies that he only reluctantly completed the novel and tellingly blames its imperfect structure on the literary market:

The fragments attempted here by the author are obedient to the capricious laws of taste and to the convenience of merchants. Some journal asked for a piece that would not be too long, and would not be too short, that would be able to fit in so many columns for such a price. . . . Artists, for fear of getting nothing published, are obliged to begin several things in order to succeed with one of them here or there. . . . If you find in this story many employees and few superior women, this fault is due to the reasons I have been underlining: the employees were ready, at the right length, and finished, while the superior woman has yet to be painted. (890, 893)

This allusion to the market conditions that determined the novel's publication (and explicitly underlie the shift from superior protagonist to a multitude of characters) harks back to the subject at hand. Like the employees in the story— stuck in small, compartmentalized jobs and competing for better salaries— Balzac's novel is reduced to the space that it takes up and the price it can command. Perhaps the flaws and the ambitions of this novel are not at odds. As his first extended story to concentrate so much attention on wage labor and the urban middle class, *Les Employés* is oddly compelling to the modern reader. Watching it sputter along, we can read the precarious engagement of the nineteenth-century imagination with the essential banality of alienated labor, of human mediocrity, of bureaucratic waste. And then, as we become attuned to the pathos inherent in the novel's form, the text suddenly appears more clever, sharper at the edges; we realize that the novelist has inscribed this very difficulty into the story itself. *Les Employés* becomes an extremely unstable text: like those optical illusions—where a young girl suddenly turns into an old witch—it gets harder to say which parts of the novel are "boring and insipid" and in which parts the narrative is most accomplished.

I want to briefly trace this by looking once more at the tension between the two modes of characterization that this study has scrutinized. While novels often posit the central interiority of one protagonist against the fragmented exteriority of many minor characters, *Les Employés* actually revolves around this situation, as it tells the story of how Xavier Rabourdin (the hero of the story) tries and fails to reduce the number of government employees in Paris (the novel's minor characters). Rabourdin's heroism lies primarily in the painstaking proposals for government reform on which he has been working for many years. This report, summarized at length early in the novel, centers on the conviction that there are simply *too many people* working in the bureaucratic system, and suggests a two-edged policy of downsizing coupled with pay raises: "The ministers diminished the salaries and augmented the number of employees, believing that the more people employed by the government, the stronger the government will be. The contrary law is an axiom inscribed into the universe: there is only energy when the number of principal actors is small. . . . Employ few people, triple or double the pay and suppress the pensions, take young employees . . . these were the main points of a reform plan as useful to the state as to the worker" (46, 49).

Rabourdin's perception of the superfluity of government employees is intricately connected with the narrative's own treatment of its minor characters. It is this point of connection between Rabourdin's fictional enterprise and Balzac's own fictive enterprise that is the central achievement of *Les Employés*. Launching into the description of Rabourdin's painstaking memorandum about Parisian government, Balzac writes: "It is difficult to account in detail, chapter by chapter, for a plan which embraced the whole budget and descended into the infinite details of the Administration in order to synthesize them, but perhaps an indication of the principal reforms will suffice" (49). Like Balzac's work, Rabourdin's massive treatise on government (which has taken ten years to write [95] and would take twenty to implement [55]) is a subtle play of the local and the global. Starting from the perspective of the whole, he descends into countless administrative details in order to synthesize them back into a totality. Similarly, *in this very same sentence*, Balzac tries to find a synthesis between "recounting in detail" and "indicating the principal reforms" of Rabourdin's treatise.

This balancing act of synthesizing the infinitely particular and the global is the process that underlies Balzacian typification, and Rabourdin tacks onto his report, as the concrete manifestation of his engagement with the "infinite details of the Administration [infiniment petits de l'Administration]," a series of character sketches:

> Sébastien had committed the imprudent act of bringing to the office the record of the most dangerous work, planning to copy it there. This was a general memorandum about the employees in Paris, with indications of their present and future situations, and their personal interests outside of work. . . . Beyond this information, Rabourdin's memorandum examined the moral capacities and physical faculties necessary to understand which men possessed the intelligence, aptitude and health indispensable in the people that were supposed to carry the burden of public affairs, who needed to do everything quickly and well. (95)

This memorandum resembles the novel's own enormous digression, when, "avant d'entrer dans le drame," Balzac pauses and runs through a series of thumbnail descriptions of the employees in Rabourdin's office. Balzac's sketches, like Rabourdin's, focus on the workers' personal interests outside of their employment ("leurs enterprises personnelles"), and the juxtaposition of public role and private hobbies is almost a parodic simplification of the way that the Balzacian type balances exterior and interior identity.

Later the novel more insistently associates Rabourdin's sketches with Balzacian characterization, when Dutocq, who has copied Rabourdin's secret memo, brings it to des Lupeaulx and reveals what Rabourdin has said about the secretary-general. "Des Lupeaulx was succinctly analyzed in five or six sentences, the quintessence of the biographical portrait placed at the beginning of this story. From the first words, the secretary-general felt judged by a man stronger than himself; but he wanted to give himself time to examine the whole work, which ranged far and wide" (168). While the secretary-general considers Rabourdin "stronger than himself," the narrator suggests that Rabourdin's description is even stronger than its *own* portrait of des Lupeaulx "placed at the beginning of this story." Rabourdin captures "the quintessence" of Balzac's already compressed, and essentializing, portrait of des Lupeaulx in only "five or six sentences." This comparison between the two descriptions of des Lupeaulx might make us forget that the portrait which begins the story and Rabourdin's briefer encapsulation of this portrait are *both* written by Balzac. The novelist has purposefully inscribed his omniscient narrative into the story that it surrounds, comparing his own caricatures with one of his fictional characters' caricatures.[22]

By adding the appendix to Rabourdin's treatise, Balzac aggressively connects his own fictional project with Rabourdin's bureaucratic one, specifically highlighting *La Comédie humaine*'s distinctive way of representing character-types. The long catalog description in "Quelques employés vus de trois-quarts" is thus explicitly tied to Rabourdin's report, even as it also fits into the novel's position within *La Comédie humaine*:

> Before entering into the drama, it is necessary to paint here the silhouettes of the principal actors in the division of La Billardière, who will provide, moreover, several varieties of the Clerk species, and justify not only the observations of Rabourdin, but also the title of this Study, which is essentially Parisian. (118)

This sentence is quite important. If the novel accentuates the link between these workers' compartmentalized positions and their personal characteristics (as we have seen in the example of Poiret), this passage highlights the *position* of the descriptions themselves within the overall narrative. On the one hand, these portraits are a "necessary" interruption that will delay the essential "drama" of the novel—the story of Rabourdin's struggle for a promotion. On the other hand, the portraits slot into, and confirm, *Les Employés*'s taxonomic function within Balzac's oeuvre. By justifying the novel's "essentially Parisian" title, the chapter—which functions as a digression—becomes essential to the narrative. And because of this Parisian anchoring, the novel itself becomes essential to "Scènes de la vie parisienne," which is, in turn, essential to *La Comédie humaine* as a whole. At the same time, the descriptions serve to justify *Rabourdin's* observations, so that they are torn between their fictional and metafictional status, referencing both the imagined situation of Rabourdin and the actual configuration of *La Comédie humaine*.

The beginning of part 2 has three different openings. We read the section's title, "Les Bureaux," the chapter title, "Quelques employés vus de trois-quarts," and then come to an abrupt sentence: "In Paris, nearly all the offices resemble each other [A Paris, presque tous les bureaux se ressemblent]." The offices resemble each other *because* there are so many of them, just as it is the multiplicity of the bureaucrats which assures that they will be viewed only in "three-quarter portraits." This term highlights the descriptive process underlying minor characters: their inflection into a crowded narrative space assures a distended and distorted portraiture, the "silhouette" that is generated when we squeeze a full human personality into a limited role. The multiplicity that underlies and generates this kind of condensed typification is emphasized at the end of the long catalog of descriptions that make up this chapter, when Balzac adds to his portraits of Billardière, de La Brière, Antoine, Dutocq, du Bruel, Godard, Phellion, Vimeux, Bixiou, Minard, Colleville and Thullier, Chazelle and Paulmier, Poiret, Fleury, Desroys, and le petit La Billardière a final overview:

> These were the principal physiognomies of the Billardière division, where you could also find several other employees whose habits or figures more or less approached or diverged from the ones listed here. (141)

The sentence is deliberately imprecise: the workers more or less come toward or go away from these traits. And such imprecision is necessarily plural: if only *one* bureaucrat remained, it would not make sense to avoid defining him.

The passage then does begin to describe these extraneous employees, but with each random detail our impression becomes oddly less specific:

> In Baudoyer's office one came across some workers who were balding, icy, bundled up in flannel, perched on the fifth floor and growing flowers there, had pine walking sticks, threadbare clothes, and were never without an umbrella. These people, who hold the ground between happy caretakers and disgruntled workers, too far removed from the administrative center to hope for any advancement, represent the pawns in the bureaucratic chess game. . . . In the face of the various aspects of these strange figures, it is difficult to decide if such pen-holding mammals become morons because of their jobs, or if they do these jobs because they are a little moronic from birth. (141)

Just as nondescript pawns are so anonymous *because* they are the most common chess pieces, so the strange physiognomy of these employees is connected both to their functionality and to their very mass identity. (The system of chess—which insistently links together the position and the "personality" of the pieces—is actually a suggestive analogue to my model of characterization.)[23] Returning to the chapter's beginning, we can note how, immediately after the opening sentence, Balzac emphasizes the *strangeness* of the bureaucratic setting, in a passage that again blurs the line between "realistic" and "visionary" narration: "In Paris, nearly all the offices resemble each other. In whatever ministry you go to, to ask some slight favor or get redress for the most trivial wrong, you will find obscure corridors, poorly lighted stairways, doors with oval panes of glass like eyes, just like at the theater, through which you can see fantasies worthy of Callot, and on which you find incomprehensi-

ble signs" (103). The fantastic nature of the scene is linked to its epistemological murkiness: "obscure," "poorly lighted," and "incomprehensible." We have
seen how, in Dickens, the motif of half-visibility is generated out of the
crowded social landscape, and here, too, half-visibility, which causes the apparition of an extraordinary tableau, is generated by social multiplicity and its
resultant compartmentalization. At the end of chapter 3—"Les Tarets"—Balzac motivates his turn toward *les bureaux* at the beginning of chapter 4, by
emphasizing this overcrowdedness through the image of the tiny bugs that, in
a huge number, can eat away at the wooden foundation of a structure.

> If it is possible to use the microscopic lens employed by Leuvenhoek, Malpighi, and
> Raspail in literature, as Hoffmann the Berliner has attempted to do; and if you blew
> up and sketched out the shipworms that put Holland within inches of disaster by
> eating away at her dikes, then we might see figures quite close to resembling in
> some way those of Messieurs Gigonnet, Mitral, Baudoyer, Saillard, Gaudron, Falleix,
> Transon, Godard and company, shipworms who have, what's more, demonstrated
> their power in the thirtieth year of this century. And thus, perhaps, this is the moment
> to show the shipworms who swarmed around in the offices which generate the princi-
> pal scenes of this Study. (98–99)

Balzac's blurring of realistic and visionary discourse, identified by Albert Béguin and others, is condensed in his strange analogy between scientific discovery and Hoffmann's *Contes fantastiques*. This strange synthesis—which is an
instructive framework for approaching Balzac's work in general—is here motivated by the pressure of social multiplicity, by that group of people who, once
again, cannot even be fully named (since the list ends only with "et compa-
gnie"). Later Balzac writes: "Of all the office spaces in Paris, the most grotesque are those of the municipal administration. The genius of Hoffmann, that
singer of the impossible, never invented anything more fantastic" (105).

Les Employés links Balzac's style of characterization to a specific social
context, drawing a connection between social multiplicity and literary typification that can inform our reading of other Balzac novels. To understand Balzac's representation of social multiplicity, we need to return to "le frottement
continuel des esprits et des intérêts" and to that "nature social toujours en
fusion" which dynamically organizes countless individual interests into a
seething economic structure. Multiplicity, in Balzac, is not simply the quantitative accumulation of many human beings, but rather the fracturing of many
individuals into competitive interests that are in constant struggle with each
other. For this reason, Balzac makes the "drama" of the novel revolve around
the struggle between Rabourdin and another office head to get promoted as
division chief in the Ministry of Finance, and *superimposes* this struggle upon
Rabourdin's reform project. The conflation of Rabourdin's plan to shrink government and his competition for a higher position is at the crux of the novel's
narrative logic. Of course, Balzac uses the report to emphasize Rabourdin's

qualification for the promotion. In this way, he heightens our sense of loss when Rabourdin is defeated by the machinations of Baudoyer, des Lupeaulx, and the many other characters who get involved in the story, from the aggressive intervention of Gobseck to the inadvertent participation of Rabourdin's assistant, Sébastien. Further, the report itself becomes a plot-helper, playing a decisive role in the events that lead up to Rabourdin's failure. Beyond this, however, Rabourdin's reform project and his competition with Baudoyer for a promotion constitute a kind of stereoscopic lens through which we view the space of the protagonist within the narrative. The juxtaposition of these two planes creates a dramatic connection between Rabourdin's subjective struggle as a participant within the social system and his objective diagnosis *of* this social system. And his inability to attain a promotion gets intertwined with Rabourdin's *narrative* weakness as a protagonist, a weakness that, like Rabourdin's career failure, stems from the superabundance of competing interests within which Rabourdin is positioned (that very superabundance which his reforms would have addressed).

While the struggle for social position is condensed into the central dramatic situation between Baudoyer and Rabourdin (it is not every day, the novel points out, that a division chief dies), a competitive awareness of "place" is shared by many of the book's characters. Early in the novel the notion of place is repeatedly emphasized. Célestine's mother dreams of "a duke or an ambassador, a French general or minister" who would put her daughter "in the place within society where she belongs [à la place qui lui convenait dans la société]" (37). The novel notes Célestine's failed ambition by remarking that "perhaps she would have been great in greater circumstance, perhaps she had not found her place [peut-être eût-elle été grande dans de grands circumstances, peut-être n'était-elle pas à sa place]" (40). And Célestine's ambitions carry over to her husband: "Thus, in the paroxysms of her ambition . . . Célestine attacked Xavier Rabourdin. Wasn't it up to her husband to place her properly? [N'était-ce pas à son mari de la placer convenablement?]" (41).

If a competitive sense of "place" underlies the Rabourdin household, it also underlies Rabourdin's analysis of bureaucracy. Rabourdin's central insight into the bureaucratic system is that there are simply too many people. But this excessive multiplicity is generated only through a structure of competition that puts all of the employees into a contingent position, defined in relation to other people rather than in terms of their social utility. Thus the bureaucracy first grows because of "a degenerated aristocracy . . . requiring places for its ruined children [exigeant *des places* pour ses enfants ruinés]" (46, emphasis added) and gets paralyzed because "there remains a certain quantity of indispensable clerks with extendable contracts who want to maintain their place [et qui veulent rester en place]." This competitive structure soon affects every individual, each of whom necessarily turns his attention to retaining a place: "Solely concerned with maintaining his position, drawing his pay and securing

his pension, the bureaucrat felt free to do anything to attain this great goal"
(46). And when each individual is interested only in securing, and advancing,
his place, the system as a whole—made up of hundreds of these workers—
inevitably degenerates:

> If, in subordinating everything and every person to his will, Napoleon had slowed
> down for a moment the influence of the bureaucracy—that weighty veil placed be-
> tween the good job to be done and he who can do it—it was permanently organized
> under the constitutional government, the inevitable friend of mediocrities, the enthu-
> siast for authentic documents and accounts, and as meddlesome as a petit bourgeois.
> Happy to see the various ministers constantly wrestling four hundred small spirits
> [petits esprits], with their ten or twelve ambitious and hypocritical heads, the various
> government offices hastened to make themselves indispensable in replacing real ac-
> tion with written action. (44)

In the use of that term *petits esprits* we see Balzac's dynamic kind of typification. On the one hand, this is a qualitative term, describing the mediocre characteristics possessed by the individuals. On the other hand, the term quantifies
each individual within a much larger group, suggesting that this mediocrity is
conditioned by the competitive "lutte constante." The phrase is repeated in the
same episode: "There only remained or only developed lazy, incapable or inane
people. Thus slowly the mediocrity of the French administration was established. Entirely composed of small spirits, the bureaucracy became an obstacle
to the country's prosperity" (47). *Petits esprits*, while reflecting on the individual, takes shape only in the plural form. Like the "knot of mediocrities" and the
offices that all resemble each other, this term highlights the interrelationship of
typification, competition, and multiplicity.

Rabourdin's troubles originate, in one sense, from the innocent mistake of
his loyal assistant, Sébastien de la Roche, who forgets to lock up the memorandum before leaving the office. The inflection of this character into the novel
is entirely motivated by his role within the central "drame"—his point of view
gets incorporated into the novel only because of his functional place within a
competitive struggle for a social position:

> The bureau chief could hardly bear to have this political arriviste at his house, but
> he did not want to contradict Célestine. At that moment, while he talked confiden-
> tially with a supernumerary who was destined to play a part in the intrigue brought
> about by the death of La Billardière, he kept a very distracted watch over Célestine
> and des Lupeaulx.
> Here we might take a chance to explain, as much for foreigners as for our own
> grandchildren, what a supernumerary in Paris is. (90)

The shift between these two paragraphs—highlighted, in a typically self-conscious way, by the hesitancy of "Ici, peut-être doit-on expliquer"—bridges
Sébastien's functionality within the novel's plot and his social position within

Paris. The juxtaposition suggests that Sébastien's inclusion in the story at all—which is necessitated by his inadvertent role in Rabourdin's failure—requires the incorporation of the supernumeraries, *as a class*, into the novel's comprehension of bureaucracy. The supernumeraries, however, are defined by their *lack* of position within the economic system. To let in Sébastien also means letting in the most disruptive aspect of this system, confronting the destructive effects of competition in their most naked form:

> The poor supernumerary, the true, the only supernumerary, is almost always the son of some widow of an employee who lives on a meager pension and kills herself to nourish her son until he succeeds to the place of a copy clerk, and then dies leaving him as a governmental instrument, in some place as a writing clerk, or an order clerk, or perhaps a deputy chief. . . . To go on foot, to not get muddy, to not wear out his clothing, to calculate the time he may lose standing under an overhang in case of a downpour—these are his preoccupations. . . . When, for some bizarre reason, you are in Paris at seven-thirty or eight o'clock in the morning, in the winter, and you see through the piercing cold, in the rain, or in whatever horrible weather, a pale young man appear, without a cigar, pay attention to his pocket. You will be sure to see the outline of a roll his mother has given him so that, without danger from his stomach, he can ford the nine hours that separate breakfast from dinner. (91–92)

This typifying description is again generated by the competitive jostling that reduces these workers to such a difficult and unrewarding routine. After this detailed inventory of the supernumerary's commute, Balzac notes that "three-fourths of supernumeraries quit the Administration before obtaining an appointment [as a clerk]." And, playing on the generic name, Balzac uses a mathematical metaphor to illustrate the competitive gap that underlies the supernumerary's difficult material conditions: "A young man, instructed by the glimmers of Parisian life, has soon measured the frightening distance which he finds between himself and a clerkship, that distance which no mathematician, not Archimedes, nor Newton, nor Pascal, nor Leibniz, nor Kepler, nor Laplace, could evaluate, that distance which exists between 0 and the number 1" (92). Only one minor character in a novel that features many such characters, Sébastien makes us particularly aware of the structures of superfluity and distantiation undergirding the competitive order that *Les Employés* continually illustrates. As with Topinard in *Le Cousin Pons*, we sense that Sébastien could be the hero of his own novel, rather than just a functional character who elicits a summary of supernumeraries as a class. The disjunction between Sébastien's consciousness and his place in the narrative motivates the narrator to ponder the frightening distance between zero and one. This mathematical conundrum—constitutive of the Parisian social structure—might remind us of the disturbing distinction between *la sorbonne* and *le tronche*; the gap between a man who is "everything" and a man who is "nothing," or the juxtaposition of one Rastignac against the endless stream of Poirets. Sébastien, who gets stitched into the novel's drama like a single thread, because of his one instrumental mistake, bears this weight. In *La Comédie humaine*, the stark difference between zero and one folds into the tension between one and many.

I began this section by noting how *Les Employés* seems to slot into *La Comédie humaine*, justified as an "étude sociale" within the larger representation of Parisian life. My argument proposes a different, more intriguing way this novel does slot into Balzac's fictional oeuvre: not as a novel confined—in a positivist sense—to reflecting the world of bureaucratic competition, but rather as a novel confined—in a metafictional sense—to reflecting *on* the general modalities of Balzac's fiction. Of course, what is of interest, when we try to critically integrate *Les Employés* into *La Comédie humaine*, is the way the novel synthesizes its particular focus on bureaucracy with its self-reflexive use of characterization. If *Le Père Goriot* is organized around the competition between two characters for the narrative position of protagonist, *Les Employés* titles its third and final section "A qui la place?" and concentrates its fictional story around the actual battle for a social position. Both novels highlight the relationship between their modes of characterization and the competitive social structure that their stories reflect and confront. *Le Père Goriot* maintains an intricate balance between its modulation of Goriot and Rastignac, as competing character-spaces, and its unfolding narrative of "une obscure, mais effroyable tragédie parisienne." *Les Employés* seems to dissolve as a novel, before the reader's eyes, under the pressure of narrating Rabourdin's confrontation with Parisian bureaucracy. But the generic unraveling of *Les Employés* is generated in, and lends additional weight to, the social unraveling at the heart of *Le Père Goriot*. And this minor novel—because it is so strikingly reflexive about structures of realistic characterization—gives us a lens through which to reread *Le Père Goriot*.

Afterword

Sophocles' *Oedipus* and the Prehistory of the Protagonist

> "One man cannot be the same as many."
> —*Oedipus Rex*, 850

> Oedipus says that he met Laius at a triple road, but Jocasta calls the meeting of the ways from Daulia and Delphi a split road (733, 800 ff., 1399). A *triplei odos* ("triple way") is the same as a *skistei odos* ("split way"). Two is the same as three. If one is walking a road and comes to a branching of it, there are only two ways that one can go, for the third way has already been traversed. If, however, one is not walking but simply looking at a map of such a branching, there appear to be three ways to take. Action sees two where contemplation sees three.
> —Seth Benardete, "Sophocles' *Oedipus Tyrannus*"

In chapter 1, I suggested that the character-system in *Pride and Prejudice* comes into view only as we denaturalize the overtly asymmetric structure of the novel's character-field. But why should we insist that a protagonist's centrality is contingent in the first place, against all evidence which would suggest that framing a story around a main character is not always, or even usually, very controversial? The vehicle of the protagonist seems, in many ways, to be a transhistorical legacy of literary form. Don't all kinds of narratives tell a story centered on a single protagonist without simultaneously telling the story of this individual's very construction *as* protagonist? Can't focalization be deployed as a technique without necessarily carrying the weight of its history, pointing us not merely toward a specifically individuated perspective but also toward a larger structure (the dynamically unfolding asymmetric field itself) through which this individuation takes place? Is there no such thing as an innocent protagonist?

My study recasts this question of the hero's relative innocence or guilt—which would seem to be a problem of history, of biography—as a problem of form. The character-system brings out a double movement, in which the hero's manifest history (the represented life of a central character as derived out of a novel's story) is intertwined with the implicit history of the protagonist's very centrality, a history that can be worked out only on the level of the narrative discourse. Austen's *Pride and Prejudice* offers a canonical moment in this kind of formalization: far from imposing the problem of the protagonist onto the novel, we are led to derive it out of the narrative's own dynamic construction. Austen develops a new kind of closed narrative structure (in which the comprehension of character is mediated through the charged elaboration of literary form) even as she offers a seminal formulation of the social and cultural poetics of the bildungsroman. The psychological or historical development of the hero as *youthful* character occurs in tandem with the narratological development of the protagonist as *central* character. Well before this critical study, the novel as genre has explored and, as it were, internalized the consequence of focusing a narrative around a single individual—a consequence that is felt, above all, in the very explosion of minorness around the protagonist. *Pride and Prejudice* dramatizes its formulation of the protagonist by embedding the development of Elizabeth Bennet, the remarkable central character, within a larger character-system that unfolds only as many other individuals get inflected into a network of variegated, but interconnected, character-spaces. As we have seen, the semiotics of asymmetry in this narrative hinges above all on the conversion of characters into characteristics, so that the abstraction of human beings—or, more precisely, the derivation of abstract significance out of discrete human beings—is comprehended in its full social significance.

The development of impersonal narrative and the asymmetric character-field in early-nineteenth-century fiction allows the novel to establish a particular relationship to the transhistorical category of the literary protagonist. Embodying the complicated and contradictory dynamics of nineteenth-century democratization, the novel levers itself against other genres—other vessels for or vehicles of the literary hero—by recasting history (unmediated story) *into* form. The novel offers time and again a relationship to the hero—as a psychologically delineated individual or as the bearer of cultural value—that is mediated through the simultaneous unfolding of the protagonist's centrality within the dynamically elaborated architecture of the narrative form. Any number of crucial features, as well as theories, of the novel offer fecund ground for this: from free indirect discourse to focalization to the unreliable narrator, from Lukácsian typification and Auerbach's history of a widening social mimesis to Bakhtin's heteroglossia and Girard's demonstration of triangulated desire. In other words, the *formal* problem of the hero, as central character within a manifold character-system, is intertwined with "the problematic hero," to use Lukács's term for the figure who underlies the novel's social and "philosophico-historical" modernity.

It seems, then, that there *is* no such thing as an innocent protagonist in the novel; or, at least, that such virtue is purchased, like any modern innocence, only through a partial negation of history. But in the novel our comprehension of such history is realized *in* form, not, as with so much literary theory, against form: innocence is maintained not primarily by forgetting the protagonist's guilt (a temporal or historical forgetting) but by forgetting the narrative's form.[1] As this study has consistently suggested, the early-nineteenth-century development of the strong protagonist within an omniscient narrative field is rooted in the larger philosophical, aesthetic, and ideological currents that underlie the major strands of the nineteenth-century novel (the bildungsroman, social realism, the novel of disillusionment, etc.). As the late-nineteenth-century and early modernist novel begins to contest and quarrel with these philosophical and ideological frameworks, it is not so clear that it abandons either the pitfalls or the interpretive generativity of the asymmetric character-system. While twentieth-century narratives continually define themselves in opposition to the norms of nineteenth-century realism, the twentieth-century novel will return to, elaborate, and transform the problematics of nineteenth-century character-space. The residue of Dickensian minorness in any number of twentieth-century fictions (from Conrad to Kafka to Beckett to Rushdie) is only the most evident way that the dynamics of the nineteenth-century character-system continues to inform the articulation of modern fiction. David Lodge has written:

> Character is arguably the most important single component of the novel. . . . [N]othing can equal the great tradition of the European novel in the richness, variety and psychological depth of its portrayal of human nature. (67)

Lodge's story of the novel implicitly emphasizes the centrality of nineteenth-century fiction and, in fact, rests on that "component" of the novel which I hope to have made newly, and differently, visible to contemporary literary theory: the nineteenth-century European character-system. The structural problematic actualized in the nineteenth-century novel continues to be relevant to novelistic poetics today, even when the novel polemically turns against nineteenth-century conventions of "psychological depth." The formal impact of nineteenth-century character-space on many varieties of twentieth-century fiction (and also on modern film narrative) belies the rupture that is so often posited between realist and modernist fiction.

For this reason, I am reluctant to finish my study, as many works on the nineteenth-century novel strangely do, by finishing off the object of my study, through a reading of a modernist or protomodernist text that dissolves the problematic I've been tracing even as it dissolves the nineteenth-century novel itself. My hesistancy to "complete" this analysis of the nineteenth-century character-system through a consideration of a modernist or fin de siècle fiction should not be taken to suggest that the twentieth-century novel doesn't extend, and transform, the dynamics of character-space. On the contrary, I would argue that many different strands of twentieth-century fiction manipulate these tensions in specific ways.[2] But to trace any particular manifestation, however interesting, would inevitably risk a retreat from the *conceptual encapsulation* of the dynamics of character-system in the nineteenth-century novel. The very experimental thrust of twentieth-century fiction, with its permutations and varieties of character-space, continually confirms the realist novel's achieved formulation of character-system as the ground from which all of these varieties depart. In other words, the nineteenth-century novel establishes the contingent emplacement of the protagonist, within a manifold character-field, as an essential means of narrative signification and a component part of novelistic structure.

Instead of sketching out one of these different strands, then, I want to take my leave of this study by looking back from the nineteenth-century novel's formulation of the space of the protagonist to a text that, perhaps as much as any other, might lay claim to originating the seemingly transhistorical category *of* the protagonist itself. By this turn, I do not mean to invoke Sophocles' *Oedipus* as an archetypal template for the hero or, pace Freud, for the individual subject as such. These cultural valences certainly cluster around the figure of Oedipus and, not unimportantly, readings of Oedipus's heroism often center on the eruption of guilt out of innocence. But on the contrary, this *literary-historical* movement is meant as an echo (and final enactment) of the formal movement that has been practiced throughout this study: scrutinizing the origin of the protagonist's centrality *as* contingent instead of positing it as simply natural or intrinsic to narrativity as such. Rather than configuring Oedipus as an archetypal paradigm of the protagonist, we might note that the very category "protagonist" has a specific origin and history (for which *Oedipus* and its central character are particularly important). The "first actor" in Greek drama, the protagonist (*proto-agonist*) is ushered in, significantly, only in juxtaposition with the "second" actor (*deuteragonist*) and, in the transition between Aeschylean and Sophoclean tragedy, the "third" actor (*tritagonist*). In this sense the central character originates in relation to a character-field; the contingent priority of the protagonist is built into its etymological origin.

Sophocles' addition of the tritagonist, with its consequent widening of the dramatic totality, takes place alongside a related structural change that more directly concerns the protagonist. While Aeschylus crafted three interconnected plays for the dramatic contests, forming a unified trilogy, Sophocles presented the festival with three freestanding plays, each of which is constructed as a self-sufficient and intricately patterned whole. Crucially, this allows each play to be centered on an individual in a way that was impossible with Aeschylus: while the "heroic temper" of a single figure often underlies Sophocles' drama (to use the influential phrase of Bernard Knox), Aeschylus's plays radically contextualize each individual life history within a larger sequential chain. Knox writes, "[E]very Aeschylean play we possess, except the *Persians* . . . is part of a trilogy. And every Sophoclean play is complete in itself. Sophocles' abandonment of trilogic form was probably a revolutionary step. . . . The reduction of the scope from three plays to one . . . made possible the artistic decision to present the tragic dilemma in terms of a single personality facing the supreme crisis of his life" (2–3).

If Attic drama marks a kind of conceptual and aesthetic origin for the literary protagonist in general, Sophocles' *Oedipus Rex* revolves around the birth or origin of its specific protagonist—and the problem, precisely, of how this origin is intertwined with, and looms over, the hero's projected innocence. In turning to *Oedipus*, I want to enfold the literary-historical origin of the protagonist (as formal category) within the play's own powerful interrogation of the protagonist's (biographical) origin. Just as the centrality of the protagonist is established vis-à-vis the deuteragonist and tritagonist, Oedipus's remarkable consciousness within the play (which, I will argue, is both the source *and* the consequence of his centrality) emerges in and against a much wider plain, a character-field that, as he descends into his own prehistory, finally overwhelms him. The "prehistory" in this afterword's title refers, then, both to that remote matrix of events preceding this protagonist's conscious memory (the events that cluster around Oedipus's biographical origin) and to the very emergence of the seemingly universal device of a protagonist, in relation to minor characters. Thus such a prehistory is not intended to secure a transcendent origin for the protagonist, let alone to identify a direct antecedent to the nineteenth-century novel's character-system. Rather, my reading of Sophocles' play is intended as an allegory for, and a philosophical crystallization of, the "prehistory" that becomes available through character-system itself. The afterword ends by offering a possibly new answer to the central riddle of Oedipus's identity ("who are my parents?"). If this answer revises Oedipus's history, it is placed at this study's end for a different reason: to highlight the history that is instantiated within narrative structure, through the constructed and total character-system, with its formed relationship between minor characters and the protagonist.

———

For the moment let's change our register of analysis: perhaps the problem faced by Sophocles' Oedipus is not having these *particular* parents (the mother he weds and the father he kills) but rather having any parents at all. "Not to be born is best of all," Sophocles later writes, and in a specific sense, Oedipus—like human beings everywhere—seems to give birth to himself.[3] We're not all kings, we don't all solve the riddle of the Sphinx, but all of us, like Oedipus, seem to invent the world around us, reformulating it through our minds in each reencounter with it. In a passage that dares us to postulate a summary of *Ulysses*, Joyce writes: "Every life is many days, day after day. We walk through ourselves, meeting robbers, ghosts, giants, old men, young men, wives, widows, brothers-in-love, but always meeting ourselves" (175). Oedipus is walking in this sense, on his own two feet, moving through the world only as he *walks through himself*; meeting and solving the riddles of the world with his fierce mind—the mind that has taken in the world and through which the world comes rushing in.

But before Oedipus lies the world that forms the matter of his mind: if this world only is known (and, in a political sense, only knows itself) in-and-through the king's intricate mind, it also has preceded and will exceed him, becoming the ground into which he sinks. These traces of the world—not as an object for but as the ground of consciousness—constitute the support that, according to the Sphinx, each human being needs at the two edges of life. Not always standing on our own two feet (viewing the world), we are pulled toward and become part of the world: thought itself, as much as each freestanding person, has inevitably crawled on, and will inevitably limp toward, the ground.

A central irony in *Oedipus Rex*—bitter and astounding—is that it is precisely knowledge of this condition which constitutes Oedipus's mind, as his achieved comprehension gets realized in the triumphant unraveling of the Sphinx's riddle. Oedipus's singular ability to unlock this riddle—and offer an answer that will save a city—relies on his knowledge of the relationship between human consciousness and the world. Oedipus, alone, *knows* that human beings both stand on two legs (becoming conscious of the world, grasping its riddles) and on four and three legs (preceded by and falling back into the world). Yet even as Oedipus solves the Sphinx's riddle, he gets entangled in the riddle, since the very cognitive activity that lies behind the unique solution necessarily elevates Oedipus's mind as independent *of* the world. In conceptualizing the external world as the ground for human consciousness, Oedipus's own consciousness is fully actualized: he becomes unable to recognize the ground precisely as he comprehends that it is there. For this reason, Sophocles emphasizes the self-derived nature of Oedipus's answer: the solution to the Sphinx's riddle rests entirely within himself. "But I came, Oedipus, who knew nothing, and I stopped her. *I solved the riddle by my thought alone.* Mine was no knowledge got from birds" (397–400, emphasis added).[4]

It is a commonplace to say that Oedipus knows "man" but doesn't understand "himself." He can recognize that human beings are the species with four legs in the morning, two in the afternoon, three in the evening. At the same time he cannot tease out the meaning of his own name—"swollen foot"—a name that identifies him with a specific origin, since his feet were shackled and crippled when he was left by his real parents to die. There is, of course, a noticeable continuity between the terms of the riddle and the hidden etymology of Oedipus's name: both Oedipus in particular (the person named for his wounded feet) and humankind in general (the species known by its changing number of legs) are defined by a troubled ability to become freestanding. Oedipus's wound occurs at the origin of his life, and, in an important sense, origin itself is the injury that swells up his feet. If the wound incapacitates Oedipus as a baby, this wound seems to actualize the Sphinx's riddle, which reminds us that all human beings—injured or not—are reduced to crawling or walking with a stick at either edge of our otherwise freestanding lives.

Oedipus's ability to solve the riddle and failure to understand his own name might illustrate the threatening philosophical disjunction between the general and particular, or the tension between public and private. But, as we have seen, to rigidly construct a separation between Oedipus's knowledge of the human and knowledge of the self vitiates a central irony of the play. It is ultimately Oedipus's knowledge or consciousness *of* the relationship between himself and the world that blocks him from grasping his own name's significance, as the experience of consciousness itself—in which the world gets reformulated as mind—makes it so difficult to comprehend how the world precedes and conditions the mind, conditions the very act of comprehension. It is precisely in solving the riddle that Oedipus misses his own name; in fact, just as he becomes aware of what man is (the creature with four, two, then three legs), he also offers a new definition of what man is (the creature who is *aware* that he walks on four, two, then three legs). Are these two definitions radically dissimilar? Or is the act of solving the riddle, of becoming aware, merely the exemplary event *of* standing on two legs?

Sophocles' play, of course, does not directly stage this remarkable act of ratiocination: it emerges only as one of the many recollections that occur during the duration of the play (a duration limited to one long afternoon many years later). But the play's structure does revolve around another act of ratiocination that we need to understand in terms of and juxtapose against Oedipus's experience of solving the Sphinx's riddle. This is precisely Oedipus's changing comprehension of who he is. If the story revealed by the play leads toward the past history of Oedipus's identity (an identity determined, at bottom, by the history of his parentage), the play itself defines Oedipus not by his parental identity but rather by the style of thinking that he reveals as he *contemplates* his parental identity. The character of Oedipus, limited to the short passage of time that unfolds onstage, *is* nothing other than this contemplation.

This distinction between the (sometimes contemplative) events that have made up Oedipus's life and Oedipus's contemplation of these events demonstrates the relevance of Sophocles' play to narrative theory. The tragedy of Oedipus aptly illustrates the distinction and generative interaction between story and discourse: between fictional events themselves and the mediated representation of events. *Oedipus Rex*, to put this most concisely, is the representation *of* a person's representation of the events of a lifetime. In this sense, *Oedipus Rex* functions like the detective story that Tzvetan Todorov once proposed as a heuristic template for all narrative:

> At the base of the whodunit we find a duality. . . . This novel contains not one but two stories: the story of the crime and the story of the investigation. In their purest form, these two stories have no point in common. . . . The first story, that of the crime, ends before the second begins. But what happens in the second? Not much. The characters of this second story, the story of the investigation, do not act, they

learn. . . . [T]he story of the crime—tells "what really happened," whereas the second—the story of the investigation—explains "how the reader (or the narrator) has come to know about it." But these definitions concern not only the two stories in detective fiction, but also two aspects of every literary work which the Russian formalists isolated forty years ago. . . . In the story, there is no inversion in time, actions follow their natural order; in the plot, the author can present results before their causes, the end before the beginning. (*Poetics of Prose* 45–46)

In *Oedipus Rex* we get just such a radical inversion of temporal sequence: by the end of the play we are presented with two distinct sequential chains, which contain the same events in different order. On the one hand, we can extrapolate the actual, biographical sequence of Oedipus's life—from his birth in Thebes to his self-blinding that ends the play. On the other hand, we have the reconstruction of these events as they unfold in the sequencing of the play itself. Lapsing back into a strict mode of narratology, we might chart these two temporal schemes or chronologies as follows:

STORY	DISCOURSE
1. Birth in Thebes (beginning of Oedipus)	6. The plague (beginning of the play)
1a. Given to Theban shepherd	7. Begins to investigate the prophecy
1b. Given to Corinthian messenger	5. Marries Jocasta, becomes king
1c. given to Corinthian king	4. Death of Laius at the crossroads
2. Grows up in Corinth	2. Grows up in Corinth
3. Prophecy that he will kill "father"	3. Prophecy that he will kill Laius
4. Death of Laius at the crossroads	1. Birth in Thebes
5. Marries Jocasta, becomes king	1c. Given to Corinthian king
6. The plague	1b. Given to Corinthian messenger
7. Begins to investigate the prophecy	1a. Given to Theban shepherd
8. Death of Jocasta	9. Report of Jocasta's death
9. Report of Jocasta's death	8. Death of Jocasta
10. Blinds himself (last action of Oedipus)	10. Blinds himself (last action of the play)

A major challenge for any interpretation of *Oedipus Rex* is to tease out the relationship between Sophocles' innovative method of sequential structuring and the interrogation of consciousness and selfhood underlying the play's philosophical concerns. Todorov's comment that "the characters of the second story . . . do not act, they learn" points us in an important direction. As we have seen, the crux of Oedipus's identity rests on the knotty relationship *between* thought and action—between, that is, the division of human identity into a freestanding interiority (the powerful mind that unriddles the nature of the world) and a radically contingent exteriority (the vulnerable mind that is shaped by, formulated by, and encompassed by the world).[5]

Oedipus Rex begins with a fully freestanding protagonist—and with an idealized social world in which the mind's power has been translated into *political* power, an externalized and fully actualized capability (δύνᾰμις). It is important that the audience accept Oedipus's capability as king, just as we must accept the strange logic of the Sphinx's riddle itself, where self-consciousness somehow becomes the equivalent *of* saving an entire city. In this sense, Sophocles' play points us toward an idealized ground of politics, as it emerges out of human consciousness, and human capability, itself.

We have seen how Oedipus's ability to solve the riddle "by [his] thought alone" ironically removes him from his own discovery. Oedipus has paradoxically comprehended how comprehension itself (which feeds on the world) is ultimately vulnerable to this world. The events of the play revolve not simply around Oedipus's confrontation with a different biographical matrix but also around a different kind of cognition. Coming to comprehend the nature of his own life, Oedipus is also forced into confronting a new kind of comprehension: one that is not self-sufficient or autogenerative. The crux of this new kind of comprehension rests in Oedipus's sudden dependence on a host of other persons for the information that he needs. Almost from the play's opening, Oedipus is tormented by his sudden reliance on other characters for the knowledge that he grasps after. We need to read this again on the most abstract level: in terms of the mind and the world. In the course of the play, Oedipus discovers that the world does not simply serve as material to be used by the self-actualizing mind but, instead, shapes and structures the play of mind itself. Once more the parallel between politics and thinking holds: the problematically "disobedient" subjects whom Oedipus, the king, confronts at the play's beginning stand in for a world that has suddenly become disobedient in relation to the grasping mind.

This conflation is evident in Oedipus's impatient opening lines:

The town is heavy with a mingled burden
Of sounds and smells, of groans and hymns and incense;
I did not think it fit that I should hear
Of this from messengers but came myself,
I, Oedipus, whom all men call the Great.
(3–7)

The play begins by juxtaposing two kinds of knowledge: information directly discovered by the self and information gleaned only indirectly, through other persons. These lines anticipate the play's overarching trajectory: in the course of the tragedy Oedipus will painfully come to experience and accept a knowledge (a mode of consciousness, and thus an identity) that comes out of messengers instead of himself. This is already the case when the play begins: Oedipus is awaiting first Creon's and then Teiresias's arrival. It is only through these two men that Oedipus can begin to get the answers he seeks:

You have not roused me like a man from sleep;
Know that I have given many tears to this,
Gone many ways wandering in thought,
But as I thought I found only one remedy
And that I took. I sent Menoeceus' son
Creon, Jocasta's brother, to Apollo,
To his Pythian temple,
That he might learn there by what act or word
I could save this city. As I count the days,
It vexes me what ails him; he is gone
Far longer than he needed for the journey.
(65–75)

Oedipus's decision to send Creon *begins* precisely as an extension or actualization of his thought; it is an idea that springs directly out of his mind. But as he waits, day after day, for Creon to return, he is placed in a problematically passive position. More specifically, he is placed, for the first of many times in the play, in a position of suspended or partial knowledge. Oedipus is both stuck in time and stuck waiting for someone else who is necessary for his understanding: his comprehension itself is blocked or disrupted by Creon's tardiness. It makes sense, for this reason, that Creon's own arrival is not *directly* or *immediately* comprehended, but only transmitted by Oedipus's servants, as the Priest tells him: "Thanks for your gracious words. Your servants here signal that Creon is this moment coming." Just as Oedipus must wait, stuck in time, for Creon to return with the knowledge that he seeks, so too he apprehends Creon's arrival only through "the signal" or the message of a servant. This social indirection is also, necessarily, temporal: Creon has *almost* arrived but is not quite there yet. In fact, Oedipus and the Priest continue to talk, for a tiny bit of time, *about* the tiny bit of time that still remains:

PRIEST: Thanks for your gracious words. Your servants here
    Signal that Creon is this moment coming.
OEDIPUS: His face is bright. O holy Lord Apollo,
    Grant that his news too may be bright for us
    And bring us safety.
PRIEST: It is happy news,
    I think, for else his head would not be crowned
    With sprigs of fruitful laurel.
OEDIPUS: We will know soon,
    He's within hail. Lord Creon, my good brother,
    What is the word you bring us from the God?
    (*Creon enters*)
    (78–86)

The tragedy of Oedipus subtly takes form in moments like this—in the delays (both social and temporal) that occur on the way to knowledge. This example is notable precisely in its triviality; we see Sophocles infuse temporal ephemera with significance, dramatizing Creon's approach almost in slow motion. This minute delay also operates as a dramatic encapsulation of the longer delay that Oedipus has just been experiencing *before* the play begins: the several moments that Oedipus waits *onstage* suggest the several days he has been waiting beforehand. But this scene also anticipates a number of other delays within the play itself that are still to come. As in many of the ensuing scenes, Sophocles here powerfully conflates a social process—the arrival of a character onstage—with an epistemological one. Oedipus is waiting not merely for Creon to arrive but also for his knowledge itself to accrue—knowledge that, however, he can get at only *through* Creon and thus through the passage of time. But what happens to Oedipus himself while he waits?

The delay of information is first extended when Creon reveals the Oracle's admonition that Laius's killer must be identified and exiled. The Chorus suggests that Oedipus should send for Teiresias, and Oedipus replies:

Even in this my actions have not been sluggard.
On Creon's word, I have sent two messengers
And why the prophet is not here already
I have been wondering.
(286–89)

Once again: delay *and* messengers. To rely on another person's words is to have one's own thought process disrupted. Oedipus points once more to his own hasty actions; and such quick action is really just the manifestation of quick thinking, or, more specifically, the effort to quickly act *on* thought, to translate thought as directly and immediately as possible *into* action. Thus the pathos obliquely suggested by Oedipus's comment that he has sent *two* messengers, one after the other.[6] To send a single messenger is, of course (as we have seen, for example, in *King Lear*), the way a king translates thought into language and then into action. The second messenger is more problematic. An option only after too much time has already opened up, sending the second messenger both establishes the king's power (the power, that is, to act upon his thoughts) and abolishes his power, since it acknowledges the dilatoriness of the previous messenger. Either the first messenger will still get to Teiresias—or *is* getting to Teiresias even in that moment when the second one is sent!—so that the second messenger is entirely useless, or the second messenger will actually deliver the king's words, so that the first messenger is useless. Chasing on each other's heels, both messengers—both messages—are, like the king's own thoughts, caught in time, revealing the problematic temporal delay that always rests between a thought and its (social) enactment.

Even as Oedipus waits for Teiresias, another social and epistemological chain has been set in motion. Creon has mentioned the single witness who survived the slaughter of Laius and now provides the first clue upon which Oedipus will work his deductive powers:

> OEDIPUS: Was there no messenger, no fellow traveler
>   Who knew what happened? Such a one might tell
>   Something of use.
> CREON: They were all killed save one. He fled in terror
>   And he could tell us nothing in clear terms
>   Of what he knew, nothing, but one thing only.
> OEDIPUS: What was it?
>   If we could even find a slim beginning
>   In which to hope, we might discover much.
> CREON: This man said that the robbers they encountered
>   Were many and the hands that did the murder
>   Were many; it was no man's single power.
>   (116–23)

Thus while waiting for Teiresias, Oedipus also begins to wait for this witness of the events at the crossroads. Delay begets delay: just as Oedipus needed to send two messengers, he now begins to wait for two separate characters. When Teiresias does arrive, their conversation develops the problematic relationship between Oedipus's creation of knowledge about the world out of his own mind and his mind's dependence on the world. Specifically, we see Teiresias talk only after Oedipus cajoles and finally commands his speech: so that it is largely through Oedipus's *own* words that Teiresias's words, about Oedipus, get created. At first Teiresias is adamantly silent: "I will not bring to the light of day my troubles" (328); "I will tell you nothing" (334); "I will say nothing further" (343). Only Oedipus's aggressive inquiries—and finally his projection of guilt onto Teiresias himself—compel the blind seer to speak.

> OEDIPUS: Indeed I am
>   So angry I shall not hold back a jot
>   Of what I think. For I would have you know
>   I think you were the complotter of the deed
>   And doer of the deed save in so far
>   As for the actual killing. Had you had eyes
>   I would have said you alone murdered him.
> TEIRESIAS: Yes? Then I warn you faithfully to keep
>   The letter of your proclamation and
>   From this day forth to speak no word of greeting
>   To these nor me; you are the land's pollution.
>   (345–53)

The exchange suggests a causal relationship between Teiresias's accusation and Oedipus's own: the seer speaks here only as a consequence of Oedipus's prompting speech. Here we can see a suggestive blurring of story and discourse: Teiresias's accusation is not motivated by Oedipus's actual misconduct, at the bloody crossroads; his changed speech is clearly in chagrined response to the speech Oedipus has *just given*, not to the murder he committed a long time ago. At this moment Sophocles seems to be suggesting a kind of repetition or reenactment of Oedipus's earlier actions: there is a relationship between the past events that will slowly be discovered in the course of the play (and which *should* motivate Teiresias's call for punishment) and the conflictual dialogue that takes place onstage (which *actually* motivates Teiresias's accusation). This conjunction between story and discourse already suggests a crucial relationship between the way that Oedipus *learns about* his past identity and the events, or prehistory, that is actually discovered.

The accusation that erupts out of this dialogue is caused not merely by Oedipus's flawed relationship to Teiresias but by his problematic relationship to dialogue itself. More specifically, in Teiresias's accusation we see, once again, Oedipus's limited control over the construction of knowledge. Out of his own mind he summons and then commands another person to speak, but if this speech *emerges* out of Oedipus's own speech (and, finally, Oedipus's own thought), it is also radically distinct from Oedipus. The very nature of dialogue—or the emergence of knowledge out of dialogue—problematizes the model of cognition, of riddling, that Oedipus brings to the play. This does not occur only with Teiresias. Throughout the play, Oedipus has to rely on information—evidence, messages, and speech—made by and derived through other people. Each such event is, implicitly, an "accusation" as much as Teiresias's overt accusation—an accusation against the model of self-consciousness that forms the core of Oedipus's identity. The actual accusations that pile up in the course of the play are motivated by and, finally, indistinct from the accusatory nature of these dialogues themselves. As we have seen, these dialogues do not directly lead to Oedipus's knowledge about himself—the play is constituted almost entirely by delay and by partial knowledge. Without these delays, without these conversations that are means toward an end (the end of absolute self-knowledge), what kind of play would still remain? In fact, Oedipus arrives at a different understanding of himself as he undergoes the dialogues, not just once he has finished them: his tragic identity emerges not when all the conversations are done (and a complete knowledge has been reached) but precisely in the course of the conversations, and in his painful confrontation with a knowledge that *is* only partial, bounded in time, and socially mediated.

In his controversial book *Sophocles' Oedipus: Evidence and Self-Conviction*, Frederick Ahl argues that this conversation with Teiresias—as well as most of the other conversations that Oedipus has in the course of the play—

produces unreliable information. Ahl notes how the proof of Oedipus's guilt as the murderer of Laius is circumstantial, arising at the intersection of a number of different perspectives and stories, none of which can point directly to the crime itself. Ahl's chief claim—that Sophocles has intentionally hidden a suggestion that Oedipus, in fact, was *not* the child of Laius and Jocasta, and thus, while a murderer, is not guilty of the more shocking actions for which he comes to accept blame—has been greeted with valid skepticism by most critics of the play. But the larger framework that structures Ahl's argument is more important than this polemical claim about guilt and innocence: the crucial point is that Oedipus's guilt—which is to say both his past *and* present identity—depends on a series of conversations with different minor characters, each of which has a dramatic logic of its own, and offers a perspective that is partially independent of Oedipus's own consciousness. As Ahl argues, none of these conversations are untroubled: Oedipus bullies and cajoles his interlocutors; he distrusts them; and, as with his anger toward Teiresias, he is not above issuing threats and invective.

What is the origin of Oedipus's anger? We have already seen that it is rooted in his impatience—more specifically, in his epistemological impatience, his discomfort with any kind of partial knowledge, with a world that will not immediately yield itself up to his ratiocination. Throughout most of the play Oedipus experiences just such partial knowledge, and, increasingly, he confronts a more troublingly partial *self*-knowledge. But this is inevitable: since Oedipus's self is defined through knowledge (the nexus of knowledge and power that revolves around the Sphinx's riddle), a crisis of epistemology necessarily becomes a crisis of identity; the failure of comprehension quickly extends to both the object and the process of self-comprehension. The delay that structures this play does not just create suspense about the final result or final configuration of Oedipus's identity (both past and present) but rather configures this identity itself.

Delay—as with Creon, the messengers, the servants, and Teiresias—is not merely temporal but also social. Oedipus is blocked from full access to or knowledge of the world because he must go through other characters, must rely on indirect information, acknowledging not simply the message but the person who transmits the message. He is therefore constantly waiting for someone to *arrive* onstage, and such impatient waiting does not end when a character finally does arrive, but merely gets absorbed into the conversations themselves, which are also driven by delay and impatience. For Oedipus the journey back into his past self, or toward comprehension of his past self, is also the widening *of* comprehension, which now comes to depend on a number of witnesses. The confusion that triggers this influx of other persons begins with the discrepancy between two accounts of the murder at the crossroads, a discrepancy prompting Oedipus's angry non sequitur that "one man cannot be the same as many." But Oedipus's growing dependence on other characters, which accelerates at this precise point in the play, suggests a way to resolve this paradox, as his consciousness, and self-consciousness, become imbricated with many other persons.

The stark contradiction between the servant's account—that there were many robbers at the crossroads—and Oedipus's knowledge that he was alone is never resolved in *Oedipus Rex*. Rather, this contradiction is conspicuously dropped. Oedipus and Jocasta await the "messenger" who was a witness to the murder of Laius—they hope he will sort out this contradiction between the one and the many. While they are waiting—into this period of suspended judgment and this space of partial knowledge—another messenger enters, with the news that the king of Corinth has died. The Corinthian messenger unfolds the story of how Oedipus was, in fact, not born of the king, and, for the second time in the play, goes back to Oedipus's name, to the swollen feet that rest at the heart of the dramatic plot. Now Oedipus's own birth is called into question, and the murder of Laius is subsumed by this deeper, more remote matrix of events. As knowledge is gained, more knowledge is required: the Corinthian messenger can confirm Oedipus's connection with the king and queen of Corinth but has no knowledge about his actual origins. Another witness is needed, the Theban herdsman who has no knowledge of where Oedipus was raised but might confirm his own encounter with the Corinthian messenger. Oedipus is now entirely reliant on secondhand sources of information, substituting for his own direct knowledge—of the events at the crossroads—the indirect knowledge (of much earlier events) that he can glean from these messengers. Trying to derive his vulnerable origins, Oedipus is, in fact, as helpless as the child who is handed from parent to herdsman to messenger to foster parent. Just as the baby, who could not walk, relies on these outside figures for survival, so Oedipus now relies on outside figures for comprehension, for self-comprehension.

This parallel between story and discourse is not simply abstract: in fact, the very *same* people provide for both the infant's survival and the adult's consciousness. This fact seems to me of great importance to the tragedy. The minor characters who are radically implicated into the *discourse* (as absolutely intrinsic to Oedipus's discovery of his vulnerable birth) are in precisely the same way implicated into the *story* itself (intrinsic to his survival at his birth). Such a convergence ties together the two registers of representation in Sophocles' play. Both Oedipus's origin and Oedipus's conscious knowledge (*of* his origin) come to revolve around the contingent activity of these two minor characters: before (or, in the discourse, after), as they provide the necessary links in a social chain of parenting (as the baby is handed over from person to person), and after (or, in the discourse, before) as they provide the necessary links in a circumstantial chain of evidence that ultimately reveals Oedipus to himself. The two temporally distinct roles of the characters in fact merge: exactly as Oedipus's *comprehension* of his past identity gets radically dispersed—dependent on these minor figures and no longer autoconstitutive—his past identity also gets reconfigured, beholden to these same minor figures, not as providers of knowledge but as the intermediate caretakers who actually enabled the abandoned baby to survive. Only such a conjunction—between discourse and story, between the very act of consciousness (in the present) and the events that are cognized (in the past)—can allow Oedipus to grasp the element of reality, of history, that had eluded him. Oedipus's consciousness, transfixed on the belated comprehension of his own prehistory, relies on the selfsame world that is implicated in this prehistory.[7]

Let's recall again the displacement that occurs as these two characters—the Corinthian messenger and the Theban herdsman—enter the play and enter into both Oedipus's unfolding chain of reasoning and the bygone social chain that this reasoning will finally uncover. It is the moment of suspension par excellence. Unnerved by the terrifying similarity between the murder of Laius and Oedipus's own confrontation with an old man as he was on the road to Thebes, both Oedipus and Jocasta await a witness who might bring more certainty to the relationship between these two events. The two scenes are riddled with contradictions: Oedipus remembers being the sole attacker at a trifurcated road and leaving no survivors; the messenger has survived an attack by many people at a bifurcation. Two roads or three? One assailant or many? An attack that kills everybody or an attack with a single survivor? The scene at the crossroads seems marked, above all, by numerical confusion.

This inscribed event—a scene of physical violence which seems to stand in stark contrast to the intellectual activity that has just come to define Oedipus—presents a negative version of the core confrontation between reflection and social action that underlies Sophocles' play. In a kind of universal nightmare, we find here the clash of mind against world: self-assertion becomes brutalized and murderous in the competition for space; the arrangement of a king and his adjuncts breaks down even as the social world gets transformed into two clashing one-way streets. As Seth Benardete suggests, the confusion over the number of roads stems from Oedipus's inability to locate himself within the world he observes: he thus ignores or abstracts himself when he sees the third road, which is lying under his feet. In a similar way, one person might be confused with many, and Oedipus's claim that "I killed everyone there" is technically false since he himself (*as well as* the messenger who comes back into the social and evidentiary chain) is still alive to make this claim. For these reasons the unanswered questions have always disturbed but never really disrupted the play's dramatic unity and narrative logic. On the contrary, the effectiveness of the messenger and the herdsman is framed by the confusion that they enter into—a confusion, we need to remember, that is constituted not just by the different numbers that get mixed up at the crossroads, but also by the delay in Oedipus's knowledge itself. The numerical contradictions are resolved precisely as Oedipus's closed process of self-comprehension gets transformed in this period of suspense, a transformation that is completed by the radical implication of these two minor characters simultaneously into both his comprehension and the self that is finally understood.

At this point, of course, Oedipus's wondrous kingship—resting on the synthesis of knowledge and power—breaks down. Political authority, that idealized mode of capability, is shattered at the play's end. In becoming blind, Oedipus gains more knowledge but less power: capability is severed into its two component parts. And yet the defining moment in Oedipus's life has already, silently, passed before us. In some ways the blinded Oedipus returns to his own freestanding self: he has become a coherent, if markedly diminished, whole. Many more years will now pass him by, just as Oedipus had ruled, capably and on his two feet, for quite a long time. The volatile subjectivity of the play, on the other hand, was unique and extraordinary. In his impatience and partial knowledge, in the comprehension that became momentarily available through radical incomprehension: it is in these guises, above all, that Oedipus endures as a literary representation. Such comprehension depends, as we have seen, on the piling up of confusion and alarm, as well as on the entry of ever more people into the play, and into the fabric of self-consciousness. *The messenger and the herdsman* are, in fact, the final and most troubling parents of Oedipus: it is through these two figures that the social chain is revealed in its full open-endedness, and with these two minor characters that Oedipus—the great protagonist of Sophoclean drama—discerns the dispersed if not infinite social world that precedes and stands before him.

Notes

Prologue
The *Iliad*'s Two Wars

1. English translations are based on Lattimore's *Iliad of Homer*, with some modifications.

2. For an example of how critics read the opening in terms of the epic's unity, see Redfield, 95: "The proem thus states in brief compass the whole of which it is the introductory part. It is a kind of lyric at the head of the piece, a masterpiece of compression; here even more than elsewhere, every word is made to tell." See also Griffin and Hammond, 67–68: "A poem as long as the *Iliad*, if it was to be a unity and not a mere train of events, needed a good deal of introduction. . . . The first seven lines form a clearly defined proem, which has a structure . . . and which states the subject matter of the epic."

3. For a fine example of how richly a minor character in the *Iliad* can bear upon an interpretation of the epic's thematic and structural totality, see Laura Slatkin, *The Web of Thetis: Allusion and Interpretation in the* Iliad.

4. Kirk (138) points to another rhetorical strategy that simultaneously emphasizes Thersites within the *Iliad*'s discursive structure and subordinates him within its fictional universe: "He is the only character in the *Iliad* to lack both patronymic and place of origin—some minor characters are given only one or the other, but he, who is not exactly minor, receives neither. This is usually taken to mean that he is a common soldier, a member of the *plathus* ('multitude', 143) or *demos* ('people', 198), who are left unnamed by the poet." For an extended study of Homer's description of Thersites, in the context of the *Iliad* as a whole and the Greek literary tradition, see Eddie R. Lowry, *Thersites: A Study in Comic Shame*.

5. Aristotle continues, "Here again, then, the transcendent excellence of Homer is manifest. He never attempts to make the whole of the war of Troy the subject of his poem, though that war had a beginning and an end . . . he detaches a single portion, and admits as episodes many events from the general story of the war—such as the Catalogue of the Ships and others—thus diversifying the poem." Aristotle's particular example takes on more significance in light of this relationship between social and compositional unity. By choosing this specific digression as his exemplary episode, Aristotle once again links formal diversity to social multiplicity. Ironically, the Catalogue, which so noticeably fails to stand in for all the people it tries to recount, is here made to stand in for the diversity of episodes in general.

6. On this point, see Postlethwaite's astute reading, which concludes that "Thersites has in fact voiced the disappointment and frustration felt by them all. . . . The speech represents the demoralization of the ordinary soldiers after the withdrawal of Achilles" (93–95).

7. The *aristeiai* are an important formal device in the *Iliad*, designating varied episodes in which a specific character achieves his highest or "best" accomplishment in

battle, an accomplishment that tends to reflect—and concisely actualize—his most essential virtues and characteristics.

8. See Auerbach, *Dante*. Auerbach argues that Dante's conception of the afterlife, far from transcending the actuality of "secular" human experience, ironically provides an opportunity to more fully encapsulate ordinary life as embodied in human personality. In Dante's new vision of eternity, the fleeting qualities of each individual are not transcended after death but get distilled and presented in a stable and essential framework. Auerbach writes: "However, the individual figures, arrived at their ultimate, eschatological destination, are not divested of their earthly character. Their earthly historical character is not even attenuated, but rather held fast in all its intensity and so identified with their ultimate fate" (86). The threshold between earth and heaven that Dante's characters bridge might reflect on the threshold of literary characterization itself, as it places a discrete, contingent fictional self within an abstracted and unchangeable narrative economy. What's thematized in the *Inferno*—the static emplacement, or imprisonment, of a changeable human—holds true, in an important sense, for *any* literary character, as he or she is circumscribed into a delimited, and permanent, configuration within a larger narrative structure.

9. Auerbach writes of Homeric characters: "Their living presence and diversity stem, as we can everywhere perceive, from the situation they inevitably get involved in, and it is the situation that prescribes their actions and their suffering" (*Dante* 2).

10. Lukács's influential conception of the character-*type* also reflects the fusion of interiority and exteriority that we can see in the "first fighters" of the *Iliad*. See especially *Studies in European Realism*. The convergence between Lukács's theory of typification and Auerbach's dialectical reading of character in Dante suggests an important affinity between these two seminal twentieth-century theories of literary realism.

11. To see how far the realist novel travels from this kind of characterization, we can note the subordinated position of the *Cénacle* within Balzac's *Lost Illusions*, a group of talented artists and thinkers who befriend Lucien de Rubempré and who bear a striking (structural) resemblance to the circle of fighters. The *Cénacle* is depicted insistently in terms of two qualities: it puts all the members of the tightly knit group in an organic relationship with each other, and it actualizes the uniqueness of each individual, who is defined by his distinct aesthetic talents or political viewpoint. As Balzac writes: "Each of them, like d'Arthez, bore on his forehead the stamp of his own particular genius. . . . These nine people composed a fraternity in which esteem and friendship kept peace between the most conflicting ideas and doctrines . . . all of them [were] equally proficient in their respective sphere of knowledge" (216–22).

Balzac deliberately embeds this artistic circle within his scathing depiction of Restoration Paris's culture industry. As with the circle of first fighters, the virtues of these artists and thinkers can't be dissociated from their social configuration, as a limited and coherent group. But the fate of this small group *within* the narrative as a whole demonstrates how little the band of nineteenth-century intellectuals has in common with the circle of Greek soldiers. The *Cénacle* is simply a weak foil in the dominant plot of *Illusions perdues*; far from determining the protagonist's fate, it becomes an early casualty of Lucien's Parisian misadventures and is soon neglected by the narrative. The small group of unbroken personalities are forced *outside* of society (and the novel), rather than, as in the *Iliad*, holding society together. While the *Cénacle* exists only as it is detached from both society and the novel's main plot, the circle of fighters in the

Iliad has form and meaning only because it *encompasses* the rest of society and stabilizes the epic's compositional structure.

12. For an analysis of related passages, see Benardete, "Aristeia of Diomedes," 35: "Homer now presents for the first time a list of those whom Odysseus and Hector killed without saying anything about them except their names; indeed not one of the men that Odysseus killed receives either patronymic or epithet. This increasing anonymity . . . does not reach its height until much later, when Antilochus kills the nameless charioteer of Asios and Homer has Patroclus kill twenty-seven men in four words."

13. Achilles' explicit subordination of Lykaon—"Patroklos . . . who was better by far than you are"—is elaborated through the poetic density of his reply, which flows into and develops the central protagonist's essential encounter with, and gradual acceptance of, mortality. The fixed (and thus delimited) location of Lykaon's doom—*right here* and *right now*—is subordinated to the extraordinary rendering of Achilles' mortality as indefinite, to take place, unimaginably, at "a dawn or an afternoon or a noontime."

14. On the ethical imagination of the *Iliad*'s narrator, see Simone Weil, "The *Iliad*: A Poem of Force," 3–29.

Introduction
Characterization and Distribution

1. "The Knight's Tale," 1334: "Now will I stop (speaking of) Palamon for a while." To "stynte" here means primarily "to stop" or to "turn away from," while also suggesting the more modern sense of "depriving." The word has a complicated history: in the relation of the obsolete definitions of "to cut short, to stop" and "to cease speaking of" with the modern sense of "to limit unduly in supply, to keep on short allowance, to scant," we can see the narrative logic that underlies distribution (*Oxford English Dictionary*). Chaucer's rich use of the term recurs several times in the tale, as in "But *stynte* I wole of Theseus a lite / And speke of Palamon and of Arcite" (2093–94). The kind of self-conscious awareness about narrative distribution that this term implies runs throughout "The Knight's Tale" (and other sections of *The Canterbury Tales*). For instance, the narrator comments: "Greet was the strif and long bitwix hem tweye, / If that I hadde leyser for to seye, / But to th'effect. It happed on a day, / To telle it yow as shortly as I may . . ." (1187–90); or, again: "And in this wise I lete hem fightyng dwelle, / And forth I wole of Theseus yow telle" (1661–62). The Chaucerian narrator is frequently concerned with the problem of *arranging* and *distributing* narrative around multiple characters, as is made so evident in the structure of the *General Prologue*—a wonderful, and pathbreaking, formulation of the character-system—as well as in the structure of *The Canterbury Tales*, which is divided not by theme or chronological sequence but merely by persons.

2. Gogol parodies this same tension in "The Overcoat": "Of this tailor, of course, not much should be said, but since there exists a rule that the character of every person in a story be well delineated, there's no help for it, let us have Petrovich here as well" (400). In *The Three Clerks* (a novel structured around both narrative *and* social competition) Trollope elaborates on the pressure that an expansive aesthetics of characterization puts on narrative coherence: "We need not give any detailed description of Charley's prison house. He was luckily not detained there so long as to make it necessary that we should become acquainted with his fellow-captives, or even have much intercourse

with his jailers" (340). In both of these examples, attention to a new character inevitably threatens to lead out toward other characters. This narrative connection follows the basic structure of economic exchange in Gogol's example (the tailor is clearly a *functionalized* minor character); in Trollope, the character's very detainment, in the story, is ironically a site for narrative expansion. Characters can, in fact, be "detained" either within the story or in the narrative itself. As Stendhal writes in *The Charterhouse of Parma*, precisely as the narrative shifts away from the putative protagonist: "Mais pour le moment, nous sommes obligés de laisser Fabrice dans sa prison, tout au faite de la citadelle de Parme; on le garde bien, et nous l'y retrouverons peut-être un peu changé" (276). (Imprisonment in this sense, like exile—which I will discuss below—operates at the threshold *between* narrated world and narrative structure.)

For a comic account of how the pressures of distribution intersect with—and indeed help formulate—narrative praxis, see Twain's preface to *Those Extraordinary Twins*, which gives a genealogy of how the tale arose out of the composition of *Pudd'nhead Wilson*: "I *lavishly elaborated these people and their doings*, of course. But the tale kept spreading along and spreading along, and other people got to intruding themselves and taking up more and more room with their talk and their affairs. Among them came a stranger named Pudd'nhead Wilson, and a woman named Roxana; and presently the doings of these two *pushed up into prominence* a young fellow named Tom Driscoll, *whose proper place was away in the obscure background*. Before the book was half finished those three were taking things into their own hands and working the whole tale as a private venture of their own—a tale which they had nothing at all to do with, by rights." This conflict between character-space and narrative coherence hinges on Twain's subtle suggestion of the implied person's agency ("people got to intruding themselves," etc.). Later in the preface, Twain describes the guilt he feels toward a character who had since been abandoned—and the extreme remedy (in the story) he deploys for this (discursive) problem: "Yes, here she was, stranded with that deep injustice of hers torturing her poor torn heart. I didn't know what to do with her. I was as sorry for her as anybody could be, but the campaign was over, the book was finished, she was sidetracked, and there was no possible way of *crowding her in*, anywhere. . . . I finally saw plainly that there was really no way but one—I must simply give her the grand bounce. . . . [I] began the next calender with this statistic: 'Rowena went out in the back yard after supper to see the fireworks and fell down the well and got drowned' " (230–32, emphases added). As the preface continues, Twain employs this new solution on a number of troublesome figures—plunging character after character "down the well."

3. Forster also speaks to the crucial difference between how a flat character might represent an abstract idea and how the character himself can become *abstracted into* an idea: "It is not his idée fixe, because there is nothing *in him into which* the idea can be fixed. He is the idea, and such life as he possesses radiates from its edges and from the scintillations it strikes when other elements in the novel impinge" (104, emphasis added).

4. See Hélène Cixous, "The Character of 'Character' "; Alain Robbe-Grillet, *Pour un nouveau roman*; Roland Barthes, "Introduction à l'analyse structurale des récits" and *S/Z*; A. J. Greimas, *Sémantique structurale: Recherche de méthode*; Philippe Hamon, "Pour un statut sémiologique du personnage." See also Nathalie Sarraute, *L'Ère du soupçon: Essais sur le roman*. For an interesting limit case of this method, see

Roland Le Huenen and Paul Perron, *Balzac. Sémiotique du personnage romanesque: L'exemple d'*Eugénie Grandet. For American narratology in this vein, see Thomas Docherty, *Reading (Absent) Character: Towards a Theory of Characterization in Fiction*. For a recent reconsideration of the eighteenth-century British novel that offers a much more historically nuanced analysis of characterization in fiction, see Catherine Gallagher, *Nobody's Story: The Vanishing Acts of Women Writers in the Marketplace, 1670–1820*, which ingeniously positions the rise of credible characters and *readerly* investment in these new kinds of characters within a much larger socioeconomic framework involving new forms of credit and financial investment. Gallagher's study suggests a new way of putting the literary character back into relation with contemporary theory. See also Diedre Shauna Lynch, *The Economy of Character: Novels, Market Culture, and the Business of Inner Meaning*, which explicitly aims to historicize the method of Barthes and Cixous (14–20).

5. See Vladimir Propp, *Morphology of the Folktale*, and see Greimas, 172–92. Greimas establishes six actants: Sujet, Objet, Destinateur, Destinataire, Opposant, and Adjuvant. For a more recent typology of minor characters that eclectically encompasses work in this direction, see David Galef, *The Supporting Cast: A Study of Flat and Minor Characters*, who divides minor characters into seven "structural types"—Narrators and Expositors; Interrupters; Symbols and Allegories; Enablers or Agents of Action; Foils and Contrast; Double or Dopplegangers; Emphasizers—and four "mimetic types"— Eccentrics, Friends, and Acquaintances; Family; People, Chorus, Upper and Lower Classes, Background; Subhuman: Animal Objects, Places (15–25).

6. Most notably, James Phelan tries to construct a heterogeneous theory of character in *Reading People, Reading Plots: Character, Progression and the Interpretation of Narrative*. Phelan's renewed insistence on a mimetic effect (in juxtaposition with the "thematic" and "synthetic" aspects of the literary character) is suggestively linked to the ethical dimension of narrativity by Adam Zachary Newton in *Narrative Ethics*. See also Shlomith Rimmon-Kenan's *A Glance beyond Doubt: Narration, Representation and Subjectivity*, which meditates on the status of referentiality within narratology. (The title itself suggests the horizon of this project: isn't a glance necessarily doubtful?) For other works that react, in varying ways, to the formalist or structuralist de-emphasis of character, see W. J. Harvey, *Characters and the Novel*; Martin Price, *Forms of Life: Character and Moral Imagination in the Novel*; Baruch Hochman, *Character in Literature*; Brian Rosenberg, *Little Dorrit's Shadows: Character and Contradiction in Dickens*; and Irving Howe, *A Critic's Notebook* 36–117.

7. See de Man on this "recurrent debate" in *Allegories of Reading*, 3–5.

8. On the relation of distribution and characterization, see Hamon's insightful *Texte et idéologie*. Hamon, by accounting for the way that the distributed weight of attention to different individuals can organize narrative structure, provides an excellent example of efforts to reconsider structuralism's excision of the human from *within* a narratological framework. Hamon analyzes how novels construct univalent and polyvalent ideological fields through this hierarchical arrangement of characters—what Hamon calls "la poétique d'échelle." He traces the nineteenth-century shift from a central protagonist to more dispersed character-systems as the registering of ideological uncertainty: "On passe ainsi d'une esthétique de l'intensité, de la concentration, de la focalisation idéologique . . . à une esthétique de la neutralisation normative . . . d'une certaine 'ère du soupçon' idéologique" (102). Hamon's *end* is ideological, but his means of arriving at

the text's ideological signification is through characters' referentiality. At certain points—as though reacting against the implications of his own model—Hamon de-emphasizes the suggestive specificity of these means. Most notably, he compares the dispersion of attention to many characters with the loss of meaning that accompanies free verse's dispersion of the rhyme away from line ends (73). A shrewd comparison—but one that bluntly disregards how rhyme organizes structure (through literal, phonic similarity) and how characters organize structure (through their implied referential weight). See also Hamon's *Le Personnel du roman*.

9. Needless to say, the necessary relation between character-spaces is frequently intertwined with the actual relations between characters in the story-world itself, but the variations in how these two planes interact are immense. Throughout this study I will try to develop analyses of specific novels in terms of how the relationship between character-*spaces* (in the discourse) underlies or is in tension with the relationship between characters (in the story). To fully see this interaction, however, we need to *conceptually* disaggregate the two entwined strands of characterization.

10. It is notable, in this context, that Greimas's actantial model of characterization—which is one of the crucial schemes for antireferential character theories—radically distinguishes the humanness of central and peripheral characters. Subordinate characters, defined as "adjuvants" and "opposants," get reduced to an adjectival function, and the noun that they modify turns out to be, finally, a human subject, now presented on a strictly psychological register: "l'adjuvant et l'opposant ne soient que des projections de la volonté d'agir et des résistances imaginaires du sujet lui-même, jugés bénéfiques ou maléfiques par rapport à son désir" (180). Greimas's interpretive structure does not abolish reference but configures it in a particular way—as a central interiority, defined by *desire*, that absorbs all other individuals into its own perspective. (As with Aristotle's theory of the unified form, the most we end up with in Greimas is a "single organism"). Such a model obscures the many ways a literary text might resist this arrangement, and misses a larger structural field within which the dynamic relationship between reference and symbol can itself be scrutinized. For a related analysis of Greimas, see Jameson, 122–23.

Giamatti's seemingly conservative notion of epic allegory also resonates improbably with Cixous's influential avant-garde critique of characterization. Like Greimas, Cixous does not ultimately eliminate the relationship between literary structure and the human, but merely insists that narrative can represent only *one* individual, who is projected in various ways into the subordinated population of the text. Giamatti's "hero" becomes Cixous's psychoanalytic "subject," whose "decentered" and polyvalent selfhood is ramified through the allegorical operations of the character-system. This psychoanalytic approach is already anticipated in Freud's 1908 essay "The Relation of the Poet to Day-Dreaming," in which he argues that all popular fiction relies on (or, in rare cases, strains against) an "egocentric" structure with "a hero who is the centre of interest," and minor characters who are defined in relation to this central figure. Freud then goes on to address the way that such egocentric structure travels from romance to realism by taking a *discursive* rather than plot form: while romance fiction places the hero "under the protection of a special providence" (recovering from a sword wound, escaping from a shipwreck, to use Freud's examples), modern psychological fiction takes a more subtle form: "It has struck me in many so-called psychological novels, too, that only one person—once again the hero—is described from within; the author dwells in his soul and looks upon the other people from outside" (180).

11. Tasso writes: "A poem can be formed in which, as in a microcosm, there would be read here arrays of armies, here battles on land and sea, here stormings of cities, skirmishes and joustings, here descriptions of hunger and thirst, here storms, conflagrations, prodigies; there would be found seditions, discords, errors, adventures, magic spells; there deeds of cruelty, of audacity, of courtesy, of generosity; there experiences of love, sometimes happy, sometimes unhappy, sometimes joyous, sometimes pathetic; but may the poem that contains so great a variety of matter be one in form and soul, and may all its elements be put together in such a way that if one part is taken away, or its position changed, all is destroyed" (from *Torquato Tasso: Prose*, ed. Ettore Mizzali [Milan, 1959], 589, quoted in Ryding, 15).

12. This reinterpretation of realist detail opens up questions that this study can only touch on. The "detail" is central to discussions of realism because it bears directly on the tension between totality and particularity, or metaphor and facticity, which is at the heart of much theorization of the novel. McKeon's ambitious dialectical account of the novel centers on such a tension, as it is manifested in the seventeenth-century conflict between traditional, authoritarian modes of epistemology and the rising awareness and comprehension of historicity. Empiricism catalyzes narrative forms that are plagued by the potentially disruptive effect of the details they now incorporate, by "problems of how to achieve quantitative completeness and how to justify factual selectiveness" (93). As McKeon quotes John Foxe, "To express every minute of matter in every story, what story-writer in all the world is able to perform it?" (93). Such an excess of reality is often understood in its temporal and spatial dimensions. With the new authenticity of factual details, where does descriptive absorption end? With the contemplation of ever more discrete units of time, what instants will be excluded? I want to ground the realist dialectic not in its confrontation with too much time, or too many spatial details, but as it comprehends too many *human beings*, who crowd into the narrative and demand attention. This shift from problems of detail to problems of social inclusion is suggested by McKeon's comment on a new "responsiveness to the factuality of *individual life* so intense that the dominance of over-arching pattern is felt, in varying ways, to be quite problematic" (98, emphasis added). Behind realism's urge toward precision—that obsessive tendency to include all the details of life—is an urge to include people (*each* of whom has a detailed consciousness of life). Barthes's reality-effect might then relate to what Demetz, discussing Balzac's realism, calls "a socially-more inclusive literature, giving voice to multitudes speechless in the dark" (418).

We might also note that a tension between detailed precision and *imprecision* in the realist novel resembles the way that the inclusion of minor characters is typically intertwined with their distortion. Three examples might suggest the nature of this connection between precision and the poetics of social inclusion. Consider these two passages from Elizabeth Gaskell's *Mary Barton* in which, respectively, descriptive detail is intertwined with the novel's incorporation of traditionally unrepresented lower-class characters and descriptive *im*precision is connected to—and, I would argue, motivated by—excluded human beings who cannot fully enter the narrative frame:

Her little bit of crockery-ware was ranged on the mantelpiece, where also stood her candlestick and box of matches. A small cupboard contained at the bottom coals, and at the top her bread and basin of oatmeal, her frying-pan, tea-pot, and a small tin saucepan, which served as a kettle, as well as for cooking the delicate little messes of broth which Alice was sometimes able to manufacture for a sick neighbor. (15)

You went down one step even from the foul area into the cellar in which a family of human beings lived. It was very dark inside. The window-panes were many of them broken and stuffed with rags, which was reason enough for the dusky light that pervaded the place even at mid-day. . . . Quickly recovering themselves, as those inured to such things do, they began to penetrate the thick darkness of the place, and to see three or four little children rolling on the damp, nay wet, brick floor, through which the stagnant, filthy moisture of the street oozed up; the fireplace was empty and black; the wife sat on her husband's lair, and cried in the dank loneliness. (66)

It is in the imprecise "three or four children"—effaced as individuals in their needy multiplicity—that we can locate exclusion, and the social grounds for the blurred visual field. A fuller analysis might link this dialectic between detail and blur (which runs through the narrative) with the structure of the novel's character-system. Finally, consider the precise details that surround the description of Father Time's suicide and murders in *Jude the Obscure* ("done because we are too menny"): "At the back of the door were fixed two hooks for hanging garments, and from these the forms of the two youngest children were suspended, by a piece of box-cord round each of their necks, while from a nail a few yards off the body of little Jude was hanging in a similar manner. An overturned chair was near the elder boy, and his glazed eyes were slanted into the room; but those of the girl and the baby were closed" (355). In this case, the passage's intrusive details—"a piece of box-cord," "from a nail a few yards off," "an overturned chair"—work to tragically stand in for the specificity of the murdered children; narrative attention toward these children—annihilated because of their social extraneousness—produces the details that powerfully suggest, in their empiric singularity, the destruction of singularity which has just occurred.

13. See Forster, 100–118. Forster's theory is unique in its popularity among both referential and formal theories of characterization.

14. Such a conflation would suggest a fuller theory of James's own characterization, which links the pressures of distributing attention to James's protomodernist stylistic innovations. A similar connection, between the difficulty of representing minor characters and crucial stylistic developments that flow into modernism, can be found within Joseph Conrad's fiction. *Lord Jim*, perhaps most strikingly, thematizes the conflict between the one and the many in the parable of Jim's cowardly abandonment of the pilgrims aboard the *Patna*. Marlow's inability to communicate adequately with Jim or to coherently narrate Jim's story is directly related to the impossibility of comprehending the mass of humanity whom Jim abandons, and who are so incompletely registered within the narrative itself. As Marlow writes, in an image that concisely grounds Conrad's impressionism in this social crisis: Jim, the endangered protagonist of the novel, is "blurred by crowds of men as by clouds of dust" (202).

15. And what is a spasm here develops more fully in a later passage where "[in] an extravagant pitch of fury, Newman Noggs jerked himself about the room with the most eccentric motion ever beheld in a human being" (485).

16. Critics have observed this distinction between two inverse kinds of subordinate characters, without analyzing these as the dialectical results *of* subordination. Besides

Greimas's "adjuvant" and "opposant," see Harvey, on the "card" and the "ficelle," 62–63.

17. The distinction between story and discourse, crucial terms in this study, is summarized in Seymour Chatman, *Story and Discourse*. Discourse refers to the actual language and structure of the narrative, story to the fictional events that we extrapolate from the discourse. For my own discussion of these terms, see the final section of this introduction.

18. Bertha has the distinction of being near the center of both the fictional *and* the critical-theoretical reconfiguration of nineteenth-century minorness. She is the surprising protagonist of Jean Rhys's *Wide Sargasso Sea*, one of the first novels to hinge on rewriting a literary character-system to change the modalities of dominant and subordinate character, and the eponymous hero of Gilbert and Gubar's foundational *The Madwoman in the Attic*, which established a tradition of bringing out the radical perspectives of female writers vis-à-vis heightened attention to minor characters.

19. By linking them together in later scenes, Brontë insists on a structure that transcends the oddity of either character. As Jane's understanding of Bertha grows clearer, Grace remains on the scene, shadowing the increasingly direct encounters between the protagonist and her fragmentary double: "A woman did, I doubt not, enter your room: and that woman was—must have been—Grace Poole. You call her a strange being yourself: from all you know, you have reason to so call her. . . . In a state between sleeping and waking, you noticed her entrance and her actions; but feverish, almost delirious as you were, you ascribed to her a goblin appearance different from her own: the long disheveled hair, the swelled black face, the exaggerated stature, were figments of imagination, results of nightmare" (271). And again: "In a room without a window, there burnt a fire, guarded by a high and strong fender, and a lamp suspended from the ceiling by a chain. Grace Poole bent over the fire, apparently cooking something in a saucepan. In the deep shade, at the farther end of the room, a figure ran backwards and forwards. What it was, whether beast or human being, one could not, at first sight, tell" (278).

20. English translation based on C. K. Scott Moncrieff and Terence Kilmartin, *Remembrance of Things Past*, vol. 1 (New York: Random House, 1981), 12.

21. See Marx, 186: "In this case, the utility relationship has a quite definite meaning, namely, that I derive benefit for myself by doing harm to someone else. . . . All this is actually the case with the bourgeois. For him only one relation is valid on its own account—the relation of exploitation; all other relations have validity for him only in so far as he can include them under this one relation."

22. See Moretti, *The Way of the World*.

23. Film narrative opens a rich and complicated terrain for character-space and character-system. In film the dynamics of narrative subordination, attention, and neglect can always be potentially literalized in the spatial organization of the screen itself. More specifically, the continual interaction and tension between mise-en-scène and camera shot offers an opportunity for *doubling up* character-space: the relative minorness or centrality of characters (within the story) can be consolidated and elaborated, or ironized and critiqued, *both* in the dynamic positioning of the characters within a scene's staging and in the translation of the scene, through camera, onto screen-space. For a seminal analysis of interaction between mise-en-scène and screen space, see Bazin. Essential aspects of traditional film syntax can be read in terms of character-space

and character-system—from the development of montage (explicitly in relation to the problematics of social multiplicity) to the use of close-up (as a device that so often either emphasizes *or* fragments the human form) to the conventions of shot-reverse-shot (which simultaneously distributes two radically different *kinds* of attention to two characters in a series of shots, potentially stabilizing—or undermining—both the relationship between the two individuals and the configuration of each person as alternately subject and object).

24. The structure of the novel here resembles Macpherson's definition of nineteenth-century liberal democracy as "the combination of an ethical principle of equality with a competitive market model of man and society" (25).

25. The Austen chapter is therefore more extensive than other readings in the book; I am not trying to apply terms here but to derive them in interplay with the narrative itself. For the most part, then, the key terms of the study (such as "character-space" and "character-system") do not play a major role in this chapter; they are rather a destination to which the chapter, and the novel, lead.

26. This play of permutation is notably apparent in Austen's own novels—no two central positions (nor any two central *characters*) are alike: her closed structures allow for a remarkable elaboration and investigation of—and finally, a profound brooding over—the very nature of centrality. Most saliently, we might note how, in tandem, *Mansfield Park* and *Emma* unravel the achieved construction of centrality that has just taken place in *Pride and Prejudice*. Fanny's modesty and Emma's self-centeredness can be seen not merely in a *psychologized* relationship to Elizabeth Bennet's character but also as a double challenge to the structural principles underlying *Pride and Prejudice*'s formulation of character-*space*. *Mansfield Park* brilliantly places a socially minor character *into* the central position—putting massive pressure on *Pride and Prejudice*'s elaborate double motivation of centrality in story and discourse. *Emma*, on the other hand, hypostatizes the protagonist's centrality, which, in comparison to Elizabeth Bennet's, is *unearned*: in both discourse (unlike *Pride and Prejudice* the narrative *immediately* focuses on the central figure—not just with the famous first sentence but, of course, with the title itself) and story (in the privileged social position that *Emma* starts in, rather than attains—a privilege that is continually implicated in her problematic love of self). These two novels—which cannot be fully considered in this study—are a remarkable artistic response to the author's own achievement; and the three novels together forcefully demonstrate how the dynamic configuration of a protagonist's centrality (or character-space) is a crucial aspect of fiction itself.

27. See Forster, 103–4: "In their purest form, [flat characters] are constructed round a single idea or quality: when there is more than one factor in them, we get the beginning of the curve toward the round. . . . The really flat character can be expressed in one sentence."

28. In this study I will often use the terms *histoire* and *discours*, instead of story and discourse, to convey the formal sense of the distinction, since "story" and "discourse" have such broad colloquial meaning.

29. Rimmon-Kenan, *Narrative Fiction* 3.

30. This relationship between compression and centrality is further elaborated when Bulkington makes his second and final appearance in "The Lee-Shore"—that notable *and* notably brief chapter in *Moby Dick*. Here Bulkington is granted *symbolic or thematic* centrality even while the chapter literalizes his diminutive *narrative* space: "Won-

derfullest things are ever the unmentionable; deep memories yield no epitaphs; *this six-inch chapter is the stoneless grave of Bulkington*" (97, emphasis added). This sentence—and the chapter as a whole—blur structure and reference by making the material composition of the narrative discourse (those six inches of print) stand in for the fictional character's unjustly constricted position within the story. Bulkington's strange character-space, of course, has plenty of company and competition in *Moby Dick*, one of the most compelling character-systems—both aesthetically and politically—in the nineteenth-century American novel. Melville's *Benito Cereno*, with its three competing and problematically connected character-centers, also dramatically demonstrates how the literary character emerges only in the interaction *between* story and discourse. The novella, I would argue, places the three component elements of a character-system—narrator, hero, minor character—into an unstable, triangulated relationship: Cereno, the eponymous protagonist (and *putative* captain of the *San Dominick*); Delano, the focalizing agent or inscribed narrator par excellence (who is also a *visiting* captain); and Babo, a parodically minor character and servant to the captain who covertly controls the ship (and is thus the *actual* captain, although his power is never directly registered in the discourse). The remarkable tale is structured around the three characters' continual shifts in *centrality* (as potential protagonists within the discourse) and *power* (as potential captains within the story).

Chapter One
Narrative Asymmetry in *Pride and Prejudice*

1. I take this phrase from Dickens's *Bleak House*, where Esther Summerson (at once a startlingly major and minor character, collapsing the terms of this study in on themselves) writes, "So strangely did I hold my place in this world that until within a short time back I had never, to my own mother's knowledge, breathed—had been buried—had never been endowed with life—had never borne a name" (569).

2. This is already a theme in one of the first important essays on Austen's work. In his unsigned 1815 review of *Emma*, Walter Scott writes of Austen's presentation of Mr. Bennet and Mr. Collins in *Pride and Prejudice*: "This is one of the portraits from ordinary life which shews our author's talent in a very strong point of view. A friend of ours, whom the author never saw or heard of, was at once recognized by his own family as the original of Mr. Bennet, and we do not know if he has yet got rid of the nickname. A Mr. Collins, too, a formal, conceited, yet servile young sprig of divinity, is drawn with the same force and precision" (reprinted in Littlewood, 293). In the subtle play *between* "force" and "precision," we can already sense the same dynamics of caricature—while precision implies the author's holding back in relation to the object, force implies the opposite.

3. As I discuss in the introduction, Dorothea's ambiguous but finally resilient centrality in *Middlemarch* is one of the more important examples of the dynamics of the protagonist's space in Victorian fiction. Ironically, this very passage helps *construct* Dorothea's central space on one narrative register, even while it explicitly motivates a shift toward Casaubon. The double reference to Celia and Sir James builds the larger symbolic opposition between their two different types of superficiality against Dorothea's depth of character; thus the narrator's negative judgment of Celia and Sir

James—ostensibly invoked to pull attention away from Dorothea—also develops her centrality on the symbolic plane.

4. It is also clear that in one important sense Harding's model cannot be the basis for a structural understanding because this "implicit agreement," if it could actually be followed, would drain caricature of any force—would, in fact, make caricature disappear as a descriptive category. If we were actually to become fully oblivious to the wholeness of a human personality, we would be unable to recognize a representation *as* caricature. Even to make Harding's division between characters and caricatures relies, finally, on the comparison to real people that he then wishes to deny.

5. Lionel Trilling, "A Portrait of Western Man," *The Listener*, June 11, 1953, 970; quoted in Butler, 202.

6. In fact, the putatively subtle distinction between Elizabeth and Jane *is* pointedly ironic: the rhetoric of balance ("more" than, "less" than) obscures how *both* Elizabeth's surfeit of quickness and lack of pliancy work to suggest that Jane is simply not as smart. Furthermore, the identification of Elizabeth with "more quickness" directly echoes Mr. Bennet's claim that Elizabeth has "something more of quickness than her sisters" in chapter 1, which, we will see, both sets in motion and anchors the basic asymmetric elaboration of the character-system. To repeat this general claim in *specific* reference to Jane helps enfold the sister who might seem to partially challenge Elizabeth's lock on narrative centrality safely within the asymmetric structure. The subordinate clause in this sentence—"and with a judgment too unassailed by any attention to herself"—is also fascinating. Here the emphatic negative ("too unassailed") even more successfully conceals the actual charge of this sentence—not just less intelligent, Jane, distracted by the attention she receives, is somewhat self-absorbed, a combination that is usually quite fatal in an Austen novel. This clause also deviously increases the narrative attention *toward* Elizabeth precisely in terms of her own meritorious self-neglect.

7. A wonderfully elongated sentence from *Northanger Abbey* illustrates how this double-edged comparison propels the energy of Austen's early work: "Mrs. Thorpe, however, had one great advantage as a talker, over Mrs. Allen, in a family of children; and when she expatiated on the talents of her sons, and the beauty of her daughters,— when she related their different situations and views,—that John was at Oxford, Edward at Merchant-Taylors', and William at sea,—and all of them more beloved and respected in their different stations than any other three beings ever were, Mrs. Allen had no similar information to give, no similar triumphs to press on the unwilling and unbelieving ear of her friend, and was forced to sit and appear to listen to all these material effusions, consoling herself, however, with the discovery, which her keen eyes soon made, that the lace on Mrs. Thorpe's pelisse was not half so handsome as that on her own" (32). This sentence, with its twenty clauses, shows a young writer experimenting with structure and taking pleasure in the "effusions" of fictional language. The sentence flows seamlessly between two kinds of comparison or discrimination: the "different situations" or "different stations" generated out of the dynamic structure of social reality, and the *interior elaboration* of this, in the comparison (through Mrs. Allen's free indirect discourse) that brings the sentence to a halt.

8. It is this abstraction that leads to the remarkable number of transitive verbs that "character" is coupled with in the novel. At various points character—always as the abstract qualities *of* a person—is described as something that can be considered (125), decided (11), developed (213), drawn (264), enquired of (206), exposed (174), fixed

(231), given (258), illustrated (93), known (143), mistaken (258), misunderstood (273), praised (143), questioned (206), reestablished (227), respected (212), restored (326), sketched (94), studied (23), sunk (149), understood (22), unfolded (191), and valued (85). This relentless solidification of an abstraction is purchased only by the demateria-lization of actual persons, who are subsumed into their characteristics.

9. The entail, an emblem of *old* property relationships, is transformed by Austen into a means to symbolically comprehend a historically new kind of economic insecu-rity. More generally, *Pride and Prejudice* takes essential elements of an archaic eco-nomic world—most notably the entail and primogeniture—and uses them to describe and confront emergent economic structures. Thus while the competition among sisters for an elder son *could* have informed much earlier literature, it is Austen who makes it the central situation of a nineteenth-century literary work. The entail, in *Pride and Prejudice*, takes on meaning only in relation to Mrs. Bennet's middle-class, nonlanded economic background. The nuanced condensation of archaic and emergent forms (which resembles the stylistic synthesis of fairy tale and realism) is well suited to the dynamic, transitional nature of the novel's socioeconomic period.

10. The problem of disinheritance, which underlies all the economics of marriage in *Pride and Prejudice*, is even more visibly—and structurally—present in Austen's previous novel, which begins by positing a kind of absolute rupture between landed wealth and financial insecurity. The opening lines of *Sense and Sensibility* present the clearest image of the disinherited ground in Austen; crucially, landed wealth is consoli-dated in—and formulated in relation to—the *centered individual*, "long settled" in Sus-sex, with a large estate, and a residence "in the centre of [his] property." Similarly, *dis*inheritance will be comprehended in the very *shared* status of Elinor and Marianne as potential co-protagonists in the novel, a doubling of character-space that amplifies the sisters' newly insecure social positions in terms of their insecure narrative positions.

11. This relationship illustrates Goldmann's theory about the "rigorous homology" between capitalism, as a social structure, and the novel, as a narrative form. Goldmann asserts that it is unproductive to look only for a "relation between certain elements of the *content* of fictional literature and the existence of a social reality." Such an analysis, never accounting for either the novel's totality or the totality of a social system, cannot lead us to account for a connection between the two. Rather, we must look at "the relation between the *novel form* itself and the *structure of the social* environment in which it developed, that is to say, between the novel as a literary genre and individualis-tic modern society. . . . The novel form seems to me, in effect, to be *the transposition on the literary plane of everyday life in the individualistic society created by market production*" (6–7, Goldmann's emphasis). In *Pride and Prejudice* we can see a specific example of this link, in the relationship between asymmetry, the disintegration of a fixed, hierarchal social order, and the resulting tension between the one and the many.

12. Is Jane in the room? This unanswerable question, in fact, leads into several oth-ers: Why wouldn't Jane be there—is there any textual evidence *included* that motivates her exclusion? If Jane *is* in the room (in the story), why doesn't she get incorporated into the narrative discourse? Or has Austen simply forgotten the character or not even considered this question? This third suggestion seems least likely: the rigorous config-uration of "the girls" as a unit in the beginning of the narrative is necessarily reinforced by this final extreme of neglect, the lack of *any* attention directed toward the eldest sister, so that we don't even know whether she is present in the scene.

13. The constant use of italics for personal pronouns and, frequently, for facilitating a comparison between different characters, is a strong example of how the tension between "character" as interior quality and "character" as (a) social being manifests itself on the syntactic level in *Pride and Prejudice*. Italics, of course, contribute crucially to the narrator's ironic tone; they are perhaps the most ironic of all syntactic devices. In general italics create implication, suggesting something beyond the normal meanings of a word. But in Austen italicization that conveys an excess of tone or implication is constantly merged with italicization that conveys social distinction. I offer two of the many examples. Darcy says to Elizabeth: "But your *family* owe me nothing. Much as I respect them, I believe, I thought only of *you*" (375). Again, the narrator describes Elizabeth's recognition that Collins might want to propose to her: "It now first struck her, that *she* was selected from among her sisters as worthy of being the mistress of Hunsford Parsonage." Here italicization inevitably contributes to the growing sense of singularity, distinction, and centrality that Collins's "selection" helps facilitate. We could compare these italicized terms to an example that is more clearly semantic. Elizabeth thinks about Darcy, "Perhaps he had been civil, only because he felt himself at ease; yet there had been *that* in his voice, which was not like ease" (274). Italics thus encapsulate the tension we have been examining: they enable qualitative distinctions, such as between "ease" and "*that*" which is not ease; but they also facilitate social distinctions, allowing the individual to define him- or herself against others.

14. This particular technique—of promoting a protagonist's centrality by making him or her the center of *other* people's thoughts—is notably used in *Le Rouge et le noir*. Stendhal distributes interior discourse among many different characters besides Julien Sorel but makes the vast majority of all the other characters' thoughts revolve around Julien. Thus we often see Mme Renal's thoughts indirectly represented or even directly quoted, but only as they relate to her relationship with Julien. Perhaps the best—because briefest—example of this process is when Julien enters a café and the omniscient narrator breaks from the central protagonist's point of view to give us a fragment of what the waitress is thinking: "But the young lady behind the bar had noticed the charming figure of this young country bourgeois who, arrested three feet from the stove, and with his little parcel under his arm, examined a fine white plaster bust of the king. . . . This little air of authority pleased Amanda. This young man isn't a nobody, she thought" (370, 372). This is the only thought of Amanda's that the narrator describes, moving the narrative simultaneously away from and toward Julien.

15. Is this a pattern? Do characters who are introduced later in a narrative often get externalized in this way, so that, among other things, they are much more likely to be depicted without narrative amplification of their interiority or point of view? This question itself suggests the kind of artistic choice and signifying field that become visible through the structural dynamics—and varieties—of character-system. It's a problem that quickly leads out to other novels: how could we correlate, for instance, the ascribed interiority (or focalizing *weight*) of characters in relation to their relatively early or late arrival into the narrative in *Middlemarch*? Or *Germinal*?

16. This is precisely the passage with which Harding begins his essay on caricature, noting, "If we were to object that this surely is rather unlikely—two or three minutes perhaps but hardly a quarter of an hour—it would be a misreading; we should be missing the fact that this is a convention of joking exaggeration" (83). But we can now see this moment within a narrative continuum and understand it as a specific narrative

choice made as the system of asymmetry is developing. Collins isn't simply "unreal" but is rather *derealized* in a specific way that develops and functions in relation to the novel as a whole.

17. In fact Charlotte's problematic status is indissociably bound up *in* her three different kinds of help, which variously point us toward the character or toward the narrative structure. Thus, as we have seen, "plot-help" is essentially structural (it can take place regardless of the character's personality), while "psychological help" displaces this structural utility of the narrative helper (i.e., facilitating the progress of the protagonist) into the individualized characteristics *of* the helper. But the final level of Charlotte's help—the "symbolic help" accomplished through juxtaposition—trumps these characteristics, returning us to the hard lesson of structure. This return to structure is ultimately bound up in the collapse of the friendship itself, a collapse which is embedded within a larger tension that we need to understand in terms of the story/discourse disjunction: as a youthful character, the bildungsroman protagonist *needs* close friends; as a central character, *she can't really have them.*

18. The grammatical status of "dwelling" is important—the narrative consistently pushes us toward structure, so that here what the word is about *is* in large part its own syntactic modality. Each participial construction in the passage, in fact, has a hidden (or syntactic) connotation ("to dwell") that underlies its intentional denotation. But in this case the syntactic connotation of these participles (merely *as* participles) isn't the end point either. If Greimas argues that characters inevitably fit into a grammatical structure, here the participial construction itself (even as it absorbs the discrete signification of specific verbs) is motivated by, and serves to elaborate, the emplaced protagonist as such (whose achieved centrality is the final result of the "dwelling" that is here signified on the level of both semantic denotation and syntactic connotation).

19. English versions from Richard Miller's translation of *S/Z* (New York: Hill and Wang, 1974), with some modifications.

20. We will see this tendency of the character-system to proliferate more markedly in *Great Expectations*, where, as in many of Dickens's novels, minorness seems to always create more minorness. But Fitzwilliam's small space within *Pride and Prejudice*'s complicated economy of character is instructive, precisely because it *is* so limited. Clearly not necessary in the way of a Lydia or a Mr. Collins, Fitzwilliam is a fine example of one kind of superfluous character, as the dynamic inflection of the character creates a sense of widening that takes form only against the intricate bounding of the character-system as a whole. To put this another way: the inflection of Fitzwilliam's character-space into the novel transiently widens the *discourse* in much the same way as his arrival at Rosings, within the story, casually widens Elizabeth's own social possibilities. Like the character himself, the character-space is somewhat flirtatious: Fitzwilliam dangles a vague significance, what we might call a kind of structural innuendo (how can the reader make this character mean something within the novel as a whole?).

21. "Multiplicity" is different from other themes (associated with Wickham) that might be sustained *by* the metonymic construct, because this theme, unlike all the others, redounds directly *back onto* the socionarrative structure that subtends it. It is *only* this aspect of Wickham, in other words, that can comprehend the profound relationship between vehicle and tenor (rather than merely instrumentalizing the way in which Austen constructs a stable "value system"). Multiplicity, then, is both a "value" produced

through the asymmetrical character-system and one that is bound within the very construction and organization *of* the character-system.

22. If the analysis has traced how Wickham's subordination is not just embedded within, but serves to thematize, multiplicity, a similar argument can be made about Darcy's singular wealth. In this way it is appropriate that Darcy's socionarrative value—contingent on the crowding out of other persons—is ultimately manifested, in the referenced world of the story itself, as the ability of the landed person to *replicate himself*. This is in the end what wealth attains in *Pride and Prejudice*, either the aggressive expansion of a Lady Catherine or, more valorously, the cultivated replication of a Darcy. In this sense Darcy's wealth offers a *social* version of the expansion of Elizabeth's character-space that we have traced in terms of *consciousness*. This is most evident during the famously pivotal Pemberley episode at the beginning of volume 3. Pemberley enables a union not just of the two central characters but of their two modes of self-expansion, fusing together Elizabeth's reflection and Darcy's self-replication (a replication that the novel persuasively embeds within the very idea of property).

To begin with, Austen makes it clear that Pemberley offers an external field for Elizabeth's play of consciousness: "Every disposition of the ground was good; and she looked on the whole scene, the river, the trees scattered on its banks, and the winding of the valley, *as far as she could trace it*, with delight. As they passed into other rooms, these objects were taking different positions; but from every window there were beauties to be seen" (246, emphasis added). These views, offering a mobile interaction between subject and objects, spatialize that profusion of consciousness ("from *every* window") which we have already seen in Elizabeth's reading and reflection ("[h]er astonishment . . . was increased by *every* review of it"; "she studied *every* sentence"; etc.). In other words, Darcy's cultivated estate produces a spatial ground *for* the expansion of consciousness. Soon after this, Elizabeth is presented with two miniatures that offer "likenesses" of Wickham and Darcy. These representations, of course, help stage the now shifting battle between the two persons. Of Darcy, Mrs. Reynolds notes that "I am sure *I* know none so handsome; but in the gallery up stairs you will see a finer, larger picture of him than this" (247). In the same way as there are different views of Darcy's landscape from every window, these images offer more than one view of Darcy himself. If portraiture can offer enhanced (i.e., enlarged) and *multiple* versions of a single, irreplaceable person, the field of property, this episode soon informs us, can too. Just as there are *two* different portraits of Darcy, so he has more than one *home*:

> "Is your master much at Pemberley in the course of the year?"
> "Not so much as I could wish, Sir; but I dare say he may spend half his time here; and Miss Darcy is always down for the summer months." (248)

Two pictures (one large, one small); "half" his time at Pemberley: the episode suggests an equivalency between portrait and property as two sites that replicate or externalize a person beyond his intrinsic, bodily limitation. This doubling of portrait and property in relation to the person forms the context for the "recognition" scene, as Elizabeth's reevaluation of Darcy (itself another sign of *her* distinctive and ever growing self-consciousness) is threaded through both painting *and* estate: "The picture-gallery, and two or three of the principal bed-rooms, were all that remained to be shown. . . . In the gallery there were many family portraits, but they could have little to fix the attention of a stranger. Elizabeth walked on in quest of the only face whose features would be known to her. At last it arrested her—and she beheld a striking resemblance of Mr. Darcy, with such a smile over the face, as she remembered to have sometimes seen, when he looked at her. She stood several minutes before the picture in earnest contemplation. . . . There was certainly at this moment, in Elizabeth's mind, a more gentle sensation towards the original, than she had ever felt in the height of their acquaintance" (250). In this passage, the narrative brilliantly reverses the priority of original and replication, so that Elizabeth's sensation toward—or memory of—the "original" (i.e., the actual *person*) is facilitated through her encounter with the "resemblance" (the aesthetic replication). As with painting, where the replication of personhood stares us, literally, in the face, so with property, except that with ownership, such replication is highly mediated. (In this way a house doesn't literally resemble a person, but you can find "characteristics" of a person *in* his house, or in other possessions that serve to actualize him.) Such mediation, however, is necessary *to* that other form of self-replication which the novel traces: consciousness, interiority itself. The passage we are considering thus marks a conjuncture of Darcy's property and Elizabeth's reflective capability: the portrait gallery (a constitutive element of the estate) opens up a space wherein reflection can take place—attention is fixed; memory is facilitated; for "several minutes" the portrait (and the space between reflection and person) allows "contemplation" that, as the narrative pointedly mentions, all takes place "in Elizabeth's mind." Again: "[A]s she stood before the canvas, *on which he was represented*, and fixed his eyes upon herself, *she thought* of his regard with a deeper sentiment of gratitude than it had ever raised before" (251, emphases added). It is this relationship between reflection and property (as two conjoined and mutually constitutive modes of self-representation or self-replication) that underlies the suddenly energized relationship between Elizabeth and (the actual) Darcy; we might say it is this relationship between reflection and property that constitutes the ultimate "marriage" of the novel.

And then, in a brilliant stroke, Austen disjunctively frames an encounter between the person in his own right and the wealth that, in the portrait gallery, consolidates the abstractions of a person (through "character," "resemblance," "memory," and "property"): "As they walked across the lawn towards the river, Elizabeth turned back to look again; her uncle and aunt stopped also, and while the former was conjecturing as to the date of the building, *the owner of it himself* suddenly came forward from the road, which led behind it to the stables" (251, emphasis added). Surely one of the great sentences in the novel, this abrupt clash between person and property confirms the reversed priority we have just seen in the portrait gallery: as Elizabeth recognized the original through the resemblance (rather than the other way around), we here recognize Darcy only *through* his property, since Darcy's "sudden" emergence, in his own right, is legible only as we link the pronoun that identifies him ("the owner of *it*") to the "building" that precedes him. It is the contrast between this syntactic mediation (we move from the building, to the owner, to Darcy) and the stated suddenness of the encounter that makes this moment of "recognition" so fitting for the Pemberley episode, which relentlessly mediates Elizabeth's encounter with Darcy (through property, through aesthetic representation, and, not least of all, through her own reflexive consciousness). In the end, wealth is a happy version of that abstraction, or dematerialization, which attaches to the functionalized minor character: wealth expands the human being (you can be in *more* than one place at a time); functionality constricts him (you are "always moving from place to place"; you are "laughed out of existence").

23. See particularly his discussion on 3–23.

24. An important exception is Mrs. Reynolds, who does not seem notably distorted. Mrs. Reynolds, Darcy's *chief* helper, is the servant who gets drawn into the sphere of the protagonist's centrality, like a magnet picking up some of this central charge. In this way, Reynolds's distinction from the other servants nuances but also confirms the overall asymmetric structure. By having *one* servant who is more fully humanized, the novel makes an exception that proves the rule: the relatively harmonious configuration of Mrs. Reynolds's personality calls even more attention to the other servants' distortion.

Chapter Two
Making More of Minor Characters

1. Thus: "The central problem of *Dombey and Son, a problem faced by all the characters*, is how to break through the barriers separating one from the world and from other people" (146, emphasis added); "*David Copperfield* repeats in several minor stories the theme of marriage (Annie and Dr. Strong, Traddles and Sophy, the bad marriage of Betsey Trotwood . . .)" (150); "Krook, Snagsby, Mrs. Snagsby, Guppy, Esther Summerson, Tulkinghorn, Inspector Bucket, Hortense, Lady Dedlock, all of these characters seek or fear some kind of clarity, some knowledge about themselves or about one another, some revelation of a mystery" (168). Notice in this last example how the protagonist is sandwiched in among all these minor characters! In *Little Dorrit*, Miller comments that "all the many forms of imprisonment in this novel are primarily spiritual rather than physical," and then lists, as examples, Miss Wade, Merdle, Flora Casby, Blandois, John Chivery, Pancks, Mrs. Merdle, Ferdinand Barnacle, Tip Dorrit, and Mr. Dorrit (230–31). Miller's study offers perhaps the most comprehensive account of the intersection of character and theme in Dickens's novels.

2. This attention stands out against whatever thematic frame the reader scrambles to construct around them. We might consider again Frank's discussion of Silas Wegg. Like much of the best Dickens criticism, this interpretation moves from implied person to thematic abstraction, disembodying Wegg in discovering what Wegg, as distorted minor character, "embodies." In one sense, there is a similar play between the corporeal (embodied) and the abstract (disembodied) anytime a character is made to stand for a theme. But here the wooden leg, neither bodily nor strictly unbodily, literally enacts this tension within the narrative itself. In other words, Wegg's emblematic wooden leg doesn't only stand for both petrification and fragmentation but also stands *as* a product of the clash between embodiment and disembodiment that is produced *by* a character's standing for such abstractions in the first place. Wegg, of course, can't stand his narrative position nor, in certain memorable passages, stand up at all. ("Involuntarily making a pass with his wooden leg to guard himself as Mr. Venus springs up . . . Mr. Wegg tilts over on his back, chair and all"[297].) Wegg's leg both demonstrates how Dickens's minor characters signify (here connoting Frank's "petrification" and "fragmentation") and suggests that these very connoted qualities might be the result *of* signifying, the consequences of Wegg's abstraction and absorption, as minor character, into the narrative and thematic totality. The wooden leg is both a vehicle for and a result of Wegg's minorness.

3. This dispersed eccentricity, the product of compression, itself becomes compressed into one repeated speech tag ("I'll eat my head") with which "Mr. Grimwig back[s] and confirm[s] *nearly every* assertion he ma[kes]" and a specific, defining physical feature (his own "particularly large" head). Finally these two distinct qualities become merged into one paradigmatic synecdoche: the exaggerated, distorted head that, as any reader of *Oliver Twist* can remember, is an emblem of Grimwig's fictional being.

4. For instance, Grimwig's "jerk" and "convulsion" might remind us of these descriptions of the human tugboat, Mr. Pancks, smoking, in *Little Dorrit*: "Indeed, he was fearful of something happening to Mr. Pancks in the violent conflict that took place between the breath he jerked out of himself and the smoke he jerked into himself" (641). "In his great self-satisfaction he put his cigar to his lips (being evidently no smoker), and took such a pull at it, with his right eye shut up tight for the purpose, that he underwent a convulsion of shuddering and choking" (431). In turn, Pancks's "right eye shut up tight" can set off a chain of associations hinging on a similar distortion: from John Chivery in the same novel ("One of his eyes . . . was also weak, and looked larger than the other as if it couldn't collect itself" [255]), to Mr. Murdstone in *David Copperfield* ("he had that kind of shallow black eye—I want a better word to express an eye that has no depth in it to be looked into—which, when it is abstracted, seems from the peculiarity of light to be disfigured" [71]), to the literally one-eyed Squeers in *Nicholas Nickleby*.

5. Golding defines the idiolect, such a crucial method of characterization for Dickens, as "the totality of speech habits of a single person at a given time" (1). About Flora, Golding notes, "In respect of surface interest, no other idiolect in *Little Dorrit* comes anywhere near that of Flora Finching" (165).

6. The weakness of the protagonist in Dickens manifests itself in any number of ways. While Arthur Clennam has a notably passive personality, as though acquiescing psychologically in his (narrative) condition, John Harmon is literally drowned, suffering perhaps the most violent consequences of his weak centrality. If Harmon's drowning is both literal and thematic, it is also *narrative*: Harmon is brilliantly constructed as a submerged protagonist, deriving a fully actualized centrality only at the novel's *midpoint* ("A Solo and a Duet"), even as Harmon's (alleged) *corpse* is present in the very opening scene. The first-person narrators—David Copperfield, Esther Summerson, and Pip—are also overwhelmed by minor characters and by the larger narrative, even while they are all in obvious ways more active in their own interest. Much has been written about David Copperfield's vexed psychological—and narrative—relationship with minor characters. In one astute reading of the novel, Welsh analyzes the novel's "passive-aggressive" structure by looking at the different ways that David is positioned vis-à-vis the many compelling minor characters (*From Copyright to Copperfield*, 141–55). In *Bleak House*, such a conflict is, of course, powerfully literalized in the divided structure of the novel itself: this radical narrative form is in large part motivated by Esther's shifting position as alternately marginal and central. I will discuss Pip's particular status as a Dickensian protagonist in chapter 3. In *Barnaby Rudge*, to touch on one more variation, being a pawn of history not only threatens the formal grip of the protagonist (one of the least narratively powerful in Dickens) but also turns him into a literal idiot. It is in this novel, as well, that Dickens first extravagantly confronts his fears of the crowd, a mass of persons that has both social and narrative bearing.

7. "Oliver Twist and his companions suffered the tortures of slow starvation for three months, at last they got so voracious and wild with hunger, that one boy, who was tall for his age, and hadn't been used to that sort of thing (for his father had kept a small cookshop), hinted darkly to his companions, that unless he had another basin of gruel per diem, he was afraid he might some night happen to eat the boy who had slept next him, who happened to be a weakly youth of tender age. He had a wild, hungry eye; and they implicitly believed him. A council was held; lots were cast who should walk up to the master after supper that evening, and ask for more; and it fell to Oliver Twist" (56).

8. This small passage already suggests the contours of Dickens's system of characterization, in the imprecisely registered "eight or ten fat gentlemen" toward whom Oliver's bewildered consciousness is directed, and the "particularly fat gentleman with a very round, red face" who then condenses this exteriority, and, through this condensation, verges on caricature.

9. Picaresque fiction, we might argue, is structurally divided between passive and active versions of the protagonist, alternatively emphasizing individual agency and social contingency. Auerbach identifies this split structure in comparing twelfth-century quest narratives about knights' adventures with *Don Quixote*. Both the active and passive sides of these narratives are determined by social asymmetry. On the one hand, the structure of characterization in quest narrative is class-determined. "Only members of the chivalric-courtly society are worthy of adventure, hence they alone can undergo serious and significant experiences. Those outside this class cannot appear except as accessories, and even then generally in merely comic, grotesque and despicable roles" (*Mimesis* 139). On the other hand, in *Don Quixote*'s modern rendition of this, we see the spiritual result of the *contingency* that underlies this structure: "By his detailed description of the circumstances of his hero's life, Cervantes makes it perfectly clear, at the very beginning of his book, where the root of Don Quixote's confusion lies: he is the victim of a social order in which he belongs to a class that has no function . . . he has no role and no mission. He feels his life running meaninglessly out, as though he were paralyzed" (137).

10. See J. H. Miller, 11–12: "*The Pickwick Papers* is a long succession of scenes in which Pickwick and his friends meet, one after another, characters who surge up suddenly and vividly within the field of our immediate vision, command all of our attention for a brief span of time, and then disappear altogether, never, for the most part, to reappear. . . . Each specimen can only be defined by its queerness, by its deviation from any type." This summary emphasizes the strong connection between minorness and caricature, although Miller does not focus his analysis on this connection.

11. The minor characters in these examples range from unnamed strangers who quickly leave the novel, to the more important Bob Sawyer and Jack Hopkins, to Sam Weller, when he is first introduced through his "singular catalogue of visitors." (It makes sense that Sam seems most singular in this first appearance, as he soon becomes a kind of intermediary between Pickwick and minorness, functioning somewhat in the manner of Jane in *Pride and Prejudice*.)

12. Note the passive construction in the following sentence: "And the first cab having been fetched from the public-house, where he had been smoking his first pipe, Mr. Pickwick and his portmanteau *were thrown into* the vehicle." Like the description of the waterman, this brief action encapsulates the essentially passive status of the protagonist,

dependent on others *even* to be set in motion. Mr. Jingle himself repeats this action several pages later: " 'Up with you,' said the stranger, assisting Mr. Pickwick on to the roof with so much precipitation as to impair the gravity of the gentleman's deportment very materially" (78).

13. In a later scene Mr. Tupman stares at Joe, and the narrator, once again, links the minor character's attention-compelling singularity to his effaced interiority: "Mr. Tupman looked round. There was the fat boy, perfectly motionless, with his large circular eyes staring into the arbour, but without the slightest expression on his face that the most expert physiognomist could have referred to astonishment, curiosity, or any other known passion that agitates the human breast. Mr. Tupman gazed on the fat boy, and the fat boy stared at him; and the longer Mr. Tupman observed the utter vacancy of the fat boy's countenance, the more convinced he became that he either did not know, or did not understand, anything that had been going forward" (172).

14. Most dramatically, perhaps, when the guns in a military procession that Pickwick is leisurely observing suddenly turn upon him—and charge: "[T]he command 'eyes front' had been given, and all the spectator saw before him was several thousand pair of optics, staring straight forward, wholly divested of any expression whatever. . . . Mr. Pickwick *gazed through his spectacles for an instant upon the advancing mass*, and then fairly turned his back and—we will not say fled; first, because it is an ignoble term, and, secondly, because Mr. Pickwick's figure was by no means adapted for that mode of retreat" (118–19, emphasis added). In the emphasized phrase, Dickens literalizes the potential inversion between the "spectator" and the object of observation (an inversion already suggested in the rendering of observation as "all that [Pickwick] saw before him was," rather than the more direct "all that Pickwick saw was").

15. As I have suggested, Emma's centrality, unearned in comparison to Elizabeth Bennet's, might be equated with her unearned wealth. The novel prods us to ask questions *about* centrality similar to those we might ask about wealth: What is its history? What is its origin? On whose work does it rest? And how does it distort its holder's relationship to the world? *Emma*, in fact, raises nearly every problem of narrative centrality we can imagine. Let me give two examples of this. Above all, Austen's novel defines narrative centrality by the configuration of a person *into* an observing subject— as with *Pride and Prejudice*, the space of the protagonist depends in large part (but not entirely or exclusively) on focalization, or the inflection of the third-person narrative through the inscribed perspective of a character. (It is in this way that *Emma*, Austen's most rigorous exploration of the space of the protagonist, is also considered her most significant exploration of free indirect discourse.) But the novel forcefully scrutinizes the dialectics of observation that sustain the space of the protagonist, showing how Emma's very need to *be* a focalizer ultimately makes her beholden to the objects (which is to say, the persons) that she perceives. (Again, this problem doesn't apply only to Emma but, in fact, might apply to any central protagonist.) The problematization of focalization occurs both on the level of plot (for instance, in Jane and Frank's deliberate duplicity) and also in particular scenes. For example, as the social confusions mount up, Austen describes Emma as "necessarily overhearing the discourse of Mrs. Elton and Miss Fairfax, who were standing a little way behind her" (324) and again notes how "Emma was obliged to overhear what Mrs. Elton and Jane Fairfax were talking of" (359). It's difficult to convey the effect of these passages, after hundreds of pages where Emma's ability *to* focalize—to hear and see the events of the novel—has been

so profoundly linked to her powerful narrative centrality and agency. These passages, however, convert agency into *necessity*, as the very power of observation subtly subordinates the focalizer to the object. (As another passage notes, "Mr. Elton was so near, that she heard every syllable" [327].) Later the narrative famously transforms the other pole of Emma's centrality: not the ability to *give* attention (as the focalizing subject), but the ability to *command* the attention of others. Thus at Box Hill the most basic experience of centrality—the self beholding itself beheld—is converted into a source of profound shame: " 'Your gallantry is really unanswerable. But (lowering her voice)—nobody speaks but ourselves, and it is rather too much to be talking nonsense for the entertainment of seven silent people' " (369). If these scenes render the two constitutive elements of Emma's centrality (the intensification of *her* attention and her ability to *command* attention) as placing her at a disadvantage to the persons whom she observes or who observe her, this never breaks the narrative's essential structure, which, beginning with the title (which collapses novel into character), consistently works to center Emma.

16. See the fine discussion of this mediation in D. A. Miller, 1–20.

17. Again, I want to suggest that this misperception can't be reductively extracted as a character flaw of Emma's but instead is instantiated as a flaw in structure itself, in Emma's very discursive emplacement as central character. This discursive emplacement is then wonderfully confirmed *by* all coordinates of the story-world, which immediately immerses its locus of interest in a prehistory of privilege, "handsome, clever and rich."

18. Consider, for example, how the image surfaces in two essential narrative planes of *The Pickwick Papers*: the interpolated tale ("He died one morning of apoplexy, as he was going to open his outer door. Fell with his head in his own letter-box, and there he lay for eighteen months" [361]) and the "Wellerism," or Sam's continually outrageous metaphors ("It's over, and can't be helped, and that's one consolation, as they always says in Turkey, ven they cuts the wrong man's head off" [398]).

19. Many critics have seconded Orwell's sense that Dickens's fraught critique of social structures takes a moral rather than political form. While often explicitly depicting institutional and economic ills, Dickens's novels rarely convey a dynamic sense of the larger structure that produces these institutions and economic conditions in the first place. In *The City of Dickens*, for example, Welsh writes: "The alienation of urban life, the unrelatedness of people and the interrelatedness of the city as a functional system, the sense that the problems are too many and too complex, that they grow at a rate with which it is impossible to keep up, throw a heavy burden on political organization. But in the metropolis there is no political organization to receive the burden; and still less confidence in politics. What is yearned for is a confidence that will transcend uncertainty and pain. . . . Everything points to some religious solution" (52).

20. Welsh aptly pinpoints this two-step dance in his comment about the original title of *Little Dorrit*: "Dickens's inability to find a political creed finally comes down to the doubly ironic proposition that whatever is wrong is 'Nobody's Fault.' 'Nobody' is ironic because it stands for somebody, and doubly ironic because Dickens finally does not know who that somebody may be: it may as well be nobody after all" (*City of Dickens*, 51). Moretti also identifies this tension on a structural level, in the interplay between Dickens's representation of urban complexity and his recourse to family romance: "Time after time, the family romance acts thus as Dickens' fundamental scaffold, whose structuring power is never equaled by the plot's sociological axis. . . . It is

a further instance of the tentative, contradictory path followed by urban novels: as London's random and unrelated enclaves increase the 'noise,' the dissonance, the complexity of the plot—the family romance tries to *reduce* it, turning London into a coherent whole" (*Atlas of the European Novel*, 130). Moretti is arguing that Dickens's marriage plots work against and deflect his tendency toward sociological analysis. In chapter 3, I will consider the tension between *Great Expectations*'s probing social realism and conservative metaphoric frame.

21. What do we learn about a world that appears in this way: not merely as it is visually represented *in* the appearances but as it motivates such a particular mode of representation in the first place? By stressing the "concreteness of his vision" and the "power of evoking visual images," Orwell's description seems at first glance to simplify Dickens's achievement. But his analysis also suggests that such evocation is not so simple after all. In fact, we need to read Orwell's comment that "the concreteness of [Dickens's] vision is a sign of what is missing" in two different ways. On the one hand, this seems to highlight a specific failure of the novels: concreteness is a sign, for the *critic*, of what is otherwise missing from the novel itself. Throughout his essay, Orwell (like so many Dickens critics after him) does try to build a critical paradigm that can discern and distinguish what is comprehended in Dickens's world (individuals, images, appearances) and what is excluded (history, processes, structures). But Orwell's phrase might also suggest that "what is missing" gets powerfully *signified* in the narrative itself. In this reading, the heightened appearance of the Dickensian minor character (*as* merely appearance) intrinsically signals his or her obscuring (as fully realized person). The simple "concreteness" of Dickens's vision, I have been arguing, is embedded within a complicated scrutinization and staging of social observation and interaction. The compelling and detailed "appearance" that pulls attention away from the narrative center relies on, even as it subsumes, a sequence of processes: narrative delimitation triggers descriptive distortion; the implied individual is squeezed and becomes distorted within his delimited space while attracting attention as a "character," as someone who offers himself up as a "sight" or a "scene." The person disappears into the "appearance" of the character, but the concrete—and distorted—appearance is "a sign" of this disappearance.

22. This description of laughter is extended in *Nicholas Nickleby*'s repeated passages about John Browdie, one of the most endearing of Dickens's minor characters: "If there could only have been somebody by, to see how the bed-clothes shook, and to see the Yorkshireman's great red face and round head appear above the sheets every now and then, like some jovial monster coming to the surface to breathe, and once more dive down convulsed with the laughter which came bursting forth afresh—that somebody would have been scarcely less amused than John Browdie himself" (596); "Never was man so tickled with a respectable old joke, as John Browdie was with this. He chuckled, roared, half suffocated himself by laughing large pieces of beef into his windpipe, roared again, persisted in eating at the same time, got red in the face and black in the forehead, coughed, cried, got better, went off again laughing inwardly, got worse, choked, had his back thumped, stamped about, frightened his wife, and at last recovered in a state of the last exhaustion and with water streaming from his eyes" (631). These distended sentences show Dickens following the logic of his briefer description of Mr. Weller: the profusion of small clauses is a formal extension of the dispersion they are describing. As with Weller's "internal laughter," John Browdie moves from "laughing inwardly" toward convulsion and dispersion: notice how Browdie's "great red face and

round head" appear by themselves in the first description, and how the second description ends "with water streaming from his eyes." Convulsion is, in this rare case, a kind of expression *of* these characters' interior beings, so that Dickens works through his caricatures—and the highly particular idiolects of these two minor characters—to almost arrive at a realignment of surface and depth. More often, of course, this dispersion functions not as an *elaboration* of "internal" sentiment but as a graphic symbol of the gap between a minor character's interior and outer being.

23. This passage is suggestively illuminated by Benjamin's discussion of gambling in "On Some Motifs in Baudelaire." Gambling, Benjamin writes, "certainly does not lack the futility, the emptiness, the inability to complete something which is inherent in the activity of a wage slave in a factory. Gambling even contains the workman's gesture that is produced by the automatic operation, for there can be no game without the quick movement of the hand by which the stake is put down or a card is picked up. The jolt in the movement of a machine is like the so-called *coup* in a game of chance. The manipulation of the worker at the machine has no connection with the preceding operation for the very reason that it is its exact repetition" (177).

24. I take this phrase from James A. Davies, *The Textual Life of Dickens's Characters*.

Chapter Three
Partings Welded Together: The Character-System in *Great Expectations*

1. For a general description of the distinction between these two kinds of characters, see Bal's discussion of focalization, 100–118.

2. In his essay "Toward a Definition of the Picaresque" Guillen succinctly describes the social conditions of the picaresque novel as "the decline of the ancient concept of the polis, of social man, of the communal structure of the Middle Ages; the rise of the modern metropolis, the bourgeoisie, shifting social classes" (102).

3. Bakhtin uses the category "adventure novel of everyday life" in "Forms of Time and Chronotope in the Novel" (111).

4. Hamon captures the asymmetric basis of characterization in picaresque fiction nicely, writing of "le héros picaresque, qui traverse des nébleuses de personnages qui ne réapparaitront plus, et qui n'existeront que le temps de la recontre" ("Pour un statut sémiologique du personnage," 16).

5. For another scene that resonates with this passage in *Gil Blas*, consider *Madame Bovary*'s inflection of the blind beggar, a crucial minor character who is painfully subordinated—yet strangely significant—in both the story and the discourse.

6. This passage is also an extreme example of what Lambert calls the "suspended quotation"—where a character's speech is interrupted and (usually briefly) delayed by narrative description. Lambert's clever and understated study of Dickensian stylistics opens up suggestive lines of inquiry into the Dickensian narrator's relationship to characters and to the *narrated world* in general.

7. Twice Pip's consciousness seems to literally collapse, so that he retrospectively writes: "As I came to myself (with the aid of a heavy thump between the shoulders, and the restorative exclamation 'Yah! Was there ever such a boy as this!' from my sister), I found Joe telling them about the convict's confession, and all the visitors suggesting different ways by which he had got into the pantry" (72); and "I caught the

coach just as it came out of the yard. I was the only inside passenger, jolting away knee-deep in straw, when I came to myself" (430).

8. Thus:

"Now you see, Joseph and wife," said Pumblechook, as he took me by the arm above the elbow, "I am one of them that always go right through what they've begun. This boy must be bound, out of hand. That's my way. Bound out of hand." (132)

And here I may remark that when Mr. Wopsle referred to me, he considered it a necessary part of such reference to rumple my hair and poke it into my eyes. I cannot conceive why everybody of his standing who visited at our house should always have put me through the same inflammatory process under similar circumstances. Yet I do not call to mind that I was ever in my earlier youth the subject of remark in our social family circle, but some large-handed person took some such ophthalmic steps to patronize me. (106)

As it turned out, however, that he only wanted me for a dramatic lay-figure, to be contradicted and embraced and wept over and bullied and clutched and stabbed and knocked about in a variety of ways, I soon declined that course of instruction; though not until Mr. Wopsle in his poetic fury had severely mauled me. (137)

Pumblechook's despicable aggression toward Pip cannot be dissociated from his caricatured exteriority: the rudeness of his flatness produces both his violence and his ridiculousness.

The worst of it was that that bullying old Pumblechook, preyed upon by a devouring curiosity to be informed of all I had seen and heard, came gaping over in his chaise-cart at tea-time, to have the details divulged to him. And the mere sight of the torment, with his fishy eyes and mouth open, his sandy hair inquisitively on end, and his waistcoat heaving with windy arithmetic, made me vicious in my reticence. (95)

9. For a recent overview of this question see Newsom, who encapsulates the many different dimensions of Dickens's interest in, and fictional elaboration of, childhood. Newsom's emphasis on the "limited consciousness" (98) or "limited perspective" (98) of the Dickensian child resonates with my narrative argument.

10. "Covent Garden market, and the avenues leading to it, are thronged with carts of all sorts, sizes and descriptions, from the heavy lumbering waggon, with its four stout horses, to the jingling of the costermonger's cart with its consumptive donkey. The pavement is already strewed with decayed cabbage-leaves, broken haybands, and all the indescribable litter of a vegetable market; men are shouting, carts backing, horses neighing, boys fighting, basket-women talking, piemen expatiating on the excellence of their pastry, and donkeys braying. These and a hundred other sounds form a compound discordant enough to a Londoner's ears, and remarkably disagreeable to those of country gentlemen who are sleeping at the Hummums for the first time" ("The Streets—Morning" 70—71).

11. And *Nicholas Nickleby* hardly changes the matter: in this staged encounter between the bildungsroman and a dispersed and highly "peculiar" Dickensian character-system, it is clear who wins. Dull Nicholas is toppled over by Smike, Squeers, Newman Noggs, etc.

12. This peripherality also seems to seep into the clothes themselves: Trabb touches Pip "on the outside of each elbow," so that in this instant of servitude, the tailor also oddly enacts the way that minor characters continually exceed the protagonist (here hovering around the outside of a paradigmatic "extremity" in the novel). A similar dialectic is suggested in the way that, as Pip writes, "Mr. Trabb measured and calculated me."

13. For example, Welsh argues that Uriah Heep functions as a displacement of those negative characteristics which David wants to repress or deny: Heep is "a true Doppelgänger, whose main function . . . is to embody sexual longing and to take the offensive against the father who stands in its way" (*From Copyright to Copperfield*, 144).

14. A realist novel might explore a more romantic idiom through a secondary character, or a novel of manners might condense a more tragic interest through a minor figure. A writer can use a subordinate character in one novel to negotiate with a past project (think of Shem the Penman in *Finnegans Wake*) or anticipate a future one (as when a minor character in *The Adventures of Tom Sawyer* leads out into the counternarrative of *Huckleberry Finn*). With Twain, the complicated negotiation of minorness facilitates the dynamic relationship between the radically different literary registers of two novels. A similar process drives Virginia Woolf's transition from *The Voyage Out* to *Mrs. Dalloway*—a transition that also carries clear stylistic and aesthetic weight. Our understanding of the character-systems in both *Huckleberry Finn* and *Mrs. Dalloway* must begin with the remarkable way that the central protagonists emerge *out of* previously minor positions. In a different way, Dostoevsky uses the arrangement of characters to fuse together two competing narratives into one, interweaving his interest in an (unfinished) project called *The Drunks* into the *second* scene of *Crime and Punishment*, in which Raskolnikov encounters Marmeladov in the tavern after rehearsing the crime that he will eventually enact at the end of volume 1. To return to Dickens—the subordinate role of Bradley Headstone in *Our Mutual Friend* is a notable example of this kind of minorness; a number of critics have argued that Bradley's character opens up a whole series of thematic and narrative possibilities—almost an entirely different novel—that Dickens adjudicates over not merely in punishing Headstone but also in attempting to contain the subplot of Headstone-Eugene-Riderhood more generally. For a study of embedded genre shifts within the nineteenth-century novel, see Keen.

15. The history of the thematization of the character-system would clearly constitute a book in itself. To give one recent instance in this larger history, Cohen, in her reconstruction of the poetics of nineteenth-century sentimental fiction, elaborates her interpretation of the ethical thematics of *Claire d'Albe* (as it builds an opposition between collective welfare and individual freedom) through the novel's character-system: "Cottin uses the delineation of character to reinforce her text's organizing double bind. The two principal secondary characters each embody one of the opposing moral imperatives tearing Claire apart" (36). Cohen casts the sentimental novel in explicit distinction *to* nineteenth-century realist fiction, offering the most important recent model of nineteenth-century narrative poetics not derived from—and in fact formulated *against*—social realism. Her brief thematization of the character-system (in the novel that she uses as a model for sentimental fiction) shows how essential the organization of character is to narrative signification—operating effectively both in conventional realist poetics and in Cohen's quite *different* narrative modeling of a decanonized fictional genre.

16. A fine example would be Bourdieu's analysis of the character-system in Flaubert's *L'Éducation sentimentale* as a field of ideological signification. Bourdieu ana-

lyzes how the novel's minor characters map the delimited possible roles within the Parisian social and cultural field during the years around the revolution of 1848, while the very *negative* space of the protagonist (who performs *no* social role, and does *nothing*) opens a possibly oppositional space for *art itself* within the sociocultural field. Bourdieu's essay forcefully demonstrates how individual characters can get structured into a character-field that, through its distributional organization, reflects social reality (as it is constituted through competing socioideological positions and stances). Crucially, Bourdieu's ideological analysis (like Cohen's in the previous example) also accounts for the specifically asymmetric structure of Flaubert's character-system, by highlighting Frédéric Moreau's qualitative differentiation *from* the larger character-field that, however, simultaneously defines him.

17. This discussion draws above all on Brooks's discussion of *Great Expectations* in *Reading for the Plot*. Brooks's analysis is distinct among psychoanalytic criticism of the novel for its attention to the psychodynamics *of* narrative structure itself. For an important psychological analysis of the disjunction between the narrator and the protagonist, which recasts Pip's memoir as a projection, see Jordan, "The Medium of *Great Expectations*." For Jordan, Pip's interactions with minor characters take place along the spectrum of self-assertion and self-punishment.

18. Thus Brooks describes how *many different* minor characters are all linked together within a single repressive chain of associations that have their origin in the "binding" of Pip's consciousness: "Repression plays a dominant role in the theme of education which is so important to the novel, from Mrs. Joe's bringing up by hand, through Mrs. Wopsle's aunt's schoolroom, to Mr. Pocket's career as a 'grinder' of dull blades (while his own children meanwhile are 'tumbling up'). Bringing up by hand in turn suggests Jaggers's hands . . . Jaggers's sinister hand-washings point to the omnipresent taint of Newgate, which echoes the earlier presence of the Hulks, to which Mrs. Joe verbally assigns Pip" (*Reading for the Plot* 120). Alternatively, Brooks observes that "the question of texts, reading and interpretation is . . . consistently thematized in the novel" (131), and argues, for example, that "Mr. Wopsle's career may stand as a figure for Pip's" (134).

19. If this seems too boldly stated—the character isn't literally inside Pip, of course—we need only consider Van Ghent's comment in one of the great essays on this novel: "Pip . . . carries the convict inside him . . . Magwitch is the concretion of his potential guilt" (65).

20. For a foundational distinction between metaphor and metonymy, see Roman Jakobson, "Two Aspects of Language and Two Types of Aphasic Disturbances," in Jakobson and Hale, 55–82. My analysis also draws on de Man's method in *Allegories of Reading*, which suggests that while literary language always strives to build metaphoric meaning through metonymic constructions, literary criticism can work to reveal the metonymic operations behind metaphor: "[T]he assertion of the mastery of metaphor over metonymy owes its persuasive power to the use of metonymic structures" (15). For a related analysis of metaphor and metonymy in *Great Expectations*, see Connor, 109–44.

21. For an important, and related, theory of the literary character, see Phelan. Phelan insists on the multidimensional nature of the literary character: to roughly cast my study in his terms, I am looking at how a specific aspect of the synthetic dimension of characters—their relative domination or subordination within the narrative—is intertwined with their mimetic and thematic significance.

22. The following discussion draws on valuable criticism that has elucidated *both* the metaphoric and metonymic economies of *Great Expectations*. In addition to Brooks's and Connor's essays (which both focus primarily on metonymic chains of association), I have benefited from Schor's discussion of Pip's deployment of metaphor, 153–77. My discussion tries to amplify these important critical elaborations of the novel's figurative economy by framing metaphor and metonymy as *competing* descriptive drives that can be understood and put in relation to each other through the overall character-system. Schor's analysis already suggests the strong relationship between figuration and characterization as it grounds the deployment of metaphor in the narrator's relationship to *specific* characters in the novel.

23. This makes sense insofar as a hand—the bodily extremity that is employed either to grasp or to push away other people—enables both fragmentation and connection, exemplifying, like the leg-chain-and-iron, the very metonymic processes that it fulfills in the novel's figurative economy.

24. Immediately after this, Miss Havisham more insistently dephysicalizes herself, through the use of a clichéd metaphor:

> "Do you know what I touch here?, she said, laying her hands, one upon the other, on her left side.
> "Yes, ma'am." (It made me think of the young man.)
> "What do I touch?"
> "Your heart."
> "Broken!" (88)

25. This insight is already suggested by Van Ghent, who insists that the reader of *Great Expectations* must *hesitate* before simply reading persons through the objects they are associated with: "This device of association [of a person with a thing] is a familiar one in fiction; what distinguishes Dickens' use of it is that the associated object acts not merely to *illustrate* a person's qualities symbolically—as novelists usually use it—but that it has a necessary metaphysical function in Dickens' universe . . . objects actually usurp human essences" (63, Van Ghent's emphasis).

26. As Goffman writes, "Urban life would become unbearably sticky for some if every contact between two individuals entailed a sharing of personal traits, worries, and secrets" (49).

27. Pylades, the companion of Orestes, has the odd privilege of speaking exactly *once* in Aeschylus's *Libation Bearers*, despite being onstage for much of the play. What makes Pylades such a limit point of dramatic minorness is not simply that he speaks the least amount possible while still *having* a voice, but that the words he does say are utterly consequential: he intercedes just as Orestes briefly hesitates before killing his mother, coming in at the protagonist's one moment of self-doubt (or, you might argue, one moment of actual self-consciousness). In his rewriting of Aeschylus's play, Sophocles seems attuned to Pylades' dramatic minorness: the character is still part of the cast, and continually accompanies Orestes through the *Electra*, but now he has *no* lines at all. (The function of interlocutor, meanwhile, passes on to the much more voluble tutor who also accompanies Orestes in Sophocles' version.)

28. Magwitch's face, "very near to mine," resembles Levinas's description of the keyword "visage." (More generally, Levinas's meditation on the relationship between consciousness and exteriority is a suggestive intertext with *Great Expectations*.) Levi-

nas invokes the notion of the "visage" as that aspect of other human beings which is irreducibly exterior: "The way in which the other presents himself, exceeding *the idea of the other in me*, we here name face. This *mode* does not consist in figuring as a theme under my gaze, in spreading itself forth as a set of qualities forming an image. The face of the Other at each moment destroys and overflows the plastic image it leaves me, the idea existing to my own measure and to the measure of its *ideatum*—the adequate idea. It does not manifest itself by these qualities, but *kath'auto*. It expresses itself" (50–51). Furthermore, Levinas insists that the self's encounter with the visage has a priority over consciousness itself. If Pip, remembering his early encounter with Magwitch, notes that compared to the "theme" of Estella, "the event . . . had impended over me longer yet," Levinas argues for the priority of exterior experience over metaphoric construction: "Every recourse to words presupposes the comprehension of the primary signification, but this comprehension, before being interpreted as 'consciousness of,' is society and obligation . . . the face to face founds language . . . the face brings the first signification, establishes signification itself in being" (206–7).

29. We can see this in his dialect too—even the famous repetition of "warmint" is both a hardening and an eccentricity. See my discussion of idiolects in chapter 2.

30. Consider this passage:

Suddenly, he clapped his large hand on the housekeeper's, like a trap, as she stretched it across the table. So suddenly and smartly did he do this, that we all stopped in our foolish contention.

"If you talk of strength," said Mr. Jaggers, "*I'll* show you a wrist. Molly, let them see your wrist."

Her entrapped hand was on the table, but she had already put her other hand behind her waist. "Master," she said, in a low voice, with her eyes attentively and entreatingly fixed upon him. "Don't."

"I'll show you a wrist," repeated Mr. Jaggers, with an immoveable determination to show it. "Molly, let them see your wrist."

"Master," she again murmured, "Please!"

"Molly," said Mr. Jaggers, not looking at her, but obstinately looking at the opposite side of the room, "let them see *both* your wrists. Show them. Come!"

He took his hand from hers, and turned that wrist up on the table. She brought her other hand from behind her, and held the two out side by side. The last wrist was much disfigured—deeply scarred and scarred across and across. (236)

31. Consider, by way of contrast, Dickens's comments about the composition of *Barnaby Rudge*: "It is almost indispensable in a work of fiction that the characters who bring the catastrophes about, and play important parts, should belong to the Machinery of the Tale—and the introduction towards the end of a story where there is always a great deal to do, of new actors until then unheard of, is a thing to be avoided, if possible, in every case" (739). This passage demonstrates Dickens's sense of the dynamic tension between the claims of characters and the exigencies of narrative structure.

32. As I have suggested, one of the great examples of this process would certainly be Huck Finn, a minor character in Twain's *Adventures of Tom Sawyer*, through whom, in his very disruptive minorness, Twain is able to imagine a different novel that in so many ways transcends the original. But if a minor character and, arguably, the character's very minorness, leads Twain from *Tom Sawyer* to *Huckleberry Finn*, the latter

novel sees Tom Sawyer, now himself temporarily reduced to narrative minorness, return at the end of the story to assert his ancient narrative and social privilege. Tom's return as competing protagonist comes at the cost of Huck's narrative, and most particularly at the cost of Jim, who emerges, in *Huck's* novel, as one of the most achieved, and troubling, minor characters in American literature.

33. To pile even more significance onto this minor minor character, we can note how he frames the relationship between clothing and economic exchange that we have already examined in its most grisly dimensions: if Pip's clothing requires an ever more dispersed chain of specialized, fragmented labor, the Jack literally puts together a wardrobe by picking up fragments of clothing from human corpses. He is not the first character we've seen who seems to clothe himself in this way. When Pip first arrives in London and walks by Newgate prison, he encounters just such a character, "an exceedingly dirty and partially drunk minister of justice" (165) whom he describes as follows: "[T]hen he showed me the Debtor's Door, out of which culprits came to be hanged: heightening the interest of that dreadful portal by giving me to understand that 'four on 'em' would come out at that door the day after tomorrow at eight in the morning, to be killed in a row. This was horrible, and gave me a sickening idea of London: the more so as the Lord Chief Justice's proprietor wore (from his hat down to his boots and up again to his pocket-handkerchief inclusive) mildewed clothes, which had evidently not belonged to him originally, and which, I took into my head, he had bought cheap of the executioner. Under these circumstances I thought myself well rid of him for a shilling" (166). This "gentleman's" clothing is like a nightmarish analogue to Pip's own new suits; while the "hatter" and "bootmaker" and "hosier" (as well as the Trabb's boys of the world) rest behind Pip's clothes, the "proprietor" depends on (soon-to-be) human corpses for his "hat" and "boots" and "pocket-handkerchief." The proprietor buys these goods "cheap" from the executioner, just as Pip himself gets "rid" of this character through an economic exchange. Like Pip, this minor character gets his suit from a multiplicity of different persons, even as he gives a "sickening idea" of London in the depiction of a *group* of criminals who are facing execution and will be "killed in a row." (This ghoulish economy is itself inverted, and elaborated, in Wemmick's mourning rings and jewelry, which, for the most part, seem to be purchased by contributions from criminals who are awaiting execution.)

34. The excess of feeling that is always hidden behind function is suggested again near the novel's end, when Pip awakens from his illness to find Joe by his bedside. Joe's return to Pip is a crucial element of narrative closure, and Pip is curious to find out how Joe learned of his illness.

"How long, dear Joe?"

"Which you meantersay, Pip, how long have your illness lasted, dear old chap?"

"Yes, Joe."

"It's the end of May, Pip. To-morrow is the first of June."

"And have you been here all the time, dear Joe?"

"Pretty nigh, old chap. For, as I says to Biddy when the news of your being ill were brought by letter, which it were brought by the post and being formerly single he is now married though underpaid for a deal of walking and shoe-leather, but wealth were not a object on his part, and marriage the great wish of his heart—"

"It is so delightful to hear you, Joe! But I interrupt you in what you said to Biddy."

"Which it were," said Joe, "that how you might be amongst strangers, and that how you and me having been ever friends, a wisit at such a moment might not prove unacceptabobble." (463–64)

Here the closing in of friends—the reunification of Pip and Joe—is accomplished literally by the parting of the postman, whose own story gets crowded out as he conveys the message that reunites Pip and Joe. The inclusion of the postman's story halts Pip's, generating a tension underlined by the way that Joe's description (of the postman's marriage and job) seems to grammatically (and thematically) proliferate. Dickens's subtle gesture toward the postman's experience—note how Pip misunderstands his own interruption—demonstrates an ambition not just to represent different characters but to inscribe the way that certain characters *won't* be represented. The postman is reduced to both a paradigmatic *narrative* functionality (in the reunion of Joe and Pip) and a social functionality, in a job that is "underpaid for a deal of walking and shoe-leather." This actual underpayment suggests here the underrecognized experience that constitutes *any* narrative help (since by definition the significance of the narrative helper's activity is derived primarily in relationship to another, more central character). If this analysis of the postman, the Jack, or Mike seems to spend too much time on truly insignificant characters (unlikely to survive, like the novel's great minor characters, in the reader's affective memory of the novel), we need to see how this is the exact opposite of an argument that would grant thematic signficance to one or several characters but remain unconvinced about a *structure* of minorness. These glimmerings of persons are, in this sense, crucial to the problem of asymmetric characterization as such—and besides, who would confidently put a precise limit on the impact that might result when a reader lights upon any particular person within the narrative form?

35. Interestingly, Moynahan makes several comments about the character-system that resonate with a reading focused on the socionarrative elaboration of Pip's problematic centrality. On Orlick himself, for example, Moynahan astutely notes that "Orlick's end is missing from the book . . . it seems that Orlick simply evaporates into thin air after his punitive role has been performed" (161). As in Duckworth's comments on *Pride and Prejudice*, we can see referentiality here emerging through the very figures used to unfold an allegorical or symbolic reading—the force of symbolic utility pushes the character "out of existence," or in this case causes him to "evaporate into thin air."

36. Thus: " 'More than that,' said he, folding his arms on the table again, 'I won't have a rag of you, I won't have a bone of you, left on earth. I'll put your body in the kiln—I'd carry two such to it, on my shoulders—and, let people suppose what they may of you, they shall never know nothing' " (436).

Chapter Four
A qui la place?: Characterization and Competition in *Le Père Goriot* and *La Comédie humaine*

1. See Pasco's overview of this controversy, 22–23 and 154–55. While P. G. Castex, Charles Gould, Martin Turnell, Jean-A. Ducourneau, and others argue for Goriot's centrality, Pierre Barbéris, Anthony R. Pugh, André Le Breton, Maurice Bardèche, Nicole Mozet, and others take Rastignac as the dominant figure.

2. In a recent example, Beizer notes how the novel "continually shifts focus" among Rastignac, Goriot, and Vautrin, and then comments that "[t]he three points which vie for a position of centrality in the novel are in fact variations on a theme" (354).

3. For translations of *Le Père Goriot* I have consulted *Old Goriot*, trans. Marion Ayton (Crawford, Middlesex: Penguin, 1951).

4. These examples vary significantly. For example, while *Anna Karenina*'s fascinating division between Karenina and Levin typically motivates alternating series of chapters, and is not marked by the two characters' extensive association in the social world of the story itself, *Sense and Sensibility* features two individuals who are locked into an extremely close relationship both as sisters *and* as fictional centers of narrative attention. The different refraction of the co-protagonists in story and discourse, and the thematic elaboration of discursive tensions within the story (or vice versa), might be the starting point for this kind of analysis. *Blood Meridian*, somewhat like *Le Père Goriot*, is divided between a central *focalizer* (the unnamed Kid) and a central actor (the grotesque and enormous Judge). This structure resembles that of several other canonical American novels, such as *Moby Dick* (Ishmael watches Ahab act) and *The Great Gatsby* (Carraway slowly uncovers Gatsby's life). (We might also think, here, of *Citizen Kane*.) In most of these examples the doubly configured relationship (how the two characters are arranged and juxtaposed in the story and the discourse) leads out into a more intricate character-system that incorporates a number of other characters into this already divided structure.

5. See also Demetz's discussion of Balzacian typification: "[T]he modern novelist, Balzac implies, follows the methodological example of the natural scientist by closely observing a multitude of individuals, isolating their common traits, separating them from the individual case, and concentrating them in a new model inclusive of all the individuals of the group or class" (407).

6. It is this "middle" class that provokes Balzac's most acute awareness of multiplicity. In the second rung of the social ladder discussed in the opening to *La Fille aux yeux d'or*, the syntactic dilation that we see in the description of César's friends is expanded to encompass the entire social class to which he belongs: "That kind of ambition brings our attention to the second of the spheres of Paris. . . . Wholesale merchants and their staff, government employees, the men of the little bank and great integrity, swindles and damned souls, the senior and the junior clerks, the clerks to the bailiff, to the solicitor, to the notary, in short the bustling, wary, speculative members of this petite bourgeoisie which nourishes the interests of Paris and makes them grow, makes corners in commodities, stores the products made by the proletariat, takes charge of the fruit from the South, the fish from the sea, the wines of every sun-drenched hill slope," etc., etc. (364–65). Before noting the specific content of Balzac's description, we must pay attention to the bulged form of this sentence. The form itself highlights the multiplicity of the enterprises, regardless of the descriptions of the particular enterprises that are actually enumerated.

7. This synthetic analysis addresses a methodological suggestion by Erich Auerbach: "[I]t is . . . difficult to describe with any accuracy the intellectual attitude which dominates Balzac's own particular manner of presentation. The statements which he himself makes on this subject are numerous and provide many clues, but they are confused and contradictory; the richer he is in ideas and inspirations, the less is he able to separate

the various elements of his own attitude . . . [W]hat is needed to explain his realistic art is precisely a careful separation of the currents which mingle in it" (*Mimesis*, 474).

8. Martin Kanes describes these two schools of criticism while noting the way that many of Balzac's most probing interpreters cross the boundaries of these perspectives.

> Balzac made his entry into academic precincts where his work was studied for its conformity to accepted literary standards and frequently for its accuracy as a mimetic transcription of reality. But at the same time, philosophical interpretation flourished, rooted in the insights of a previous era. Downplaying questions of biography, mimesis, politics or textual characteristics, it was concerned with the theoretical view of human nature to be found in *La Comédie humaine* taken as a finished product. . . . The greatest commentators on Balzac have always seen, of course, that there was no contradiction between Balzac the visionary and Balzac the secretary to society. (7, 10)

Crossing the boundaries is not equivalent to obliterating them; we can, indeed, identify these two strains of Balzac's style.

9. Barbéris talks about "les tensions . . . entre expérience de la division et recherche de l'unité" (194). Richard writes: "Elle pose la vie, à travers de multiples rêveries pourtant sur la chair, l'objet, le héros romanesque, comme le produit d'une poussée unique. Mais elle envisage *en meme temps* comme le résultat d'une série d'oppositions complexes, 'une suite de combinaisons qu'il faut étudier, suivre, pour arriver à se maintenir toujours en bonne posture.' [*Eugénie Grandet*]"(135). More recently, Mozet comments that "[L]'écriture balzacienne est écriture de la différenciation et de la nuance, dans une tension permanente entre le désir de vérité et d'unité et la multitude des expérimentations et des points de vue . . . cette contradiction fondamantale entre une intention totalitaire et l'éclatement kaléidoscopique des realisations" (9–10).

10. Rastignac's reveries—revolving around his ambition to get launched within the high Parisian social circles—and his agitated thoughts about Goriot are not qualitatively dissimilar. Both trains of thought are signs of his outer-directed consciousness, a relationship that is made clear at the end of the scene, in a passage which returns to Rastignac's interiority and shows its essentially shallow nature: "Distrait par les soupçons qui lui venaient sur le compte du Père Goriot, *plus distrait encore* par la figure de Mme de Restaud, qui de moments en moments se posait devant lui comme la messagère d'une brillante destinée, il finit par se coucher et par dormir à poings fermés" (77, emphasis added).

11. This play on the connection between the visual and cognitive aspects of "apercevoir" and "s'apercevoir" continues in this section. The phrase is attributed twice more to Rastignac: "Trop attentif pour s'apercevoir qu'il n'était pas seul, Eugène entendit tout à coup la voix de la comtesse" (96), and "Quand Eugène mit le pied sur le perron, il s'aperçut qu'il pleuvait" (102).

12. See Barbéris, 45–59.

13. See the use of this relationship as a main example in the theory of the double plot, in Levin, 1–20. For a seminal account of the double plot, see Empson.

14. See Shell, especially 24–47.

15. Of course, many interpretations of *King Lear* center on the play's political and ideological structure and significance. For a recent political interpretation of *King Lear*, see Kahn, who suggests that criticism of *King Lear* must "turn from psychology to political psychology" (179). For other divergent interpretations of *King Lear* as a repre-

sentation of monarchical ideology, see Halpern, 215–69, and Moretti, "The Great Eclipse: Tragic Form as the Deconsecration of Sovereignty," in *Signs Taken for Wonders*, 42–82.

16. Kent's doomed effort to reestablish the unity of thought, language, and action through disguise follows from Lear's horrific failure to comprehend Kent's loyalty: when Kent desperately tries to preserve the unified state (which depends on nothing other than the king's actualized centrality), Lear bitterly accuses him, as we have seen, of attempting "[t]o come betwixt our sentence and our power" (1.1.171). This tangled miscommunication between man and king—sadly echoed and amplified in the paradox of Kent, the most direct of men, forced into disguise—cannot be attributed to a personal failing of either man; rather, it results from the structure of kingship's disintegration before their eyes. It is particularly poignant that the separation of the king's words from his power is placed on the shoulders of the subject who most consistently tries to ground speech in thought (as he says later in the scene, "I can . . . deliver a plain message bluntly" [1.4.33]).

17. It is interesting to note, in the context of Lear's entanglement with his rebelling servant's language, that the king never speaks alone. In this sense, Lear does not have a real soliloquy, since all his monologues are performed in the presence of at least one other character. This is a strong indication of the particularly social status of language for Lear (since speech is, precisely, what translates consciousness into action, interior thought into social power). The *real* soliloquy is displaced onto Edmund, whose villainy rests precisely in his *peculiarity*, in the root sense of the word. In this somber play, the only real alternative to deriving identity through the king is to generate it, impossibly, through one's own individuality: "I must have your land" (1.2.16) and "Let me, if not by birth, have land by wit" (1.2.181).

18. In his major essay on characterization, Lukács briefly alludes to this scene, together with some scenes in *Hamlet*, as exemplifying how a field of literary characters dramatically embody comprehensive worldviews. See "The Intellectual Physiognomy," in *Writer and Critic*, 159–60: "The typical does not exist in isolation. . . . A character becomes typical only in comparison with and in contrast to other characters who, with more or less intensification, evoke other phases and aspects of the same contradictions, contradictions decisive to their lives and careers also. Only through a complicated dialectic rich in intensified contradictions can a character be elevated to typicality. Take a character generally recognized as typical, Hamlet. Without the contrast with Laertes, Horatio and Fortinbras, Hamlet's typicality could not be revealed. . . . Rastignac's inner conflicts are those of the entire younger generation in the post-Napoleonic period, a fact which is made clear in his contrasting discussions with Bianchon." I am less interested in the relationship between character and worldview (what Lukács, beginning with Plato's *Symposium*, calls "intellectual physiognomy") than in the dynamic notion of typification that leads Lukács to Rastignac's encounter with Bianchon in the Luxembourg Gardens.

19. For a reading of Pons's death that places responsibility on a *single* minor character rather than a group of them, see Marcus, 51–80. Marcus, however, reads Cibot *not* as an individual but rather as a site of transgression within a much larger, and historically specific, sociocultural discursive elaboration. The "female porter who successfully schemes to expose her tenant's most private space" (3), Cibot is significant as an *embodiment of* the "overlooked crossings that . . . undermined" the putative nineteenth-

century "separation of public and private realms" (7). Interestingly, Marcus's reading relies on, even hinges on, the implications of centrality and marginality for implied personhood. In Marcus's reading, the narrative enacts a chiasmus across the boundaries of minorness and centrality through which the charged ideological conflict between resident bachelor and *portière* is elaborated: Cibot becomes the privileged focalizer, while Pons (and Schmucke) are drained of interiority. "Even the narrator's description of Pons's apartment building emerges from Cibot's presence, contributing further to Cibot's appropriation of Pons's place as a central character whose point of view should focalize descriptive passages" (72). If Marcus's reading of *Le Cousin Pons* demonstrates the very heuristic consequences of minorness *for* ideological thematics, my reading of *Le Père Goriot* might return the favor, embedding this critical practice itself (point of view, character centrality) *within* the charged interaction between "city" and "home" for which Marcus provides a cultural geography.

20. We can see this in Topinard's conversations with Gaudissard and Schmucke:

"I gave you a day job, cleaning the lamps in the wings, and now you're in charge of the music scores. And that's not all. You make a franc a day extra working the monsters and organizing the demons when we put on a scene from Hell. That's a position envied by all the backstage hands. There are jealous people in this theater, my friend, and you have made enemies." (358)

—Me? In old Baudrand's place?

—*Yes.*

—Who told you that?

—*M. Cautissard!*

—Oh! It's enough to drive me mad with joy . . . Rosalie, did you hear that; this will make them envious at the theater." (374, Balzac's emphasis)

21. See Lotte, 474–76.

22. The original description of des Lupeaulx is, for Balzac, typically typical, defining him in terms of a more general social category and highlighting his functional position within the overall story: "At the ministry, there flourished as secretary-general a certain Clément Chardin des Lupeaulx, *one of those* characters that the flood of political events pull into the stream for several years. . . . [S]ince he was one of the principal actors in this drama, he merits a description which should be even more extensive because the July revolution has suppressed this post so eminently useful to constitutional ministers. . . . [T]his secretary-general *resembled all the mediocrities [ressemblait à toutes les médiocrités]* who form the knot of the political world" (59–60, emphasis added).

23. Three hierarchical scales of quantity (and thus social position)—the multiplicity of the pawns, the duality of the knights, bishops, and rooks, and the singularity of the king and queen—correspond to and motivate the "characteristics" of these pieces: the freedom of the royalty; the "eccentricity" of the knight, or "single-minded intensity" of the rook, or "black-or-white moralism" of the bishop; and the flatness of the pawn, who can go only in a single direction but might be transformed, through promotion, into a unique being. The elegance of the best pieces, furthermore, does not exist in-and-of-itself but can be conceived only comparatively—we see how powerful the queen is by the way she encompasses the functions of the other pieces. (Like Elizabeth Bennet, the queen has "something more of quickness.") Reference and structure are indissociable.

Afterword
Sophocles's *Oedipus Rex* and the Prehistory of the Protagonist

1. For a valuable recent discussion of the constructed opposition *between* history and form as a metastructure of contemporary literary theory, see Kaufman.

2. For one example of such a strand, we might consider the canonical moment in the modern African-American novel encapsulated in the triad of Wright, Baldwin, and Ellison. The interrelationship of their most important novels (*Native Son, Go Tell It on the Mountain, Another Country, Invisible Man*) can be suggestively illustrated through consideration of the space of the protagonist. *Native Son*—an inevitable source of departure for Ellison and Baldwin—offers a brilliant example of a protagonist whose strong *narrative* centrality is unfolded in continual contrast to his social or referenced *minorness*. This doubleness is grimly embedded within Bigger Thomas's very name, a name that begs the question: bigger than, or in terms of, what? If Wright's novel memorably transforms the privilege of narrative centrality into a form of *suffocation*, such a transformation highlights larger questions about characterization that are essential to the very project of the African-American novel: What kind of narrative centrality is possible for characters who are structurally subordinated within the social system? And (as with Balzac's and Dickens's divergent efforts to make more of minor characters) how should the modern novel negotiate the configured relationship between minority characters and minor characters: by devising new permutations of asymmetry or by abandoning the structural premises of asymmetry altogether? Baldwin's *Another Country* offers a unique answer to these questions and demonstrates the kind of imaginative *permutation* that sustains the relevance and power of character-system. The first quarter of the novel deliberately replicates the suffocating centrality of Bigger Thomas (displaced onto the musician Rufus Scott); but then, as the apparent protagonist commits suicide, the novel shifts toward a decentered and carefully balanced character-system, whose seemingly equitable distribution among a diverse group of characters is tarnished only by the sense that the characters (and character-spaces) revolve around an empty center, constituted by the mourned absence of Rufus himself. (To return to our discussion of *Pride and Prejudice*—Baldwin thus manages to configure the space of the protagonist as precisely *"one-quarter"* of the novel, in contrast to Butler's "three-quarters.") Ellison's *Invisible Man*, on the other hand, pushes asymmetry even further, drawing (like *Great Expectations*) on the episodic poetics of the picaresque novel to reframe and radically ironize the disjunction between narrative centrality and social minorness that organizes *Native Son*.

3. *Oedipus at Colonus*, 1410.

4. Translations from David Grene, with some modifications.

5. The question of consciousness and the question of structure converge around Oedipus's problematic dramatic centrality. For this reason, the divide between the Aeschylean and Sophoclean protagonist gets ramified in the complicated temporal structure of *Oedipus Rex*. We might fruitfully compare Sophocles' organization of his play to Aeschylus's sequentially narrated trilogy about Oedipus. Besides *The Seven against Thebes*, this trilogy includes the lost plays *Laius* and *Oedipus*. As we can tell from the title alone, Aeschylus front-loads the Sophoclean backstory into the first play, eliminating the dialectics of discovery and recognition that are so crucial in Sophocles' version while foregrounding the transgenerational sweep of events.

6. Jebb notes that this line can be translated as either "I have twice sent a man to bring him" or "I have sent two sets of messengers to bring him" (39). This ambiguity broadens the sense of confusion generated by the plurality.

7. In Dawe's authoritative commentary on *Oedipus Rex*, he is driven to make this extravagant comment about lines 924–1224 (which contain the two scenes centered on the messenger and herdsman): "With the possible exception of some scenes in Homer, the next three hundred lines constitute the finest achievement in Greek poetic technique to have survived to our era" (190). Charles Segal notes that Sophocles "probably invented the figure of the Corinthian Messenger" (95) in his revision of the Oedipal myth. Segal also notes another Sophoclean innovation that intensifies the importance of these two minor characters to the protagonist's survival: "Sophocles adds the detail that Laius pierces the feet, presumably to discourage passersby from rescuing the child, and this is the first time that this motif appears in the myth" (29).

Works Cited

Ackroyd, Peter. *Dickens*. New York: Harper Collins, 1990.

Ahl, Frederick. *Sophocles' Oedipus: Evidence and Self-Conviction*. Ithaca, N.Y.: Cornell University Press, 1991.

Altman, Charles. "Medieval Narrative vs. Modern Assumptions: Revising Inadequate Typology." *Diacritics* 4.2 (1974): 12–19.

Aristotle. *Poetics*. Trans. S. H. Butcher. New York: Dover Publications, 1951.

Armstrong, Nancy. *Desire and Domestic Fiction: A Political History of the Novel*. New York: Oxford University Press, 1987.

Auerbach, Erich. *Dante: Poet of The Secular World*. 1929. Trans. Ralph Manheim. Chicago: University of Chicago Press, 1961.

———. *Mimesis: The Representation of Reality in Western Literature*. 1946. Trans. Willard D. Trask. Princeton: Princeton University Press, 1953.

Austen, Jane. *The Novels of Jane Austen*. Ed. R. W. Chapman. 3d ed. 5 vols. Oxford: Oxford University Press, 1932–1934.

Bakhtin, M. M. *The Dialogic Imagination*. Trans. Michael Holquist. Austin: University of Texas Press, 1981.

Bal, Mieke. *Narratology: Introduction to the Theory of Narrative*. Trans. Christine van Boheemen. Toronto: University of Toronto Press, 1985.

Balzac, Honoré de. *Avant-propos de "La Comédie humaine."* 1842. *La Comédie humaine*, Pléaide I. Paris: Éditions Gallimard, 1976.

———. *César Birotteau*. 1837. Paris: Éditions Gallimard, 1975.

———. *La Cousine Bette*. 1846. Paris: Éditions Gallimard, 1972.

———. *Le Cousin Pons*. 1847. Paris: Flammarion, 1993.

———. *Les Employés*. 1836. Paris: Éditions Gallimard, 1985.

———. *Eugénie Grandet*. 1834. Paris: Éditions Gallimard, 1972.

———. *Histoire des treize*. 1834. Paris: Librairie Général Française, 1983.

———. *Illusions Perdues*. 1843. Paris: Flammarion, 1990.

———. *Le Père Goriot*. 1834. Paris: Flammarion, 1995.

———. *Preface de la première édition*, *Les Employés*, 879–96. 1838. *La Comédie humaine*, Pléaide VII. Paris: Éditions Gallimard, 1977.

———. *Preface de la première édition*, *Une Fille d'Ève*, 261–72. 1839. *La Comédie humaine*, Pléaide II. Paris: Éditions Gallimard, 1976.

Barbéris, Pierre. *Le Père Goriot de Balzac: écriture, structures, significations*. Paris: Librairie Larousse, 1972.

Barthes, Roland. "Introduction à l'analyse structurale des récits." *Communications* 8 (1977): 1–27.

———. "The Reality Effect." 1968. In *The Rustle of Language*, trans. Richard Howard, 141–48. Berkeley and Los Angeles: University of California Press, 1986.

———. *S/Z*. Paris: Éditions du Seuil, 1970.

Bazin, André. *What Is Cinema?* Vol. 1. Trans. Hugh Gray. Berkeley and Los Angeles: University of California Press, 1969.

Béguin, Albert. *Balzac lu et relu*. Paris: Éditions du Seuil, 1965.

Beizer, Janet L. *Family Plots: Balzac's Narrative Generations*. New Haven: Yale University Press, 1986.

Benardete, Seth. "The Aristeia of Diomedes and the Plot of the *Iliad*." *Agon: A Journal of Classical Studies* 2 (1968): 10–38.

———. "Sophocles' *Oedipus Tyrannus*." In *Sophocles: A Collection of Critical Essays*, ed. Thomas Woodard, 105–22. Englewood Cliffs, N.J.: Prentice-Hall, 1966.

Benjamin, Walter. *Illuminations*. 1955. Trans. Harry Zohn. New York: Schocken Books, 1968.

Berger, Harry. *The Allegorical Temper*. New Haven: Yale University Press, 1957.

Bloom, Harold. *The Western Canon: The Books and School of the Ages*. New York: Harcourt Brace & Company, 1994.

Booth, Wayne. *The Rhetoric of Fiction*. 1961. Chicago: University of Chicago Press, 1983.

Bourdieu, Pierre. *Les Règles de l'art: Genèse et structure du champ littéraire*. Paris: Éditions du Seuil, 1992.

Brontë, Charlotte. *Jane Eyre*. 1848. New York: Bantam Books, 1981.

Brooks, Peter. *The Melodramatic Imagination: Balzac, Henry James, Melodrama, and the Mode of Excess*. New Haven: Yale University Press, 1976.

———. *Reading for the Plot: Design and Intention in Narrative*. New York: Alfred A. Knopf, 1984.

Butler, Marilyn. *Jane Austen and the War of Ideas*. Oxford: Oxford University Press, 1975.

Chatman, Seymour. *Story and Discourse*. Ithaca, N.Y.: Cornell University Press, 1978.

Chaucer, Geoffrey. *The Complete Poetry and Prose of Geoffrey Chaucer*. Ed. John H. Fisher. New York: Holt, Rinehart and Winston, 1977.

Cixous, Hélène. "The Character of 'Character.' " *New Literary History* 5 (1974): 383–402.

Cohen, Margaret. *The Sentimental Education of the Novel*. Princeton: Princeton University Press, 1999.

Connor, Steven. *Charles Dickens*. Oxford: Basil Blackwell, 1985.

Conrad, Joseph. *Lord Jim*. 1900. London: Penguin Classics, 1986.

Culler, Jonathan. *Structuralist Poetics: Structuralism, Linguistics and the Study of Literature*. London: Routledge, 1975.

Davies, James A. *The Textual Life of Dickens's Characters*. London: Macmillan, 1989.

Dawe, R. D. *Oedipus Rex*. Cambridge: Cambridge University Press, 1982.

de Man, Paul. *Allegories of Reading: Figural Language in Rousseau, Nietzsche, Rilke and Proust*. New Haven: Yale University Press, 1979.

———. *Blindness and Insight: Essays in the Rhetoric of Contemporary Criticism*. Minneapolis: University of Minnesota Press, 1983.

Demetz, Peter. "Balzac and the Zoologists: A Concept of the Type." In *The Disciplines of Criticism: Essays in Literary Theory, Interpretation and History*, ed. Peter Demetz, Thomas Greene, and Lowry Nelson, Jr., 397–419. New Haven: Yale University Press, 1968.

Descombes, Vincent. *Objects of All Sorts: A Philosophical Grammar*. 1983. Trans. Lorna Scott-Fox and Jeremy Harding. Baltimore: Johns Hopkins University Press, 1986.

Dickens, Charles. *Bleak House*. 1853. London: Penguin Books, 1985.
———. *David Copperfield*. 1850. London: Penguin Books, 1985.
———. *Dombey and Son*. 1848. London: Penguin Books, 1985.
———. *Great Expectations*. 1861. London: Penguin Books, 1965.
———. *Hard Times*. 1854. Oxford: Oxford University Press, 1989.
———. *Little Dorrit*. 1857. Baltimore: Penguin Books, 1967.
———. *Martin Chuzzlewit*. 1844. London: Everyman, 1994.
———. *Nicholas Nickleby*. 1839. London: Penguin Books, 1986.
———. *The Old Curiosity Shop*. 1841. London: Everyman, 1995.
———. *Oliver Twist*. 1837. London: Penguin Books, 1985.
———. *Our Mutual Friend*. 1865. London: Penguin Books, 1985.
———. *The Pickwick Papers*. 1837. London: Penguin Books, 1986.
———. *Sketches by Boz*. 1836. London: Penguin Books, 1995.
Docherty, Thomas. *Reading (Absent) Character: Towards a Theory of Characterization in Fiction*. Oxford: Oxford University Press, 1983.
Dostoevsky, Fyodor. *The Double: A Poem of St. Petersburg*. Trans. George Bird. 1846. In *Great Short Works of Fyodor Dostoevsky*, 3–144. New York: Harper and Row, 1968.
———. *The Idiot*. 1869. Trans. Henry and Olga Carlisle. New York: New American Library, 1969.
Duckworth, Alistair. *The Improvement of the Estate*. Baltimore: Johns Hopkins University Press, 1972.
Eliot, George. *Middlemarch*. 1872. New York: Bantam Books, 1985.
Empson, William. "Double Plots: Heroic and Pastoral in the Main Plot and the Sub-Plot." 1935. In *Some Versions of Pastoral*, 27–86. London: Hogarth Press, 1986.
Engels, Friedrich. *The Condition of the Working Class in England*. 1845. Trans. W. O. Henderson and W. H. Chaloner. Stanford: Stanford University Press, 1958.
Erlich, Victor. *Russian Formalism: History—Doctrine*. 1955. New Haven: Yale University Press, 1981.
Flaubert, Gustave. *L'Éducation sentimentale*. 1869. Paris: Éditions Gallimard, 1965.
Forster, E. M. *Aspects of the Novel*. 1927. London: Edward Arnold Publishers, 1958.
Frank, Lawrence. *Charles Dickens and the Romantic Self*. Lincoln: University of Nebraska Press, 1984.
Freud, Sigmund. *The Interpretation of Dreams*. 1900. Trans. James Strachey. New York: Avon Books, 1965.
———. "The Relation of the Poet to Day-Dreaming." 1908. In *Collected Papers*, trans. Joan Riviere, 4:173–83. London: Hogarth Press, 1925.
Galef, David. *The Supporting Cast: A Study of Flat and Minor Characters*. Pennsylvania: Pennsylvania State University Press, 1993.
Gallagher, Catherine. *Nobody's Story: The Vanishing Acts of Women Writers in the Marketplace, 1670–1820*. Berkeley and Los Angeles: University of California Press, 1994.
Gaskell, Elizabeth. *Mary Barton*. 1848. Oxford: Oxford University Press, 1987.
———. *North and South*. 1855. Oxford: Oxford University Press, 1998.
Giamatti, A. Bartlett. *Play of Double Senses: Spenser's* Faerie Queene. New York: W. W. Norton and Company, 1975.

Gilbert, Sandra M., and Susan Gubar. *The Madwoman in the Attic: The Woman Writer and the Nineteenth-Century Literary Imagination*. New Haven: Yale University Press, 1979.

Goffman, Erving. *The Presentation of Self in Everyday Life*. New York: Doubleday, 1959.

Gogol, Nicolai V. "The Overcoat." 1842. In *The Collected Tales of Nicolai Gogol*, trans. Richard Peaver and Larissa Volokhonsky, 394–424. New York: Pantheon Books, 1998.

Golding, Robert. *Idiolects in Dickens: The Major Techniques and Chronological Development*. London: Macmillan Press, 1985.

Goldmann, Lucien. *Towards a Sociology of the Novel*. Trans. Alan Sheridan. London: Tavistock, 1962.

Greimas, A. J. *Sémantique structurale: Recherche de méthode*. Paris: Librairie Larousse, 1966.

Griffin, Jasper, and Martin Hammond. "Critical Appreciation, Homer, *Iliad* 1.1–52." In *Homer*, ed. Ian McAuslan and Peter Walcot, 65–95. Oxford: Oxford University Press, 1999.

Guillen, Claudio. *Literature as System: Essays toward the Theory of Literary History*. Princeton: Princeton University Press, 1971.

Halpern, Richard. *The Poetics of Primitive Accumulation: English Renaissance Culture and the Genealogy of Capital*. Ithaca, N.Y.: Cornell University Press, 1991.

Hamon, Philippe. *Le Personnel du roman: Le système des personnages dans les Rougon-Macquart d'Emile Zola*. Geneva: Librairie Droz, 1983.

———. "Pour un statut sémiologique du personnage." In *Poétique du récit*, ed. Gérard Genette and Tzvetan Todorov, 115–80. Paris: Éditions du Seuil, 1977.

———. *Texte et idéologie: Valeurs, hiérarchies et évaluations dans l'oeuvre littéraire*. Paris: PUF, 1984.

Harding, D. W. "Character and Caricature in Jane Austen." In *Critical Essays on Jane Austen*, ed. B. C. Southam, 83–105. London: Routledge and Kegan Paul, 1968.

Hardy, Thomas. *Jude the Obscure*. 1895. London: Macmillan, 1974.

Harvey, W. J. *Character and the Novel*. London: Chatto & Windus, 1965.

Hochman, Baruch. *Character in Literature*. Ithaca, N.Y.: Cornell University Press, 1985.

Homer. *Iliad, I and II*. Ed. David B. Monro and Thomas W. Allen. Oxford Classical Texts. Oxford: Oxford University Press, 1902; reprint, 1990.

———. *Iliad of Homer*. Trans. Richmond Lattimore. Chicago: University of Chicago Press, 1951.

Howe, Irving. *A Critic's Notebook*. San Diego: Harcourt Brace & Company, 1994.

Hunt, Herbert J. *Balzac's* Comédie Humaine. London: University of London, Athlone Press, 1959.

Jaffe, Audrey. *Vanishing Points: Dickens, Narrative and the Subject of Omniscience*. Berkeley and Los Angeles: University of California Press, 1991.

Jakobson, Roman, and Morris Hale. *Fundamentals of Language*. The Hague: Mouton, 1956.

James, Henry. "Preface to the New York Edition." 1907. In *Wings of the Dove*, 35–51. London: Penguin Books, 1986.

Jameson, Fredric. *The Political Unconscious: Narrative as a Socially Symbolic Act.* London: Routledge, 1981.

Jebb, Richard. *The Oedipus Tyrannus of Sophocles.* Cambridge: Cambridge University Press, 1958.

Johnson, Claudia. *Jane Austen: Women, Politics and the Novel.* Chicago: University of Chicago Press, 1988.

Jordan, John. "The Medium of *Great Expectations.*" *Dickens Studies Annual* 11 (1983): 73–88.

Joyce, James. *Ulysses.* 1922. Ed. Hans Walter Gabler. New York: Vintage Books, 1986.

Kafka, Franz. *The Trial.* Trans. Willa and Edwin Muir. New York: Random House, 1964.

Kahn, Paul W. *Law and Love: The Trials of* King Lear. New Haven: Yale University Press, 2000.

Kanes, Martin, ed. *Critical Essays on Honoré de Balzac.* Boston: G. K. Hall & Co., 1990.

Kantorowicz, Ernst Hartwig. *The King's Two Bodies: A Study of Medieval Political Theology.* Princeton: Princeton University Press, 1957.

Kaufman, Robert. "Red Kant, or, The Persistence of the Third *Critique* in Adorno and Jameson." *Critical Inquiry* 26.4 (Summer 2000): 682–724.

Keen, Suzanne. *Victorian Renovations of the Novel: Narrative Annexes and the Boundaries of Representation.* Cambridge: Cambridge University Press, 1998.

Kirk, G. S. *The Iliad: A Commentary.* Vol. 1. Cambridge: Cambridge University Press, 1985.

Knights, L. C. *How Many Children Had Lady Macbeth? An Essay in the Theory and Practice of Shakespeare Criticism.* Cambridge: The Minority Press, 1933.

Knox, Bernard. *The Heroic Temper: Studies in Sophoclean Tragedy.* Berkeley and Los Angeles: University of California Press, 1964.

Kroeber, Karl. "*Pride and Prejudice*: Fiction's Lasting Novelty." In *Jane Austen: Bicentenary Essays*, ed. John Halperin, 144–56. London: Cambridge University Press, 1975.

Lambert, Mark. *Dickens and the Suspended Quotation.* New Haven: Yale University Press, 1981.

Le Huenen, Roland, and Paul Perron. *Balzac. Sémiotique du personnage romanesque: L'exemple d'*Eugénie Grandet. Montreal: Les Presses de l'Université de Montréal, 1980.

Lesage, Alain-René. *Histoire de Gil Blas de Santillane.* 1715. Paris: Société des Belles Lettres, 1935.

Levin, Richard. *The Multiple Plot in English Renaissance Drama.* Chicago: University of Chicago Press, 1971.

Levinas, Emmanuel. *Totality and Infinity: An Essay on Exteriority.* 1961. Trans. Alphonso Lingis. Pittsburgh: Duquesne University Press, 1969.

Littlewood, Ian, ed. *Jane Austen: Critical Assessments.* East Sussex: Helm Information, 1998.

Lodge, David. *The Art of Fiction.* London: Penguin Books, 1992.

Lohner, Edgar. "The Intrinsic Method: Some Reconsiderations." In *The Disciplines of Criticism: Essays in Literary Theory, Interpretation and History*, ed. Peter Demetz,

Thomas Greene, and Lowry Nelson, Jr., 147–72. New Haven: Yale University Press, 1968.

Lotte, Fernand. *Dictionnaire biographique des personnages fictifs de* La Comédie humaine. Paris: Librairie José Corti, 1952.

Lowry, G. S. *Thersites: A Study in Comic Shame*. New York: Garland Publishers, 1991.

Lukács, Georg. *Goethe and His Age*. 1947. Trans. Robert Anchor. New York: Grosset and Dunlap, 1969.

———. *History and Class Consciousness: Studies in Marxist Dialectics*. 1922. Trans. Rodney Livingstone. Cambridge: MIT Press, 1971.

———. *Studies in European Realism*. Trans. Edith Bone. London: Hillway Publishing Company, 1950.

———. *The Theory of the Novel*. 1920. Trans. Anna Bostock. Cambridge: MIT Press, 1971.

———. *Writer and Critic and Other Essays*. Trans. Arthur D. Kahn. New York: Grosset and Dunlap, 1970.

Lynch, Deidre Shauna. *The Economy of Character: Novels, Market Culture, and the Business of Inner Meaning*. Chicago: University of Chicago Press, 1998.

Macpherson, C. B. *The Life and Times of Liberal Democracy*. Oxford: Oxford University Press, 1977.

Marcus, Sharon. *Apartment Stories: City and Home in Nineteenth-Century Paris and London*. Berkeley and Los Angeles: University of California Press, 1999.

Marcus, Steven. *Dickens: From Pickwick to Dombey*. London: Chatto & Windus, 1965.

Marx, Karl. *Selected Works*. Ed. David McLellan. Oxford: Oxford University Press, 1977.

Mayhew, Henry. *London Labour and the London Poor*. 1861. New York: Dover Publications, 1968.

McKeon, Michael. *The Origins of the English Novel 1600–1740*. Baltimore: Johns Hopkins University Press, 1987.

Melville, Herman. *Moby Dick: An Authoritative Text*. 1851. Ed. Harrison Hayford and Hershel Parker. New York: W. W. Norton and Company, 1967.

Mill, John Stuart. "Thoughts on Parliamentary Reform." 1859. In *Collected Works of John Stuart Mill*, 19:313–39. Toronto: University of Toronto Press, 1977.

Miller, D. A. *Narrative and Its Discontents: Problems of Closure in the Traditional Novel*. Princeton: Princeton University Press, 1981.

Miller, J. Hillis. *Charles Dickens: The World of His Novels*. Cambridge: Harvard University Press, 1965.

Moretti, Franco. *Atlas of the European Novel*. London: Verso, 1998.

———. *Signs Taken for Wonders: Essays in the Sociology of Literary Forms*. London: Verso Classics, 1997.

———. *The Way of the World: The Bildungsroman in European Culture*. London: Verso, 1987.

Moynahan, Julian. "The Hero's Guilt: The Case of *Great Expectations*." In *Assessing Great Expectations*, ed. Richard Lettis and William E. Morris, 149–68. San Francisco: Chandler Publishing Company, 1960.

Mozet, Nicole. *Balzac au pluriel*. Paris: PUF, 1990.

Mudrick, Marvin. *Irony as Defense and Discovery*. Princeton: Princeton University Press, 1952.

Newsom, Robert. "Fictions of Childhood." In *The Cambridge Companion to Charles Dickens*, ed. John Jordan, 92–105. Cambridge: Cambridge University Press, 2001.

Newton, Adam Zachary. *Narrative Ethics*. Cambridge: Harvard University Press, 1995.

Orwell, George. "Charles Dickens." In *Dickens, Dali and Others*, 1–76. New York: Harcourt, Brace and World, 1946.

Pasco, Allan H. *Balzacian Montage: Configuring* La Comédie humaine. Toronto: University of Toronto Press, 1991.

Phelan, James. *Reading People, Reading Plots: Character, Progression and the Interpretation of Narrative*. Chicago: University of Chicago Press, 1989.

Poovey, Mary. *The Proper Lady and the Woman Writer: Ideology as Style in the Works of Mary Wollstonecraft, Mary Shelley, and Jane Austen*. Chicago: University of Chicago Press, 1984.

Postlethwaite, N. "Thersites in the *Iliad*." In *Homer*, ed. Ian McAuslan and Peter Walcot, 83–95. Oxford: Oxford University Press, 1998.

Poulet, Georges. *La Distance intérieure*. Paris: Librairie Plon, 1952.

Prendergast, Christopher. *The Order of Mimesis: Balzac, Stendhal, Nerval, Flaubert*. Cambridge: Cambridge University Press, 1986.

Price, Martin. *Forms of Life: Character and Moral Imagination in the Novel*. New Haven: Yale University Press, 1983.

Propp, Vladimir. *Morphology of the Folktale*. Trans. L. Scott. Austin: University of Texas Press, 1968.

Proust, Marcel. *Du côté de chez Swann*. 1919. Paris: Flammarion, 1987.

Pugh, Anthony. *Balzac's Recurring Characters*. Toronto: University of Toronto Press, 1974.

———. "Personnages reparaissants avant *Le Père Goriot*." In *L'Année Balzacienne 1964*, 215–39. Paris: Editions Garnier Frères, 1964.

Rabel, Robert J. *Plot and Point of View in the* Iliad. Ann Arbor: University of Michigan Press, 1997.

Redfield, James. "The Proem of the *Iliad*: Homer's Art." *Classical Philology* 74 (1979): 95–110.

Richard, Jean-Pierre. *Études sur le romantisme*. Paris: Éditions du Seuil, 1970.

Rimmon-Kenan, Shlomith. *A Glance beyond Doubt: Narration, Representation and Subjectivity*. Columbus: Ohio State University Press, 1996.

———. *Narrative Fiction: Contemporary Poetics*. London: Routledge, 1983.

Robbe-Grillet, Alain. *For a New Novel*. 1963. Trans. Richard Howard. Evanston: Northwestern University Press, 1965.

Robbins, Bruce. *The Servant's Hand: English Fiction from Below*. Durham, N.C.: Duke University Press, 1993.

Rosenberg, Brian. *Little Dorrit's Shadows: Character and Contradiction in Dickens*. Columbia: University of Missouri Press, 1996.

Ryding, William W. *Structure in Medieval Narrative*. The Hague: Mouton, 1971.

Sarraute, Nathalie. *L'Ère du soupçon: Essais sur le roman*. Paris: Éditions Gallimard, 1956.

Schiller, Friedrich. *On the Aesthetic Education of Man*. Trans. Elizabeth M. Wilkinson and L. A. Willoughby. Oxford: Clarendon Press, 1982.

Schor, Hilary. *Dickens and the Daughter of the House*. Cambridge: Cambridge University Press, 1999.

Segal, Charles. *Oedipus Tyrannus: Tragic Heroism and the Limits of Knowledge.* 2d ed. New York: Oxford University Press, 2001.

Sell, D. Roger. *Great Expectations: New Casebooks.* London: Macmillan, 1994.

Shakespeare, William. *King Lear.* The Arden Shakespeare, 3d ser. Ed. R. A. Foakes. Surrey: Thomas Nelson and Sons, 1997.

Shell, Marc. *Money, Language and Thought: Literary and Philosophical Economies from the Medieval to the Modern Era.* Berkeley and Los Angeles: University of California Press, 1982.

Slatkin, Laura. *The Web of Thetis: Allusion and Interpretation in the* Iliad. Berkeley and Los Angeles: University of California Press, 1991.

Smith, Adam. *The Wealth of Nations.* 1776. New York: Modern Library, 1937.

Sophocles. *Sophocles I: Oedipus the King, Oedipus at Colonus, Antigone.* Trans. David Grene. Chicago: University of Chicago Press, 1991.

Stendhal. *Romans et nouvelles I.* Paris: Éditions Gallimard, 1952.

Tanner, Tony. *Jane Austen.* Cambridge: Harvard University Press, 1986.

Thackeray, William Makepeace. *Vanity Fair.* 1848. New York: Random House, 1958.

Todorov, Tzvetan. *The Poetics of Prose.* 1971. Trans. Richard Howard. Ithaca, N.Y.: Cornell University Press, 1977.

———. *Qu'est-ce que c'est la structuralisme?* Paris: Éditions du Seuil, 1973.

Tomachevski, Boris. "Thematique." 1925. In *Théorie de la literature: Textes des formalists russes,* ed. Tzvetan Todorov, 263–307. Paris: Éditions du Seuil, 1966.

Trollope, Anthony. *Barchester Towers.* 1857. London: Penguin Books, 1983.

———. *The Three Clerks.* 1858. London: Penguin Books, 1993.

Twain, Mark. *Pudd'nhead Wilson* and *Those Extraordinary Twins.* New York: Penguin Books, 1969.

Tynianov, Yuri. *The Problem of Verse Language.* 1924. Trans. Michael Sosa and Brent Harvey. Ann Arbor: Ardis, 1981.

Van Ghent, Dorothy. *The English Novel: Form and Function.* New York: Holt, Rinehart and Winston, 1953.

Vygotsky, Lev. *The Psychology of Art.* Trans. Scripta Technica. Cambridge: MIT Press, 1971.

Watt, Ian. *The Rise of the Novel: Studies in Defoe, Richardson and Fielding.* London: Chatto & Windus, 1957.

Weil, Simone. "The *Iliad*: A Poem of Force." 1941. Trans. Mary McCarthy. In *The Proper Study: Essays in Western Classics,* ed. Quentin Anderson and Joseph Mazzeo, 4–29. New York: St. Martin's Press, 1962.

Welsh, Alexander. *The City of Dickens.* Oxford: Clarendon Press, 1971.

———. *From Copyright to Copperfield: The Identity of Dickens.* Cambridge: Harvard University Press, 1987.

Wilde, Alan. "Mr. F's Aunt and the Analogical Structure of *Little Dorrit.*" *Nineteenth Century Fiction* 19 (1964): 33–44.

Williams, Raymond. *The English Novel from Dickens to Lawrence.* London: Chatto & Windus, 1970.

———. "Introduction." In *Dombey and Son,* ed. Peter Fairclough. London: Penguin Books, 1970.

———. *Marxism and Literature.* Oxford: Oxford University Press, 1977.

Acknowledgments

Like others before it, this is a twice-told tale. The initial development of this argument benefited from the ideas and responses of many interlocutors at Yale University. Peter Brooks, in his own work and through his generous engagement in this project, has been my long-standing model for the theoretical encounter with European narrative. Carla Kaplan helped sharpen the claims and arguments of this project; her keen insights and rigorous questions improved this book in numerous ways. My first thanks goes to these supportive and thoughtful advisers. I also owe special thanks to Franco Moretti, who played a crucial intellectual role in the earliest formulation of this project and then (as though in a final demonstration of structuralism's claim) combined two character-functions in one, as a valued reader at the book's end.

Acknowledgments with too many thanks, like a novel with too many characters, can become ungrateful through their very inclusiveness. Over the years, this work has been supported by many teachers, friends, and colleagues in different places. For ideas about reading that I hope are reflected in these pages, I'd like to thank Susan Winnett, Richard Brodhead, Geoffrey Hartman, and Stephen Schwartz. For particularly helpful responses to this manuscript, I want to single out John Bender, Ilya Bernstein, Terry Castle, Natalka Freeland, Pericles Lewis, Michael Holquist, Leah Price, David Quint, David Riggs, Aidan Wasley, and Ruth Yeazell. In finishing this project at Stanford University, I've benefited deeply from the responses, friendship, and intellectual energy of Jay Fliegelman, Rob Kaufman, Paula Moya, Sianne Ngai, and Rob Polhemus. Detailed readings by Garrett Stewart and Regenia Gagnier reflected this project back to its author in a way that really mattered. And D. A. Miller, in the book's final stages, was always willing to offer something more of his quickness. Finally, Charles Baraw has been an invaluable and reliably perceptive friend to both this project and its author.

This book had the good fortune to find excellent editors. I'd like to thank Mary Murrell for her belief in this project and her professional fairness and acumen. Lauren Lepow did an amazing job in copyediting the manuscript, and her hand has left its mark on many of its pages.

Finally, it is a pleasure to acknowledge Karla Oeler, whom I want to thank for the sustained correspondence, in all the different senses of the word, and one particularly wise P.S. She lived with, and helped me think through, this book, and it would not be the same without her involvement.

This book is dedicated, with cheerful affection, to my parents, Isser Woloch and Nancy Spelman Woloch, and to my brother David.

Index

character-space (*cont'd*)

Huckleberry Finn, 362n.14, 365–66n.32; in *Another Country*, 372n.2; in *Barchester Towers*, 12–13; in *Benito Cereno*, 347n.30; in the bildungsroman, 29–30, 176, 320, 351n.17; in *Blood Meridian*, 368n.4; in *The Canterbury Tales*, 339n1; and chess, 313, 371n.23; in *Citizen Kane*, 368n.4; and collective groups, 6–7, 62–63, 64–65, 185–86, 246–47, 292, 298, 338–39n.11, 349n.12; compressed, 68–75; and co-protagonists, 36, 244–46, 265–82, 368n.4; in *David Copperfield*, 146, 148–49, 171–76; in *The Divine Comedy*, 338n.8; of the double, 238–43; in *Emma*, 146–48, 357–58n.15; in *Les Employés*, 303–35; in epic poetry, 18–19; externalized, 82–88, 201–3, in film narrative, 345–46n.23; and funerals, 301; in *Gil Blas*, 180–82; in *Great Expectations*, 177–243, passim; in *The Great Gatsby*, 368n4; in *Henry IV*, 86–87; in the *Iliad*, 1–11; in *Illusions perdues*, 338–39n.11; and inequality, 8–11, 43, 58–60, 64–7, 80, 86–87, 97, 123–24, 129, 143–44, 192, 219–23, 271; in *Invisible Man*, 372n.2; in *Jane Eyre*, 25–26, 345n.18–19; in *King Lear*, 278–80, 282–88; late in narratives, 233–37, 302–3, 350n.15, 365n.31; in *The Libation Bearers*, 364n.27; in *Little Dorrit*, 131–32, 165–66, 168–69, 170–71; in *Lord Jim*, 344n.14; in *Mansfield Park*, 39, 346n.26; in *Middlemarch*, 31–32; of minor minor characters, 116–22, 232–37, 365n.31, 366–67n.34; in *Moby Dick*, 39–40, 347–47n.30, 368n.4; in *Native Son*, 372n.2; in the nineteenth-century novel, 32–37, 307, 321–22; in *Oedipus Rex*, 319–35; in *Oliver Twist*, 128–31, 132; in *Our Mutual Friend*, 126, 155, 236, 354n.2; in *Le Père Goriot*, 244–318, passim; in the picaresque novel, 180–82, 356n.9; in *The Pickwick Papers*, 133–44, 152–53; in *Pride and Prejudice*, 33–34, 43–124, passim; and recurring characters, 290, 291–96; in the realist novel, 19–21, 34, 43–45, 245–46, 246–55, 338–39n.11; in *Romeo and Juliet*, 37; in *Le Rouge et le noir*, 46–47, 350n.14; in *Sense and Sensibility*, 349n.10; and servants, 28, 119–22, 140–43, 228, 232–33, 274, 354n.24; sporadically appearing, 167–68, 171; in the twentieth-century novel, 321–22, 372n.2; in *Vanity Fair*, 39; and weak protagonists, 35, 125–33, 134–36,

143–44, 178–80, 185–87, 188–92, 202, 217–23, 355n.6; in *The Wings of the Dove*, 21–24

The Charterhouse of Parma (Stendhal), 340n.2

Chatman, Seymour, 14

Chaucer, Geoffrey: *The Canterbury Tales*, 12, 339n.1

Cixous, Hélène, 16, 342n.10

Claire d'Albe (Cotin), 362n.15

Cohen, Margaret, 362n.15

Collins, Wilkie, 35; *The Moonstone*, 245

La Comédie humaine (Balzac): critical reception of, 258, 369n.8; and *Les Employés*, 307, 308–9, 312, 318; origins of, 289–95; Parisian social framework in, 249, 256–57; preface to, 256–57; recurring characters in, 35–36, 293–94, 295; typification in, 255, 256–57, 312

Conrad, Joseph: *Lord Jim*, 344n.14

Contes fantastiques (Hoffmann), 314

Cotin: *Claire d'Albe*, 362n.15

La Cousine Bette (Balzac), 261, 304

Le Cousin Pons (Balzac), 261, 262, 299–303, 299–304, 370–71nn.19–20

Crime and Punishment (Dostoevsky), 33, 362n.14

Culler, Jonathan, 14

Daniel Deronda (Eliot), 245

Dante Alighieri: *Inferno*, 7, 338nn.8–10

David Copperfield (Dickens): 125, 146, 148–49, 155, 171–76, 354n.1, 355n.4, 355n.6, 362n.13

Dawe, R. D., 373n.7

de Man, Paul, 16, 17, 363n.20

Demetz, Peter, 343n.12, 368n.5

Descombes, Vincent, 293–94

Dickens, Charles: *Barnaby Rudge*, 149, 355n.6, 365n.31; *Bleak House*, 126, 145, 150–52, 153, 155–56, 159–61, 166, 221, 347n.1, 355n.6; *David Copperfield*, 125, 146, 148–49, 155, 171–76, 354n.1, 355nn.4 and 6, 362n.13; *Dombey and Son*, 24–25, 30, 354n.1; *Little Dorrit*, 126, 131–32, 151, 154, 155–56, 158–59, 165–66, 168–69, 170–71, 222, 354nn.1–2, 355nn.4–5, 358n.20; *Martin Chuzzlewit*, 153, 154; *Nicholas Nickleby*, 24–25, 125, 151, 154–55, 160, 166, 167, 344n.15, 355n.4, 359–60n.22, 361n.11; *The Old Curiosity Shop*, 170; *Oliver Twist*, 128–32, 138–39, 145,